THE INTERNATIONAL DEFENSE
OF WORKERS

WOODROW WILSON CENTER SERIES

W W | Wilson Center

WOODROW WILSON CENTER SERIES

The Woodrow Wilson International Center for Scholars was chartered by the U.S. Congress in 1968 as the living memorial to the nation's twenty-eighth president. It serves as the country's key nonpartisan policy forum, tackling global challenges through independent research and open dialogue. Bridging the worlds of academia and public policy, the Center's diverse programmatic activity informs actionable ideas for Congress, the administration, and the broader policy community.

The Woodrow Wilson Center Series shares in the Center's mission by publishing outstanding scholarly and public policy-related books for a global readership. Written by the Center's expert staff and international network of scholars, our books shed light on a wide range of topics, including U.S. foreign and domestic policy, security, the environment, energy, and area studies.

Conclusions or opinions expressed in Center publications and programs are those of the authors and speakers and do not necessarily reflect the views of the Center staff, fellows, trustees, advisory groups, or any individuals or organizations that provide financial support for the Center.

Please visit us online at www.wilsoncenter.org.

Margarita M. Balmaceda, *Russian Energy Chains: The Remaking of Technopolitics from Siberia to Ukraine to the European Union*

Abraham M. Denmark, *U.S. Strategy in the Asian Century: Empowering Allies and Partners*

Samuel F. Wells Jr., *Fearing the Worst: How Korea Transformed the Cold War*

Donald R. Wolfensberger, *Changing Cultures in Congress: From Fair Play to Power Plays*

William H. Hill, *No Place for Russia: European Security Institutions Since 1989*

THE INTERNATIONAL DEFENSE OF WORKERS

Labor Rights, U.S. Trade Agreements, and State Sovereignty

KEVIN J. MIDDLEBROOK

Columbia University Press

New York

Columbia University Press
Publishers Since 1893
New York   Chichester, West Sussex
cup.columbia.edu

Library of Congress Cataloging-in-Publication Data
Names: Middlebrook, Kevin J., author.
Title: The international defense of workers : labor rights, U.S. trade
  agreements, and state sovereignty / Kevin J. Middlebrook.
Description: New York : Columbia University Press, [2024] | Series: Woodrow
  Wilson center series | Includes bibliographical references and index.
Identifiers: LCCN 2023027341 (print) | LCCN 2023027342 (ebook) |
  ISBN 9780231213424 (hardback) | ISBN 9780231213431 (trade paperback) |
  ISBN 9780231559881 (ebook)
Subjects: LCSH: Employee rights—United States. | International trade. |
  Collective labor agreements—United States. | Social responsibility of
  business—United States.
Classification: LCC HD6971.8 .M54 2024 (print) | LCC HD6971.8 (ebook) |
  DDC 331.01/10973—dc23/eng/20231204
LC record available at https://lccn.loc.gov/2023027341
LC ebook record available at https://lccn.loc.gov/2023027342

Cover design: Chang Jae Lee
Cover image: Diego Rivera, *Miners in Guerrero* (c. 1936) © 2023 Banco de México Diego
Rivera Frida Kahlo Museums Trust, Mexico, D.F. / Artists Rights Society (ARS),
New York

To Mariel

Contents

List of Acronyms and Abbreviations   ix

1. The International Defense of Labor Rights: Concepts, Policy Arenas, and the Challenge of State Sovereignty   1

2. Pathways to the North American Agreement on Labor Cooperation: From Multilateral Proposals to Unilateral Actions Linking Labor Rights and Trade Agreements   39

3. Context and Constraints: The Origin and Negotiation of the North American Free Trade Agreement's Labor Rights Provisions   68

4. The North American Agreement on Labor Cooperation in Principle and in Practice, 1994–2020   118

5. Legacies of the North American Agreement on Labor Cooperation: Labor Rights, U.S. Free-Trade Agreements, and U.S.-Mexican Negotiations over the Trans-Pacific Partnership, 2001–2017   189

6. Renegotiating the North American Free Trade Agreement: Labor Rights and the United States-Mexico-Canada Agreement, 2017–2019   245

7. Labor Rights, Trade Agreements, State Sovereignty: Past Record and Future Prospects   289

Acknowledgments   319

*Appendix A: Statistical Analysis of U.S. Generalized System of Preferences Cases,
1985–1995   321*

*Appendix B: Annotated List of NAALC Public Communications Submitted
to the Canadian, Mexican, and U.S. National Administrative Offices (NAOs),
1994–2020   325*

*Appendix C: Annotated List of Public Submissions to the U.S. Office of Trade
and Labor Affairs (OTLA), 2008–2016   339*

*Appendix D: Annotated List of Rapid Response Mechanism Petitions Concerning
Mexico Submitted to the U.S. Interagency Labor Committee for Monitoring
and Enforcement, 2021–2022   343*

Notes   349

Bibliography   491

Index   543

Acronyms and Abbreviations

ACHR	American Convention on Human Rights
AFL-CIO	American Federation of Labor-Congress of Industrial Organizations
ANAD	Asociación Nacional de Abogados Democráticos / National Association of Democratic Lawyers
ASPAM	Asociación Sindical de Pilotos Aviadores de México / Mexican Association of Airline Pilots
ASSAM	Asociación Sindical de Sobrecargos de Aviación de México / Mexican Association of Airline Flight Attendants
CAW	Canadian Auto Workers
CBERA	Caribbean Basin Economic Recovery Act
CBI	Caribbean Basin Initiative
CCC	Clean Clothes Campaign
CCCs	corporate codes of conduct
CCE	Consejo Coordinador Empresarial / Private Sector Coordinating Council
CEACR	Committee of Experts on the Application of Conventions and Recommendations (ILO)
CEDAW	Convention on the Elimination of All Forms of Discrimination Against Women
CFA	Committee on Freedom of Association (ILO)
CFCRL	Centro Federal de Conciliación y Registro Laboral / Federal Center for Conciliation and Labor Registration
CFE	Comisión Federal de Electricidad / Federal Electrical Commission

CIDE	Centro de Investigación y Docencia Económicas / Center for Economic Research and Teaching
CIOAC	Central Independiente de Obreros Agrícolas y Campesinos / Independent Central of Agricultural Workers and Peasants
CIPM	Coordinadora Inter-sindical Primero de Mayo / May 1 Inter-Union Coordinating Network
CJM	Coalition for Justice in the Maquiladoras
CLC	Canadian Labour Congress
CNDH	Comisión Nacional de Derechos Humanos / National Human Rights Commission
CNTE	Coordinadora Nacional de Trabajadores de la Educación / National Coordinating Committee of Education Workers
COPARMEX	Confederación Patronal de la República Mexicana / Mexican Employers' Confederation
CROC	Confederación Revolucionaria de Obreros y Campesinos / Revolutionary Confederation of Workers and Peasants
CROM	Confederación Regional Obrera Mexicana / Mexican Regional Labor Confederation
CSQ	Centrale des Syndicats du Québec / Quebec Labor Central
CSR	corporate social responsibility
CTM	Confederación de Trabajadores de México / Confederation of Mexican Workers
CUSFTA	Canada-United States Free Trade Agreement
CUSWA	United Steelworkers-Canada
CWA	Communications Workers of America
DR-CAFTA	Dominican Republic-Central America-United States Trade Agreement
EAP	economically active population
EPZ	export-processing zone
ETI	Ethical Trading Initiative
EU	European Union
FAT	Frente Auténtico del Trabajo / Authentic Labor Front
FESEBS	Federación de Sindicatos de Empresas de Bienes y Servicios / Federation of Unions of Goods and Services Enterprises
FLA	Fair Labor Association
FLOC	Farm Labor Organizing Committee

FSM	Frente Sindical Mexicano / Mexican Union Front
FSTSE	Federación de Sindicatos de Trabajadores al Servicio del Estado / Federation of Public Service Workers' Unions
FTA	free-trade agreement
FTQ	Fédération des travailleurs et travailleuses du Québec / Québec Workers Federation
GATT	General Agreement on Tariffs and Trade
GDP	gross domestic product
GSP	generalized system of preferences
GUF	global union federation
IACtHR	Inter-American Court of Human Rights
IAMAW	International Association of Machinists and Aerospace Workers
IBT	International Brotherhood of Teamsters
ICCPR	International Covenant on Civil and Political Rights
ICEM	International Federation of Chemical, Energy, Mine and General Workers' Unions
ICESCR	International Covenant on Economic, Social and Cultural Rights
ICFTU	International Confederation of Free Trade Unions
IFA	International Framework Agreement
IFTU	International Federation of Trade Unions
ILC	International Labour Conference (ILO)
ILCME	Interagency Labor Committee for Monitoring and Enforcement
ILO	International Labour Organization
ILRERF	International Labor Rights Education and Research Fund (1986)
ILRF	International Labor Rights Forum (1996)
ILWU	International Longshore and Warehouse Union
IMF	International Metalworkers' Federation
INEGI	Instituto Nacional de Estadística, Geografía e Informática / National Institute of Statistics, Geography, and Informatics
ITGLWF	International Textile, Garment and Leather Workers' Federation
ITO	International Trade Organization

ITS	international trade secretariats
ITUC	International Trade Union Confederation
IUF	International Union of Food, Agricultural, Hotel, Restaurant, Catering, Tobacco, and Allied Workers' Associations
IWMA	International Working Men's Association
JFCA	Junta Federal de Conciliación y Arbitraje / Federal Conciliation and Arbitration Board
JLCA	junta local de conciliación y arbitraje / local conciliation and arbitration board
LFT	Ley Federal del Trabajo / Federal Labor Law
LFTSE	Ley Federal de los Trabajadores al Servicio del Estado / Federal Law for Public Service Workers
LyFC	Luz y Fuerza del Centro / Central Light and Power
MORENA	Movimiento Regeneración Nacional / National Regeneration Movement
MSN	Maquila Solidarity Network
NAALC	North American Agreement on Labor Cooperation
NACLC	North American Commission on Labor Cooperation
NAFTA	North American Free Trade Agreement
NAO	national administrative office
NGO	nongovernmental organization
NLRB	National Labor Relations Board
OCAW	Oil, Chemical, and Atomic Workers
OECD	Organization for Economic Co-Operation and Development
OPIC	Overseas Private Investment Corporation
OTCA	Overseas Trade and Competitiveness Act (1988)
OTLA	Office of Trade and Labor Affairs (U.S. Department of Labor)
PACE	Paper, Allied-Industrial, Chemical, and Energy Workers
PAN	Partido Acción Nacional / National Action Party
PANAL	Partido Nueva Alianza / New Alliance Party
PRD	Partido de la Revolución Democrática / Party of the Democratic Revolution
PRI	Partido Revolucionario Institucional / Institutional Revolutionary Party

RMALC	Red Mexicana de Acción frente al Libre Comercio / Mexican Action Network Against Free Trade
SCJN	Suprema Corte de Justicia de la Nación / Mexican Supreme Court
SCMW	Support Committee for Maquiladora Workers
SEIU	Service Employees International Union
SINTTIA	Sindicato Independiente Nacional de Trabajadores y Trabajadoras de la Industria Automotriz y las Adhesivas / National Independent Union of Automotive and Related Industry Workers
SME	Sindicato Mexicano de Electricistas/Mexican Electricians' Union
SNTMMSRM	Sindicato Nacional de Trabajadores Mineros, Metalúrgicos y Similares de la República Mexicana / National Union of Mexican Mineworkers and Metalworkers
STIMAHCS	Sindicato de Trabajadores en la Industria Metálica, Acero, Hierro, Conexos y Similares / Union of Workers in the Metal, Iron, Steel, and Related and Similar Industries
STPS	Secretaría del Trabajo y Previsión Social / Ministry of Labor and Social Welfare
STRM	Sindicato de Telefonistas de la República Mexican / Mexican Telephone Workers Union
SUTSP	Sindicato Único de Trabajadores de la Secretaría de Pesca / General Union of Workers at the Ministry of Fishing
TPP	Trans-Pacific Partnership Agreement
UAW	United Automobile, Aerospace, and Agricultural Implement Workers of America
UDHR	Universal Declaration on Human Rights
UE	United Electrical, Radio, and Machine Workers of America
UFCWIU	United Food and Commercial Workers International Union
UN	United Nations
UNITE!	Union of Needletrade, Industrial, and Textile Employees
UNT	Unión Nacional de Trabajadores / National Union of Workers
UPIU	United Paperworkers International Union
USAS	United Students Against Sweatshops

U.S. DOL	U.S. Department of Labor
U.S. GSP	U.S. Generalized System of Preferences
USMCA	United States-Mexico-Canada Agreement
USTR	Office of the United States Trade Representative
USW	United Steelworkers (United Steel, Paper and Forestry, Rubber, Manufacturing, Energy, Allied Industrial and Service Workers International Union)
WFTU	World Federation of Trade Unions
WRC	Worker Rights Consortium
WTO	World Trade Organization

THE INTERNATIONAL DEFENSE OF WORKERS

CHAPTER 1

The International Defense of Labor Rights

Concepts, Policy Arenas, and the Challenge of State Sovereignty

Efforts to define and defend workers' rights are as old as wage labor itself. Although these struggles have always been centered principally in the workplace and in national public policy arenas, debates concerning the legitimate scope of labor rights and the means for advancing them have become increasingly international. This process has been driven forward both by key events and pressures from entrepreneurs and labor organizations themselves, and it has been strongly reinforced by an expanding international consensus in support of human rights more generally.[1] Since its creation in 1919, the International Labour Organization (ILO)—the only survivor among the international organizations established under the Treaty of Versailles and the principal norms-setting agency on labor rights—has been the main forum for discussions among labor organizations, business groups, and national governments regarding which worker protections enjoy broad support and how best to ensure them in practice.[2] The growing post-World War II international consensus in favor of human rights (including core labor rights) bolstered the ILO's position. In the late twentieth and early twenty-first centuries, deepening concerns about the social justice consequences of intensified international economic competition gave new prominence to such matters as forced labor, child labor, the freedoms to organize and bargain collectively, and workplace safety and health.

Despite a strengthening consensus over time in favor of an expanding range of worker protections, international actions to defend labor rights are politically sensitive because, with the partial exceptions of cross-border solidarity initiatives launched by labor organizations and corporate social responsibility campaigns undertaken by nongovernmental groups, these efforts often centrally engage the question of state sovereignty. The creation of the ILO marked an important step away from the most traditional conceptualizations of state sovereignty, which held that states had absolute authority over their domestic affairs. The decision-making model employed by the ILO mitigates sovereignty concerns because its labor rights conventions become legally binding only when member states formally ratify and adopt them into domestic labor legislation. Even so, it was the post–World War II sea change in international norms regarding human rights that pushed back sovereignty limits and expanded the ILO's scope for action.[3] Quite tellingly, it was only after the United Nations General Assembly published the Universal Declaration of Human Rights in 1948 that the ILO adopted landmark conventions regarding the politically intrusive issues of workers' rights to organize and bargain collectively.

Embedding labor rights provisions in trade agreements has often been particularly controversial. Although debates regarding links between trade and labor standards date from the early nineteenth century, formal recognition of this linkage in a multilateral agreement came only in the 1948 Havana Charter, which was negotiated as the basis for a proposed international trade organization. Yet despite persistent lobbying by labor organizations and some national governments, no such provision was ever included in the General Agreement on Tariffs and Trade (GATT). Beginning in the early 1980s, increasing international economic competition led organized labor movements in industrialized countries to promote labor rights provisions in generalized system of preferences (GSP) programs, preferential trade agreements that industrialized countries established under the GATT to give developing countries expanded access to their markets.[4] The labor provisions in these programs were somewhat less contentious as a means of advancing labor rights because, even though industrialized countries retained full autonomy in the terms under which they granted market access, participation in them was on a bilateral basis. However, sovereignty concerns resurfaced prominently when the focus of debate shifted back to a rights-based social charter in a multilateral trade agreement. Indeed, labor rights advocates failed in their efforts to insert a social charter into the agreement establishing the World Trade Organization (WTO), which was created in 1995 to replace the GATT. The principal opposition came from many developing country governments that feared that labor organizations in industrialized countries would turn any such worker-protection provisions into a disguised form of protectionism and thereby undercut their national comparative advantage as low-wage economic competitors.

In this context, the adoption of the North American Agreement on Labor Cooperation (NAALC) in 1993 as a side agreement to the North American Free Trade Agreement (NAFTA) constituted a watershed in the international promotion of labor rights. Even with growing international consensus in favor of worker protections, the NAALC set several important historical precedents. Not only was it the first occasion on which labor rights provisions were linked to a U.S. free-trade agreement, but the labor complaints filed under NAALC procedures also elicited significant displays of cross-border solidarity among North American trade unions and labor- and human-rights groups. Many observers have criticized the NAALC for its constrained dispute-resolution procedures and its very limited capacity to correct rights violations in the workplace. Nonetheless, it established a crucial precedent for embedding labor rights protections in preferential trade agreements and set the terms of debate for all the free-trade agreements (FTAs) subsequently negotiated by the United States with developing countries. Moreover, although some complaints were lodged under the labor rights provisions of later U.S. FTAs, the significantly larger number of complaints filed under the NAALC concerning alleged rights violations in Canada, Mexico, and the United States constitute an indispensable empirical base for addressing the broader research question posed in this book: Under what conditions are the labor provisions in U.S. preferential trade agreements an efficacious strategy for defending worker rights internationally? For all these reasons, the NAALC is an important object of scholarly investigation.

This book analyzes the NAALC experience as a foundational (substantively important) case in the evolution of debates over the labor rights/trade linkage in U.S. policy and the international defense of workers' rights.[5] It examines the political origins of the agreement both in earlier twentieth-century efforts to insert labor-standards provisions into multilateral and U.S. preferential trade agreements and in the 1990–1992 negotiations over the NAFTA; the intense political controversies that arose in 1993 among Canada, Mexico, and the United States over the NAALC's scope and institutional design; its operation in practice between 1994 and 2020 and its principal successes and failures; and the longer-term policy legacies of the NAALC both in subsequent U.S. FTAs and in the 2017–2019 negotiations over revising the NAFTA and the labor rights provisions of the successor United States-Mexico-Canada Agreement (USMCA). There is extensive literature on the diplomatic negotiations among Canada, Mexico, and the United States over the adoption of the NAFTA, as well as on many of the individual labor rights complaints filed under the NAALC. Publications on the NAALC range from a plethora of law review articles written in the 1990s assessing its potential importance to a series of reports by U.S. and Canadian trade unions and labor-rights groups critically examining the outcome of early complaints and questioning the agreement's practical impact on rights violations in Mexico. Many of these initial assessments accurately highlighted the NAALC's restricted enforcement provisions, but they were perhaps too quick to dismiss its longer-term political legacies. Nor do previous studies examine in depth the impact of NAALC complaints on the politics of labor law reform and policy enforcement in Mexico.

Attaching labor rights protections to trade agreements is a relatively new phenomenon in international affairs, which makes the NAALC and its legacies a subject worthy of close analysis. However, trade agreement–linked labor provisions such as the NAALC are not the only arena for the international defense of workers' rights, nor was the NAFTA the only U.S. trade agreement to include labor protections. This book therefore establishes a comparative context for an assessment of the NAALC experience in two different ways. First, this introductory chapter briefly overviews three alternative international arenas for the promotion of labor rights: cross-border union solidarity actions, initiatives undertaken by the ILO, and corporate social responsibility campaigns.

Second, later chapters examine the negotiation, content, and implementation of labor rights provisions included in the U.S. GSP program (chapter 2), post-NAFTA U.S. free-trade agreements (chapter 5), and the USMCA (chapter 6). Because the content of these provisions and the terms for their implementation evolved significantly between 1984 and 2019, this case selection permits a structured, focused comparison of the policy impact of the labor protections in different U.S. trade agreements, which constitute the principal international examples of labor rights/trade linkage.[6]

The tension between state sovereignty and the international promotion of labor rights lies at the heart of this analysis. The positions that developing country governments adopt vis-à-vis international labor rights norms can vary greatly depending upon differences in domestic political and economic circumstances and the specific rights in question. However, national political authorities' resistance to international norms—both to adopting them as law and to implementing them in practice—has historically been strongest with regard to freedom of association and the rights to organize and bargain collectively. If sovereign resistance poses a substantial obstacle to the international promotion of these rights, then logically, the potentially most influential strategies available to rights promoters in an international system of states would be those that leverage state sovereignty to positive effect—that is, strategies that bring one (generally more powerful) state's sovereign rights to bear against those of another (generally weaker) state. Yet, as a later section of this chapter shows, actions undertaken in other international labor rights arenas generally pose only oblique challenges to state resistance to rights promotion. In contrast, both negotiations over a developing country's participation in a U.S. trade agreement (in which the fulcrum of U.S. sovereignty leverage is the government's decision whether to grant another country access to the U.S. domestic market) and the subsequent implementation of its labor provisions place workers' rights, including the freedom of association and the right to collective bargaining, at the center of state-to-state interactions. A detailed reconstruction of U.S. negotiations with Mexico over the Trans-Pacific Partnership agreement (chapter 5) and the USMCA (chapter 6) and with several other developing-country trade partners (chapters 5 and 7) and a careful analysis of the implementation of U.S. GSP labor provisions (chapter 2) show that the United States is particularly capable of exercising its sovereignty leverage to positive effect when access to the U.S. market is at stake.

This book's most important research contribution is its systematic assessment of the efficacy of the NAALC and the labor-rights provisions in other U.S. trade agreements as means for defending workers' rights, with particular reference to the freedom of association and the rights to organize and bargain collectively. However, it also contributes to broader debates concerning the international promotion of human rights by focusing on the role of state actors. Research on nongovernmental norms entrepreneurs, epistemic communities, and transnational human rights action networks has substantially reshaped the study of international relations.[7] National governments form part of these rights-promotion chains, but they are often presented as little more than black boxes where internal decision-making processes and state-to-state interactions are concerned.[8] Because trade agreements are formal intergovernmental accords, they "bring the state back in" and necessarily make national governments central actors in the implementation of their labor rights provisions.[9] There certainly is scope for debate whether placing governments in this position is, on balance, a positive or negative factor for labor rights promotion. Yet the key role that governments play in this process does mandate close attention to the broad range of national interests involved and the character of these state-to-state interactions.

Because the progressively greater acceptance of labor rights as human rights helped establish the political conditions leading to the insertion of labor protections into U.S. trade agreements and has strongly influenced such rights-promotion strategies as corporate social responsibility campaigns, this chapter begins by tracing the evolution of this debate from the late nineteenth through the twentieth centuries. It also examines the tension—both in international law and in political and social practice—between state sovereignty and the international promotion of workers' rights. The following section then compares alternative international policy arenas for the defense of labor rights in terms of several issues that will be central to both an examination of the NAALC experience and the promotion of labor rights under other U.S. trade agreements: the sociopolitical actors typically involved; the principal object of their actions (for instance, private companies or national governments); the main issues generally in contention; and the typical policy impacts of actions undertaken in these different arenas, especially with regard to the capacity of labor organizations and labor-rights groups to challenge sovereignty obstacles and advance freedom of association and the rights to organize and bargain collectively. The final section of this chapter develops an analytic framework for assessing the conditions under which sovereignty leverage can be employed to advance labor rights internationally and discusses the principal research methods and data sources employed in this book.

THE INTERNATIONALIZATION OF LABOR RIGHTS

The internationalization of labor rights has been closely linked to an expanding international consensus in favor of human rights more broadly defined. These processes have been driven forward both by continuing campaigns by major sociopolitical actors and by the events-based international moral shocks that have been decisive in the emergence and evolution of human rights regimes.[10] Labor organizations' efforts to establish international worker-rights protections have often reflected a combination of material self-interest and ethical commitment.

The internationalization of labor rights arguably began with efforts by the International Working Men's Association (also known as the First International) in the 1860s to promote demands for the eight-hour working day among its West European affiliates.[11] However, the formation of the ILO in 1919—a development that was in significant part a capitalist-state response to the fears of worker unrest unleashed by the first successful socialist revolution in Russia in 1917—was particularly significant in this regard.[12] The formal adoption and enforcement of the ILO's principal policy statements (conventions) fall to sovereign states. Yet the tripartite structure—unique among major international organizations—of the chief ILO decision-making bodies (with government, labor, and employer representatives) and the consensual process through which ILO policies are formulated imbue them with considerable international legitimacy.[13] The degree of acceptance or legitimacy expands as more states subscribe to them.

The creation of the ILO certainly reflected the growing political influence of organized labor movements in West European countries, but it also coincided with—and greatly benefited from—initial shifts in international sentiment concerning the sovereign rights of states. Until the negotiation of the Treaty of Versailles in 1919 and related interstate treaties protecting the rights of minority populations in European countries, the strong consensus in international law was that the way in which national governments treat their citizens or subjects was "not a subject of legitimate international concern."[14] For this reason, the fact that the League of Nations Covenant included among its stated goals "fair and humane conditions of labour for men, women and children" represented an important departure. Indeed, some advocates for the ILO argue that the body's tripartite approach "implied that conditions of labour and social policy were recognized from the beginning of the new era of international organizations as appropriate subjects for interstate action."[15] The league did not, however, go so far as to establish "meaningful international rights or obligations which protect human beings as human beings," and colonial powers blocked other international human rights initiatives during the interwar period.[16]

For these reasons, in its first two decades, the ILO focused principally on important but relatively narrow individual worker rights and such social issues as working time, social security, child labor, employment policy, and wages. Of the sixty-seven conventions adopted by the ILO between 1919 and 1939, a total of thirty conventions (44.8 percent of the total) addressed working time and social security (fifteen each), and another twelve conventions (17.9 percent) focused on issues affecting seafarers. Only one of the eight conventions that the ILO subsequently characterized as "fundamental" (no. 29, concerning forced or compulsory labor in the private sector) was adopted during this period (in 1930), and the ILO rarely invoked moral standards or specifically employed "rights" language in the conventions it adopted before World War II.[17] Similarly, even though the preamble to the ILO's 1919 constitution had recognized "the right of association for all lawful purposes by the employed as well as by the employers" as one of its general principles, only one of the actionable conventions adopted before World War II and the consequent shift in international attitudes regarding the limits of state sovereignty addressed collective labor rights (no. 11, stating that agricultural workers should have the same right to association as industrial workers).[18] In fact, of the nine principles specified in the ILO's original constitution, five focused on such issues as wages, working time, child labor, and policy enforcement.[19]

The decisive institutionalization of international labor rights occurred in conjunction with the creation of the United Nations human rights system. Debates about international human rights began with the outbreak of World War II and were pushed forward by U.S. President Franklin D. Roosevelt's "Four Freedoms" State of the Union address on January 6, 1941, and by the Atlantic Charter, the document signed on August 14, 1941, in which Roosevelt and British Prime Minister Winston Churchill defined Allied powers' goals for the postwar world.[20] The charter's principles, including "human rights and justice," were endorsed by 26 Allied states in the January 1–2, 1942, declaration by the United Nations and by all states forming the United Nations Organization in August 1945.[21] The ILO contributed significantly to this normative shift by issuing the Declaration of Philadelphia on May 10, 1944, which reiterated its commitment to promoting social justice as a basis for ensuring international peace, reaffirmed freedom of association and the right to collective bargaining as fundamental principles underpinning the ILO (sections I[b], III[c]), and underscored the close links between labor rights and human rights more generally.[22] Some analysts mark the declaration as the first assertion of "universal social rights of the individual."[23]

Although the Universal Declaration of Human Rights (UDHR) that the United Nations General Assembly adopted on December 10, 1948, was a nonbinding resolution, it marked a crucial advance in codifying evolving international understandings regarding human rights.[24] For example, in addition to stipulating that "everyone has the right to life, liberty and security of the person" (article 3), precluding torture and degrading treatment or punishment (article 5), and barring arbitrary arrest or detention (article 9), the declaration guarantees the freedoms of expression, assembly, and association (articles 19, 20 [1]).[25]

Reflecting the ILO's work over preceding decades, it also recognizes a broad range of economic, social, and political rights for workers, including the rights to work, equal pay for equal work, just remuneration, limitations on working hours, paid holidays, and so forth (articles 23-25). Article 23(4) states unequivocally that "everyone has the right to form and to join trade unions for the protection of his interests."[26]

The United Nations adopted two further key agreements on December 16, 1966, both of which came into force following ratification by thirty-five member states: the International Covenant on Civil and Political Rights (ICCPR, in effect since March 23, 1976), and the International Covenant on Economic, Social and Cultural Rights (ICESCR, in effect since January 3, 1976).[27] Both covenants, reflecting the norms established by the ILO and the political influence of organized labor in democratic capitalist societies, directly address labor rights.[28] In its substantial list of civil and political rights, the ICCPR's article 22(1) restates the UDHR's guarantee of freedom of association and "the right to form and join trade unions." Indeed, article 22(3) explicitly endorses the ILO's convention no. 87 (adopted in 1948) concerning the freedom of association and the right to organize.[29] The ICESCR, in turn, includes among its expansive list of rights "the right of everyone to form trade unions . . . for the promotion and protection of his economic and social interests" (art. 8(1)[a]).[30] Like the ICCPR, the ICESCR's article 8(3) specifically reaffirms ILO convention no. 87.

Some analysts argue that fundamental human rights have *jus cogens* status— that is, they are "part of international law to which states commit irrespective of whether or not they are party to individual treaties."[31] Others, however, emphasize that the UDHR did not formally impose binding obligations on states and that the multiple rights detailed in the ICCPR and the ICESCR are obligatory only for states that voluntarily accede to them.[32] Even in the case of fundamental rights of the individual, none of the rights articulated in these documents is absolute or unconditional. Their exercise can be limited by states, either to protect the rights and freedoms of others or in the public interest (for instance, in order to safeguard public order or national security).[33] The fact that the ICESCR only requires each signatory state to meet its obligations progressively over time "to the maximum of its available resources" (art. 2[1]) clearly limits the practical realization of the rights it articulates.[34]

Nevertheless, by the time the ICCPR and the ICESCR came into force, there was a clear international consensus in favor of broadly defined human rights, including core labor rights. For example, in April–May 1968, the World Conference on Human Rights in Tehran declared (the Proclamation of Tehran) that the UDHR is "a common understanding of the peoples of the world concerning the inalienable and inviolable rights of all members of the human family and constitutes an obligation for the members of the international community."[35] Risse and Ropp (2013: 9) note that "in the twenty-first century, there is not a single state left in the international system that has not ratified at least one international human rights treaty."[36] By 2021, 173 of the United Nations' 193 member states (89.6 percent) had become parties to the ICCPR, and 171 of the member states (88.6 percent) were parties to the ICESCR.[37]

STATE SOVEREIGNTY VERSUS LABOR RIGHTS: THE DOUBLE HELIX

There is no doubt, then, that there is an extensive international consensus in support of human rights, including labor rights broadly defined.[38] Nevertheless, as Donnelly (2007) cogently argues, "Enforcement of authoritative international human rights norms . . . is left almost entirely to sovereign states" (283) . . . "Except in cases of genocide, sovereignty still ultimately trumps human rights" (289).[39] Indeed, despite evolution over time in the meanings of sovereignty and the growing importance of nonstate actors in defining international human rights norms, state sovereignty significantly shapes the recognition of human rights and the implementation of rights guarantees in at least three ways.[40]

First, Westphalian sovereignty—the central idea that states as political organizations are "based on the exclusion of external actors from authority structures within a given territory"—limits the overall expansion of human rights regimes.[41] A state may voluntarily accede to a human rights agreement under which it pledges to observe certain standards, thus placing domestic practices under external scrutiny. The actual challenge that such agreements pose to Westphalian sovereignty depends upon the impact they have in practice on domestic authorities' political control.[42] Yet the de facto segmentation of international human rights regimes reflects states' overall sensitivity to such potential risks to the autonomy of domestic authority. For example, Donnelly's characterization of human rights regimes differentiates among declaratory, promotional, implementation, and enforcement regimes. This spectrum ranges from the simple

articulation of widely accepted norms (declaratory), to international information exchanges and nonintrusive assistance (promotional), to policy coordination and weak monitoring procedures (implementation), to strong monitoring
and authoritative international decision making (enforcement).[43] States have
generally successfully resisted the shift from promotional to implementation and
enforcement regimes.[44] Despite advances involving the International Criminal
Court, human rights agreements that empower supranational judicial authorities
to enforce rights guarantees are rare precisely because they directly impinge on
Westphalian sovereignty.[45]

Second, because of sovereignty concerns, the international consensus in favor
of (and the degree of national resistance to) rights varies in practice across different kinds or categories of rights. The debate over international humanitarian
intervention illustrates this point. Both the concept and practice of international
humanitarian intervention date from the 1990s; some analysts identify it as a
post–Cold War phenomenon and an example of the strengthening ideological
hegemony of human rights, reinforced by the international moral shocks produced by genocide in Bosnia, Rwanda, Kosovo, and East Timor.[46] Its merits are
still much debated because the United Nations' commitment to the principle
of Westphalian sovereignty is clear.[47] Nonetheless, even the strongest advocates
of forceful international action to block gross human rights violations by a sovereign state accept that the practice is restricted to the extreme case of genocide.[48] No human rights advocate seriously suggests action of this kind to prevent
such rights violations as a national government's suppression of the rights of free
speech, assembly, or association.

The concept of rights derogation further illustrates the way in which state sovereignty concerns establish a de facto internal hierarchy among different human
rights.[49] The preamble of the 1948 UDHR refers to "the equal and inalienable
rights of all members of the human family," and the 1993 Vienna Declaration
and Programme of Action—the product of a more inclusive, post–Cold War
deliberative process that was adopted by consensus by the representatives of 172
states—declares that "All human rights are universal, indivisible, and interdependent and interrelated" (paragraph 5).[50] In strict international law terms, then,
there is no agreed rights hierarchy.[51] Yet foundational human rights documents
do distinguish between those rights that states can and cannot derogate. The
ICCPR, for example, recognizes (article 4) that states can derogate from their
obligations "in time of public emergency which threatens the life of the nation

and the existence of which is publicly proclaimed." However, article 4(2) stipulates that states cannot derogate from certain core individual rights: the inherent right to life (article 6); freedom from torture or cruel, inhuman, or degrading treatment or punishment (article 7); the prohibition against slavery and servitude (article 8); rights to due legal process (articles 11, 15, 16); and the freedoms of thought, conscience, religion, and expression (article 18). These provisions reflect the simple reality that there is, in effect, greater international consensus in favor of some rights (particularly those "core rights which are directly related to human existence,"[52] such as the prohibition against genocide or torture) than others (for instance, a broad range of social rights and more recent issues such as the "rights of peoples").

Finally, Weberian (domestic) sovereignty, "the ability of public authorities to exercise effective control within the borders of their own polity,"[53] is also of crucial importance where the implementation of rights guarantees is concerned.[54] Even though a state may accede to human rights treaties and recognize rights in principle, effective implementation of these commitments depends upon its ability to do so. This is generally a question of legal authority and practical administrative capacity. However, different kinds of rights engage domestic sovereignty in different ways, and they pose distinctive political and legal challenges. Special difficulties may arise in federal systems in which different governmental units exercise independent legal authority. In recognition of this constraint, the federal governments of Canada, Mexico, the United States, and several other countries have made recognition of these jurisdictional boundaries a condition of their accession to international agreements.[55]

In the specific case of labor rights, tensions clearly exist between state sovereignty and the recognition and implementation of different rights guarantees. Donnelly (2013: 246) maintains that "the area of worker rights remains the domain of internationally recognized human rights where standards are most fully developed and multinational monitoring is most advanced."[56] In part, this reflects the fact that core worker rights have long enjoyed broad international legitimacy; indeed, they are a prime example of a "script of modernity" that all modern states follow.[57] The very longevity of the ILO and its unique tripartite structure—an established forum in which an active consensus can be formed through the regular interaction of government, labor, and business representatives—are also important in this regard. Yet it is also the case that ILO conventions do not frontally challenge Westphalian sovereignty because they become legally binding only when states voluntarily ratify and adopt them as domestic labor law.[58] A national government responsible for gross violations of workers' rights may face ILO censure and intense international condemnation, but its sovereignty is not directly at stake.

Even so, the interplay between Westphalian and Weberian sovereignty concerns does shape states' external recognition and domestic implementation of different labor rights—in effect, segmenting individual and "collective-action" rights, the term adopted here to refer jointly to the freedom of association and the rights to organize and bargain collectively.[59] The strongest international consensus around workers' rights involves those issues most closely associated with the welfare of the human person, including such issues as forced and compulsory labor, child labor, discrimination in employment, workplace safety and health, wages and employment conditions, and so forth. The rights to organize and bargain collectively are, strictly speaking, also individual rights in the sense that they involve actions taken by individuals; the ICCPR and ICESCR recognize the rights to organize and bargain collectively as core rights, but they do not award special status to the collective worker organizations that are the product of such actions.

However, collective-action rights pose a much greater potential challenge than individual worker rights to state officials' exercise of their public authority. All labor rights inherently have both political and economic dimensions, and in capitalist democracies, collective-action rights in particular link both the public and the private sectors because they are invoked in the context of worker-employer relations and struggles over the organization of economic production in the workplace. In some cases, union ties to opposition political forces—or even the mere existence of independent organized groups—may also pose a threat to those in power. As a consequence, there has been notably less international consensus regarding (and greater state resistance to) the adoption and international monitoring of collective-action rights than individual labor rights because the former cut to the heart of state sovereignty in the classic Weberian meaning of the term.[60] It is significant in this regard that the ILO conventions concerning freedom of association (no. 87, which held in articles 2 and 3(2) that workers and employers have the right to form organizations without previous authorization or interference by public authorities) and the right to collective bargaining (no. 98) were only adopted in 1948 and 1949, respectively, following the proclamation of the UNDR and a historic shift in international support for human rights broadly defined.[61]

Debates within the ILO regarding the right to strike offer a particularly instructive example of the way in which long-standing sovereignty concerns shape the articulation of international labor rights. Some analysts maintain that the ILO, in effect, has always recognized the right to strike. For example, Bellace (2014: 32–33) argues that the authors of the ILO's 1919 constitution employed the phrase "freedom of association" (recognized as a key principle in the preamble to the constitution) synonymously with "trade union rights," which they understood to include collective bargaining and industrial action. The ILO Committee of Experts on the Application of Conventions and Recommendations maintains that parts of convention no. 87 (articles 2, 3, 8, 10) establish a basis for the right to strike, and the Committee on Freedom of Association (CFA, created in 1951 to examine allegations of violations of conventions nos. 87 and 98) has, since 1952, taken the position that the right to strike is an essential element of trade union rights.[62] Indeed, in what was no doubt a significant moral and political victory for labor rights advocates, conventions nos. 87 and 98 were the first two listed in the ILO's Declaration on Fundamental Principles and Rights at Work in 1998.

Nevertheless, even though the ICESCR and regional social charters include protection of the right to strike in their guarantees of freedom of association,[63] there is no ILO convention specifically protecting the right to strike.[64] In fact, the ILO has, over the course of several decades, shied away from taking such a high-profile stance on the matter. In ILO debates about the right to strike that took place in 1926 and 1927, "some governments believed it an aspect of national sovereignty to maintain the ability to regulate workers' associations and their activities, because workers engaged in demonstrations and strikes for political purposes."[65] Employer representatives were opposed to ILO action on the question because they feared it would increase labor power; worker representatives were concerned that a formal statement might, in some ways, limit what labor organizations could do in exercising freedom of association. In its preparatory paper preceding the adoption of convention no. 87 in 1948, again in discussions concerning the CFA's mandate, and yet again in 1959 and 1970, the ILO declined to adopt a formal convention on the right to strike because of sovereignty objections.[66]

In summary, the relationship between state sovereignty and labor rights can be envisioned as a double helix—two intertwined (interrelated and mutually reinforcing) and descending hierarchies. Westphalian sovereign resistance is strongest where the recognition of collective-action rights is concerned because acceding to international standards in this area invites substantially closer international scrutiny of the established domestic political and economic order. This resistance diminishes with regard to individual labor rights about which there is near-universal consensus, such as the prohibition against the worst forms of child labor and minimum standards of workplace safety and health. Similarly, in the case of Weberian sovereignty, there is generally greater resistance to the enforcement of collective-action rights guarantees than to individual rights because the former are central elements of national political economy.

ALTERNATIVE INTERNATIONAL ARENAS FOR ADVANCING LABOR RIGHTS

Over time, international efforts to define, promote, and defend labor rights have played out in four principal policy arenas. Listed in terms of the approximate chronological order in which they came to prominence, these are: (1) cross-border, union-to-union solidarity actions, in which trade unions and their members in one or more countries offer moral and/or material solidarity support to fellow workers whose rights are under threat; (2) the International Labour Organization, the principal international norms agency responsible for defining different labor rights and encouraging member countries to ratify and implement them as national law; (3) the fora created by embedding labor rights in nonreciprocal preferential and free-trade agreements (of which the U.S. GSP program and the NAFTA/NAALC are but two of several examples);[67] and (4) corporate social responsibility (CSR) campaigns, through which labor rights activists exert pressure on transnational companies to adopt voluntary codes of corporate conduct and ensure compliance with basic labor rights across what are often far-flung supply chains and production networks.

Although these are the principal international arenas for the defense of labor rights broadly defined (that is, including both individual and collective-action rights), they are certainly not the only ones.[68] For example, several United Nations (UN) committees—the UN Human Rights Committee, the UN Committee on Economic, Social, and Cultural Rights, the UN Committee on the Elimination of Discrimination against Women, and the UN Committee on the Rights of the Child, among others—are empowered to hear complaints involving different labor rights. Yet, in practice, most such cases within the United Nations system are directed to the ILO because it is the principal UN specialized agency in the field.[69] Similarly, although regional human rights bodies such as the Inter-American Court of Human Rights (IACtHR) often hear labor cases, most of the complaints filed with the IACtHR involve individual labor rights (for example, the forced disappearance, extrajudicial execution, or assassination of trade union leaders or members); cases involving the rights to organize, bargain collectively, and strike rarely (if ever) come before them.[70] There have even been instances in which foreign labor organizations have sued U.S. transnational corporations in U.S. domestic courts, although this constitutes a comparatively restricted arena for the international defense of labor rights.[71]

Each of the international policy arenas discussed here is distinct, but labor rights actions undertaken in one or more of them often overlap. For instance, ILO-defined labor standards may constitute the basis for complaints filed under the labor provisions of U.S. preferential or free-trade agreements; indeed, the U.S. government has sometimes cited ILO conventions in complaints it has pursued under the NAALC and U.S. FTA labor rights procedures even when the United States itself had not ratified the ILO convention in question.[72] Cooperation on preparation of the complaint and lobbying for favorable U.S. government action in support of it may also help the submitting organizations develop sociopolitical networks and tactical experience that may later permit them to organize an effective CSR campaign.[73] Over time, the evolution of international rights promotion strategies—from, for example, cross-border union solidarity initiatives in the nineteenth and twentieth centuries to CSR campaigns in the late twentieth and early twenty-first centuries—has often encouraged rights advocates to act in multiple international arenas either at the same time or in close sequence.

What is particularly important in the context of the preceding discussion of labor rights and state sovereignty is that the rights/sovereignty interface differs substantially across these arenas. The greatest difference is between government-to-government interactions in the fora created by U.S. preferential and free-trade agreements and initiatives undertaken by the ILO. In the former, interactions between states necessarily engage sovereignty issues, even if the significance of sovereignty obstacles varies depending on the nature of the labor rights (individual versus collection-action) in contention. In contrast, because the ILO's constitution establishes that its conventions are only binding when formally ratified and adopted into national law by its member states, government-to-government confrontations rarely arise over them. Both union-to-union solidarity initiatives and CSR campaigns can, in principle, openly challenge a national government's overall labor policies. However, as the following discussion will show, sovereignty questions arise much less frequently in these arenas because, in practice, more contentious collective-action rights are rarely the principal focus of actions undertaken in them.

Sociopolitical actors' ease of access to these distinct arenas also differs considerably. The decision to initiate a cross-border union solidarity action or a CSR campaign lies entirely with those sociopolitical actors that are directly involved. Both labor (and employer) organizations and member states have regular access to ILO complaint procedures. In contrast, the U.S. government is the central player in labor rights complaints filed under U.S. preferential and free-trade agreements. Although the complaint procedures established by these agreements are broadly open to trade unions, human- and labor-rights groups, and even individuals, U.S. government officials hold final decision-making authority over whether to pursue allegations of rights violations lodged against other governments.

Chapters 2, 4, and 5 examine in depth the labor rights complaints filed under U.S. preferential and free-trade agreements between the mid-1980s and the late 2010s. The discussion in this section places that analysis in comparative context by briefly assessing cross-border union solidarity actions, efforts by the ILO to promote international labor standards, and CSR campaigns. The focus is on how these alternative international arenas compare in terms of: (1) the principal sociopolitical actors involved; (2) the main object of their actions (for instance, private companies or national governments); (3) the range of issues generally in contention, with particular attention to the relative prominence of collective-action rights; and (4) the typical policy impacts of initiatives undertaken in these different arenas, especially with regard to the capacity of labor organizations and rights activists to challenge sovereignty barriers and advance collective-action rights.

Cross-Border Union Solidarity Actions

Cross-border union solidarity actions, characteristically involving one or more trade unions or national labor organizations providing moral and material support to counterparts in another country, constitute the oldest and most frequented international arena for the defense of workers' rights. Indeed, as Hyman (2005: 137) notes, "Labour movement internationalism is as old as the idea of a labour movement itself." Documented examples stretch from the mid-nineteenth to the twenty-first centuries and span the compass in terms of the national base from which they emanate and the geographic location of solidarity counterparts: North-North, North-South, South-South, and even South-North.[74] This subsection briefly overviews the range of sociopolitical actors typically engaged in such actions and how this has evolved over time; the principal targets (for example, individual private companies and/or national governments) and issue foci of international solidarity initiatives; and the ways (if any) in which these cross-border actions may confront obstacles posed by state sovereignty to the promotion of collective-action rights.

Some of the earliest recorded instances of cross-border labor solidarity are among the most notable examples of activities undertaken in this arena. The international socialist movement was among the earliest proponents of cross-border cooperation among emergent working-class organizations.[75] The International Working Men's Association (IWMA) was formed in September 1864 to coordinate strike actions in Western Europe, but it also sought to shape broader international debates concerning workers' rights. For instance, delegates to its first international congress (held in Geneva in September 1866) adopted resolutions calling for a maximum eight-hour workday as an international standard and condemning excessively long working hours for children and women's employment in manufacturing activities.[76] Karl Marx, the IWMA's de facto leader until 1872, and Friedrich Engels also promoted networking on labor rights issues through communist correspondence societies and the formation of working-class political parties.[77]

Creating the capacity to initiate cross-border solidarity actions was a principal motivation for founding some of the earliest international labor organizations. Indeed, nineteenth-century solidarity movements had two lasting organizational legacies. First, international trade secretariats (ITSs), primarily Western Europe-centered international associations of national trade unions, formed to share information concerning wages and working conditions and coordinate transnational actions by workers in particular occupations and industries. For instance, glass bottle makers formed an international trade association in 1886 that united these skilled workers in a number of West European countries. The International Trade Secretariat, established in 1889, linked international federations of typographers and printers, hatters, cigar makers and tobacco workers, and boot and shoemakers.[78] Over time, these ITSs (known after 2002 as global union federations, GUFs) frequently reorganized and consolidated their memberships;[79] in 2022, there were a total of sixteen GUFs representing an international constellation of national unions in diverse occupations and industries.[80] One of the most prominent examples was the IndustriALL Global Union, which was formed in 2012 through a merger of the International Metalworkers' Federation; the International Federation of Chemical, Energy, Mine and General Workers' Unions (ICEM); and the International Textiles, Garment and Leather Workers' Federation (ITGLWF).

Second, in parallel with the formation of the ITSs, national labor organizations joined forces in overarching international labor confederations. West European unions formed an International Trade Union Secretariat in 1901, which regrouped as the International Federation of Trade Unions (IFTU) in 1913.[81] In turn, the World Federation of Trade Unions (WFTU), established in London in October 1945, replaced the IFTU and played an important role in lobbying the new United Nations' Economic and Social Council to provide broad guarantees for the exercise and development of trade union rights.[82] Cold War tensions split the WFTU in 1949, with West European and U.S. national trade union confederations seceding and creating the International Confederation of Free Trade Unions (ICFTU, whose motto was "Bread, Peace, Freedom." In 2006, the ICFTU merged with the social Christian-influenced World Confederation of Labour to form the International Trade Union Confederation (ITUC).[83] Other examples include the Christian-oriented World Organization of Workers and the anarcho-syndicalist International Workers' Association.

Over time, in conjunction with the internationalization of labor rights and the growing prominence of nongovernmental organizations (NGOs) committed to promoting human rights more generally, international labor- and human-rights groups and cross-border solidarity networks proliferated. Particularly after the 1970s, many of these groups and networks formed without formal ties to major trade unions, although leading unions and labor federations/confederations often constitute crucial allies and financial supporters.[84] They became especially active in defending the rights of women workers and workers in *maquiladora* (in-bond manufacturing) industries in developing countries. Some of them (for example, the Washington, DC-based International Labor Rights Forum [ILRF] and the Toronto, Canada-based Maquila Solidarity Network [MSN], founded in 1994) have regularly filed labor complaints—often in conjunction with trade unions but sometimes acting alone—under U.S. GSP and NAALC procedures.[85] Other important examples, among many more, include the U.S.-based Coalition for Justice in the Maquiladoras (CJM, San Antonio, Texas, 1989), United Students Against Sweatshops (Washington, DC, 1998), the Europe-based Clean Clothes Campaign (Amsterdam, 1989), and Ethical Trading Initiative (London, 1998).[86] The Women Working Worldwide network (Manchester, England, 1987) has sometimes even stood in for trade unions in organizing workers in union-hostile export-processing zones.[87] In other instances, NGOs have cooperated with trade unions to advance common goals (in, for example, an international antisweatshop campaign during the 1990s),[88] and they have also provided assistance to improve union capacity in developing countries.[89]

Because trade unions and their national and international organizations are central actors in this arena, freedom of association and the rights to organize and bargain collectively are consistently high issue priorities. In practice, however, international solidarity actions, both historical and contemporary, are frequently reactions to particular crises or events. They range from quite spontaneous manifestations of moral support, to pressures against a private firm or a national government to settle a protracted conflict over the terms of employment at a particular work site, to protests against the policies pursued by individual private companies or national governments.

- In May 1920, militant East London dockworkers refused to load arms and ammunition onto the S.S. *Jolly George* because they suspected that the cargo would, with the tacit support of British government authorities, help sustain Polish military attacks against Bolshevik Russia.[90]
- From the 1970s into the early 1990s, the ICFTU and ITSs played prominent roles in the international anti-apartheid campaign against white minority rule in the Republic of South Africa. These labor allies provided direct financial and advisory support to South African unions; lobbied for the release of imprisoned Black leaders; mobilized international opposition against restrictive domestic labor legislation; organized boycotts of South African products and monitored different countries' embargoes of South African imports; demanded that transnational companies alter their employment practices in South Africa; and brought sustained pressure to bear on different countries

to adopt anti-apartheid foreign policy measures, including economic sanctions.[91]

- In the course of a January 1990 work stoppage organized by dissident workers at Ford Motor Company's manufacturing plant in Cuautitlán, Mexico, to protest cuts in employment and fringe benefits and an unrepresentative union leadership, armed thugs hired by the company-aligned union local shot and killed one protesting worker and wounded eight others. In response, activist Ford workers in the United States and Canada publicly denounced the killing and formed the North American Ford Workers Solidarity Network. Three Minnesota-based labor activists highlighted the Ford-Cuautitlán case in the complaint they filed in 1991 challenging Mexico's designation as a U.S. GSP beneficiary.[92]
- In the early 1990s, concerted support from major U.S. textile and garment workers' unions and the ITGLWF helped employees at the Bibong Apparel Co.'s subsidiary in the Dominican Republic win a three-year struggle to obtain the first precedent-setting collective bargaining agreement in the country's export-processing zone.[93]
- In 1997 and 1998, dockworkers in Australia, Canada, Denmark, France, Japan, Sweden, and the United States demonstrated their solidarity with locked-out Liverpool dockworkers by providing financial assistance and coordinating disruptive tactics that targeted shipping companies using the Port of Liverpool.[94]

The number, occupational range, and geographic scope of cross-border solidarity actions such as these are great.

The motivations behind these actions often bridge the ideological or humanitarian appeal of worker-to-worker solidarity and material interests based in trade union efforts to assert control over labor markets and economic competition. For example, U.S. trade unionists defending freedom of association and the collective bargaining rights of workers in Mexico and other developing countries frequently act on the assumption that unions that represent their members and engage in more effective collective bargaining will, over time, raise domestic wage levels and thereby protect U.S. unionized jobs by reducing the incentive that U.S. companies have to shift production to lower-wage countries.[95] Calculations of this kind are perhaps most obvious in cases of within-company solidarity in which workers resist employer efforts to pit some employees against others, such as Mercedes-Benz and Volkswagen workers in Brazil refusing to expand auto-mobile production in order to meet unfulfilled demand and thereby undercut Volkswagen workers on strike in South Africa in the late 1990s.[96]

As noted, cross-border actions are typically undertaken by one or more trade unions (and sometimes even by individual company- or plant-level union sections or groups of dissident workers within them, in what some analysts label "grassroots solidarity") or by national labor federations or confederations. Information provided by global union federations often informs these initiatives, and GUFs can play important roles by publicizing conflicts and mobilizing international support for investor protests or consumer boycotts of individual firms.[97] For the most part, however, GUFs do not provide financial support for individual solidarity actions, and they rarely become involved in negotiating collective bargaining agreements or resolving workplace conflicts.[98] Similarly, the ICFTU/ITUC has mainly operated as a clearinghouse for information concerning union organization, labor legislation, wages and working conditions, and labor rights violations in different countries, as well as a general promoter of labor standards before international organizations.[99] Direct involvement by GUFs or the ICFTU/ITUC in specific conflicts has generally consisted of initiatives such as filing complaints with the ILO's Committee on Freedom of Association concerning the broader issues at stake (see below).[100]

The international framework agreements that different global union federations have negotiated with individual transnational companies constitute an exception in this regard. Since the late 1980s and early 1990s, GUFs have signed over a hundred of these agreements (the first union-company agreements negotiated at the international level), mainly with Western Europe–based transnational firms in the metalworking, chemical, construction, food processing, telecommunications, and service industries, in order to formalize codes of corporate conduct.[101] They differ from regular codes of conduct in that they are explicitly bilateral agreements and, often citing ILO conventions, specifically address core labor standards, typically committing companies (and generally the firms' suppliers) to respecting freedom of association and the right to collective bargaining. In principle, the agreements give GUFs a role in monitoring their implementation, and by legitimating core labor standards, they may strengthen national unions' positions in subsequent bargaining interactions with the signatory companies.[102] They do not, however, constitute legally binding industrial relations agreements. In part for this reason, implementation has been spotty in practice, and their application has proved impossible when their content conflicts with national laws and policies concerning unionization and collective bargaining.[103]

Cross-border union solidarity initiatives often confront multiple obstacles. Internet communications and increased ease of international travel have greatly reduced the traditional barriers posed by geography, and "just-in-time" production arrangements and global supply chains potentially increase the leverage that can be exerted by unionized workers through solidarity actions undertaken at different points in these chains. There are, however, persistent challenges: variations in the structure of national collective bargaining systems (centralized versus industry-wide versus enterprise- or plant-specific) and forms of trade union organization (national versus sectoral versus company by company); differences in union history and ideological orientation; trade union concerns about international competition for jobs and investment; limits on, and competing claims for, unions' financial and organizational resources; some union leaders' concern that their own negotiations with a transnational firm might be complicated by support given to protest actions undertaken by workers employed by the firm's subsidiaries in other countries; and language differences, racial and cultural stereotypes, and nationalist sentiments. Moreover, both employers and governments may actively resist solidarity actions such as synchronized collective bargaining or sympathy strikes. In some developing countries, national law may actually bar local unions from affiliating with international labor organizations, participating in sympathy strikes or boycotts, or even sending delegates to international labor conferences. In industrialized countries as well, bans on secondary or sympathy strikes may hamstring national and international solidarity support in some conflicts. Even more broadly, because national governments remain the principal focus of trade union efforts to shape public policy, many labor organizations may view international solidarity actions as necessarily a lower priority.[104]

Democratic internal governance in the unions on both sides of a cross-border alliance can be an underappreciated necessary condition for effective international solidarity action. The leading Northern labor organizations that are most prominently engaged in this arena are, in principle, democratically constituted membership organizations, and the literature on international solidarity emphasizes the importance of generating rank-and-file backing for initiatives that draw on finite financial and organizational resources to support activities that at best hold uncertain prospects of material gain and which could otherwise be devoted to initiatives of more immediate importance to union members.[105] In contrast, consolidated internal democracy is not necessarily an initial requirement in Southern unions receiving international solidarity support; indeed, many such actions are undertaken specifically to back dissident worker groups seeking to establish democratic union governance. However, the longer-term potential of these cross-border interactions may be undercut if incumbent union leaders are unaccountable to rank-and-file members and instead are aligned with government and/or employer interests. In fact, they may actively oppose any international contacts that would, in effect, challenge their position by promoting workers' rights. Moreover, in the absence of internal democracy, unions in developing countries are highly unlikely to engage in South-South or South-North cross-border solidarity.

It is difficult to draw overall conclusions concerning the typical outcomes of union-to-union, cross-border solidarity actions. However, the author's necessarily partial review of the voluminous literature on this subject published since the 1990s found few examples of solidaristic unions succeeding in mobilizing significant state-to-state pressures in support of their demands. Even then, the focal point was often quite specific: a demand that a target government compel a private company to respect national labor law or intervene to resolve a particular workplace conflict, free union leaders held as political prisoners, or curtail threats and/or actual physical violence against trade unionists. There are documented examples of cross-border solidarity campaigns coinciding with supportive state action against a common target undertaken through U.S. GSP and NAALC complaints procedures, cases in which rights activists could argue that the labor violations they were protesting in a specific company or workplace formed part of a pattern of violations of the labor protections embedded in these trade agreements.[106] Of course, there may be union-to-union solidarity actions that led directly to significant changes in a target country's laws and policies concerning freedom of association and the rights to organize and bargain collectively, or to strong external governmental pressures in support of such demands. They are, nevertheless, vanishingly rare.

The International Labour Organization

The International Labour Organization is both the principal norms-setting agency on labor rights and an important forum for addressing complaints from both workers' organizations and member states concerning violations of international standards. Its leading role as a promoter of labor standards formally derives from its status since 1946 as a specialized agency within the United Nations system.[107] The adoption of labor rights provisions in the ICCPR and the ICESCR undoubtedly strengthened the ILO's position in this regard. It has, however, continued to set the pace in the definition of international norms on such broad questions as indigenous peoples' rights (conventions numbers 107 and 169, adopted in 1957 and 1989, respectively).[108] The legitimacy of its role rests not only on its near-universal membership and its unique tripartite governance structure but also on the fact that the conventions it has adopted on issues other than core labor (human) rights are generally more procedural than substantive in focus.[109] For example, although the ILO insists on the importance of minimum wage standards, it has sought to avoid controversy over the question by generally not attempting to define actual minimum wage levels in different countries.[110] Similarly, although the assumption is that observing the rights to organize and bargain collectively will, over time, produce rising wages, the ILO further defers to national sovereignty by accepting some degree of national legal regulation of union formation.

The ILO employs conventions, recommendations, and other instruments to advance labor rights.[111] The most important of these are conventions, major policy positions adopted by a two-thirds majority of all delegates attending the annual International Labour Conference (ILC). Between 1919 and 2021, the ILO adopted a total of 190 conventions on a broad range of issues.[112] On June 18, 1998, it took the further step of adopting the Declaration on the Fundamental Principles and Rights at Work and its follow-up, a statement that highlighted the principles expressed in eight fundamental conventions—those regarding freedom of association and the right to collective bargaining, abolition of forced or compulsory labor, prohibition of the worst forms of child labor, minimum wages, and equal remuneration and nondiscrimination in employment—as core international labor standards.[113] Table 1.1 lists the full titles of these eight conventions and the dates on which they were adopted; they typically took effect two years after adoption.

The 1998 declaration was historically important because, whereas conventions enter into effect only when member states formally ratify them and adopt the labor legislation required to implement their contents, the ILO affirmed that the declaration's core standards are binding on all member states, regardless of whether they have ratified the individual conventions that underpin them.[114]

TABLE 1.1 Fundamental Labor Rights Conventions Adopted
by the International Labour Organization

Fundamental Conventions

No. 29: Convention concerning Forced or Compulsory Labour (1930)

No. 87: Convention concerning Freedom of Association and Protection of the Right to
Organise (1948)

No. 98: Convention concerning the Application of the Principles of the Right to
Organise and to Bargain Collectively (1949)

No. 100: Equal Remuneration Convention (1951)

No. 105: Abolition of Forced Labour Convention (1957)

No. 111: Convention concerning Discrimination in Respect of Employment and
Occupation (1958)

No. 138: Minimum Wage Convention (1973)

No. 182: Convention concerning the Prohibition and Immediate Action for the Elimination
of the Worst Forms of Child Labour (1999)

Declaration on Fundamental Principles and Rights at Work (1998)

Freedom of association and the effective recognition of the right to collective bargaining

Elimination of all forms of forced or compulsory labour

Effective abolition of child labour

Elimination of discrimination in respect of employment and occupation

---

Source: International Labour Organization, "ILO Declaration on Fundamental Principles and Rights at
Work," accessed October 4, 2022, www.ilo.org/declaration/lang--en/index.htm.

Note: The ILO amended the declaration in 2022 and added "a safe and healthy working environment" to
the list of fundamental principles.

Of particular note, the two fundamental rights given priority of place in the
declaration are freedom of association and the right to collective bargaining, an
emphasis that increases the legitimacy of actions taken in defense of them across
all the other rights-promotion arenas examined here. The fact that the declaration and/or the core conventions it cites have been formally adopted as evaluative standards in the labor provisions of, for instance, the European Union's
Generalized System Preferences program, all the bilateral free-trade agreements
negotiated by the United States since 2007, the International Finance Corporation's Performance Standards on Environmental and Social Sustainability,
and the United Nations Global Compact, demonstrates the ILO's success in its
norms-setting role.[115]

Yet the actual enforcement of international labor standards remains the most difficult challenge facing the ILO.[116] All member states are required to submit newly adopted conventions to domestic decision-making bodies for consideration between twelve and eighteen months after they are approved by the ILC. Thereafter, members are required to report regularly on the steps they have taken to implement in domestic labor law all of those conventions they have ratified.[117] At least in principle, member states that have not ratified a particular core convention are required to file an annual report outlining the extent to which national law addresses the issues raised in it and the reasons for not ratifying the convention. These reports are shared for comment with leading worker and employer organizations in the country in question and then reviewed by the Committee of Experts on the Application of Conventions and Recommendations (CEACR), an independent panel established in 1926 that is comprised of twenty international jurists appointed to three-year terms by the governing body. In addition, the CEARC and the tripartite Conference Committee on the Application of Standards review complaints alleging that a member state has not complied with a ratified convention. Complaints may be filed either by a labor or employer organization ("representations of non-observance of conventions"), or by an ILC worker or employer delegate, another member state that has also ratified the convention at issue, or the governing body in its own capacity ("complaints of non-observance").[118]

Because of the central importance that the ILO attaches to freedom of association and the right to collective bargaining, it has established special procedures to protect these fundamental rights. The CEACR regularly conducts general surveys of countries' labor laws to determine whether they conform to the provisions of conventions nos. 87 and 98, and it undertakes more detailed studies of the labor rights situation in particular countries if the situation warrants. Since 1964, it has published an annual register of "cases of progress" to create positive incentives for member states to ratify and implement these two conventions. In addition, the ILO complaint system includes separate procedures for investigating alleged violations of them. The tripartite Committee on Freedom of Association, established in 1951 and comprised of nine members of the governing body, meets three times each year to consider complaints against any member state, regardless of whether the country involved has formally ratified conventions nos. 87 and 98.[119] The target state has the right to reply to these complaints and submit evidence in its own defense. However, the governing body can also appoint an independent commission of inquiry to gather further evidence concerning the issues in dispute before it issues a final report, although it has rarely taken this step. Complaints to the CFA typically involve such matters as violations of the right to establish trade unions, the content of union statutes, employer obstruction of union activities, and a government's suspension or dissolution of labor organizations.[120]

Nevertheless, because the ILO itself has no binding legal or sanctioning authority over member states' actions, political persuasion and moral sanction are its principal enforcement instruments.[121] Its inclusive membership and tripartite governance structure greatly enhance the credibility of the positions it adopts, and as scholarship in other fields has shown, moral authority can be a consequential power resource.[122] Like signing international human rights treaties more generally, adopting ILO conventions can influence state policies by shifting public expectations and validating the demands of domestic rights advocates.[123] Conventions set standards for domestic labor legislation, and they are frequently cited as key points of reference by national and international judicial authorities. In conjunction with its 1998 declaration, the ILO has sought to maximize the impact of its international standing by adopting follow-up procedures to track those member states that have yet to ratify one or more of the fundamental conventions cited in the declaration. It has also published successive annual "global reports" on the status of each of the core labor standards highlighted there.

There are a number of documented cases in which the ILO has quite effectively used its powers of moral suasion to protect trade unionists (for example, by successfully lobbying governments for the release of imprisoned union activists or the reinstatement of workers fired by employers for their union activities) and to effect positive change regarding collective-action rights (for instance, by persuading a government to modify labor legislation on the basis of CFA recommendations).[124] Its most conspicuous success in this regard may have been its ability to persuade Poland's Communist government to grant legal recognition to the Solidarity trade union movement in November 1980.[125] Nonetheless, there are also many examples of the ILO failing to curtail rights abuses when confronted by strong sovereign resistance from member states.

The case of Myanmar illustrates the significant difficulties the ILO sometimes faces even in addressing such a fundamental question as serious, persistent violations of the prohibition against the use of forced labor.[126] In response to a complaint filed in June 1996 by twenty-five ILC worker delegates alleging that

Myanmar systematically violated convention no. 29 (Forced Labour Convention, 1930), the governing body appointed a formal commission of inquiry in March 1997. However, the Myanmar government invoked its right under the ILO constitution to deny the fact-finding panel physical access to the country, and it later rejected the commission's recommendations. It also rebuffed a condemnatory resolution adopted in June 1999, finding "that the attitude and behaviour of the Government of Myanmar are grossly incompatible with the conditions and principles governing membership of the Organization."[127] Only the ILO's historically unprecedented decision to invoke constitutional article 33, which authorizes it to take any "such action as it may deem wise and expedient to secure compliance," forced the Myanmar government to grant an inspection mission access to the country in September–October 2001 and to undertake limited legal reforms to ban the use of forced labor. Still, the ILO concluded that violations persisted in many parts of the country. Both the European Union and the United States cited the ILO's findings in their decisions, respectively, to suspend Myanmar's GSP trade preferences and to bar all imports from the country. Yet even with these supportive actions, the ILO was unable to resolve the problem fully.[128]

Corporate Social Responsibility Campaigns

Beginning in the late 1980s and early 1990s, both labor- and human-rights NGOs and trade unions increasingly turned to corporate social responsibility (CSR) campaigns to confront challenges posed by the progressive globalization of economic production. They pressured private firms to address these issues by adopting corporate codes of conduct (CCCs) that addressed labor rights. These initiatives built on precedents set by historic consumer boycotts (for instance, campaigns against the consumption of California table grapes headed by the United Farm Workers of America in the 1970s and against Nestlé's aggressive marketing of breast milk substitutes in developing countries in the late 1970s and early 1980s) and several important international efforts, often led by the ICFTU/IFTU and ITSs/GUFs, to establish global codes of conduct for transnational companies.[129]

Corporate codes are voluntary agreements. They specify the ethical principles that are to guide a company's conduct and its relations with stakeholders, state the obligations the firm incurs, and outline potential sanctions for company employees who fail to act in accordance with them.[130] First-generation CCCs were written and implemented by individual transnational firms such as Levi

Strauss & Co. (1991) and Nike (1992) acting on their own. Over time, however, the center of gravity shifted to multistakeholder model codes that were progressively more aligned with core ILO conventions and United Nations declarations on labor rights. They generally featured independent third-party monitoring of code enforcement by U.S. and European labor-rights NGOs, for-profit and not-for-profit specialized auditing groups, and/or labor-rights NGOs in host countries. In some cases, these groups certified individual production facilities as compliant with international labor standards. Supportive national government policies have often been important in the development of these initiatives, and in some instances, governments have directly encouraged them. For example, U.S. officials brought together leading brand-name apparel and footwear companies, national trade unions, human-rights NGOs, and consumer advocates to establish the Apparel Industry Partnership in 1996, which gave rise to the Fair Labor Association (FLA) in 1999. Similarly, the British government helped create the multisector stakeholder Ethical Trading Initiative (ETI) in 1998 and even provided direct financial support for it.[131]

Among the most active promoters and monitors of CCCs addressing labor issues have been the U.S.-based FLA (Washington, DC), Social Accountability International (New York City, 1997), Worker Rights Consortium (WRC, Washington, DC, a group created in 2000 by United Students Against Sweatshops), Verité, Inc. (Amherst, Massachusetts, 1995), and, in Europe, the ETI, Clean Clothes Campaign (CCC), and Fair Wear Foundation (Amsterdam, 1999).[132] Trade unions have often joined NGOs in CSR initiatives.[133] However, because differences in organizational histories, strategic goals, and core constituencies have at times created significant tensions among them,[134] NGOs have frequently acted alone in negotiating with transnational firms over the content of CCCs, monitoring companies and certifying that different production sites meet agreed labor standards, and promoting consumer boycotts to compel company compliance. Indeed, it was the rise of labor- and human-rights NGOs during the 1980s and 1990s that expanded CSR campaigns into a new arena for the international defense of labor rights.

Contemporary corporate codes generally endorse the ILO core conventions, including those concerning freedom of association and the right to collective bargaining. Their main focus, though, is most commonly on individual labor rights and such issues as low wages, excessive working hours, occupational safety and health, sexual harassment and other forms of workplace discrimination, and especially child and forced labor.[135] This emphasis often reflects strong employer resistance (particularly by supplier firms in global industries in which competitive pressures are intense) to making concessions on collective-action rights that would directly affect their control over business operations and the organization of production at the plant level. However, CSR initiatives are also more likely to emphasize labor-rights-as-human-rights issues because their main goal is to alter corporate conduct by redirecting consumer and investor preferences and, if necessary, mobilizing public support for company-specific boycotts through name-and-shame campaigns. Publicly highlighting the disturbing discrepancy between what workers in poor countries earn as a proportion of a luxury product's final sale price (for instance, in 1999, young El Salvadoran women were paid US$0.84 for sewing jackets that Liz Claiborne retailed in the United States for US$194),[136] or publicizing images of children working under very harsh conditions, are far more effective political tactics in this regard than condemning a developing country's labor laws on freedom of association that allow a transnational firm to avoid unionization of its far-flung employees.[137] The targets of these initiatives are often image-conscious, brand-name transnational companies whose market identity and concern for their international reputation make them (and their principal suppliers) more potentially vulnerable to social movement campaigns organized along these lines.[138]

Corporate responsibility campaigns are, by definition, focused on the actions of individual private companies, not on a host country's underpinning labor laws and policies. Nevertheless, in some instances, they have raised broader issues and brought considerable pressure to bear on government policies that systematically violate labor rights. One of the most prominent CSR campaigns mobilized in the wake of the Rana Plaza tragedy, a building collapse at a garment-producing complex in Dhaka, Bangladesh, in April 2013 that killed 1,129 people and injured over 2,000 more—the deadliest workplace tragedy in the history of the global apparel industry. A coalition comprised of two GUFs (IndustriALL and UNI Global Union), four labor-rights NGOs (CCC, ILRF, MSN, WRC), and more than 180 brand-name apparel companies based in some twenty countries quickly negotiated an Accord on Building Safety in Bangladesh.[139] The initial five-year agreement, which covered some 1,600 factories and two million workers, required signatory firms to maintain their purchasing volumes in Bangladesh for two years and make substantial annual payments into a centralized program that provided for workplace safety training, regular plant-level inspections, and the publication of all inspection reports. In addition, the agreement provided for binding arbitration of disputes over its implementation, which made its provisions legally binding on signatory companies.[140] The Rana Plaza accord was, however, exceptional in this regard.

The very large number of extant CCCs, substantial differences in code provisions and the form and effectiveness of enforcement mechanisms, and significant limitations on the capacity to monitor company compliance along sometimes lengthy supply chains in such globally dispersed industries as apparel and footwear production, all make it difficult to assess their overall impact.[141] Certainly, the most important consequence of successful CSR campaigns has been to persuade leading transnational corporations in consumer-driven industries that they must devote serious attention to working conditions and labor rights in their supplier firms. These campaigns can also bolster workers' morale and political resolve in struggles over labor rights and even heighten local factory managers' awareness of labor laws. Indeed, in countries where trade unions are weak and the state's labor enforcement capabilities are limited, CCCs can sometimes be employed as a valuable tool in collective bargaining, and they may allow rights advocates to address problems in industries or production centers such as export-processing zones that would otherwise be beyond their reach.[142] There have been cases in which the effective implementation of CCCs notably improved working conditions in specific companies and their supplier networks.[143] Moreover, there is some consensus that they have generally raised international business standards in developing countries where child labor, forced labor, and occupational safety and health are concerned.[144]

Nonetheless, in part because of the priority given to individual labor rights and plant-level working conditions in the implementation of many corporate codes, there are few documented instances in which CSR campaigns and CCCs substantially strengthened collective-action rights.[145] Some CCCs, particularly those promoted by private industry associations, defer to host countries' local labor laws whether or not they are in accordance with ILO standards.[146] And, as in the case of cross-border union solidarity actions, the author's review of the extensive literature on these topics published since the 1990s found no evidence that CSR campaigns influenced a national government's laws and policies concerning freedom of association and the right to collective bargaining unless they operated in parallel with labor rights complaints pursued through such state-to-state vehicles as the U.S. GSP program, the NAALC, and U.S. FTA complaint procedures.[147]

SOVEREIGNTY LEVERAGE, U.S. TRADE AGREEMENTS, AND THE DEFENSE OF LABOR RIGHTS

A Framework for Analysis

Negotiations over, and subsequent implementation of, labor rights provisions in trade agreements constitute two distinct political moments when *sovereignty leverage* can theoretically come into play. Again, this term refers to one (generally more powerful) state's ability to bring its sovereign rights to bear against those of another (generally weaker) state in order to induce change in the latter's behavior. In negotiations between the United States and another country over either the content of a trade agreement's labor rights provisions or preaccession changes that the United States seeks in the prospective trade partner's labor laws and/or policies, the fulcrum of leverage is the U.S. government's decision whether to grant the other country enhanced export access to its domestic market.[148] If that country later fails to comply with its agreed labor rights obligations, then the U.S. government's principal point of leverage in subsequent interactions with its counterpart lies in its capacity to levy financial penalties, impose trade-linked sanctions, or, if the terms of the agreement so stipulate, possibly suspend or terminate privileged access to the U.S. market.

At both moments, a diverse set of factors determines whether, when, and how the United States might exercise its potential leverage. In principle, sovereignty leverage should be greatest during initial trade negotiations when the terms of the agreement itself are at issue and its final approval remains uncertain. Even in these circumstances, however, it is difficult to predict the extent of U.S. leverage vis-à-vis a prospective trade partner because the character of a particular foreign policy relationship or negotiating process may be shaped by many elements. The choices that political leaders make, the bargaining tactics that negotiators employ, and the relative negotiating skills of the government officials involved are all major considerations in this regard. Because the object of negotiations is a special trade agreement, the nature of the existing economic relationship between the United States and a potential partner is certainly an important part of the equation, but the economic benefits to be derived from liberalizing trade ties may vary greatly in significance for both the United States and the other party. Even when a developing country's government calculates that very substantial benefits can be derived from expanded access to the U.S. market, its willingness to ratify and then implement strong new labor standards may be constrained by the perceived political and economic costs of adopting measures that might seriously threaten existing production arrangements in key industries. At a minimum, based on the double-helix model outlined earlier in this chapter, one might anticipate that the most difficult state-to-state bargaining would be over collective-action rights because of the core political economy issues they pose. In the evocative image conjured by international relations theorist Stanley Hoffman (1966: 884), "As the artichoke's heart gets more and more denuded, the governments' vigilance gets more and more alerted."

Following adoption of a trade agreement, the leverage that the U.S. government can potentially exert to ensure compliance with agreed labor rights provisions depends heavily on the institutional design of dispute-settlement procedures and, of course, on U.S. government officials' political commitment to achieving that goal. How the signatories' labor obligations are defined, the openness of complaints procedures to trade unions and other nongovernmental actors, the nature and severity of the penalties that can be levied for rights violations, and the target of those penalties (national governments or private companies) are all important considerations. Whether a trade partner's economic access to the U.S. market can, in principle, be suspended or terminated as a penalty for severe, persistent labor rights violations may prove to be especially important in this regard.

As Putnam (1988) so compelling demonstrates in his analysis of international diplomacy as a two-level game, the (sometimes shifting) alignment of domestic sociopolitical forces in the countries involved is of central importance in both the preagreement negotiation and postagreement implementation moments. In the United States, trade unions have, since the 1970s, regularly criticized trade agreements with developing countries because increased market competition from lower-labor standards, lower-wage producers threatens the employment stability, wages, and working conditions of union members. However, the U.S. labor movement's capacities to influence trade negotiations, the content of trade agreement-linked labor provisions, and the actual enforcement of these provisions once an agreement comes into effect have varied considerably over time in line with its overall political influence and the partisan identity and political orientation of different presidential administrations. In developing countries, there is more likely to be a broad initial consensus in favor of joining a preferential or free-trade agreement with the United States because of the substantial economic gains that may flow from it. Yet the longer-term alignment of domestic sociopolitical forces in partner countries is important because U.S. sociopolitical actors may be more effective in enforcing another government's compliance with trade agreement-linked labor obligations if they can identify and mobilize allies in the country where rights violations occur.

This analytic framework structures the empirical analysis and the arguments developed in this book. As previously noted, the chapters that follow examine in depth U.S.-Mexico negotiations over labor rights questions associated with the NAFTA (1993), the Trans-Pacific Partnership agreement (2012–2016), and the revised NAFTA, the United States–Mexico–Canada Agreement (2017–2019). The assessment of the implementation of trade agreement-linked labor standards includes a subset of U.S. GSP labor complaints filed between 1985 and 1995 (the period in which U.S. GSP labor provisions were most intensively employed) and the universe of labor rights complaints filed under both the NAALC (1994–2020) and post-NAFTA U.S. free-trade agreements (2008–2016). This combination of cross-case comparison and within-case analysis in both negotiations over, and the implementation of, trade agreements' labor protections constitutes a broad comparative basis on which to evaluate different dimensions of the NAALC experience and to draw more general conclusions regarding the conditions under which trade agreement-linked labor provisions constitute an efficacious means of defending workers' rights internationally.[149]

The empirical materials examined in chapters 2 through 6 and the conclusions drawn in chapter 7 do, however, broadly validate the lines of argument highlighted by the analytic framework presented above. The record shows that, on balance, the U.S. government's capacity to exercise sovereignty leverage has been greatest during preagreement state-to-state bargaining with prospective trade partners when future access to the U.S. market—the fulcrum point of U.S. sovereignty leverage—is at stake. Over time, U.S. government officials demonstrated political learning by expanding the scope of negotiations to include both the trade agreement's labor provisions and the labor law and policy reforms that prospective partner governments were required to undertake as a condition for accession to the agreement. Yet despite a number of successes in these areas, securing actual implementation of agreed labor reforms has frequently proved difficult because U.S. leverage over a free-trade partner government markedly declines once an agreement takes effect.

Still more, because U.S. free-trade agreements institutionalize government-to-government interactions over the signatory countries' compliance with their labor rights obligations, U.S. bargaining leverage in resolving labor complaints is constrained. A comparative assessment of U.S. GSP labor rights petitions over the 1985–1995 period and the labor complaints filed under the NAALC and post-NAFTA FTAs shows that the former were notably more effective than the latter in promoting reforms in labor law and policy in developing countries concerning collective-action rights (freedom of association and the rights to organize and bargain collectively). Significant variations in the design of these agreements' complaint procedures and sanctions provisions are the most probable explanation for these different outcomes. Whereas the threat of market-access suspension or termination has sometimes caused developing countries to promise important policy reforms in response to U.S. GSP petitions, the U.S. government has no authority to exclude a partner country from a free-trade agreement even for serious, persistent labor rights violations. In fact, over the 1994–2022 period, the U.S. government never levied economic sanctions of any kind against an FTA partner country for rights violations. Even the political impact of local sociopolitical alliances mobilized in the target country by U.S. labor rights petitioners differed between the U.S. GSP petitions, on the one hand, and NAALC and U.S. FTA complaints, on the other, because of these differences in institutional design.

Research Methods and Data Sources

The principal research methods employed in this book are comparative case studies and process-tracing. Close analysis of carefully selected case studies is a well-established qualitative method for examining complex sociopolitical phenomena.[150] For instance, assessing a target government's responses to labor rights complaints filed under the provisions of a U.S. trade agreement and the terms on which they are resolved requires attention to multiple factors and possible interactions among them. Significant changes in a country's labor laws and policies concerning unionization and collective bargaining may reflect intersecting domestic and/or international forces, ranging from partisan alternation in government or regime change to external diplomatic pressures focused on the legal obligations the country incurred under the terms of a trade agreement. Differentiating among these factors and determining their relative causal importance in explaining observed changes require an understanding of the sociopolitical, economic, and foreign policy circumstances in which these legal and/or policy reforms occur. Case studies facilitate this kind of in-depth, contextualized analysis. Examining the resolution of labor rights complaints filed under different U.S. trade agreements (the GSP program versus the NAALC versus post-NAFTA free-trade agreements) is a form of structured cross-case comparison that highlights the importance of changes over time in the content of different agreements' labor rights provisions and their application.

The arguments developed earlier in this chapter suggest that because trade agreement-linked labor provisions generally give high priority to collective-action rights and because potential sovereignty leverage constitutes an integral element in these state-to-state accords, external pressures exercised over (preagreement bargaining) or through (dispute resolution processes) these provisions are more likely to advance collective-action rights in developing countries than are actions undertaken through alternative rights-promotion arenas. However, because sovereign resistance to external pressures is also likely to be strongest where collective-action rights are concerned, external pressures may also be less likely to effect significant policy change in this area than, for instance, in the case of individual labor rights.[151] No previous study has systematically examined either the outcomes of government-to-government bargaining over labor rights in association with U.S. preferential trade agreements or the results of the labor complaints subsequently filed under dispute resolution procedures linked to, or embedded in, these agreements (from the U.S. GSP program through the NAALC to post-NAFTA FTAs). Moreover, because sovereignty leverage as a causal mechanism is likely to operate differently in these distinct contexts, between different countries and across different complaint processes, and over time,[152] it is difficult to predict these outcomes a priori.[153] For these reasons, the case studies presented here should be considered exploratory (or heuristic) in character.[154]

Process-tracing is an appropriate means of analyzing both preagreement U.S. bargaining over labor rights with Mexico and other prospective trade partners and the subsequent implementation of agreement-linked labor provisions through dispute-settlement procedures. This within-case mode of analysis focuses primarily on identifying and assessing the significance of possible causal links between independent and dependent variables.[155] Because the central U.S. goal in both preagreement bargaining and dispute-resolution processes is to persuade a target government to change established labor law and/or policy, it is imperative to establish as clearly as possible the specific causal processes involved. For example, the historical reconstruction of state-to-state bargaining processes and the identification of those factors that shaped government officials' negotiating goals, changing bargaining positions, and tactical decisions require close attention to national context and often shifting domestic political circumstances. Similarly, in order to formulate an adequate explanation of how a developing country's government responds to labor rights complaints filed under a U.S. trade agreement, it is necessary to draw upon multiple kinds of evidence to weigh the relative importance of external pressures exerted through agreement-linked labor provisions against other possible explanations for any observed policy change concerning collective-action rights (multicausality or equifinality).

The research findings presented here are based on a variety of sources. These include: the extensive secondary literature published on the several topics addressed in this introductory chapter; public documents and internal reports by the U.S., Mexican, and Canadian governments, several international agencies, and labor- and human-rights nongovernmental organizations; NAALC and U.S. FTA labor complaint case files; and both English- and Spanish-language newspapers and journals, among other sources. In addition, the author compiled and analyzed (employing statistical tests when it was feasible to do so) original data sets concerning a subset of the labor rights petitions filed under the U.S. GSP program and all the complaints registered under both the NAALC and post-NAFTA U.S. free-trade agreements.

This book also draws extensively on 122 semi-structured interviews that the author conducted (principally between 2004 and 2022) with former and serving senior government labor and trade policy officials, trade union representatives, and labor- and human-rights activists in the United States, Mexico, and Canada. All interviewees were selected based on their occupational position and their degree of involvement in the trade negotiations and labor rights complaint processes examined here.[156] Because of the sensitivity of the issues involved, many of the interviewees requested anonymity.[157] They are, therefore, identified in the text only by their general occupational position. On points of particular importance, the author systematically sought confirmation from more than one interview source, and whenever possible, the author triangulated the interview materials used as evidentiary sources by supplementing them with information drawn from documentary reports and journalistic accounts.

CHAPTER 2

Pathways to the North American Agreement on Labor Cooperation

From Multilateral Proposals to Unilateral Actions Linking Labor Rights and Trade Agreements

M any studies of the North American Agreement on Labor Cooperation (NAALC) limit their discussion of labor rights/trade linkage in U.S. foreign economic policy to that agreement alone. As noted in chapter 1, the NAALC was indeed innovative in several important ways. Its formulation was, however, part of a decades-long attempt by U.S. labor organizations and supportive government policymakers to link labor standards to trade agreements. This chapter establishes an essential historical context for understanding the debates surrounding the negotiation of the NAALC by examining the longer-term trajectory of those efforts.

These U.S. initiatives reanimated older debates concerning the merits of linking labor standards and trade.[1] Although several authors have addressed competing views on this issue by assessing the likely economic impact of embedding labor standards in multilateral trade agreements,[2] there is no simple resolution of the question on its own terms. In the end, what counted in the formulation of U.S. policy in this area were the shifting terms of domestic political debate. The U.S. policy-making process was shaped primarily by heightened concerns about the negative impact of intensified international economic competition on the wages and employment security of unionized workers. The proponents of attaching labor-rights conditionality provisions to trade agreements did, however, draw some political benefit from the expanding international consensus in favor of labor rights broadly defined.

The first part of this chapter traces the evolution of both international and U.S. domestic debates concerning whether to embed labor rights provisions in trade agreements. Sovereignty concerns strongly underpinned international debates about labor rights/trade linkage. Repeated efforts to establish enforceable labor standards in multilateral trade agreements failed primarily because of many states' resistance to the loss of sovereignty over an issue with broad domestic economic and political ramifications. Developing countries, the bloc of states most consistently opposed to this linkage in multilateral trade fora, sometimes explicitly opposed such proposals on sovereignty grounds. However, even when developing country governments, often seeking to protect private-sector interests, argued for the right to maintain their international comparative economic advantage as low-wage producers, or maintained that universal standards would not respect differences in cultural understandings about labor rights, the underpinning concern was national sovereignty.

The second section analyses complaints filed between 1985 and 1995 under the labor rights provisions of the U.S. Generalized System of Preferences (GSP) program, which offers nonreciprocal, duty-free access to the U.S. marketplace for specified products from designated developing countries.[3] This program is of particular interest for two reasons: It was the first trade agreement to institute sovereignty leverage (the U.S. government's authority to suspend or terminate beneficiary countries' market access) as a means of defending labor rights internationally, and more labor complaints have been filed under it than under any other U.S. trade agreement. Because of the volume of labor complaints filed under the program and because of significant differences in institutional design between this program and the NAALC concerning the potential application of trade-linked sanctions in response to documented labor rights violations, the record of U.S. GSP complaint resolution constitutes a valuable empirical baseline against which to assess the NAALC experience.

THE LONG MARCH: EVOLVING APPROACHES TO LABOR RIGHTS/TRADE LINKAGE

From the mid-twentieth century onward, labor organizations and their political allies actively sought to expand their scope of action beyond traditional union-to-union, cross-border solidarity actions and International Labour Organization (ILO) initiatives by embedding worker protections in trade agreements. These efforts were often framed in terms of core worker rights and fair labor standards, and some advocates explicitly defended these proposals on the grounds that they advanced democratic principles, international solidarity, and social justice in all countries.[4] However, the consistent underlying rationale was to protect workers in more economically advanced countries from the competitive pressures posed by goods imported from countries with less rigorous worker protections and lower wages.[5] The centrality of material interests in many of these initiatives led opponents to label them "protectionist."[6] Yet this emphasis was only natural given that the labor organizations seeking to link labor rights and trade agreements acted in defense of, and were broadly accountable to, their members' interests and preferences.[7]

Early Multilateral Initiatives

Although debates regarding labor rights and trade became particularly intense in the late twentieth century, this issue had a much older heritage. Indeed, British, French, and Belgian social activists made several specific proposals in this area during the 1830s and 1840s.[8] Their principal motivating concern was that, in the absence of international agreements on matters such as hours of work and child labor, foreign economic competition would inevitably undermine national efforts to establish minimum labor standards. Proposals of this kind multiplied during the second half of the nineteenth century in response to intensifying industrialization and expanding trade, and the various international congresses organized between 1876 and 1913 to discuss workplace safety and health and minimum labor standards constituted important precedents for the creation of the ILO in 1919.[9] The Treaty of Versailles acknowledged this heritage in its statement that "the failure of any nation to adopt humane conditions of labour is an obstacle in the way of other nations which desire to improve the conditions in their own countries."[10] The ILO's constitution did not explicitly recognize trade sanctions for labor rights violations—but neither did it rule them out as part of the "measures of an economic character" that one member state might take against another when other means of redressing rights violations had been exhausted.[11]

The first invocation of labor standards in a multilateral trade agreement came at the United Nations Conference on Trade and Employment, which was held in Havana, Cuba, from November 1947 through March 1948 to establish an International Trade Organization (ITO).[12] On at least two contemporary occasions, leading U.S. labor organizations—the Congress of Industrial Organizations (1943) and the Textile Workers Union of America (1945)—had called for an agreement explicitly linking fair labor standards and international trade.[13] Yet the only reference to labor issues in the initial draft of the ITO charter produced by the U.S. government was a provision permitting member countries to bar imports of goods produced by prison labor; the broader subject of fair labor standards arose only in deliberations by the ITO Preparatory Committee (October-November 1946) in London.[14] Representatives of the World Federation of Trade Unions and the American Federation of Labor participated in the London meetings,[15] but the available documentary record indicates that the Cuban delegation was the leading advocate of a more general labor standards provision.[16] In the Preparatory Committee negotiations, the Cuban delegation argued that the tariff advantages associated with "most favored nation" status should be linked to a country's observance of fair labor standards. This position was, however, opposed by delegates from the United States, the United Kingdom, and India.[17] At the Havana conference, Colombia, Mexico, and Uruguay all submitted proposals that would have permitted a member state to take "reasonable and equitable measures to protect its industry from the competition of like products produced under substandard conditions of labour and pay."[18] These different initiatives informed article 7 of the final Havana Charter, which stated in part:

> The Members recognize that unfair labour conditions, particularly in production for export, create difficulties in international trade, and, accordingly, each Member shall take whatever action may be appropriate and feasible to eliminate such conditions within its territory.[19]

The article did not, however, authorize importing countries to impose domestic restrictions on imports from countries where unfair labor conditions prevailed.[20]

The inclusion of a reference to labor standards in the Havana Charter was no doubt politically significant. However, the ITO project ultimately failed. In the United States, competing international priorities (the 1948 Marshall Plan for postwar European reconstruction, the creation of the North Atlantic Treaty Organization in 1949, and the outbreak of the Korean War in 1950), partisan struggles over U.S. trade policy, reservations about ways in which commitments made in the Havana Charter (for example, affirmative provisions regarding full employment) might circumscribe U.S. sovereignty, and concerns that article 7 would lead the ITO to assume responsibilities already encharged to the ILO, all worked to sideline the initiative.[21] Indeed, the U.S. House of Representatives Committee on Foreign Affairs delayed hearings on the ITO charter until April 1950, and the Senate Foreign Relations Committee never scheduled hearings on the matter.[22] Other countries eventually followed the United States in dropping consideration of the charter.[23] The General Agreement on Tariffs and Trade (GATT, adopted on October 30, 1947, as part of the broader ITO initiative and in effect from January 1, 1948) permitted countries to block imports produced by prison labor (article XX[e]), but it otherwise omitted any specific link between trade and social issues.[24]

Yet this certainly did not end international debate on the question.[25] In 1953, the U.S. government, seeking to win domestic and international support for Japan's accession to the GATT, advocated inserting a labor standards provision in the agreement that closely paralleled the Havana Charter's article 7.[26] Although that initiative failed (other parts of the GATT were amended instead), labor organizations remained actively engaged in this area. In 1960, for example, the influential International Metalworkers' Federation (IMF) adopted a resolution that criticized "instances of unfair competition in international trade, based upon [the] low level of labour conditions in exporting industries." The IMF explicitly reaffirmed its support for international trade liberalization. However, it argued that all GATT member states should have an obligation to eliminate unfair labor conditions, especially restrictions on freedom of association and collective bargaining, and that the GATT should adopt complaint procedures that would allow labor and employer organizations in importing countries (working through their national governments) to address the social effects of market disruptions caused by exports from countries with unjustifiably low wage levels.[27] In 1976, the IMF proposed that the GATT's "escape clause" (article XIX) be expanded so as to allow a country to suspend imports temporarily when domestic production and employment were disrupted by low-wage imports. It also called for the creation of a tripartite commission to supervise this new "social clause." And in May 1978, the International Confederation of Free Trade Unions (ICFTU) adopted a "development charter" that explicitly linked fair labor standards to North-South trade liberalization.[28]

From Multilateralism to Unilateralism in U.S. Trade Policy (and Back Again)

From the 1960s onward, U.S. labor organizations were particularly active in seeking to link labor standards to trade agreements.[29] They did so principally in response to growing economic competition from lower-wage countries. The American Federation of Labor-Congress of Industrial Organizations (AFL-CIO, the largest and most politically important U.S. labor organization) unsuccessfully sought to include a fair labor standards provision in the U.S. Trade Expansion Act of 1962.[30] In October 1969, the AFL-CIO adopted a policy resolution calling on the U.S. government to promote international negotiations to develop "workable international fair labor standards in international trade . . . not only to protect U.S. workers against unfair competition, but also to assure workers in other countries a fair share of the increased returns resulting from expanded trade."[31] The AFL-CIO pressed this point at hearings on trade policy held by the U.S. House of Representatives Committee on Ways and Means in May–June 1970. International trade still represented a comparatively small proportion of total U.S. gross national product.[32] However, the AFL-CIO justified its proposals as a response to the economic challenges facing U.S. workers as a consequence of multinational companies expanding overseas investment and their subsequent importation into the U.S. market of goods produced in lower-wage countries without strong worker protections.[33]

At the time, the AFL-CIO focused primarily on possible actions (including complaints procedures and annual reports on countries' labor standards) by international organizations, particularly the GATT.[34] In doing so, it built upon a 1969 report by the U.S. Office of the Special Trade Representative for Trade Negotiations (the Roth Report) that advocated U.S. efforts "to develop international agreement upon a workable definition of fair labor standards and upon realistic means for their enforcement. This effort should be made through the GATT and the International Labor Organization (ILO) and possibly under other international organizations as well."[35]

The AFL-CIO framed its proposals in these terms at least in part because there was uncertainty about how the United States could use domestic legislation to promote labor standards in other countries.[36] Nonetheless, from the outset, both AFL-CIO officials and sympathetic U.S. legislators outlined their positions on this question in terms that presaged later debates regarding labor rights provisions in the generalized system of preferences legislation: "Any exploration of preferences on semi-manufactured or manufactured products from developing countries should include appropriate mechanisms for preventing market disruption and adequate fair labor standards."[37]

The GATT remained the principal focus of the U.S. labor movement's attention in legislative debates leading to the adoption of the Trade Act of 1974, the legislation that introduced GSP provisions into U.S. trade policy.[38] The initial bill submitted by the administration of President Richard M. Nixon (1969–1973, 1973–1974) to the House of Representatives (House Resolution 6767, April 10, 1973) made no reference to labor standards of any kind. Early in the proceedings, however, labor-allied legislators introduced an amendment calling on the president to "require fair labor standards in international trade to prevent unfair competition."[39] The prominent U.S. union leaders who testified in favor of embedding fair labor standards in trade agreements negotiated by the United States specifically cited the Havana Charter as a point of reference.[40] They suggested that such provisions should be part of the GATT rather than U.S. domestic legislation, but they accepted that in order to enforce international fair labor standards, the United States would have to bar imports from countries that failed to observe them.[41] The final House report on the measure argued that existing GATT provisions were outdated because they failed to adequately address "trade issues arising from the utilization of the labor of low-wage countries without regard to acceptable or equitable fair labor standards," and it advocated amending the GATT to include "international fair labor standards and procedures to enforce them."[42] Section 121(4) of the final legislation listed among the steps to be taken toward GATT revision "the adoption of international fair labor standards" and procedures to enforce them.[43]

However, none of these initiatives found sufficient international political traction, and so when the GSP provisions of U.S. trade legislation came up for renewal in 1983–1984, U.S. labor organizations and their political allies shifted the focus of their lobbying efforts from the GATT to domestic law.[44] Like the Nixon administration's proposal in April 1973, the initial GSP renewal bill submitted by the administration of Ronald Reagan (1981–1985, 1985–1989) to the U.S. Senate contained no labor provisions.[45] This omission (and the Reagan administration's later "vehement" opposition to labor provisions in the legislation) was curious in view of the fact that the administration's Caribbean Basin Initiative (CBI), a program offering duty-free entry into the U.S. market for most products from designated Caribbean and Central American countries, had from the outset (identical bills submitted to the Congress on March 18, 1982, as H.R. 5900 and S. 2237) included labor rights conditions.[46] The 1983 Caribbean Basin Economic Recovery Act incorporated that same language: "In determining whether to designate any country a beneficiary country under this title, the President shall take into account . . . the degree to which workers in any country are afforded reasonable workplace conditions and enjoy the right to organize and bargain collectively."[47]

Nevertheless, in March 1984, the substantive focus of legislative debate changed markedly when Representative Donald Pease (Democrat-Ohio) submitted a proposal for GSP renewal that made the protection of "internationally recognized worker rights" a mandatory criterion in U.S. government decisions regarding whether to extend tariff preferences to developing countries.[48] In defending his initiative, Representative Peace linked the international defense of core labor rights and the economic interests of U.S. workers: "The rights of American workers will be more secure and U.S. industrial health will be more effectively advanced by a positive, aggressive effort to extend those labor rights to workers in all of the countries with which we must compete in the global marketplace. Quite honestly, no worker is free until all workers are free."[49]

His bill defined "internationally recognized worker rights" to include "the freedom of association, the right to organize and bargain collectively, a prohibition on the use of any form of forced or compulsory labor, the prohibition and elimination of discrimination in respect of employment and occupation, the establishment of a minimum age for the employment of children, and the delineation of acceptable conditions of work with respect to minimum wages, hours of work, and occupational safety and health."[50] A developing country would be ineligible for designation as a GSP beneficiary "if that country has not adopted laws that extend internationally-recognized worker rights in that country and is not enforcing those laws." In addition, Pease's bill prohibited a beneficiary country from excluding workers employed in so-called special economic or export-processing zones from the protections offered by its national labor legislation, and it gave labor rights advocates legal standing to participate in the U.S. government's annual review of a country's GSP beneficiary status.[51]

Pease's bill received strong support from the most powerful U.S. unions and Americas Watch, a leading human rights group.[52] In fact, representatives of the AFL-CIO, who were highly critical of the GSP program's impact on U.S. employment in industries facing intense competition from lower-wage foreign exporters, indicated that organized labor's support for renewal of the GSP program was contingent upon inclusion of labor rights provisions in revised legislation.[53] However, in order to win this key point, they accepted compromise language that acceded to Reagan administration concerns on several other important issues. The final bill (House Resolution 6023, October 3, 1984) eliminated antidiscrimination guarantees from the list of protected labor rights, required only that developing countries demonstrate that they were "taking steps toward ensuring internationally recognized worker rights" as a condition for gaining or retaining GSP beneficiary status, and permitted the federal executive to waive these labor rights conditions when the president determined it was in the national interest to do so.[54]

Specialists in international human rights law sharply criticized the legislation for the ambiguity of its language, its failure to align U.S. standards more explicitly with those articulated by ILO conventions, and the lack of transparency and the great discretion afforded the executive branch in evaluative procedures. They argued that because the legislation did not reflect the concerns of contemporary U.S. human rights policy, its principal motivations were most likely protectionist in nature.[55] Nonetheless, the labor provisions in the final legislation were a significant political victory for worker rights advocates and an important point of inflection in long-standing national and international efforts to link labor rights to trade agreements.

Indeed, the Generalized System of Preferences Renewal Act of 1984 established a major precedent. In the years that followed, the same set of labor rights and evaluative procedures were incorporated into a number of pieces of U.S. legislation. These included: legislation regulating the Overseas Private Investment Corporation (OPIC, 1985); the 1988 congressional authorization for the executive to negotiate multilateral trade agreements on a "fast track" basis (a procedure permitting the Congress to approve or reject a proposed trade agreement but not amend its content); the Omnibus Trade and Competitiveness Act (OTCA) of 1988; the 1990 renewal of the Caribbean Basin Initiative and the 2000 Caribbean Trade Partnership Act; the Andean Trade Preference Act of 1991; a 1992 bill that barred the Agency for International Development from expending funds for U.S. investment promotion in countries failing to meet stipulated labor rights standards; and the African Growth and Opportunity Act in 2000. In addition, after 1994, the U.S. directors of the International Monetary Fund and the World Bank were required to use their "voice and vote" to screen loan proposals for their effects on workers' rights.[56]

Inserting labor rights considerations into the OTCA, an action that was facilitated by Democrats' majority control of both the U.S. House of Representatives and the Senate in 1988 but which was also backed by a large proportion of Republican legislators,[57] was particularly significant in political and symbolic terms.[58] Labor rights violations by a foreign country were henceforth included among the "unreasonable" acts, policies, and practices subject to the full range of U.S. trade sanctions under Section 301. Whereas previous legislation (the CBI, the amended 1984 trade act, and OPIC) applied these conditions only to developing countries, the provisions of the OTCA apply to all U.S. trading partners, and trade sanctions can be directed at the specific industries or products where worker rights violations are concentrated.[59] Moreover, the legislation required the U.S. Department of State to prepare in-depth annual reviews of a "country's laws, enforcement of those laws, and practices with respect to internationally recognized worker rights" in "each country with which the United States has an economic or trade relationship" and "the conditions of worker rights in any sector which produces goods in which United States capital is invested."[60]

The World Trade Organization and Labor Rights

During the late 1980s, in parallel with their domestic legislative victories, U.S. labor organizations and their political allies renewed their efforts to embed labor rights provisions in multilateral trade agreements.[61] They faced persistent opposition from developing countries, which viewed such provisions as protectionist measures designed to cancel their comparative advantages in international economic competition. Nevertheless, in 1986–1987, 1990, and again in 1994, the United States proposed GATT working groups on labor rights issues. In an effort to build international support for these initiatives, in 1990, the U.S. government dropped from its list of five "core" rights a prohibition against child labor and guarantees of minimum conditions of work, thereby reducing its list to freedom of association, the rights to organize and bargain collectively, and freedom from forced or compulsory labor.[62] The United States also clarified that it was not seeking to negotiate an international minimum wage.[63]

The focus of these efforts shifted to the World Trade Organization (WTO) when this body was created on January 1, 1995, to replace the GATT as the principal promoter of international trade liberalization.[64] The efforts the United

States made to place the labor rights issue on the agenda of the WTO Ministerial Conference held in Singapore in December 1996 had been backed by Belgium, France, Norway, and both the European Commission and the European Parliament, although Australia, Germany, and the United Kingdom dissented.[65] At the time, the understanding among these supporters was that a WTO "social clause" would not mimic U.S. domestic legislation by including trade sanctions for labor rights violations.[66] Nonetheless, strong, consistent opposition from developing country governments blocked action at the Singapore meeting.[67] Although the final Singapore declaration was the first official WTO document to mention labor standards, it only reaffirmed WTO members' "commitment to the observance of internationally recognized core labour standards" and their belief that "the International Labour Organization (ILO) is the competent body to set and deal with these standards."[68]

In the run-up to the December 1999 WTO ministerial meeting in Seattle, Washington, U.S. unions and labor rights groups again exerted strong pressures on the administration of William J. (Bill) Clinton (1993–1997, 1997–2001) to lobby for the inclusion of a "social clause" in the agreement governing the WTO. Organized labor's political leverage within the Democratic Party was enhanced by the approach of the 2000 presidential election. The Clinton administration responded by renewing its push for the creation of a working group that would define a set of core labor standards that would subsequently be embedded in all multilateral trade agreements. Groups such as the ICFTU actively supported a "social clause," but developing countries (led by India, Egypt, Pakistan, Brazil, and Thailand) again articulated their vigorous opposition to this proposal.[69] What derailed the U.S. initiative was near-unanimous international opposition to Clinton's statement that countries failing to meet basic labor standards should be subject to trade sanctions. The European Union sharply rejected this position and advocated what had emerged as the de facto minimum international consensus position on the subject: closer WTO-ILO cooperation on labor issues.[70] Of course, this outcome greatly strengthened the ILO's legitimacy as the principal labor rights norms-setting agency and the importance of its 1998 Declaration on Fundamental Principles and Rights at Work. However, the WTO's perfunctory affirmation of the Singapore declaration in 2001 effectively suspended the decades-long debate about linking labor rights provisions to multilateral trade agreements.[71]

IMPLEMENTING THE LABOR RIGHTS PROVISIONS OF THE U.S. GENERALIZED SYSTEM OF PREFERENCES PROGRAM

Adding labor rights-conditionality provisions to the U.S. GSP program was a key point of inflection in the evolving debate over labor rights/trade linkage. This section assesses the efficacy of U.S. GSP procedures as a means of defending labor rights in developing countries, with particular reference to freedom of association and the rights to organize and bargain collectively. A number of countries operate GSP programs.[72] However, only those established by the United States and the European Union (EU) contain labor rights-conditionality provisions.[73] The authority to suspend or terminate a developing country's enhanced market access because of serious, persistent labor rights violations constitutes a basis for exercising sovereignty leverage to advance collective-action rights.

The analytic framework formulated in chapter 1 identified the negotiations over a trade agreement and the subsequent implementation of its labor rights provisions as two distinct political moments when sovereignty leverage can potentially come into play. In the case of the U.S. GSP program, the program had already been in existence for nearly a decade when labor rights provisions were adopted in the amended Trade and Tariff Act of 1984. When the legislation took effect on January 3, 1985, the Reagan administration certified all countries that then held beneficiary status, pending a mandatory review by the Office of the United States Trade Representative (USTR). The 1985–1986 review led to the exclusion of Nicaragua and Romania and the suspension of Chile and Paraguay on labor rights grounds,[74] but thereafter, the USTR generally initiated reviews of GSP beneficiaries' labor laws and practices only in response to specific petitions alleging rights violations filed by trade unions and/or labor- and human-rights nongovernmental organizations (NGOs).[75] The following discussion assesses the implementation of the GSP program's labor rights provisions as a test of the extent to and the conditions under which sovereignty leverage can be deployed effectively.

U.S. GSP Review Procedures and Complaint Petitions

Regulations governing the USTR, the agency principally responsible for overseeing compliance with the labor rights provisions of U.S. trade law, offer interested parties (including labor- and human-rights NGOs) an annual opportunity to petition for the review of labor practices in any country that is a recipient of GSP benefits.[76] The GSP Subcommittee of the USTR's Trade Policy Staff Committee (comprised of representatives of twenty different federal departments and agencies) examines the petition and decides whether it merits formal review.[77] If it agrees to conduct a review, the USTR may draw upon Department of State and Department of Labor country reports and any other source of information it deems appropriate. In addition, it holds public hearings and a public consultation on the matter before reaching a final determination, which, in principle, occurs within a year after the petition was filed. If the USTR finds that a country's labor practices violate U.S. law where "internationally recognized worker rights" and prohibitions against the worst forms of child labor are concerned (regardless of whether such practices have a direct impact on the U.S. economy or employment),[78] it may then recommend to the president one of several possible actions. These range from dismissing the petition on the grounds that a country is already "taking steps toward ensuring internationally recognized worker rights," to extending the review while compliance negotiations with the beneficiary country proceed, to suspending or terminating some or all GSP benefits for the target country.[79] Although the country involved has the opportunity to defend its position during the USTR review, it cannot appeal the final U.S. decision. It can, however, later petition for the restoration of GSP benefits.

The GSP review process embodies (and has often been criticized for) broad executive-branch discretion. This discretion derives in part from the amended 1984 Trade and Tariff Act's failure to invoke specific ILO conventions in its definition of "internationally recognized worker rights," the absence of clear criteria by which the USTR is to judge what constitute acceptable variations in minimum labor standards and the severity of rights violations in different countries, and the ambiguity of the "taking steps" determination.[80] Executive discretion informs USTR decisions regarding which petitions to accept for formal review and especially the president's decision whether to suspend or terminate a particular country's GSP eligibility. Indeed, as noted above, the relevant legislation permits the executive branch to waive labor-conditionality requirements altogether when the president determines it is in the national interest to do so.[81] The president must provide a written report to Congress on all final decisions, but the decisions cannot be appealed.[82] The multiagency composition of the USTR's Trade Policy Staff Committee virtually guarantees that the decisions to undertake a labor rights review or to suspend or terminate a country's GSP eligibility are framed by broader U.S. foreign policy considerations.

Between 1985 and 2011 (the most recent date for which complete information is readily available), the USTR received at least 188 petitions concerning alleged labor rights violations in fifty-four different GSP beneficiary countries. It accepted ninety-one of those petitions (48.4 percent) for review.[83] The petitioners included major U.S. labor organizations—particularly the AFL-CIO but also several national industrial unions—and NGOs focusing on labor and human rights issues.[84] The focus of these petitions (many of which cited more than one issue) ranged from generally repressive political conditions to specific violations of individual and collective-action rights.[85] The incidence of filings was greatest during the 1980s and 1990s, tailing off in the early 2000s. Analysts attribute this decline to "complainant fatigue" with USTR procedures (aggravated by lapses and short-term renewals of the GSP program in the mid-1990s, which made it difficult to predict the USTR's review schedule), labor activists' shift toward other modes of action (particularly corporate social responsibility campaigns), and the growing number of U.S. free-trade agreements with developing countries (which generally make participating countries ineligible for GSP benefits).[86]

Although the USTR reviewed ninety-one of the labor rights petitions it received between 1985 and 2011, in only fourteen instances did the United States suspend or terminate a country's GSP eligibility. The countries affected were: Bangladesh (2013), Belarus (2000), Central African Republic (1989), Chile (1988), Liberia (1990), Maldives (1995), Mauritania (1993), Myanmar (1989), Nicaragua (1987), Pakistan (1996), Paraguay (1987), Romania (1987), Sudan (1991), and Syria (1992).[87] It was far more common for the U.S. government to use the review process as a forum for bilateral negotiations over labor rights practices in the target country.

An Analysis of U.S. GSP Labor Rights Petitions, 1985–1995

Several analysts have examined the motivations behind U.S. GSP filings (whether, for example, trade union petitioners typically seek to block competing imports from developing countries) and the factors shaping USTR decisions to accept or reject them for review.[88] Yet, no previous study has systematically analyzed the actual impact of USTR reviews on labor rights law and practice in a range of targeted countries.[89] Examining review impact in all the countries targeted since 1985 would constitute a most daunting task. There is, however, a substantial body of qualitative research available on petition processes and evolving labor rights conditions in a subset of these countries. Drawing on this material, this section assesses causal links between USTR pressures, target governments' responses, and collective-rights outcomes in fifteen countries between 1985 and 1995: Chile, Colombia, Costa Rica, Dominican Republic, El Salvador, Guatemala, Haiti, Honduras, Indonesia, Malaysia, Nicaragua, Pakistan, Panama, Paraguay, and Peru.[90]

The selection criterion employed in compiling this original dataset was the ready availability of sufficient information for an in-depth examination of the impact of GSP petitions and U.S. government efforts to promote collective-action rights (freedom of association and the rights to organize and bargain collectively) in a target country. Because of the particular interests of the authors whose research constitutes the basis for this analysis, Latin American and Caribbean countries comprise a disproportionate share of this subset (twelve of fifteen countries).[91] Nevertheless, the petitions filed against these fifteen countries ($N = 64$) comprise 52.5 percent of the 122 labor rights petitions filed between 1985 and 1995, the period of most intense GSP petitioning. Equally important, these country cases offer a significant range of variation in the independent variables that might determine the efficacy of the petition process in advancing collective-action rights in the countries involved: the number of trade unions and labor- and human-rights NGOs filing petitions; the extent of political support that U.S.-based petitioners were able to mobilize among trade unions and/or labor rights groups in the target country; the target country's export sensitivity to potential GSP sanction; whether there was a change of political regime in the targeted country during the course of the USTR review; and whether GSP eligibility was suspended or terminated as a consequence of the USTR review. The GSP petitions alleged a broad range of labor rights violations, but collective-action rights in the private and/or public sectors were central issues in all the countries targeted.

The outcomes that GSP petition processes produced in the target countries (the dependent variable) also varied considerably.[92] Observed outcomes were coded on a five-point scale ranging from 0 (no observed changes regarding freedom of association and the rights to organize and bargain collectively, even if there were improvements in other labor rights areas during the USTR review) to 4 (evidence that by the end of the USTR review, there was generally effective implementation in practice of freedom of association and the rights to organize and bargain collectively, including in the public sector and in any export-processing zones).[93] Employing this original coding scheme permits a more fine-grained, contextual assessment of changes in collective-action rights resulting from USTR reviews than what would be possible using the worker rights data compiled by Mosley (2011b) and by Cingranelli, Richards, and Clay (2014), although the outcome results reported in table 2.1 were cross-checked against both these datasets.[94] Distinguishing between collective-rights outcomes resulting from USTR reviews and those occurring as part of broader processes of sociopolitical change in the target countries is sometimes difficult. As a partial control, the outcomes recorded were those evident within three years after the USTR initiated its review process (or, in the case of multiple petition acceptances, within three years after the final petition acceptance).[95]

The AFL-CIO was by far the most active petitioner. Acting either on its own ($N = 29$) or in alliance with other unions or NGOs ($N = 8$), it was involved in thirty-seven (57.8 percent) of the sixty-four petitions filed between 1985 and 1995 (see table 2.1). Indeed, the AFL-CIO participated in GSP procedures involving all the countries listed in table 2.1, and in the Indonesian case, it filed five solo petitions alleging violations of GSP labor-rights conditionality. The two most active NGOs were the International Labor Rights Education and Research Fund (ILRERF) and Americas Watch (a division of Human Rights Watch), although in some filings—particularly those involving El Salvador and Guatemala—several other labor rights groups also appeared as copetitioners. In several instances, there was close cooperation and mutual support among trade unions and labor- and human-rights NGOs, but in only four country cases (Colombia, El Salvador, Guatemala, Pakistan) did they appear as copetitioners.

The USTR accepted for review thirty-seven (57.8 percent) of the sixty-four petitions it received regarding alleged rights violations in the fifteen countries under discussion here.[96] Labor organizations (particularly the AFL-CIO) were more successful in this regard than NGOs; 67.6 percent of the petitions they filed were accepted for review, whereas the USTR accepted only 31.3 percent of the petitions filed by NGOs. When NGOs partnered with labor organizations, their acceptance rate rose to 63.6 percent.[97] Trade unions might have enjoyed greater credibility or exercised more political leverage as advocates of labor rights, or the staff of the AFL-CIO and major industrial unions might have had access to more resources or have been more proficient in preparing GSP petitions than their NGO counterparts. The petition acceptance rate for NGOs might also have been

TABLE 2.1 Selected U.S. generalized system of preferences labor rights petitions, 1985–1995

Country	Petitioners Unions	NGOs	Both	Petitioners per filing	Political support in target country	USTR Response: Accept	USTR response: Reject.	Export Sensitivity of target country	Regime change	Policy impact
Chile	3	0	0	1.3	Weak	2	1	1.2/1.2	No	0
Colombia	0	1	2	2.0	Weak	0	3	3.6/3.6	No	0
Costa Rica	1	0	0	1.0	Moderate	1	0	3.0/17.8	No	1
Dominican Republic	2	3	0	1.0	Strong	4	1	8.6/22.4	No	3
El Salvador	4	4	3	2.2	Strong	8	3	1.4/6.2	Yes	2
Guatemala	5	2	5	3.0	Strong	4	8	4.3/9.9	Yes	3
Haiti	6	0	0	2.0	Weak	4	2	16.0/75.6	Yes	0
Honduras	1	1	0	1.0	Moderate	1	1	1.8/9.8	No	1
Indonesia	5	3	0	1.3	Weak	4	4	0.7/0.7	No	0
Malaysia	2	2	0	1.0	Weak	1	3	3.0/3.0	No	1
Nicaragua	1	0	0	1.0	Weak	1	0	1.4/1.4	No	0
Pakistan	0	0	1	3.0	Weak	1	0	1.5/1.5	No	0
Panama	2	0	0	1.0	Strong	2	0	9.2/14.1	No	2
Paraguay	3	0	0	1.0	Weak	3	0	1.0/1.0	Yes	2
Peru	2	0	0	1.0	Weak	1	1	6.4/6.8	No	0

Sources: USTR 2005. Chile (Dorman 1989: 13–14; Adams 1990; Frundt 1998: table 4.1, 94–95; Compa and Vogt 2001: 209–12; Morley and McGillion 2015: 253–55), Colombia (Frundt 1998: table 4.1, 98), Costa Rica (Frundt 1998: table 4.1, 228–37), Dominican Republic (Frundt 1998: table 4.1, 207–27; Douglas, Ferguson, and Klett 2004: 277–81); El Salvador (Dorman 1989: 11–12; B. Davis 1995; Frundt 1998: table 4.1, chaps. 5–6; Douglas, Ferguson, and Klett 2004: 281–84; Athreya 2011: 33–44), Guatemala (Frundt 1998: table 4.1, chap. 7; Compa and Vogt 2001: 212–22; Douglas, Ferguson, and Klett 2004: 288–91), Haiti (National Labor Committee 1993; Frundt 1998: table 4.1, 99–100; Tsogas 2000: table 1; Arthur 2003), Honduras (Frundt 1998: table 4.1, 192–206; Athreya 2011: 44–54), Indonesia (Compa and Vogt 2001: 222–28, Athreya 2011: 23–33), Malaysia (Dorman 1995: 12–13; Tsogas 2000: table 1; Compa and Vogt 2001: 222–28; Athreya 2011: 15–23), Nicaragua (Frundt 1998: table 4.1, 248–52), Pakistan (Compa and Vogt 2001: 228–31; Candland 2007: 41; Athreya 2011: 63–65), Panama (Frundt 1998: table 4.1, 237–46), Paraguay (International Confederation of Free Trade Unions 1997; Frundt 1998: table 4.1, 96; Cook 2007: 55–56), Peru (Frundt 1998: table 4.1, 97; Cook 2007: 53, 120–27).

(continued)

TABLE 2.1 (*Continued*)

Coding scheme for political support in target country:

Weak = nominal (if any) trade union and/or labor rights NGO support for a GSP petition because of government intimidation or repression, overall labor movement weakness, or the absence or weakness of politically independent unions.

Moderate = trade union and/or labor rights NGO public endorsement of a GSP petition, sometimes including involvement in petition design and documentation.

Strong = active trade union and/or labor rights NGO engagement with the GSP petition process, with some unions publicly calling for a USTR review, signing or cosigning a GSP petition, pressing for domestic legal and policy reforms, and monitoring reform implementation in coordination with the USTR.

Measures of export sensitivity of target country:

This column reports two measures (in percent) of a target country's export sensitivity to possible GSP suspension or termination: GSP-eligible exports to the United States as a proportion of the target country's total world exports in the year that the USTR first accepted a labor rights petition for review ("GSP"), and all exports to the United States that were subject to U.S. labor rights conditionality (under the GSP program and any other preferential trade agreement) as a proportion of the target country's total world exports in that same year ("GSP +"). Author's calculations based on U.S. import data from the Center for International Data, University of California-Davis, accessed July 10, 2023, https://cid.ucdavis.edu/usixd; and World Trade Organization/World Bank export data, accessed July 10, 2023, https://data.worldbank.org.

Coding scheme for observed policy impact:

0 = no observed changes regarding freedom of association and the rights to organize and bargain collectively within three years after the USTR initiated its review process, even if there were improvements in other labor rights areas during the USTR review.

1 = modest policy change regarding unionization and collective bargaining rights during the specified period.

2 = modification of labor code provisions regarding unionization and collective bargaining rights during the specified period.

3 = extension of favorable formal labor code provisions to the public sector and any export-processing zones during the specified period.

4 = evidence that within three years after the USTR initiated its review process that there was generally effective implementation in practice of the freedom of association and the rights to organize and bargain collectively, including in the public sector and any export-processing zones.

Notes: "Petitioners per filing" (author's calculation) is the mean number of petitioners per filing. USTR acceptances include those petitions filed while a formal USTR review was already under way and which were "continued" by the USTR. "Regime change" refers to significant political and/or regime change occurring during the USTR review period. NGOs = nongovernmental organizations; USTR = Office of the United States Trade Representative.

lowered somewhat by the fact that groups like the ILRERF were sometimes the first to employ the GSP process against countries with poor labor (and human) rights records, sometimes under inauspicious political circumstances. For example, America's Watch, the ILRERF, and allied labor rights groups filed several petitions against El Salvador (1987–1989) during the final years of the Cold War and under presidents Ronald Reagan and George H. W. Bush (1989–1993), both Republican administrations that only moderately supported labor rights petitions.[98] At the time, the USTR adopted a controversially narrow definition of labor rights violations, arguing that the assassination or kidnapping of trade unionists did not necessarily violate GSP conditionality requirements because the crimes were committed against individuals engaged in opposition political activities rather than in trade union work in a more limited sense.[99]

The degree of pressure that GSP petitioners were able to bring to bear on target countries through the USTR review process—a combination of the number of petitions filed against a particular country, the number of petitioners involved, and the extent of political support among trade unions and/or labor rights groups in the target country—varied considerably, not least because mobilization by petitioners and their target-country allies did not automatically translate into equivalent pressure by the U.S. government.[100] The number of petitions filed against the fifteen countries under examination ranged from one (Costa Rica, Nicaragua, Pakistan) to twelve (Guatemala) (table 2.1). The mean number of petitioners per filing ranged from one to three; in the petitions against Guatemala in 1991 and 1992, a total of ten union and labor rights NGOs were involved.[101]

In several cases (Chile, Haiti, Indonesia, Malaysia, Pakistan, Paraguay), persistent government repression made it impossible for U.S.-based petitioners to mobilize any substantial political support in the targeted country.[102] In El Salvador and Malaysia, government officials and business groups argued that U.S. labor organizations sought to deprive their country of GSP benefits simply to protect their own market position against lower-cost competition, and they were initially successful in dissuading domestic labor groups from backing the USTR review.[103] The absence of credible support in the target country was important because it sometimes undercut petitioners' position vis-à-vis the USTR by making it harder for them to document their claims in persuasive detail.[104]

Yet in six countries (Costa Rica, Dominican Republic, El Salvador, Guatemala, Honduras, and Panama), there was moderate domestic support (public endorsement of a GSP petition by trade unions and/or labor rights groups, sometimes including their involvement in petition design and documentation) or strong support (active trade union and/or labor rights NGO engagement with the GSP petition process, with some unions and/or labor rights groups publicly calling for a USTR review, signing or cosigning a petition, pressing for domestic legal and policy reforms, and monitoring reform implementation in coordination with the USTR) for the GSP petition process (table 2.1).[105] This was particularly impressive in El Salvador and Guatemala, countries that were at the time engulfed in violent civil conflict. In El Salvador, the Union Federation of Salvadoran Workers (Federación Sindical de Trabajadores Salvadoreños, FSTS) bolstered continuing efforts by its U.S. allies by filing its own GSP petition in 1990.[106] In Guatemala, substantial numbers of labor organizations actively backed U.S. GSP petitions in 1986 and 1992 (documenting labor code violations and labor court failings), and in 1993 and 1994, they demanded that the USTR extend its review until the national government enacted meaningful reforms.[107] In addition to bringing some domestic political pressure to bear on the target government, support of this kind increased petitioners' credibility with the USTR.[108]

The data presented in table 2.1 evidence a close association between petitioner pressure and observed positive changes in collective-action rights. However, the volume of petitions filed and the number of petitioners involved were not in themselves determinative in this regard. The total number of petitions filed in the five countries with outcomes coded 2 or 3 (Dominican Republic, El Salvador, Guatemala, Panama, Paraguay) ranged from two (Panama) to eleven (Guatemala); the mean number of petitioners per filing ranged from 1 (Dominican Republic, Panama, Paraguay) to 3.2 (Guatemala).

The data in table 2.1 indicate a stronger relationship between the strength of political support mobilized in the target country and observed outcomes rated 2 or 3.[109] Indeed, in four of these five cases (Dominican Republic, El Salvador, Guatemala, Panama), there was a close association between target-country domestic support for GSP action and the outcomes achieved. Only in the Dominican Republic and Panama were national labor movements comparatively strong at the time the GSP petitions were filed.[110] As noted above, the cases of El Salvador and Guatemala demonstrate that it was possible for GSP petitioners to mobilize meaningful domestic political support for their initiatives even in countries without a strong labor movement or an established democratic tradition. On the basis of the information available, it is not possible to determine the frequency with which U.S. actors' decision to file a GSP petition reflected prior communications with labor unions or NGOs in the target country, or whether pre-existing binational alliances played a role in this regard. In the cases of El Salvador and Guatemala, however, the binational ties forged among human rights activists during civil conflicts in these countries in the 1980s and early 1990s did underpin GSP-centered collaboration.[111] The strength of those networks may, in part, explain the volume of GSP petitions filed against the two countries.

Nonetheless, one cannot necessarily conclude that U.S. pressures backed by substantial target-country domestic support were by themselves always sufficient to effect significant change in collective-action outcomes. In three of the five countries with outcomes coded 2 or 3 (El Salvador, Guatemala, Paraguay), democratic regime change was of equal (or greater) importance than external pressures per se in bringing about observed changes in collective-action rights.[112]

In both El Salvador and Guatemala, U.S. trade unions and labor- and human-rights NGOs used GSP procedures to campaign intensively, over a sustained period, against egregious rights violations, many of which were linked to government attacks on opposition forces during prolonged civil conflicts. These initiatives received strong support from—and, in turn, bolstered—besieged labor movements in these countries, and in Guatemala, they contributed to a gradual shift over time in private sector attitudes regarding the merits of consultation and negotiation with unions. However, progress on collective-action rights was closely bound up with broader efforts to negotiate national peace agreements, establish more democratic forms of governance, and address pending socio-economic demands in these war-torn societies. Indeed, the USTR extended its reviews of rights violations in El Salvador and Guatemala until peace processes were further advanced. In El Salvador, the 1992 peace accords created an Economic and Social Forum to discuss, among other topics, labor rights. Similarly, in Guatemala, the Tripartite Commission that—bolstered by insistent USTR pressures—significantly advanced collective-action labor rights implementation was a product of the 1996 peace settlement.

In Paraguay, the AFL-CIO filed GSP petitions to protest labor rights violations under General Alfredo Stroessner's long-lived authoritarian regime, and in 1987, the U.S. government suspended the country's GSP eligibility. However, government repression and the extreme weakness of the national labor movement precluded the mobilization of significant domestic political support. It was the overthrow of the Stroessner regime in 1989 that opened the way for extensive labor reforms under a new democratic government.

The core assumption underpinning GSP labor-conditionality provisions and U.S. efforts to leverage state sovereignty to positive effect through this program is that a target country will be willing to remedy rights violations in order to protect its tariff-free access to the U.S. marketplace.[113] Among the countries examined here, there was some variation in target countries' export sensitivity to the potential suspension or termination of GSP benefits. However, in fourteen of these fifteen countries, GSP-eligible exports to the United States in the year in which the USTR first accepted a labor rights petition for review (or, in the case of Colombia, the year the first petition was filed) constituted less than 10 percent of the country's total worldwide exports.[114] This proportion ranged from 0.7 percent in Indonesia (1989) to 16 percent in Haiti (1988) (table 2.1, column 6, lefthand score). In and of itself, then, countries' sensitivity to the potential loss of GSP benefits does not clearly explain differences in their responses to USTR pressures.[115]

It is important to note, however, that eight of the countries under discussion here (Costa Rica, Dominican Republic, El Salvador, Guatemala, Haiti, Honduras, Panama, Peru) were also beneficiaries of other U.S. preferential trade agreements—the Caribbean Basin Economic Recovery Act (CBERA, 1983, 1990) and the Andean Trade Preference Act of 1991—that also included labor rights-conditionality provisions.[116] Combined exports to the United States under the GSP and these other programs (hereinafter GSP+[117]) as a proportion of worldwide exports varied from a low of 6.2 percent in El Salvador (1990) to 75.6 percent in Haiti (1988) (table 2.1, column 9, righthand score). Yet of the four countries with the highest GSP+ export sensitivity (Costa Rica, Dominican Republic, Haiti, Panama), only in the Dominican Republic and Panama (where domestic political support was strong and democratic regime change was not a factor) did USTR pressures produce an observed outcome in collective-action labor rights policy in the 2–3 range.

However, even this expanded measure of export sensitivity may not fully describe a country's vulnerability to GSP or GSP-related penalties or indicate how sensitive governing political and economic elites may be to strong external pressures. A country's exports to the United States under the GSP program may, for instance, be concentrated in industries judged particularly important for a country's development strategy (for example, the electronics sector in Malaysia).[118] In the case of Chile, the suspension of GSP eligibility in 1988 affected exports valued at US$87 million, but it also led to the loss of Overseas

Private Investment Corporation insurance coverage valued at US$750 million, affecting US$1 billion in U.S.-origin foreign direct investment. In El Salvador, the country's political and economic elites were greatly concerned about the negative political symbolism that a GSP suspension would entail. The USTR's ongoing review of petitions filed by the AFL-CIO, Americas Watch, and the FSTS in 1990 gave Salvadoran labor organizations increased political leverage in their demands for labor law reform and national ratification of several ILO conventions. Impending USTR decision deadlines in February and November 1993 were the impetus for last-minute government and business concessions in negotiations over the content of a new national labor code—legislation that was enacted in May 1994 and constituted the basis for the USTR's final "taking steps" finding in July 1994.[119]

Because of such considerations, in some instances, the mere threat of a GSP petition or USTR action can cause a government to make important policy concessions regarding labor rights.[120] In Honduras in the early 1990s, the threat of a GSP petition led the government to undertake extensive negotiations with U.S. authorities that led to a November 1995 memorandum of understanding addressing freedom of association issues, labor inspection, and the country's overall capacity to improve its labor practices.[121] Even more dramatically in the case of Guatemala, the national business community was greatly concerned that GSP sanctions would harm the country's overall international reputation. These fears were so strong that U.S. government threats to suspend GSP eligibility mobilized strong business opposition against President Jorge Serrano's unconstitutional seizure of enhanced executive authority in May 1993, leading to his resignation and the restoration of democratic governance.[122]

Overall, the data presented in table 2.1 indicate that the extent of domestic actors' political support for USTR initiatives—and thus perhaps stronger or more sustained GSP-centered actions by the U.S. government—was more important than export sensitivity in inducing target-country governments to respond to U.S. pressures by adopting policy changes in the area of collective-action labor rights. This conclusion was confirmed through a statistical analysis employing Bayesian logit and ordered-logit regressions (see appendix A).[123] The regression results reported in table A.1 indicate that there was consistently a statistically significant relationship (at either the $p < 0.05$ or $p < 0.01$ thresholds) between "political support" and "observed outcomes," whereas other possible explanatory factors (the aggregate number of petitions filed against a country, the

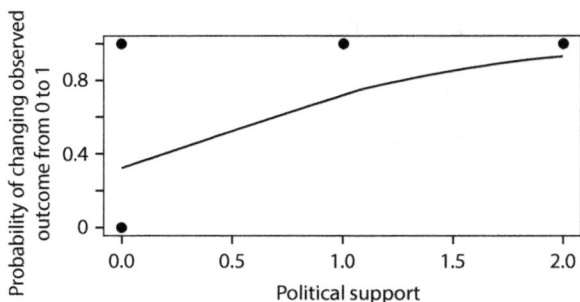

2.1 Probability that increased political support in the target country for USTR actions will produce positive change in collective-action labor rights

Source: Table A.1 (model 1, dataset A)

Notes: "Political support" values are 0 (weak), 1 (medium), and 2 (strong). USTR = Office of the United States Trade Representative

target country's export sensitivity, whether the country experienced democratizing regime change, the target country's economic size and level of socioeconomic development at the time GSP petitions were filed against it, and whether the country is in the Caribbean Basin or in the Latin American region, areas of historically strong U.S. political and economic influence) were not statistically significant. Figure 2.1 graphically depicts the probability that an increase in domestic political support for USTR actions will lead to a more positive observed outcome in collective-action rights.

A visual inspection of the data in table 2.1 might suggest the presence of interaction effects among key factors. For example, six of the eight countries in which GSP-centered U.S. pressures produced any observed change in collective-action labor rights—Costa Rica, Dominican Republic, El Salvador, Guatemala, Honduras, and Panama—were democratic or democratizing countries (a factor partially represented by the strength of domestic political support for GSP petitions) located in the Caribbean Basin (a region in which U.S. political and economic influence has historically been especially strong) with comparatively small economies.[124] Conversely, three of the six countries with no observed change in collective-action rights (Chile, Indonesia, Peru) were under authoritarian rule,[125] located outside the Caribbean Basin, and among the larger economies in this group of GSP target countries—all factors that may have somewhat increased their capacity to resist U.S. sovereignty leverage.[126] However, perhaps because of the small number of cases ($N = 14$),[127] regression analysis identified no statistically significant interaction effects among any of the independent variables examined.

Target-country governments, typically invoking claims to national sovereignty, frequently resisted USTR pressures because of strenuous private sector opposition to labor reform. Although it varied in intensity and in form of expression, such opposition was a constant in all the countries under discussion here and was particularly strong where collective-action rights were concerned. This had two major consequences. First, private sector resistance significantly constrained what concessions target-country governments were prepared to make in their negotiations with U.S. officials. There were several instances in which a government responded to USTR pressures (or the threat of a USTR review) by making limited policy changes. For example, the Guatemalan and Indonesian governments enacted increases in the minimum wage.[128] In Colombia, the government restricted pregnancy testing as a condition of employment in high-risk jobs.[129] And in Peru, the government adopted legislation regulating hours of work and promised to provide compensation to employees who were unjustly dismissed.[130] These policy changes clearly benefited workers, but they fell far short of substantial changes in law and/or in practice regarding freedom of association and the rights to organize and bargain collectively.

Second, even when the exercise of U.S. sovereignty leverage produced important legal reforms strengthening collective-action rights, private sector opposition persisted and made implementation of agreed reforms a major challenge in almost all the cases examined here. Opposition was often particularly intense to extending collective-action rights in export-processing zones (EPZs), areas frequently regarded as central to a developing country's promotion of nontraditional exports and in which low production costs are a key factor in international economic competitiveness. In Pakistan and Panama, these areas were formally exempt from national labor law.[131] In the Dominican Republic, Guatemala, Haiti, Honduras, and elsewhere,[132] employers strenuously resisted unionization efforts, government officials tolerated the illegal firing of workers attempting to form trade unions, and strikes were officially or unofficially banned. Governments often failed to enforce laws requiring employers to respect labor rights as a condition for acquiring export permits. The immense challenge of effectively enforcing collective-action rights in EPZs is a principal reason why table 2.1 contains no observed outcomes rated 4.[133]

Although the political disposition of national governments was the main factor determining the outcome of GSP petition processes, limited state capacity in target countries also constituted a major barrier to advancing collective-action rights. In almost all the cases examined here, problems such as governments' limited capacity to inspect workplaces throughout the national territory, judicial authorities' incapacity to resolve individual and collective labor disputes expeditiously, and corruption of administrative and judicial authorities were significant constraints on the exercise of labor rights in practice.[134] These difficulties, coupled with persistent employer opposition to the legal adoption and subsequent implementation of collective-action labor rights, meant that enforcement remained a major challenge both during and after USTR investigations, even where external pressures had prompted countries to adopt important legal reforms.

External actors addressed these problems in different ways. For example, at the same time that the USTR pressured El Salvador and Guatemala to adopt and implement meaningful labor reforms, the U.S. Agency for International Development (joined in the case of Guatemala by Spain, the ILO, and the Organization of American States) made substantial investments in these countries' administrative and judicial capacity to regulate worker-employer relations and enforce national law, including both expanded material resources and enhanced personnel training.[135] The USTR's formal reviews of El Salvador and Guatemala remained open for extended periods, and in both countries, it organized follow-up missions to ensure that promised labor reforms were being implemented in practice.[136] The case of Indonesia illustrates how important such continued external supervision can be: After the USTR terminated its review in 1995, government repression of independent trade unionists resumed.[137] Yet, in the end, just as domestic political support was important to achieving some degree of success through the GSP petition process, it was undoubtedly the most important factor in effective long-term national enforcement of labor rights in compliance with international norms.

CONCLUSION

In Krasner's terms, trade agreements like the U.S. GSP program do not violate a participating state's international legal sovereignty because they are contracts that are entered into voluntarily. The program's labor rights–conditionality provisions do, however, compromise Westphalian sovereignty because they subject "domestic institutions and personnel to external influence."[138]

This chapter has shown that sovereign resistance, frequently reflecting strong employer opposition to rights enforcement, poses major obstacles to international efforts to advance collective-action rights. In the fifteen countries examined here, national governments were generally less opposed to the formal adoption of international norms than they were to their implementation in practice. Only four of these states (Chile, El Salvador, Indonesia, Malaysia) had failed to ratify both core ILO collective-action rights conventions (nos. 87 and 98) prior to the first GSP filings against them.[139] In contrast, albeit with important differences in degree and in form, all these countries resisted U.S. efforts to employ GSP conditionality to ensure compliance with these norms. The resulting modal pattern was sustained bilateral negotiation over labor rights issues.

These cases also demonstrate that the GSP petition process can, by providing labor rights proponents with a fulcrum of sovereign leverage against rights violators, constitute a means of advancing collective-action rights in developing countries. The assumption underpinning the U.S. GSP labor-conditionality provisions is that a target state will be willing to correct serious rights violations in order to protect its access to the U.S. marketplace. Yet at least in the fifteen countries examined here over the 1985–1995 period, export sensitivity alone did not have a clearly significant impact on observed policy outcomes. Nor, in this set of cases, did actual suspension or termination of GSP benefits produce an immediate breakthrough regarding collective-action rights.[140] In Guatemala and Honduras, however, U.S. threats to suspend GSP eligibility did register strongly with political and economic elites concerned about their country's general international reputation. Indeed, because suspension or termination of benefits was always a potential economic sanction (with possibly substantial spillover effects through, for instance, the loss of OPIC coverage of U.S. foreign direct investment), this dimension of the U.S. GSP program may have influenced target governments' political calculations more frequently than the available secondary literature directly documents.[141]

In some countries, U.S. pressures contributed both to important legal reforms and a generally heightened awareness of labor rights issues in government and employer circles. The success rate was, nevertheless, modest. None of the observed outcomes merited a rating of 4 (table 2.1). In only five of the countries (Dominican Republic, El Salvador, Guatemala, Panama, Paraguay) were there observed outcomes in the 2–3 range, and in El Salvador, Guatemala, and Paraguay, petition-centered pressures were a contributing factor to rights advances achieved through broader democratization processes. In the cases of Costa Rica, Dominican Republic, El Salvador, and Pakistan,[142] U.S. GSP petitions followed or overlapped with ILO pressures to correct serious rights violations. It is particularly noteworthy that there was a close association between the strength of political support that GSP petitioners were able to mobilize in the target country and positive changes in collective-action rights. This association was closer than that between observed outcomes and either the aggregate number of petitions filed against a target country, the number of petitioners involved, or that country's export sensitivity.

The finding that U.S. GSP petitioners' success in mobilizing domestic political support in target countries significantly enhanced the effectiveness of external pressures sheds new light on how state sovereignty can, in practice, be leveraged to promote labor reforms in developing countries. Even in countries without a strong labor movement or a consolidated democratic political order, the engagement of local trade unions and/or labor rights NGOs can sometimes heighten pressures on national governments to introduce legal and policy reforms. Local allies may prove important for the purposes of gathering information on actual labor rights conditions and developing concrete proposals for inclusion in GSP petitions.[143] However, evidence of local support for GSP petitions may have been even more significant in enhancing the perceived validity of these claims in the eyes of U.S. government officials and thereby galvanizing their political will to act upon them. This point is especially important because the GSP review process reserves broad discretion to the U.S. federal executive and, because the target of potential trade penalties is another national government, broader foreign policy considerations necessarily inform U.S. government responses to GSP labor rights petitions.

Over the 1985–1995 period, the GSP petition process was open to a wide range of sociopolitical actors (so long as, in view of the USTR's general policy of not self-initiating reviews of labor practices in beneficiary countries, they were prepared to bear the sometimes considerable resource costs involved). Moreover, in the cases examined here, civil society actors themselves often absorbed enduring lessons from participating in it. Not only did they gain experience in how to formulate labor rights petitions to U.S. government authorities, but they also learned how important it was to build collaborative alliances among potential trade union and NGO allies both within the United States and in the country where labor rights violations occurred. In fact, the ties forged between several U.S. labor- and human-rights NGOs and trade unions in the course of GSP petition processes directly underpinned several of the labor rights complaints that were later filed against Mexico under the NAALC (see chapter 4).

Finally, although the conclusions reached in this chapter are based on cases from 1985–1995, they remain directly relevant to contemporary U.S. GSP labor rights petition processes. Neither petition procedures nor the political obstacles that rights advocates confront in developing countries have changed since then.[144] The proliferation of U.S. free-trade agreements (which generally state that the reciprocal benefits they contain replace participating countries' GSP eligibility), the growing prominence of corporate social responsibility campaigns, the smaller size of the U.S. labor movement and a consequent decline in the resources dedicated to international initiatives, and a shift in major U.S. trade unions' international focus away from GSP-eligible economic activities, all mean that U.S. unions and labor rights activists initiate GSP petitions less frequently than they once did.[145] Nonetheless, the GSP petition process remains an important strategic option for them, and recourse to it is far more common than are labor rights complaints filed under the provisions of U.S. free-trade agreements.

CHAPTER 3

Context and Constraints

The Origin and Negotiation of the North American Free Trade Agreement's Labor Rights Provisions

T he North American Free Trade Agreement (NAFTA) was historically significant for three main reasons. First, it was the first free-trade agreement negotiated between economically advanced countries and a developing country, linking states with vastly different power capabilities, distinctive foreign policy trajectories, and economies that varied greatly in size and competitiveness. Because Canada and the United States had recently adopted a bilateral free-trade agreement, the negotiations over the NAFTA focused principally on how to integrate a newly industrializing country into a trade accord between two advanced industrial economies. These negotiations were only possible in political terms because the Mexican government had recently embraced promarket policies that opened up new opportunities for economic integration on a continental scale.

Second, the agreement represented a major shift in Mexico's foreign alignment. Although Canada also had a complicated history of unequal interaction with its more powerful North American neighbor,[1] Mexico's past relationship with the United States had been particularly traumatic. The loss of over half of its territory to the United States between 1835 and 1855,[2] and especially its humiliating defeat in the Mexican-American War (1846–1848), engendered strong nationalist sentiments and cast a long shadow over bilateral relations throughout the late nineteenth and most of the twentieth centuries. Mexico's long-standing advocacy of a strict policy of nonintervention and binding principles in international affairs (particularly juridical equality among states and the peaceful settlement of international disputes) derived from its core interest in defending its sovereignty and constraining U.S. power.[3] Indeed, from the mid-nineteenth century until the outbreak of World War II, Mexico had maintained a carefully calculated political distance from "the colossus of the North"—a policy based in part on geographical barriers (the less populated, arid areas of northern Mexico and the southwestern United States) to closer interaction. Despite a record of effective bilateral collaboration during World War II, Mexico sought to safeguard its national sovereignty during post-war decades by adopting a de facto policy of "bargained negligence" vis-à-vis the United States. Thus, Mexico's proposal in 1990 for a free-trade agreement with the United States constituted a remarkable break with a long foreign policy tradition and a decisive step toward the institutionalization of closer bilateral ties.[4]

Third, the NAFTA included, albeit as a supplemental agreement, explicit provisions concerning workers' rights, the North American Agreement on Labor Cooperation (NAALC). This international agreement marked a significant departure from past efforts to link labor rights protections to trade agreements, which had focused either on attempts to establish a "social clause" in the multilateral General Agreement on Tariffs and Trade (GATT) or on the U.S. Generalized System of Preferences program (chapter 2). In fact, the NAALC constituted a key precedent that shaped negotiations over all subsequent trade agreements to which the United States became a party through 2020.

Yet despite the importance of this precedent, the scope of covered labor rights and the dispute-settlement provisions in the NAALC were quite restricted. Its provisions were, in fact, far weaker than those first proposed by U.S. negotiators, who sought to shore up domestic political support and win legislative approval of the NAFTA by initially calling for the creation of a powerful, quasi-supranational trilateral secretariat that would ensure respect for broadly defined worker rights in the three signatory countries, especially in Mexico. This outcome was surprising because of the substantial asymmetries in power capabilities between the United States and its NAFTA partners.[5] Following an overview of the historical circumstances that led to the NAFTA and the initial controversies over worker rights that surrounded its negotiation, this chapter examines in depth the domestic and international political bargaining that occurred in 1993 over attaching labor rights provisions to the accord. It seeks to explain the puzzling nature of the NAALC outcome and why the U.S. government was unable to deploy its sovereignty leverage more effectively in the negotiations by focusing on the structure of the negotiating process, the alignment of domestic sociopolitical actors in the three countries, and the ways in which sovereignty concerns shaped the parties' negotiating positions.

THE NORTH AMERICAN FREE TRADE AGREEMENT

Although the NAFTA originated in the specific confluence of economic and political conditions prevailing in Mexico, the United States, and Canada in the late 1980s and early 1990s, the idea of institutionalized North American economic integration was not new. A combination of geographical contiguity (Canada and the United States share a 3,987-mile land border, while Mexico and the United States share a 1,935-mile land border) and Canada-U.S. and Mexico-U.S. market integration from the nineteenth century onward defined the potential basis for enhanced policy coordination in economic affairs.[6]

These were, however, highly asymmetric economic relationships. The economic size of the United States (with a gross domestic product [GDP] of US$5,465 billion in 1990) dwarfed that of Canada (with a GDP of US$516.7 billion in that year) and especially Mexico (with a GDP of US$236 billion in 1990).[7] Moreover, even though Canada and Mexico were significant foci of U.S. trade and investment, both countries were far more economically dependent on the United States than the United States was on either of them. For example, whereas in 1985, U.S. goods exports to Canada represented 21.9 percent of all U.S. goods exports, and U.S. goods imports from Canada constituted 20.4 percent of all such imports,[8] in 1988, the U.S. market absorbed 72.8 percent of all Canadian merchandise exports and the United States was the source of 65.5 percent of all Canadian merchandise imports.[9] Similarly, whereas in 1989, U.S. goods exports to Mexico constituted 6.9 percent of all U.S. goods exports, and imports from Mexico represented 5.7 percent of total U.S. goods imports,[10] the United States was the destination for 69.1 percent of all Mexican goods exports and the source of 69.3 percent of all goods imported into Mexico.[11] The United States was also the source of nearly two-thirds of the total stock of direct foreign investment in both Canada and Mexico.[12]

Such marked disparities in economic size and in trade and investment dependence, combined with histories of politically charged bilateral relations, long gave both Canada and Mexico pause when proposals for institutionalized integration arose. For this reason, the 1965 Canada-United States Automobile

Products Trade Agreement, which stimulated integrated automotive production in the transborder region surrounding final-assembly plants in Detroit, Michigan, was a particularly important development.[13] With that agreement as a precedent, and with an eye on Mexico's strategically important petroleum reserves, on November 13, 1979, U.S. presidential candidate Ronald Reagan called for a "North American accord" to promote a freer flow of goods, services, and people among Canada, Mexico, and the United States. As president, in January 1981, Reagan again proposed a North American common market.[14] The idea fell flat, however, as the Mexican and Canadian governments both hastened to demur.[15] Nevertheless, by the end of Reagan's terms in office (1981–1985, 1985–1989), the United States and Canada had successfully negotiated the far-reaching Canada-United States Free Trade Agreement (CUSFTA, 1989).[16] George H.W. Bush, Reagan's vice president, sought to carry the momentum forward by promising during his own presidential campaign in 1988 that he would seek to create a continental free-trade zone.[17]

Whereas over the course of the 1980s, consecutive U.S. presidential administrations consistently favored closer North American economic integration, prevailing views in Ottawa and Mexico City shifted substantially. In his 1983 campaign to lead the Progressive Conservative Party, Brian Mulroney (Canada's prime minister between September 1984 and June 1993) strongly opposed a free-trade agreement with the United States. By 1985, however, worsening bilateral trade tensions had produced a cross-party consensus in favor of a comprehensive agreement that would protect Canada's access to the vital U.S. market and establish reliable dispute-settlement mechanisms.[18] On September 26, 1985, therefore, the Mulroney government formally proposed a free-trade agreement with the United States. Talks opened in Ottawa on May 21, 1986, and negotiations finally concluded on October 3, 1987. The CUSFTA was signed on January 2, 1988, and took effect on January 1, 1989.[19]

Where Mexico was concerned, the country's 1982 foreign debt crisis was the crucial catalyst for a radical transformation of official views concerning national development strategy and economic relations with the United States.[20] A sharp rise in international oil prices after 1973 and the discovery of substantial new petroleum reserves in the mid-1970s sparked rapid economic growth and permitted Mexico to borrow heavily in international capital markets. However, when oil prices fell in 1981–1982, and rising U.S. interest rates significantly raised the costs of servicing its U.S. dollar-denominated debt, Mexico found itself unable either to meet its debt payment obligations (thus detonating the Latin American debt crisis of the 1980s) or to secure the foreign exchange necessary to finance essential imports.

The administrations of Miguel de la Madrid Hurtado (1982–1988) and Carlos Salinas de Gortari (1988–1994) were, therefore, compelled to implement structural adjustment policies and an increasingly radical series of market-oriented reforms that included trade, exchange-rate, and industrial policy liberalization; deregulation of foreign investment flows and domestic commercial and financial activities; and the large-scale privatization of state-owned enterprises. In April 1985, Mexico and the United States signed a bilateral agreement designed to reduce Mexican export subsidies and limit U.S. countervailing duties on Mexican imports, the first comprehensive trade agreement between the two countries since 1950.[21] In August 1986, Mexico acceded to the GATT.[22] Following this key step, Mexico and the United States signed two bilateral agreements designed to promote economic cooperation: a Framework of Principles and Procedures for Consultation Regarding Trade and Investment Relations in November 1987, and an Understanding Regarding Trade and Investment Facilitation Talks in October 1989.[23] By 1989, "Mexico's average weighted tariff was 6.2 percent, and 96 percent of Mexican imports were free of quotas."[24]

Salinas, in particular, made the deepening of domestic economic reform, a reduction in Mexico's foreign debt burden, and the promotion of direct foreign investment central axes of his presidential agenda. Under the terms of the 1987 framework agreement with the United States, Mexico had agreed to pursue bilateral trade-liberalization negotiations in several key economic areas, and by June 1990, the two countries had reached sectoral agreements on steel, textiles, agriculture, alcoholic beverages, automobile engines, customs proceedings, and intellectual property.[25] Yet Salinas's initial commitment was principally to multilateral trade policy options and the diversification of Mexico's external economic ties.[26] In fact, when the presidents-elect of Mexico and the United States met on November 22, 1988, in Houston, Texas, Salinas rejected an initial, informal proposal from George H. W. Bush (1989–1993) to pursue bilateral free-trade negotiations with the United States on the grounds that Mexico's first priority was reducing its foreign-debt obligations.[27]

For these reasons, real drama attended Salinas's historic decision to recast economic relations with the United States by proposing a bilateral free-trade agreement. His initiative followed a period of heightened tension in Mexico-U.S.

relations during the mid-1980s, originating in strong U.S. opposition to Mexico's activist foreign policy during the Central American crisis and criticism of Mexico over trade, immigration, drug trafficking, and domestic political issues.[28] Moreover, Salinas's decision broke with the public positions he had taken on the subject throughout 1989.[29] As late as February 1, 1990, in the keynote address he gave to the World Economic Forum in Davos, Switzerland, Salinas argued that a "common market" between Mexico and the United States was "inadvisable" because of differences in the two countries' level of development.[30] Nevertheless, Salinas awakened his secretary of commerce and industrial development, Jaime Serra Puche, in the early hours of February 2 to announce his decision to pursue a free-trade agreement with the United States.[31]

It was Salinas's "Davos conversion" that caused Mexico to redirect its trade and investment strategy. Between January 25 and February 4, 1990, Salinas led a high-level delegation of cabinet ministers and national business leaders on a trip to Portugal, the United Kingdom, the Federal Republic of Germany, Belgium, and Switzerland to promote investment opportunities in Mexico. However, the delegation's presentations in national capitals and at the World Economic Forum met with a disappointing response. Salinas and his advisers found that, in the immediate aftermath of the fall of the Berlin Wall in November 1989, Western European investors were primarily focused on emerging opportunities in Eastern Europe, not faraway Mexico. Confronted by this new reality, and in line with the counsel he received during his tour from Portugal's President Mario Soares and German Chancellor Helmut Kohl, Salinas concluded that Mexico's most viable strategic option was to pursue deeper economic integration with the United States, its principal trade and investment partner. From his perspective, a free-trade agreement offered a historic opportunity to redefine the two countries' complicated, often tendentious bilateral relations.[32]

While still in Davos, Secretary Serra Puche alerted U.S. Trade Representative (USTR) Carla Hills of the Mexican government's interest in seeking a free-trade agreement with the United States.[33] In late February 1990, Salinas dispatched Serra Puche and Chief of Staff José Córdoba Montoya on a secret mission to Washington, DC, to gauge the Bush administration's reactions.[34] They reported that President Bush, U.S. Secretary of State James Baker, and other senior officials expressed enthusiasm for the initiative, and on March 8, Salinas telephoned Bush to confirm the latter's personal support.[35] News of these discussions appeared in the *Wall Street Journal* on March 27,[36] and on June 11, Bush and Salinas publicly announced their support for bilateral free trade during Salinas's visit to Washington, DC.[37] However, it was not until August 21 that Salinas formally wrote Bush requesting trade negotiations.[38] President Bush then officially notified the U.S. Congress—in the form of letters to Representative Dan Rostenkowski (Democrat-Illinois), chair of the House Committee on Ways and Means, and Senator Lloyd M. Bentsen Jr. (Democrat-Texas), chair of the Senate Committee on Finance, on September 25, 1990—that he intended to enter into negotiations with Mexico.[39]

Canada was a reluctant participant in this process. Prime Minister Mulroney, himself a late convert to the idea of a free-trade agreement with the United States, had won the heated 1988 general election debate about trade policy, and with a solid parliamentary majority, his Progressive Conservative Party had implemented the CUSFTA in January 1989. However, in early 1990, the Canadian economy was entering a recession. Many of Mulroney's critics blamed the CUSFTA for significant domestic job losses, and his public approval ratings were at a historic low.[40] In view of the small volume of Canadian trade with Mexico, Mulroney was hesitant to reopen a bitter domestic debate about trade policy. Yet he was committed to safeguarding Canada's diplomatic parity vis-à-vis the United States and preventing Mexico from securing access to the U.S. market on terms more favorable than those established in the CUSFTA. After he learned of the Mexico-U.S. discussions in mid-March 1990, Mulroney oversaw extended government deliberations regarding the alternatives open to Canada, and on September 24, 1990, he concluded that the negotiations should be conducted on a trilateral basis.[41]

Preliminary meetings among Mexican, U.S., and Canadian representatives to establish the parameters of negotiations began on September 20, 1990.[42] Mexican officials had, for some time, expressed reservations about Canadian participation in the negotiations, but Salinas began to give ground on the matter in November 1990. Although USTR Carla Hills had initially favored a bilateral Mexico-U.S. agreement, Canada's participation in the U.S.-led military coalition in the 1991 Persian Gulf war made it politically impossible for President Bush to deny Canada an equal role in free-trade negotiations.[43] On February 5, 1991, Bush, Mulroney, and Salinas publicly announced their intention to negotiate a free-trade agreement and officially confirmed that the negotiations would indeed be conducted on a trilateral basis.[44]

Formal negotiations began on June 12, 1991, in Toronto, Canada; a draft text was in circulation by mid-January 1992. Negotiations on the main text concluded on August 12, 1992, in Washington, DC. Bush, Mulroney, and Salinas witnessed their trade ministers formally initial the agreement on October 7, 1992, in San Antonio, Texas, and there were coordinated signing ceremonies in all three national capitals on December 17. Canada's House of Commons (by a vote of 140 to 124) and Senate (by a vote of 47 to 30) approved implementing legislation on, respectively, May 27 and June 23, 1993, and Canada's governor general (the head of state and representative of the Queen of England) assented to (signed) the treaty on June 23.[45] Final approval of implementing legislation in the U.S. House of Representatives (by a vote of 234 to 200) and Senate (by a vote of sixty-one to thirty-eight) came, respectively, on November 17 and 20, 1993, and President William J. (Bill) Clinton (1993–1997, 1997–2001) signed the measure into law on December 8.[46] The Mexican Senate ratified the agreement on November 22, 1993, by a vote of fifty-six to two, and it became law following its publication in the *Diario Oficial de la Federación* on December 20–21.[47] The NAFTA formally entered into effect on January 1, 1994.[48]

The final text, encompassing twenty-two chapters and seven annexes, extended to more than two thousand pages.[49] The negotiating parties conspicuously excluded several politically sensitive issues from consideration (including the free movement of labor across national borders and foreign investment in the extraction and processing of Mexican oil and natural gas), and in some sectors, transition periods extended to fifteen years. However, the agreement largely eliminated tariff and nontariff barriers to trade among the signatory countries (with a specified tariff-reduction schedule, carefully defined rules-of-origin requirements, and separate chapters on such sectors as agriculture, automobiles, financial services, and textiles), protected intellectual property rights, and established detailed procedures for the resolution of trade and investment disputes.[50] Among its most important provisions, the NAFTA guaranteed Canadian and U.S. investors in Mexico the same legal protections available to Mexican companies, including an explicit safeguard (article 1110[1]) against arbitrary expropriation or nationalization. Some critics argued that in failing to establish political preconditions for expanded Mexican access to their domestic markets, Canada and the United States missed an opportunity to advance democratization in Mexico.[51] Nevertheless, the agreement accelerated North American economic integration and marked a watershed in the institutionalization of relations among the three signatory countries.

AFTERSHOCK: THE ORIGIN OF THE NAFTA'S
LABOR RIGHTS PROVISIONS

Although trilateral bargaining over the main NAFTA text ended in August 1992, the negotiating process was not over. Between March and August 1993, Canadian, Mexican, and U.S. officials struggled to address environmental and labor rights concerns in the context of the agreement. These protracted negotiations produced the North American Agreement on Environmental Cooperation and the North American Agreement on Labor Cooperation, two "side-agreements" to the NAFTA.[52]

The standard account is that NAFTA-related labor issues arose in the context of the 1992 U.S. presidential campaign as Democratic Party candidate Clinton sought to reassure his party's traditional union supporters that their interests would be protected once the trade agreement went into effect.[53] The position that Clinton articulated during the campaign was highly significant because it laid down a political marker and established the context for subsequent negotiations over a supplemental labor agreement to the NAFTA. However, labor issues had, in fact, been at the center of debate from the very first discussions about a possible North American free-trade agreement. As early as June-July 1990, U.S. Secretary of Labor Elizabeth Dole—reflecting opposition from the U.S. labor movement to a trade agreement with Mexico—argued against taking up the NAFTA before the results of the GATT's Uruguay Round trade negotiations had been debated in Congress, sometime in late 1991. Representative Rostenkowski, chair of the powerful House Committee on Ways and Means, took the same position for similar reasons.[54]

The prospective impact of trade and investment liberalization on workers in both the United States and Mexico was one of the most contentious issues raised in the U.S. congressional debate over whether to authorize the Bush administration's trade negotiations with Mexico.[55] In the U.S. Trade Act of 1974, Congress granted the executive branch the authority to negotiate trade agreements on a fast-track basis (meaning that Congress can, within 90 legislative days, approve or disapprove a proposed trade pact but cannot amend or filibuster it).[56] Congress must periodically renew this authority, and on March 1, 1991, President Bush formally requested that it do so. The U.S. labor movement had begun lobbying against fast-track authorization during the autumn of 1990,[57] and opponents of a trade agreement with Mexico chose this legislative juncture as their first battleground.[58]

In response to pressure from labor (and environmentalist) opponents, and with the support of Bush administration officials seeking to ensure sufficient political support to win congressional approval, on March 7, 1991, Representative Rostenkowski and Senator Bentsen wrote letters to President Bush stressing the importance of both environmental protection and workers' rights in Mexico and insisting that these issues be addressed either in the text of the trade agreement or in close conjunction with the negotiations.[59] Similarly, House Majority Leader Representative Richard Gephardt (Democrat-Missouri) wrote to President Bush on March 27, 1991, to express deep concern about the human rights situation in Mexico and wage disparities between Mexico and the United States. He also insisted that any free-trade agreement between the two countries establish "acceptable conditions with respect to wages and hours of work" and other labor rights protections.[60]

In the course of a heated debate about the anticipated impact of a free-trade agreement with Mexico, U.S. labor opponents of the initiative won three concessions. First, in response to criticisms that a free-trade deal would harm U.S. workers by undercutting employment in agriculture, the textile industry, and other low-wage economic activities and would encourage businesses to relocate production to lower-wage sites in Mexico, on May 1, 1991, the Bush administration announced an "action plan" that included, among other measures, assistance for dislocated workers.[61] At the same time, President Bush sent letters to Senator Bentsen, Representative Rostenkowski, and all other members of Congress in which he assured them that:

> Mexico's laws provide comprehensive rights and standards for workers in all sectors, including the maquiladoras. . . . While enforcement problems have resulted largely from a lack of resources, a NAFTA would both raise living standards and create resources for enforcing existing laws.[62]

In January 1992, the administration followed up with the announcement of an expanded federal job-training program. And on August 24, 1992 (after the NAFTA negotiations had concluded and shortly before the full text of the agreement was unveiled to the public on September 6), it proposed a five-year, US$10 billion worker adjustment program—up to one-third of whose benefits were specifically reserved for workers adversely affected by the NAFTA—that included both retraining assistance and temporary income support.[63]

Second, on May 3, 1991, U.S. Secretary of Labor Lynn Martin and Mexican Secretary of Labor and Social Welfare Arsenio Farell Cubillas signed a memorandum of understanding that outlined a five-year program of bilateral cooperation, consultations, and information exchanges on child labor, workplace safety and health, working conditions and the enforcement of labor standards, collective bargaining agreements, procedures for resolving labor conflicts, and a range of associated issues.[64] All these activities were to be undertaken through the existing U.S.-Mexico Bilateral Commission. There were bilateral cooperative exchanges on labor matters and agreements on such technical issues as training in industrial hygiene techniques in September and October 1991 and again in February, June, and October 1992.[65]

Then, on September 14, 1992, the Mexican and U.S. governments signed a second framework agreement that extended bilateral cooperative activities and established a "consultative commission" cochaired by the two countries' secretaries of labor (or their designees). This high-level body, which offered a general forum for bilateral consultations (as well as, on the U.S. side, labor, business, and academic input) on labor matters, was to meet annually to review the full range of cooperative activities undertaken by Mexico and the United States.[66] It is noteworthy that, even though the commission merely had coordinating and consultative functions, Mexico expressly stipulated:

> This agreement does not empower one Party's authorities to undertake, in the territorial jurisdiction of the other, the exercise and performance of the functions or authority exclusively entrusted to the authorities of that other Party by its national laws or regulations (article 10).

In the August negotiations over the constitution of the consultative commission, Mexican negotiators strongly rejected a U.S. proposal that the commission be empowered to receive public complaints about either country's failure to enforce its labor laws.[67]

Third, while acceding to President Bush's request for a two-year extension of fast-track negotiating authority, on May 24, 1991, the U.S. House of Representatives also adopted (nonbinding) House Resolution 146 by an overwhelming margin of 329 to 85.[68] This measure, known informally as the Gephardt-Rostenkowski resolution in reference to Representatives Gephardt and Rostenkowski, identi-fied the objectives to be achieved in conjunction with a trade agreement with Mexico. In addition, it stipulated that, whatever the specific contents of such an agreement, the United States would be permitted to maintain its own work-place safety and health standards and adopt measures to minimize the dislo-cation of U.S. workers in agriculture and industry. In essence, it established political conditions for the negotiations by confirming that in negotiating the NAFTA, the Bush administration would fulfill the commitments made in the May action plan concerning "environmental protection, health and safety standards, labor and industry adjustment (including worker adjustment assis-tance), and worker rights."[69]

Even though President Bush took several steps to mollify labor opponents of the NAFTA, it is an open question whether, had he won a second presidential term in November 1992 and carried forward the domestic political campaign in favor of the accord, an expanded worker adjustment program would have been sufficient to win the Democratic congressional votes necessary for the agreement's final approval. Some Bush administration officials were apparently encouraged to believe so by the fact that the American Federation of Labor-Congress of Industrial Organizations (AFL-CIO), the principal U.S. labor confederation, had pushed strongly for such a program from the outset of the NAFTA debate.[70] However, the intensity of rank-and-file union opposition to a free-trade agree-ment with Mexico made the political prospects of such a deal—union support for the measure in exchange for expanded worker-adjustment assistance—unlikely.[71] The Bush administration had included worker-adjustment assistance in the May 1991 action plan in response to pressure from Bentsen, Gephardt, and Rosten-kowski, but Bush's credibility on this point was, in fact, somewhat suspect. His 1992 budget bill had proposed elimination of the Trade Adjustment Assistance Program established in 1962, and the U.S. General Accounting Office concluded that his August 1992 proposal for an expanded program was inadequate to address the dislocations that U.S. workers were likely to suffer as a consequence of liberalized trade with Mexico.[72]

It is understandable that the NAFTA, negotiated by three center-right, pro-business administrations at a time when there was no precedent for embed-ding worker rights in a free-trade agreement, contained no labor provisions beyond the preamble's general objectives: "create new employment opportu-nities and improve working conditions and living standards," and "protect,

enhance, and enforce basic workers' rights." Nonetheless, given the importance that President Bush and his senior officials attached to the NAFTA,
the strong opposition voiced by the U.S. labor movement and major portions
of the Democratic Party,[73] and the hard political fact that Republicans were
in the minority in both the House of Representatives and the Senate, it is
somewhat puzzling that the Bush administration did not take bolder action
on the issue. Some Bush administration officials believed that, even though
their cooperative and consultative agreements with Mexico were unlikely to
satisfy the concerns of labor opponents, they would at least give the labor
movement's Democratic congressional allies sufficient political cover that the
administration could assemble a legislative coalition broad enough to prevail
on the issue.[74] In the end, mainly because they were concerned about strong
Republican resistance,[75] in the end, Bush administration officials did not propose anything as ambitious as a separate trilateral accord on labor issues, even
though an agreement between Mexican and U.S. officials in late May 1991 that
labor (and environmental) concerns would not be addressed in the body of any
free-trade agreement implicitly raised this possibility.[76] Part of the rationale was
that Mexico's legal standards were already strong and that NAFTA-induced
economic growth would generate the financial resources required to improve
labor law enforcement.[77]

In the event, of course, the challenge of winning congressional approval of
the NAFTA did not fall to Bush. At the outset of negotiations, U.S. officials had
judged that negotiators would need to reach a final agreement by early 1992 in
order to avoid the likely political complications associated with the U.S. presidential election campaign and win congressional approval of an agreement
before the end of President Bush's term in office.[78] However, because the negotiations covered multiple sectors and confronted divergent national interests, and
because of the delaying tactics employed at different times by the negotiating
parties,[79] there was insufficient time remaining after the conclusion of trilateral
negotiations for Bush administration officials to secure congressional ratification
before the U.S. presidential election in early November 1992. When Bush lost,
President-elect Clinton agreed that Bush should sign the agreement on December
17, 1992, at the end of the maximum ninety-day period that had begun when Bush
had notified Congress of his intention to do so. Thereafter, Congress had ninety
legislative days in which to vote the measure up or down, a requirement that
established the time frame for the side-agreement negotiations.

THE BACKGROUND TO THE LABOR RIGHTS NEGOTIATIONS

The U.S. Congress decided the fate of the NAFTA, which made political maneuvering in the United States over labor (and environmental) matters and final legislative approval of the agreement the central focus of attention. However, domestic political considerations in Mexico and Canada—particularly deep-seated concerns about national sovereignty in both countries, counterbalanced in Mexico by the Salinas administration's intense interest in winning approval of the NAFTA—also had a significant impact on negotiations over the labor rights accord. In Canada, moreover, the constitutional division of authority between federal and provincial governments over labor matters was a major factor shaping Canadian negotiating positions.

Organized labor's position vis-à-vis the NAFTA and a prospective worker rights side-agreement varied greatly among the three countries. In both the United States and Canada, declines in the national labor movements' size and economic bargaining strength made them perceive a free-trade agreement with Mexico as a major threat, the potential risks of which could not be adequately counterbalanced by a supplementary labor-rights agreement. Nonetheless, the Clinton administration's need to win Democratic congressional support for the NAFTA compelled U.S. negotiators to push hard for side-agreement provisions designed to safeguard workers' rights in the hope that these provisions might muffle organized labor's vociferous criticisms of a trade agreement with Mexico. In contrast, the Progressive Conservative Party's solid parliamentary majority meant that Canadian negotiators had little need to pay heed to the interests of a politically marginalized labor movement. In Mexico, the organized labor movement, which had also lost strength since the early 1980s, stood to gain substantially from industrial expansion and employment growth generated by the NAFTA. The Confederation of Mexican Workers (Confederación de Trabajadores de México, CTM) and other parts of the official, government-aligned labor movement were, however, viscerally opposed to labor side-agreement terms that would undercut their position by permitting any external intervention in domestic labor affairs that might strengthen the position of union rivals. Although the political position of government-allied labor organizations had eroded under the De la Madrid and Salinas administrations, they retained significant bargaining leverage within the governing Institutional Revolutionary Party (Partido Revolucionario Institucional, PRI) coalition.

United States

The NAFTA and its implications for U.S. workers were among the most contentious issues in the 1992 presidential election. Most conspicuously, flamboyant independent candidate H. Ross Perot made the agreement a centerpiece of his populist campaign, warning during a televised presidential debate on October 15 that a free-trade agreement with Mexico would produce "a giant sucking sound" as U.S. companies shifted investment and jobs to lower-cost production sites in Mexico.[80] However, President Bush equally sought to exploit the issue for electoral advantage. Administration officials pushed to conclude the NAFTA negotiations before the Republican National Convention (at which the president was to be nominated for a second term) on August 17 so that Bush could claim success on a major foreign policy initiative. On September 18, with the election campaign in full swing, he notified Congress of his intention to sign the agreement, thus setting into motion the timetable on which legislation to implement the proposed treaty would be debated and voted. And on October 7, in an obvious effort to burnish his credentials as a statesman, Bush met with Mulroney and Salinas in San Antonio, Texas, to witness trade ministers from the three signatory countries initial the final NAFTA text.[81]

At the same time, the Bush administration attempted to use the NAFTA as a wedge issue to appeal to Hispanic voters and to divide the Democratic Party. Although general public opinion on the agreement was quite evenly divided,[82] some members of the U.S. Hispanic community—traditionally aligned with the Democratic Party—supported a free-trade agreement with Mexico. One of the principal goals of the dedicated NAFTA office that the Mexican government established in Washington, DC, in autumn 1990 was to cultivate the support of Hispanic organizations such as the National Council of La Raza and the Hispanic Chambers of Commerce, which eventually advocated approval of the agreement.[83] Moreover, Bush partisans sought to attract centrist Democrats by portraying anti-NAFTA elements as captives of "protectionist" forces such as organized labor.[84]

In part because of this Republican critique, the NAFTA posed a particularly delicate issue for Democratic presidential candidate Clinton. On the one hand,

Clinton (a prominent member of the centrist Democratic Leadership Council and its chair in 1990–1991) had sought to build a national political reputation by portraying himself as a "New Democrat" who, in contrast to the Republican caricatures of his party as unremittingly "protectionist," did not necessarily oppose free trade.[85] Indeed, he described himself as "a free-trader at heart."[86] Yet, on the other hand, Clinton also badly needed the support of organized labor and other traditional Democratic constituencies that were inexorably opposed to the NAFTA.

Clinton, therefore, positioned himself so as to offer conditional support for a major U.S. trade initiative while simultaneously shoring up support from the labor and environmental groups that formed the core of the campaign against the NAFTA.[87] In a speech titled "Expanding Trade and Creating American Jobs" that he delivered at North Carolina State University in Raleigh, North Carolina, on October 4, 1992, just prior to the official initialing of the final NAFTA text and the first televised candidate debate of the 1992 campaign, Clinton declared:

> The issue here is not whether we should support free trade or open markets. Of course, we should. The real question is whether or not we will have a national economic strategy to make sure we reap the benefits, and the answer today is, we don't. . . . As president, I will seek to address the deficiencies of the North American Free Trade Agreement through supplemental agreements with the Canadians and the Mexican government and by taking several key steps here at home. I will not sign legislation implementing the North American Free Trade Agreement until we have reached additional agreements to protect America's vital interests. But I believe we can address these issues without renegotiating the basic agreement.[88]

In addition to other proposed modifications to the NAFTA package (on such matters as safeguards against import surges), Clinton advocated the negotiation of supplemental environmental protection and labor rights agreements with Canada and Mexico that ensured "easy access to the courts, public hearings, the right to present evidence, streamlined procedures and effective remedies" to violations of national law.[89] Among other specific measures, he called for the creation of trilateral environmental and labor commissions with the authority to develop minimum standards, resolve disputes, and adopt remedies in order to ensure enforcement of a signatory country's own laws.[90] In a televised debate with Bush and Perot on October 19, Clinton further elaborated his position regarding the proposed free-trade agreement by stating:

> I say on balance it does more good than harm "if"—if we can get some protection for the environment so that the Mexicans have to follow their own environmental standards, their own labor law standards and if we have genuine commitment to re-educate and re-train the American workers who lose their jobs and reinvest in this economy.[91]

These commitments sufficed to defuse the NAFTA issue during the 1992 presidential campaign. Following his election, however, Clinton faced the daunting challenge of securing majority congressional support for the agreement. Although Clinton did eventually stake considerable political capital on winning approval of the NAFTA, the depth of his support was in doubt for several months as his newly inaugurated administration wrestled with cabinet appointments and competing policy priorities, especially a deficit-reduction bill and health-care reform legislation.[92] His senior advisers were, in fact, sharply divided over the merits of pursuing the NAFTA. Some of them argued that it was reckless to devote time and effort to pushing through a Bush-era agreement; others emphasized the costs of severely dividing Democrats in Congress at the very outset of the Clinton administration.[93]

The main obstacle that Clinton faced was, of course, staunch opposition to the NAFTA from the U.S. labor movement. During the 1950s and 1960s, when international trade still represented a comparatively small proportion of the United States' gross national product and manufactured imports posed few threats to domestic production and employment,[94] organized labor generally supported proposals to liberalize international trade because such measures promised to create larger export markets for U.S. producers and thereby promote employment growth.[95] For example, the AFL-CIO actively supported passage of the tariff-reducing Trade Expansion Act of 1962.[96] Beginning in the late 1960s and early 1970s, however, the labor movement began to confront a dramatically altered environment because of increasing international economic competition. Unions responded to the resulting company bankruptcies and job losses by calling for tariff and/or nontariff barriers to protect the domestic market.[97]

More broadly, the decline of the U.S. manufacturing sector undercut the labor movement's size and influence. Union membership as a proportion of private-sector employment peaked at 35.7 percent in 1953 and then fell almost continuously thereafter, reaching 11.7 percent in 1991. The declines in both aggregate membership and union density (the proportion of unionized employees in the labor force) had been particularly sharp during the 1980s and were concentrated in manufacturing industries.[98] Indeed, the AFL-CIO, whose membership declined from 16.4 percent of the U.S. labor force in 1975 to 11 percent in 1993, and its largest affiliates suffered some of the greatest membership losses.[99] Whatever representational problems might have existed within particular unions, these were at root organizations whose leaders were ultimately accountable to rank-and-file members. As a consequence, they were highly sensitive to the risk of further membership losses resulting from the surge in low-cost manufactured imports and relocation of U.S. manufacturing facilities that were likely to result from a free-trade agreement with Mexico.

The position that the U.S. labor movement adopted regarding the NAFTA was strongly conditioned by its experience with Mexico's fast-growing *maquiladora* (in-bond processing) sector. The Mexican government had established the Border Industrialization Program (BIP) in 1966 to ameliorate unemployment in the Mexico-U.S. border region following the termination of the 1942–1964 Bracero Program, a contract-labor program under which Mexican workers were sent to work temporarily in the United States, principally in the agricultural sector. The so-called maquiladora program permitted the duty-free import of materials that were to be assembled or processed in Mexico for subsequent re-export, exempting firms from national restrictions on foreign ownership but prohibiting them from selling their finished products in the domestic market.[100] The BIP took advantage of provisions in the U.S. tariff code (items 806.30 and 807.00) that levied customs duties only on the value added in Mexico.[101] From modest beginnings, the maquiladora sector expanded rapidly during the 1980s, from 585 plants employing 127,048 workers in 1982 to 2,042 plants employing 486,210 workers in 1992.[102]

Some of the employment losses that occurred in the U.S. manufacturing industry during the 1970s and 1980s no doubt resulted from corporate decisions to shift production to countries other than Mexico. Nevertheless, especially during the early years of the Border Industrialization Program, U.S. companies (including manufacturers of apparel, automobile parts, and consumer electronics) were far and away the most numerous and largest employers in the maquiladora sector.[103] Between 1986 and 1991, Mexican employment in U.S. firms in the transportation-equipment and electronics industries grew at the same time as U.S. employment in these sectors declined.[104] Because unionized workers in the United States have long enjoyed significant wage and fringe-benefits premiums, and because companies with unionized employees have therefore faced higher wage and benefits expenses than their nonunionized competitors, firms operating in industries in which labor costs represent a significant proportion of total production costs have had a clear financial incentive to relocate production to nonunionized sites. In some industries, the advantages of having component suppliers located close to final-production sites have often been a more important consideration.[105] Mexico's northern border region, however, offered the simultaneous attractions of substantially lower labor costs, very low union density, and geographic proximity (and reliable transportation links) to the U.S. market.[106] For these reasons, the NAFTA—and the prospect that U.S. companies would take advantage of its strong investor protection provisions and commercial dispute-resolution mechanisms to shift additional production to Mexico, where political constraints on union organizing and collective bargaining might constitute an unfair competitive advantage by keeping labor costs low—posed a palpable threat to a number of major U.S. trade unions.[107]

Under these circumstances, it is hardly surprising that U.S. labor organizations were overwhelmingly opposed to a free-trade agreement with Mexico.[108] They had, in fact, opposed Mexico's maquiladora program from its beginning and had lobbied unsuccessfully for the abolition of the U.S. tariff code provisions that underpinned its growth.[109] As noted above, unions and their political allies in Congress lobbied vigorously in 1990 and 1991 against the extension of fast-track trade negotiating authority, and during the bitter debate over approval of the NAFTA, the labor movement strongly mobilized against the agreement. The most outspoken labor critics characterized the measure as a "life-and-death issue" and announced their intention to deny future organizational and financial support to Democratic members of Congress who voted for it. Groups such as the American Federation of State, County, and Municipal Employees and the American Federation of Teachers, whose public-sector membership was not directly vulnerable to potential job losses resulting from the NAFTA, took a less aggressive opposition stance. However, the AFL-CIO Executive Council and the leaders of the most powerful U.S. industrial unions (including those organizations representing electrical workers, garment workers, machinists, and others) staunchly opposed the agreement.[110] Whereas several leading environmental organizations expressed their willingness to support the NAFTA so long as the Clinton administration negotiated a separate agreement with Canada and Mexico that addressed their most pressing concerns, the U.S. labor movement sought to defeat it outright.[111]

Labor opposition to the NAFTA strongly registered in the U.S. Congress. A significant number of Democratic members of both the House of Representatives and the Senate relied heavily on the AFL-CIO for financial and organizational support during election campaigns.[112] Unrelenting opposition from a core Democratic Party constituency, combined with tepid overall public support for the agreement, defined the magnitude of the political challenge facing President Clinton as he sought to win congressional approval of the NAFTA.[113]

Mexico

In Mexico, ratification of the NAFTA was never in doubt. The long-ruling PRI held an overwhelming majority (sixty-one of sixty-four seats) in the federal Senate,[114] and the most important mass-media companies (especially Televisa, which controlled four-fifths of the national television audience) were firmly aligned with President Salinas de Gortari and the PRI.[115] Moreover, from early 1990 onward, Salinas sought both to neutralize potential domestic opposition to the agreement and shift general public opinion in favor of it by working assiduously to reassure traditional Mexican nationalists that the final terms of a free-trade agreement with the United States would safeguard the country's sovereignty.[116] Toward this end, Mexican negotiators explicitly excluded from the bargaining agenda those issues most likely to produce a nationalist backlash. Foremost among these was the continued state monopoly on exploration for and production of oil and natural gas.

Nevertheless, increasing public awareness in the United States and Canada of labor rights problems in Mexico clearly placed the Salinas administration on the defensive in negotiations over a labor accord. At root, Mexican officials viewed U.S. demands for such an agreement as an inappropriate intrusion on national sovereignty.[117] However, they grudgingly but pragmatically accepted that it was a necessary price to pay in order to secure U.S. congressional approval of the NAFTA.[118] The free-trade agreement was, after all, President Salinas de Gortari's highest foreign policy priority and a linchpin in his program of market-oriented economic reform.[119] Failure to secure its approval would have constituted a major political defeat.[120]

Mexican officials, therefore, approached the side-agreement negotiations with two main goals. First, they sought to ensure that these negotiations would not lead to the unraveling of the entire free-trade agreement, either via the reopening of negotiations over the main NAFTA text or its eventual defeat in the U.S. Congress. From the moment of Clinton's election on November 3, 1992, Mexican officials anxiously sought to confirm his commitment to the agreement.[121] In Salinas's congratulatory telephone call to Clinton on November 5, he urged the president-elect to proceed with ratification of the NAFTA without any significant modifications.[122] In an interview with the *New York Times* published on November 21, Salinas signaled his willingness to negotiate agreements to address Clinton's concerns with the NAFTA, but he reiterated his opposition to reopening negotiations over the main text.[123] Later that month, Salinas dispatched Chief of Staff Córdoba to Washington, DC, to meet with senior Clinton advisors, whom he pressed for the early signature of the free-trade agreement. At the same time, Mexican officials advised Clinton's team that a major delay in ratifying the agreement might undermine Mexico's economic and political stability, issues that were of significant concern to U.S. officials.[124]

At Salinas's request, he and Clinton met briefly on January 8, 1993, in Austin, Texas, where Clinton reassured Salinas that he remained committed to the NAFTA and that environmental and labor side-agreements would neither necessitate a reopening of general NAFTA negotiations, constitute disguised protectionism, nor infringe upon Mexican sovereignty.[125] Nevertheless, as the weeks slipped by following Clinton's inauguration as president on January 20, 1993, without any further communication, Mexican officials grew concerned that the NAFTA would not be approved before the end of the year. They feared that a lengthy delay, or the eventual defeat of the measure in the U.S. Congress, would greatly complicate Mexico's 1994 presidential succession process.[126]

Second, although the Salinas administration was willing to make some concessions in order to prevent the collapse of side-agreement negotiations, Mexican officials vigorously sought to protect from external scrutiny or challenge an established system of state-labor relations that was a pillar of Mexico's postrevolutionary regime. Side-agreement negotiators' defense of this system was couched in terms of national sovereignty, and they stressed the extensive worker rights formally guaranteed by the Mexican Constitution and federal labor law. As a practical matter, however, they were mainly concerned with protecting arrangements of vital domestic political and economic importance.

The state-labor relations regime forged in the decades after the Mexican Revolution of 1910–1920 combined both constitutional and legal protections of key labor rights and significant legal and administrative controls on worker participation.[127] Article 123 of the 1917 Constitution raised social reforms to the level of constitutional guarantees, addressed the emerging organized labor movement's principal policy demands, and legitimated expanded state involvement in worker-employer affairs. Its provisions recognized the rights to unionize and to strike; established regulations governing minimum wages, working hours and overtime pay, workplace conditions (including occupational safety and health measures), and worker-employer contracts; and created tripartite (labor-government-business) conciliation and arbitration boards to mediate worker-employer conflicts. The 1931 Federal Labor Law (Ley Federal del Trabajo, revised in 1970) and subsequent legislative reforms further expanded the range of legal arrangements favorable to workers, including the requirement that an employer sign a collective agreement when an officially registered union solicited one, the recognition of both "closed shop" provisions in worker-employer contracts and industry-wide collective bargaining agreements, procedural safeguards of workers' right to strike, such as a ban on the hiring of replacement workers while a legally recognized strike was in progress, and the stipulation that employers automatically deduct union dues from workers' paychecks and distribute the proceeds to union officers.

Nevertheless, in the ongoing debates during the 1920s and 1930s regarding the appropriate extent of state authority over labor affairs, the labor movement was forced to accept a number of significant legal and administrative controls on various forms of worker participation.[128] For example, although under the 1931/1970 federal labor law, a group of at least twenty workers had the legal right to form a union without prior authorization, a union could not negotiate a collective contract with an employer or engage in other activities such as strikes until it was officially registered by either a state-level conciliation and arbitration board or, in the case of unions operating in federal-jurisdiction economic activities, the Ministry of Labor and Social Welfare (Secretaría del Trabajo y Previsión Social, STPS). Registration procedures were, in principle, relatively straightforward. In practice, however, they were subject to purposeful administrative delay and political abuse—and unions that ceased to meet various legal requirements could lose their registration. Moreover, unions were required to report changes in their membership and leadership within specified time periods, and union officials were not empowered to act until their election was acknowledged by state labor authorities. There was no compulsory arbitration of worker-employer conflicts, but federal labor law imposed a number of procedural restrictions on strikes.

In addition to constitutional and legal provisions such as these, the Mexican system of state-labor relations rested on a durable alliance that postrevolutionary political leaders formed with working-class organizations as a means of marshaling support and exercising power. This alliance, whose most important labor proponents and beneficiaries were the Mexican Regional Labor Confederation (Confederación Regional Obrera Mexicana, CROM) during the 1920s and the Confederation of Mexican Workers (CTM) after its formation in 1936, provided government-aligned unions with diverse benefits. Union leaders won privileged access to national, state, and local elective offices and prominent positions in labor-related governmental agencies, as well as the opportunities for (often illicit) material gain that these posts offered.[129] The CTM, as the official labor sector of the governing PRI, virtually monopolized labor representation on institutions like the Mexican Social Security Institute (Instituto Mexicano del Seguro Social), the National Minimum Wage Commission (Comisión Nacional de los Salarios Mínimos), and the National Commission for Worker Profit-Sharing (Comisión Nacional para la Participación de los Trabajadores en las Utilidades). For their part, members of government-aligned unions benefited disproportionately from some publicly financed social welfare programs, including subsidized access to basic commodities, housing, and consumer credit. For example, for many years, the CTM claimed the lion's share of the benefits provided by the National Worker Housing Institute (Instituto del Fondo Nacional de la Vivienda para los Trabajadores) and the Workers' Bank (Banco Obrero). In exchange, the CTM and other government-allied labor organizations reliably delivered large-scale electoral support for the PRI's candidates and provided reliable backing for PRI governments during periods of economic or political crisis.

This was, nonetheless, a highly unequal alliance. Linking the CTM to the "official" party symbolized organized labor's inclusion in Mexico's postrevolutionary governing coalition. However, legal restrictions on union formation, internal union activities, and strikes—backed by the political elite's control over the means of coercion and state officials' willingness to use force when necessary to achieve their objectives—established the de jure and de facto parameters of labor action. Unions' dependence on legal, financial, and political subsidies, and union leaders' consequent greater reliance on political alliances than on the mobilization of rank-and-file support, made them vulnerable to government pressure. Indeed, the ability of government-allied labor organizations to preserve their preferential access to public resources depended primarily on their willingness to control the actions of rank-and-file union members. This dependence was accentuated by the labor movement's own weaknesses, including its heterogeneous organizational composition, the comparatively small size of many unions, and the frequent absence of effective representational arrangements linking labor leaders with union members.

Mexico's organized labor movement suffered significant reversals after the country's 1982 foreign debt crisis. As a consequence of stringent post-1982 government austerity measures, the subsequent closure or privatization of many state-owned enterprises, and other historic shifts in government policy toward labor, the labor movement declined substantially in size, bargaining strength, and political influence.[130] Nevertheless, the government-allied labor organizations remained a fundamental part of Mexico's governing political coalition, and their proven willingness to control workers' economic and political demands in exchange for access to diverse legal, financial, and political subsidies in effect underpinned a significant share of the economic benefits that Mexico expected to derive from the NAFTA because foreign investors highly valued assurances of continued "labor peace."[131] The preservation of the established state-labor relations regime was, therefore, a central goal of Mexico's side-agreement negotiators.

The Salinas administration also had more specific reasons to be concerned about the content of any labor side-agreement negotiated with the United States and Canada. Fidel Velázquez Sánchez, the nonagenarian leader of the CTM, had initially raised objections to the idea of a free-trade agreement with the United States, reflecting the CTM's broader concerns about the negative effects that economic liberalization policies had on employment and wages in some sectors of the Mexican economy.[132] He later changed his position, and the CTM endorsed the NAFTA in late 1991 based on the prospect that substantial additional foreign investment in Mexico, which would lead to the creation of new enterprises and additional employment opportunities.[133] Yet, when the prospect of a labor

side-agreement arose, the implicit quid pro quo for Velázquez's continued support became government officials' willingness to defend the state-labor relations
regime from which the CTM and other old-guard labor organizations benefited
so substantially. Moreover, at the time, Velázquez and his labor allies held real
bargaining leverage on two different fronts. First, labor's participation after 1987
in regularly renewed tripartite economic stabilization pacts (*pactos*) was a central element of government macroeconomic policy. Second, in 1993, Salinas was
increasingly focused on the complex dynamics surrounding the selection of the
PRI's next presidential candidate and the imperative of maintaining party unity
before the 1994 presidential election. Support from Velázquez and other national
labor leaders for the PRI's presidential candidate—which had faltered in 1988,
when government-aligned unions found it difficult to mobilize their members'
electoral support for a party responsible for years of declining inflation-adjusted
wages and serious job losses in key industries[134]—was a vital element in Salinas's
political calculations.[135]

Although the government-allied labor movement, Mexico's principal business associations, and the mainstream mass media all supported the NAFTA,
there was, in fact, some domestic political opposition to a free-trade agreement with the United States.[136] However, it posed no significant constraint on
Mexican negotiators, and it had no impact on eventual approval of the final
agreement. The most publicly visible coalition of opposition forces was the
Mexican Action Network on Free Trade (Red Mexicana de Acción Frente al
Libre Comercio, RMALC), a coalition modeled on Canada's Pro-Canada/Action
Canada Network (see below) that grouped some dissident labor organizations
and a large, diverse array of civil society groups.[137] It was formed in April 1991
with the assistance of Canadian groups that had opposed the CUSFTA, with
the broad goals of defending Mexican sovereignty against "U.S. imperialism"
and promoting an alternative model of national economic development to the
market-focused strategy advanced by the Salinas administration.[138] Among the
RMALC's labor supporters, the most prominent organization was the Authentic Labor Front (Frente Auténtico del Trabajo, FAT), a small social-Christian
labor confederation founded in 1960 that claimed some thirty thousand affiliates.[139] The FAT's role in anti-NAFTA debates gained it new allies among labor
groups in the United States and Canada,[140] and the RMALC won considerable
public attention by convening events such as an "alternative summit" in Zacatecas, Mexico (October 1991), during the NAFTA negotiations. Its activism did

gain the RMALC an audience with Mexico's NAFTA negotiating team and the opportunity to outline its position. Nevertheless, its actions had no discernible impact on national policy.

Canada

Of the three countries involved, Canada had the least at stake in the negotiations over a labor side-agreement to the NAFTA. Even if failure to secure agreement over the terms of a labor (or environmental) accord ultimately led to defeat of the NAFTA in the U.S. Congress, Canada's core interests were protected by its existing free-trade agreement with the United States. This circumstance had initially led to considerable debate within the Mulroney government about what position to adopt regarding Mexico-U.S. trade negotiations (whether to decline to participate, participate only as an observer, or engage fully in the process), and to some extent, it colored other participants' perceptions of Canada as a negotiating partner.

Canadian trade unions and civil society organizations, however, were certainly not ambivalent about the NAFTA. The Canadian labor movement had long opposed free-trade initiatives. The Canadian Labour Congress (CLC) had, for example, formed an important part of the broad-based Pro-Canada Network formed in 1987 to oppose a bilateral free-trade agreement with the United States.[141] This experience, and labor organizations' conviction that the Canada-United States Free Trade Agreement had contributed to significant job losses in the manufacturing sector and accentuated the negative impact of the 1991 recession in Canada, strongly shaped labor's position concerning the NAFTA.[142]

Like their U.S. counterparts, Canada's principal labor organizations feared that the agreement would directly harm their material interests because they, too, faced the threat of long-term membership decline. The proportion of unionized employees in the labor force (including the public sector) fell significantly after the late 1980s, from 35.9 percent in 1989 to 30.7 percent in 1998. The greatest declines were among male employees and in goods-producing industries.[143] Acting on these concerns, the CLC played a very active role in the Common Frontiers anti-NAFTA coalition formed in early 1991 after Canada formally joined the tripartite negotiations.[144] Leading elements of the organized labor movement—including the CLC, the Québec-based Confederation of National Unions (Confédération des Syndicats Nationaux), and the Canadian Auto

Workers—also collaborated with U.S. unions in opposing a free-trade agreement with Mexico.[145] They argued that a number of U.S.-owned manufacturing plants in Canada had closed as investment capital shifted to Mexico's maquiladora industry, and they predicted that NAFTA would have significant negative consequences for employment and social protections in Canada.[146]

The fact that Canada's leading labor organizations were politically aligned with the opposition New Democratic Party meant that they had little incentive to muffle their dissent. By the same token, however, because the Progressive Conservative Party held solid majorities in both the House of Commons and the Senate and because it did not rely on the political support of organized labor, the Mulroney government could, in the main, afford to ignore labor opposition to the NAFTA. In practice, CLC representatives attended government-convened meetings concerning the side-agreement negotiations, but they made no significant contributions to them.[147] That position, together with the overall intransigence of the Canadian labor movement (like their U.S. counterparts, Canadian trade unionists did not believe that the threats posed by the NAFTA could be substantially ameliorated by a supplemental agreement addressing labor rights issues), reduced the likelihood that Canadian negotiators would tailor their bargaining positions over the content of a side-agreement in an attempt to win labor support.

In some ways, then, the Mulroney government had substantial political leeway in the side-agreement negotiations.[148] Canadian negotiators were, however, constrained by the country's constitutional arrangements concerning the implementation of treaty obligations. Under the Constitution Act, 1867, federal and provincial governments have exclusive authority to legislate (and implement international treaty obligations) in specified subject areas. With the exception of federal-jurisdiction economic activities such as navigation and shipping, labor matters fall within the legal jurisdiction of the ten provinces.[149] Thus, unlike their Mexican and U.S. counterparts, Canadian negotiators could not agree to side-agreement terms that would constitutionally bind provincial governments. Moreover, any agreement the federal government reached would not become binding (except in those economic activities that fell under the specific jurisdiction of federal authorities) until appropriate enabling legislation was ratified by each provincial government. For these reasons, federal-provincial relations were central to Canada's approach to the labor side-agreement negotiations, as they had been in the earlier negotiations over the CUSFTA.[150]

NEGOTIATING THE NORTH AMERICAN AGREEMENT
ON LABOR COOPERATION

Because the epicenter of debate over approval of the NAFTA was Washington, DC, the political impetus in the labor side-agreement negotiations lay with U.S. officials.[151] Negotiators representing the United States, led by the Office of the United States Trade Representative (USTR), sought an agreement whose terms would fulfill President Clinton's campaign promises. However, differences of opinion within the Clinton administration about how best to achieve this goal delayed for several months the drafting of a formal proposal.[152] From the outset, there were voices warning that sovereignty concerns—not only in Canada and Mexico but also in the United States—would constrain the authority of any new institutions created under the NAFTA. For example, the Department of State opposed "supranational enforcement authority" on the basis of "serious Constitutional concerns." At least in public statements, Republicans expressed these reservations more loudly than Democrats.[153]

Domestic political calculations influenced the conduct of U.S. negotiators. At least initially, their proposals for a North American accord on worker rights were strongly prolabor in content. Over several months, USTR Michael (Mickey) Kantor insisted, with President Clinton's support, that any agreement have "teeth," particularly in the form of trade-based sanctions imposed on a country that systematically violated labor rights.[154] However, as the trilateral negotiations dragged on into late summer 1993, Clinton administration officials became increasingly convinced that they could not win the backing of influential Democratic legislators like House Majority Leader Gephardt. Even though the Democrats held a 259-175 majority in the House of Representatives, widespread Democratic opposition meant that, in practice, congressional approval of the NAFTA would require substantial Republican support.[155] For this reason, administration officials ceded ground on some positions that had met substantial opposition from Republican legislators and their allies in the private sector.

Although strong opposition to the NAFTA from most U.S. unions was the principal reason the side-agreement negotiations took place, the U.S. labor movement played a rather ambivalent role in the actual negotiating process. Labor leaders initially took the position that any North American labor accord should establish common rights and standards. The Clinton administration ruled out that possibility, both because higher international standards might conceivably become grounds for challenging U.S. laws and because Clinton had already assured President Salinas de Gortari that any side-agreement to the NAFTA would not infringe upon Mexican sovereignty—meaning that the enforcement of existing national laws, not the setting of new labor standards, would be the focus of negotiations.[156] However, U.S. labor leaders were insistent that any trilateral agreement recognize such core rights as the freedom of association and the right to bargain collectively, granting workers the quality of protection that the NAFTA gave to intellectual property rights.[157]

Yet, in the main, U.S. labor leaders did not want to participate so fully in the give-and-take of negotiations that Clinton administration officials would presume they were willing to give final approval to the NAFTA in exchange for specific concessions to them.[158] Unlike a number of leading U.S. environmental organizations (which endorsed the Clinton administration's efforts to secure a strong environmental side-agreement with an independent trilateral environmental commission), the AFL-CIO took the position that the negative impact the NAFTA was likely to have on unionized U.S. workers could not be substantially ameliorated by a trilateral agreement on labor standards.[159] An AFL-CIO representative, therefore, attended meetings of the Labor Advisory Committee on Trade Negotiations and Trade Policy (a body mandated by Congress and jointly sponsored by the USTR and the Department of Labor), but the confederation did not contribute actively to the formulation of side-agreement proposals.[160]

Opening Negotiating Positions

From the outset, debates about a potential labor side-agreement focused mainly on three central issues: the scope of any potential accord on labor rights (that is, the labor rights that would be recognized and protected under the terms of an agreement); the design and authority of any new North American institutions created to implement the agreement; and how persistent rights violations in any of the signatory countries would be sanctioned.

In an initial framing of options for the Clinton administration in late February 1993, a National Economic Council (NEC) interagency working group established on February 3 laid out three possibilities.[161] The first option featured a small continental commission with a trilateral dispute-settlement mechanism but only weak enforcement powers that, while recognizing the core rights of freedom of association and collective bargaining, would primarily promote minimum standards on nonpolitical labor issues such as those concerning child labor, minimum wages, and workplace safety and health. As a second option, the working group proposed a trilateral commission with an independent secretariat that, in addition to the responsibilities outlined in the first option, would be authorized to analyze issues such as protections against "downward harmonization" in social conditions, worker participation and representation, and the relationship between wages and productivity in the three countries. It would also have overall responsibility for promoting trilateral dialogue to define minimum continental standards for nonpolitical labor issues, political worker rights (freedom of association and the rights to organize and bargain collectively), and minimum wages, including the promotion of labor-management dialogue in key sectors, such as automobiles, apparel, and electronic products. Under the final option, a trilateral commission would have a similarly broad substantive mandate and the authority to levy trade-related sanctions or adopt "border measures" as a means of enforcement.[162] The focus in all three options was on "national enforcement of labor laws." Although Secretary of Labor Robert Reich favored the third, institutionally more robust option, the interagency task force charged with negotiating a labor side-agreement reached no firm consensus on its goals prior to the actual start of negotiations with Canada and Mexico.[163]

Inside U.S. Trade, a Washington, DC-based specialist newsletter, published a leaked copy of the "NEC NAFTA Work Group Draft on Labor" (dated February 25, 1993),[164] and Herminio Blanco Mendoza, Mexico's undersecretary of commerce and industrial development and lead NAFTA negotiator, transmitted both the original text and a Spanish-language translation of the document to Norma Samaniego de Villareal, undersecretary of labor and social welfare and Mexico's chief labor side-agreement negotiator, on March 10, 1993. The Mexican government framed its initial negotiating positions based on the NEC document. Most important, it outright rejected the idea that any trilateral labor commission would have the authority to receive public communications (*planteamientos del público*), alleging that a NAFTA country had failed to implement its national labor laws.[165]

Formal negotiations over a supplemental labor accord began with a preliminary trilateral meeting in Arlington, Virginia, on March 17–18, 1993.[166] At this meeting, the U.S. team called for an agreement containing a charter of principles (among which would be a mutual commitment to improving North

American labor standards over time), the creation of a trilateral commission to oversee implementation of the agreement, and measures adequate to ensure the reliable domestic enforcement of labor rights (without any mention of trade-based sanctions).[167] More detailed discussions, focused principally on initial proposals from the United States and Canada, were held in Mexico City on April 13-15. Even though U.S. negotiators did not stake out a strong position regarding possible sanctions of rights violations because of continuing debates within the Clinton administration over this issue, at both meetings, Mexican negotiators registered their strong opposition to the idea that a trilateral institution might investigate a signatory country's labor record and impose trade-linked sanctions for rights violations.[168] However, the three governments did not formally table written proposals until the third session, which was held on May 19-21 in Hull, Ontario.[169]

The U.S. proposal began with a lengthy "Statement of Labor Principles" that explicitly called on all three countries to "recognize that their mutual prosperity depends on the promotion of competition based on raising productivity, quality, and the rate of innovation, rather than keeping labor and environmental standards low."[170] It then listed two sets of principles: six "internationally-recognized labor rights" ("freedom of association; freedom to organize and bargain collectively; prohibition of forced labor; a minimum age for the employment of children; minimum standards governing hours of work, wages, and health and safety conditions; the elimination of employment discrimination on the basis of race, color, sex, religion, political opinion, national or social origin") and nine principles that could help the signatory countries "achieve the shared goal of high-productivity economic development."[171] The draft acknowledged that the actual placement of these principles in an agreement (whether in the preamble or in an annex at the end) was under discussion. However, placing them at the very beginning of a proposed text clearly signaled U.S. negotiators' intent to secure an agreement that was broad in scope.

The U.S. draft proposed that a labor rights accord be administered by a Labor Commission comprised of a governing council (whose members were the three signatory countries' labor ministers/secretaries or their designees), a secretariat, and a public advisory council (articles 8-13). The secretariat was to provide general administrative support and report to the council "annually on the labor enforcement activities of the Parties." In order to bolster the secretariat's autonomy and independence, the U.S. draft stipulated that the council could remove its executive director only for cause and that "any government or any other authority external to the Commission" was not to seek to influence its activities (articles 11 [1, 3, 4], 12 [1b]). The trilateral Public Advisory Committee was to be comprised of six nongovernmental representatives from each country serving three-year terms; it was to meet annually before regular council sessions and offer advice on any matter "within the scope of this Agreement" (article 13).

For the most part, the emphasis was on domestic enforcement of existing national labor law.[172] However, the U.S. proposal also envisioned "the negotiation of labor standards in the free trade area with a view to adoption in the Parties' laws of any standards agreed in such negotiations," and it permitted the council (by a two-thirds vote) to make recommendations to a signatory country on any labor-related matter (article 10 [2b, 9]). The principles that would guide all of the institutions created under a potential agreement were consensus, the promotion of cooperation among the signatory parties, transparency, and public access (articles 9, 10 [2]).

Although the U.S. proposal stressed the importance of cooperation among the NAFTA partners in safeguarding workers' rights and improving labor standards, it also recognized that violations of labor rights might occur in one or more countries. The document, therefore, included a separate chapter on dispute settlement, and it authorized the secretariat to "receive and consider submissions from any person or nongovernmental organization of a Party regarding labor matters," including "a claim that a Party has failed to enforce its labor laws" (article 12 [3, 8a]).[173] An annex to the proposal ("Criteria for Evaluating Public Submissions") required the secretariat to determine that a submission "demonstrates a persistent and unjustifiable pattern of failure by the Party to enforce its labor law," that "local avenues of relief have been exhausted or it would be futile to initiate or pursue them," and that "the submission appears to be primarily aimed at the encouragement of labor law enforcement rather than the protection of a domestic industry" (annex, points 2, 3, 8, respectively). Yet when the secretariat's investigation found evidence of "a persistent and unjustifiable pattern of non-enforcement" of labor law, the council was required to consider the matter in a special session. If the council was unable to resolve the dispute within thirty days, it could, by a two-thirds vote, convene an arbitral panel (similar in composition and mode of operation to arbitral panels established in NAFTA chapter 20) to examine the matter (article 16 [1, 3, 4]. Finally, if the arbitral panel concluded that a signatory party had, in fact, failed to enforce its labor laws properly and a further special meeting of the council failed to reach a consensual agreement on the matter within thirty days, the complaining party could "suspend an appropriate level of benefits under the NAFTA until such action is initiated" (article 16 [4h]).[174]

Like their U.S. counterparts, Canadian negotiators tabled a detailed draft text at the May meeting.[175] It shared with the U.S. proposal a commitment to broadly framed labor rights and a deep commitment to transparency and public access in the proceedings of new North American labor institutions.[176] In fact, in some areas, it went beyond the U.S. proposal. For example, an annex added to the U.S. list of labor rights principles explicitly guarantees the right to strike, equal pay for men and women, and compensation in cases of work accidents or occupational diseases. Even more than the U.S. text, the Canadian document stressed the importance of cooperation among the NAFTA partners and transparency in all labor-related matters (preamble, articles 1–3, 7, 11). In its advocacy of transparency, the Canadian government went so far as to propose that each NAFTA country be required to share with its partners, at their request, a copy of any contemplated change in federal labor law or "a labour regulation of general application at the federal level" and to take into account any comments on the measure that its partners might make (article 2 [1,2]).[177] Under the terms of article 11 (b, c), a new North American Labour Commission (comprised of cabinet-level national representatives or their designees) was required to prepare an annual public report that, among other topics, covered "the actions taken by the Parties to meet their obligations under this Agreement" and "relevant views and information received from nongovernmental organizations and the public."

At the same time, though, the Canadian government's proposal contained provisions that reflected its underlying sovereignty concerns and the importance of federalist arrangements in Canadian labor law.[178] For example, it called for an administrative secretariat comprised of different national sections, which each of the three signatory countries would staff and finance (article 8). The document also proposed three national governmental councils comprised of representatives of federal and state or provincial governments (article 9) and three separate advisory councils comprised of "non-governmental representatives of industry, labour, and other interested communities" (article 10). Moreover, although it contained a requirement that signatories ensure that labor standards were met by state or provincial governments (article 2 [5]), the Canadian proposal explicitly stated that the agreement would not necessarily alter a country's existing distribution of federal and state/provincial authority in labor matters. It allowed any party, at the time of its accession to the envisioned trilateral labor accord, to declare to which territorial units it would apply (article 20).

The Canadian document, like the U.S. proposal, also recognized that significant violations of labor rights might occur in one or more of the signatory countries. However, in marked contrast to the U.S. position, the Canadian approach to addressing such potential problems relied entirely on good-faith communications among the NAFTA partners and the dissuasive effect that public scrutiny and condemnation of rights violations might have.

Allegations of persistent labor rights violations could be lodged either by a national government (in the form of a request for government-to-government consultations[179]) or by any interested person or nongovernmental entity in the signatory countries (in the form of "communications" submitted to national sections of the secretariat[180]). In the first instance, the complaining government could also request consultations with the commission on the issue. If these discussions failed to produce a satisfactory outcome, the commission could appoint an evaluation panel to assess the merits of the allegation and make suggestions about how to resolve the matter (articles 13 [1], 14).[181]

In the second instance, the Canadian document proposed (article 15 [1]):

> Any person or group of persons within the territory of a Party who have direct and reliable knowledge of a situation that allegedly demonstrates a consistent pattern of non-enforcement, on the part of another Party, of its labour laws or the obligations set out in Part Two [of the agreement], in relation to workplaces, firms or companies that produce goods or services traded between the Parties or that compete with goods produced or services provided from another Party, may submit a Communication, including supporting information and documentation, to the section of the Secretariat located in the territory of such person or group.[182]

If deemed admissible by the government of the country in which the complaint originated, that government was obligated to forward the communication to its advisory council and, if applicable, to its governmental council as well. These bodies could express their views on the matter and recommend that the case be brought before the North American Labour Commission (articles 16 [1], 17).

National sections of the secretariat could assist evaluation panels created by the commission in their examination of such claims. However, in contrast to the powers granted to the secretariat in the U.S. proposal, they had no independent authority to initiate investigations of labor rights violations (articles 8, 15).

Following any investigation it undertook of nonenforcement allegations, the commission could "make recommendations to the Parties that will be made public, as may assist the Parties to reach a mutually satisfactory resolution of the matter at issue and promote continued improvement in labour laws and their enforcement" (articles 13 [2c]). However, the Canadian proposal did not specify any means of definitively resolving disagreements over alleged labor rights violations. The findings of evaluation panels were normally to be made public within thirty days after they were submitted to the commission, but thereafter the only action the commission could take was to "keep the matter under review" (article 14 [5]).

Far more than the Canadian proposal, the Mexican draft accord tabled at the May negotiating session sought to protect national sovereignty over labor issues and win recognition of Mexico's particular development circumstances.[183] For example, after reaffirming the broad goals shared by the NAFTA partners ("common interest in ensuring improved working and living conditions, more and better employment opportunities, increased productivity, and rising income levels for the workers of the three countries"), the preamble stated that the parties to any labor accord would be resolved to "reaffirm their respective territories" and safeguard (unspecified) labor rights "within the framework of their respective laws." Article 1 ("General Commitments") further committed the signatory countries to "confirming their full respect for each Party's constitutional and legal framework and recognizing their differences in terms of economic development and resource endowment."[184]

The specific provisions of the Mexican proposal also differed substantially from those tabled by the U.S. and Canadian governments. First, the document implicitly sought to limit sharply the scope of any North American labor accord. The preamble stated that the NAFTA partners should:

Enhance regional competitiveness, based on higher levels of productivity, quality and innovation, by promoting . . . a suitable context for strengthening labor-management relations, which would promote the dialogue between workers and employers, lead to the active participation of labor organizations, and thus stimulate the creativity and involvement of workers.

However, there was no reference in the document to any of the collective-action rights (the freedom to organize, the right to bargain collectively, the right to strike) that were given a prominent place in the U.S. and Canadian proposals.[185] Indeed, the only specific discussion of labor rights anywhere in the proposal appeared in an annex discussing the kinds of "bilateral or trilateral joint cooperation programs" that might be pursued by a North American labor commission. The eight-point list included occupational safety and health, child labor, and migrant workers.[186]

Second, the Mexican proposal called for new North American labor institutions with far less expansive authority than the initial U.S. proposal envisioned. In parallel with the U.S. and Canadian drafts, the Mexican document proposed a North American Labor Commission comprised of an executive committee (labor ministers/secretaries or their designees), a secretariat, and national advisory councils (articles 3-6). Although the executive committee could provide support for consultations among the signatory parties (see below), its principal responsibilities were to "establish priorities for cooperative action and develop bilateral and trilateral work and technical assistance programs" (article 4 [2f]). Similarly, the secretariat was to support the executive committee and any technical working groups that it might establish. However, the secretariat had no authority to report on labor rights enforcement in signatory countries or to initiate investigations of alleged rights violations (article 5).[187] Separate labor and business advisory panels could offer advice on any issue relevant to the agreement—but only at the invitation of a country's executive commissioner (article 6).

The principal institutional innovation in the Mexican proposal was its call for the NAFTA governments to rely on the International Labour Organization (ILO) to oversee their enforcement of labor law. This was an unprecedented proposal because the ILO had never previously played such a role. It was, in effect, a further effort to block U.S. or Canadian intrusion into Mexico's domestic affairs. Under the terms of the proposal, the three governments would negotiate an agreement with the ILO that would draw on its "expertise and independence" to "systematically document, through periodic reports, efforts by the Parties to secure enforcement" of labor rights (article 1[3]).[188]

By including an article on trilateral "consultations," the Mexican document recognized that allegations of labor rights violations might arise. Yet it restricted trilateral attention to the "persistent and systematic failure by one Party, occurring after the entry into force of this Agreement, to secure the effective enforcement of its labor laws and regulations with respect to health and safety in the workplace" (article 7[1]). The proposal did not indicate what procedures a NAFTA government—and, in contrast to what was permitted under the U.S. and Canadian proposals, only governments could initiate such complaints—should follow to arrive at such a conclusion. However, if bilateral consultations on the issue proved unsuccessful and if the Executive Committee also proved unable to resolve the matter within ninety days, the committee could publish a report containing relevant evidence from both the complaining party and the party complained against (article 7[2–5]). The Mexican proposal did not contemplate any further formal action at all in response to alleged violations of labor rights, much less the imposition of trade-linked sanctions against the offending party.

Thus the Mexican proposal, like the draft accord tabled by the Canadian government, relied exclusively on negative public attention to encourage effective government enforcement of labor laws. It did, however, go notably further than the Canadian proposal in imposing additional constraints on foreign intervention into a NAFTA country's internal affairs. For example, the document specified (article 7[6]) that no complaint could be legitimately lodged against a country for "(a) the authorities' reasonable exercise of their investigatory or prosecutorial discretion, based on the merits of each case in light of existing evidence; or (b) bona fide decisions of the authorities regarding the allocation of enforcement resources to violations of health and safety rights determined to have higher priority."[189]

Table 3.1 summarizes the U.S., Canadian, and Mexican governments' initial proposals for a NAFTA labor side-agreement.

Prolonged Negotiations, Shifting Political Calculations

The short composite draft accord that was compiled following the May negotiating session clarified (article 2[a]) that a list of recognized labor rights would appear in an annex rather than in the preamble of a final agreement, but it otherwise reflected little progress in resolving the main issues at stake.[190] Over the course of the next three meetings (in Washington, DC, on June 8–9; in Cocoyoc, Mexico, on July 8–10; and in Ottawa, Canada, on July 19–22), the principal lines of division among Canadian, Mexican, and U.S. negotiators concerned precisely which labor rights would be formally recognized in a prospective trinational agreement, the institutional design and specific authority of new North

TABLE 3.1 Initial proposals by the U.S., Canadian, and Mexican governments and final agreement on a NAFTA labor side-agreement, 1993

	United States	Canada	Mexico	Final Agreement
Scope of covered labor rights	Broad (including collective-action rights)	Broad (including collective-action rights)	Narrow (cooperation on safety and health, child labor, migrant workers)	Broad statement of principles (including collective-action rights)
Governance structure	Trilateral commission and autonomous secretariat with broad investigatory authority	Trilateral commission; secretariat comprised of national sections with limited authority	Trilateral commission and secretariat with limited authority	Trilateral commission and secretariat; separate NAOs with investigatory authority
Dispute settlement	Public submissions to secretariat; submission of trade benefits if national labor laws not enforced	Government consultations in commission; public submissions to national secretariats; public suasion if national labor laws not enforced	ILO reports on national labor law enforcement; government consultations on safety and health violations, but no further action	Public submissions to NAOs; fines if national labor laws not enforced; trade sanctions if fines not paid (except for Canada)
Labor rights violations subject to sanctions	Broad (including collective-action rights)	Broad (including collective-action rights); but subject only to public suasion	None	Occupational safety and health, minimum wages, child labor

Notes: The U.S., Canadian, and Mexican governments tabled initial written proposals at the May 19-21, 1993, negotiating session in Hull, Ontario. The three draft texts were published in *Inside U.S. Trade*, May 21, 1993. ILO = International Labour Organization; NAFTA = North American Free Trade Agreement; NAO = national administrative office

American labor institutions, and what penalties (if any) would be levied against countries where labor rights violations occurred.[191]

Mexican negotiators endorsed proposals to address occupational safety and health issues in a prospective accord because they believed that Mexico could benefit substantially from external assistance with training and the development of workplace standards.[192] They were, however, often on the defensive in the side-agreement debates. They resented being drawn into negotiations driven mainly by U.S. domestic political considerations; they took the position that the Mexico-U.S. memorandum of understanding on labor cooperation that had been negotiated during the 1991 U.S. fast-track debate already addressed the relevant issues; they were concerned that U.S. demands for enhanced labor standards and trade-linked sanctions constituted thinly disguised protectionism; and, on sovereignty grounds, they strongly resisted any external intervention in Mexico's domestic labor affairs.[193] Mexican officials were quickly disabused of their initial belief that, despite the intense political controversies that had arisen in the United States in 1991 over labor issues in the context of free-trade negotiations, any conditions placed on the NAFTA agreement after the U.S. presidential election would be largely cosmetic.[194] Yet even as their concerns about the fate of the NAFTA grew (reflecting their doubts about the Clinton administration's willingness to push hard to win congressional approval of the agreement), Mexican negotiators held firmly to their initial positions.[195]

The positions taken by Mexican officials in the labor side-agreement negotiations largely reflected both their deeply held concerns about safeguarding national sovereignty and their keen awareness of the political and economic importance of their country's established state-labor relations regime.[196] However, Mexican labor leaders themselves contributed to the formulation of Mexican negotiating positions. A labor delegation led by the CTM's Moisés Calleja García, a former Supreme Court justice and CTM legal counselor, participated formally in the negotiations.[197] Fidel Velázquez (secretary-general of the CTM during 1941–1946 and then continuously from 1950 until his death in 1997, at the age of ninety-seven) and other national labor leaders had endorsed the NAFTA. Nevertheless, they rejected the idea of a supranational labor rights commission with authority over such political issues as freedom of association and collective bargaining practices because they feared that such an arrangement would, in practice, undercut the legal supports provided by Mexico's existing federal labor law. The strength of their opposition constrained Mexican government representatives in their negotiations over the scope of a trinational labor accord.[198]

Mexican representatives did enjoy several important advantages in the prolonged side-agreement negotiations. First, international law and the principle of state sovereignty were on their side in the sense that there was no precedent for establishing a supranational labor-rights entity with the authority to override Mexico's national laws and regulations or to compel an expansion of existing labor rights. Any agreement would be framed in terms of confirming each signatory country's responsibility to implement effectively its own labor rights protections. The Mexican government's negotiating stance centered on this principle.[199]

Second, the Mexican government could claim to occupy comparatively high legal ground where worker rights were concerned. As a practical matter, the core issue underlying the NAALC negotiations (and the stated reason for U.S. and Canadian labor advocates' concerns about the negative consequences of establishing a free-trade agreement with Mexico) was the well-documented fact that political controls on unionized workers were deeply embedded features of Mexico's postrevolutionary authoritarian regime. Yet, in formal legal terms, Mexican workers' strong constitutional guarantees and labor law protections were, in many ways, more favorable than those enjoyed by Canadian and U.S. workers.[200] For example, Mexico's 1970 Federal Labor Law prohibited employers from hiring strikebreakers, guaranteed a three-month maternity leave, and established both minimum and seniority-based payments when workers with permanent employment status were fired without just cause. Mexican officials fully appreciated that comparatively superior legal provisions such as these would strengthen their bargaining position because U.S. officials were highly unlikely to offer to match Mexican standards in these areas in exchange for revisions of Mexican labor law and practice in the areas of greatest U.S. concern.[201]

Moreover, Mexico entered the side-agreement negotiations having ratified a substantially larger number of ILO conventions (seventy-six by September 1992) than either Canada (twenty-seven) or the United States (eleven).[202] Most important, Mexico had ratified five of the seven conventions then in effect that the ILO later characterized as "fundamental" (see table 1.1), whereas the United States had ratified only one of them.[203] As noted in chapter 1, ILO conventions acquire binding legal status when formally adopted by a signatory state, and the number and range of conventions a country has adopted are often viewed as measures of its commitment to internationally recognized labor rights. During the NAFTA debate, the AFL-CIO had called for U.S. ratification of a number of key ILO conventions, including nos. 87 (on freedom of association and the right to organize), 95 and 131 (on minimum wages), 98 (on the right to organize and bargain collectively), 100 and 111 (on equal remuneration and non-discrimination in employment), 29 (on forced or compulsory labor), 138 (on child labor), and 155 (on occupational safety and health).[204] The fact that the United States had not done so gave Mexican negotiators a strong defense against U.S. and Canadian charges that Mexico failed to respect internationally recognized labor rights.[205]

Third, Mexico held a somewhat better tactical position where the timeframe for side-agreement negotiations was concerned. During the main NAFTA negotiations, neither U.S. nor Canadian negotiators found reason for haste. In essence, U.S. officials sought to take advantage of the facts that the Mexican government had formulated the initial proposal for free-trade negotiations and had a larger political stake in securing an agreement by, on different occasions, slowing discussions so as to extract further concessions from their Mexican counterparts. Similarly, because Canada already had in place a free-trade agreement with the United States, its representatives at the bargaining table had an interest in reaching a trilateral accord only if its provisions were at least as favorable as those in its existing bilateral agreement.[206] With the side-agreement negotiations, however, the Mexican and U.S. positions were essentially reversed. The Clinton administration faced growing pressures to secure labor (and environmental) accords as a means of building congressional support for a controversial measure that, under U.S. law, required final ratification no later than autumn 1993. The Salinas administration was also anxious to see the NAFTA ratified by the end of 1993 so as to avoid any complications in the delicate presidential succession process. Mexican negotiators were, however, prepared to play for time, with the goal of making only the minimum concessions required to facilitate eventual ratification of the NAFTA.[207] Indeed, because Salinas personally controlled Mexico's presidential succession process, he had the capacity to postpone the date on which the PRI's 1994 presidential candidate was announced in order to reduce time pressures on Mexican side-agreement negotiators.[208]

Finally, several of the positions adopted by Mexican negotiators were strongly supported by their Canadian counterparts, although the two negotiating teams did not coordinate their bargaining positions in advance.[209] Despite express assurances to the contrary in the initial U.S. written proposal,[210] the Canadian government and private sector both feared that trade-linked sanctions of labor rights violations would function as a form of protectionism, and Canadian side-agreement negotiators flatly refused to accept them.[211] In addition, they strongly defended the principle of national sovereignty by continuing to emphasize the constraints they were under because of Canada's federalist arrangements. Because most Canadian labor law came under provincial jurisdiction, representatives of the federal government considered it constitutionally impermissible to agree to binding labor standards that might contravene provincial laws.[212]

In the end, shifting political calculations in the United States and Mexico forced both parties toward compromise. Key figures in the Clinton administration (including Secretary of Labor Reich) had favored a strong, enforceable agreement on labor matters, and for some members of Congress and their labor allies, trade-linked sanctions constituted a litmus test in this regard.[213] By late June 1993, however, as the likelihood of winning support from leading Democrats like Representative Gephardt waned, Clinton administration officials acknowledged that the ultimate passage of the NAFTA would require a labor accord acceptable to Republicans. Business interests and Republican legislators had, since January, consistently opposed a side-agreement that granted supranational authority to trilateral institutions, gave them significant investigatory and enforcement powers, and included trade-linked sanctions of labor rights violations. On several different occasions, they had openly challenged President Clinton on these issues, threatening to vote against the NAFTA if their concerns were not adequately addressed.[214] Persistent opposition along these lines clearly constrained U.S negotiators and pushed them toward accommodation with their Canadian and Mexican counterparts.[215]

The Salinas administration, too, was prepared to make concessions as the price necessary to win ratification of the NAFTA. At inconclusive rounds of negotiation in early June, early July, and late July, Mexican negotiators accepted that some form of sanctions regime would be necessary, although they proposed fines (either on governments that did not enforce their own laws or directly on the offending companies, with the proceeds directed to programs designed to ameliorate the originating problems) rather than trade-linked penalties.[216] However, they continued to resist U.S. proposals for an autonomous trilateral institution with the authority to investigate and punish the perpetrators of labor rights violations. Instead, in line with the initial Canadian proposal, they favored national secretariats responsive to their respective governments. In repeated debates about the scope of an agreement and which labor rights would be recognized in it, Mexican (and Canadian) negotiators insisted that existing national laws should constitute the basis of a trilateral accord.[217]

Negotiators discussed institutional arrangements in detail from July 8 through early August, agreeing to establish a trilateral labor commission and secretariat (initially called an international coordinating secretariat) and a special national office in each of the three countries (initially called national administrative units"). What was notable was that the authority and functions of these new institutions would differ sharply from those outlined in the initial written U.S. side-agreement proposal. There would, for instance, be no trilateral public advisory committee to bolster the commission's authority, nor would it have responsibility for promoting improved or minimum continental labor standards. Similarly, the secretariat would have no independent investigatory authority. Rather, its functions were limited to coordinating trilateral cooperative activities, preparing background reports on such topics as labor regulations and labor market conditions in the signatory countries, and otherwise supporting administratively the implementation of the side-agreement.[218] Moreover, the three government-operated national administrative offices, rather than an autonomous trilateral secretariat, would receive and be responsible for addressing public communications concerning alleged violations of labor rights occurring in another NAFTA country.[219]

By July 23, the date on which the negotiating teams compiled the first extended draft of the agreement, they had also formally agreed on ten of the eleven labor principles that would underpin the agreement (see table 4.1). However, they did not reach a consensus on the final principle (concerning the rights of migrant workers) until the end of the month.[220]

There was a seventh round of negotiations in Washington, DC, on July 29–30, and talks continued there starting on August 4. The thorniest issue facing negotiators during this arduous final phase concerned dispute-settlement procedures, particularly the labor rights violations potentially subject to penalties and the character of the penalties that might be applied to a country that failed to enforce effectively its labor laws. Indeed, prior to August 9, none of the draft texts in circulation had contained any language at all addressing dispute-settlement questions. Throughout the negotiations, Mexican officials had staunchly resisted external scrutiny of national enforcement of labor laws on any issues other than those concerning safety and health in the workplace.[221] Their modest concession in the August 9 draft text was to expand this to the "non-adversarial" examination of " other technical labor standards," a formulation that referred to labor issues other than collective-action rights.[222] Even at that late date, however, the draft agreement circulated among the three negotiating teams included no language at all regarding the kinds of labor rights violations that might be subject to sanction or the penalties a signatory country would face if a specially appointed dispute-settlement panel found that it had "persistently failed to enforce its laws" and subsequently failed to adopt appropriate corrective measures under an agreed "action plan."[223]

Final compromises brought the bargaining process to a conclusion in Ottawa early on August 13, one year following the end of the NAFTA negotiations.[224] As part of a final set of trade-offs with the United States, Mexico accepted the possibility of trade-linked sanctions (trade-based penalties would apply only if a sanctioned country failed to pay an assessed fine) as the price of securing U.S. congressional approval of the NAFTA.[225] A turning point on this issue came after a meeting between Secretary Serra Puche and Representative Gephardt on August 6, in which Gephardt made it clear that trade-linked sanctions were essential if congressional approval were to be secured.[226] His position was understandable in the context of the labor-conditionality provisions that the U.S. Congress had attached to trade legislation since 1984, which consistently included the option of imposing trade-based sanctions as a penalty for serious, persistent labor rights violations. Yet Canadian negotiators—with the personal support of Prime Minister Kim Campbell, who conveyed this position directly to President Clinton in a telephone conversation—adamantly refused to go along. Trilateral negotiations were, at this point, close to breaking down.[227]

In an effort to resolve persistent disagreements regarding the character of a sanctions regime, Canadian negotiators finally agreed to a special provision in the side-agreement in which Canada's Federal Court could fine the federal government or provincial governments for a persistent failure to enforce its/ their own labor laws. In exchange, Canada was exempted from the trade-linked sanctions that formally applied to Mexico and the United States.[228] Canada also won agreement that provinces representing 35 percent of its national labor force would have to approve the provisions of the labor accord before they took final effect.

As part of their final deal with Mexican officials, U.S. negotiators dropped their demand that the labor rights whose violation would be subject to fines or trade-linked sanctions include "industrial relations" (for example, the freedom of association and the rights to organize and bargain collectively).[229] Alleged violations in a particular country of any of the eleven labor rights principles listed in the agreement's annex 1 would be open to scrutiny by other signatory governments. However, only a restricted subset of them would be subject to grievance procedures that might conclude with the levy of fines or trade-linked sanctions.[230] Renewed, intense U.S pressures on August 11–12, at the very end of the negotiating process, led the Mexican government to add child labor laws and minimum wage standards to workplace safety and health measures as the rights subset whose violation could be sanctioned by fines or trade-linked penalties (see table 3.1).[231] Including minimum wage standards in this category, which may, in fact, have been the final concession made by Mexican negotiators,[232] allowed Clinton administration officials to claim that the side-agreement did address wage issues in Mexico, albeit in restricted fashion.

In the course of a telephone conversation on the evening of August 12 in which Presidents Clinton and Salinas de Gortari confirmed these various understandings, Salinas also committed his government to linking future minimum wage increases to productivity gains in order to help undercut arguments by NAFTA opponents that Mexico would enjoy unfair competitive economic advantages under the agreement.[233] This was a politically important concession for two reasons. First, the wage-productivity link had been the focus of U.S. concerns and U.S.-Mexico bilateral discussions throughout the negotiations.[234] The preambles to the side-agreement proposals initially tabled by the U.S. and Canadian governments in May had both highlighted the issue,[235] but the final NAALC preamble simply reaffirmed the parties' (somewhat ambiguous) goal of "promoting higher living standards as productivity increases." Second, Salinas had previously rejected an overall wage-productivity link in negotiations with the CTM over a National Accord for the Elevation of Productivity and Quality.[236] At Clinton's urging, Salinas publicly announced this commitment in a televised address on August 13. He was responding in part to Gephardt's demand during the last phase of negotiations that average wages in Mexico be linked to productivity gains.[237]

The North American Agreement on Labor Cooperation was signed on September 14, 1993.[238] The Clinton administration then turned to the political management of the labor (and environmental) side-agreements.[239] At the time they were publicly announced on August 13, President Clinton issued only a brief statement claiming that the NAFTA was now also a "fair trade agreement."[240] The administration had delayed the signing until after a congressional vote on politically divisive balanced-budget legislation so as to preserve as much Democratic Party unity as possible when the NAFTA debate began in earnest.[241] Nevertheless, the side-agreements immediately met with significant dissent. Former independent presidential candidate Perot condemned the accords and urged Congress to reject the NAFTA. Democratic Majority Leader Gephardt, whose 1988 presidential candidacy had highlighted trade issues and whose position on the NAFTA was thought to be capable of swaying the votes of approximately seventy Democratic representatives, concluded:

> The announced side agreements fall short in important respects, and I am not optimistic that these defects can be successfully resolved. I cannot support the agreement [NAFTA] as it stands.[242]

Lane Kirkland, president of the AFL-CIO, dismissed the labor side-agreement as a "bad joke . . . a Rube Goldberg structure of committees all leading nowhere."[243] The situation was also clouded by doubts about how much political capital President Clinton was prepared to invest in winning approval of the NAFTA, a question that continued to divide his top advisers.[244]

In the end, President Clinton did devote significant effort to winning public support for and congressional approval of the NAFTA. One of the public relations strategies he adopted was to highlight Salinas's (never fulfilled) pledge to link future minimum wage increases in Mexico to productivity gains, going so far as to cite (inaccurately)

> a dramatic and unprecedented commitment by the Government of Mexico to tie their minimum wage structure to increases in productivity and growth of the Mexican economy and to make that a part of the trade agreement, so that failure to do that could result in fines and ultimately trade sanctions.[245]

Administration officials also won over some Democratic congressional votes by offering particularistic side-deals, including last-minute restrictions on sugar, vegetable, and citrus imports from Mexico.[246] For others, however, the NAALC (and the environmental side-agreement), as well as President Clinton's public promise that the United States would withdraw from the NAFTA if Canada or

Mexico withdrew from either side-agreement, provided essential political cover.[247] The vote in the House of Representatives on November 17, 1993, was 234 in favor and 200 against, with Democratic members splitting 102 in favor and 156 against. The Senate approved the agreement by a 61–38 vote on November 20.[248]

CONCLUSION

Formal approval of the NAFTA did not end political debate in Washington, DC, over labor rights issues in Mexico. Indeed, in January 1995, as U.S. policymakers debated the terms of a financial rescue package during Mexico's 1994–1995 "peso crisis," Representative David Bonior (Democrat-Michigan and Democratic whip in the House of Representatives) and other liberal Democrats sought to condition U.S. assistance on significant changes in Mexican politics and labor policy, including strengthening workers' rights to organize, bargain collectively, and strike and formally linking wage increases to productivity gains. And again, in October 1995, U.S. congressional critics of the NAFTA introduced a "NAFTA Accountability Act" that required democratization in Mexico as a condition for continuation of the free-trade agreement.[249]

The NAALC on its own nonetheless constituted a major departure in the ongoing debate about linking labor rights to trade agreements. Yet despite its importance in this regard, the rights guarantees and dispute-settlement provisions included in the accord were restricted and the object of much subsequent criticism. Even at the time the NAALC was announced, the AFL-CIO denounced it as a step backward from existing U.S. legislation, such as the Generalized System of Preferences (GSP) program, because it weakened the U.S. government's capacity to sanction Mexico—previously a leading U.S. GSP beneficiary—for worker rights violations. Not only were collective-action rights excluded from the NAALC's penalty regime, but potential NAALC sanctions were far less severe than the possible suspension or termination of trade and investment benefits under the U.S. GSP scheme and related legislation.[250] One key question, then, is whether even more intense pressure from the United States might have pushed Mexico into accepting an agreement in which sanctions could have been applied against violations of a much broader range of worker rights.

Some analysts have underscored the relevance of this question by noting that, even though labor and environmental issues were paired for political reasons in the initial trilateral exchanges about possible side-agreements to the NAFTA and in formal negotiations between March and at least late July 1993,[251] the North American Agreement on Environmental Cooperation (NAAEC) was, in several ways, a more robust international agreement.[252] A comparison of the NAALC and the NAAEC is in some ways instructive, but it does not necessarily demonstrate conclusively that a substantially different labor accord was within the reach of U.S. negotiators. As noted above, there is evidence that even the U.S. Department of Labor and some U.S. trade unions preferred nationally controlled offices rather than a single, autonomous trilateral institution to monitor signatories' enforcement of their labor obligations. Even more important, however, it was much easier for U.S. and Mexican negotiators to find common ground on environmental questions than on labor rights issues. The Salinas administration was very willing to address environmental problems in the Mexico-U.S. border region; in fact, there was a significant record of bilateral cooperation in this area dating from the 1983 La Paz agreement, and environmental groups in Mexico favored a trilateral environmental agreement.[253] In contrast, even though Mexico had previously qualified its Westphalian sovereignty by acceding to numerous ILO conventions, national labor law and policy were strategic issues that cut to the core of the country's political economy and its Weberian sovereignty.[254] Indeed, President Salinas de Gortari, in the account of events he prepared for the historical record, strongly implied that he would have walked away from the NAFTA had he been required to make concessions in the NAALC negotiations that in any way infringed upon Mexican sovereignty.[255]

In reality, though, senior Mexican and Canadian NAALC negotiators and a former high-level Mexican elected official have acknowledged that the Mexican government would almost certainly have made further concessions in response to U.S. labor demands if that had been the price for securing final U.S. congressional ratification of the NAFTA.[256] It is highly unlikely that Mexican negotiators, given their own concerns about potential disguised U.S. protectionism and Canada's adamant, sovereignty-based position on the issue,[257] would have conceded to U.S. calls for a strong trade-based sanctions regime for rights violations. Yet they might well have given ground by adding "industrial relations" issues (including freedom of association and the rights to organize and bargain collectively) to the list of workers' rights whose violation was potentially subject to external penalty. A concession along these lines was, in fact, under active discussion among senior Mexican government officials when NAALC negotiations appeared to have deadlocked in early August 1993.[258] There was, of course, vigorous opposition to the idea from representatives of both Mexican organized labor and the national business community. However, given the strong executive authority that Salinas exercised throughout his term in office, it is certainly possible that he could have compelled domestic agreement on the issue if that had been necessary to achieve his larger strategic goal of a continental free-trade agreement. Had this been the course he adopted, Salinas would presumably have relied on the length and complexity of NAALC dispute-settlement procedures to limit Mexico's political exposure to any U.S. and/or Canadian complaints that it failed to enforce core labor rights.

Given the substantial power asymmetries that characterized U.S.-Mexico bilateral relations and the Salinas administration's overriding political interest in winning approval of the NAFTA, why were U.S. negotiators unable to secure a labor side-agreement on these counterfactual terms? The two most important factors were the alignment of domestic sociopolitical actors in the United States and the structure of and the U.S. legislative calendar for the NAALC negotiations.

In marked contrast to the broad unity that President Salinas de Gortari forged and maintained among domestic interest groups throughout the NAALC negotiations, different political constituencies in the United States remained divided over both the overall merits of a labor side-agreement and its content. The opposition voiced by U.S. business interests and Republican legislators against a labor side-agreement was not surprising. In the end, the political imperative of securing congressional Republicans' support for the NAFTA was an important factor constraining U.S. negotiators pushing for a stronger NAALC.

The impact of the U.S. labor movement's at best ambivalent stance in the NAALC negotiations is more difficult to assess. One observer has argued that if leading U.S. labor organizations had adopted the same strategy as a number of prominent environmental groups and signaled a willingness to back the NAFTA if the Clinton administration effectively addressed their principal concerns, then U.S. negotiators might have secured a final agreement that more closely resembled their initial proposals.[259] A contemporary report did suggest that U.S. negotiators, under intensifying pressure to bring the side-agreement negotiations to a conclusion, may have agreed to the exclusion of "industrial relations" rights violations from external sanction because they believed that most major U.S. unions were unlikely to back approval of the NAFTA regardless of the NAALC's specific contents.[260] In those circumstances, given that senior Mexican officials were considering whether to make a last-minute concession on this issue, it is possible that a more engaged negotiating posture by U.S. labor organizations might have produced a different NAALC outcome. It is, though, questionable whether U.S. unions could have easily adopted a different position in a political context defined by Perot's 1992 populist presidential campaign against the "giant sucking sound" created by low-wage economic competition from Mexico. Labor leaders were certainly in no position to reassure skeptical rank-and-file union members that a mere side-agreement to the NAFTA would hold back the tidal undertow of continental free trade. The dynamics of the negotiations were, nevertheless, paradoxical: concessions that U.S. negotiators made on the pivotal issue of trade-related sanctions for violations of collective-action rights only reinforced the reservations that U.S. trade unions—the intended beneficiaries of the NAALC—had about the likely efficacy of the side-agreement, which, in turn, increased business and Republican influence as Clinton administration officials calculated how to assemble a majority congressional coalition in a close, high-stakes vote on the NAFTA.

The structure of, and the U.S. legislative calendar for, the side-agreement negotiations were, however, even more important elements in determining the final NAALC outcome. First, President Clinton, probably more because of the competing demands of his ambitious domestic policy agenda than because of insistent Mexican lobbying, planned from the outset to hold side-agreement negotiations without reopening the NAFTA text. This decision, in effect, deprived U.S. NAALC negotiators of their most important point of potential sovereignty leverage. As a consequence, the dynamics of the negotiations were very different than they would have been if discussions over labor rights had been bound up with the content of the trade agreement itself.[261] Second, the fact that these were trilateral negotiations may have reduced U.S. bargaining leverage vis-à-vis Mexico because on several important issues Mexican and Canadian negotiators took similar positions and often combined forces against U.S. demands. Finally, the tight U.S. legislative calendar for a final congressional vote on the NAFTA enhanced Mexican officials' negotiating leverage and increased the potential pay-offs from delays and resistance to a more expansive NAALC. As the legislative clock ran down, U.S. negotiators were forced to make significant concessions in order to close the deal.

CHAPTER 4

The North American Agreement on Labor Cooperation in Principle and in Practice, 1994–2020

This chapter presents the first systematic assessment of the North American Agreement on Labor Cooperation (NAALC), in principle and in practice, over the entire period it was in effect, 1994–2020.[1] The first section overviews both the institutions created by the NAALC, the trilateral Commission on Labor Cooperation (the only international body other than the International Labour Organization devoted exclusively to labor rights and labor-related matters) and national administrative offices in the three signatory countries, and the eleven labor principles that underpinned their operation. The agreement did not explicitly establish common minimum labor standards that were binding on Canada, Mexico, and the United States. Rather, it emphasized national sovereignty in this area, only requiring that each country enforce its own labor laws.[2] The NAALC did, however, impinge upon traditional conceptions of state sovereignty by legitimating close external attention to national labor law and policy. Although under certain narrow conditions, the agreement formally provided for monetary or trade-linked penalties against a member country, the public attention and international pressure generated by external scrutiny were, in practice, the strongest sanctions imposed by the NAALC against violations of its agreed labor principles.

The discussion then turns in sections two through four to a detailed analysis of the forty-six public communications (grievance petitions) submitted to the Canadian, Mexican, and U.S. national administrative offices (NAOs) between 1994 and 2020. These submissions were framed in terms of one or more of the NAALC's eleven labor principles and addressed alleged labor rights violations in diverse circumstances, ranging from individual companies and specific work-places, to broad policy areas affecting entire industries or economic sectors, to the content of national labor law itself. This examination goes beyond previous studies of NAALC public communications by combining a rigorous evaluation of both the petitions filed with the Canadian and/or U.S. NAOs concerning labor rights in Mexico with an assessment of submissions to Mexico's NAO regarding the rights of Mexican migrant workers in the United States and Canada. It engages the politics of the NAALC at two levels. First, the discussion devotes particular attention to the process of submitting and resolving public communi-cations, focusing on the type and number of sociopolitical actors involved (trade unions and/or labor-, human-, and migrant-rights nongovernmental organiza-tions), whether they constituted binational or trinational coalitions, the specific NAALC principles the submissions invoked, the time that NAOs required to process the petitions, the final case outcome, and whether the public communi-cations produced any observed policy impact (that is, changes in labor law and/ or government policy) in the target country. Second, the analysis considers both the domestic and foreign policy factors that shaped member states' responses to NAALC public communications.

The fifth section examines the impact of the NAALC public communications process in three key areas: the understanding of comparative labor law and labor rights problems that developed in the three signatory states and its longer-term importance in defining the agenda for subsequent U.S.-Mexican negotiations over labor rights issues; the construction of transnational social capital in the form of binational and trinational coalitions mobilized to defend workers' rights, especially in Mexico and the United States; and the impact of NAALC public communica-tions on labor rights law and policy in Mexico. On this last topic, the discussion focuses especially on the ways that different presidential administrations in the United States and Mexico engaged NAALC processes and the consequences for the implementation of, for example, a bilateral ministerial agreement under which the Mexican government agreed to provide public access to union registration and collective contract information and promote secret balloting in representation elections to determine legal control over a worker-employer contract.

The conclusion assesses the overall NAALC experience in terms of the limited sovereignty leverage that the United States was able to bring to bear on Mexico and the factors that explain the overall (in)effectiveness of NAALC procedures in effecting significant changes in Mexican labor law and policy.

THE NAALC's INSTITUTIONAL ARCHITECTURE
AND UNDERPINNING LABOR PRINCIPLES

In Mexico and the United States, the NAALC took full effect along with the North American Free Trade Agreement (NAFTA) on January 1, 1994.[3] However, because the Canadian federal government's jurisdiction over labor matters is limited to federal employees, three federal territories, and specified economic activities of interprovincial and international importance (banking, telecommunications, shipping and transportation, grain handling, uranium mining), labor law enforcement in Canada is primarily a sovereign provincial responsibility.[4] Therefore, in order to take binding effect, the NAALC required ratification by a sufficient number of provinces so that, along with workers under federal government jurisdiction, they together constituted at least 35 percent of the national labor force.[5] Ratifications by Alberta (1995), Manitoba (1997), and Québec (1997) fulfilled this requirement.[6] Even then, however, the NAALC applied only in those provinces that had ratified it. Ontario, Canada's most populous province, and four others never ratified the agreement.

The NAFTA's stated objectives were, among others, to "improve working conditions and living standards in [the three countries'] respective territories, and protect, enhance and enforce basic workers' rights" (NAALC preamble). Toward these ends, the NAALC established new trilateral and national institutions and recognized a significant range of labor rights. The underpinning principles were "respect for each Party's constitution and law" (preamble) and an explicit recognition of each signatory's right "to establish its own domestic labor standards" (article 2). Indeed, the agreement's overall objectives included promoting "compliance with, and *effective enforcement by each Party of, its labor law*" (article 1, emphasis added).[7] Article 5(8) underscored national sovereignty concerns by stipulating:

> For greater certainty, decisions by each Party's administrative, quasijudicial, judicial or labor tribunals, or pending decisions, as well as related proceedings shall not be subject to review or reopened under the provisions of this Agreement.

Similarly, article 42 stated clearly, "Nothing in this Agreement shall be construed to empower a Party's authorities to undertake labor law enforcement activities in the territory of another Party."[8]

The NAALC created two sets of new institutions.[9] First, a trilateral North American Commission for Labor Cooperation (NACLC) comprised of a governing council of ministers and a secretariat had overall responsibility for implementing the agreement (articles 8–14). The council was to meet in an annual regular session and in special session at the request of any signatory state, with decisions generally reached by consensus.[10] The specific functions of the commission, whose annual budget (US$1.8 million during 1994–1999 and US$2.1 million after 1999[11]) was funded equally by the three countries, included promoting a wide array of cooperative activities addressing occupational safety and health, child labor, migrant workers, employment standards, workplace gender equality, worker-employer cooperation, and "legislation relating to the formation and operation of unions, collective bargaining and the resolution of labor disputes."[12] The secretariat, whose executive director was appointed by the council to a renewable three-year term and rotated by nationality consecutively among the NAALC signatories, was responsible for such activities as preparing background reports on labor law, labor market conditions (employment rates, average wages, labor productivity), and human resource development in the member countries. Its fifteen-member staff, recruited on an equitable basis from nationals of each member state, was not to receive instructions from any government or authority external to the council (articles 12–14).[13]

Second, the NAALC required each signatory country to establish a national administrative office at the federal government level, with each country responsible for its staffing and operational costs.[14] These offices were principal points of contact on NAALC matters for other national governmental agencies, the other signatories' NAOs, and the secretariat. The NAOs had operational responsibility for organizing a range of cooperative activities, with lead responsibility for coordinating trinational programs initially rotating among the three offices.[15] However, their most conspicuous public role was to address allegations of labor rights violations under the NAALC's provisions. The U.S. officials who negotiated the accord purposefully defined this function in quite general terms so that the U.S. government had flexibility in designing its own NAO and establishing its internal procedures:[16]

> Each NAO shall provide for the submission and receipt, and periodically publish a list, of public communications on labor law matters arising in the territory of another Party. Each NAO shall review such matters, as appropriate, in accordance with domestic procedures. (Article 16[3])

Underpinning Commission and NAO operations were the eleven labor principles recognized in NAALC annex 1 (see the text box). The list gave a pre-eminent place to freedom of association and the rights to organize and bargain collectively, and it reaffirmed the long-standing international prohibition on forced labor. However, in explicitly recognizing the right to strike, equal pay for women and men, and the protection of migrant workers, the annex went beyond both the list of core labor rights later highlighted by the International Labour Organization's (ILO) Declaration on Fundamental Principles and Rights at Work (1998) and the "internationally recognized worker rights" promoted in prior U.S. trade legislation.[17] Few analysts have given the NAALC its due for these advances.

NORTH AMERICAN AGREEMENT ON LABOR COOPERATION:
LABOR PRINCIPLES

The following are guiding principles that the Parties are committed to promote, subject to each Party's domestic law, but do not establish common minimum standards for their domestic law. They indicate broad areas of concern where the Parties have developed, each in its own way, laws, regulations, procedures and practices that protect the rights and interests of their respective workforces.

1. **Freedom of association and protection of the right to organize**
    The right of workers exercised freely and without impediment to establish and join organizations of their own choosing to further and defend their interests.

2. **The right to bargain collectively**
    The protection of the right of organized workers to freely engage in collective bargaining on matters concerning the terms and conditions of employment.

3. **The right to strike**
    The protection of the right of workers to strike in order to defend their collective interests.

4. **Prohibition of forced labor**
    The prohibition and suppression of all forms of forced or compulsory labor, except for types of compulsory work generally considered

---

acceptable by the Parties, such as compulsory military service, certain civic obligations, prison labor not for private purposes and work exacted in cases of emergency.

5. **Labor protections for children and young persons**

The establishment of restrictions on the employment of children and young persons that may vary taking into consideration relevant factors likely to jeopardize the full physical, mental and moral development of young persons, including schooling and safety requirements.

6. **Minimum employment standards**

The establishment of minimum employment standards, such as minimum wages and overtime pay, for wage earners, including those not covered by collective agreements.

7. **Elimination of employment discrimination**

Elimination of employment discrimination on such grounds as race, religion, age, sex or other grounds, subject to certain reasonable exceptions, such as, where applicable, *bona fide* occupational requirements or qualifications and established practices or rules governing retirement ages, and special measures of protection or assistance for particular groups designed to take into account the effects of discrimination.

8. **Equal pay for women and men**

Equal wages for women and men by applying the principle of equal pay for equal work in the same establishment.

9. **Prevention of occupational injuries and illnesses**

Prescribing and implementing standards to minimize the causes of occupational injuries and illnesses.

10. **Compensation in cases of occupational injuries and illnesses**

The establishment of a system providing benefits and compensation to workers or their dependents in cases of occupational injuries, accidents or fatalities arising out of, linked with or occurring in the course of employment.

11. **Protection of migrant workers**

Providing migrant workers in a Party's territory with the same legal protection as the Party's nationals in respect of working conditions.

Source: Reproduced from *International Legal Materials* 32, no. 6 (1993): 1515–16 (North American Agreement on Labor Cooperation, annex 1).

In terms of possible enforcement actions, however, NAALC labor rights were ordered hierarchically in three tiers.[18] Each NAO could accept public communications concerning alleged violations of any of the eleven rights recognized in annex 1 that occurred in another NAALC country (a limitation that avoided jurisdictional overlap by precluding submitters from employing NAALC procedures to file complaints against their own government).[19] Moreover, an NAO could at any time request consultations with another NAO regarding " the other Party's labor law, its administration, or labor market conditions in its territory."[20] If the government pursuing the issue subsequently judged that its concerns had not been adequately addressed, it could then proceed to request ministerial-level consultations with the counterpart government on any of the eleven recognized labor principles.[21] If the matter in question could not be satisfactorily resolved at the ministerial level, the government pursuing the issue could request, by giving notice to the NACLC secretariat, that the council establish an independent, three-member (one from each NAALC signatory) evaluation committee of experts (ECE) to examine "patterns of practice by each Party in the enforcement of its occupational safety and health or other technical labor standards," so long as the matter was trade-related and covered by "mutually recognized labor laws" in the countries involved.[22] These conditions, in effect, established a second tier of labor rights, prioritizing a range of individual rights while excluding alleged violations of collective-action rights (the rights of freedom of association and collective bargaining and the right to strike) from further enforcement action.

If the ECE's final report to the council determined that a signatory state had persistently failed to enforce effectively its "occupational safety and health, child labor or minimum wage technical labor standards" (article 27[1]), and if the council itself was unable to reach a satisfactory resolution of the dispute within sixty days, it could, by a two-thirds vote, initiate the final stage of NAALC enforcement procedures by convening an arbitral panel (AP)—in effect creating a third tier of protected labor rights.[23] The independent, five-member panel had a maximum of 240 days to present its final report and recommendations (articles 36, 37). If the panel also found a "persistent pattern of failure" by the defendant government, and if the parties in dispute were unable to agree on the terms and implementation of a mutually satisfactory action plan to correct the demonstrated rights violations, the council could reconvene the AP. At this stage, if the panel determined that the defendant party had not taken adequate steps to remedy the pattern of nonenforcement, it could impose a "monetary enforcement assessment" not to exceed 0.007 percent of the total trade in goods between the disputing parties.[24] If the panel subsequently found that the party in question had failed to pay the fine within 180 days, the complaining party(ies) could suspend the defendant country's NAFTA tariff benefits annually in an amount no greater than the fine that had been levied.[25] The suspension was to last until the defendant country either paid the fine or took satisfactory remedial action or the complaining party(ies) had collected the amount of the unpaid fine.[26]

Critics of the NAALC have repeatedly noted that, although the agreement addressed each of these possible enforcement procedures in careful detail, no public communication in Canada, Mexico, or the United States ever reached the ECE or AP stages.[27]

NAALC PUBLIC COMMUNICATIONS: AN OVERVIEW

Within the broad mandate established by NAALC article 16(3), each signatory country adopted its own internal guidelines setting the terms for receiving and reviewing public communications alleging labor rights violations in another NAALC country.[28] For this reason, the procedures followed by each NAO differed somewhat.[29] For instance, the U.S. NAO (US NAO) regulations in effect between January 1994 and December 2006 normally required a public hearing as part of each review process. The Canadian NAO (CAN NAO) guidelines emphasized that reviews would ensure "an accessible, open and transparent examination of the issues," but public meetings or consultations were only one of several investigative options. The Mexican NAO (MEX NAO) guidelines referred only to the possibility of organizing "informative sessions."[30] Yet despite such differences, all three countries' administrative guidelines generally evidenced flexibility and openness.[31]

Most important, all three NAOs accepted submissions from a range of labor organizations and labor-, human-, and migrant-rights groups, regardless of whether the submitter(s) were based in the NAO's own country or in other NAALC countries. As a consequence, even though the overall number of public communications filed with the three NAOs between 1994 and 2020 was modest (forty-six submissions: Canada, seven; Mexico, fourteen; United States, twenty-five), the total number of Canadian, Mexican, and U.S. sociopolitical actors involved in NAALC processes (259) was substantial (table 4.1; see appendix B for an annotated

TABLE 4.1 NAALC public communications to the Canadian, Mexican, and U.S. national administrative offices (NAOs), 1994-2020

NAO case number	Type and number of submitters			Binational (BN) or trinational (TN) coalition	NAALC principle(s) cited	Case duration (in days)	Final case outcome	Observed policy impact
	Unions	NGOs	Total					
CAN 98-1 (Echlin/Itapsa)	29	14	43	TN	1, 9	295	MC	0
CAN 98-2 (Yale / Immigration and Naturalization Service)	2	17	19	No	6, 11	211	D	0
CAN 99-1 (Labor Policy Association / EFCO Corporation)	0	1	1	No	9	62	D	0
CAN 2003-1 (Puebla garment producers)	0	3	3	TN	1, 6, 9	586	MC	0
CAN 2005-1 (Aviacsa pilots)	1	0	1	No	1, 2	238	D	0
CAN 2008-1 (North Carolina public employees)	56	2	58	TN	1, 2, 6-10	NA	R	NA
CAN 2011-1 (SME)	63	23	86	TN	1-3, 9	NA	R	NA
MEX 9501 (Sprint Corp)	1	0	1	No	1	111	MC	0
MEX 9801 (Solec International)	2	2	4	BN	1, 6, 7, 9, 10	505	MC	1 + 2
MEX 9802 (Washington State apple growers and producers)	3	1	4	No	1, 2, 6, 7, 9-11	462	MC	1 + 2
MEX 9803 (DeCoster Egg Farm)	1	0	1	No	6, 7, 9-11	486	MC	2
MEX 9804 (Yale / Immigration and Naturalization Service)	2	17	19	No	6, 11	779	MC	2
MEX 2001-1 (New York State workers' compensation)	0	4	4	No	9-11	744	MC	0
MEX 2003-1 (H-2A visa migrant workers, North Carolina)	1	1	2	BN	1, 2, 4, 6, 7, 9-11	3565	MC	1 + 2
MEX 2005-1 (H-2B visa migrant workers; various states)	2	10	12	BN	4, 6, 9-11	2773	MC	2
MEX 2006-1 (North Carolina public employees)	56	2	58	TN	1, 2, 6-10	2220	R	0
MEX 2011-1 (H-2B visa migrant carnival and fair workers)	1	13	14	BN	6, 11	423	MC	2
MEX 2012-1 (Alabama anti-immigrant law)	1	1	2	BN	1, 2, 6, 7, 9-11	NA	W	0

Case								
MEX 2015-1 (US Department of Labor)	0	0	1	No	7	1146	R	0
MEX 2016-1 (gender discrimination, H-2A and H-2B female migrant workers)	3	25	28	TN	7, 8	1447	R	0
MEX 2016-2 (gender discrimination, female migrant agricultural workers in Canada)	2	7	9	TN	7, 8	NA	R	NA
US 940001 (Honeywell, Inc.)	1	0	1	No	1, 2	240	R	0
US 940002 (General Electric Co.)	1	0	1	No	1, 2	240	R	1
US 940003 (Sony Corp)	0	4	4	BN	1, 2	238	MC	0
US 940004 (General Electric Co.)	1	0	1	No	1, 2	NA	W	0
US 9601 (SUTSP, Ministry of Fishing)	0	3	3	BN	1	228	MC	0
US 9602 (Maxi-Switch)	3	0	3	BN	1	NA	W	1
US 9701 (pregnancy testing)	0	4	4	BN	7	241	MC	2
US 9702 (Han Young)	4	5	9	TN	1, 9	235	MC	1 + 3
US 9703 (Echlin–Itapsa)	24	14	38	TN	1, 9	228	MC	3
US 9801 (Aeroméxico flight attendants)	1	0	1	No	3	63	D	0
US 9802 (child labor in tomato production)	0	1	1	No	5	NA	CC	0
US 9803 (St.-hubert McDonald's)	3	1	4	BN	1, 2	NA	W	0
US 9804 (Canadian rural mail carriers)	18	5	23	TN	1, 2, 7, 9, 10	61	D	0
US 9901 (TAESA flight attendants)	2	0	2	BN	1, 2, 6, 9	240	MC	0
US 2000-01 (Auto Trim / Custom Trim)	3	21	24	TN	9, 10	277	MC	0
US 2001-01 (Duro Bag Manufacturing Co)	2	0	2	No	1, 2	238	D	0
US 2003-01 (Puebla garment producers)	0	3	3	TN	1, 2, 6, 9	308	MC	0
US 2004-01 (Yucatán apparel producers)	0	2	2	BN	6, 9	NA	W	0
US 2005-01 (Federal Labor Law reform, 2002)	20	2	22	TN	1-3	369	D	0

(continued)

TABLE 4.1 (Continued)

| NAO case number | Type and number of submitters | | | Binational (BN) or trinational (TN) coalition | NAALC principle(s) cited | Case duration (in days) | Final case outcome | Observed policy impact |
	Unions	NGOs	Total					
US 2005-02 (Aviacsa pilots)	1	0	1	No	1, 2	406	D	0
US 2005-03 (Rubie's de Mexico)	1	2	3	BN	1–7, 9, 10	686	R	0
US 2006-01 (SNTMMSRM and Pasta de Conchos)	1	0	1	No	1, 6, 9	295	D	0
US 2011-02 (SME)	69	23	92	TN	1–3, 9	3150	R	0
US 2015-04 (Chedraui retail stores)	2	2	4	BN	1, 2, 6, 7, 9, 10	239	R	0
US 2018-01 (Federal Labor Law reform, 2018)	2	0	2	BN	1, 2, 9	152	D	0

Sources: Author's content analysis of public communications to, and public reports by, the Canadian, Mexican, and U.S. national administrative offices (NAOs); U.S. NAO 1999; Compa and Brooks 2019: 95–97, 106, 112–17, 120–22, 126–30, 133–36, 138, 140, 142–43; González Graf 2009: 149, 152–53; Finbow 2006: 116; Brower 2008: 174; Graubart 2008: 77; Aspinwall 2013: 103.

Notes: NAALC = North American Agreement on Labor Cooperation; NGOs = nongovernmental organizations; NA = Not available. See the list of acronyms for other acronyms and appendix B for a summary description of each public communication.

Type and number of submitters: This column reports the number of labor organizations (individual trade unions and labor federations or confederations) and labor-, human-, and migrant-rights NGOs filing public communications under the NAALC. The total number of labor unions endorsing a communication does not include individual union locals (or sections) listed in the submission documents if the corresponding national union did so. However, in those cases in which Canadian and U.S. national divisions of the same union endorsed a communication, both divisions were counted as separate submitters. See appendix 3 for the national distribution of the unions and NGOs enumerated here. In the absence of detailed information concerning two public communications to the Canadian NAO, the author drew on parallel submissions to the Mexican and U.S. NAOs: US 2005-02 / CAN 2005-1 and CAN 2008-1 / MEX 2006-1.

In several cases (MEX 2001-1, MEX 2005-1, MEX 2011-1, MEX 2016-2, US 2000-01), individual migrant workers or former employees were listed among the submitters. In MEX 9803 and MEX 2005-1, respectively, the Government of Mexico and an Idaho-based private law firm representing immigrant workers appeared as a copetitioners. A single former employee of the U.S. Department of Labor filed MEX 2015-1. In US 9804 and CAN 99-1, a private company (one in each case) appeared as a copetitioner. These submitters were excluded from the total number of unions and NGOs reported in the table.

NAALC principles cited: In cases in which there was a discrepancy between the NAALC principles identified in the submitters' public communication and in the final NAO report, the principles listed here are those appearing in the NAO report. In MEX 9804, US 9802, and US 2018-01, the author identified the NAALC principles based on information included in the public communication.

Case duration: "Case duration" is the time between the submission of a public communication and the NAO's formal decision regarding the case (or, in MEX 2016-1, the termination of NAALC jurisdiction on July 1, 2020). In cases in which the NAO produced more than one report (CAN 98-1, MEX 2001-1, US 9702), the author selected the date midway between the issuance of the reports as the termination date. In the cases (MEX 2003-1, MEX 2006-1, MEX 2011-1, MEX 2015-1) in which the available sources identify only the month in which the NAO final report was issued, the author employed the midmonth day (15) in the calculations.

Final case outcome: The NAO's final disposition of the case: D = declined for review; R = accepted for review; MC = ministerial consultations recommended; CC = case closed (inactive); W = submitters withdrew the case.

Coding scheme for observed policy impact:

0 = no observed changes;

1 = modest changes advancing labor rights at the workplace level (including, for example, legal recognition of a politically independent union)

2 = modification of government policies regarding individual worker rights and workplace practices (for example, occupational health and safety, employment discrimination, or immigration enforcement policies)

3 = modification of formal government policies affecting freedom of association and the right to collective bargaining

4 = effective implementation in practice of the rights to association and collective bargaining

In CAN 98-1, the policy impact is rated "0" because Canada was not party to the U.S.-Mexican ministerial agreement that addressed the parallel submission US 9703. In CAN 98-2, the policy impact is rated "0" because the Canadian NAO declined to review the submission, even though the parallel submission MEX 9804 achieved a positive policy effect. In US 940004, the public communication contributed to the negotiation of a favorable private settlement, after which the submitters withdrew the submission.

roster of all NAALC public communications, 1994–2020).[32] The forty-six public communications were filed by a total of 135 labor organizations (individual trade unions and labor federations and/or confederations) and 124 labor-, human-, and migrant-rights nongovernmental organizations (NGOs) based in the three NAALC countries.[33] Eleven of the public communications were filed by a single organization, but in fourteen cases, there were more than ten cosubmitters.[34] The largest transnational coalitions were those mobilized in parallel submissions CAN 2011-1 / US 2011-02 (with, respectively, eighty-six and ninety-two cosubmitters) protesting the Mexican government's assault on the democratic Mexican Electricians Union (Sindicato Mexicano de Electricistas, SME), and MEX 2006-1 / CAN 2008-1 (both with fifty-eight cosubmitters) concerning legal limitations on the collective bargaining rights of public employees in the state of North Carolina (table 4.1).[35]

The largest numbers of participants were in the United States and Mexico, with unions (a shorthand reference to all labor organizations) outnumbering NGOs in Canada and Mexico and NGOs predominating in the United States: Canada (17 unions, 10 NGOs; total = 27), Mexico (83 unions, 26 NGOs; total = 109), United States (35 unions, 88 NGOs; total = 123).[36] One important indication of the inclusiveness of NAO proceedings is that a significant proportion of these submitters only participated in a single NAALC filing: Canada, 9 of 27 (33.3 percent), Mexico, 24 of 109 (22.0 percent), United States, 61 of 123 (49.6 percent).

From the outset, sociopolitical actors in all three countries employed NAO processes to address alleged violations of a broad range of NAALC labor principles. Two or more principles were invoked in a substantial majority of the public communications: CAN NAO (six of seven, 85.7 percent); MEX NAO (twelve of fourteen, 85.7 percent), US NAO (twenty of twenty-five, 80 percent) (table 4.1). And, as table 4.2 shows, principles no. 1 (freedom of association and the right to organize) or no. 2 (the right to bargain collectively) were invoked in, respectively, 67.4 percent and 47.8 percent of all NAO submissions. Alleged violations of freedom of association and the right to organize (mainly in Mexico) featured in 80 percent of all US NAO submissions and in 71.4 percent of the CAN NAO cases, but principle no. 1 was also invoked in 42.9 percent of the MEX NAO submissions (generally focused on the rights of Mexican migrant workers in the United States). Similarly, cases involving principle no. 2 ranged from 28.6 percent of the MEX NAO submissions to 60 percent of the US NAO submissions. Perhaps not surprisingly, principles nos. 6 (minimum employment standards) and

TABLE 4.2 NAALC principles invoked in public communications to the Canadian, Mexican, and U.S. national administrative offices (NAOs), 1994–2020 (number of times invoked and as a percentage of all submissions to each NAO)

NAALC principle	Canadian NAO		Mexican NAO		US NAO		Overall total	
	Number	Percent	Number	Percent	Number	Percent	Number	Percent
No. 1	5	71.4	6	42.9	20	80.0	31	67.4
No. 2	3	42.9	4	28.6	15	60.0	22	47.8
No. 3	1	14.3	0	0	4	16.0	5	10.9
No. 4	0	0	2	14.3	1	4.0	3	6.5
No. 5	0	0	0	0	2	8.0	2	4.3
No. 6	3	42.9	9	64.3	7	28.0	19	41.3
No. 7	1	14.3	9	64.3	4	16.0	14	30.4
No. 8	1	14.3	3	21.4	0	0	4	8.7
No. 9	5	71.4	8	57.1	12	48.0	25	54.3
No. 10	1	14.3	8	57.1	4	16.0	13	28.3
No. 11	1	14.3	8	57.1	0	0	9	19.6

Source: Author's calculations based on information presented in table 4.2. The total public communications to each NAO were: Canada, 7; Mexico, 14; United States, 25 (total = 46).

Note: See table 4.1 for the full statement of NAALC principles. Vertical columns do not add to 100 because the public communications generally invoked more than one NAALC principle.

7 (employment discrimination) featured most prominently in submissions to the MEX NAO concerning the rights of Mexican migrant workers in the United States and Canada, with each of them featured in 64.3 percent of all MEX NAO cases (table 4.2).

As noted above, the NAALC restricted possible monetary or trade-linked sanctions to persistent violations of a signatory country's laws regarding child labor (principle no. 5), minimum wages (principle no. 6), and workplace health and safety (principle no. 9, occupational injuries and illnesses). Both principles nos. 6 and 9 featured prominently in NAO submissions, with no. 6 raised in 41.3 percent of all public communications (ranging from 28 percent of US NAO submissions to 64.3 percent in MEX NAO cases; table 4.2) and workplace health and safety matters addressed by 54.3 percent of all submissions (ranging from 48 percent in US NAO cases to 71.4 percent in CAN NAO cases).[37] However, only three submissions (CAN 99–1, US 9802, US 2004-01) were limited to principles nos. 5, 6, and/or 9 (table 4.1).[38]

The next two sections assess in detail the public communications filed with the three NAOs over the 1994–2020 period. With the exception of CAN 99-1(filed by the Labor Policy Association and the EFCO Corporation), the communications to the CAN NAO were parallel submissions that were generally filed first with the US NAO or the MEX NAO.[39] For this reason, the following discussion focuses principally on the U.S. and Mexican NAO cases, with attention to CAN NAO submissions where appropriate.[40] In addition to an overall examination of how the three NAOs handled the public communications they received and conducted their review processes, the analysis considers case duration, final outcomes of NAALC processes, and related matters.

U.S. AND CANADIAN PUBLIC COMMUNICATIONS ON LABOR RIGHTS ISSUES IN MEXICO

The US NAO received a total of twenty-five public communications between 1994 and 2020, twenty-three alleging labor rights violations in Mexico and two involving NAALC-related issues in Canada (table 4.1, appendix B).[41] It only reviewed thirteen of these submissions, all involving alleged labor rights violations in Mexico.[42] In eight of the reviews the U.S. NAO conducted (61.5 percent), it concluded the process by recommending ministerial consultations with Mexican labor authorities, and U.S. and Mexican authorities subsequently negotiated government-to-government agreements addressing the issues raised by the submissions.[43] The U.S. NAO declined to review seven of the public communications filed with it. In four other instances, the sociopolitical actors involved withdrew their submission. In US 9802 (one of only two NAALC public communications involving alleged violations of principle no. 5 concerning child labor), the party involved failed to follow up on the matter at issue. After a year, the U.S. NAO closed the file.[44]

How the U.S. NAO responded to the public communications it received varied depending on the legal and substantive matters at issue, but NAO officials were also attuned to the political dimensions of each case.[45] In US 2011-02, the Mexican Electricians Union (SME), joined by sixty-one other North American unions (Mexican, thirty-two; U.S., nineteen; Canadian, ten), twenty-three NGOs (U.S., fourteen; Mexican, six; Canadian, three), and seven international labor organizations, filed a complaint condemning the Mexican government's abrupt decision to close the state-subsidized and heavily indebted Central Light and Power Company (Luz y Fuerza del Centro) on October 11, 2009. The government's action led to the immediate dismissal of some 44,000 unionized workers and the de facto dismemberment of one of Mexico's oldest democratic unions.[46] The SME, seeking to gain a degree of international leverage in its settlement negotiations with the government of Mexico, reportedly requested that U.S. NAO officials postpone their final report on the submission.[47] Quite fortuitously, this request allowed the U.S. NAO to avoid overt controversy with the Mexican government over a politically charged conflict in which it had few prospects of meaningfully influencing the outcome.[48] However, by the time a final report was issued—a full 8.6 years after the case was filed (table 4.1) and the day before the NAALC's jurisdiction expired on July 1, 2020—developments in Mexico had made moot some of the SME's initial claims. This allowed U.S. NAO officials to conclude that the Mexican government's controversial actions in the conflict had not violated any of its NAALC obligations[49]—no doubt an outcome the original submitters would not have desired.

The number of sociopolitical actors engaged in public communications to the U.S. and Canadian NAOs ranged greatly, from one to ninety-two (table 4.1). There were nine cases in which a single labor union acted by itself, and in another nine communications, the submitters were all NGOs. In ten instances, more than twenty unions and NGOs formed a trinational coalition to pursue a particular case, and as noted above, parallel submissions regarding the SME (CAN 2011-1 and US 2011-02) mobilized larger coalitions than any other NAALC public communication over the 1994–2020 period. The public communications these sociopolitical actors filed with the U.S. NAO invoked nine of the eleven NAALC principles (tables 4.1, 4.2). However, in both US NAO and CAN NAO public communications, principles nos. 1, 2, 6, and 9 were particularly prominent. In fact, as previously reported, principle no. 1 was at issue in fully 80 percent of US NAO and 71.4 percent of CAN NAO submissions (table 4.2).

The NAALC's provisions provided the U.S. and Canadian national administrative offices with broad justification to undertake detailed examinations of Mexican government labor law, policy, and enforcement.[50] However, especially in the early US NAO public communications, the individual private employers involved, the U.S. Council on International Business, the U.S. National Association of Manufacturers, and even Mexican NAO officials sometimes identified grounds on which to argue that the U.S. NAO exceeded its jurisdiction and the scope of the NAALC in accepting the submissions for review.[51] Nonetheless, in the thirteen public communications reviewed by the U.S. NAO and in the two submissions on which the Canadian NAO published final reports, the offices conducted in-depth examinations of both the submitters' allegations and relevant Mexican labor law and policy. Although the NAOs could not compel testimony or subpoena evidence, officials from both the United States and Canada frequently posed follow-up questions to or met with the submitters and other interested parties (including, for example, representatives of the firms where the alleged rights violations occurred and/or their international business partners, incumbent Mexican union officials, and federal and state labor and/or occupational safety and health authorities) in order to clarify their understanding of the facts of the cases they reviewed. In addition, they regularly consulted with the Mexican NAO and sometimes with other Ministry of Labor and Social Welfare (Secretaría del Trabajo y Previsión Social, STPS) officials regarding the content and correct interpretation of Mexican labor law.[52] In some instances, the U.S. NAO commissioned independent analyses of key issues under consideration,[53] and U.S. and Canadian officials often consulted with Mexican labor attorneys with relevant expertise on specific legal questions.[54]

These investigations were often highly detailed. For example, in US 9901 (a communication alleging that Mexico's privately-owned Executive Air Transport, Inc., had systematically violated occupational safety and health and minimum employment standards for flight attendants), U.S. NAO personnel closely examined company records of overtime pay, payroll contributions to the Mexican Social Security Institute (Instituto Mexican del Seguro Social) and the National Worker Housing Institute (Instituto del Fondo Nacional de la Vivienda de los Trabajadores), and reports of on-board safety problems.[55] In US 2000-01 (a complaint charging that Mexican federal government agencies had repeatedly failed to enforce occupational safety and health laws or provide adequate compensation for workplace injuries and illnesses at two auto-parts plants owned by Florida-based Breed Technologies, Inc., in the Mexican state of Tamaulipas), the U.S. NAO-led delegation that conducted a site visit in January 2001 included industrial hygienists from the U.S. Occupational Safety and Health Administration and the National Institute for Occupational Health and Safety.[56] Similarly, in CAN 98-1 (a submission that, along with allegations of violations of freedom of association, charged that workers at Itapsa, S.A. de C.V., a brake-system

manufacturing plant in the state of México owned by Connecticut-based Echlin, Inc., were exposed to asbestos and other toxic substances without adequate
personal protective equipment), an industrial hygiene engineer from Human
Resources Development Canada (Labour Branch) joined the Canadian NAO site
visit to the plant.[57]

The procedural guidelines under which the U.S. NAO operated before
December 21, 2006, required it to hold public hearings as part of its review, and over
the 1994–2004 period, it held ten such hearings in California (San Diego), Texas
(one in Brownsville, two in San Antonio), and Washington, DC (six hearings).[58]
The hearings (with, after the first hearing, simultaneous English-Spanish translation available) offered the submitters, the witnesses they called in support of
their allegations (sometimes including Mexican workers who, for instance, had
been fired because of their organizing activities or personally affected by occupational safety and health violations),[59] and other interested parties a public forum
in which to detail their allegations. Employer representatives sometimes filed
written responses to claims made in their communications,[60] but they generally
did not appear in person at the public hearings.[61] In US 2005-03 (a case involving
a challenger union's failed efforts to win legal registration at Rubie's de México,
a Hidalgo-based textile firm producing costumes, masks, and pet outfits for U.S.
companies such as Mattel, Inc.), the US NAO substituted a site visit in Mexico
for a public hearing in the United States. During the March 6–15, 2006, visit
to Mexico City and Hidalgo, U.S. NAO personnel met with MEX NAO and
other STPS officials, the president of the Local Conciliation and Arbitration
Board that had ruled against the challenger union's registration petition, plant
managers and attorneys representing Rubie's, workers affiliated with both the
incumbent and the alternative unions, and independent labor law experts with
knowledge of the case.[62]

The time required for the U.S. NAO to complete its assessment of public communications varied considerably, ranging from 61 days (US 9804) to 3,150 days
(US 2011-02, 8.6 years) and averaging 407 days (13.6 months, $N = 20$) (table 4.1).[63]
Some of the cases in which the U.S. NAO eventually decided not to conduct a
formal review actually took longer to resolve (see, for example, US 2005-01 and
US 2005-02) than the submissions it did review. In the thirteen communications
in which the U.S. NAO completed a formal review, case duration ranged from
228 days (US 9601, US 9703) to 3,150 days (US 2011-02) and averaged 504 days

(1.4 years, N = 13). In US 2005-03, the lengthy duration was caused in part by the Mexican NAO's long delay (454 days) in responding to US NAO enquiries concerning the case. As noted above, the extreme delay in terminating US 2011-02 was due in part to the SME's request that the U.S. NAO postpone its public report. Setting aside these two outlying cases, the mean duration of reviewed submissions was 247 days (8.2 months, N = 11). The operational guidelines in effect before December 21, 2006, allowed the U.S. NAO a maximum of 240 days (including a possible sixty-day extension) in which to resolve a case. In eleven of the fifteen submissions (73.3 percent) it concluded between October 1994 (US 940001/940002) and July 2006 (US 2005-02), it met, or very nearly met, that deadline. Even under the new guidelines, it resolved US 2015-04 in 239 days.

The public reports issued by both the U.S. and Canadian NAOs at the end of their reviews provided objective, balanced assessments of the matters before them. In format, each report began with an overview of relevant NAALC provisions, the NAO's jurisdiction, and the terms under which it conducted the review; summarized the principal issues raised in the public communication and relevant sections of Mexico's domestic law and, where appropriate, international treaty obligations;[64] reported on what steps the NAO had taken to investigate allegations of labor rights violations and Mexican government responses as well as its findings; and concluded by recommending whether or not national labor authorities should seek ministerial consultations with their Mexican counterparts.

Even in cases in which U.S. and Canadian NAO officials did not recommend ministerial consultations, they sometimes signaled that they found the submitters' claims credible.[65] In other public communications, however, they concluded that the complainants had not adequately pursued redress through existing institutional channels, a point of particular importance given the NAALC's focus on the effective enforcement of national law.[66] For instance, in US 940003 (a complaint that the incumbent union, plant managers, and the state-level conciliation and arbitration board had conspired to block formation of an alternative, independent union at the Sony Corporation manufacturing facility in Nuevo Laredo, Tamaulipas), the U.S. NAO found that workers at the plant had not requested that labor authorities be present to witness the contested union representation election, nor had they filed any complaint thereafter with Mexican labor officials.[67] Similarly, in CAN 98-1 (Echlin/Itapsa), a submission that otherwise offered a persuasive example of the inherent conflict of interest embedded in a conciliation and arbitration board's tripartite structure (see below) and its bias in favor of the government-allied Confederation of Mexican Workers (Confederación de Trabajadores de México, CTM), the Canadian NAO noted that the independent union that lost a recount election to determine which of two rival unions would have legal control over the collective bargaining agreement had not requested that Federal Conciliation and Arbitration Board (Junta Federal de Conciliación y Arbitraje, JFCA) authorities employ a secret ballot.[68] In US 2005-03 (Rubie's de México), the U.S. NAO investigation forced the complainants to admit that they had pursued their case before a JFCA special board that clearly lacked jurisdiction in the matter only after the jurisdictionally appropriate state-level conciliation and arbitration board had repeatedly denied their union registration petition—information that had presumably been purposefully omitted in their NAALC public communication.[69] Moreover, in this case, U.S. NAO authorities concluded that the challenger union "appears to have attempted to circumvent established legal procedures in Mexico" and that its "legal strategy appears to have contributed in part to the confusion and delays in processing their petitions."[70]

Indeed, in several cases, U.S. and Canadian NAO authorities found that, contrary to what the submitters had alleged, the Mexican government had not failed to enforce adequately existing national labor law. In CAN 98-1 (Echlin/Itapsa), for example, Canadian NAO officials concluded that "[occupational safety and health] inspections were carried out routinely at the plant. Correctives [sic] measures were ordered and follow-up inspections for compliance were conducted."[71] In US 2005-03 (Rubie's de México), the U.S. NAO found no conclusive evidence that "the Government of Mexico failed to enforce its child labor laws in connection with alleged illegal hiring of minors."[72] In these situations, however, U.S. and Canadian officials usually sought to identify some points in the submitters' original claims that they could endorse. For instance, the Canadian NAO's public report on occupational safety and health issues at Echlin/Itapsa noted that hazardous materials should have been labeled in Spanish and that some workers who were exposed to these materials did not have adequate personal protective equipment. Similarly, in US 2005-03, even though U.S. NAO officials criticized the submitters' initial legal strategy, they also found fault with the state-level conciliation and arbitration board's reliance on technical legal errors as grounds on which to deny the challenger union legal registration.[73]

Principal Issues in U.S. and Canadian Public Communications Regarding Mexico

The main thrust of both U.S. and Canadian public communications and final NAO public reports regarding Mexico was a sustained critique of the substantial obstacles that workers faced in attempting to exercise their rights to unionize and bargain collectively (NAALC principles nos. 1 and 2) and the absence, in practice, of an impartial, independent labor justice system (NAALC Article 5[4]).[74] Both Mexico's 1917 Constitution (articles 9 and 123[XVI]) and the 1970 Federal Labor Law (articles 354–58) guaranteed freedom of association and the right to organize. Moreover, Mexico had ratified ILO convention no. 87 (in April 1950) on the freedom of association and the right to organize (but not convention no. 98 on the rights to organize and bargain collectively). Nevertheless, so-called employer protection contracts (*contratos de protección patronal*) and constraints on workers' capacity to freely choose their union representatives constituted major barriers to their effective exercise of these rights.

By the 1990s, it had become common practice in Mexico for an employer to sign a collective bargaining agreement with a compliant government-aligned union or a spurious union leader even before a workforce was hired. These agreements nominally met the minimum terms of federal labor law, but once in effect, they gave an employer virtually untrammeled control over workplace affairs. A protection contract also safeguarded an employer against the risk of an indefinite strike declared by a rival union seeking to win legal control over the contract.[75] Because the export-led development model that Mexico adopted after the mid-1980s relied on low labor costs as a basis of international comparative advantage, many employers regarded control over unionization and workplace relations as vital to their economic success. Agreements of this kind became ubiquitous in some of the country's most important economic activities, including the auto-parts industry, commercial aviation, banks, and especially maquiladora (in-bond processing) plants.[76]

Rank-and-file workers or a rival labor organization that contested an incumbent union's control over a protection contract and sought to revise its terms faced major legal hurdles. They were first required to petition the tripartite (comprised of labor, government, and business representatives) conciliation and arbitration board (*junta de conciliación y arbitraje*) that had originally registered the contract for approval to hold a recount election (*recuento sindical*) to determine which union would have legal title to the agreement.[77] However, juntas generally shunted aside threats to an incumbent union's workplace control by, for instance, identifying legal technicalities on which to rule against challengers.[78] If a junta did grant the challengers the right to a recount election, they faced a second potential barrier: The terms under which the election was conducted were generally set by existing union statutes, which normally required workers to cast voice votes openly—often with incumbent union officials and/or employer representatives present—rather than by secret ballot.[79] Before a 2012 reform of the Federal Labor Law eliminated so-called separation exclusion clauses (*cláusulas de exclusion de separación*) in collective contracts, an employer was obligated to dismiss any worker who lost her or his union membership if the existing collective bargaining agreement so stipulated.[80] Dissenting workers who challenged incumbent union leaders therefore faced very real risks of being expelled from the union and, as a consequence, losing their jobs.[81]

As many as twelve of the thirty-two (37.5 percent) U.S. and Canadian public communications concerning Mexico that were filed between 1994 and 2020 addressed the issue of protection contracts.[82] Both the submissions and the NAO public reports on these cases noted that workers often did not have access to the collective bargaining agreements that defined their working conditions and that Mexican labor law did not require union leaders to share the agreements or their contents with their members.[83] The fact that local affiliates of Mexico's two largest labor confederations, the CTM and the Revolutionary Confederation of Workers and Peasants (Confederación Revolucionaria de Obreros y Campesinos, CROC), were the incumbent unions involved in these cases highlighted the likely ubiquity of protection contracts and the obstacles that many government-aligned unions posed to the effective exercise of workers' rights. Moreover, the problems existed in both local (state-level)- and federal-jurisdiction economic activities.[84] As the number of NAALC communications focusing on protection contracts mounted, the U.S. and Canadian NAOs repeatedly advocated the creation of a public registry of unions and contracts to address the problem.[85] The U.S. NAO could have declined to review US 2015-04 (a case involving protection contracts and alleged violations of minimum employment standards by Grupo Comercial Chedraui, Mexico's third-largest retail chain) on the grounds that the submission did not raise any significant new issues concerning labor law and policy in Mexico.[86] However, the U.S. NAO accepted it for review with the explicit intention of highlighting the issue of protection contracts and necessary labor reforms during contentious U.S.-Mexican negotiations in 2015 over Mexico's accession to the Trans-Pacific Partnership agreement.[87]

As noted above, not only did dissident workers and external union organizers who contested protection contracts and sought to form alternative, politically independent unions face strong, sometimes violent opposition from employers and incumbent unions,[88] but they also often confronted major obstacles in resolving their complaints through the established labor justice system. The impartiality of conciliation and arbitration boards—especially whether their actions complied with the NAALC requirement that "tribunals . . . are impartial and independent and do not have any substantial interest in the outcome" (article 5[4])—in cases involving freedom of association and the right to collective bargaining was a central issue in numerous public communications filed with the U.S. and Canadian NAOs.[89]

One of the submitters' main arguments in these cases was that the tripartite composition of conciliation and arbitration boards meant that a challenge to an incumbent union's workplace authority was inevitably judged by a panel in which two of the three members might have a direct stake in the outcome. First, the elected labor representative was consistently a member of a union that was also affiliated with the CTM, CROC, or the Mexican Regional Labor Confederation (Confederación Regional Obrera Mexicana, CROM).[90] Second, the appointed government representative's priority was generally to maintain stability in workplace relations. Moreover, government representatives on the boards, especially in local-jurisdiction economic activities like those in which maquiladora plants were most prominent, were sometimes closely aligned with business interests. Over the 1994-2020 period, at least fifteen US and CAN NAO public communications (46.9 percent, $N = 32$) specifically addressed this structural conflict of interest and/or questioned the impartiality of state-level and federal conciliation and arbitration boards.[91]

The boards were specifically charged with conducting the recount elections, whose purpose was to resolve rival labor organizations' conflicting claims to legal control over workplace representation. Under established junta procedures, however, secret ballots could be employed only if both parties agreed to do so.[92] As noted above, dissident workers who voted for an alternative union by voice or raised hand in an open meeting, often with representatives of the incumbent union and/or the employer present, revealed their identity publicly and thereby incurred the risk of being dismissed as a union member and then fired.

For example, in public communication US 9703 (Echlin/Itapsa), the submitters alleged that the JFCA special board had, at the incumbent CTM union's request, postponed a scheduled recount election on short notice and failed to notify the challenger union, the Union of Workers in the Metal, Iron, Steel, and Related and Similar Industries (Sindicato de Trabajadores en la Industria Metálica, Acero, Hierro, Conexos y Similares, STIMAHCS).[93] As a consequence, when STIMAHCS supporters arrived to vote at the originally scheduled time, they found themselves the only Itapsa workers present—making it easy for incumbent union leaders to identify them as dissidents. When the recount election was eventually held, CTM loyalists threatened and intimidated STIMAHCS supporters, and one STIMAHCS representative was beaten by thugs hired by the incumbent CTM union. Nonetheless, the JFCA special board formally accepted election results that favored the CTM union.[94] In its public report on this case, the Canadian NAO argued that failure to conduct secret-ballot elections in neutral locations (that is, not in the workplace) seemingly contradicted Mexico's obligations under article 25(b) of the International Covenant on Civil and Political Rights, which stipulated that public elections be conducted by secret ballot.[95]

More broadly, a number of the public communications that U.S. and Canadian unions, labor- and human-rights NGOs, and their Mexican allies filed with the U.S. and Canadian NAOs challenged Mexican law and policy regarding the procedures employed to legally register trade unions and the number of unions officially recognized in a single company or workplace. Union registration procedures in Mexico were, in principle, straightforward in administrative terms, but in practice, both federal and state-level labor authorities regularly obstructed the formation of politically independent unions and favored government-aligned labor organizations.[96] Moreover, although the Federal Labor Law in effect at the time formally acknowledged the possibility that there might be more than one labor organization in a particular company or workplace (article 388), it was long-standing Mexican government policy to grant legal representational rights to only one union in a given private-sector enterprise or workplace.[97] In the public sector, however, this limitation was embedded in law. Until the late 1990s, the Federal Law for Public Service Workers (Ley Federal de los Trabajadores al Servicio del Estado, LFTSE) barred more than one union in a federal government workplace. It also restricted federal government unions' affiliations to the Federation of Public Service Workers' Unions (Federación de Sindicatos de Trabajadores al Servicio del Estado, FSTSE).[98] Because of the political sensitivity of union activity in the public sector, independent labor organizations faced great obstacles in challenging the FSTSE's representational monopoly.

Only one of the US NAO public communications (US 940003) obliquely addressed the Mexican government policy precluding legal recognition of more than one labor organization in a given company or workplace.[99] However, US submission 9601 directly questioned legal restrictions on the unionization rights of federal government employees. In this communication, a binational coalition of labor- and human-rights NGOs—the U.S.-based International Labor Rights Education and Research Fund (ILRERF) and Human Rights Watch/Americas, and Mexico's National Association of Democratic Lawyers (Asociación Nacional de Abogados Democráticos, ANAD)—challenged legal restrictions on freedom of association and the right to organize in the case of the General Union of Workers at the Ministry of Fishing (Sindicato Único de Trabajadores de la Secretaría de Pesca, SUTSP). The SUTSP, which as the representative of some 2,300 Ministry of Fishing employees had been the largest politically independent union of federal government workers in Mexico, lost its workplace representational rights (although, following lengthy judicial proceedings, not its legal recognition at the time of the US NAO submission) when a new union was formed and registered to represent employees at a reorganized Ministry of the Environment, Natural Resources, and Fishing. The submitters argued that the Federal Conciliation and Arbitration Tribunal (Tribunal Federal de Conciliación y Arbitraje, TFCA) could not serve as an impartial arbiter in the matter because the federal government and the FSTSE together selected six of its ten members.

Following its review, the U.S. NAO generally endorsed the submitters' claims and proposed ministerial consultations on the status of Mexico's international treaty obligations and constitutional provisions regarding freedom of association.[100] The three NAALC labor ministers agreed to exchange information on these questions, and they jointly sponsored a public seminar on the issues in Baltimore, Maryland, in December 1997. However, the Mexican government undertook no reforms of the LFTSE in response.[101] In 1999, the Mexican Supreme Court (Suprema Corte de Justicia de la Nación, SCJN) ruled that those provisions of the LFTSE that barred more than one union in a federal government workplace and limited public-sector unions' affiliation options to the FSTSE were unconstitutional because they violated the obligations Mexico had assumed when it ratified ILO convention no. 87. The government subsequently ceased enforcing the problematic provisions of the LFTSE, but it delayed reform of the law itself through at least 2016.[102]

The U.S. NAO may have accepted US 9601 for review in July 1996 because it perceived an opportunity to address freedom of association and labor tribunal impartiality issues in Mexico in a case on which other significant actors had already taken clear positions. For instance, the ILO Committee of Experts on the Application of Conventions and Recommendations had, between 1981 and 1995, repeatedly criticized provisions of the LFTSE that violated convention no. 87. Perhaps even more significant, the labor- and human-rights NGOs that initiated the public communication noted in their filing that the Mexican Supreme Court had, in May 1996, ruled unconstitutional a law in the state of Jalisco that, like the LFTSE, barred more than one union in any given government entity.[103] By bringing the matter before the three NAALC labor ministers, the U.S. NAO was, in effect, joining efforts to change Mexican law and policy at a time when the established practice of dominant Mexican labor organizations (including the FSTSE) of automatically affiliating their members to the long-ruling Institutional Revolutionary Party (Partido Revolucionario Institucional, PRI) was under attack.[104]

The Limits of Success: Case Studies of US NAO Submissions 9701 (Pre-Employment Pregnancy Testing) and 9702 (Han Young)

Two US NAO submissions—a 1997 case regarding gender discrimination in the Mexican maquiladora industry and a 1998 case involving freedom of association and occupational safety and health at the Han Young auto-parts plant in Tijuana, Baja California—reveal both the strengths and limitations of the NAALC public communications process.[105] The gender-discrimination filing was the first to address a NAALC principle other than freedom of association and the right to collective bargaining, and it contributed to significant change in Mexican public policy regarding workplace gender discrimination. It was, moreover, among the US NAO cases submitted by labor rights NGOs without the formal involvement of major trade unions. The Han Young case was among the most controversial of the many US NAO submissions highlighting freedom of association issues in Mexico. It was also the first NAO filing to address occupational safety and health issues, one of the three NAALC principles violations of which might lead to monetary penalties or trade-linked sanctions.

The Fight Against Gender Discrimination in the Maquiladora Industry

On May 16, 1997, a coalition of four U.S. and Mexican human- and labor-rights groups (the Women's Rights Project and Americas divisions of Human Rights Watch, the International Labor Rights Forum, and the National Association of Democratic Lawyers) filed a public communication with the U.S. NAO alleging discrimination against women workers in the maquiladora plants concentrated along the Mexico-U.S. border.[106] Although the gender composition of the maquiladora workforce changed over time as the proportion of male employees in these plants increased, employers in the sector traditionally recruited young female workers on the assumption that they constituted a more deferential, pliant labor force and were likely to demonstrate greater tolerance for and physical dexterity in low-wage assembly tasks.[107] However, hiring young women posed a potential cost risk because Mexican law guaranteed a twelve-week paid maternity leave and other postmaternity benefits. Many maquiladora employers had sought to avoid this risk by requiring that female job applicants take a pregnancy test as a condition of employment or by harassing and intimidating female employees who became pregnant in the hope that they could be forced to resign their position before they gave birth.

An investigative report published by Human Rights Watch, a New York-based NGO, extensively documented discriminatory acts of this kind.[108] The authors found evidence of widespread gender discrimination in employment practices at thirty-eight of the forty-three maquiladora firms studied in five northern cities (Tijuana, Baja California; Chihuahua, Chihuahua; and Matamoros, Reynosa, and Río Bravo, Tamaulipas). A number of these companies were subsidiaries of such major transnational firms, including American Telephone and Telegraph, General Motors, Johnson Controls, Matsushita, Sanyo, Sunbeam-Oster, Teledyne, TRW, W. R. Grace, and Zenith. Prospective female employees were required to take pregnancy tests or answer intrusive questions about their personal lives in order to determine whether they were or were likely to become pregnant, and pregnant applicants were routinely denied employment. Women who became pregnant after they were hired were often verbally abused, given difficult job assignments or less favorable work shifts, or otherwise harassed by supervisors in concerted efforts to provoke their resignation. As a consequence, female employees concealed their pregnancies and accepted unsafe work assignments (involving, for example, exposure to industrial chemicals or other hazardous materials) in order to avoid dismissal. Women workers felt unable to challenge these practices for fear of being blacklisted and denied future employment in the maquiladora sector.[109]

The public communication that the submitters filed with the U.S. and Mexican NGOs in May 1997 was based on this report.[110] As required by the NAALC, the complainants charged that the Mexican government had failed to enforce effectively its own laws (article 3[1]) prohibiting gender discrimination or to provide adequate access to administrative, quasi-judicial, or labor tribunals to enforce the law (article 4[1, 2]). The submitters also noted that NAALC principle no. 7 specifically barred employment discrimination on the basis of race, religion, age, sex, or other grounds. Moreover, they argued that gender discrimination in hiring and employment violated the ILO's convention no. 111 (Discrimination in Respect of Employment and Occupation), the United Nations International Covenant on Civil and Political Rights and the Convention on the Elimination of All Forms of Discrimination Against Women (CEDAW), and the American Convention on Human Rights, all of which had been ratified by Mexico.

The U.S. NAO agreed on July 14, 1997, to investigate the case (designated US 9701), and on November 19, 1997, it held a public hearing in Brownsville, Texas, on the issues in dispute. Witnesses at the hearing included both experts on Mexican labor law and employer practices and five women workers employed in maquiladora plants. Two elements made this a notable case: It was the first submission the U.S. NAO had considered that did not allege violations of freedom of association and/or the right to collective bargaining, and it was one of six US NAO public communications filed by human- and labor-rights NGOs rather than by trade unions or union-NGO coalitions (table 4.1).

In its responses to the U.S. NAO, Mexico's NAO denied that pregnancy testing in the maquiladora industry was as widespread as Human Rights Watch alleged. The main point of controversy, however, concerned the legality of pre-employment pregnancy testing. Mexican officials argued that national labor law did not expressly prohibit screening of this kind and that it was impossible for anyone to pursue a claim of gender discrimination prior to the existence of a formal employment relationship.[111] Nor, under these circumstances, could institutions such as conciliation and arbitration boards be faulted for failing to enforce the law adequately. The U.S. NAO had, therefore, exceeded the scope of its mandate under the terms of the NAALC.

The U.S. NAO issued findings and recommendations on January 12, 1998, that broadly endorsed the complainants' charges. It reaffirmed that posthire discrimination against pregnant women was clearly illegal under Mexican law while acknowledging differing views among Mexican officials (and some ambiguity in ILO convention no. 111 and the CEDAW) concerning the legal status of pre-employment pregnancy screening. Nevertheless, the U.S. NAO argued that under the terms of the NAALC, the matter was an appropriate subject of ministerial consultations between the United States and Mexico. It based this conclusion in part on evidence it received that senior Mexican labor officials had themselves sought the voluntary cooperation of maquiladora employers to end a practice that they considered inappropriate, even if technically legal.[112] The U.S. NAO found particularly telling an analysis of women's issues prepared in 1996 by the Ministry of the Interior (Secretaría de Gobernación), which concluded, "Women workers are frequently subjected to discriminatory practices in obtaining employment and in dismissal from employment for reason of pregnancy or because they are nursing."[113]

Javier Bonilla García, Mexico's secretary of labor and social welfare, initially declined his U.S. counterpart's request to consult on the matter, saying that female workers were already amply protected under Mexican labor law. However, under presidential instructions, he eventually agreed to do so.[114] On October 21, 1998, the two labor ministries signed an implementation agreement that provided for a series of cooperative outreach activities designed to counter gender discrimination in the workplace and raise public awareness of the problem.[115] These actions did not, however, address the issue of pre-employment discrimination because the Mexican government insisted that this would, in effect, constitute an expansion of labor rights and exceed the NAALC's mandate to focus on the enforcement of existing national laws. The Mexican government also blocked publication of a North American Commission on Labor Cooperation investigative report on pregnancy testing and employment.[116]

Nevertheless, by significantly increasing public awareness of the issue, the NAO proceedings did contribute to policy change in Mexico.[117] The Human Rights Watch initiative sparked a national campaign in Mexico focused on pre-employment pregnancy screening and the reproductive rights of working women.[118] At a trinational conference convened in March 1999 in Mérida, Yucatán, to examine pregnancy-based discrimination in the workplace and gender discrimination in the three NAFTA countries, Mexican labor officials publicly acknowledged for the first time that employment discrimination on the basis of gender and pregnancy (both pre- and posthire) was illegal under

Mexican law.[119] They also announced the creation of a new women's bureau, the Equity and Gender Policy Unit, at the STPS. There was, at the time, no amendment of the Federal Labor Law specifically to ban pre-employment pregnancy screening, but in September 1999, Rosario Robles, the first female governor of the Federal District, amended the district's penal code to bar pregnancy-based discrimination.[120] Moreover, the Ministry of Public Education (Secretaría de Educación Pública) ended pregnancy tests as a condition of employment.[121] Between 1997 and 2000, there were at least six bills submitted to the federal legislature addressing pregnancy-related discrimination, and in 2003, Congress unanimously passed a broad antidiscrimination law that explicitly prohibited gender- or pregnancy-based discrimination in hiring.[122] The 2012 reform of the Federal Labor Law adopted this prohibition.[123]

The resonance of NAO proceedings concerning US 9701 may have been amplified by the fact that there was already an awareness of the issue in Mexican policymaking circles and an emerging commitment to address the problem of pregnancy-based discrimination. Although changes in employer practices were slow and uneven, the subsidiaries of some major U.S. corporations (including General Motors, ITT Industries, Motorola, and Zenith) did alter their employment policies as a result of the negative publicity generated by the Human Rights Watch report and the US NAO case.[124] The administration of President Vicente Fox Quesada (2000–2006) strongly condemned pregnancy testing, and his administration took several steps (including negotiating agreements with the National Council of the Maquiladora Industry and state governments) to eliminate the practice.[125] And beginning in 2015, the U.S. Department of Labor and the STPS collaborated on a US$1.389 million project to improve the tools available to Mexican labor inspectors to combat gender discrimination (including pregnancy discrimination) in the workplace and to increase workers' awareness of their rights.[126]

The Struggle for Freedom of Association at Han Young

No less than twenty of the twenty-five public communications filed with the US NAO between 1994 and 2020 alleged violations of Mexican workers' freedom of association. Indeed, before the submission on gender discrimination in May 1997 (US 9701), all of the US NAO filings had addressed this issue as U.S. unions and their Mexican allies employed NAALC procedures to challenge the foundation of Mexico's established state-labor relations regime. Many of these early actions focused particularly on unionization efforts in the maquiladora industry, a sector whose growth was fueled in significant part by U.S. manufacturing companies moving production (and jobs) to Mexico and in which politically independent trade unions were virtually nonexistent.[127] The Han Young case, therefore, formed part of a much broader, concerted effort by Mexican and U.S. labor organizations to promote independent unionism in the maquiladora industry. The US NAO submission was nonetheless notable both for the range of U.S. and Mexican trade unions and labor rights groups involved and for the exceptionally high level of political attention it received.

The conflict began in April 1997 when a group of workers at Han Young de México, a Korean-owned company in Tijuana, Baja California, employing approximately 120 people in the assembly of truck chassis for Hyundai Precision America (a subsidiary of Hyundai Corporation), sought to organize an independent union.[128] They acted out of mounting discontent with their existing union, an affiliate of the Revolutionary Confederation of Workers and Peasants (CROC, one of Mexico's major government-aligned labor confederations) that had failed to secure improved wages and working conditions or to address very serious workplace safety and health problems. Although workers at the plant were regularly exposed to airborne toxic contaminants as a result of welding and other manufacturing processes, there was insufficient exhaust ventilation, exposure monitoring, occupational safety and health training, or other hazard-control measures. Nor did the company provide workers with adequate personal protective equipment, such as safety shoes and glasses, respirators, face shields, and chemical-resistant gloves.

On June 2, 1997, the dissident Han Young employees conducted a one-day work stoppage in support of their demands, but they suspended the action the next day when company managers evidenced some willingness to address their concerns. Two weeks later, federal labor inspectors responded positively to a petition from the workers and conducted a health-and-safety inspection of the plant, after which they notified the company that it would have to rectify twenty-three deficiencies (including inadequate ventilation, electrical hazards, unsafe materials handling, and lack of personal protective equipment for workers) within twenty-five working days at most.[129] However, worker-employer relations worsened in mid-July when the company's new director of human resources began a systematic campaign of harassment against the protest organizers. In early

August, some workers (including the three union representatives on the newly created employer-worker safety and health committee) were fired, and the company offered them severance payments in an unsuccessful effort to dissuade them from filing reinstatement claims with the state-level Local Conciliation and Arbitration Board (Junta Local de Conciliación y Arbitraje, JLCA).

At about this time, the Han Young employees suspended their independent unionization efforts and agreed to affiliate themselves with the Authentic Labor Front's (FAT) Union of Workers in the Metal, Iron, Steel, and Related and Similar Industries (STIMAHCS). On August 6, the STIMAHCS formally petitioned the JLCA to replace the CROC's José María Larroque Union of Workers in Various Occupations (Unión de Trabajadores de Oficios Varios "José María Larroque") as the legally recognized collective bargaining representative at Han Young. Company managers responded by bringing in some twenty new employees in an attempt to dilute workforce support for the STIMAHCS, and CTM representatives visited the plant in an effort to win workers' support and prevent the STIMAHCS from consolidating its position. Nevertheless, the JLCA proceeded to schedule a recount election on October 6 to determine which union—the CROC affiliate or the STIMAHCS—enjoyed majority worker support.[130]

Despite serious irregularities in the representation election, the STIMAHCS won the contest by a vote count of 54–34. However, company managers continued to fire supporters of the independent union and hire nonunion replacement workers. Then, on November 10, the three-member JLCA—reportedly comprised of a Baja California state labor official, an affiliate of the CROC, and an employer representative with ties to Han Young[131]—declared that the STIMAHCS was ineligible to represent Han Young workers on the grounds that it was registered as a national union in the metallurgical sector rather than in the automotive sector. It annulled the results of the recount election and ruled that the CROC retained legal control over the collective bargaining agreement.

On October 30, as the conflict at Han Young escalated and gained increasing international notoriety, a coalition of four U.S. and Mexican labor rights groups filed a public communication with the U.S. NAO alleging systematic violations of Han Young workers' right to choose which union would represent them and the Mexican government's failure to ensure the fairness and impartiality of its labor tribunals. The complainants were: the San Diego, California-based Support Committee for Maquiladora Workers (SCMW), whose director had been involved from the outset in efforts to organize an independent union at

Han Young; the STIMAHCS; the International Labor Rights Education and Research Fund; and Mexico's National Association of Democratic Lawyers.[132] (The Berkeley, California-based Maquiladora Health and Safety Support Network formally joined the case in December 1997, and in February 1998, it filed a supplemental submission alleging serious occupational safety and health problems at the Han Young plant.) This action was endorsed by Worksafe! Southern California and three of the most powerful U.S. and Canadian labor unions: the United Automobile, Aerospace, and Agricultural Implement Workers of America (UAW), the United Steelworkers (USW), and the Canadian Auto Workers (CAW), all of which joined the case as cosubmitters.[133] The U.S. NAO formally accepted the public communication (designated US 9702) for review on November 17, 1997.

Even as the US NAO proceedings began, the Mexican federal government intervened in an effort to mediate the Han Young conflict. Federal and state labor officials together reached an agreement with workers and managers that included convening a new representation election in the understanding that Baja California officials would formally recognize the winner. The second election was held on December 16, now with a CTM-affiliated local union facing off against the STIMAHCS in a secret ballot vote. Company managers offered payoffs to workers willing to vote in favor of CTM representation, but the STIMAHCS again prevailed by a narrow margin.[134]

On January 12, 1998, the JLCA granted registration to the Han Young workers' independent "October 6" Union of Industrial and Commercial Workers (Sindicato de Trabajadores de la Industria y del Comercio "6 de octubre") and recognized it as the legal bargaining representative at the plant, making Han Young the only one of Baja California's 790 maquiladora plants represented by an independent union.[135] All but one of the workers who had been dismissed for union organizing activities accepted reinstatement. Nevertheless, in subsequent months, plant managers continued to harass and sometimes dismiss union activists, hired nonunion replacement workers in an attempt to undercut the new union, and conspired with the CROC and the CTM to convene yet a third union representation election that might return control over the company's collective contract to a more pliant labor organization.[136]

On February 18, 1998, the U.S. NAO held a public hearing on the case in San Diego, at which it heard testimony from the complainant organizations, twenty-seven Han Young workers, employer representatives, and expert witnesses called to testify about union organizing conditions in the maquiladora industry. Han Young's owner and managers summarily denied the allegations made against them. They claimed that they were not opposed to any union, whatever its organizational affiliation, so long as it clearly enjoyed majority worker support. Moreover, they denied that anyone had been fired for union organizing activities; employees who had been dismissed either had failed to perform their jobs satisfactorily or had violated company policies. Han Young managers also asserted that safety and health conditions were perfectly adequate, noting that the plant had been subject to frequent state inspections.[137]

The U.S. NAO issued two reports on the Han Young case, the first on freedom of association issues (April 28, 1998) and the second on occupational safety and health questions (August 11, 1998). The reports dismissed several of the complainants' allegations (concerning, for example, some employment practices at the Han Young plant), but on balance, the U.S. NAO found that their claims had merit. Although US NAO officials recognized that Hyundai Precision America had played a positive role by pressuring Han Young managers to correct serious workplace safety and health problems and by recognizing workers' legal right to organize their own union, they were not persuaded by the employer's testimony in the case.[138] They expressed serious doubts about the impartiality of the JLCA at different junctures, and they were also troubled by the JLCA's unexplained decisions in November 1997 to reverse itself on the question of STIMAHCS eligibility to represent Han Young workers and to annul the October 6 election. Moreover, the U.S. NAO's public report on occupational safety and health issues noted that, although plant inspections had been thorough and consistent with Mexican laws and regulations, it was unclear whether Han Young had ever paid the various fines levied against it for workplace safety and health violations.[139]

The U.S. NAO did, however, acknowledge that the JLCA's conduct in September and October 1997 was, on the whole, appropriate and reasonable, and it applauded both the Mexican federal government's efforts to resolve the Han Young conflict and ongoing federal programs designed to improve the functioning of conciliation and arbitration boards (including the consistency with which they applied juridical criteria). It also recognized that, although some safety and health problems still existed at the plant, the negative publicity generated by the case and pressures from federal labor authorities had led to significant improvements in workplace conditions at Han Young.[140] Yet despite these findings, the U.S. NAO went on to recommend binational ministerial consultations on Mexico's legal provisions for union representation elections, the conduct of tripartite conciliation and arbitration boards, and ways of improving the effectiveness and deterrent effect of workplace inspections.[141]

An extensive solidarity movement in the United States and Canada had mobilized behind the Han Young workers' demands. International observers organized by the SCMW had been present at the October 6 union representation election,[142] and, in November 1997, U.S. and Canadian supporters conducted a one-day fast in solidarity with four Han Young workers who had gone on hunger strike to pressure the Baja California conciliation and arbitration board to recognize the October 6 election victory.[143] Solidarity protests targeted Hyundai automobile dealerships in a number of U.S. cities in late 1997 and early 1998. From July through September 1998, trade unions and labor rights activists organized similar actions throughout the United States and Canada, culminating in a "Han Young Action Day" on September 19.[144]

The Han Young case attained such prominence in part because it coincided with an intense political battle in the United States over presidential authority to negotiate free-trade agreements, a debate that, in large part, replayed the controversy over "fast track" reauthorization that had occurred around initial NAFTA discussions in 1991.[145] As noted in chapter 3, the U.S. Trade Act of 1974 required periodic congressional renewal of the executive branch's authority to negotiate trade agreements on a so-called fast-track basis (meaning that Congress can approve or disapprove of proposed trade pacts but cannot amend or filibuster them). Many congressional Democrats opposed renewing presidential fast-track authority in 1997–1998 unless the legislation required U.S. trade negotiators to include strong environmental and labor rights safeguards in any future trade agreements. In their fight against the renewal bill, several members of Congress with close ties to the U.S. labor movement (including Representative Richard Gephardt [Missouri], the Democratic majority leader in the House of Representatives and an aspirant to the Democratic presidential nomination in 2000, and David Bonior [Michigan], the Democratic majority whip in the House) cited the Han Young case as an example of the NAALC's failure to protect workers' rights.[146] In an effort to assuage congressional criticism, both President William J. (Bill) Clinton (1993–1997, 1997–2001) and Vice President Albert Gore responded to strong concerns expressed by senior Democratic congressional leaders and as many as thirty other House members by discussing the Han Young case directly with Mexican President Ernesto Zedillo Ponce de

León (1994-2000) during Zedillo's official working visit to Washington, DC on November 13-14, 1997.[147]

The political pressures generated by the transnational Han Young solidarity movement no doubt had a significant impact on both the U.S. NAO's commitment to the case and the Mexican federal government's efforts to resolve the festering conflict.[148] However, despite the international support they received in their protracted struggle for a politically independent, representative union and improved wages and working conditions, Han Young workers found it impossible to defend their hard-won gains in the workplace. Other maquiladora employers and Baja California state government officials, fearing the precedent of an independent union and its possible impact on the local investment climate, urged Han Young's owner not to negotiate with the new union.[149] In March 1998, even before the U.S. NAO issued its first report on the case, the company changed its legal name to Traho Services, announced it would relocate its plant to another part of Tijuana, and began to lay off workers.[150]

In an effort to defend their movement and their jobs, on May 22, 1998, Han Young workers maneuvered to freeze company assets by declaring a strike before the factory closed. However, the night before their planned action, CTM enforcers occupied the plant in order to keep it open.[151] The JLCA later claimed that the CTM had won a new union representation election and declared the Han Young workers' strike action illegal on a technicality.[152] Federal court judges in the state issued three separate injunctions against the bogus representation election and ordered the JLCA to respect Han Young workers' right to strike.[153] Nevertheless, the Tijuana police blocked Han Young employees' attempts to regain control of their workplace, and their efforts to shut down the new manufacturing site in eastern Tijuana were unsuccessful. The struggle continued through at least July 2000, but it eventually failed.[154]

Although NAALC procedures and international solidarity actions could not protect a local independent union over the longer term, the Han Young case did contribute to modest nominal changes in Mexican government policies regarding freedom of association and the right to collective bargaining. The US NAO's call in April 1998 for ministerial consultations on the issues raised by US 9702 initially drew a sharp rebuttal from STPS officials, who said that the U.S. NAO was "supporting the demands of one side in this dispute, stirring up emotions and generating hopes that go beyond the terms of the North American Free Trade Agreement."[155] Nonetheless, STPS Secretary Bonilla did eventually acquiesce (perhaps as early as October 1998) to consultations with U.S. Secretary of Labor Alexis Herman.[156] A formal agreement outlining the Mexican government's response was, however, delayed until May 18, 2000. At that time, the U.S. Department of Labor and Mexico's Ministry of Labor and Social Welfare issued a joint statement on both the Han Young and the Echlin/Itapsa (US 9703) submissions.

In this four-page agreement, the two governments pledged, "In a spirit of cooperation and complete respect for the sovereignty of each country regarding labor law and practice on the principles of freedom of association and protection of the right to organize," to address the main issues raised in the two cases.[157] Specifically, they agreed to develop an action plan to be implemented over a fifteen-month period.[158] Under its terms, the STPS agreed to "continue promoting the registry of collective bargaining contracts in conformity with established labor law" and to make efforts "to promote that workers be provided information pertaining to collective bargaining agreements existing in their place of employment." Most important, in recognition that the right to organize "can only be assured when workers are able to freely choose their representatives," the STPS also committed itself to "promote the use of eligible voter lists and secret ballot elections in disputes over the right to hold the collective bargaining agreement." This was the first time that Mexican labor authorities publicly agreed that secret voting procedures would be employed in future recount elections to resolve conflicts over title to collective bargaining agreements. They also agreed to combat employer protection contracts by promoting access to information concerning collective contracts, thereby supplementing an STPS website displaying information regarding registered federal-jurisdiction unions.[159] On this basis, the observed policy impacts of US 9702 and US 9703/CAN 98-1 are coded 3 in table 4.1.

MEXICAN PUBLIC COMMUNICATIONS ON LABOR RIGHTS ISSUES IN THE UNITED STATES AND CANADA

The Mexican NAO received a total of fourteen public communications between 1994 and 2020, thirteen alleging labor rights violations in the United States and one concerning alleged violations in Canada (table 4.1, appendix B). The Service Employees International Union (SEIU) eventually withdrew MEX 2012-1 (regarding an Alabama law that discriminated against undocumented immigrant workers).[160] The Mexican NAO accepted the remaining thirteen submissions for review, and in nine of these cases (69.2 percent), at the end of the review process, it recommended formal consultations between the Mexican and U.S. secretaries of labor.[161] In eight of these nine cases (88.9 percent), the Mexican and U.S. secretaries of labor subsequently announced joint declarations and formulated work plans to address the issues raised by the submissions.[162]

The number and identity of the sociopolitical actors that filed public communications with the Mexican NAO varied greatly (table 4.1, appendix B). A single union or labor confederation filed MEX 9501 (Mexican Telephone Workers Union, STRM) and MEX 9803 (CTM), but national, binational, or trinational coalitions mobilized behind all the other submissions. The number of organizations participating in these coalitions ranged from two (MEX 2003-1, MEX 2012-1) to fifty-eight (MEX 2006-1) and averaged twelve across the thirteen submissions in which unions and/or NGOs were involved.[163] Overall, NGOs (eighty-three) slightly outnumbered labor organizations (seventy-five), and a number of these coalitions were tilted heavily toward either NGOs (MEX 9804, MEX 2001-1, MEX 2005-1, MEX 2011-1, MEX 2016-1) or unions (MEX 2006-1). The submitters included some of the organizations that repeatedly engaged in NAALC processes over a number of years, including the Support Committee for Maquiladora Workers, the binational Center for Migrant Rights (Centro de Derechos del Migrante), the ILRERF/International Labor Rights Forum, the National Association of Democratic Lawyers (ANAD), FAT, SEIU, the United Electrical, Radio, and Machine Workers of America (UE), and the Union of Needletrade, Industrial, and Textile Employees (UNITE!). Only on occasion did national-level labor organizations initiate (the CTM in MEX 9803) or join these coalitions as cosubmitters: Mexico's National Union of Workers (Unión Nacional de Trabajadores, UNT[164]) in MEX 9802, MEX 2005-1, and MEX 2006-1/CAN 2008-1; the Canadian Labour Congress (CLC) in MEX 2006-1/CAN 2008-1; and the AFL-CIO in MEX 2011-1.[165] In three instances, the petitioning coalitions were comprised of exclusively Mexican (MEX 9802) or U.S. (MEX 9804, MEX 2001-1) sociopolitical actors.[166]

All the MEX NAO submissions except MEX 2006-1 / CAN 2008-1 (North Carolina Public Employees) and MEX 2015-1 (U.S. Department of Labor) in some way addressed the labor rights of Mexican migrant workers. However, they varied considerably in scope, ranging from grievances concerning labor practices at a particular employer to de facto class action complaints regarding immigration law and law enforcement across broad sectors of the U.S. and Canadian economies.[167] In MEX 9801, for example, a four-member Mexican-U.S. binational coalition protested systematic attempts by Solec International, Inc. (a Japanese-owned, California-based manufacturer of solar panels) to block formation of a union that promised to protect the employees' workplace rights regarding such matters as occupational safety and health. Similarly, MEX 9803 was a complaint against DeCoster Egg Farm, a large Maine egg producer, for violations of migrant labor rights, minimum employment standards, discrimination in employment, and occupational safety and health violations. In contrast, a number of other public communications were much broader in scope. They involved workers employed by apple growers and packers in the state of Washington (MEX 9802); a challenge to U.S. government migration law enforcement practices that discouraged undocumented migrant workers from filing wage and hour complaints for fear that doing so would expose them to the risk of deportation (MEX 9804); a complaint that the U.S. federal government and the state of New York failed to effectively enforce laws governing compensation to workers who suffered occupational injuries (MEX 2001-1); the rights of H-2A visa migrant agricultural workers in the state of North Carolina (MEX 2003-1), H-2B visa nonagricultural workers in various U.S. states (MEX 2005-1), and H-2B visa workers employed in traveling carnivals and fairs (MEX 2011-1); an anti-immigrant law in the state of Alabama (MEX 2012-1); and gender discrimination against vulnerable Mexican female migrant workers in the United States (MEX 2016-1) and Canada (MEX 2016-2). Although the filings were generally framed in terms of violations of migrant workers' rights in particular companies or states, the submitters employed the public communications as vehicles through which to highlight broad inequities in U.S. and Canadian migration law and law enforcement in major industries or economic sectors that employed large numbers of Mexican migrant workers.[168] In at least two cases (MEX 9501 and MEX 9802), the sociopolitical actors involved submitted communications to the Mexican NAO concerning matters on which they had already filed complaints with the U.S. National Labor Relations Board (NLRB).[169]

Although the MEX NAO submissions were heavily focused on the labor rights of Mexican migrant workers, they did not always specifically invoke NAALC principle no. 11 (protection of migrant workers) (table 4.1). Freedom of association and the right to organize (principle no. 1) were central issues in MEX 9501

(Sprint Corporation) and 9801 (Solec International, Inc.). Public communications MEX 9802 (Washington State apple producers and packers), MEX 2003-1 (H-2A visa migrant workers in North Carolina), and MEX 2012-1 (anti-immigrant legislation in Alabama) did cite principle no. 11. Yet here, too, U.S. law and law enforcement practices that obstructed efforts by migrant workers to organize in defense of their workplace rights were among the principal issues.[170] In MEX 2016-1 and MEX 2016-2, the workers in question were temporary female migrants to, respectively, the United States and Canada. However, the submitters chose to frame these cases in terms of employment discrimination (principle no. 7) and equal pay for women and men (principle no. 8).

In the course of their reviews, Mexican NAO officials regularly engaged in detailed consultative communications with their U.S. counterparts about U.S. labor law and policy.[171] However, even though the Mexican NAO's administrative guidelines authorized them to organize "informative sessions" as part of their review process, they did not do so.[172] Indeed, the public record of MEX NAO public communications contains evidence of only three occasions on which Mexican officials met personally with complainants or sent written questions to them (MEX 9802, MEX 9804, MEX 2001-1).[173] In MEX 9802, STPS officials held a private hearing in Mexico City on December 2, 1998, to solicit direct testimony from workers (the majority of whom were either from Mexico or of Mexican descent) employed in apple orchards and packing sheds in the state of Washington.[174] In contrast, in their review of MEX 9501 (concerning the Sprint Corporation's attempt to block an organizing campaign by Latino workers at its San Francisco–based telemarketing facility by closing the facility just prior to a scheduled union representation election), Mexican NAO officials met with Sprint corporate attorneys in late March 1995 during a previously scheduled trip to Washington, DC, for a trilateral government-to-government meeting on freedom of association and the right to organize. There is, however, no evidence that they met with the workers or union leaders involved in the case, nor did they make any effort to secure additional testimony from the submitters.[175] None of the Mexican NAO's final reports include anything similar to the highly detailed investigative findings produced by the Canadian and U.S. NAOs.

Resource constraints could certainly have influenced the character of the Mexican NAO's reviews in this regard. However, another plausible explanation is that the Mexican government did not want to undertake any action that would even implicitly endorse the legitimacy of external monitoring of a country's domestic labor affairs. As noted at the beginning of this chapter, national sovereignty concerns clearly underpinned (and constrained) the NAALC. Each Mexican NAO public report underscored the centrality of state sovereignty by including, either in these same words or in very similar terms, language employed in the MEX 9802 report (p. 15):

> The Mexico NAO notes that the NAALC does not provide a basis for questioning the Parties' legal framework, and it reiterates its permanent respect for the Constitution and laws of each of the Parties, and in particular respect for their sovereignty.

By restricting to a bare minimum its engagement with NAALC public communications, the Mexican NAO's operational conduct both reflected and reinforced the Mexican government's traditional defense of national sovereignty.[176]

The Mexican government did, however, seek to employ NAO reviews to pursue its foreign policy priority of defending the rights of Mexican migrant workers in the United States and Canada. As noted above, except in two instances (MEX 2006-1, a complaint against the significant legal restrictions on the rights of North Carolina public employees, and MEX 2015-1, a case in which an anonymous former employee charged the U.S. Department of Labor with discrimination against minority employees in its hiring and promotion practices), all of the public communications submitted to the Mexican NAO addressed, in one form or another, the rights of Mexican migrant workers in the United States or Canada. The available evidence indicates that these submissions were almost all voluntary initiatives undertaken by sociopolitical actors that identified the Mexican NAO as the most logical NAALC forum in which to highlight the labor rights violations suffered by Mexican migrant workers.[177]

The Zedillo administration may have encouraged the initial NAO submissions on migrant worker rights both as a way of counterbalancing the early rush of US NAO public communications alleging widespread labor rights violations in Mexico and as a means of promoting a long-standing Mexican policy priority.[178] The most likely such case was MEX 9803 (DeCoster Egg Farm), in which the submitter was the government-allied Confederation of Mexican Workers (CTM), and the government of Mexico appeared as cosubmitter.[179] It is probable, however, that MEX 9803 case was an exception in this regard.[180] In MEX 9804 (a case submitted during the Zedillo administration that challenged U.S. government migration law enforcement practices) and MEX 2001-1 (New York State workers' compensation), all the submitters were U.S. labor- and migrant-rights NGOs without any known political connection to the Mexican government. Similarly, many of the public communications regarding migrant worker rights that were submitted to the Mexican NAO during the 2000s-2010s (for instance, MEX 2003-1, MEX 2005-1, MEX 2011-1, MEX 2012-1, MEX 2016-1, and MEX 2016-2) were filed by binational or trinational coalitions comprised of activist groups that the Mexican government would have found difficult to coordinate.[181]

The administrative guidelines under which the Mexican NAO operated set no maximum time for the completion of its reviews, and in practice, the duration of cases varied greatly—from 111 to 3,565 days (9.8 years). Some of these delays were extraordinary, given the generally formulaic character of the Mexican NAO's reviews, but not all of them were the result of its own administrative inefficiencies. In some submissions (MEX 2001-1, MEX 2005-1, MEX 2006-1, MEX 2015-1, MEX 2016-1), the delays in bringing the cases to conclusion were caused, in part, by the U.S. NAO's failure to respond, or extreme tardiness in responding, to standard MEX NAO cooperative consultation requests. No public information is available concerning MEX 2016-2. However, the mean duration time for the remaining cases was 1,222 days (3.3 years, $N = 12$). The duration period generally lengthened over time, although the pattern in this regard was not completely consistent (table 4.1).[182]

The Mexican NAO's final reports on the public communications it reviewed generally followed the same overall format adopted by the U.S. and Canadian NAOs: a summary of the complainant allegations, a statement of the NAALC articles and principles at issue, and a review of relevant national law and, in some instances, international treaty obligations (see, for example, MEX NAO public report 9803). The reports were, however, much more formulaic than those issued by its North American counterparts. In several instances (MEX 9501, MEX 9803, MEX 2011-1), the Mexican NAO's review of the communication consisted simply of a recitation of the various allegations made by submitters concerning violations of NAALC principles and the relevant provisions of applicable U.S. laws.

Consistent with its overall low-intensity engagement with NAALC procedures, the Mexican NAO's final reports rarely called for specific U.S. remedial actions or legal reforms.[183] Some reports were guardedly critical of U.S. enforcement of labor and immigration law (see, for example, MEX NAO public report

2006-1). Others cited reports by a U.S. federal or state government agency and/or independent groups that acknowledged the existence of labor law enforcement problems like those indicated in the petitioners' submission.[184] For the most part, however, they simply summarized extant U.S. law and requested that the U.S. government carefully consider the issues raised in the submission at hand. For instance, the Mexican NAO's recommendations regarding communication MEX 2011-1 (concerning H-2B visa migrant workers employed in traveling carnivals and fairs) included these summary statements:

> [The Mexican NAO] calls to the attention of the U.S. Department of Labor this review report so that it can, in conformity with its internal procedures, determine what course of action is appropriate in terms of its own legislation and internal practices to address the arguments posed by the petitioners regarding whether the rights of migratory workers with H-2A and H-2B visas have been violated. . . . Mexico's NAO abstains from making pronouncements with regard to the dispositions that according to the petitioners limit the rights of workers in the agricultural sector and of migrant workers. . . . Similarly, in accordance with NAALC article 2, Mexico's NAO makes no pronouncements on U.S. labor law now in effect, based on the right of the Parties to establish internally their own labor norms and, for that reason, to adopt or modify their labor laws and regulations.[185]

Similarly, in its final report on MEX 2015-1 (a case involving alleged employment discrimination in the U.S. Department of Labor), the Mexican NAO carefully observed:

> This review is not intended to establish supra-national mechanisms inasmuch as, pursuant to the NAALC, the role of the NAO is not to judge or modify the laws of the other Parties. In accordance with the NAALC, the purpose of the MEX NAO review report is to call attention to U.S. labor authorities to matters regarding an alleged failure to comply with labor laws, as described in Public Communication MEX 2015-1. . . . [The MEX NAO review report] is brought to the attention of the U.S. DOL [Department of Labor] so the latter can determine, in accordance with its rules and internal practices, how to address the petitioners' arguments concerning violation of Labor Principle No. 7 on elimination of employment discrimination, as well as the alleged

violation of U.S. domestic law concerning compliance with the Merit System Principles and regulations of the U.S. Federal Government on Prohibited Personnel Practices.[186]

Despite the Mexican NAO's cautious posture, many of the MEX NAO submissions did heighten political awareness of the labor rights challenges confronting Mexican migrant workers in the United States and Canada.[187] For instance, in parallel to MEX 9803 (DeCoster Egg Farm), MEX 2003-1 focused on the status of migrant agricultural workers in North Carolina, at the time, the U.S. state with the largest number of H-2A visa workers. The submitters underscored that these workers regularly faced employer discrimination or reprisals for their efforts to organize and bargain collectively, but they were excluded from the protections of the National Labor Relations Act and the U.S. Migrant and Seasonal Agricultural Worker Protection Act.[188] Moreover, funding from the U.S. Legal Services Corporation was not available to lawyers representing migrants, an issue that was also a central focus of MEX 2005-1. The complainants maintained that the United States was, therefore, in violation of eight of the eleven NAALC principles (table 4.1).[189]

In MEX 9802 (Washington State apple producers and packers), the submitting organizations may have been more focused on indicting aspects of U.S. labor law and practice than on achieving any specific policy change. They highlighted the serious obstacles that agricultural workers faced in attempting to exercise their right to organize, and they criticized the U.S. government for failing to ratify ILO convention no. 87 on the rights to organize and bargain collectively. Yet even though their submission did not detail any specific corrective actions, it did bolster local unionization efforts and elicit positive policy responses from both the state of Washington and the U.S. Department of Labor.[190] In two other cases, the complainants apparently sought to employ the public communication process to gain additional publicity for and leverage in their unionization campaigns. Solec International workers (MEX 9801) eventually succeeded in winning NLRB certification of their union, and in the wake of the conflict that was the focus of MEX 2003-1, the Farm Labor Organizing Committee successfully negotiated a collective bargaining agreement for more than eight thousand H-2A Mexican workers employed by the Mount Olive Pickle Company.[191] In terms of the observed policy impact of NAALC procedures, these three cases are coded 1 in table 4.1.

More broadly, several MEX NAO public communications contributed to policy changes that modestly benefited Mexican migrant workers.[192] In most instances, the U.S. Department of Labor (U.S. DOL) accepted a Mexican request for ministerial consultations,[193] and, as a result, on several occasions, the two governments negotiated memoranda of understanding addressing the issues raised in MEX NAO submissions. On May 18, 2000, they subscribed to a memorandum concerning MEX 9801, MEX 9802, and MEX 9803; on April 15, 2002, the U.S. DOL and the STPS issued a joint declaration committing the two governments to protecting workers' rights regardless of their migrant status; and in response to MEX 2003-1, MEX 2005-1, and MEX 2011-1, on April 3, 2014, the two ministries issued a joint declaration concerning H-2A and H-2B visa migrant workers.[194] These agreements called upon the U.S. government to hold public outreach sessions to educate migrant workers regarding their labor rights in such areas as occupational safety and health and gender and ethnic discrimination.[195] For example, in conformance with the May 2000 memorandum, the U.S. DOL held public outreach sessions of this kind with migrant workers and employers in Yakima, Washington, in 2001 and in Augusta, Maine, in 2002, as well as government-to-government meetings in Washington, DC and Mexico City.[196] Similarly, as part of the 2014 agreement, the U.S. and Mexican governments reaffirmed the 2004 Consular Partnership Program between the U.S. Department of Labor, the Mexican Ministry of Foreign Affairs, and Mexican consulates in the United States, under which U.S. authorities conducted outreach activities for Mexican migrant workers, and they agreed to expand the role that the consulates played in educating Mexican migrant workers regarding their labor rights and how to exercise them. The extensive program of outreach activities included training programs (developed in consultation with Mexican and U.S. immigrant rights groups) for H-2A and H-2B visa holders in agriculture, food packing, forestry, and traveling carnivals and fairs, as well as information and consultation sessions in fifteen U.S. and seven Mexican states from July 2014 through February 2015.[197] On this basis, seven Mexican NAO cases are coded 2 in terms of their observed policy impact (table 4.1).[198]

The clearest example of the U.S. government making a significant change in immigration law enforcement was in response to public communication MEX 9804.[199] On September 17, 1998, a U.S. national immigrant rights coalition comprised of the Yale Law School Workers' Rights Project, the International Labor Rights Forum, fifteen other U.S. human- and migrant-rights NGOs,[200] and two major U.S. unions (SEIU and UNITE!) submitted a complaint to the Mexican NAO against the U.S. DOL and the U.S. Immigration and Naturalization Service (INS). Their communication focused on a June 11, 1992, joint enforcement memorandum that required Department of Labor officials investigating a wage and working hours (overtime) complaint to inspect employer records (I-9 forms) concerning the immigration status of employees.[201] If, in the course of their inspection, they found evidence that employees lacked appropriate legal documentation, inspectors were required to report the matter to the INS. The submitting organizations argued that the memorandum violated the U.S. DOL's guarantee of the full payment of wages to all workers, regardless of citizenship or immigration status, and that the memorandum resulted in the systematic underenforcement of U.S. minimum wage and maximum working hours laws (and therefore violated NAALC principles nos. 6 and 11) because it subjected undocumented workers to the risk of deportation when they reported rights violations. The Mexican NAO formally accepted the submission for review on November 22, 1998, and in apparent response,[202] the U.S. government immediately reversed course. On November 23, the U.S. DOL and the U.S. Department of Justice signed a new memorandum of understanding stating that henceforth U.S. DOL officials would not review I-9 forms as part of workplace inspections undertaken in response to workers' complaints.[203]

The Clinton administration's commitment to the success of the NAALC may have made the U.S. government especially responsive to Mexico's use of NAALC procedures. For instance, the U.S. Department of Labor agreed to a government-to-government meeting in response to the MEX 9801 (Solec International) public communication even though the submission mainly originated in local union organizers' frustration that repeated appeals by Solec corporate attorneys had produced continued delays in the scheduling of a union representation election by the National Labor Relations Board.[204] Even more indicative in this regard, there was a positive observed policy impact in four of the five Mexican NAO public communications filed between 1994 and 1998 (table 4.1). The United States did not amend the law limiting the organizing rights of farmworkers employed under H-2A visas. However, the Clinton administration acted quickly to correct a federal administrative policy on workplace inspections and immigration law enforcement, and it was willing to undertake extensive public education and outreach initiatives and strengthen the role of Mexican diplomatic authorities in protecting the rights of Mexican migrant workers. As the next section shows, the U.S. government's commitment to the NAALC weakened under the successor administration of George W. Bush (2001–2005, 2005–2009). Nonetheless, Mexican NAO public communications concerning the rights of Mexican migrant workers in the United States continued to yield positive policy impacts (see table 4.1) in a political context in which the Bush administration gave high priority to migration issues in bilateral relations with Mexico.[205]

ASSESSING THE IMPACT OF NAALC PUBLIC COMMUNICATIONS

The stated purpose of the NAALC was to promote labor rights in North America. In practice, did the public communications filed with NAOs and reviewed over the 1994–2020 period advance this goal? This section examines this central question by analyzing the impact of public communications in three areas: deepening mutual understanding of labor law and labor rights challenges among the NAALC signatory states; strengthening the social capital that trade unions and labor-, human-, and migrant-rights NGOs could deploy in the international defense of worker rights; and influencing the content of labor law and government policy, particularly in Mexico.

DEEPENING UNDERSTANDING OF COMPARATIVE LABOR LAW AND LABOR RIGHTS PROBLEMS

In the process of assessing NAALC public communications, Canadian, Mexican, and U.S. government officials greatly expanded their mutual understanding regarding labor law and policy in all three countries.[206] The U.S. NAO's comment on the first two submissions it received (US 940001 and US 940002) is illustrative in this regard: "There is a dearth of practical knowledge in each of the three signatory countries to the NAALC about legislation in the other countries that guarantees the right of freedom of association and the right to organize."[207] At a time when the NACLC secretariat was not yet operational, the U.S. NAO addressed this problem by proposing a trinational government-to-government seminar (with participation from state or provincial authorities) on freedom of association and public information and educational initiatives to communicate to the general public details regarding the content of the NAALC and how it would operate.[208] A parallel example is the Mexican NAO's first public report (MEX 9501), which indicated how limited Mexican officials' initial understanding of U.S. labor law was by addressing such topics as the definition of a "bargaining unit," the authority exercised by the National Labor Relations Board, and whether foreigners could become union members or serve as union officers.[209]

Several of the early NAO public reports and ministerial joint declarations called upon the NACLC secretariat to undertake systematic research on topics such as the impact of plant closings on freedom of association, labor and employment laws for migrant workers, and so forth. Certainly, the secretariat's most enduring contribution was to publish studies that improved mutual understanding of comparative labor and industrial relations law in the NAALC signatory countries.[210] Even though the numerous public seminars and educational outreach activities organized on such topics as Mexican labor law and policy and U.S. immigration law and enforcement practices did not alter the material circumstances that gave rise to specific NAALC public communications, they did improve government officials' understanding of the constitutional, legal, and policy context framing the issues involved.[211] Over time, the NAO public reports themselves came to constitute something equivalent to "case law" that both submitters and NAO officials could cite to demonstrate that the matter under consideration indeed formed part of a broader pattern of labor rights violations.[212] For example, in its public report on US 9703 (Echlin/Itapsa), the U.S. NAO referred to seven previous submissions detailing (often successful) attempts by employers and incumbent trade unions to prevent dissident workers from organizing an alternative union.[213]

More broadly, although NAALC procedures themselves led to only limited changes in Mexican labor law and practice (see below), the public communications assessed by the U.S. and Canadian NAOs between 1994 and 2020 were instrumental in setting the agenda for future U.S. and Canadian negotiations with Mexico concerning labor rights issues. As chapters 5 and 6 will show, long-standing obstacles to Mexican workers' effective exercise of freedom of association and the right to bargain collectively—in particular, the legal status of employer protection contracts, the absence of any requirement for secret balloting in contract recount elections, and the structural bias embedded in the tripartite composition of labor conciliation and arbitration boards—were central issues in U.S.-Mexican bargaining between 2012 and 2016 over Mexico's accession to the Trans-Pacific

Partnership free-trade agreement (chapter 5) and in U.S. (and Canadian) negotiations over the revision of the NAFTA between 2017 and 2019 (chapter 6). It is
unlikely that there would have been such widespread consensus among U.S. and
Canadian government officials and legislators regarding the need for fundamental labor reform in Mexico had it not been for lessons learned in preceding years
through NAALC public communications. Their positions on this question differed dramatically from the focus on simple "enforcement of national law" that
had informed the original NAALC negotiations in 1993 (chapter 3).

BUILDING SOCIAL CAPITAL IN THE INTERNATIONAL
DEFENSE OF LABOR RIGHTS

One of the most notable aspects of NAALC public communications was frequent
cross-border collaboration among Canadian, Mexican, and/or U.S. sociopolitical
actors in defense of labor rights, including the rights of migrant workers. This
phenomenon has led several authors to argue that one of the NAALC's most
important legacies was to build transnational social capital.[214] Labor organizations (individual trade unions and labor federations and/or confederations)
and/or labor-, human-, and migrant-rights NGOs did indeed form binational
or trinational coalitions to advance their claims in a significant proportion of
the public communications filed with all three national administrative offices:
Canada, four of seven submissions (57.1 percent); Mexico, eight of fourteen
submissions (57.1 percent); the United States, seventeen of twenty-five submissions (68.0 percent) (table 4.1).[215] However, the social capital-building effects of
the NAALC were not distributed equally. Of the 135 labor organizations and
124 NGOs engaged in public communications between 1994 and 2020, substantial
numbers only participated in a single submission: Canada, nine (33.3 percent);
Mexico, twenty-four (22.0 percent); United States, sixty-one (49.6 percent).[216]
The bulk of the communications were, in fact, filed by a relatively small number
of sociopolitical actors in all three countries.

The following text box lists by country of origin the sixteen unions and
NGOs most actively involved in NAALC public communications and the submissions in which they participated.[217] These sixteen organizations together
participated in thirty-two of the total forty-six (69.6 percent) communications
filed. All sixteen of them mobilized against the Mexican government's assault

on the historically democratic Mexican Electricians' Union in 2011 (CAN 2011-1/ US 2011-02), and a large proportion of them participated in the parallel submissions concerning Echlin/Itapsa (US 9703 / CAN 98-1; twelve organizations, 75 percent) and North Carolina public employees (MEX 2006-1 / CAN 2008-1; ten organizations, 62.5 percent). Across the three NAALC signatory countries, the most active organizations were the Canadian Labour Congress (eight communications), Mexico's National Union of Workers (UNT) (twelve communications), and, in the United States, the International Labor Rights Education and Research Fund / International Labor Rights Forum and the United Electrical, Radio, and Machine Workers of America (UE) (ten communications each).

LEADING SUBMITTING ORGANIZATIONS AND PUBLIC COMMUNICATIONS TO THE CANADIAN, MEXICAN, AND U.S. NATIONAL ADMINISTRATIVE OFFICES (NAOS), 1994–2020

CANADA

Canadian Labour Congress (8): CAN 2011-1/US 2011-02, MEX 2006-1/ CAN 2008-1, US 9703/CAN 98-1, US 9804, US 2005-01

Canadian Association of Labour Lawyers (7): CAN 2011-1/US 2011-02, MEX 2006-1/CAN 2008-1, US 9703/CAN 98-1, US 9804

Canadian Automobile Workers (7): CAN 2011-1/US 2011-02, MEX 2006-1/ CAN 2008-1, US 9703/CAN 98-1, US 2005-01

Maquiladora Solidarity Network (5): CAN 2011-1/US 2011-02, US 2000-01, US 2003-1/CAN 2003-1

Workers' Federation of Québec (FTQ, 5): CAN 2011-1/US 2011-02, MEX 2006-1/ CAN 2008-1, US 9803

MEXICO

National Union of Workers (UNT, 12): CAN 2011-1 /US 2011-02, MEX 9802, MEX 2005-1, MEX 2006-1/CAN 2008-1, MEX 2016-1, MEX 2016-2, US 9703/ CAN 98-1, US 2005-01, US 2018-01

(continued on next page)

(*continued from previous page*)

National Association of Democratic Lawyers (ANAD, 10): CAN 2011-1/
US 2011-02, MEX 2012-1, US 940003, US 9601, US 9701, US 9702, US 9703/
CAN 98-1, US 9804

Authentic Labor Front (FAT, 9): CAN 2011-1/ US 2011-02, MEX 9802,
MEX 2005-1, MEX 2006-1/CAN 2008-1, US 9703/CAN 98-1, US 2015-04

Mexican Telephone Workers' Union (STRM, 7): CAN 2011-1/US 2011-02,
MEX 9501, US 9602, US 9703/CAN 98-1, US 9804

Union of Workers in the Metal, Iron, Steel, and Related and Similar Industries
(STIMAHCS, 6): CAN 2011-1/US 2011-02,
MEX 9802, MEX 2006-1/CAN 2008-1, US 9702

UNITED STATES

International Labor Rights Education and Research Fund / International Labor
Rights Forum (10): CAN 2011-1/US 2011-02, MEX 9804/CAN 98-2,
US 940003, US 9601, US 9701, US 9702, US 9803, US 9804

United Electrical, Radio, and Machine Workers of America (UE, 10):
CAN 2011-1/US 2011-02, MEX 2006-1/CAN 2008-1, US 940002, US 940004,
US 9703/CAN 98-1, US 2000-01, US 2005-01

UNITE! (10): CAN 2011-1/US 2011-02, MEX 9804/CAN 98-2, MEX 2006-1/
CAN 2008-1, US 9703/CAN 98-1, US 2004-1, US 2005-01

American Federation of Labor-Congress of Industrial Organizations (9):
CAN 2011-1/US 2011-02, MEX 2011-1, MEX 2016-1, US 9703/CAN 98-1,
US 2000-01, US 2001-01, US 2018-1

United Steelworkers (9): CAN 2011-1/US 2011-02, MEX 2006-1/CAN 2008-1,
US 9703/CAN 98-1, US 9804, US 2005-01, US 2006-1

International Brotherhood of Teamsters (8): CAN 2011-1/US 2011-02, US 940001,
US 9703/CAN 98-1, US 9803, US 9804, US 2005-01

Source: Author's examination of public communications to the Canadian, Mexican, and U.S.
national administrative offices (NAOs).

Notes: Public communications are listed in alphabetical order by the NAO to which they were
submitted (that is, CAN, MEX, and US) rather than in chronological order. Parallel submissions
to two different NAOs are linked in the table and were counted as separate submissions. See the
list of acronyms for some organizations' full names and appendix B for a summary description of
each communication. The International Labor Rights Research and Education Fund changed its
name to International Labor Rights Forum in 1996. UNITE! became UNITE HERE! in 2004.

Yet even among these leading participants, there was considerable variation in their involvement. Of the thirty-two public communications in which one or more of these organizations was involved, twelve (37.5 percent) were filed by one of these unions or NGOs acting alone (see the previous text box). In part, this reflected the fact that some submissions focused on issues of special concern to a particular union or NGO. For example, both the UE and the International Brotherhood of Teamsters (IBT) had lost union members in the United States as major U.S. corporations shifted production to lower-cost, nonunionized maquiladora plants in northern Mexico.[218] It was therefore logical that they turned to the new NAALC complaint process to support the FAT-affiliated STIMAHCS in its efforts to organize workers in these facilities in support of their demands for higher wages and improved working conditions, efforts which (if successful) might have reduced these plants' low-wage competitive advantage. The IBT filed US 940001 in support of the STIMAHCS at Honeywell Corporation's electronic manufacturing plant in Ciudad Chihuahua, Chihuahua, and the UE submitted US 940002 and US 940004 to protest employer opposition to the STIMAHCS unionization campaign at a General Electric Co. electrical motor plant in Ciudad Juárez, Chihuahua.[219] The Mexican Telephone Workers Union (STRM) was similarly motivated to protest the Sprint Corporation's employment practices at its San Francisco subsidiary (MEX 9501) because it was concerned that the telecommunication company might adopt similar policies following its announced expansion into Mexico.[220] It was understandable that some of the earliest public communications were filed by a single organization as different unions tested the practical efficacy of NAALC procedures.[221] However, this practice did not entirely disappear over time; five later submissions (US 9801, US 9802, US 2005-02 / CAN 2005-1, US 2006-01) were also filed by a single union or NGO (table 4.1).[222]

Nevertheless, the evidence of active cross-border collaboration in NAALC public communications is strong. A total of eight of the thirty-two submissions (25 percent) listed in the previous text box engaged two of these leading NAALC participants, and another thirteen of these communications (40.6 percent, $N = 32$) involved three or more of them.[223] The U.S.-based International Labor Rights Education and Research Fund / International Labor Rights Forum, which had a long-established record of solidarity actions and engagement with trade agreement-linked labor rights matters (including the U.S. Generalized System of Preferences labor complaints analyzed in chapter 2) and Mexico's National

Association of Democratic Lawyers (ANAD) were the principal submitters on four different occasions (US 940003, US 9601, US 9701, US 9702). Similarly, the Toronto-based Maquila Solidarity Network was actively engaged in NAALC public communications focused on workers' rights in maquiladora plants in Mexico (US 2000-01, US 2003-1 / CAN 2003-1).

Collaborating across borders to identify cases for potential NAO review, formulating the required submission documents and preparing public testimony, and sometimes coordinating related support campaigns in one or more of the NAFTA countries all undoubtedly strengthened cooperative ties and constructed valuable shared social capital among these labor organizations and NGOs. However, it is important to note that in several instances, solidarity interactions and cooperative ties originated in the 1991–1993 anti-NAFTA mobilizations or even earlier (and thus predated the NAALC per se) or had been formulated prior to collaboration on a NAALC public communication. Several U.S. and Mexican labor organizations (including the AFL-CIO, Communications Workers of America [CWA], UE, STRM, and FAT) interacted through the MacArthur Foundation–funded Mexico-U.S. Diálogos networking project starting in 1991.[224] The UE and the FAT had, in February-March 1992, signed a "Strategic Organizing Alliance" centered on UE-represented manufacturing facilities in the United States that had shifted production to Mexico, particularly to maquiladora plants in the state of Chihuahua.[225] Similarly, the CWA and the STRM had (along with the Communication and Electrical Workers of Canada [CEWC]) signed collaboration agreements in December 1991 and February 1992. This was the basis for the CWA's informal assistance to STRM in its MEX 9501 submission (Sprint Corporation) and their joint submission of US 9602 (Maxi-Switch), a case in which the STRM-created Federation of Unions of Goods and Services Enterprises (Federación de Sindicatos de Empresas de Bienes y Servicios, FESEBS) led the local unionization campaign.[226] The large trinational coalition that mobilized in US 2000-01 (Auto-Trim / Custom-Trim) included fourteen U.S. and five Mexican labor rights NGOs, many of which had an established tradition of collaborative action in support of maquiladora workers in the U.S.-Mexico border region.[227] The cosubmitters of MEX 2006-1 / CAN 2008-1 (North Carolina public employees) could not have assembled a trinational coalition involving thirty-five Mexican unions (appendix 3), twenty-nine (82.9 percent) of which had not previously joined a NAALC public communication, without turning to pre-existing solidarity networks.[228]

The phenomenon of cross-border collaboration in NAALC public communications developed as a social practice rather than in response to an institutional requirement.[229] As previously noted, the NAALC specified that each signatory country's national administrative office would receive public communications concerning labor rights issues in another country. Some sociopolitical actors' established alliances or ideological motivations may have particularly inclined them to seek international partners; others may have found it especially useful to forge ties with unions and/or labor-, human-, or migrant-rights NGOs in another country in order to ensure that the factual and legal bases of their NAALC communications were as persuasive as possible. However, despite variations among the three countries in the procedural guidelines each government established for its NAO, none of them required submitters to coordinate their efforts across national borders.[230] Indeed, seventeen of the total forty-six NAALC public communications (36.9 percent) were filed with an NAO by one or more sociopolitical actors based exclusively in that same country (table 4.1). This proportion did not vary greatly among submissions to any of the three NAOs: Canada (42.9 percent), Mexico (42.9 percent), and the United States (32.0 percent).

One of the most significant examples of cross-border trade union collaboration to emerge from the NAFTA / NAALC experience was the alliance between the AFL-CIO and the UNT. From the 1950s through the mid-1990s, the AFL-CIO maintained an exclusive formal alliance with the government-allied Confederation of Mexican Workers.[231] However, because of the imminent threat that the NAFTA and expanded off-shore manufacturing production posed to unionized U.S. workers,[232] the two confederations' sharply different official positions in the NAFTA debate,[233] and CTM affiliates' position as incumbent unions in many Mexican production facilities governed by employer protection contracts, the AFL-CIO reassessed its position and acknowledged the importance of building cross-border ties with democratically organized unions actively committed to raising wages and improving working conditions in Mexico.[234] In January 1998, AFL-CIO president John Sweeney traveled to Mexico City to inaugurate an American Center for International Labor Solidarity office established to promote cross-border labor collaboration, including through NAALC public communications.[235] While in Mexico, Sweeney conspicuously met not only with CTM representatives but also with the leaders of several politically independent labor organizations, including the FAT, STRM, and UNT.[236] The AFL-CIO first participated formally in a NAALC public communication in the Echlin/Itapsa case, where it joined the third-largest trinational coalition assembled over the entire 1994–2020 period.[237] For its part, the UNT also joined in NAALC public communications beginning with US 9703 / CAN 98-1 (Echlin/Itapsa), and, acting either alone or in coalition, it participated more frequently in these initiatives than any other Canadian, Mexican, or U.S. labor organization (a total of twelve submissions). In September 1999, the AFL-CIO and the UNT signed a formal collaboration agreement, and they worked together in the CAN 2011-1/ US 2011-02 and MEX 2016-1 communications. They were the sole cosubmitters in the complaint filed with the U.S. NAO (US 2018-01) against a 2017 controversial Mexican labor law reform proposal.

EVALUATING THE POLICY IMPACT OF NAALC PUBLIC COMMUNICATIONS

A central question regarding the labor rights provisions of any U.S. trade agreement is whether the complaints filed under dispute-settlement procedures have a positive impact by promoting changes in labor law and policy in the target countries where rights violations occur, either immediately or over the longer term. An analysis of the data presented in table 4.1 employing multiple ordered-logit regression models found that the only statistically significant relationship was between final case outcome (whether the NAO receiving the public communication accepted it for review and, in due course, recommended ministerial consultations on the issues involved) and observed policy impact.[238] This result is not surprising because, with the exceptions of US 940002 and US 9602, only public communications that ended in ministerial consultations produced any observed policy impact. Several other independent variables—a dummy variable representing the country where the public communication was submitted, the type of submitting organization (trade union, NGO, or both), the number of submitters, whether or not the submitters constituted a binational or trinational coalition, and the case duration (in days)—had no overall statistically significant impact on observed policy impact at the conventional $p < 0.05$ confidence interval. A separate Bayesian ordered-logit regression analysis of US NAO submissions did, however, find a weak but still positive association ($p < 0.1$) between coalition type (that is, whether or not a binational or trinational coalition made the submission) and final case outcome.[239]

Because collective-action rights (NAALC principles nos. 1–3) were a principal focus in many public communications, and because, in some instances, the submitters acted strategically by invoking principles nos. 5, 6, and/or 9 in order to ensure that cases involving collective-action rights would potentially qualify for financial or trade-linked sanctions against the target government, the regression analysis also employed dummy variables to test whether there was any significant relationship between the invocation of principles nos. 1–3 alone, or "strategic" submissions invoking one or more of principles nos. 1–3 *and* one or more of principles nos. 5, 6, and 9, and observed policy impact. There were no such relationships across all the NAALC filings. However, multiple Bayesian logit and ordered-logit regression analyses of MEX NAO public communications found a weak but positive association ($p < 0.1$) between the "strategic action" dummy variable and the observed policy impact.[240]

An aggregate statistical analysis cannot, however, address all the relevant questions concerning the policy impact of NAALC public communications, in part because the small number of cases involved precludes equivalent analyses of the records compiled by all three individual NAOs acting separately. Because the preceding section assessed the effects of Mexican NAO submissions on U.S. law and policy concerning migrant workers, and because neither the Mexican nor the U.S. NAOs issued public reports on the three submissions concerning Canada (MEX 2016-2, US 9803, US 9804), the principal focus here is on the impact of NAALC procedures on labor rights in Mexico. This subject has been the most controversial issue in previous analyses of the NAALC experience.

The NAALC Policy Impact Record Regarding Mexico

One of the principal criticisms lodged against the NAALC, particularly by U.S. and Canadian unions, was that the public communications process did not provide an effective remedy for the specific labor rights violations in Mexico that gave rise to NAO submissions.[241] As membership organizations, the litmus test for trade unions was whether NAALC procedures could, for example, protect fellow labor activists in Mexico who risked their jobs by conducting unionization campaigns.[242] However, the NAALC's jurisdictional mandate—promoting the effective enforcement of national law by the signatory states—precluded NAO authorities from taking actions that would have, for instance, led to the immediate reinstatement of individual workers who had been fired for exercising their rights to freedom of association and collective bargaining.[243] Moreover, U.S. NAO officials themselves perceived their role as international support for the rule of law rather than as arbiter of specific labor conflicts.[244] Even if the U.S. and Canadian NAOs had had the authority to rectify labor rights violations in particular circumstances, and even if they had always completed their reviews within the periods stipulated by their operational guidelines, their actions would almost certainly have come too late to protect dismissed Mexican workers facing great economic duress.[245] Because of the lengthy delays sometimes involved in scheduling and conducting ministerial consultations,[246] any actual change in government policy resulting from NAALC processes generally took even longer.

Nor did NAALC procedures provide strong protection overall for union organizing efforts in Mexico, even though the U.S. NAO went to some lengths to promote public dialogue regarding union organizing and representation.[247] As discussed above, the U.S. NAO declined to engage with the high-profile SME submission (US 2011-1), which raised broad questions concerning freedom of association and the right to collective bargaining in Mexico. In several cases, filing a public communication with the U.S. NAO did at least temporarily strengthen union organizers' negotiating position vis-à-vis the employer. In US 940002 (General Electric Co.), the union reached an agreement with company managers to hold a secret-ballot election at General Electric Co.'s electrical motor plant in Ciudad Juárez, Chihuahua. In US 9803 (St.-Hubert McDonald's), the government of Québec agreed that the provincial council would examine anti-union company shutdowns like the closing of a McDonald's franchise in St.-Hubert. On that basis, the binational submitter coalition agreed to withdraw the complaint, although, in the end, provincial government officials refused to make any change in labor law or enforcement policy.[248] However, only in the Maxi-Switch (US 9602) and Han Young (US 9702) cases did a local independent union in Mexico win legal recognition because of the international pressures generated by U.S. NAO proceedings. On these bases, the observed policy impacts of the US 940002, US 9602, and US 9702 communications are coded 1 in table 4.1., even though in both the Maxi-Switch and Han Young cases, the employer succeeded over time in undercutting the local union.[249]

In those public communications they did review, the U.S. and Canadian NAOs faced at least three major barriers in their efforts to promote Mexican workers' rights to freedom of association and collective bargaining. First, as noted above, employer protection contracts were not illegal prior to the April 30, 2019, reform of federal labor law. Second, ten of the twenty-two communications (45.5 percent) to these two NAOs that cited NAALC principles nos. 1 and/or 2 with reference to Mexico involved maquiladora plants.[250] Especially in garment production and other light manufacturing activities, employers often preferred to close the facilities and relocate their operations, either elsewhere in Mexico or in other low-wage developing countries, rather than accede to contract negotiations with a politically independent union.[251] This was, for example, the employers' response to unionization campaigns at Han Young in the state of Baja California (US 9702), Matamoros Garment and Tarrant in the state of Puebla (US 2003-01 / CAN 2003-1), and Rubie's de México in the state of Hidalgo (US 2005-03).[252] Third, a large proportion of maquiladora production in Mexico was in local (state-level)-jurisdiction economic activities. As the case study of the Han Young conflict demonstrated, state-level labor conciliation and arbitration boards were often strongly allied with local employer interests. In the core maquiladora production centers along the Mexico-U.S. border, maquiladora employer associations lobbied vigorously to preserve a no-union, protection-contract business environment.[253]

Overall, NAALC public communications had the greatest impact as catalysts for change in Mexico by influencing Mexican government policies in two different areas: pre-employment pregnancy testing and public access to union registration and collective contract information and adoption in principle of secret balloting in contract representation elections.[254] Because a preceding section discussed the first topic in detail, the focus here is on the longer-term impact of the May 18, 2000, bilateral agreement on public accessibility to union registration and collective contract information and secret balloting in recount elections that the Mexican and U.S. ministers of labor negotiated to address issues raised by the US 9702 (Han Young) and US 9703 / CAN 98-1 (Echlin/Itapsa) cases. On both these issues, NAALC procedures and the ministerial agreement bolstered domestic calls for policy reform.

The STPS had created an internet site that listed legally registered federal-jurisdiction labor organizations as early as 1998.[255] However, the May 2000 ministerial agreement marked the Mexican government's first explicit commitment to creating a public registry of all officially registered unions and collective bargaining agreements. The proposals for improving access to labor justice that the STPS had developed in conjunction with the 1995–2000 National Development Plan had not included an initiative of this kind.[256] There were, though, domestic proponents of such a measure. Two politically independent labor groups, the

FESEBS and the "Union Movement and the Nation" Forum (Foro El Sindicalismo ante la Nación), had called for the creation of a national public union registry (Registro Público Nacional Sindical) in August 1997, even before public communication US 9702 (Han Young) was filed.[257] The labor law reform bill that the center-left Party of the Democratic Revolution (Partido de la Revolución Democrática, PRD) proposed in 1998 had also advocated creating a public registry of all registered unions and collective contracts.[258]

Yet despite these combined domestic and external pressures, actual policy change in this area was slow and partial. The STPS and the Federal Conciliation and Arbitration Board (JFCA) did create internet sites providing access to, respectively, federal-jurisdiction union registration documents and collective contract information.[259] However, the union registration information was not accessible by employer name (making it impossible to determine whether a union was present at a particular production site),[260] and U.S. labor officials, therefore, continued to press for full implementation of the 2000 ministerial agreement at both the federal and state levels.[261] It was not until 2012 that the Federal Labor Law required the STPS and state-level labor conciliation and arbitration boards to publish key information concerning all officially registered unions: the union's name, address, and registration number; the names of executive committee members and their terms of office; the number of union members; the union's statutes; and the name of any federation and/or confederation with which the union was affiliated—but explicitly *not* the economic activity in which the union's members were engaged.[262] Similarly, the 2012 labor law reform required (article 391bis) federal- and state-level labor conciliation and arbitration boards to publish information concerning all collective bargaining agreements they registered. In both instances, the crucial impetus for change was the 2002 Federal Law on Transparency and Access to Governmental Public Information. This measure, adopted unanimously by both chambers of the federal Congress, granted (albeit only in response to specific requests) broad public access to all government records.[263] But as a practical matter, even in the late 2010s, only the STPS and local labor conciliation and arbitration boards in the Federal District and the state of San Luis Potosí published union registration information, and only the JFCA and the Federal District local board regularly published collective bargaining agreements.[264]

The Han Young and Echlin/Itapsa cases also contributed significantly to an emerging national policy debate over secret balloting in recount elections.

Although the JFCA sometimes employed secret balloting in recount elections even prior to the 2000 ministerial agreement,[265] Mexico's federal labor law had historically given labor conciliation and arbitration boards broad discretion in how they determined whether a union held majority status and thus legal title to a collective bargaining agreement.[266] The first major labor law reform initiative formulated during the 1990s (by the center-right National Action Party [Partido Acción Nacional, PAN] in July 1995) did not introduce any change in this regard.[267] However, the PRD's 1998 labor law reform proposal did call for secret voting in recount elections.[268] The practical experience of Arturo Alcalde Justiniani, a prominent pro-union democracy labor lawyer who had represented the STIMAHCS in the Echlin/Itapsa conflict and who was one of the coauthors of this reform initiative, inspired the PRD's proposal on the issue.[269]

Control over internal election procedures was, however, a lynchpin of government-allied unions' dominance in workplace affairs, and the resistance to policy change in this area was persistent and strong.[270] In June 2001, the AFL-CIO and the PACE (Paper, Allied-Industrial, Chemical, and Energy Workers) International Union sought to test the Mexican government's May 2000 commitment to promote secret balloting in recount elections by filing a public communication with the U.S. NAO (US 2001-1) that addressed developments at the Duro Bag Manufacturing Corporation's plant in Río Bravo, Tamaulipas. In March 2001, Duro Bag workers represented by a recently registered independent union had been compelled to cast recount ballots publicly, in front of representatives of both the local CROC union and the company, in an election the independent union lost.[271] The facts of the case were clear. Nonetheless, the U.S. NAO declined to review the communication because Mexican labor law did not require secret balloting, and U.S. officials sought to maintain a dialogue on the issue with their Mexican counterparts.[272]

In December 2002, the Mexican government did comply with the letter of the May 2000 ministerial agreement when the PAN, PRI, and Mexican Ecologist Green Party (Partido Verde Ecologista de México) submitted a proposed labor law reform bill to Congress. The bill, commonly known as the "Proyecto Abascal" in reference to STPS Secretary Carlos Abascal Carranza, included a provision requiring a secret vote in recount elections.[273] However, the practical effect of this provision was nullified by an additional requirement that a union seeking legal control over a collective contract submit to a labor conciliation and arbitration board a signed list of its members, therewith revealing the names of those workers who were likely to support a challenger union to the board officials responsible for conducting a recount election.[274] Critics feared that, in a polarized workplace environment, this requirement would, in practice, make dissident workers vulnerable to unjustified harassment or dismissal by employers.[275]

The Fox administration's plans for labor law reform ended in a stalemate.[276] As a consequence, there was no actual policy change concerning voting in recount elections before the Mexican Supreme Court ruled in decisions on September 10 and October 1, 2008, that conducting contract recount elections by a "personal, free, direct, and secret vote" constituted a basic element in the "democratic life of the worker."[277] The Federal Labor Law did not specify the procedures that labor conciliation and arbitration boards should follow to resolve disputes over legal title to a collective bargaining agreement (the term *recount* appeared only in article 931, concerning procedures employed in determining the legality of labor strikes), and nowhere in the law was there any requirement for secret balloting. In justifying its decision, the court made reference to the May 2000 Mexican-U.S. agreement regarding recount elections. Yet it framed its central argument in terms of "the democratic rule of law" guaranteed by the 1917 Constitution and Mexico's obligations under international treaties, especially ILO conventions nos. 87 and 98 and the Universal Declaration of Human Rights.[278]

However, even though the court's second ruling was binding (*jurisprudencia definida*) in all future court cases, it did not immediately compel federal- and state-level labor conciliation and arbitration boards to employ secret balloting in recount elections because SCJN decisions resolving controversies among lower courts over *amparo* decisions did not, at that time, have general legal effect.[279] It was certainly noteworthy in this regard that the 2012 federal labor law reform did not alter established provisions that gave labor conciliation and arbitration boards wide discretion in how they assessed whether a union retained majority status and thus legal title to a collective contract.[280] In fact, it was not until September 29, 2015, that the JFCA adopted criteria codifying how federal-jurisdiction boards would henceforth comply with the Supreme Court's 2008 decision.[281]

Explaining NAALC Policy Outcomes in Mexico

Apart from the inherent limitations of the NAALC as an instrument for defending labor rights, shifts over time in U.S. and Mexican political leaders' commitment to NAALC procedures were crucial in shaping the agreement's effectiveness in advancing labor rights in Mexico.

Having staked considerable political capital on a labor "side-agreement" in the negotiations over U.S. congressional approval of the NAFTA, President Clinton was under pressure to demonstrate that NAALC procedures could, in fact, effectively address complaints regarding labor rights violations in Mexico.[282] The Clinton administration was, at the outset, braced for a flood of public communications. Indeed, four digits followed the year-date marker (for example, "940001") in the initial case numbering system, an arrangement that would have accommodated up to 9,999 communications.[283] The administration, therefore, sought to bolster the U.S. NAO's credibility by appointing individuals with strong U.S. labor backgrounds to senior staff positions. Secretary Irasema T. Garza, formally appointed in July 1994, had past experience with the United Auto Workers (where she interned while attending the University of Michigan Law School) and the American Federation of State and Municipal Employees (where she had served for seven years on the executive board of Local 2733).[284] Some U.S. unions criticized Garza for scheduling a public hearing on the first public communications (US 940001 and US 940002) in Washington, DC, thereby making participation more difficult for workers from the General Electric and Honeywell plants to be cited in the submissions. However, she won praise for intervening with both the U.S. Border Patrol and Magnéticos de México plant managers to ensure that thirteen Mexican workers could cross the U.S. border to testify at the public hearing held in San Antonio, Texas, on the Sony case (US 940003).[285] Similarly, apparently because of political fallout from public criticism of the U.S. NAO's decision not to seek ministerial consultations following its review of US 940001 and US 940002,[286] the office recommended ministerial communications in all the public communications it accepted for review throughout the remainder of the Clinton administration (table 4.1).[287] Moreover, as previously noted, U.S. NAO officials proactively sought to expand their understanding of Mexican labor law and practice by supplementing the more general comparative labor law studies undertaken by the NACLC secretariat with specially commissioned research on the character and scope of rights violations in Mexico.[288]

It was certainly no coincidence that the only US NAO public communications that resulted in at least nominal government policy change regarding collective-action rights in Mexico (US 9702 and US 9703) were backed by strong U.S. diplomatic pressures. Both the U.S. union submitters and the Clinton administration understood well the symbolic importance of the Han Young and Echlin/Itapsa cases in the intense political maneuvering around the 1997 U.S. congressional vote to reauthorize "fast track" trade-agreement negotiation authority, which explains why both President Clinton and Vice President Gore were willing to discuss the Han Young case directly with President Zedillo. Yet, these were the only US NAO submissions in which the White House ever became directly involved. The Clinton administration might have enjoyed special influence with the Mexican government because of the extraordinary steps it had taken to engineer an international financial rescue package valued at up to approximately US$49.5 billion during Mexico's severe 1994–1995 financial crisis.[289] It is, moreover, certainly possible that President Zedillo's positive response to U.S. pressures over the Han Young case reflected his gratitude for timely U.S. financial and political support.

There is, however, no direct evidence indicating that these considerations affected either U.S. or Mexican government handling of US NAO communications more generally.[290] At least, senior officials in Mexico's Ministry of Labor and Social Welfare felt no special pressures regarding their handling of US NAO submissions during this period.[291] It is perhaps telling in this regard that, although the Zedillo administration exerted direct pressures on Baja California state labor officials to resolve the Han Young controversy expeditiously, the Mexican and U.S. governments did not reach a ministerial agreement on the issues raised by the US 9702 and US 9703 submissions until three years after the Han Young conflict began. Even then, the Mexican government symbolically reaffirmed its national sovereignty in such matters by linking the public announcement of this agreement to a parallel announcement on the same day (May 18, 2000) of a bilateral ministerial agreement in which the U.S. government agreed to address the issues raised by the MEX 9801, MEX 9802, and MEX 9803 public communications by expanding programs to improve migrant workers' understanding of their labor rights in such areas as occupational safety and health and gender and ethnic discrimination.

The political pressures on the Clinton administration to demonstrate the effectiveness of NAALC procedures placed the Mexican government on the defensive in responding to US NAO public communications concerning labor rights violations in Mexico.[292] The persistent failure of the Zedillo administration (and of all its successors through 2018) to undertake major reforms to safeguard workers' formal guarantees of freedom of association and the right to collective bargaining and to ensure the independence and impartiality of the labor justice system fundamentally reflected a sufficient lack of political will.[293] However, in order to explain more fully NAALC policy outcomes in Mexico, it is also important to understand that even when some senior Mexican government officials accepted that US NAO communications raised legitimate issues regarding national labor law and policy,[294] the government's responses to these cases were constrained in four major ways.

First, in straightforward political terms, the barriers to undertaking major labor law and constitutional reforms were high. In fact, a series of labor law reform initiatives under consideration between 1989 and 2010 all eventually failed.[295] Even when the administration of President Felipe Calderón Hinojosa (2006–2012) did manage to enact a reform measure at the end of his term, it did not alter union and contract registration procedures. Moreover, because federal and state-level labor conciliation and arbitration boards had been established by article 123 of the 1917 Constitution, restructuring the labor justice system would have required a constitutional amendment—the formal requirements for which (passage by two-thirds majorities in both chambers of the federal Congress and adoption by a majority of state legislatures) constituted an even greater political hurdle. The overall political weakness of President Zedillo throughout his term in office effectively precluded actions of this magnitude.[296]

Second, from the mid-1990s into the 2000s, the political dynamics of Mexico's governing coalition blocked progressive labor reform initiatives. The CTM and CROC were both dominant national labor confederations and mainstays of the PRI-led coalition. Over time, the influence of government-aligned labor organizations would fade, and business opposition would become the main obstacle to significant labor law reform. However, even though President Zedillo was often at odds with old-guard elements of the PRI coalition, during his presidency, these groups still enjoyed considerable political influence because of their support for the tripartite macroeconomic pacts that had stabilized the Mexican economy in the aftermath of the 1994–1995 financial crisis.[297] In fact, in the established sexenal rhythm of national electoral politics during the PRI era, their policy leverage increased as the next presidential election approached and the PRI sought to mobilize its traditional constituencies and preserve its majority at the polls. This was certainly the case in the run-up to the 2000 presidential election because the intensity of multiparty electoral competition was increasing sharply.[298]

The Mexican unions and labor rights NGOs available as coalitional allies in US NAO public communications during and after the 1990s, while sufficient in number and importance to demonstrate that an independent labor movement did exist in Mexico, lacked the membership size and political influence required to act as effective counterweights to government-aligned labor organizations like the CTM and the CROC.[299] There is ample evidence that mobilizing binational and/or trinational coalitions that included pro-union democracy elements in Mexico increased U.S. submitters' capacity to formulate well-documented public communications and reinforced the credibility of their claims in the eyes of U.S. NAO officials.[300] However, unlike in some of the U.S. Generalized System of Preferences labor rights complaints examined in chapter 2, organizations like the FAT were too small and politically marginal to exercise any substantial lobbying weight in domestic debates over labor law and policy.

Indeed, the composition of some US NAO submitter coalitions may actually have worked against them politically in Mexico. For example, from the perspective of Mexican government officials, the FAT-affiliated STIMAHCS (which played a leading role in five of the ten US NAO submissions addressing NAALC principles nos. 1 and 2 in maquiladora plants)[301] was hardly a disinterested defender of labor rights. Rather, it was engaged with its U.S. and Canadian partners in strategic organizing campaigns whose explicit goals were to expand the FAT's membership and influence vis-à-vis government-aligned labor organizations and, by improving working conditions and raising wages in Mexico, to reduce the competitive threat that maquiladoras posed to unionized jobs in the United States.[302] Some Mexican labor officials were therefore inclined to view US NAO communications, whatever their substantive merits, as vehicles through which domestic union rivalries were internationalized. From their perspective, in many of these cases, they were asked to intervene in support of political opponents like the FAT against long-term government allies like the CTM and the CROC.[303]

Third, like any Mexican president, President Zedillo was constrained by the jurisdictional boundaries imposed by Mexican federalism. Although the Federal Labor Law was national in scope, the federal government's direct administrative authority over labor matters was restricted to federal-jurisdiction industries and, in state-jurisdiction economic activities, workplace safety and health measures and occupational training.[304] Sociopolitical actors in the United States—both those groups submitting US NAO public communications and the U.S.

government officials responsible for addressing the substantive issues in dispute—may have assumed that the federal executive's historic dominance in Mexican politics translated into easy control over state government labor authorities. The Han Young case demonstrated that high-level U.S. diplomatic pressure could, in fact, motivate Mexican federal officials to intervene in state-jurisdiction labor disputes. However, this was an exceptional situation. In many instances, the relative autonomy that state-level legal jurisdiction granted state government officials, in effect, protected their alliances with local business and labor groups linked to the maquiladora industry, which were doggedly committed to maintaining workplace control in an important economic activity.[305] More generally, the fact that seven of the twenty-five (28.0 percent[306]) US NAO public communications concerning Mexico addressed alleged labor rights violations in state-jurisdiction maquiladora plants posed a difficult political paradox: In their efforts to address the issues these submissions raised, U.S. officials sought to pressure the Mexican federal government, the responsible party under the NAALC, to correct labor rights violations in the area in which its legal authority and practical operating capacity were the most limited.

Finally, the Zedillo administration's response to US NAO public communications was strongly shaped by issue salience—that is, the relative political sensitivity of the different NAALC principles involved. Mexican government labor officials consistently resisted U.S. pressures to reform labor law provisions concerning collective-action rights that would endanger established political controls over workplace affairs. It is significant in this regard that the US NAO public communication that contributed to the most durable policy change in Mexico was US 9701 (pregnancy testing), a case that fundamentally involved individual rather than collective-action labor rights. This was also an issue about which Zedillo administration officials may have been particularly sensitive to potential damage to Mexico's international reputation and in which the U.S. petitioners could tap into an emerging domestic consensus in favor of policy change.

The U.S. government's commitment to NAALC procedures and the intensity of diplomatic pressures on Mexico declined appreciably under the administration of President George W. Bush.[307] It was perhaps natural that, with the passage of time, other bilateral foreign policy priorities gained in relative importance. More specifically, however, Elaine L. Chao, U.S. secretary of labor between 2001 and 2009, substantially downplayed the importance of labor rights issues in interactions with her Mexican counterparts.[308] Certainly, the proportion of public communications involving Mexico that the U.S. NAO declined to review was substantially higher during the Bush years (50.0 percent, $N = 8$) than during the Clinton administration (11.1 percent, $N = 9$).[309] In part, this change may have reflected a purposeful shift in the U.S. NAO's evaluative criteria, with the office insisting that complainants exhaust domestic avenues of redress before initiating NAALC procedures—a conservative departure in U.S. NAO policy long advocated by the U.S. private sector.[310] Nor did any of the US NAO submissions regarding Mexico that were filed during the Bush administration yield any positive observed policy impact (table 4.1). These developments, combined with a growing conviction that scarce financial and staff resources might be more effectively employed by pursuing other labor-rights promotion strategies that promised to yield more tangible results, discouraged U.S. and Canadian unions and labor- and human-rights NGOs from filing public communications concerning Mexico.[311]

During the Bush administration, U.S. labor authorities were also sometimes less responsive in interactions with their Mexican counterparts than Clinton administration officials had been. In public communication MEX 2001-1 (New York State workers' compensation), the U.S. Department of Labor tabled the STPS request for ministerial consultations and suggested consultations between either NACLC council designees or the U.S. and Mexican NAOs.[312] As a consequence, no ministerial consultations were ever held.[313] In MEX 2006-1 (North Carolina public employees), the U.S. NAO did not respond in a timely fashion to standard Mexican government enquiries regarding the case,[314] which accounted at least in part for the very long case duration time (table 4.1).

Mexican resistance to NAALC procedures also increased during this period.[315] The Ministry of Labor and Social Welfare's distinctly different responses to requests for ministerial consultations in US 940003 (Sony Corporation) and US 2003-01 / CAN 2003-1 (Puebla garment producers), both of which addressed freedom of association issues, is highly indicative in this regard. In the former case (the first such U.S. request under the NAALC), STPS Secretary Santiago Oñate Laborde quickly agreed to a request for ministerial consultations from U.S. Secretary of Labor Robert B. Reich dated April 11, 1995. The two ministers signed an agreement on May 30, 1995, in which, in addition to a program of three joint public seminars on union registration and certification procedures at the federal and state levels in all three NAALC countries, the Mexican government agreed to commission a study of these issues by independent Mexican labor law experts and to discuss union registration questions both with Magnéticos de México (Sony) workers and managers and with labor authorities in the state of Tamaulipas.[316] In sharp contrast, Mexican labor authorities delayed ministerial consultations with their U.S. and Canadian counterparts on US 2003-01/CAN 2003-1 from October 29, 2004, until April 24, 2008 (1,273 days; 3.5 years). In the end, they agreed to trilateral consultations only because incoming president Barack Obama (2009–2013, 2013–2017) had, as a presidential candidate, raised the possibility of renegotiating the NAFTA, and they wished to resolve the case before he took office.[317] Similarly, in US 2005-03 (Rubie's de México), the Mexican NAO did not respond to U.S. NAO enquiries concerning the case for an extraordinary 454 days (1.2 years).[318]

At least in part, Mexico's declining responsiveness may have been a consequence of the lower priority that U.S. government officials gave to NAALC procedures. However, the center-right, pro-business administrations of Vicente Fox and Felipe Calderón also delayed their resolution of public communications filed with the Mexican NAO concerning the rights of migrant workers in the United States. The three MEX NAO public communications with the longest case duration times (MEX 2003-1, MEX 2005-1, MEX 2006-1) were filed during the administration of President Fox and not resolved until near the end (November 2012) of the succeeding administration of President Calderón.

CONCLUSION

The NAALC established a major historical precedent by linking labor rights protections to a free-trade agreement for the first time. Because of shared sovereignty concerns among the three signatory states, the agreement focused on the effective implementation of national labor law rather than the definition of common labor standards in the NAFTA countries. Nevertheless, the NAALC greatly expanded potential external scrutiny of domestic labor law and policy in Canada, Mexico, and the United States.[319] Its most important contribution was the international attention it focused on such issues as the practical constraints on freedom of association and collective bargaining in Mexico and the rights of Mexican migrant workers in the United States and Canada. In some instances, international condemnation and strong diplomatic pressures did succeed in advancing workers' rights.

Yet NAALC procedures generally had very limited policy consequences. The favorable impact that Mexican NAO public communications had on U.S. immigration enforcement policies and U.S. attention to the rights of Mexican migrant workers may have been one of the most unexpected outcomes of the NAALC—indeed, an unanticipated outcome in view of the overall asymmetries in power capabilities between Mexico and the United States and the Mexican government's distanced approach to NAALC proceedings. However, for most of the sociopolitical actors engaged in NAALC public communications, it was far more important that the U.S. and Canadian submissions did little either to correct the specific labor rights violations that gave rise to public communications or to alter Mexico's established model of state-labor relations.[320] Even though the U.S. and Canadian NAOs actively promoted public dialogue regarding freedom of association and the right to collective bargaining, NAALC procedures notably failed to provide strong protection overall for union organizing efforts in Mexico.

The principal constraint on NAALC procedures focused on labor rights in Mexico was that, from the time the agreement was signed in September 1993, U.S. sovereignty leverage over Mexico greatly declined. Mexico's trade dependence on the United States remained high, but as a confirmed NAFTA partner, its overall economic relationship with its northern neighbor was never at risk in disputes over labor rights. By explicit prior agreement, the potential financial or trade-related penalties under the NAALC were modest.[321] Still more important, the fact that it was the Mexican government (and not the individual companies that were actually responsible for labor rights violations) that was liable intrinsically linked any debate over sanctions to the overall character of the U.S.-Mexico bilateral relationship. Even at a time when the political imperative to demonstrate the efficacy of NAALC procedures was high, the Clinton administration backed away from a high-profile public communication (US 9801 / Aeroméxico flight attendants) that explicitly challenged the authority of the Mexican presidency.[322] The Clinton administration was similarly respectful of Mexico's sovereignty sensibilities in the ways it addressed other submissions as well.[323] During the George W. Bush administration, the conviction that issues other than NAALC labor rights communications were of greater importance in bilateral relations grew even stronger. The priority that both the U.S. and Mexican governments gave to the overall bilateral relationship is the most probable explanation for why the procedures employed to address NAALC public communications never graduated to the appointment of an evaluation committee of experts, much less an arbitral panel.[324]

These overall political constraints on NAALC procedures explain why U.S. and Canadian unions and labor- and human-rights NGOs had so little success in employing public communications to advance workers' rights in Mexico (and why their engagement with NAALC procedures declined over time).[325] Although participating in these actions certainly strengthened social capital among North American defenders of labor rights, neither the number of submitters engaged in particular communications nor the transnational character of many submitter coalitions had any clear impact on either final case outcome or observed policy impact. The most successful U.S. submission (US 9701/pregnancy testing) involved only four U.S. and Mexican NGOs. In contrast, the large trinational coalition assembled in US 2005-01 (Federal Labor Law reform, 2002) was unable to win even a formal review by the U.S. NAO. Perhaps even more important, because of the continuing political influence of old-guard labor organizations such as the CTM and the CROC, none of the NAALC coalitions, regardless of size, was able to mobilize strong domestic lobbying pressures to reform labor law and policy on freedom of association and the right to collective bargaining in Mexico.

The impact of NAALC procedures concerning Mexico was further constrained by a combination of issue salience and established legal jurisdiction. Given the character of the political coalition that underpinned Mexico's state-labor relations regime, it was in no way surprising that the Mexican government strongly and consistently resisted U.S. and Canadian pressures to modify labor law provisions and policies concerning freedom of association and the rights to organize and bargain collectively. The comparatively rapid steps that the federal government took to address pregnancy testing as a condition of employment contrast sharply with the absence of any real policy change concerning the use of secret ballots in recount elections to resolve competing unions' rival claims to workplace representation. And even when Mexican federal labor officials were prepared to back some independent unions' demands for legal recognition, their authority over developments in state-jurisdiction economic activities was constrained. In this regard, there was an underlying asymmetry in a number of the NAALC public communications. The strategic interest of many U.S. and Canadian unions lay in promoting independent union-led organizing campaigns in the maquiladora plants that posed the most immediate threats to their members.

These were, however, workplaces controlled by government-aligned unions and located in states where the maquiladora sector was of vital economic importance. Even when federal labor authorities accepted that real rights violations had occurred, these circumstances tested both their political loyalties and their jurisdictional mandate.

Despite its limitations, the NAALC experience was fundamentally important in establishing the terms of subsequent political debate in the United States regarding how to link labor rights protections to both bilateral and multilateral free-trade agreements. It also centrally defined the issue agenda in U.S-Mexican bargaining between 2012 and 2016 over Mexico's accession to the Trans-Pacific Partnership agreement and in trilateral negotiations between 2017 and 2019 over the labor provisions of the United States-Mexico-Canada Agreement that replaced the NAFTA in 2020.

CHAPTER 5

Legacies of the North American Agreement on Labor Cooperation

Labor Rights, U.S. Free-Trade Agreements, and U.S.-Mexican Negotiations over the Trans-Pacific Partnership, 2001–2017

The principal legacy of the North American Agreement on Labor Cooperation (NAALC) was the link it established between labor rights and free-trade agreements. Indeed, the precedent so clearly redefined the terms of political debate in the United States that, whereas the NAALC was a "side-agreement" to the North American Free Trade Agreement (NAFTA), all subsequent U.S. bilateral and multilateral free-trade agreements embedded labor provisions in the agreement itself.

Negotiations between the U.S. government and domestic labor rights advocates, on the one hand, and between the United States and the countries that were parties to these free-trade agreements (FTAs), on the other, produced variations in the specific terms of these provisions. Nevertheless, the NAALC experience shaped the subsequent U.S. approach to the labor provisions in these agreements in three broad ways. First, whereas the NAALC signatories' obligations were limited to the enforcement of existing national labor laws, post-NAFTA agreements made the principles articulated in the International Labour Organization's (ILO) 1998 Declaration on Fundamental Principles and Rights at Work the benchmark for assessing domestic labor rights and standards. Second, whereas the NAALC ordered possible enforcement actions in a three-tier hierarchy, U.S. FTAs negotiated or amended after 2007 made all covered labor rights (including collective-action rights) fully enforceable.[1] Third, in partial reaction to the NAALC experience, over time, the U.S. government shifted toward a strategy of pressuring potential FTA partners to adopt significant labor reforms in line with the ILO declaration as a precondition for accession to the agreement under negotiation.

This chapter examines the NAALC's legacies across different moments in which they influenced U.S. approaches to labor provisions in FTAs. The first section analyzes the labor rights provisions of the U.S. free-trade agreements that came into force between 2001 and 2012. It notes two important points of inflection in the evolving political debate over trade and labor rights: the ways in which the 1998 ILO declaration shifted the terms of reference concerning benchmark labor standards in these agreements and the impact of a 2007 U.S. bipartisan congressional-executive agreement that established a consensus concerning the core labor rights obligations in U.S. FTAs and defined the criteria by which labor complaints would be assessed in dispute-settlement procedures. This section also includes a detailed analysis of all the labor rights complaints filed under these post-NAFTA agreements between 2008 and 2016, including the controversial case involving Guatemala that severely tested the viability of these procedures.

None of these changes over time in the U.S. approach to the content and implementation of FTA labor provisions addressed unresolved questions concerning labor rights in Mexico. However, both the lessons U.S. stakeholders had absorbed from the NAALC experience itself and the NAALC legacies manifested in post-NAFTA FTAs set the terms for U.S.-Mexican interactions between 2012 and 2016 over Mexico's accession to the Trans-Pacific Partnership (TPP), a multilateral agreement to promote trade among twelve Pacific Basin countries. The second part of this chapter examines these intense, prolonged negotiations in depth, the result of which was the historically important reforms of the Mexican Constitution in 2017 that significantly strengthened the legal basis for democratic worker rights. These constitutional amendments opened, in turn, a debate about far-reaching reform of Mexican federal labor law that culminated in U.S.-Mexican negotiations between 2017 and 2019 over the labor provisions of a revised NAFTA, the United States-Mexico-Canada Agreement (chapter 6).

The negotiations and labor rights complaints discussed in this chapter constitute different tests of the United States' capacity to maximize its trade leverage to advance worker rights in developing countries. These include (1) the definition of the formal terms of labor provisions in bilateral or multilateral FTAs, including signatory parties' labor obligations and the criteria for resolving labor complaints; (2) U.S. pressures for potential trade partners to adopt significant domestic labor reforms as a prior condition for acceding to these agreements;

and (3) labor rights complaints procedures as a mechanism to ensure effective implementation of FTA labor provisions. The conclusion offers a comparative assessment of these different tests and lessons that can be drawn from them.

LABOR RIGHTS PROVISIONS IN POST-NAFTA U.S. FREE-TRADE AGREEMENTS: AGREEMENT CONTENT AND COMPLAINT RESOLUTION

Between the time the NAFTA took effect in 1994 and 2012, the United States negotiated bilateral or multilateral free-trade agreements with fourteen countries in which labor rights were a potentially controversial subject (listed in chronological order by the year in which the agreement entered into force): Jordan (2001), Chile (2004), Bahrain (2006), El Salvador (2006), Guatemala (2006), Honduras (2006), Morocco (2006), Nicaragua (2006), Dominican Republic (2007), Costa Rica (2009), Oman (2009), Peru (2009), Colombia (2012), and Panama (2012).[2] This section begins by examining key developments during this period that shaped the labor contents of these agreements, focusing particularly on the precedents set by the United States-Jordan Free Trade Agreement and the bipartisan congressional-executive agreement that Democrats and Republicans reached in 2007 concerning labor provisions in future U.S. free-trade agreements.

The second part of this section analyzes the eight labor rights submissions filed with the U.S. Department of Labor's Office of Trade and Labor Affairs (OTLA) under these post-NAFTA agreements between 2008 and 2016 against (in alphabetical order) Bahrain, Costa Rica, the Dominican Republic, Guatemala, Honduras, and Peru. In parallel with the assessment of NAALC public communications in chapter 4, this analysis considers the sociopolitical actors involved and the substantive focus of these complaints, the terms on which they were resolved, and the policy impact they had on collective-action labor rights in the target countries. The discussion concludes with a detailed examination of the labor complaint that was lodged against Guatemala in 2008 and finally resolved in 2017. This was the only complaint that proceeded through all stages of the dispute-settlement process. The failure of the U.S. government to win a favorable judgment against Guatemala, despite evidence of extensive labor rights violations and strong support from U.S. and Guatemalan labor organizations, raised serious questions about the enforceability of standard U.S. FTA labor provisions and significantly influenced the terms of debate over labor issues when NAFTA renegotiations began in 2017 (chapter 6).

The Context and Content of U.S. FTA Labor Rights Chapters

The NAFTA/NAALC experience left pending three major issues that shaped discussions over the labor contents of subsequent U.S. free-trade agreements. The first of these—whether labor rights provisions would henceforth constitute a regular part of the agreement—was the simplest to resolve in political terms. The NAALC's position as a side-agreement had arisen from the timing of its negotiation following the conclusion of negotiations over the NAFTA. The U.S. domestic debate over the merits of including labor (and environmental) provisions in trade agreements continued, but if they were included, no major stakeholder could easily justify relegating labor rights to a lesser formal status than investment protections or intellectual property rights.[3] As a consequence, beginning with the 2001 U.S.-Jordan agreement (where the discussion of labor issues was limited to a single page), all later U.S. FTAs included a separate labor chapter. By extension, this meant that alleged labor rights violations would henceforth be addressed through procedures established in the agreement's chapter on dispute settlement, which also constituted a significant departure from the separate public communication process created by the NAALC.

Two other questions were, however, more difficult to resolve: how to define the labor rights and standards that were to be protected under the agreement and what criteria would determine whether labor violations would incur monetary and/or trade-linked sanctions.

The NAALC had avoided the issue of common labor rights and standards by merely requiring that Canada, Mexico, and the United States each enforce their own labor laws without any obligation to improve them over time (chapter 4). Both national sovereignty considerations in what were then novel discussions about the appropriate extent of external involvement in sensitive domestic affairs and negotiation time pressures made that the simplest position to adopt. At the time, this approach seemed defensible because Mexico's constitution and federal labor law formally offered strong labor protections; the principal concern was effective labor law enforcement.[4] It was, however, impossible to make a similar claim for some of the developing countries with which the United States subsequently negotiated free-trade agreements.

The U.S.-Jordan agreement, the first U.S. FTA negotiated after the NAFTA, reflected the emerging international consensus that the ILO's 1998 Declaration on Fundamental Principles and Rights at Work defined an appropriate set of fundamental labor rights (see table 1.1).[5] The agreement retained the NAALC's key formulation that each party's principal obligation was the effective enforcement of its own labor laws.[6] However, it qualified this formulation by referencing the parties' commitments under the ILO declaration (article 6.1) and by defining "labor laws" as those statutes and regulations directly related to freedom of association, the rights to organize and bargain collectively, a prohibition on the use of any form of forced or compulsory labor, a minimum age for the employment of children, and acceptable conditions of work with respect to minimum wages, hours of work, and occupational safety and health (article 6.6). The inclusion of "acceptable conditions of work," drawn from language in the U.S. Generalized System of Preferences (GSP) program and other U.S. trade legislation, went beyond the 1998 ILO declaration. Yet the U.S.-Jordan agreement (and other U.S. FTAs that entered into force before 2007) omitted the declaration's reference to "elimination of discrimination in the workplace."[7] Most notably, the U.S.-Jordan FTA (and all subsequent trade agreements the United States negotiated before the revision of the NAFTA in 2019) failed to follow the NAALC precedent in explicitly recognizing the right to strike, compensation for workplace injuries, and the protection of migrant workers.

The United States was prepared to define labor rights in line with the 1998 ILO declaration because its language paralleled the "internationally recognized worker rights" included in the labor provisions of existing U.S. trade legislation. Invoking the ILO declaration was an important political advance for labor rights advocates.[8] Yet observing those rights was not a binding legal obligation under the terms of the U.S.-Jordan agreement; the parties only agreed to "strive to ensure that such labor principles and the internationally recognized labor rights . . . are recognized and protected by domestic law" (article 6.1). The United States and Jordan did agree (article 6.2), however, that "it is inappropriate to encourage trade by relaxing domestic labor laws." Moreover, they agreed to "strive to ensure" that they did not waive or otherwise derogate from these labor standards in order to promote trade (a phrase that in later U.S. FTAs was expanded to include investment).

The U.S.-Jordan FTA also set significant precedents regarding the criteria to be employed in resolving labor rights disputes.[9] Most important, article 6.4(a) stated:

> A Party shall not fail to effectively enforce its labor laws, through a sustained or recurring course of action or inaction, in a manner affecting trade between the Parties.

The "in a manner affecting trade" wording had originally arisen in the contentious 1997–1998 debate over the U.S. congressional renewal of presidential authority to negotiate trade agreements on a "fast-track" basis. Officials in President William J. (Bill) Clinton's administration (1993–1997, 1997–2001) sought language that would bridge the political gap between organized labor's and congressional Democrats' insistence on including labor (and environmental) provisions in future FTAs and staunch business and Republican opposition to any such action.[10] The provision containing this formulation in the U.S.-Jordan agreement, which in later U.S. FTAs was also expanded to include investment, did not distinguish (or create an enforcement hierarchy) among recognized labor rights as the NAALC had done. Nevertheless, it established an enforcement standard more stringent than that employed by the U.S. GSP program, under which claims of labor rights violations need not demonstrate any economic effect, or the review procedures for public communications regarding most of the recognized labor principles in the NAALC. In effect, it was more restrictive than even the limiting criterion (that the labor violation in question be trade-related) the NAALC set for a public communication involving occupational safety and health, child labor, or minimum wage issues to go before an evaluation committee of experts and an arbitral panel (chapter 4). In determining whether a government had systematically failed to meet its labor obligations, the U.S.-Jordan agreement, like the NAALC (article 49.1), recognized a country's right to exercise discretion in its allocation of labor enforcement resources (article 6.4(b)).

The emerging political consensus around these issues in the United States coalesced in the Bipartisan Trade Promotion Authority Act of 2002 (the legislation that renewed presidential authority to negotiate trade agreements on a fast-track basis)[11] and particularly in the Bipartisan Agreement on Trade Policy (BATP) reached by the George W. Bush administration (2001–2005, 2005–2009) and congressional Democrats and Republicans on May 10, 2007.[12] Democrats, who had not controlled the U.S. House of Representatives since January 1995, won a 233-202 majority in the 2006 midterm elections. In 2005, the Dominican Republic-Central America-United States Trade Agreement (DR-CAFTA) sparked intense controversy because, with the possible exception of Costa Rica, it included countries with notably poor labor rights records for which the standard "effective enforcement of domestic labor law" obligation was highly questionable.[13] Moreover, because the free-trade agreement removed these countries from the U.S. GSP program, it eliminated the main U.S. enforcement mechanism for addressing labor rights problems in them.[14] As a consequence, Democrats were strongly committed to strengthening the labor provisions in U.S. FTAs. Confronted by a legislative stalemate over pending agreements with Colombia, Panama, Peru, and the Republic of Korea,[15] and with President Bush's fast-track trade negotiating authority set to end on June 30, 2007, Republicans—despite continued opposition from business organizations[16]—acceded to Democrats' demand that free-trade agreements henceforth negotiated by the United States include "an enforceable commitment to adopt and effectively enforce . . . basic labor standards."[17]

What became widely known as the "May 10 agreement" stipulated that U.S. trade agreements would incorporate an:

> enforceable obligation for the countries to adopt and maintain in their laws and practice the five basic internationally-recognized labor principles, as stated in the ILO Declaration on Fundamental Principles and Rights at Work.[18]

These five principles were: "freedom of association; the effective recognition of the right to collective bargaining; the elimination of all forms of forced or compulsory labor; the effective abolition of child labor and a prohibition on the worst forms of child labor; and the elimination of discrimination in respect of employment and occupation." However, some U.S. political actors and business interests remained concerned that embracing ILO conventions nos. 87 (on freedom of association and the right to organize) and particularly 98 (on the right to organize and to bargain collectively), neither of which the United States had ratified, might call into question some aspects of existing U.S. labor law.[19] At issue were the so-called right-to-work provisions of the federal Taft-Hartley Act (Labor Management Relations Act of 1947, section 14[b]) that allowed individual

U.S. states to adopt legislation permitting workers to be employed in unionized workplaces without actually joining the union or paying union dues. The May 10 agreement, therefore, emphasized that the obligation referred only to the key principles articulated in the 1998 declaration rather than to the specific ILO conventions they referenced.[20]

In addition, the agreement specified that any allegation of nonenforcement of labor obligations must demonstrate "a sustained or recurring course of action or inaction" and must occur "in a manner affecting trade or investment between the parties." It reversed the U.S.-Jordan precedent by stipulating that governmental discretion in the allocation of labor enforcement resources did not constitute a valid excuse for failing to enforce laws and regulations related to the ILO declaration principles. Furthermore, those obligations would henceforth be subject to dispute-settlement procedures and remedies (fines and/or trade-linked sanctions, based on the amount of trade injury) that paralleled commercial obligations.[21] As in the commercial provisions of trade agreements, decisions by dispute-settlement panels would not be self-executing and would not, therefore, alter any U.S. law. Finally, the agreement stipulated that only a government could invoke dispute settlement against another government for alleged violations of its labor obligations.[22]

The wording of the May 10 agreement followed the ILO declaration standards by requiring "*effective recognition of* the right to collective bargaining" and the "*effective* abolition of child labor" (emphasis added), and it specified that free-trade agreements negotiated under its terms would add "acceptable conditions of work" to the declaration principles.[23] Moreover, later agreements moved beyond the U.S.-Jordan FTA by stating that the signatory parties "shall ensure" (rather than "strive to ensure") that their domestic laws conformed to the ILO principles, with a similar change in language regarding the waiver or derogation of rights in order to promote trade or investment. Although the U.S.-Jordan agreement had not established a formal public submissions process to address alleged labor rights violations, subsequent U.S. FTAs created either a subcommittee on labor affairs (comprised of labor ministry officials) or a cabinet-level labor affairs council as permanent bodies responsible for overseeing cooperative consultations and dispute-settlement panels.[24] Each partner country established its own requirements and procedures for addressing public submissions alleging labor rights violations. (In the United States, for example, the OTLA retained the operational regulations in effect since December 2006).[25] These processes, like the NAALC, allowed a broad range of sociopolitical actors to submit complaints. All of the post-2007 U.S. FTAs also included trade-linked sanctions among the potential penalties for proven labor rights violations.[26]

One further significant development in the United States' post-NAFTA approach to labor rights/trade linkage involved the strategy employed to advance labor rights in prospective partner countries. Even during the original NAFTA debate, there had been some critics of the agreement who argued that Mexico should be required to implement major political reforms (including measures to protect labor rights) before the agreement went into effect.[27] During the 2000s, especially with regard to the controversial DR-CAFTA negotiations, the United States shifted toward this approach.[28] In the case of DR-CAFTA, the Central American countries requested that the ILO assess whether their labor laws conformed to its core standards. All of them except El Salvador had ratified the eight fundamental ILO conventions on which the 1998 Declaration was based, but the ILO concluded that labor law enforcement was a serious, unresolved problem.[29] Labor and trade officials in the DR-CAFTA countries then prepared a white paper to guide their proposed reform initiatives,[30] and the U.S. government appropriated US$180 million over a five-year period to support these efforts.[31] Similarly, in the course of final interactions with the United States over the United States-Peru Trade Promotion Agreement, the Peruvian government enacted laws to penalize employers for anti-union discrimination and interference with workers' freedom of association.[32] In addition, it reduced legal barriers to the right to strike, and it agreed to address U.S. congressional concerns about the ways that the abuse of subcontracting arrangements undercut core labor rights by creating a national oversight program to regulate temporary labor contracts and by establishing special administrative and judicial channels to benefit the workers employed on them.[33] Several other countries also adopted significant labor reforms just before or during free-trade negotiations with the United States.[34] In none of these cases was accession to the proposed trade agreement formally conditioned on prior approval of labor reforms, but the public controversies that frequently arose in the United States around these FTAs made this a practical political requirement in order to secure U.S. congressional approval.

The most prominent example of this new U.S. approach involved Colombia. Severe, persistent anti-union violence in the country sparked heated political debates in the United States over the merits of a free-trade agreement with the country.[35] On June 28, 2007, the U.S. and Colombian governments agreed to a protocol of amendment that modified the labor provisions of the prospective United States-Colombia Trade Promotion Agreement, which had been signed on November 22, 2006, in accordance with the BATP. Even then, however, the understanding among U.S. policymakers was that something more would be required in order to smooth passage of the agreement through the U.S. Congress.[36] The U.S. and Colombian governments, with only limited input from labor organizations in the two countries,[37] therefore eventually proceeded to negotiate a detailed "Colombian Action Plan Related to Labor Rights" (April 7, 2011) that addressed necessary labor rights and criminal justice reforms.

The Colombian government's commitments under the plan included (each with specified time frames and tight deadlines for implementation): reestablishing a separate ministry of labor; expanding the personal protection program operated by the Ministry of the Interior and Justice to include trade unionists under threat for their activities and augmenting the number of judicial police investigators (accompanied by an appropriate increase in available budgetary resources) assigned exclusively to criminal cases of violence against union members and activists; hiring an additional 480 labor inspectors over four years and identifying five priority sectors (palm oil, sugar, mines, ports, and the cut-flower industry) for workplace inspections; enacting legal reforms to establish criminal penalties for employers who undermined the rights to organize and bargain collectively; and adopting measures to combat employers' misuse of subcontracting arrangements to circumvent labor rights. The U.S. and Colombian governments agreed, moreover, that both technical staff and senior officials would meet several times a year during the 2011–2013 period to assess progress in implementing these measures. The Colombian government also reached agreement with private sector representatives and some trade unions to seek ILO assistance with implementing the action plan.[38] Finally, the U.S. Department of Labor (U.S. DOL) awarded Colombia grants totaling US$25 million between 2012 and 2017 to strengthen the country's labor enforcement capacity, promote workers' awareness of their rights and their ability to defend them, and reduce child labor and promote safe working conditions in the nonformal mining sector.[39]

At the time the action plan was publicly announced, President Barack Obama (2009–2013, 2013–2017) made it clear that he expected Colombia to meet the plan's targets and deadlines before he submitted the bilateral free-trade agreement to the U.S. Congress, making successful implementation of key parts of the plan a precondition for the agreement to enter into force.[40] In fact, his administration pressed to make the action plan part of the trade agreement itself. However, Republicans had regained a majority in the House of Representatives in the 2010 midterm elections, and they staunchly refused to accept any formal link between the plan and the FTA.[41] The trade agreement did finally win U.S. legislative approval,[42] yet a number of opponents cited the absence of such a link (and the fact that the U.S. government could not, therefore, formally enforce the plan's terms) as a major reason for voting against it.[43] In support of his position on this issue, Representative James McDermott (Democrat-Washington) cited the labor enforcement problems that had arisen with Mexico because of the NAALC's status as only a side-agreement to the NAFTA.[44]

Labor Complaints in Post-NAFTA Free-Trade Agreements

Over the period between 2008 and 2016, there were eight complaints filed with the OTLA concerning alleged labor rights violations in seven different U.S. FTA partner countries. In chronological order, the submissions addressed problems in Guatemala (2008), Costa Rica (2010), Peru (2010), Bahrain (2011), the Dominican Republic (2011), Honduras (2012), Peru (2015), and Colombia (2016).[45] (See appendix C for an annotated list of these submissions.) This discussion does not include the 2006 complaint against Jordan that the American Federation of Labor-Congress of Industrial Organizations (AFL-CIO) filed with the Office of the United States Trade Representative (USTR) because complete information concerning the case, including the review procedure followed, is not publicly available.[46]

The AFL-CIO was the most prominent submitter of non-NAALC labor complaints. Indeed, either acting alone (one case) or in coalition with trade unions and/or labor-rights nongovernmental organizations (NGOs) based in the target country (three cases), it was by far the most active participant in these processes (see table 5.1).[47] The International Longshore and Warehouse Union (ILWU), in alliance with two Costa Rican labor organizations, filed the 2010 complaint against Costa Rica. Labor- and human-rights NGOs participated in four of the seven submissions (57.1 percent). For example, in the 2015 submission against Peru, the U.S.-based International Labor Rights Fund (ILRF) led a coalition of seven Peruvian unions and one Peruvian indigenous-rights NGO.

TABLE 5.1 Public submissions to the U.S. Office of Trade and Labor Affairs (OTLA), 2008–2016

OTLA case number	Type and number of submitters			Binational submitter coalition	Case duration (in days)	Political support in target country	Final case outcome	Observed policy impact
	Unions	NGOs	Total					
US 2008-01 (Guatemala)	7	0	7	Yes	268	Strong	CC, DS	0
US 2010 (Costa Rica)	3	0	3	Yes	NA	Strong	W	0
US 2010-03 (Peru)	1	0	1	No	610	Strong	R	1
US 2011-01 (Bahrain)	1	0	1	No	609	Strong	CC	0
US 2011-03 (Dominican Republic)	0	1	1	No	645	Weak	R	0
US 2012-01 (Honduras)	26	1	27	Yes	1,068	Strong	CC	1
US 2015-01 (Peru)	7	2	9	Yes	239	Strong	R	0
US 2016-02 (Colombia)	5	1	6	Yes	240	Strong	CC	0

Sources: Author's review of OTLA submissions and public reports (available at U.S. Department of Labor, "Submission Under the Labor Provisions of Free Trade Agreements," accessed February 15, 2021, www.dol.gov/agencies/ilab/our-work/trade/fta-submissions); *Inside U.S. Trade*, August 13, 2010 and May 6, 2011. U.S. Department of State, "2019 Country Reports on Human Rights Practices," section 7: Worker Rights, accessed March 18, 2021, www.state.gov/reports/2019-country-reports-on-human-rights-practices/.

Notes: No case number is available for the 2010 submission concerning Costa Rica. NGO = nongovernmental organization; NA = Not available.

Coding scheme for political support in target country:

Weak = nominal (if any) trade union and/or labor rights NGO support for an OTLA petition because of government intimidation or repression, overall labor movement weakness, or the absence or weakness of politically independent unions

Moderate = trade union and/or labor rights NGO public endorsement of an OTLA petition, sometimes including involvement in petition design and documentation

Strong = active trade union and/or labor rights NGO engagement with the OTLA petition process, with some unions publicly calling for OTLA review, signing or cosigning a submission, pressing for domestic legal and policy reforms, and monitoring reform implementation in coordination with the OTLA

Final case outcome: The OTLA's final disposition of the case: CC = cooperative consultations held; DS = dispute-settlement procedures invoked; R = accepted for review; W = submitters withdrew the case.

Coding scheme for observed policy impact:

0 = no observed changes regarding freedom of association and the rights to organize and bargain collectively within two years after the OTLA issued a final report, even if there were improvements in other labor rights policies during or after the OTLA review

1 = modest policy change regarding freedom of association and the rights to organize and bargain collectively during the specified period

2 = modification of labor code provisions regarding freedom of association and the rights to organize and bargain collectively during the specified period

3 = extension of favorable formal collective-action labor code provisions to the public sector and any export-processing zones during the specified period

4 = evidence that within two years after the OTLA issued a final report there was generally effective implementation in practice of freedom of association and the rights to organize and bargain collectively, including in the public sector and any export-processing zones

Five of these submissions (62.5 percent) were filed by binational coalitions, with the AFL-CIO and the ILRF taking the lead. The complaints against Peru in 2010 and the Dominican Republic in 2011 were exceptions in this regard. The former case (US 2010-03) was filed by a single Peruvian labor organization without any U.S. allies. The latter submission (US 2011-03) was filed by Father Christopher Hartley, a British-Spanish Catholic missionary priest then associated with the Madrid-based Mission of Mercy (Misión de la Misericordia). Hartley had, since the late 1990s, worked to end the egregious labor rights violations suffered by immigrant Haitian workers employed in the Dominican Republic's sugar cane industry.

In the five cases in which the AFL-CIO (US 2008-01, US 2011-01, US 2012-01, US 2016-02) and the ILRF (US 2015-01) took the lead, the quality of the submission materials reflected their close collaboration with local trade union and NGO allies in the target country. These interactions allowed the submitters to document in persuasive detail both general patterns and specific instances of government and/or employer abuses and major failures of government labor enforcement policy. For instance, the filing against Guatemala (US 2008-01) included case studies of five individual companies in a range of export-focused economic activities, while the second submission concerning Peru (US 2015-01) referenced eight firms in the textile and garment industries and export agriculture. Similarly, the submission regarding Colombia (US 2016-02) cited examples from the oil and sugar sectors to illustrate the extent of illegal subcontracting practices.[48] The complaint against Honduras (US 2012-01) featured a total of eighteen case studies of a range of labor violations (the frequent firing of union leaders,[49] employers' abuse of subcontracting arrangements to block unionization, widespread child labor violations, and serious shortcomings in the government's labor inspection and enforcement regimes) in the apparel and auto-parts industries, export agriculture, and Puerto Cortez port facilities.

These submissions principally focused on freedom of association and the right to collective bargaining in U.S. FTA partner countries. However, the contexts and specific ways in which these rights had been infringed varied greatly. The first filing against the Peruvian government (US 2010-03) was framed quite narrowly: the National Union of United Customs and Tax Administration Workers (Sindicato Nacional de Unidad de Trabajadores de la Superintendencia Nacional de Aduanas y de Administración Tributaria) appealed to the OTLA to compel the Lima-Callao Regional Bureau of Labor and Employment Promotion to engage in collective bargaining over wage issues and, if negotiations failed, to accept binding arbitration as provided for under Peruvian law.[50] Similarly, in the case involving Costa Rica (US 2010),[51] the ILWU and its cosubmitters complained that the Costa Rican government had violated the collective-action rights of the Union of Atlantic-side Port Administration Workers (Sindicato de Trabajadores de la Junta Administradora Portuaria de la Vertiente Atlántica, SINTRAJAP) by illegally ousting its elected leadership in an attempt to undercut the union's opposition to the privatization of the Atlantic ports of Limón and Moin.

In contrast, the second filing concerning Peru (US 2015-01) and the submission against Colombia (US 2016-02) raised much broader issues by documenting widespread employer abuses of short-term or temporary labor contracts. In Peru, special export-promotion legislation in the textile and garment manufacturing industry and in export agriculture allowed companies to hire workers on an unlimited series of consecutive short-term contracts.[52] These hiring arrangements posed an obstacle to unionization because they prolonged workers' job insecurity and dissuaded them from protest. Moreover, because employers were not legally required to give any reason for failing to renew these contracts, they often manipulated short-term contracts to fire union leaders and members as a way of obstructing union formation.[53]

Similarly, in Colombia, many employers resorted to short-term contracting via so-called labor mediation arrangements (cooperatives, temporary employment agencies, and so forth) as a way of avoiding direct employment relationships and thereby blocking unionization. One of the Colombian cosubmitters, the Petroleum Industry Workers' Union (Unión Sindical Obrera de la Industria del Petróleo), had been badly undercut by extensive illegal subcontracting, systematic employer resistance to collective bargaining, and inadequate inspections and enforcement by the Ministry of Labor.[54] And in the case concerning the Dominican Republic (US 2011-03), sustained employer opposition to the unionization of migrant Haitian canecutters was closely linked to many other serious labor rights violations in the sugar industry. These included employment practices that held workers in conditions of forced or compulsory labor, extensive problems with respect to conditions of employment (minimum wages, hours of work, occupational safety and health), and violations of child labor laws.[55]

Most notably, the submissions concerning Bahrain, Colombia, and Guatemala highlighted the political repression and violence often directed against trade union leaders and labor activists in these countries.[56] Once again, however, the character of these threats differed substantially. In Bahrain, the government's campaign against trade unions (including the arrest of union leaders and the widespread firing of labor activists in both the public and private sectors) and its suspension of labor rights guarantees under a state of emergency (followed by legislation that severely restricted labor organization and representation) were linked to a specific domestic political crisis: the government of Bahrain's repression of "Arab Spring" political protests, including two general strikes, in February–March 2011. The OTLA complaint filed by the AFL-CIO, working closely with the General Federation of Bahrain Trade Unions, called upon the U.S. government to withdraw from the U.S.-Bahrain Free Trade Agreement if the Bahraini government did not cease its campaign against unions and fully restore labor rights.

In both Guatemala (see below) and Colombia, serious anti-union violence and the obstacles it posed to the exercise of freedom of association and the rights to organize and bargain collectively were long-standing human rights problems. In Colombia, the AFL-CIO and the Colombian organizations submitting the OTLA complaint reported ninety-nine murders, sixty-six attempted murders, seven forced disappearances, and six kidnappings of trade unionists between May 2012 (when the United States-Colombia Trade Promotion Agreement took effect) and April 2016, as well as many other instances of harassment and arbitrary detention.[57] Even though Colombia's Ministry of the Interior and Justice had created a National Protection Unit to safeguard potentially vulnerable individuals from threats of violence,[58] and although the number of murders of trade unionists had declined somewhat over time, Colombian police and judicial authorities had proved woefully incapable of ending the plague of anti-union violence.[59]

In all of the cases except the submissions concerning Costa Rica (US 2010), Bahrain (US 2011-01), and the first filing against Peru (US 2010-03), one of the main complaints was the ineffectiveness of governments' enforcement of existing labor law rather than the need to adopt constitutional and/or legal reforms to bring a country's domestic labor legislation in line with international norms. For example, prior to U.S. congressional approval of the United States-Peru Trade Promotion Agreement in November–December 2007, the Peruvian government had agreed to create a national oversight program to regulate temporary labor contracts and to establish administrative and judicial safeguards for the workers employed on them. However, it never acted on those commitments.[60] The Colombian government had also failed to implement laws it adopted to regulate labor intermediation, and although Colombian labor organizations had filed many complaints under a revised criminal code article that barred employer violations of workers' freedom of association, the government had not managed to win a single conviction.[61] As a consequence, in Colombia (and in other countries as well), it was common for employers simply to refuse to obey labor ministry and/ or labor court orders. Especially in labor-intensive export production, employers would frequently threaten to (or actually) close plants or reincorporate them under different names in order to avoid unionization and evade government enforcement actions.[62]

In contrast to the NAALC experience, the OTLA accepted for review all but one of the U.S. FTA labor rights complaints it received between 2008 and 2016. (In the Costa Rica case, the ILWU and its allies withdrew the submission before the OTLA reached a decision on whether to accept it for review.[63]) The OTLA acted consistently in this regard despite differences in the national identity of the submitting organization(s) or individual. Nor did it differ between the George W. Bush (2005–2009) and Obama (2009–2013, 2013–2017) administrations. In its reviews, the OTLA followed the same procedural guidelines that governed post-2006 public communications under the NAALC (one requirement of which was that it consult with both the USTR and the U.S. Department of State). Officials at the OTLA based their reviews on the submission statement and supporting documents, information they requested from the target government, and frequently on materials prepared on the same country by the ILO's Committee on Freedom of Association and Committee of Experts on the Application of Conventions and Recommendations.[64] The OTLA departed from NAALC practice by not convening public hearings on any of the U.S. FTA submissions it accepted for review. However, it conducted site visits in all of the countries involved: one each in the two submissions regarding Peru and the filing against Colombia; two each in the submissions regarding Bahrain, the Dominican Republic, and Guatemala; and four in the case concerning Honduras. During these investigative missions, OTLA officials typically met with government officials (often from several different ministries), labor organizations, employers, other stakeholders, and sometimes individual workers (including 71 workers employed in the Dominican Republic sugar sector and approximately 100 workers in several different industries in Honduras).[65] In only three of these seven submissions (42.9 percent) did the OTLA complete its review within, or close to, the stipulated target period of 240 days. Case duration times ranged from 239 days (Peru 2015) to 1,068 days (2.9 years; Honduras) and averaged 526 days (1.4 years, $N = 7$) (table 5.1).[66]

The final public reports released by the OTLA were thorough and extensively documented, often in forensic detail.[67] Most significant, the OTLA found in the complainants' favor in all seven of these submissions. Indeed, OTLA officials frequently judged the submissions sufficiently credible that in several of their public reports, they based their overall conclusions in part on the detailed information provided in the original complaints.[68] In three cases (Dominican Republic, Peru 2010, Peru 2015), the review process ended with publication of the OTLA report. In the four other cases (Bahrain, Colombia, Guatemala, Honduras), however, U.S. officials undertook cooperative consultations with their counterparts in the target countries. In the case of Guatemala (see below), they eventually initiated formal dispute-settlement procedures to resolve the issues in contention (table 5.1).

In all these cases except Peru (2010), the OTLA concluded its report with specific recommendations to the partner country that served both as a basis for subsequent bilateral discussions of the issues in question and as a checklist for follow-up OTLA monitoring.[69] For example, it called on the government of Bahrain to prohibit discrimination in employment based on political and religious opinion; repeal a ban on multisectoral labor federations; and amend the prohibitions on trade unions engaging in political activities, strikes in "strategic undertakings," and union formation in the public sector.[70] In its report on submission US 2011-03 (Dominican Republic), the OTLA listed eleven recommendations to strengthen labor inspections and law enforcement in the sugar sector,[71] and between April 2014 and May 2018, it subsequently issued six periodic reviews (each preceded by another site visit to the country) assessing progress in their implementation. Similarly, in submission US 2012-01, the OTLA first consulted with union and NGO representatives and then provided the government of Honduras with a list of seven recommendations for major policy reforms.[72] The OTLA did not recommend formal cooperative consultations with the government of Peru on US 2015-01. However, its public report recommended specific steps to strengthen the regulation of short-term work contracts,[73] and it tracked subsequent Peruvian (in)action in follow-up reports released in December 2016 and April 2018.

Only in the cases of Guatemala (see below) and Honduras did negotiations between U.S. and partner-country government officials result in formal action plans to address the labor rights violations discussed in the OTLA reports. In the latter case, the two governments released a detailed "Labor Rights Monitoring and Action Plan" in December 2015 that listed concrete actions the Honduran government would take over the period through September 2018 to ensure effective enforcement of laws related to freedom of association and collective bargaining.[74] Its principal focus was on improving the rigor of workplace inspections (including by enacting a new inspection law) and investigations of alleged incidents of unlawful dismissal of union leaders and members, employer interference in union activity, and anti-union reprisals; ensuring the consistent application of tougher sanctions on the companies where violations occurred; and eradicating child labor. In each area, the agreement specified intended outcomes, implementation time periods, and measurable criteria for evaluating progress.[75] Moreover, the Honduran government committed to sharing legislation, regulations, and other measures to improve labor enforcement with both U.S. authorities and with Honduran trade unions, NGOs, and business stakeholders organized in a tripartite follow-up commission.[76] In support of the plan, the U.S. Department of Labor funded a US$7 million project coordinated by World Vision, a religious nonprofit organization focused on child welfare, to combat exploitative child labor and improve labor rights and working conditions.

Following up on these actions, U.S. officials took several steps to promote target governments' compliance with their policy recommendations. First, following release of the final OTLA report on a particular submission, they continued negotiations with counterpart officials on a sustained basis, often in conjunction with return site visits to the country in question.[77] For instance, following agreement on a labor action plan in December 2015, U.S. labor officials held in-person technical discussions and high-level policy meetings with their Honduran counterparts on implementation actions on sixteen occasions between January 2016 and December 2018.[78] Second, in several cases, the U.S. DOL provided FTA partners with significant technical and financial assistance to strengthen their labor enforcement capacity and correct specific problems, such as the abuse of child labor.[79] For example, it granted the government of Peru US$2 million to help it improve its enforcement of regulations covering subcontracting and short-term employment contracts in nontraditional export industries.[80] The U.S. DOL also initially offered US$10 million to the Dominican Republic to combat illegal child labor and improve labor rights and working conditions in the agricultural sector, but the program was suspended in September 2014 because of the government's inadequate commitment to reform.[81] However, in 2017, it agreed to provide US$5 million in support for an ILO-coordinated project to strengthen the Dominican Republic's labor inspection capabilities.[82]

Third, in some cases, the U.S. government brought high-level diplomatic pressure to bear on a target country. For instance, in January 2014, both U.S. Secretary of Labor Thomas E. Perez and U.S. Assistant Secretary of State for Western Hemisphere Affairs Roberta S. Jacobson met with senior Honduran labor officials to discuss necessary policy reforms.[83] In August 2016, Secretary Perez led the U.S. delegation attending the second-term inauguration of Dominican President Danilo Medina (2012–2016, 2016–2020), where he underscored U.S. concerns about worker rights in the sugar industry.[84] Similarly, in November 2016, both Secretary Perez and President Obama personally raised the issues highlighted in the OTLA 2015-01 public report with Peruvian President Pedro Pablo Kuczynski (2016–2018).[85] These actions were symbolically important, but they did not always translate into a more effective reform process in the target country. In the Dominican Republic, for example, even though forced labor and child labor abuses had been central elements in both the US 2011-03 submission and the OTLA's final report on the filing, follow-up negotiations between U.S. and Dominican officials focused principally on policy reforms that granted immigrant Haitian workers access to the national social security system and measures taken by sugar companies to improve working conditions in the field (for instance, providing ready access to potable water). These were undoubtedly welcome improvements for the sugar workers affected. Nevertheless, they fell well short of resolving the most high-profile labor violations in the industry, where serious forced labor abuses persisted.[86]

Moreover, six of the seven labor complaints under discussion here (85.7 percent) received strong domestic political support in the target country (table 5.1). The coalitions of trade unions and labor- and human-rights NGOs backing the submissions against Bahrain, Colombia, Guatemala, Honduras, and Peru (2015) were particularly impressive. Of these, the case involving Honduras mobilized the largest submitter coalition, with twenty-five local labor organizations and one labor-rights NGO joining the AFL-CIO. The coalition included six national federations or confederations and unions representing workers in several important economic sectors (the garment and apparel industry, banana production, agricultural and agroindustrial activities, and railroads, ports, and the merchant marine). In all six of these submissions, local support for the OTLA complaints was presumably strong enough to register in domestic political terms. The strongest evidence of this was in Honduras, where trade unions and other labor-rights groups had sufficient credibility that the government included them on the Tripartite Follow-up Commission that negotiated a national response to the OTLA's policy recommendations and later oversaw implementation of the 2015 labor action plan.[87]

Nevertheless, despite concerted U.S. efforts and substantial domestic support in a number of target countries, the observed policy impacts of these complaints—evidence that target governments took steps to strengthen laws and/or policies concerning collective-action rights (freedom of association and the rights to organize and bargain collectively) within two years after the OTLA issued its final report—were generally disappointing.[88] Only in the first filing against Peru (US 2010-03) and in the submission involving Honduras (US 2012-01) did the OTLA process clearly contribute to modest improvements. In Peru, the government issued a series of executive decrees to strengthen collective bargaining laws by, for example, confirming that arbitration is mandatory when requested by either party in a collective labor dispute and establishing a National Registry of Collective Bargaining Arbitrators.[89] In Honduras, the government responded to U.S. pressures by adopting, in January 2017, a new law strengthening the labor inspections regime and by substantially increasing budgetary allocations to support inspection capacity. The law established significantly higher fines for labor violations and created a presumption of noncompliance if an employer blocked workplace inspections.[90] Both cases are scored "1" in table 5.1.[91]

The observed policy impacts of the other five submissions examined here (71.4 percent of the total, N = 7) are scored "0" in table 5.1. In Bahrain, although U.S. pressures (in conjunction with strong efforts by the ILO) led to the reinstatement of many (but not all) of the public sector workers who had been fired in February–March 2011, the government did not alter any of the restrictive labor laws it enacted in the wake of the 2011 crisis.[92] In several cases in which the OTLA recommended detailed steps to strengthen countries' labor enforcement capacities, the target countries adopted incremental measures to address U.S. concerns, but they were often very modest indeed. For example, in Peru (US 2015-01), despite personal interventions by President Obama and Secretary Perez, the OTLA's April 2018 progress review found little substantive progress. The government had expanded the number of department-level inspection offices and increased budgetary allocations to both the inspection program and the Ministry of Labor and Promotion of Employment. However, there had been no real changes in law or in inspection protocols to deal with the problem of employer abuse of short-term contracts to obstruct freedom of association and collective bargaining.[93]

The Colombian case is particularly instructive in this regard. As previously noted, in 2011, the U.S. and Colombian governments agreed to a detailed labor action plan that addressed key U.S. concerns regarding violence against trade unionists and the overall protection of labor rights. A subsequent five-year review of plan implementation credited the Colombian government with taking a number of important actions. These included: reestablishing an independent ministry of labor in 2011; enhancing criminal penalties for violence against trade unionists and for employer actions that undermined the right to organize and bargain collectively; substantially increasing the number of labor inspectors; cracking down on employers' creation of fake worker cooperatives to obstruct unionization; and reducing the incidence of violence against union leaders and members.[94] Yet, the review also found that, although reform measures had reduced the magnitude of major problems, all of them persisted. For example, no union member under the supervision of the National Protection Unit had been killed since its inception in 2011, but approximately three hundred union members still required armored vehicles and/or bodyguards for full-time protection.[95]

The public report the OTLA issued in January 2017 after its review of submission US 2016-02 reached similar conclusions. It criticized, and called for specific actions to remedy, the inadequacies of Colombia's labor inspection system (particularly in rural areas and with regard to abusive subcontracting arrangements), the administrative complexities and long delays involved in filing a labor complaint, and the government's overall inability to collect the fines levied against sanctioned employers.[96] The report particularly condemned "the history of and continued high rate of impunity in cases of threats and violence against unionists" and the ways in which anti-union violence undermined the freedom of association.[97]

Several factors—Colombia was a functioning electoral democracy and a close diplomatic ally of the United States, and the 2016 OTLA submission was strongly backed by the country's principal national labor organizations—favored the OTLA review process as a means of promoting further labor policy reform. Nonetheless, the process itself contributed to only modest, incremental change. In its one-year review of the steps the Colombian government had taken in response to its nineteen detailed January 2017 recommendations, the most significant action the OTLA could identify was that the Ministry of Labor had completed installation of an electronic case management system to improve its enforcement capacity.[98] It was probably small consolation to U.S. labor officials that the Colombian government took the more consequential decision to adopt stricter legislation to control employers' misuse of third-party labor intermediaries not in response to the OTLA submission but rather as part of a separate 2018 labor action plan negotiated with Canada in response to a parallel labor complaint filed by the Canadian Labour Congress and the same five Colombian labor and nongovernmental organizations under the Canada-Colombia Labor Cooperation Agreement.[99]

The Guatemala Test Case

By far the most politically significant of the U.S. FTA labor complaints under discussion here was the submission that the AFL-CIO and six Guatemalan labor organizations filed against the government of Guatemala on April 23, 2008.[100] Guatemala had long been under international pressure to address systemic labor rights violations (chapter 2), and the issues addressed by the case were perhaps the most serious of those raised in any of the NAALC or non-NAALC submissions examined in this book. Most important, however, this was the first labor complaint filed under the provisions of either the NAFTA/NAALC or later U.S. FTAs to proceed through the full dispute-settlement process. It was, therefore, a crucial test of the enforceability of the labor obligations in these agreements.

The submission focused principally on obstacles to freedom of association and the right to collective bargaining, especially those violations linked to the sustained violence (assassinations, attempted murders, coercion, and intimidation) suffered by union leaders and trade union activists. Although anti-union violence was a longstanding problem in Guatemala, the complaint highlighted developments since the DR-CAFTA had taken effect on July 1, 2006, by presenting case studies of rights violations in five different companies. These cases were selected to demonstrate that serious violations of core labor rights were common in sectors and firms (apparel manufacturing, export agriculture, food products) that either exported their production to the United States or were otherwise linked to bilateral trade (the parastatal company managing Puerto Quetzal, the country's principal port on the Pacific Ocean).[101] In detailing instances of extreme violence against trade unionists, the submission repeatedly affirmed that "the murder of the union officer violated his individual right to free association."[102] On several occasions, it quoted from an earlier ILO Committee on Freedom of Association (CFA) report on Guatemala:

> A genuinely free and independent trade union movement cannot develop in a climate of violence and uncertainty; freedom of association can only be exercised in conditions in which fundamental rights, and in particular those relating to human life and personal safety, are fully respected and guaranteed, and the rights of workers' and employers' organizations can only be exercised in a climate that is free from violence, pressure or threats of any kind against the leaders and members of these organizations, and it is for governments to ensure that this principle is respected. Moreover, the Committee recalls that the absence of judgments against the guilty parties creates, in practice, a situation of impunity, which reinforces the climate of violence and insecurity, and which is extremely damaging to the exercise of trade union rights.[103]

The submission maintained that "each of these claims, together and individually, set forth facts sufficient to establish a recurring course of action or inaction on the part of the government."[104] Its summary charge was that the "failure of the Government of Guatemala to effectively enforce its labor laws and comply with its commitments under the ILO Declaration on Fundamental Principles and Rights at Work" violated its obligations under DR-CAFTA Article 16.2.1(a).[105]

The OTLA accepted the case for review on June 12, 2008. Over the ensuing seven months, it conducted an exhaustive examination of the submitters' allegations.[106] In addition to soliciting additional information from both the complainants and the government of Guatemala, OTLA officials traveled to Guatemala on two occasions (July 20–25 and October 27–3, 2008) to interview union leaders, workers, employers, government officials, and other relevant parties.

The public report that the OTLA issued on January 16, 2009, strongly favored the complainants. The report credited the government of President Álvaro Colom (2008–2012) for its willingness to discuss the issues raised by the submission, and it applauded the government's decision in November 2008 to reactivate the cabinet-level Multi-Institutional Commission on Labor Relations that had been established by presidential decree in 2003. The OTLA also conditionally accepted the Guatemalan government's position that trade unionists might have been victims of generalized violence rather than attacks specifically directed at them for their union activities. Nevertheless, the OTLA report concluded, "When a union leader is violently attacked with total impunity, the crime's impact can reach beyond the individual and cast a shadow of fear upon others, weakening the right of association and collective bargaining."[107] It went on to detail the many employer practices that obstructed Guatemalan workers' freedom of association and right to collective bargaining, including large-scale firings of union organizers, refusal to grant labor inspectors access to work sites, and persistent refusal to comply with labor court orders.[108] After making a number of specific recommendations to the Guatemalan government concerning how to remedy significant weaknesses in labor law enforcement (including strengthening the Special Prosecutor's Unit for Crimes Against Trade Unionists), the OTLA recommended continued informal government-to-government collaboration to address the issues at stake rather than formal cooperative consultations under DR-CAFTA article 16.6.1.

However, extended discussions between January 2009 and July 2010 among the U.S. Departments of Labor and State, the USTR, and the government of Guatemala did not produce any tangible results. As a consequence, on July 30, 2010, USTR Ron Kirk and U.S. Secretary of Labor Hilda L. Solis wrote their Guatemalan counterparts to request formal consultations concerning the government of Guatemala's failures to enforce its DR-CAFTA obligations related to the freedom of association, the rights to organize and bargain collectively, and acceptable conditions of work.[109] Yet these consultations, held between September 8–9 and December 6, 2010, also failed to resolve the principal U.S. concerns, and so on May 16, 2011, the USTR requested a meeting of the DR-CAFTA Free Trade Commission. When ministerial consultations in Guatemala City on June 7, 2011, did not resolve the matters in dispute, on August 9, 2011, the U.S. government officially requested the establishment of an arbitral panel under DR-CAFTA article 20.6.1. The panel was formally constituted on November 30, 2012,[110] but at the request of the parties, it immediately suspended its operations while the two governments negotiated an enforcement action plan.

Guatemalan and U.S. officials eventually reached agreement on a fourteen-page document (dated April 25, 2013) that listed in great detail, with specified time periods for implementation, the steps the Guatemalan government agreed to take in order to improve enforcement of its labor laws.[111] These actions were in five principal areas: (1) strengthening the Ministry of Labor's capacity to enforce labor laws, including the budgetary resources required for effective enforcement, improved access to information concerning firm ownership and potential plant closings, new legislation to expedite the transfer of confirmed cases of rights violations to labor courts for sanction, standardized time frames for labor inspections, hiring additional labor inspectors, and labor inspectors' enhanced access to police assistance to ensure their access to work sites; (2) taking multiple steps to improve the enforcement of labor court orders, including better training of judges and regular monitoring of the labor courts to ensure that criminal charges were pursued when employers violated court orders, as well as the systematic review of judges' enforcement of their rulings (and possible disciplinary action against judges who failed to do so); (3) adopting new annual reporting procedures to ensure that export companies complied with national labor laws (including at least one annual inspection of all companies located in export-processing zones, EPZs) and the revocation of firms' EPZ tax benefits as a penalty for labor law violations; (4) instituting measures to ensure that workers received final wage and benefit payments when factories closed unexpectedly, including creation of a rapid-response team to prevent or oversee the closure of companies in EPZs and regulations requiring the Ministry of Labor to ensure proactively that social security and other payments were made to workers when companies closed; and (5) enhancing transparency and coordination among government agencies, including widespread publication of the enforcement plan, meetings of the Tripartite Commission on International Labor Affairs to monitor its implementation, and publication of disaggregated statistics on different aspects of labor law enforcement. The plan did not, however, specifically address the ongoing problem of anti-union violence in Guatemala.

The enforcement plan suspended arbitral panel proceedings for six months (with the possibility of a second six-month suspension if both parties agreed). However, its wording allowed the United States to employ resumption of panel proceedings as a penalty if the government of Guatemala failed, for example, to enact legislation strengthening labor enforcement procedures within a specified time period. In the event, following two further suspensions of panel proceedings, a meeting between USTR Michael B. G. Froman and Guatemalan President

Otto Pérez Molina (2012–2015) in Washington, DC, in July 2014, and a trip by Ambassador Froman to Guatemala later that same month to address issues such as pending legislation to sanction companies for labor law violations, in mid-August 2014 U.S. officials concluded that Guatemala had still failed to take adequate corrective actions.[112] As a result, the arbitral panel finally initiated its proceedings on September 19, 2014.

Over the course of thirty-three months, the three-member arbitral panel (initially comprised of members from Guatemala,[113] the United States, and Canada) reviewed multiple written submissions and rebuttals. It also heard oral arguments from both U.S. and Guatemalan government representatives at a hearing in Guatemala City on June 2, 2015. In addition, the panel considered letters regarding the case from the AFL-CIO, the International Trade Union Confederation, four Guatemalan labor organizations, two Guatemalan NGOs, and four employers' associations.[114]

The initial U.S.-written submission to the panel focused on the government of Guatemala's alleged failure to enforce its laws related to freedom of association and the rights to organize and bargain collectively by not securing compliance with labor court orders and by not registering unions or instituting concilia-tion procedures in a timely manner. It also charged that the Guatemalan gov-ernment failed to enforce its labor laws concerning acceptable conditions of work by not conducting adequate workplace inspections or imposing obligatory penalties. The U.S. submission cited examples of these enforcement failures in eighteen specific companies and two sectors (coffee farms and African palm oil plantations), only two of which had featured in the 2008 OTLA (US 2008-01) submission.[115] The U.S. government argued that, overall, the documented labor rights violations in the apparel and steel industries, shipping and port services, agriculture, and coffee and palm oil production "influenced the conditions of competition (specifically, the supply of, and relationship to, labor) of Guatema-lan companies that engage in trade, including exports, with CAFTA-DR Parties such as the United States."[116] However, despite frequently expressed U.S. gov-ernment concerns about the extent of anti-union violence in Guatemala and the fact that the 2008 OTLA case had focused principally on this issue, the U.S. submission to the arbitral panel did not address the question. At the time, USTR officials continued to view this as a question of criminal (rather than labor) law, and they were unwilling to pursue a matter outside their traditional areas of expertise that would be difficult for them to document convincingly.[117]

In response, the Guatemalan government's initial written submission critiqued the probative value of the evidence submitted by the United States (portions of which included, in order to protect witnesses from possible recrimination, anonymous statements and exhibits with redacted information). It also rebutted U.S. claims regarding the enforcement of labor law in individual companies, especially with regard to whether the alleged failures resulted from a deliberate policy of neglect and thereby constituted "a sustained or recurring course of inaction."[118] In addition, the submission argued that the United States had failed to demonstrate that the alleged failings of the Guatemalan government to enforce its laws had any effect on trade among DR-CAFTA member states, in part because the U.S. submission cited trade data for entire sectors rather than trade effects attributable to the individual companies it referenced.[119]

The panel finally ended its lengthy quasi-judicial proceedings in late September 2016,[120] and it issued its final report on June 14, 2017.[121] The report broadly endorsed U.S. claims that the Guatemalan government had failed to secure compliance with labor court orders, and it agreed that these cases might constitute a recurring course of inaction.[122] Nevertheless, it identified only one instance (Avandia, a garment manufacturer) in which the Guatemalan government's failure to enforce applicable labor laws gave the employer a competitive trade advantage.[123] With regard to labor inspections and the imposition of penalties for labor law violations, the arbitral panel found only one case (Fribo, an apparel manufacturer) in which the government had failed to conduct proper workplace inspections.[124] Furthermore, the panel determined that it did not have jurisdiction to address U.S. claims concerning union registration processes in Guatemala because this issue had not been included in the original U.S. government request to establish an arbitral panel.[125] Overall, therefore, it concluded that the United States had not proven that Guatemala had failed to conform to its obligations under DR-CAFTA article 16.2.1(a).[126]

Reactions to the arbitral panel's report from U.S. unions and labor-rights groups were immediate and incredulous. Some analysts criticized different aspects of the U.S. government's handling of the case, including the failure to include in the initial U.S. call to establish the panel either union registration issues or supporting statements by the ILO and other labor-rights organizations regarding the general labor rights environment in Guatemala.[127] However, most responses focused on the possibly precedent-setting approach the panelists took to the "in a manner affecting trade" benchmark that had become a standard provision in U.S. FTA labor chapters:

> An interpretation of Article 16.2.1(a) that treated as a violation every failure, through a sustained or recurring course of action or inaction, to effectively enforce labor laws simply because it occurred in a traded sector, or with respect to an enterprise engaged in trade, would not be consistent with its wording. It would require no proof of influence or material impression upon the cross-border exchange of goods and services. It would simply require proof of some effect on an employer or economic sector engaged in trade. This is not the same thing as an effect on trade.[128]
>
> The Panel does not agree with this approach [that advocated in the U.S.-written submission] to determining whether a failure to effectively enforce labor laws affects conditions of competition. We are of the view that such an interpretation would drain the phrase "affecting trade" of its ordinary meaning, and effectively equate it with the term "trade-related." We have determined that in order for a failure to enforce to affect trade it must change conditions of competition by conferring a competitive advantage upon an employer engaged in trade.[129]

At the time the USTR-formulated "in a manner affecting trade" provision was inserted in the U.S.-Jordan FTA, there had been no significant discussion among U.S. stakeholders about the evidentiary standards it might establish in grievance proceedings. In fact, the AFL-CIO had accepted this language without dissent.[130] However, requiring that a complainant produce firm-level data showing that labor rights violations significantly reduced an individual employer's labor costs and thereby gave the company a measurable competitive advantage in export markets hugely increased the required burden of proof. That conclusion, and the inability of the U.S. government to prevail in a nine-year effort to hold Guatemala—which, between 1990 and 2013, had been called before the ILO's Committee on the Application of Standards on twenty-one occasions, more frequently than any other country[131]—to account for systemic labor rights violations, greatly disillusioned the international labor rights community. The outcome placed the viability of labor provisions in free-trade agreements as a means for advancing workers' rights in developing countries in grave doubt. Moreover, the case cast a long shadow over ongoing negotiations among Canada, Mexico, and the United States to revise the NAFTA's labor provisions (chapter 6).

U.S.-MEXICAN NEGOTIATIONS OVER THE TRANS-PACIFIC PARTNERSHIP AND DEMOCRATIC LABOR REFORM IN MEXICO

The legacies of the NAALC experience, the precedents set in the labor chapters included in post-2007 U.S. free-trade agreements, and the lessons the U.S. government learned in addressing FTA labor complaints all shaped the Obama administration's approach to, and negotiations over, the multilateral Trans-Pacific Partnership trade agreement.[132] For the U.S. government, bilateral negotiations with Mexico over its accession to the agreement offered a new opportunity to press for reforms of its labor justice system and for the effective protection of freedom of association and the rights to organize and bargain collectively that had not been achieved through the NAALC's public communications procedures. In the end, Obama administration officials proved willing to bring strong diplomatic pressures to bear on the Mexican government in order to secure historically important constitutional reforms that significantly strengthened the legal basis for democratic worker rights in Mexico.

The Trans-Pacific Partnership, the United States, and Mexico

The Trans-Pacific Partnership (TPP), negotiated by twelve Pacific basin states between February 2008 and October 2015, was, without doubt, one of the most ambitious free-trade agreements.[133] The thirty-chapter accord promoted trade among countries that together accounted for approximately 40 percent of global commerce.[134] Proponents maintained that the TPP was especially innovative in its advocacy of international labor (and environmental) standards. Indeed, the U.S. decision in 2008 to join what had originally been a more limited free-trade initiative made labor (and environmental) issues key topics in the multilateral negotiations.[135]

The final TPP text included a separate chapter 19 on labor rights that largely replicated the provisions in U.S. FTAs finalized after the May 10 agreement in its definition of labor obligations and its somewhat simplified dispute-settlement arrangements.[136] It did separate the "acceptable conditions of work" requirement from the ILO fundamental labor rights principles and, in recognition of the development status of some TPP member states, specify that these conditions were to be "determined by [each] party" (article 19.3.2n5)—although presumably still in compliance with ILO norms. However, the agreement also required signatory parties to adopt measures to discourage the importation of goods produced in whole or in part by forced or compulsory labor (article 19.6), and it specifically stipulated that the nonderogation provisions in article 19.4 applied to any "special trade or customs area, such as an export processing zone or foreign trade zone." Article 19.9.2 on public submissions permitted each party to require that a complainant indicate how the issue in dispute affected trade or investment among the TPP parties, but it placed no nationality requirements on submitters.[137]

Of particular note, the U.S. government built on its previous FTA experience by negotiating separate bilateral labor rights agreements with Brunei, Malaysia, and Vietnam that were to be implemented *before* the TPP took effect.[138] These so-called labor consistency plans, all dated November 2015, addressed in detail highly sensitive issues, including freedom of association and the right to collective bargaining, trade union leadership, strikes, forced labor and human trafficking, child labor, employment discrimination, acceptable conditions at work, labor inspection procedures and complaint mechanisms, and labor subcontracting and outsourcing arrangements. The plans frequently cited specific provisions of domestic labor law and regulations that were to be modified to be consistent with ILO standards. In all three cases, the agreements established timetables for these reforms and annual reviews by special bilateral committees to evaluate progress in bringing them about. This intrusive approach regarding countries with notoriously poor labor rights records significantly shaped U.S.-Mexico interactions around the TPP.

The Mexican government announced in November 2010 that it would not take part in the TPP.[139] Yet only a year later, it reversed its position because of concerns that U.S. membership in the pact would allow economic competitors around the Pacific Rim to undercut its position in its principal export market, the United States. Mexico joined the fifteenth round of multilateral negotiations in December 2012.[140] The United States, the largest economy among TPP states and the most insistent advocate of labor rights provisions in the agreement, was the de facto gatekeeper in these multilateral talks. The Mexico-U.S. negotiating agenda over the TPP included several difficult issues (concerning, for example, automotive industry rules of origin, patent protection for pharmaceutical products, and sanitary and phytosanitary measures affecting agricultural products).[141] Labor rights in Mexico were a major point of contention.

Opening Negotiating Positions: United States

Both the content of the May 10, 2007, executive-congressional agreement concerning labor rights provisions in U.S. FTAs and domestic political constraints shaped the way the Obama administration approached bilateral negotiations over labor rights in Mexico. In political terms, the principal challenge facing the administration was winning congressional approval of the TPP. A substantial majority of Democrats in the House of Representatives had voted against approval of the NAFTA in 1993 (chapter 3). President Obama faced an even more uphill struggle in this regard because of the U.S. labor movement's unrelenting opposition to the TPP and many congressional Democrats' backing of U.S. labor demands, in part because of their continued reliance on trade unions for financial and organizational support during election campaigns. Congressional Democrats' capacity to place labor rights issues at the center of FTA negotiations had been amply demonstrated when they compelled the George W. Bush administration to renegotiate accords with Colombia, Peru, and the Republic of Korea following adoption of the May 10 agreement.[142] Indeed, one telling indication of Obama administration sensitivity to the issue was that U.S. officials had decided not to support Colombia's candidacy to join the Organization of Economic Co-Operation and Development because of continuing concerns about the labor rights situation in the country.[143] Whether significant numbers of congressional Democrats would ever have voted for the TPP remains an open question because organized labor's opposition to the agreement went well beyond specific objections to its labor rights provisions (including, for example, investor-state dispute-settlement arrangements).[144] Nonetheless, Obama administration officials clearly understood that demonstrating firmness over labor issues in bilateral negotiations with Mexico was essential to winning congressional approval of the TPP.[145]

The commitment that President Obama, Vice President Joseph R. Biden Jr., and senior Obama administration officials shared regarding the importance of Mexican labor rights was strongly reinforced by past bilateral interactions under the NAALC.[146] A wide range of U.S. sociopolitical actors—government officials, trade unions, and labor-rights advocates—questioned the efficacy of NAALC procedures as a mechanism for addressing rights violations in Mexico. Over time, their concerns had come to focus on two main issues: respect in practice for constitutionally and legally guaranteed collective-action rights (freedom of association and the rights to organize and bargain collectively) and the political independence of tripartite (comprised of labor, government, and business representatives) conciliation and arbitration boards (*juntas de conciliación y arbitraje*). As discussed in chapter 4, federal and state-level juntas were responsible for resolving worker-employer conflicts and legally registering collective contracts and, in economic activities under state-level jurisdiction, trade unions. In practice, both federal and state-level authorities regularly obstructed the formation of politically independent unions (and favored government-aligned labor organizations). Moreover, because government-allied unions dominated labor representation on juntas, rank-and-file challenges to their workplace control and efforts to win higher wages, improved fringe benefits, and better working conditions often failed. For the Obama administration, therefore, the TPP negotiations with Mexico offered an opportunity to strengthen NAFTA/NAALC labor provisions, as Obama had repeatedly promised to do during his 2008 presidential-primary campaign.[147]

Opening Negotiating Positions: Mexico

Mexican government officials understood from the outset that labor rights issues would arise during the TPP negotiations. They had discussed the matter in general terms with senior U.S. officials even before Mexico formally sought to join the negotiations, and they initially expressed willingness to adopt new labor measures under TPP auspices. Mexican officials were, furthermore, aware of the multilateral debate already underway regarding the content of a proposed labor chapter in the agreement (whether, for instance, labor obligations would be subject to binding dispute-settlement procedures). However, even though they knew how sensitive labor rights questions concerning Mexico were in some U.S. political circles, they did not anticipate how important the issue would become in bilateral interactions with the United States.[148] They may also have assumed that the defensive positions Mexico had previously taken regarding its state-labor relations regime might still hold. For example, during negotiations over the NAALC in 1993, Mexican officials had successfully invoked claims to national sovereignty and parried many specific U.S. demands by insisting that Mexico's federal labor law offered stronger formal protections in some areas than did U.S. law.[149] They had argued, moreover, that Mexico had ratified and still adhered to a substantially larger number of ILO conventions (seventy-six) than the United States (eleven), including five of the seven conventions then in effect that the ILO later characterized as "fundamental" (versus only one for the United States).[150] Several members of Mexico's TPP negotiating team had participated in the NAFTA negotiations and had witnessed how the administration of President Carlos Salinas de Gortari (1988–1994) had deflected U.S. pressures for a stronger NAALC. Even though some of these officials recognized the existence of serious domestic labor rights problems, they may have assumed that they, too, could address U.S. demands without fundamentally altering the labor relations status quo.[151]

Furthermore, Mexico's TPP negotiators could accurately claim that undertaking major reforms of national labor legislation would be difficult politically. The 1970 Federal Labor Law (Ley Federal del Trabajo) was revised in 2012 only after multiple unsuccessful attempts to do so, dating back to the late 1980s.[152] In the case of the junta system, because tripartite conciliation and arbitration boards had been established by the 1917 federal constitution (article 123, clause XX), any fundamental changes would require constitutional reforms— and thus the support of two-thirds majorities in both chambers of the federal Congress and a majority of state legislatures.

Equally important, both government-aligned labor organizations and the private sector had long defended the legal status quo. Most unions remained dominated by leaders whose entrenched position was underpinned by labor law provisions that effectively blocked rank-and-file efforts to hold them accountable. The labor movement was weaker in organizational and political terms in the 2010s than it had been in 1993 when opposition from the Confederation of Mexican Workers (Confederación de Trabajadores de México, CTM) had strongly influenced Mexican government opposition to a more expansive NAALC. Nevertheless, the CTM held a long record of successfully opposing labor law and political reforms that threatened its dominant position in industrial relations and its status as the official labor sector of the once-hegemonic Institutional Revolutionary Party (Partido Revolucionario Institucional, PRI).[153]

Preserving the established state-labor relations regime was also very important to Mexican business interests. The willingness of government-aligned unions to moderate wage demands and limit strikes had for decades been a pillar of the country's political economy. Moreover, as discussed in chapter 4, over time, the private sector had become increasingly reliant on so-called employer protection contracts (*contratos de protección patronal*). These agreements formally met minimum legal requirements, but, in practice, they gave employers unchallenged control over workplace affairs. Once in place, the force of law protected employers from workers' attempts to negotiate a new contract. Because Mexico's established export-led development model relied on low labor costs as a basis of international comparative advantage, many employers regarded control over unionization and workplace relations as vital to their economic success. The nature of business interests thus substantially raised political barriers to domestic labor reform.

The PRI administration of President Enrique Peña Nieto (2012–2018) was not unconditionally opposed to change in labor law and policy. Senior administration officials evidenced some sensitivity to the sustained criticism that the ILO had voiced regarding protection contracts and restrictions on freedom of association.[154] For instance, in March 2015, Alfonso Navarrete Prida, head of the Ministry of Labor and Social Welfare (Secretaría del Trabajo y Previsión Social, STPS), assured representatives of several international labor organizations that Mexico would ratify ILO convention no. 98 on the rights to organize and bargain collectively. In June 2015, he and twenty-five state-government labor ministers "categorically rejected" protection contracts, and in November 2015, Navarrete announced a new labor inspection protocol to verify that workers were aware of contract negotiations undertaken on their behalf.[155] Pressure on the government over this issue was also building from international brand-name companies with manufacturing operations in Mexico. Under the leadership of the Maquiladora Solidarity Network, a Canadian NGO promoting international labor rights, such internationally prominent clothing and footwear companies as Adidas, New Balance, Nike, Patagonia, Puma, and Walt Disney had openly condemned protection contracts and worked to ensure that the agreements they signed with Mexican suppliers met their own codes of corporate conduct and international labor rights standards.[156] Nonetheless, domestic opposition to major reforms that would alter the state-labor relations status quo remained strong.

The Character and Outcome of Bilateral Negotiations

In the United States, the USTR had statutory responsibility for TPP negotiations.[157] However, with USTR concurrence, senior Department of Labor officials were centrally engaged in bilateral negotiations with Mexico over labor rights.[158] The Department of State and the U.S. embassy in Mexico City played supporting roles.

The AFL-CIO, the largest and most politically influential U.S. labor organization, and several national industrial unions held seats on the USTR's Labor Advisory Committee for Trade Negotiations and Trade Policy, but by convention, they were not directly involved in the negotiations. They did, however, maintain a steady drumbeat of highly public denunciations of labor rights violations in Mexico, which, they argued, unfairly placed U.S. workers at a competitive disadvantage and resulted in depressed wages.[159]

In Mexico, the Ministry of the Economy (Secretaría de la Economía) took the lead in TPP negotiations. Once labor rights became a central issue, senior STPS officials became actively involved as well. The Ministry of Foreign Relations (Secretaría de Relaciones Exteriores) also followed the negotiations closely because of its statutory authority in trade negotiations, and the Mexican embassy in Washington, DC, was well-positioned to gauge the U.S. domestic political environment. The CTM and other old-guard labor organizations, despite having had representation in the NAALC negotiations, played no formal part in the unfolding bilateral discussions.[160]

Bilateral TPP negotiations were conducted in both Washington, DC, and Mexico City. At first, Mexican trade negotiators tried hard to avoid in-depth engagement with their U.S. counterparts on labor rights questions. Concerns about the TPP's prospective labor provisions had initially led Mexican business organizations to oppose Mexico joining the multilateral negotiations, and they subsequently argued that any final agreement should recognize the existing NAALC as the framework governing labor issues in the North American context. This "carve out" arrangement would have greatly reduced the range of labor rights obligations whose violation was potentially subject to trade-linked sanctions under the terms of the TPP's labor chapter. Mexican government officials initially adopted this position as their own in order to gain bargaining time.[161]

When U.S. pressures finally forced their hand, Mexican negotiators then shifted to a second strategy, differentiating among actions the Mexican government was prepared to take to address the labor rights problems highlighted by the United States. For instance, they noted that Mexico had recently enacted reforms raising the legal working age to fifteen and that the government was collaborating with the ILO to combat child employment problems.[162] They also stressed the Peña Nieto administration's commitment to gender equality in the workplace and enhanced workplace inspections. Mexican negotiators indicated, moreover, that the Mexican government was prepared to make legal and procedural changes that would improve the operations of conciliation and arbitration boards. However, they persistently resisted constitutional reforms of the junta system,[163] and they ruled out as entirely unacceptable in domestic political terms the U.S. demand to sign a separate labor consistency plan like the bilateral accords the United States was negotiating with Brunei, Malaysia, and Vietnam.[164] The USTR was under public pressure from Democratic congressional representatives to reach a TPP-linked agreement with Mexico like those it eventually signed with these three countries.[165] Nonetheless, Mexican officials held firm on this point, arguing that the U.S. demand clearly infringed upon Mexico's national sovereignty.[166]

Obama administration officials fully understood that they were discussing politically sensitive issues with a NAFTA partner and valued ally. They nevertheless insisted on major labor reforms that would both satisfy TPP requirements (regarding, for example, the impartiality of labor tribunals) and improve the political odds for U.S. congressional approval of the TPP—a concern that U.S. officials openly shared with their Mexican counterparts.[167] In fact, U.S. negotiators maintained their demand for a labor consistency plan until near the end of the multilateral TPP negotiations, perhaps, in part, as a tactic to extract Mexican concessions on other important issues.[168] In the end, however, they accepted a Mexican offer to formulate independently significant labor reforms.[169] The U.S. side also agreed to Mexican negotiators' request that bilateral discussions on the matter be closely held and that their joint public position would be that any reforms Mexico enacted were undertaken entirely at the initiative of the Mexican government. The U.S. negotiators took these crucially important decisions— in effect, endorsing Mexico's third bargaining strategy—because they sought to expand the Peña Nieto administration's capacity to address labor rights issues and avoid nationalist "negative reverberation" in domestic politics that would have narrowed the possible "win-set."[170]

Yet Mexican negotiators still sought to prevent labor questions from complicating interactions with the United States over their TPP trade priorities, and in December 2014, they proposed that U.S. DOL and STPS officials meet to discuss those matters outside the regular TPP process.[171] The two labor delegations proceeded to hold in-depth discussions throughout 2015 over reforms to Mexico's Federal Labor Law. The monthly negotiating sessions were conducted either by telephone and video conference calls or in face-to-face meetings in Mexico City or Washington, DC. The Mexican team prepared legislative drafts, shared them with their U.S. counterparts, and then negotiated over the proposals line by line.[172] At the same time, U.S. DOL officials consulted selectively with independent labor law experts in Mexico to deepen their understanding of specific legal provisions and their likely impact on worker-employer relations.[173]

Throughout this period, consensus on the U.S. side regarding the importance of labor rights placed the issue at or near the top of its TPP agenda with Mexico.[174] The Obama administration demonstrated strong credibility in pushing its agenda because, unlike in the 1993 NAALC negotiations, the grounding for its demands (particularly the May 10 agreement and the legislative requirement enacted on June 29, 2015, that the president submit to Congress "a meaningful labor rights report" on all countries joining the TPP[175]) and the secrecy in which negotiations were conducted left little room for significant internal or public dissent on the matter.[176] On this basis, as multilateral negotiations over the TPP's chapter 19 neared completion in June-July 2015, U.S. officials pressed their Mexican counterparts harder. Although the intrusive demands that White House Chief of Staff Denis McDonough presented in a testy June 2015 telephone call offended the Mexican recipient and his senior colleagues (and reportedly prompted President Obama to telephone President Peña Nieto shortly thereafter to calm matters),[177] the exchange underscored the depth of U.S. commitment on the issue.

These intense, sustained U.S. pressures continued after the formal conclusion of multilateral TPP negotiations.[178] In response, in late 2015, the Mexican government took two important actions to address U.S. demands. First, on November 30, 2015, despite strong resistance from leading Mexican business organizations, President Peña Nieto submitted ILO convention no. 98 to the federal Senate for ratification.[179] Second, on December 4, 2015, he announced that he intended to reform the labor justice system.[180] These actions were, however, insufficient to satisfy Obama administration officials, who were increasingly concerned about the passage of time and decreasing prospects for enacting the TPP before the end of President Obama's term in office.[181] The beginning of the 2016 Democratic presidential primary season also raised the prospect that candidates might face criticism from U.S. trade unions over the administration's failure to address adequately their concerns about "labor dumping" by Mexico—that is, labor rights abuses that prevented wages from rising in line with productivity increases and thereby placed U.S. workers at a competitive disadvantage.[182]

The Obama administration, therefore, took several additional steps to underscore both the utmost seriousness of the U.S. commitment on labor rights issues and the urgent need for decisive action by the Peña Nieto government. First, during a negotiating session with his senior Mexican counterparts in Washington, DC, in mid-February 2016, Secretary of Labor Perez, for the first time, explicitly demanded that Mexico adopt constitutional reforms as the means for resolving labor justice problems. He was blunt in stating that the Mexican proposals for labor law reform that had been agreed with U.S. negotiators would not suffice; constitutional reforms were necessary to eliminate the tripartite juntas and give full autonomy to labor justice institutions.[183] Second, Vice President Biden, during a trip to Mexico City in late February to cochair a meeting of the U.S.-Mexico High Level Economic Dialogue created when Obama visited Mexico in May 2013, also stressed the importance of constitutional reforms. He did so both in his interactions with cabinet-level Mexican officials and directly with President Peña Nieto in a private, after-dinner conversation on February 25, 2016.[184]

Third, U.S. Secretary of the Treasury Jacob Lew, working in close consultation with USTR Froman and Secretary Perez, telephoned Secretary of Finance and Public Credit (Secretaría de Hacienda y Crédito Público) Luis Videgaray Caso to argue that it was essential for the Mexican government to undertake constitutional reforms of the labor justice system if the Obama administration were to have any real chance of winning U.S. congressional approval of the Trans-Pacific Partnership agreement. Lew and Videgaray had an established, positive working relationship,[185] and final adoption of the TPP was a high policy priority for both of them. However, neither of these two senior officials had previously been involved in the bilateral negotiations over labor issues. From the perspective of the Obama administration, Lew's communication with Videgaray was an attempt to break the impasse between U.S. and Mexican labor and trade officials and move the constitutional reform issue "up the ladder" in Mexican decision-making circles.[186]

Videgaray had reason to take Lew's intervention on the question extremely seriously because it coincided with word from the International Monetary Fund that the Obama administration (Lew served as the official U.S. representative to the fund) had expressed reservations about what had previously been the standard biannual renewal of Mexico's flexible line of credit. The fund had, with strong U.S. support, first approved this "hard," reserves-backed flexible credit line for US$47 billion in April 2009 during the global financial crisis.[187] Mexico suffered a sharper economic decline during the crisis than any other Latin American country,[188] and its access to the fund's financial reserves played a crucial part in reassuring its international creditors. In early January 2016, the Peña Nieto administration had sought to safeguard the country's financial stability against any potential threat posed by Mexico-bashing Republican presidential candidate Donald J. Trump by requesting a significant increase in the line of credit from the US$70 billion agreed in 2014 to $100 billion.[189] Germany had long resisted continuation of this special arrangement, but senior Mexican officials were shocked when International Monetary Fund sources informed them in late February of sudden, unanticipated U.S. reservations about their renewal request. The stated U.S. concern was that the fund lacked sufficient available funds and that the size of the requested increase might disadvantage more financially vulnerable countries.[190]

Whether some senior Mexican officials actually perceived at least an implicit quid pro quo in the Lew-Videgaray conversation (U.S. support for Mexico's line-of-credit request in exchange for the Mexican government undertaking constitutional labor reforms) or whether they claimed there was issue linkage in an attempt to advance their own goals, cannot be determined conclusively. However, any uncertainty about renewal of the International Monetary Fund line of credit threatened to raise international concerns about the country's longer-term financial stability. For that reason, these developments altered both the focus of internal Mexican government policy debates and their dynamics by bringing Videgaray—Peña Nieto's most influential senior policy adviser and someone who, in the context of U.S.-Mexico negotiations over revising the NAFTA (chapter 6), later publicly expressed openness to labor rights reforms—into the discussion.

Within twenty-four hours after Mexican officials confirmed that the Obama administration had expressed reservations about the government's line-of-credit renewal request, President Peña Nieto convened a meeting with his closest senior advisers to discuss how they would respond. Peña Nieto had previously rejected advice from his senior legal advisers to address labor rights problems through constitutional reforms in part because of the political challenges of doing so late in his administration. Confronted by these new circumstances, however, he quickly reversed his position.[191] Immediately thereafter, STPS Secretary Navarrete telephoned his U.S. counterpart, Secretary Perez, to communicate the substance of the decision.[192] Peña Nieto presumably reaffirmed his decision to President Obama himself when Obama, acting on the recommendation of Secretary Perez, telephoned him around March 1, 2016, to confirm matters.[193]

Although Peña Nieto acceded to reforming constitutional article 123, the content of the amendment(s) remained open to internal debate and bilateral negotiation. Beginning in early March 2016, the Office of Legal Counsel to the Presidency (Consejería Jurídica de la Presidencia, CJP) began drafting possible reforms to article 123. These drafts were shared with U.S. DOL and other U.S. government officials, and, as they had done in negotiations over federal labor law reforms, the Mexican and U.S. teams then debated them in telephone calls, video conferences, and face-to-face meetings.[194] The discussions were intense and detailed, focusing on both general issues and the specific, line-by-line language of different reform proposals. Although Mexican negotiators sought throughout to maintain as much executive authority as possible,[195] their position on the terms of constitutional reforms evolved significantly as the negotiations progressed.

There was apparent agreement from the outset, based on prior bilateral negotiations,[196] that a revised article 123 would include a clear statement of the principles or "fundamental propositions" that would henceforth underpin the Mexican labor justice system. The text of a proposed new clause XXII bis read:

> The proceedings and requirements established by law to ensure freedom of collective negotiation and the legitimate interests of employees and employers, shall guarantee, among others, an authentic representativeness of union organizations, as well as the certainty of the signature, registration and deposit of the collective labor contracts. The law shall guarantee the personal, free and secret vote of the employees to elect their leaders and in the resolution of union conflicts.[197]

Certainly, one of the most contentious questions concerned the future role (if any) for tripartite conciliation and arbitration boards, the much-criticized centerpiece of the labor justice system created by the 1917 constitution. All of the available CJP internal documents from mid-March 2016 presented the preservation of the junta system as an option. For instance, in a proposal dated March 17, Mexican negotiators presented their U.S. counterparts with six alternatives for a revised article 123 (clause XX):[198] (1) the preservation of established federal- and state-level tripartite juntas to resolve labor-capital/worker-employer conflicts, with the addition of language affirming that their "resolutions must observe the principles of impartiality, autonomy and judicial independence"; (2) obligatory conciliation by tripartite juntas, with final resolution by labor tribunals whose structure and composition would be defined later; (3) obligatory conciliation by tripartite juntas, with final resolution by labor tribunals operating under the jurisdiction of federal and state-level judicial authorities; (4) obligatory conciliation by conciliation and arbitration boards whose composition would be decided later (that is, they would not necessarily be tripartite), with final resolution by labor tribunals whose structure and composition would also be decided later; (5) obligatory conciliation by conciliation and arbitration boards whose composition would be decided later, with final resolution by labor tribunals operating under the jurisdiction of federal and state-level judicial authorities; and (6) obligatory conciliation by labor tribunals whose structure and composition would be defined later.[199] Several days later (March 21), presumably at the insistence of U.S. negotiators, Mexican officials presented a seventh option: arbitrary conciliation of labor-capital conflicts by special conciliation authorities whose character would be defined later, with final resolution by federal and state courts.[200]

The Mexican interest in preserving tripartite conciliation and arbitration boards in part reflected the daunting practical challenges involved in replacing a decades-old labor justice system. As late as early March 2016, the Peña Nieto administration sought to address U.S. criticisms by proposing a range of reforms that would enhance the boards' political impartiality (by, for example, establishing specific criteria to guide their actions) and administrative efficiency (by, for instance, defining decision time periods that would preclude purposeful delays).[201] However, the government was also strongly motivated by an underpinning commitment to tripartism that the established conciliation and arbitration boards embodied; the tripartite structure of many labor-related governmental institutions was, in fact, a principal legacy of Mexico's postrevolutionary state-labor regime.[202] As would become evident in Mexico-U.S. bilateral interactions in 2016 and again during the negotiations over revising the NAFTA / NAALC labor provisions, preserving tripartite governance of the labor justice system—and the guaranteed representation of business and old-guard labor interests that it represented—would remain both a key goal of the Peña Nieto administration and a major point of bilateral controversy.

For their part, U.S. negotiators pressed hard to eliminate the existing junta system altogether, and Mexican officials apparently conceded this point quite quickly. In fact, a CJP internal document dated March 21 refers only to "concil-iation authorities" (*instancias de conciliación*) and judicial tribunals; by April 13, these conciliation authorities were identified more specifically as "Conciliation Centers." A center in each Mexican state would examine worker-employer con-flicts in all local-jurisdiction economic activities,[203] while conflicts in federal-jurisdiction industries would be mediated by a "specialized public entity" (*ente público especializado*) whose structure and composition remained undefined. If conciliation was unsuccessful, labor tribunals established by federal and state-level judicial authorities would finally resolve disputes.[204] The April 13 draft text, in what was a further U.S. push to address the problems of employer protec-tion contracts and ghost unions, for the first time, placed mandatory review of all proposed collective contracts and legal recognition of all trade unions under the authority of the new specialized public entity.[205]

The main question then became what organizational form this new national entity would take. Obama administration officials, whose goal was to end the tripartite arrangements that permitted direct government control over worker-employer affairs,[206] argued that it should be a fully autonomous federal agency modeled on the National Institute for Transparency, Access to Information, and Protection of Personal Data (Instituto Nacional de Transparencia, Acceso a la Información y Protección de los Datos Personales). Mexican negotiators strongly objected to this proposal, noting that under Mexican law, granting such authority to an autonomous agency would, in effect, preclude the federal govern-ment from playing any significant role in labor conflicts or contract and union registration—a prospect they regarded as entirely unacceptable politically. Instead, they maintained, the new agency should be created under the terms of the Fed-eral Law on Parastatal Enterprises (Ley Federal de las Entidades Paraestatales). In taking this position, Mexican officials acceded to the U.S. demand for a new national labor contract and union registry. However, because this law does not specify the institutional design of a particular decentralized agency's governing body,[207] they kept open the possibility that the new entity would have a tripartite governance structure.[208] This was evidently President Peña Nieto's intention.[209] Obama administration officials were apparently unaware of this legal subtlety or its implications; they accepted Mexican negotiators' assurances that the entity would be independent.[210]

As these bilateral negotiations over constitutional reforms began in March, senior STPS officials opened communications about them with major Mexican business and labor organizations.[211] In their discussions with leaders of the Private Sector Coordinating Council (Consejo Coordinador Empresarial, CCE), Business Council (Consejo de Negocios), and Mexican Employers' Confederation (Confederación Patronal de la República Mexicana, COPARMEX), they openly acknowledged that President Peña Nieto's decision to proceed with constitutional reforms had resulted from U.S. pressures during the TPP negotiations. However, STPS officials adopted a very different approach in their communications with national labor leaders, drawing on the secrecy in which bilateral negotiations were conducted to manage potential domestic opposition. In justifying the proposed reforms to labor leaders, STPS officials claimed a domestic source for a decision actually taken in response to external demands. Their political cover came from the government-sponsored "Dialogues for Everyday Justice" ("Diálogos por la Justicia Cotidiana") public consultation coordinated by the Center for Economic Research and Teaching (Centro de Investigación y Docencia Económicas, CIDE).[212] The Peña Nieto administration had launched this consultation on ways to improve citizen access to justice in the immediate aftermath of the disappearance (and presumed killing) of forty-three Ayotzinapa Rural Teachers' College student trainees in Iguala, Guerrero, on September 26, 2014, an episode that sparked national and international condemnation and fundamentally challenged the government's public credibility. The purpose of the public consultation was to persuade a skeptical public of the administration's commitment to citizen justice. In the recommendations CIDE published in 2015, the labor justice panel proposed substantial reform (but not abolition) of conciliation and arbitration boards and their transfer from the executive branch to the judiciary.[213] Peña Nieto administration officials had insisted on some ambiguity in the phrasing of this recommendation precisely because they were still unsure how the TPP negotiations would evolve, and they wished to retain maximum flexibility in how they approached the matter.[214]

Leaders of the Revolutionary Confederation of Workers and Peasants (Confederación Revolucionaria de Obreros y Campesinos, CROC), the Mexican Regional Labor Confederation (Confederación Regional Obrera Mexicana, CROM), and the National Union of Workers (Unión Nacional de Trabajadores, UNT) accepted at face value the government's rationale for abolishing the juntas: the Peña Nieto administration was pursuing a demand for enhanced citizen justice in the labor arena.[215] However, STPS officials encountered strong opposition from CTM secretary-general Carlos Aceves del Olmo, whose confederation controlled a large majority of the boards' labor representatives. Whereas other labor leaders had accepted that the senior STPS official who contacted them spoke for President Peña Nieto, del Olmo insisted on speaking with the president himself.[216] Peña Nieto subsequently met privately with him on two occasions and held at least one confidential telephone conversation with him as they bargained over both the labor leader's support for constitutional reforms and, having revealed to him the real reason for the government's decision, his silence on the matter.[217] This arrangement suited both Peña Nieto and del Olmo because it protected them from nationalist criticism from other labor leaders. Indeed, del Olmo later claimed that he learned about the content of the government's reform initiatives just twenty-four hours before they were announced publicly.[218]

In the end, President Peña Nieto proposed both major constitutional and labor law reforms. The constitutional reforms abolished the tripartite conciliation and arbitration boards created in 1917 and transferred all labor justice matters from executive to judicial control at both the federal and state levels.[219] The proposed reform initiative created new federal and state-level labor tribunals to resolve strikes and adjudicate individual worker grievances falling under their jurisdiction, and it shifted the role that juntas had previously played in the conciliation of worker-employer disputes to conciliation centers established in each of Mexico's thirty-two states. Furthermore, the reforms gave constitutional recognition to freedom of collective bargaining, the need to accredit workers' consent in contract negotiations, and secret balloting in union elections.[220] Even more radically, the initiative transferred all authority to grant unions legal recognition and register collective contracts to a new national decentralized agency whose president would be selected in a procedure similar to that employed to appoint Supreme Court ministers (article 123, clauses XVIII, XX).

In turn, the proposed labor law reforms that had been negotiated with Obama administration officials over the course of 2015 introduced several measures to combat employer protection contracts.[221] Employers seeking to register a collective contract would be required to provide evidence that the workplace in question was operational, with a workforce actually present. In addition, the initiative stipulated that an employer must demonstrate that at least 30 percent of workers supported the union claiming legal control of the contract and that all employees covered by the contract had previously had access to a copy of the agreement, the union's statutes, and confirmation that the union and its leadership were officially registered with relevant labor authorities. Of particular importance, the secret-ballot procedures employed to confirm that these requirements had been fulfilled (and to resolve any dispute that might arise over which union should have legal control of an existing contract) were detailed, stringent, and designed to ensure that workers exercised a fully free vote.[222]

Peña Nieto revealed the principal elements of the constitutional reforms at a closed meeting with senior judicial authorities on April 8, 2016, but the complete contents of the constitutional and labor law reforms were not announced publicly until April 28. He submitted both initiatives to the federal Senate that same day.[223] Taken together, the constitutional and legal reforms comprehensively addressed the main points that leading U.S. trade unions had articulated regarding labor rights violations in Mexico as part of their withering December 2015 critique of the final Trans-Pacific Partnership agreement.[224] The initiatives also satisfied the Obama administration. Mexico's International Monetary Fund credit line was renewed (albeit for US$88 billion, rather than the $100 billion the Mexican government had initially requested) without controversy in May 2016.[225]

The constitutional reforms on labor rights constituted the only known instance of Mexico adopting constitutional amendments in response to an explicit external demand. Why was the Mexican government prepared to take such a momentous step after resisting for many years U.S. and ILO pressures to address persistent labor rights problems? Multiple political considerations were at play.

Most important, senior Mexican government officials concluded that making major concessions to the United States on labor rights issues was the necessary price for an outcome (accession to the TPP) that was both strategically vital for Mexico and politically important to Peña Nieto, whose personal approval ratings had fallen to historic lows.[226] They judged that, when finally confronted with the need to address questions that had long been an irritant in Mexico-U.S. bilateral relations,[227] it was preferable to adopt in-depth reforms rather than to try to defend piecemeal measures. The negative attention that ILO reports and complaints from international brand-name companies had drawn to employer protection contracts, which were increasingly identified with the endemic corruption that afflicted Mexican public affairs, was one consideration in this regard.[228] More generally, however, some key senior officials involved in internal debates over the question believed that significant labor reforms comprised part of the country's pending structural reform and democratization agendas. Although STPS officials were concerned about managing the response of old-guard labor organizations to these measures and the political turbulence that they might provoke, the senior officials engaged in the TPP negotiations found it difficult to defend the "labor dumping" status quo in interactions with their U.S. counterparts.[229]

Three political advantages underpinned President Peña Nieto's decision to proceed with the reform initiatives. First, the government counted on the closely held character of bilateral TPP negotiations over labor issues to limit domestic dissent from the Mexican labor movement. Only a small number of senior officials from the ministries directly involved were engaged in the negotiations; the issue was never discussed in a presidential cabinet meeting.[230] In part because senior Mexican officials publicly denied in the strongest terms any link between the TPP and labor reform and conceived a plausible cover rationale for the constitutional reform initiative,[231] they proved remarkably successful at keeping secret both the substance of the reforms and the circumstances that gave rise to Peña Nieto's decision. Even senior Mexican diplomats in Washington, DC, were unaware that the status of Mexico's International Monetary Fund credit line figured in the decision.[232]

Second, in implementing the initiatives, President Peña Nieto could rely on the PRI's legislative majority and strong party discipline to help win ratification of his constitutional reforms. These expectations were borne out. Despite opposition from business and old-guard labor organizations,[233] the constitutional reforms were, in the end, unanimously approved by the ninety-nine senators present on October 13, 2016, and by an overwhelming majority (379 to two, with nineteen abstentions) of those present in the federal Chamber of Deputies on November 4, 2016.[234]

Finally, senior government officials calculated they could reach side-agreements with domestic business and labor "losers" that would limit their opposition at the time President Peña Nieto announced the proposed reforms. Both government officials and business and labor opponents understood, based on their past experiences with labor law reform, that enacting constitutional changes would not necessarily overturn all elements of the status quo. The content of the secondary legislation adopted to implement the reforms would be of crucial importance. That legislation was still subject to negotiation (see below), and the text of the constitutional reforms had been drafted in a way that left open the possibility of preserving some form of tripartism in the labor justice system.[235] Moreover, the concerns of the two dominant labor confederations, the CTM and the CROC, were muffled by executive-branch assurances that their organizations would receive the lion's share of the contracts to be awarded for the construction of a new Mexico City international airport, the country's largest public infrastructure project in a century.[236]

The Transnational Defense of Mexico's Constitutional Reforms

The struggle over labor rights in Mexico did not end with congressional ratification of Peña Nieto's historic constitutional amendments. President Peña Nieto had made a personal commitment to President Obama on major labor reforms, but there was a possibility that Obama's successor might not pursue the issue with equal determination. This political calculus was the main reason Mexican officials had purposefully left undefined the institutional designs of the national union and contract registry and state-level conciliation centers,[237] and it shaped the Peña Nieto administration's actions on different fronts during Obama's final months in office.

As noted above, both chambers of the Mexican federal Congress debated and overwhelmingly approved the constitutional amendments in October-November 2016, before the end of Obama's term in office.[238] Because the process was under close U.S. scrutiny, the Peña Nieto administration pushed hard for unanimous congressional approval of the measures. In the Senate, this offered labor rights advocates unanticipated political leverage, which they used to lobby for extending the constitutional reforms' guarantee of a secret-ballot union membership vote to the initial approval of collective contracts as well. In the end, to win the backing of the center-left Party of the Democratic Revolution (Partido de la Revolución Democrática, PRD), its principal labor ally the UNT, and the Labor Party (Partido del Trabajo), Senate leaders conceded to their demand on this crucial point.[239]

The constitutional amendments then went to state legislatures for final majority approval. However, because of uncertainties regarding whether the incoming administration of President-elect Trump would seek to revise the NAFTA, the Peña Nieto administration exerted behind-the-scenes pressure to slow this process in order to keep its options open.[240] Not least, the purposeful delay in states' ratification of the constitutional amendments gave the Peña Nieto government grounds on which to deflect continued Obama administration pressures for quick congressional approval of the related labor law reforms.[241] As a consequence, the constitutional reforms were not published in the *Diario Oficial de la Federación* until February 24, 2017 (and therefore did not take effect until February 25).[242]

For the same political reasons, even though Obama administration officials pressed the Peña Nieto administration hard on the matter during the summer and fall of 2016, the Mexican Senate never took up for extended debate the proposed federal labor law reforms that Peña Nieto had announced in April and that the chamber of deputies approved in early October.[243] Instead, beginning in late 2016, STPS officials began work on alternative secondary legislation (the labor law reforms required to implement the constitutional amendments) that responded to criticisms employer organizations had voiced regarding the April initiative.[244] The STPS convened a working group comprised principally of attorneys representing leading national business organizations and representatives of the federal and state-level judiciaries. The group met daily in closed afternoon sessions over a period of eight months. One of the principal challenges its members faced was to translate the social-justice criteria and evaluative procedures that conciliation and arbitration boards had followed into the norms and procedures governing judicial tribunals. When a working draft of the proposed legislation was finally available, STPS officials began six weeks of intensive consultations with the COPARMEX, CCE, National Confederation of Chambers of Industry (Confederación Nacional de Cámaras Industriales, CONCAMIN), and Confederation of National Chambers of Commerce (Confederación de Cámeras Nacionales de Comercio, CONCANACO). Only after these consultations were over did STPS officials share a revised version of the draft legislation with attorneys representing the CTM, CROC, and CROM.[245] As with the earlier constitutional amendments, the CTM initially posed the strongest objections to some of the bill's provisions (including those that tightened legal requirements regarding strikes and relaxed the restrictions on labor subcontracting arrangements enacted in 2012). In the end, however, the CTM also assented.[246]

For reasons of political symbolism, the Peña Nieto administration tapped PRI Senators Isaías González Cuevas and Tereso Medina Ramírez (members of, respectively, the CROC and the CTM, the two largest labor confederations) to submit the initiative to the Senate's Labor Commission (Comisión del Trabajo).[247] They did so on December 7, 2017.[248] In the view of Mexican labor rights advocates, the initiative would have undercut the 2017 constitutional reforms' democratizing goals in several ways.[249] Most conspicuously, in response to insistent demands from both the business associations and old-guard labor organizations that had been consulted about the bill,[250] the Technical Council (Consejo Técnico) of the national agency responsible for officially registering all unions and collective bargaining agreements would be comprised of four labor, four business, and four government representatives (article 10)—a traditional tripartite arrangement that ensured the majority representation of those business and labor organizations.[251] Because this body would have had effective control over the agency's daily operations (including decisions over union registration and the validation of collective contracts at the national level), its proposed composition threatened more politically independent unions' organizational efforts and their ability to challenge employer protection contracts.[252]

Mexican government officials may not have fully anticipated how controversial this proposed legislation would become. In their initial communications in late 2016 and early 2017 with senior trade policy advisers to recently elected President Trump (2017–2021) regarding possible revision of the NAFTA, Mexican officials saw no indication that the new U. S. administration was particularly committed to labor rights issues.[253] However, because the submission of the González-Medina bill followed the formal launch of U.S.-Mexican negotiations to revise the NAFTA (hereinafter NAFTA 2.0) in August 2017, the legislative initiative quickly became embroiled in debates over the revised trade agreement's labor provisions. In marked contrast to Mexico-U.S. interactions over labor rights during the TPP negotiations, the political fight over the González-Medina bill was highly public.

Mexican independent unions and labor rights advocates mobilized against the proposed legislation in three ways. First, the UNT worked with the PRD to introduce its own secondary legislation initiative on February 7, 2018.[254] It forcefully rejected tripartite representation in the new national agency responsible for union and contract registration. Instead, it proposed that the agency's governing body be comprised of the heads of the National Anticorruption System (Sistema Nacional Anticorrupción), the National Human Rights Commission (Comisión Nacional de los Derechos Humanos), and the National System for Transparency, Access to Public Information, and Protection of Personal Data (Sistema Nacional de Transparencia, Acceso a la Información Pública y Protección de Datos Personales) (article 590a). The bill also underscored the importance of secret balloting in union elections and in the negotiation and approval of collective bargaining agreements.

Second, opposition forces sought to raise public awareness regarding the González-Medina initiative and its probable impact. Their principal vehicle was the Citizen Observatory on Labor Reform (Observatorio Ciudadano sobre la Reforma Laboral), a network of some 1,400 academic analysts, independent union leaders, labor lawyers, and labor rights activists formed in July 2017 to follow debates over implementation of the 2017 constitutional reforms. Their reports provided valuable, timely information to sympathetic Mexican media sources and international labor allies.

Third, Mexican unionists and labor rights advocates appealed to their international (especially U.S.) allies, drawing on the transnational social capital forged among North American labor organizations during the 1991–1993 NAFTA/NAALC debates and subsequent NAALC public communications.[255] The UNT had a formal cooperation agreement with the AFL-CIO, and on January 25, 2018, the two organizations jointly filed a NAALC communication that exhaustively critiqued the González-Medina bill and called for the U.S. Department of Labor to seek immediate ministerial consultations "with the GOM [government of Mexico] in order to dissuade it from enacting laws that violate the NAALC."[256] In a parallel action, on January 23, 183 Democratic congressional representatives published a letter to USTR Robert E. Lighthizer in which they condemned the González-Medina legislative initiative, critiqued the unfair competitive advantage Mexico derived from weak labor protections and repressed wages, and underscored the importance of strengthening NAFTA 2.0 labor standards if any final agreement were to secure Democratic legislative support.[257] In early March, Mexican unionists, federal legislators from center-left political parties, and a small group of workers with first-hand experience in fighting freedom-of-association violations discussed the dangers the González-Medina bill posed to union democracy with Democratic representatives Sander Levin (Democrat-Michigan) and Bill Pascrell (Democrat-New Jersey, then the ranking member of the House Committee on Ways and Means Subcommittee on Trade) during their visit to Mexico City for a scheduled round of NAFTA 2.0 talks.[258] Richard Trumka, president of the AFL-CIO, registered his serious concerns regarding the pending legislation directly (by letter and in person) with Ambassador Lighthizer.[259] On April 4, Trumka also wrote to Senator Ernesto Cordero Arroyo, president of the Mexican Senate's governing board, urging him to block the legislation on the grounds that it failed to comply with Mexico's obligations under the NAALC and risked undermining the NAFTA 2.0 negotiations.[260] In all these ways, the Mexico-U.S. labor rights coalition sought to take maximum advantage of the political opportunity created by the ongoing NAFTA 2.0 negotiations.[261] Their high-profile public engagement brought to bear on the Mexican and U.S. governments cross-border societal pressures that had been absent during the TPP negotiations.

In early February 2018, the authors of the controversial implementing legislation revised their initiative (eliminating provisions that permitted expanded labor subcontracting) in an effort to build political support for it. González and Medina then resubmitted it to the Senate on March 22.[262] At the time, the consensus among political observers was that the Peña Nieto administration would push the legislation forward to approval. With the July presidential elections approaching and with leftist candidate Andrés Manuel López Obrador holding a firm lead in opinion polls, the bill's business and old-guard labor supporters viewed the legislative session ending on April 30 as their last, best chance to pass the measure. Mexican and U.S. union and labor rights opponents, maintaining close communications, read the political moment in the same way. In response, they redoubled their efforts to block its approval. Over the course of just two days, the AFL-CIO and major U.S. industrial unions coordinated an urgent letter from 107 Democratic representatives and senators to Ambassador Lighthizer in which they expressed deep concern that the González-Medina bill would "gut the 2017 reform process," directly undermine "the ongoing effort to create a fair playing field for U.S. workers and U.S. businesses through NAFTA renegotiation," and pose "a potentially devastating obstacle to the success of the NAFTA renegotiation."[263] Once the letter became public (April 20), U.S. unionists worked with Mexican media contacts to ensure that it was also widely published in Mexico on the morning that the Senate convened to discuss the implementing legislation.[264]

A week before the end of the Senate's regular session, the Peña Nieto administration suspended consideration of the controversial González-Medina bill. Roberto Campa Cifrián, head of the STPS, announced that the government would hold four public consultative fora during June and July 2018 in an effort to reach broad consensus on the content of implementing legislation. The announced goal was to pass the resulting bill in a special congressional session in September.[265]

External factors were the principal determinants of the Mexican government's decision.[266] The very real prospect that approval of the González-Medina bill would heighten U.S. congressional opposition to an eventual NAFTA 2.0 agreement was of significant concern to Ambassador Lighthizer, who understood that the U.S. labor movement's demands had to be addressed if he were to achieve his goal of assembling a bipartisan congressional coalition in favor of the agreement.[267] Lighthizer made this point directly to his principal Mexican counterpart, Secretary of the Economy Ildefonso Guajardo.[268] Because Guajardo had also led the Mexican team during most of the TPP negotiations, he fully appreciated the threat that passage of controversial labor legislation might have posed to U.S. congressional ratification of a revised NAFTA.

When Campa Cifrián announced suspension of Senate consideration of the González-Medina initiative, he cited the "rarified" political environment during the final phases of the 2018 Mexican presidential campaign.[269] At the time of the decision, PRI presidential candidate José Antonio Meade Kuribreña ran third in opinion polls, and one might conclude that the Peña Nieto administration made its decision in part to prevent any possible negative publicity produced by approval of the controversial secondary labor legislation from damaging Meade's campaign. However, senior Meade campaign officials never even discussed the issue.[270] The status of the NAFTA 2.0 negotiations was far more important.[271] Given that automotive industry rules-of-origin and the content of the labor chapter had not yet been finalized, senior Mexican officials sought to avoid any additional risk in the unpredictable negotiations over a revised North American free-trade agreement,[272] a measure they judged crucially important to Mexico's economic future. It is possible, therefore, that Campa Cifrián framed his public explanation in terms that, once again, disguised the way in which external factors shaped an important domestic policy decision.

Whatever the specific calculations involved, the Peña Nieto administration's decision constituted a major political victory for prodemocracy labor forces in both Mexico and the United States. It cleared the way for the incoming López Obrador administration (2018–2024) to draft implementing legislation congruent with the goals of the 2017 constitutional reforms. That legislation was officially enacted on May 1, 2019.[273]

CONCLUSION

In the post-NAFTA bilateral and multilateral free-trade agreements examined in this chapter, the U.S. government was consistently able to employ its sovereignty leverage to embed labor rights provisions in the agreements themselves.[274] The content of these provisions changed over time in line with evolving U.S.

domestic debates concerning what should constitute signatory states' labor obligations and the evaluative criteria and dispute-settlement procedures employed to address rights violations. Perhaps the most important lesson these cases offer is that the United States was generally most successful at persuading prospective trade partners to adopt significant labor reforms when it lobbied for them during the FTA negotiations, making them a condition for accession to the agreement.[275] Among the most compelling examples were the U.S. negotiation of the 2011 labor action plan with Colombia, the potentially transformative labor consistency plan with Vietnam,[276] and the historic 2017 constitutional reforms in Mexico, which established the essential foundations for the country's democratizing May 1, 2019, Federal Labor Law. These outcomes reflected not just the United States' strategic and economic influence vis-à-vis prospective developing-country trade partners—many of them located in the Western Hemisphere, long a sphere of U.S. political predominance—but also the "up or down" nature of the accession decision-making process. The essential political requirement that both the U.S. executive and legislative branches of government endorse a free-trade agreement generally caused partner-country governments to accede even to U.S. demands regarding reforms involving collective-action labor rights, which in Weberian terms, are an area of core state sovereignty.

In marked contrast to the comparative success of market access-leverage strategies, U.S. government efforts to advance labor rights through FTA cooperative-consultation and dispute-settlement procedures produced disappointing results.[277] Only two of the eight FTA labor submissions examined in this chapter ended with *any* positive policy impact (both scored 1 on a scale of 0–4 in table 5.1). The most conspicuous failure, of course, was the 2008–2017 complaint against Guatemala, the only labor rights case ever addressed through final dispute-settlement procedures in any U.S. free-trade agreement.[278] After the U. S. government initiated formal dispute-settlement proceedings, it was able to persuade the Guatemalan government to sign a labor action plan. However, the plan achieved little in practice—so little that the U.S. government decided to move forward with dispute-settlement procedures. A particularly telling aspect of this case is that, despite intense U.S. diplomatic pressures, the Guatemalan Ministry of Labor's enforcement budget actually declined in inflation-adjusted terms between 2006 and 2010, a period during which other DR-CAFTA countries increased their labor enforcement expenditures. During this same period, the number of labor inspectors grew in every DR-CAFTA country except Guatemala, where it fell.[279]

Based on the findings from an analysis of U.S. GSP labor rights petitions reported in chapter 2, one might have predicted different results from the FTA submissions. The U.S. trade unions and labor rights NGOs that filed the OTLA submissions successfully mobilized strong support from local labor allies in almost all the target countries, the importance of which was clearly reflected in the quality of the supporting documentation. Nonetheless, the case examined in this chapter in which active local allies most clearly contributed to a positive outcome occurred outside the OTLA grievance framework: the successful transnational defense of the democratizing contents of Mexico's 2017 constitutional reforms by a coalition of Mexican and U.S. unions and NGOs. Evidence of strong local support for the OTLA complaints may also have bolstered the political commitment of the U.S. labor authorities responsible for addressing them. Yet, the fact that the OTLA accepted for review the first Peru submission (which was only tangentially related to bilateral trade issues) and the Dominican Republic submission (which was filed by a single individual) indicates that, at least during the Obama administration, this was not a necessary condition for OTLA support.[280]

In each of these cases, U.S. labor officials actively engaged in sustained bilateral negotiations over necessary legal and policy reforms in the country under review. In the complaint involving Bahrain, they apparently backed away somewhat from their initial strong demands that the Bahraini government reverse the anti-union legislation adopted in the wake of the 2011 crisis, instead focusing more on the reinstatement of public- and private-sector workers who had been fired. Moreover, in the complaints against Colombia, Guatemala, and Honduras, U.S. officials did not give priority attention to the continuing violence against trade unionists in their submission-related negotiations with these countries. In these and other instances, U.S. government support for more far-ranging reforms may, at times, have been constrained by countervailing foreign policy priorities in what were multifaceted diplomatic relationships with FTA partners. However, successive U.S. presidential administrations' demonstrated commitment to winning major labor rights improvements in Guatemala suggests that the overall U.S. failure to achieve more significant results through FTA grievance procedures cannot be attributed simply to a lack of political will.

There are two other possible explanations for the failure of U.S. FTA grievance processes to achieve better outcomes. First, compared to the possibility under the U.S. GSP program of even temporarily losing access to the U.S. market as a penalty for proven labor rights violations, the sanctions that the United States could impose on its free-trade partners were limited. Even under the terms of the FTAs that took effect following adoption of the May 10, 2007, agreement, the potential sanctions did not endanger a partner country's overall trading relationship with the United States. Moreover, the fact that governments, rather than employers, were the object of potential penalties meant that sanctions would not directly challenge the business practices that caused the rights violations in question. There is evidence that some U.S. FTA partner countries, like some participants in the U.S. GSP program, were concerned about the reputational damage that might be caused by an OTLA submission. For instance, a desire to avoid negative international publicity might have been a factor in shaping the Costa Rican government's decision to accept the August 2010 Constitutional Court ruling that reinstated SINTRAJAP union leaders. Costa Rican officials were clearly concerned enough about submission US 2010 that they took the unusual step of filing a strong rebuttal statement even before the OTLA had decided to review the complaint, and they lobbied for a rapid OTLA decision (they argued that the submission had no merit) in order to end the controversy as quickly as possible.[281] For the most part, however, reputational concerns were insufficient to overcome what was presumably strong employer opposition to legal or policy changes regarding such matters as the illegal use of subcontracting arrangements to block unionization. Only one of the four U.S. FTA labor rights submissions that ended either with cooperative consultations or with the invocation of dispute-settlement procedures produced any observed positive policy impact (table 5.1).

A second reason why U.S. FTA grievance procedures were less successful as a rights-promotion mechanism than either the U.S. GSP complaints process or U.S. pre-agreement bargaining strategies may be that the focus of the FTA cases was primarily on effective labor law enforcement rather than on partner-country legal reforms per se. Perhaps somewhat counterintuitively, it may be more difficult for external actors to influence labor enforcement policies (and strengthen the rule of law more generally) than to pressure for the adoption of legal reforms. Domestic businesses with a stake in blocking unionization and preserving uncompromised control over workplace affairs may well be less concerned about the content of labor laws than with how they are applied in practice. As a consequence, as the double-helix model outlined in chapter 1 would suggest, domestic resistance to external pressures for change may grow as the focus shifts from formal approval to effective implementation of labor laws, particularly those concerning freedom of association and the rights to organize and bargain collectively.[282] These considerations offer a possible explanation for the differences in observed policy impact reported for U.S. GSP petitions (table 2.1) and U.S. FTA submissions (table 5.1).[283] The GSP petitions examined in chapter 2 were filed between 1985 and 1995 when labor legislation in many of the target countries was particularly weak, and in several instances, their principal success was to win adoption of important legal reforms. By the time of the U.S. FTA submissions, the principal labor rights issues in these countries had evolved to the even more daunting challenge of effectively implementing existing laws despite continued business opposition.[284]

CHAPTER 6

Renegotiating the North American Free Trade Agreement

Labor Rights and the United States-Mexico-Canada Agreement, 2017–2019

At the insistence of U.S. President Donald J. Trump (2017–2021), Canada, Mexico, and the United States renegotiated the North American Free Trade Agreement (NAFTA) between August 2017 and December 2019. Labor rights were an important issue in these highly contentious interactions, as they had been in the 1990–1993 domestic and international negotiations over the NAFTA and its labor "side-agreement."[1] However, although the principal state and nonstate actors involved in these exchanges largely remained the same, the positions they adopted and the bargaining outcomes differed significantly.

Most important, whereas in 1990, it was Mexico that took the initiative in pursuing a free-trade agreement with the United States (and then Canada), in 2017, the negotiations were driven principally by the Trump administration and its dissatisfaction with the existing agreement. Previous U.S. presidential candidates (all Democrats) had also campaigned on pledges to renegotiate parts of the NAFTA, including the North American Agreement on Labor Cooperation (NAALC).[2] Trump, however, made condemnation of "the worst trade deal maybe ever signed anywhere, but certainly ever signed in this country" a central plank in his 2015–2016 presidential campaign.[3] His unanticipated Electoral College victory was based, in part, on the narrow popular-vote pluralities he won in Michigan, Ohio, Pennsylvania, and Wisconsin—all states whose substantial manufacturing workforces had suffered from the relocation of production to low-wage sites in Mexico.[4] The electoral support that Republican candidate Trump received from significant numbers of rank-and-file union members in these states reinforced his stated commitment to radically renegotiate the NAFTA in order to reduce the U.S. trade deficit with Mexico, benefit manufacturing workers by stimulating U.S. firms to shift production back to the United States, and thereby, in Trump's signature phrase, "Make America Great Again."[5] A broad bipartisan consensus among Republican and Democratic members of Congress, state governors, and the U.S. private sector strongly favored preserving the NAFTA. A range of independent assessments also stressed the importance of trade with Mexico for the U.S. economy.[6] Nonetheless, President Trump repeatedly threatened to withdraw from the agreement, in part as a bargaining tactic to press demands to which both Canada and Mexico objected.[7] In fact, in late April 2017, Trump came close to signing an executive order that would have triggered NAFTA's article 2205 and initiated U.S. withdrawal from the accord.[8]

From the outset, both the Canadian and Mexican governments expressed a willingness to reassess and "modernize" the NAFTA in order to address trade issues such as Internet commerce that had taken on new importance over time.[9] However, their relative dependence on the survival of the agreement differed substantially. Canada's negotiators strongly defended points such as "carve-outs" for its cultural industries and chapter 19 procedures to resolve trade conflicts. Yet if the negotiations had collapsed, or if Trump had followed through on his repeated threats to abrogate the trilateral accord, Canada had (as it also had in the NAFTA negotiations) a fallback position in the 1988 Canada-United States Free Trade Agreement, which had only been suspended so long as the NAFTA remained in effect. For Mexico, though, the NAFTA was of fundamental strategic economic importance. In 1993, failure to secure final approval of a free-trade agreement with the United States would have been a serious political setback for President Carlos Salinas de Gortari (1988–1994). In 2017, the NAFTA underpinned both the country's high trade dependence on the United States and its ability to attract sustained flows of foreign direct investment. As two successive Mexican presidential administrations with very different ideological profiles and political agendas demonstrated over the course of the NAFTA revision (hereinafter NAFTA 2.0) negotiations, no Mexican government could fail to energetically defend the country's stake in the agreement.[10]

The structure of the NAALC and the NAFTA 2.0 labor negotiations also contrasted greatly. Whereas in 1993, government-to-government interactions were fully trilateral, with shared draft proposals and bargaining sessions rotating among the three countries, the principal 2017–2019 interactions over labor questions were between the United States and Mexico—and among U.S. trade officials and domestic stakeholders in the labor movement and the U.S. Congress. The Canadian government offered several important labor proposals at the outset of the NAFTA 2.0 negotiations, and Mexican and U.S. negotiators kept their Canadian counterparts apprised of the issues they were debating. However, the negotiations themselves, particularly during 2018 and 2019, were more sequenced bilateral discussions (first between the United States and Mexico, and then between the United States and Canada) than trilateral exchanges. President Trump was predisposed to favor bilateral over trilateral trade negotiations because he believed it enhanced U.S. bargaining leverage,[11] and, in the final phases of the general NAFTA 2.0 negotiations, the U.S. government first sought to win concessions from Mexico that it could later impose on Canada. (Indeed, the Trump administration struck deals first with Mexico on August 27, 2018, and then with Canada on September 30, 2018.)[12] Yet in the labor rights area, this dynamic mainly reflected the fact that the 2018–2019 bilateral negotiations between the U.S. and Mexican governments were driven by long-standing concerns shared by U.S. trade unions and their Democratic congressional allies over labor rights enforcement in Mexico.

The U.S. labor movement found an unexpected ally in the Trump administration on NAFTA-related issues. Although trade union leaders opposed many of the administration's labor, healthcare, immigration, and tax policies, they shared a common opposition to the NAFTA and the NAALC.[13] Certainly, the first priority of the American Federation of Labor-Congress of Industrial Organizations (AFL-CIO) and leading industrial unions was to strengthen the NAALC's enforcement mechanisms. However, they also opposed the existing trade agreement's investor-state dispute-settlement procedures (they argued that special investment protections for transnational firms operated as a subsidy for off-shore production), and they strongly backed the Trump administration's efforts to bolster domestic-content provisions and attach a "sunset clause" to a revised NAFTA. In 1993, the AFL-CIO had mobilized to block U.S. congressional approval of the NAFTA outright, and in 2017 AFL-CIO President Richard Trumka publicly declared that "No deal is better than a bad deal."[14] Yet, in practice, given the significant integration of the U.S. and Mexican economies and North American supply chains and broad, cross-sectoral public support for preserving the agreement, ending the NAFTA was no longer a serious option.

Although there was some initial debate among U.S. labor organizations over the merits of engaging with the anti-labor Trump administration, the AFL-CIO and major unions decided early on that lobbying for a substantially revised NAFTA was the only viable course of political action available to them.[15] Throughout the process, they repeatedly signaled their willingness to negotiate seriously. In fact, the AFL-CIO prepared for the formal opening of trilateral negotiations in August 2017 by publishing a detailed policy document outlining its proposals for revising the entire trade agreement. It introduced the proposals by stating, "A better NAFTA is possible, and it should begin with a serious conversation about the recommendations set forth in this document."[16] In the final phase of negotiations, the combination of President Trump's declared willingness to scrap the NAFTA and the Democratic Party's renewed majority in the U.S. House of Representatives gave the U.S. labor movement the necessary political leverage to successfully advance many of its demands. As a consequence, the United States-Mexico-Canada Agreement's (USMCA) labor provisions were far stronger than the NAALC.

This chapter reconstructs in detail the negotiations that occurred between 2017 and 2019 over the USMCA's labor provisions. The discussion parallels chapter 3 by focusing on three main issues: the alignment of key domestic sociopolitical actors (especially in the United States and Mexico) and any important changes over time; the character of the NAFTA 2.0 negotiations over labor rights and enforcement in Mexico; and the extent to which the United States was able to deploy its sovereignty leverage to positive effect in the negotiations. The preceding analysis of NAALC public communications concerning labor rights violations in Mexico (chapter 4) and labor complaints filed under post-NAALC free-trade agreements (chapter 5) showed that, following the implementation of a trade agreement, U.S. leverage vis-à-vis its trade partners over labor questions generally declined significantly. One might have anticipated that efforts to renegotiate the long-established NAFTA / NAALC would have conformed to a similar pattern. However, Trump's repeated threats simply to withdraw from the NAFTA—threats given credibility by his unilateral abrogation in January 2017 of U.S. participation in the Trans-Pacific Partnership agreement—substantially bolstered U.S. bargaining influence.

THE NAFTA 2.0 NEGOTIATIONS OVER LABOR RIGHTS

It was obvious from the outset that negotiations over a revised NAFTA would include labor rights issues. Political consensus within the United States regarding the terms on which labor provisions were incorporated into free-trade agreements had evolved considerably since the adoption of the NAALC in 1993 (see chapter 5). At a minimum, then, any NAFTA 2.0 agreement had to reflect those changes.

There were, nevertheless, two reasons why labor issues were particularly sensitive political questions in these negotiations. First, the talks began shortly after an international arbitration panel concluded in June 2017 that the United States had not demonstrated that Guatemala's failure to enforce its labor obligations under the Dominican Republic-Central American Free Trade Agreement (DR-CAFTA) had affected bilateral trade (see chapter 5). The ruling ended a nine-year legal proceeding against a country long known for notorious labor rights violations, and it concluded the only case in which a labor rights public submission had passed through all phases of established dispute-settlement procedures in a U.S. free-trade agreement (FTA). The panel's decision not only outraged U.S. labor organizations and labor rights advocates, but it also raised fundamental questions about the practical viability of the May 10, 2007, language that had been incorporated into U.S. FTA labor rights enforcement procedures. Because the arbitration panel issued its decision on June 14, 2017, just two months before the start of the NAFTA 2.0 negotiations, it set the tone for subsequent debates over labor provisions in any revised agreement.

Second, after a quarter century of increasingly close North American economic integration, leading U.S. and Canadian industrial unions remained intently focused on the threats posed by the continued shift of manufacturing production from the United States and Canada to low-wage Mexico.[17] The NAALC had failed to establish conditions under which a representative, democratically organized Mexican labor movement could fight effectively for improved wages, benefits, and working conditions and thereby reduce the competitive economic challenges that U.S. and Canadian labor organizations faced from Mexico.[18] The NAFTA 2.0 negotiations, therefore, offered them a unique opportunity to address such issues as ineffective labor law enforcement and suppressed wages in Mexico.

The NAFTA 2.0 negotiations over labor rights proceeded in two phases.[19] During phase I (August 2017–September 2018), there were both trilateral state-to-state negotiations over the content of a revised agreement's labor chapter and exchanges among U.S. and Mexican officials and a cross-border alliance of rights activists over the labor law legislation that would implement Mexico's important 2017 constitutional reforms on labor rights (see chapter 5). These interacting negotiations ended on terms that directly linked the content of the new trade agreement's labor chapter to democratic labor law reform in Mexico. Phase II (November 2018–December 2019) effectively began when, after the Democratic Party again won majority control of the U.S. House of Representatives in November 2018, the U.S. labor movement and its Democratic congressional allies mobilized to revise key portions of the USMCA's labor chapter. The protocol of amendment to the USMCA that Democrats and the Trump administration agreed on in December 2019 significantly advanced debate over trade agreement-linked labor provisions and opened a new chapter in the international promotion of labor rights in North America.

PHASE I: RENEGOTIATING THE NAFTA / NAALC LABOR PROVISIONS, AUGUST 2017–SEPTEMBER 2018

Negotiations over the NAFTA 2.0 Labor Chapter

The first round of NAFTA 2.0 negotiations took place on August 16–20, 2017, in Washington, DC.[20] However, discussions concerning labor rights proceeded very slowly because other high-profile issues (including domestic-content rules of origin in the automobile industry, investor-state dispute-settlement procedures, patent protection for biologic drugs, and a sunset clause) took precedence. Moreover, the Office of the United States Trade Representative (USTR) and leading U.S. labor organizations entered the negotiations with substantially different goals. The USTR took the Trans-Pacific Partnership (TPP) agreement's labor chapter—which U.S. labor organizations had roundly condemned—as the logical starting point for discussions with the Canadian and Mexican governments because both these countries had ratified the TPP. The TPP had been an advance on the NAALC because its chapter 19 embraced the International Labour Organization's (ILO) 1998 Declaration on Fundamental Principles and Rights of Work, made signatories' labor rights obligations fully subject to dispute-settlement procedures, and included the May 10, 2007, language regarding rights enforcement.[21] In the wake of the Guatemala arbitration panel ruling, however, U.S. labor organizations demanded major changes in any NAFTA 2.0 labor chapter.

The TPP-based labor proposal that the USTR tabled during the third round of negotiations on September 23-27, 2017, in Ottawa, Canada,[22] immediately drew sharp criticism from U.S. labor organizations and their Democratic political allies. The AFL-CIO condemned the proposal because it retained the problematic May 10, 2007, language stipulating that alleged labor rights violations were subject to dispute-settlement procedures only when the alleged violation occurred "in a manner affecting trade or investment between the parties" and formed part of a "sustained or recurring course of action or inaction." Representative Sander Levin (Democrat-Michigan), a long-time defender of worker rights, noted that the USTR proposal was inadequate because it did not address the underlying problem of low Mexican wages resulting from the absence of effective guarantees of freedom of association. He also argued that a U.S. congressional vote on NAFTA 2.0 should be delayed until Mexico had adopted legislation implementing the country's 2017 constitutional labor reforms.[23] On November 15, 2017, sixteen Democratic senators seconded these critiques, demanding that the "in a manner affecting trade or investment" criterion be dropped from the U.S. draft and that the "in a sustained or recurring course of action or inaction" language be narrowly defined. They maintained that Mexico should implement its delayed labor law reform as a qualifying condition for NAFTA 2.0 trade benefits. In addition, they called for the creation of an "independent labor compliance and monitoring agency" to overcome weaknesses in existing dispute-settlement procedures.[24]

Some of the most innovative initial labor proposals came from the Canadian negotiating team in August 2017. Canadian negotiators argued that, whereas the TPP (and other U.S. FTA labor chapters) only called upon signatory parties to respect the "internationally-recognized labor principles" articulated in the ILO Declaration, a NAFTA 2.0 labor chapter should require all three signatory countries to adopt the eight ILO fundamental conventions on which the 1998 declaration was based (see table 1.1). The Canadian proposal also called for provisions barring violence against workers, full recognition of gender equality in the workplace (including a ban on discrimination on the basis of gender identity), and protection of indigenous peoples' rights.[25] These proposals were strongly endorsed by UNIFOR (Canada's largest private sector union), the United Steelworkers

(USW)-Canada, and, after some adjustments, the AFL-CIO.[26] They were, however, dismissed by Representative Levin on the grounds that they would be politically unviable in the United States, where adoption of ILO convention no. 87 (freedom of association and the right to organize) would challenge so-called right-to-work provisions of the federal Taft-Hartley Act (Labor Management Relations Act of 1947, section 14[b]) that allowed individual U.S. states to adopt legislation permitting workers to be employed in unionized workplaces without actually joining the union or paying union dues.[27] Levin maintained, moreover, that some of the Canadian proposals would distract NAFTA 2.0 negotiators from "the fundamental issue: Mexico's labor standards."[28] In practice, although Canadian negotiators occasionally later defended the merits of their proposals, they had only a modest impact on labor rights questions over the course of the NAFTA 2.0 negotiations.[29]

Even in the early stages of the negotiating process, U.S. labor organizations and members of the U.S. Congress publicly recognized that USTR Ambassador Robert E. Lighthizer was open to constructive dialogue on labor issues.[30] Indeed, in an August 2017 appearance before the U.S. House of Representatives Committee on Ways and Means, Lighthizer had publicly accepted that "low labor standards are an unfair trade advantage."[31] It was in this spirit that Lighthizer responded to initial criticisms of the TPP-based labor text by promising to conduct further consultations with the U.S. Congress and labor leaders and present a revised text.[32] In late November, he signaled that he agreed that labor rights violations should be subject to binding dispute-settlement provisions, and by early January 2018 (and perhaps earlier), he also indicated that he was open to modifying the initial U.S. labor proposal where May 10, 2007 language was concerned.[33] Lighthizer conveyed this position directly to members of U.S. congressional trade committees in early February, as well as his intention to seek a so-called labor consistency plan with Mexico—an idea that Mexican officials immediately rejected.[34] Nonetheless, even though 183 Democratic congressional representatives had written to Ambassador Lighthizer on January 23, 2018, to condemn Mexico's labor rights record and underscore the importance of adopting robust, enforceable labor rights provisions in a prospective NAFTA 2.0 agreement,[35] there was, at the time, no change in the USTR's formal position on these questions.[36]

One telling indication that U.S. officials understood the political importance of addressing the concerns voiced by leading labor unions and their Democratic congressional allies came in the form of a White House meeting between President Trump and senior labor leaders on February 21, 2018.[37] Following intensified consultations with U.S. labor organizations in January and February, the USTR circulated new text language on Capitol Hill and to security-cleared labor union representatives in late February 2018. It included somewhat strengthened enforcement provisions and a demand that Mexico more actively combat violence against trade unionists. Nevertheless, even though the parties involved now understood that a NAFTA 2.0 labor chapter would include a footnote specifying the meaning of "in a manner affecting trade or investment," the USTR had still not formally presented a revised labor text at the time of the seventh NAFTA 2.0 negotiating round in Mexico City on February 25–March 5, 2018.[38]

Mexico's position in these negotiations was not completely defensive. Indeed, the Ministry of the Economy's initial negotiating objectives included "strengthening compliance with national arrangements and international agreements on labor matters."[39] On September 22, 2017, at the outset of negotiations, Secretary of Foreign Relations Luis Videgaray underscored this position: "We don't want to be a country that is competitive because Mexican workers are being paid low wages. . . . If we can use the new NAFTA framework to enhance the protection of labor rights and labor conditions in the benefit of Mexican workers we are definitely going to do that."[40]

Mexican negotiators did not table their own proposed labor text until the fourth negotiating round (October 11–15, 2017, in Arlington, Virginia).[41] In doing so, they accepted that a revised NAFTA would include a separate chapter on labor rights (rather than addressing the issue in a side-agreement like the NAALC). Moreover, they assumed, like their U.S. counterparts, that the TPP's chapter 19 would be the basis for NAFTA 2.0 labor discussions.[42] For these reasons, they did not initially anticipate that labor issues would be a particularly controversial matter.[43] Nevertheless, they clearly stated early on that the U.S. call for a labor consistency plan was not acceptable. Under strong pressures from the Mexican private sector, they also flatly rejected the idea that domestic matters such as wages could be addressed through a free-trade agreement.[44]

By early April 2018, domestic-content rules of origin in the automobile manufacturing industry and labor questions had emerged as among the most challenging issues in the NAFTA 2.0 negotiations.[45] By then, there was an increasingly clear linkage between the ongoing trade negotiations and the building controversy over the labor law legislation that the administration of President Enrique

Peña Nieto (2012–2018) proposed to implement Mexico's 2017 constitutional reforms (see chapter 5), a conjuncture that U.S. labor rights activists viewed as a source of additional political leverage in negotiations over the NAFTA 2.0 labor chapter.[46] As U.S.-Mexican exchanges over these issues intensified, Secretary Videgaray, President Peña Nieto's most trusted senior adviser and the cabinet minister with the highest-level contacts in the Trump administration, assumed direct oversight over the automobile rules-of-origin and labor negotiations.[47]

In late April 2018, the USTR finally circulated a revised labor text to selected members of the U.S. Congress and other domestic stakeholders. As Ambassador Lighthizer had promised, it clarified "in a manner affecting trade or investment," but it did not eliminate all the May 10, 2007, language opposed by U.S. labor unions and rights advocates. Nor, despite strong lobbying by a number of major U.S. labor organizations, did it alter the provision specifying that the U.S. government's commitment was to the principles articulated in the ILO's 1998 declaration (and not to the underlying fundamental ILO conventions).[48] It has not been possible to determine when this text was formally tabled in the NAFTA 2.0 negotiations. The pace of negotiations did, however, slow considerably in May and June because several highly contentious issues remained unresolved (especially domestic-content rules of origin in the automobile industry, a sunset clause, investor-state dispute-settlement procedures, and intellectual property issues concerning biologic drugs[49]) and because of mounting political uncertainty surrounding the outcome of Mexico's July 1 presidential election.[50]

The labor chapter (chapter 23) that the negotiating parties finally announced on August 27, 2018,[51] paralleled the TPP's labor chapter in its overall focus and structure, including the thematic headings it employed.[52] Like the TPP's chapter 19, it framed the signatory parties' labor obligations in terms of the internationally recognized rights specified in the ILO's 1998 declaration. It also included very similar provisions concerning nonderogation of labor rights (that is, the parties agreed that it was inappropriate to weaken or reduce protections in order to encourage trade or investment), the enforcement of labor laws, cooperative activities and cooperative labor dialogue, the trinational Labor Council established to exercise oversight responsibilities and take decisions by consensus, and administrative procedures to resolve disputes arising from allegations of labor rights violations. Moreover, like all U.S. FTAs negotiated after 2007, the chapter made labor disputes that could not be resolved through consultation and dialogue fully subject to dispute-settlement procedures.

Chapter 23 did, however, depart from its TPP precedent in two significant ways. First, it strengthened and expanded labor rights guarantees. The text bolstered the right to freedom of association by explicitly protecting the right to strike,[53] strengthened language concerning the prohibition on forced or compulsory labor,[54] and clarified that "acceptable conditions of work with respect to minimum wages" included any national provisions for wage-linked social benefits (article 23.1, footnote 1). In addition, the chapter included new articles on violence against workers (article 23.7), migrant workers (article 23.8), and sex-based discrimination in the workplace, including on the basis of sexual orientation and gender identity (article 23.9).[55] Several other parts of the text reaffirmed and expanded these protections. For example, article 23.2.3 stipulated that "the Parties recognize the goal of trading only in goods that meet the obligations of this Chapter." Similarly, the chapter expanded the list of cooperative activities the signatory parties might undertake to include: strengthening compliance with ILO Convention No. 182 (Concerning the Prohibition and Immediate Action for the Elimination of the Worst Forms of Child Labor); combatting violence against workers, forced labor and human trafficking, and the movement of goods produced by forced labor; addressing gender-related issues in labor and employment and preventing gender-based violence and harassment in the workplace; and promoting the sharing of information concerning working conditions in multinational corporations operating in two or more of the NAFTA countries (article 23.12.5 [b, c, d, e, j, r]).

Second, chapter 23 addressed the labor rights enforcement problems highlighted by the 2017 Guatemala arbitration panel ruling. Article 23.3 (Labor Rights) clarified and significantly relaxed the terms under which covered rights could be enforced by including, without exception, *any* trade or investment in which the signatory countries were engaged:

> To establish a violation of an obligation . . ., a Party must demonstrate that the other Party has failed to adopt or maintain a statute, regulation, or practice in a manner affecting trade or investment between the Parties. *For greater certainty, a failure is "in a manner affecting trade or investment between the Parties" when it involves: (1) a person or industry that produces goods or provides services traded between the Parties or has investment in the territory of the Party that has failed to comply with this obligation; or (2) a person or industry that produces goods or services that compete in the territory of a Party with goods or services of another Party* (article 23.3.1 (a), footnote 4; emphasis added).

In addition, article 23.5 (Enforcement of Labor Laws) sought to clarify the meaning of the phrase ("a sustained or recurring course of action or inaction") that specified when labor rights violations would be subject to dispute settlement and potential penalty:

> For greater certainty, a "sustained or recurring course of action or inaction" is "sustained" where the course of action or inaction is consistent or ongoing, and is "recurring" where the course of action or inaction occurs periodically or repeatedly and when the occurrences are related or the same in nature. A course of action or inaction does not include an isolated instance or case (article 23.5.1, footnote 8).

The negotiating parties inserted this clarifying language into chapter 23 in several places, including in the article prohibiting violence against workers.[56]

Although low wage levels in Mexico had often been an issue in the NAFTA 2.0 negotiations, the labor chapter itself did not address the question. The only part of the overall agreement that considered wages was chapter 4 (Rules of Origin, annex 4-B, appendix), which established stringent new rules of origin in the automobile manufacturing industry. The three signatory countries agreed to a four-year transition period during which the North American regional value content (that is, the share of a vehicle's or an automotive part's value produced in Canada, Mexico, and/or the United States in order for it to qualify for duty-free export to the other countries) would rise from an existing level of 62.5 percent to 75 percent. The agreement further required that, by the end of the transition period, 40-45 percent of the labor value content of a vehicle's components be produced in factories with an average production wage rate of US$16.00 per hour, defined as "the average hourly base wage rate, not including benefits, of employees directly involved in the production of the part or component used to calculate" the labor value content.[57] In principle, the labor value content calculation would only include the wages of employees working directly on the production line. However, Mexican officials—scrambling to soften the negative impact that this change might have on its most important export manufacturing industry—successfully negotiated a provision allowing "high-wage assembly expenditures" (including expenditures on research and development or information technology) to account for up to five percentage points of the required labor value content.[58]

Annex 23-A and Democratic Labor Reform in Mexico

Including a novel provision concerning labor value content was certainly an important development in the evolution of U.S. FTAs, but by far the most politically significant labor-related portion of the revised NAFTA / NAALC accord was chapter 23's annex 23-A, titled "Worker Representation in Collective Bargaining in Mexico."[59] This document emerged as the end-product of U.S.-Mexican interactions over labor law reform in Mexico and the defeat of the controversial González-Medina initiative in spring and summer 2018 (see chapter 5).

In the final bilateral exchanges over the NAFTA 2.0 agreement in late August 2018, U.S. negotiators, responding to labor movement pressure and with an eye toward winning Democratic congressional support for the trade agreement, compelled the Mexican government to accept language designed to block any further attempts to undercut the democratizing content of Mexico's historic 2017 constitutional labor reforms.[60] Annex 23-A laid out detailed substantive requirements for secondary legislation implementing the constitutional reforms. In fact, its language closely paralleled the main provisions of the labor law reform bill the Peña Nieto administration had announced in April 2016 and later dropped in favor of the González-Medina initiative. In effect, the annex wrote into an international agreement the key reforms that U.S. government labor officials had negotiated with their Mexican counterparts during the Trans-Pacific Partnership negotiations but which the Mexican government had then sought to elude.[61]

The annex reaffirmed the terms of the 2017 constitutional amendments by requiring Mexico to "establish and maintain independent and impartial bodies to register union elections and resolve disputes relating to collective bargaining agreements," including the creation of "an independent entity for conciliation and registration of unions and collective bargaining agreements, and independent Labor Courts for the adjudication of labor disputes" (annex 23-A.2.b). It highlighted the importance of laws protecting the rights to organize and bargain collectively and prohibiting employers from interfering in union activities and/ or refusing to bargain collectively (annex 23-A.2.a). The annex also committed Mexico to creating "an effective system to verify that elections of union leaders are carried out through a personal, free, and secret vote of union members (annex 23-1.2.c). Finally, it directly addressed the problem of employer protection contracts by requiring demonstration of majority support "through exercise of a personal, free, and secret vote of workers covered by the agreement" for new collective contracts and all subsequent contract revisions addressing wages and working conditions. The independent entity responsible for registering contracts was required to confirm that the worksite was operational and that "a copy of the collective bargaining agreement was made readily accessible to individual workers prior to the vote." Moreover, all collective bargaining agreements in Mexico were to be revised at least once in the first four years after a new federal labor law took effect (annex 23-A.2.e(ii), f).[62] The U.S. authors of the annex sought to maintain pressure on Mexico by signaling that the NAFTA 2.0 trade agreement might not enter into force until after the required secondary labor legislation took effect (the target date for which was prior to January 1, 2019) (annex 23-A.3).

In formulating annex 23-A, U.S. officials adopted language similar to the April 2016 Peña Nieto labor law reform bill on the assumption that this would ease Mexican negotiators' agreement to it.[63] Yet even though the Peña Nieto administration had in 2015–2016 conceded to intense U.S. pressures and agreed to reform proposals similar to those in annex 23-A, Mexico's NAFTA 2.0 negotiating team and senior Ministry of Labor and Social Welfare (Secretaría del Trabajo y Previsión Social, STPS) officials were strongly opposed in principle to what was, in effect, a labor consistency plan like those the United States had negotiated with Southeast Asian countries (and which Mexico had successfully avoided) during the TPP negotiations.[64] However, Andrés Manuel López Obrador's landslide presidential election victory on July 1, 2018, transformed political circumstances, making it impossible for the Peña Nieto administration to have won congressional approval of secondary legislation similar to the González-Medina bill. This change, combined with explicit support for the annex's content from the López Obrador transition team and an opening statement in it clarifying that " . . . the Mexican government incoming in December 2018 has confirmed that each of these provisions is within the scope of the mandate provided to the government by the people of Mexico in the elections,"[65] led Mexican negotiators to agree to annex 23-A during the final days of U.S.-Mexican negotiations over the NAFTA 2.0 agreement in late August 2018.[66]

For the incumbent Mexican administration, this was the price to be paid in order to bring the NAFTA 2.0 negotiations to conclusion on a schedule that would permit outgoing President Peña Nieto to sign the revised trade agreement before leaving office. For the incoming López Obrador administration (2018–2024), bringing to conclusion the prolonged, controversial negotiations over issues of strategic economic importance to Mexico (amid lingering concerns that President Trump might still cancel the NAFTA) promised to remove the complicated matter from its policy agenda.[67] Moreover, the annex 23-A requirements provided the López Obrador administration with valuable political leverage in enacting a major labor law reform that was fully congruent with the 2017 constitutional reforms.[68]

PHASE II: TWO-LEVEL NEGOTIATIONS OVER LABOR RIGHTS ENFORCEMENT IN MEXICO, DECEMBER 2018–DECEMBER 2019

As previously noted, the Trump administration concluded negotiations with Mexico on August 27, 2018, and with Canada on September 30, 2018, over what was titled the United States-Mexico-Canada Agreement (USMCA). Representatives of several major U.S. unions later acknowledged that chapter 23, with modifications of the TPP template and the addition of annex 23-A, made the agreement preferable to outright U.S. withdrawal from the NAFTA and the NAALC.[69] Nonetheless, U.S. and Canadian labor organizations immediately restated their concerns about the enforcement of its labor protections.[70]

Criticisms of this kind had in the past been in vain. However, the Democratic Party won a solid majority (235 seats in a 435-seat body) in midterm elections for the U.S. House of Representatives on November 6, 2018. As a consequence, even though leaders of the Canadian, Mexican, and U.S. governments formally signed the USMCA on November 30 at a G-20 summit meeting in Buenos Aires, Argentina, the political odds against the agreement's ratification in the U.S. Congress lengthened appreciably.[71] On the same day the agreement was signed, the International Association of Machinists and Aerospace Workers (IAMAW) and the United Steelworkers announced strong opposition to it. Leo Gerard, USW president, laid down what became a key marker in negotiations over the U.S. legislation required to implement the agreements: "Only when all the issues have been resolved, and it's clear that Mexico is fully and faithfully recognizing workers' rights, should Congress vote on the agreement and implementing legislation."[72]

The USTR's Advisory Committee for Trade Policy and Negotiations and the Labor Advisory Committee on Trade Negotiations and Trade Policy (chaired by Gerard) had already issued separate reports on chapter 23 and its annex provisions that raised this same point.[73] The committees' reservations focused mainly on whether Mexico would actually implement a labor law reform bill that reflected the democratizing intent of the 2017 constitutional reforms. In addition, the Labor Advisory Committee criticized the USMCA for failing to move beyond endorsement of the ILO declaration's principles (versus the eight fundamental ILO conventions on which the declaration was based), which it argued was necessary to clarify which labor rights Mexico would be required to enforce. The committee recognized that the footnotes in chapter 23 clarifying May 10, 2007, language represented progress. However, it argued that the new language left a loophole open where the rights of public sector workers were concerned because it applied only to traded goods and services rather than to the economy as a whole.[74] A spokesperson for the AFL-CIO, in testimony given on November 15, 2018, as part of the U.S. International Trade Commission's (USITC) required public hearing on the likely economic impact of the agreement, argued that the absence of an independent labor secretariat or product-certification requirements (labels on export products certifying that they were produced under labor conditions that complied with USMCA obligations) left important questions regarding the enforcement of labor rights unresolved.[75]

These enforcement concerns centrally framed the prolonged phase II negotiations that occurred between November 2018 and December 2019, both among U.S. stakeholders (the USTR, congressional Democrats, and U.S. labor organizations) and between the United States and Mexico.[76] (Canada played virtually no role in the phase II labor rights negotiations.) Three elements were particularly important to the ultimate success of negotiations among the U.S. parties. First, Representative Nancy Pelosi (Democrat-California) returned as Speaker of the House of Representatives and exercised strong, effective leadership of the Democratic majority and Democratic legislators' negotiations with the USTR.[77] Second, USTR Lighthizer demonstrated great personal credibility in negotiations with Democratic congressional leaders and U.S. labor organizations. His honest-broker approach to the negotiations and his commitment to producing a final USMCA text capable of winning bipartisan U.S. congressional support were crucially important to the outcome.[78] And third, a focus on enforcement issues framed the phase II debates in Washington, DC, in terms with which no U.S. elected official could easily disagree. Democrats concentrated mainly on labor rights enforcement, while Republican legislators emphasized the importance of enforcing all USMCA provisions. However, no one could question the importance of "levelling the playing field [for American workers] with enforceable labor standards."[79] Indeed, in the final U.S. Senate debate on the USMCA in January 2020, no Republican spoke against enhanced labor enforcement provisions.[80]

In the aftermath of the Democrats' midterm electoral victory, Trump administration officials initially considered trying to force through congressional approval of the USMCA before new House of Representative members formally took office on January 3, 2019. In the end, they backed away from the idea because they feared a political backlash from both Democrats and Republicans.[81] Ambassador Lighthizer, facing a redefined domestic political context, immediately began informal discussions with senior House Democrats about USMCA enforcement provisions.[82] Of particular concern to USMCA critics was the fact that original NAFTA language concerning the appointment of dispute-settlement panels had not been altered, and under the NAFTA, a signatory country had been able to negate the process simply by declining to appoint its panel members or because its representative failed to attend a scheduled meeting of the three-country Free Trade Commission that authorized the appointment of the panel. In fact, in the time since the U.S. government had employed this ruse in 2000 to block the appointment of a panel to resolve a dispute with Mexico over sugar imports, no NAFTA dispute-settlement panels had been seated at all.[83] Leaders of U.S. labor organizations argued that they could have no confidence that Mexico's labor rights violations would be sanctioned under the flawed procedures incorporated into the USMCA.[84] Lighthizer quickly signaled that he was willing to work with House Democrats to address their concerns.[85]

Both U.S. labor leaders and senior House and Senate Democrats repeatedly called for the formal reopening of USMCA negotiations to address these and other matters, but USTR officials, congressional Republicans, and the Mexican government were staunchly opposed to doing so.[86] Acknowledging that the agreement's labor rights enforcement provisions needed strengthening yet resisting modifications of the USMCA, Ambassador Lighthizer floated the idea of employing section 301 of the U.S. Omnibus Trade and Competitiveness Act in cases involving labor rights violations in Mexico. Under the terms of this legislation, the U.S. government could apply a full range of trade sanctions against a foreign country for violations of international labor standards, and the sanctions could be targeted on specific industries or products where rights violations were concentrated. However, the sanctions were limited to the foreign government involved (private companies were not subject to penalty), and section 301 procedures included an injury requirement (evidence that a foreign government's "unreasonable" acts or practices constituted a burden or restriction on U.S. trade) (see chapter 2). Lighthizer's proposal was, moreover, widely dismissed as unworkable because section 301 enforcement actions were entirely at the discretion of the federal executive.[87]

The proposal that most significantly shaped the phase II debate over labor rights enforcement came from U.S. Senators Sherrod Brown (Democrat-Ohio and a member of the Senate Committee on Finance, the Senate committee with jurisdiction over foreign trade) and Ron Wyden (Democrat-Oregon and Ranking Member of the Committee on Finance). Brown initially presented his enforcement proposal to the USTR in February–March 2018, but at the time, some U.S. labor leaders were pushing their long-standing demand to create an independent labor secretariat as an enforcement mechanism. By May–June 2019, however, the Brown-Wyden proposal had moved to the center of debate among U.S. stakeholders.[88] At root, their proposed "NAFTA Labor Cooperation and Enforcement Agreement" shifted the principal focus of labor rights enforcement from the country level (in the original NAALC and in later U.S. FTAs, the country in which proven violations occurred was responsible for any fines or trade-linked sanctions) to the enterprise level.[89] Under the proposal, the U.S. government could request that the Mexican government conduct an audit of specific facilities of "producers and exporters of mined goods and producers and exporters of finished manufacturing goods with more than 100 on-site workers" in order to verify that they complied with "internationally recognized core labor standards and acceptable conditions of work." The United States could also request that U.S. officials participate in the onsite inspections. If Mexico declined to conduct the audit, or if it refused to permit U.S. officials to participate in the process, then the U.S. government could "deny USMCA preference to the shipment that is the subject of the verification." If the U.S. government later concluded that labor rights violations had, in fact, occurred, it could then deny preferential tariff treatment to export shipments originating from that facility. Goods produced with forced or child labor would be barred altogether.[90]

Brown and Wyden cited two important precedents for the production-site inspections and penalties they proposed. First, their proposal closely paralleled the terms of the Annex on Forest Sector Governance attached to chapter 18 (Environment) of the 2006 U.S.-Peru Trade Promotion Agreement. Under the terms of the annex, U.S. officials could request that the Peruvian government conduct verification inspections of individual producers or exporters in order to confirm that they were complying with Peru's forestry management practices. The U.S. request could also focus on particular shipments of forest products from Peru to the United States. If the Peruvian government denied a request that U.S. officials also take part in the site or shipment inspections, the U.S. government had the power to block entry of the products or shipment involved.[91] Second, the USMCA's chapter 6 (Textiles and Apparel) permitted an importing country's own customs officials to conduct site visits in the exporting country to determine whether particular textile and apparel goods qualified for preferential tariff treatment. If they concluded that the goods did not qualify, the importing country was authorized to bar both the particular goods in question and all "identical textile or apparel goods" coming from the same exporter or producer (article 6.6).

Senators Brown and Wyden discussed their proposal (which also called on Mexico to expand the number of trained labor enforcement personnel and proposed bilateral capacity-building measures in collaboration with the ILO) directly with Jesús Seade Kuri, Mexico's undersecretary for North American affairs and chief USMCA negotiator from April through December 2019, and Mexican Ambassador Martha Bárcena during Seade's visit to Washington, DC in early April 2019.[92] Ambassador Bárcena responded that Mexico might hypothetically be open to such an arrangement if it were fully reciprocal—and Mexican inspectors could also investigate alleged labor rights violations at U.S. production sites.[93] Ambassador Lighthizer reportedly opposed the idea of only dispatching U.S. labor inspectors to Mexican factories on the grounds that the predictable Mexican opposition to this proposal might hinder bilateral agreement on stronger labor rights enforcement measures.[94] Nonetheless, from July 2019 onward, USTR negotiations with House Democrats and U.S. unions over labor rights enforcement in Mexico focused on a facility-specific rapid response mechanism to investigate alleged violations of USMCA-covered labor rights.[95]

In parallel with their ongoing Washington, DC–centered negotiations regarding USMCA labor rights enforcement provisions, U.S. stakeholders closely monitored the progress of labor law reform legislation in Mexico. Interactions between U.S. government officials and their Mexican counterparts differed substantially in character from those that had occurred with the Peña Nieto administration (when U.S. officials negotiated the reform bill text line by line with Mexican government officials) because senior members of the López Obrador administration were seriously committed to far-reaching reform of the labor justice system. Core elements of the labor law reform proposed by López Obrador's National Regeneration Movement (Movimiento Regeneración Nacional, MORENA) originated in democratic unions' demands and opposition party reform proposals dating to the mid-1990s.[96] Nevertheless, U.S. government officials, Democratic congressional leaders, and U.S. labor representatives repeatedly stressed how important approval of the legislation was to their overall assessment of the USMCA. Indeed, USTR and U.S. Department of Labor officials communicated frequently with their Mexican government counterparts to express their concern that the final content of the legislation meet the requirements set by annex 23-A.[97] Representatives of the AFL-CIO, USW, and other U.S. industrial unions, in collaborative dialogue with Mexico's National Union of Workers (Unión Nacional de Trabajadores, UNT) and Mexican labor rights advocates, also followed evolving legislative debates in Mexico closely.[98] In fact, they reviewed, analyzed, and commented in detail on successive versions of the new federal labor legislation. In doing so, a range of U.S. stakeholders thus strongly encouraged the López Obrador administration to adopt reforms that complied with the terms of annex 23-A, especially regarding union democracy and the validation of existing collective bargaining agreements.[99]

Two examples illustrate the substantive significance of this close collaboration among U.S. and Mexican sociopolitical actors. First, there were occasions on which U.S. stakeholders directly influenced the content of the proposed reform legislation. In debating how to conduct the review of all existing collective bargaining agreements required by annex-23A (2.f), STPS officials initially proposed giving individual workers access to agreements prior to their voting to approve or revise them by posting them on a STPS website, as the Mexican government already did with federal-jurisdiction collective contracts. In the end, however, they agreed to a U.S. proposal to enhance accountability by holding the company directly involved responsible for making a printed or electronic copy of the bargaining agreement available to the workers covered by it three working days before the contract validation vote.[100] Second, in their own two-level bargaining, Mexican actors, at times, structured exchanges with their U.S. counterparts so as to advance their own reform goals. In the course of a meeting with USTR Lighthizer in late 2019 to discuss how MORENA's labor reform bill would address annex 23-A requirements concerning collective bargaining agreements, senior Mexican officials proposed adding the word *direct* to the 2017 constitutional requirement that union votes be "personal, free, and secret." Their goal was to challenge the system of indirect elections then in effect in many state-level labor federations and national industrial unions in which rank-and-file members nominally elected section delegates who, in turn, selected senior union leaders. Lighthizer endorsed the idea, and the Mexican officials involved then later justified a corresponding amendment to MORENA's legislative initiative (and overcame strong private sector and some national unions' opposition) by claiming they were responding to a U.S. demand.[101]

The initial target date for approval of legislation implementing Mexico's 2017 constitutional labor reforms was January 1, 2019. Concerns among U.S. stakeholders mounted when the legislative process bogged down in the Mexican Congress as legislators first debated educational reform legislation and other matters. Continued private sector opposition to some key provisions of the labor law bill continued to slow its progress, and the López Obrador administration felt increasing U.S. pressures to push through its final approval. Debate on the bill in the Mexican Senate was actually circumscribed in order to remove this controversial issue from the phase II USMCA negotiations and accelerate U.S. ratification of the agreement.[102]

The strong majorities that López Obrador's MORENA-led coalition held in both chambers of the Mexican Congress finally permitted official approval of the new Federal Labor Law on April 29, 2019, at the end of the regular legislative session.[103] It was enacted into law on the symbolically important date of May 1 and took effect the following day.[104] Despite broad agreement among Mexican and U.S. analysts that the legislation did indeed satisfy the requirements of annex 23-A, U.S. stakeholders remained concerned about the constitutional challenges that old-guard labor organizations quickly mounted against the law, which argued that the requirement that union members cast a direct personal vote in elections had no grounding in the 2017 constitutional reforms.[105]

As exchanges intensified between Democratic members of the House Committee on Ways and Means and the USTR over enforcement mechanisms and other USMCA issues,[106] House Speaker Pelosi responded to Ambassador Lighthizer's request for an arrangement that would help focus their negotiations by appointing (on June 13, 2019) a Trade Working Group.[107] The mandate of the working group, which was comprised of nine members of the House Democratic caucus and chaired by Richard E. Neal (Democrat-Massachusetts and chair of the Committee on Ways and Means), was to address labor, environmental, pharmaceutical, and enforcement and enforceability issues.[108] Its members met frequently with Ambassador Lighthizer, sometimes on a weekly basis, and worked closely with his staff over the following six months.[109] Members of the group also made two working trips to Mexico.[110] Between July 18 and July 22, Representative Earl Blumenauer (Democrat-Oregon and chair of the House Ways and Means Subcommittee on Trade) led a bipartisan delegation of ten representatives, including four members of the Trade Working Group, to Mexico. In Mexico City on July 19, delegation members discussed their concerns regarding the Mexican government's capacity to implement its labor justice reforms directly with President López Obrador and senior members of his administration. In San Luis Potosí, they explored the issue of employer protection contracts and expressed solidarity for Goodyear Oxo workers who had been fired by the company in 2018 in retaliation against their union organizing efforts. In Tijuana, the delegation investigated Mexico-U.S. border environmental and public health challenges.[111] On July 26, the Trade Working Group submitted a progress report to Speaker Pelosi,[112] and in early August, it sent the USTR a draft document detailing their proposals for amendments to the existing USMCA text.[113]

Senior U.S. labor leaders, principally those representing the AFL-CIO and major industrial unions,[114] were centrally engaged in these two-level negotiations over worker rights enforcement. Ambassador Lighthizer met repeatedly with AFL-CIO president Trumka and the heads of leading industrial unions during the phase II period, and senior House Democrats maintained close communications with Trumka and other union leaders as they negotiated with the USTR over labor enforcement issues.[115] On September 4, 2019, Trumka met for ninety minutes with President López Obrador and several cabinet-level Mexican officials in Mexico City to discuss the measures the Mexican government was taking to implement labor justice reform.[116] As pressures from Republicans and U.S. business associations grew in October-November 2019 to reach a final agreement on USMCA implementation legislation, Trumka publicly warned the USTR and congressional leaders not to push for a ratification vote until all labor enforcement issues had been satisfactorily addressed.[117]

During these phase II negotiations, the USTR first debated key labor enforcement questions with domestic stakeholders (House Democrats and U.S. labor leaders) and only later discussed these issues with Mexican (and Canadian) negotiators.[118] These circumstances motivated the López Obrador administration to engage with both the USTR and U.S. nongovernmental actors. Indeed, Mexican officials went to great lengths to reassure U.S. stakeholders of their commitment to implementing democratic labor reforms and upholding the country's USMCA labor obligations. In mid-March 2019, Secretary of the Economy Graciela Márquez Colín and STPS Secretary Luisa María Alcalde Luján met with USTR Lighthizer in Washington, DC, to discuss these matters.[119] A week later, Ambassador Seade traveled to New Orleans, Louisiana, to meet with U.S. labor leaders during the AFL-CIO's Executive Council meeting and discuss the USMCA labor chapter. Seade assured them that Mexico was committed to enforcing its labor obligations, and he expressed a willingness to revise the agreement's labor enforcement provisions (but not formally reopen USMCA negotiations).[120] Immediately after the official publication of MORENA's new federal labor law on May 1, 2019, Seade traveled to Washington, DC, to brief Lighthizer on the ways in which the legislation satisfied Mexico's annex 23-A obligations.[121] On June 25, STPS Alcalde sent U.S. congressional leaders a proposed three-stage "roadmap" for labor justice reform that outlined in detail the order in which selected groups of states would create new labor courts and take other steps to implement the reform.[122] Moreover, the Mexican government hosted four different U.S. congressional delegations between April and October 2019 and the Trumka visit in September.[123]

In these different meetings and in related communications, senior Mexican officials took pains to address U.S. stakeholder concerns about two specific issues: whether the Mexican government had the budgetary and administrative capacities to implement the complex, multilevel judicial reform required to replace the now-discredited labor conciliation and arbitration system,[124] and whether it would act to reduce wage disparities with the United States and Canada.

A significant bilateral controversy over the López Obrador administration's capacity to implement its labor justice reform erupted in early September 2019 when U.S. labor leaders learned that the Mexican federal government's proposed budget for fiscal year 2020 included a reported 35.8 percent cut in overall allocations to the STPS, including its funding for policy operations.[125] Representative Neal, chair of the House Democrats' Trade Working Group, and four other Democratic congressional representatives traveled to Mexico City and met with President López Obrador and senior government officials on October 8 to discuss the matter in person.[126] Mexican officials hastened to clarify that most of the reductions involved a national youth training and employment program, but in response to U.S. demands, they quickly agreed to increase the labor justice reform implementation budget by 23 percent.[127] Indeed, López Obrador went so far as to tell the Neal delegation that if Mexico did not fulfill its budgetary commitments or comply with the announced calendar for labor reform implementation, he would agree to reopen the USMCA negotiations.[128]

In addition, in a highly unusual step, López Obrador followed up his meeting with Neal's delegation by writing to both him and Speaker Pelosi (on, respectively, October 14 and 17, 2019) to confirm his administration's firm budgetary commitment to labor justice reform. He promised total expenditures of US$69,336,589 in fiscal year 2020 to initiate the process and at least US$829,099,133 in additional funding over the 2021–2023 period and subsequent years. Moreover, López Obrador promised Neal, "If more funds are needed to implement the proposed changes, you can be assured that I will take the necessary steps with Congress to guarantee the additional funds."[129] Some critics pointed out that Mexico's labor justice reform relied on state governments for some 46 percent of the total required implementation budget and that eight of the first ten states the STPS had selected to pioneer reform implementation were fully or partly controlled by opposition parties—a partisan division that was potentially very problematic because of private sector and old-guard union hostility to the reform project.[130] Nevertheless, López Obrador's personal reassurance was sufficient to assuage House Democrats' immediate reservations on the matter.

Second, the López Obrador administration sought to address long-standing U.S. concerns about wage levels in Mexico and U.S.-Mexican wage differentials. Since even before the NAFTA debate in the early 1990s, the U.S. labor movement had regularly demanded that the U.S. government eliminate tariff code provisions that gave domestic manufacturing companies an incentive to shift production to low-wage facilities in northern Mexico because of the significant threat these arrangements posed to U.S. manufacturing employment. In the final phase of U.S.-Mexican negotiations over the NAALC in 1993, President William J. (Bill) Clinton (1993–1997, 1997, 2001) extracted from President Carlos Salinas de Gortari (1988–1994) a commitment to make productivity-linked increases in minimum wages—a (never fulfilled) pledge that Clinton then aggressively peddled to NAFTA opponents as evidence of his administration's commitment to protecting U.S. workers against unfair economic competition from Mexico (see chapter 3).

Both U.S. and Canadian stakeholders and trade negotiators pressed Mexican officials hard on wage questions from the outset of the NAFTA 2.0 negotiations. Under pressure from major U.S. (AFL-CIO), Canadian (UNIFOR), and Mexican

(UNT) labor organizations, negotiators discussed the problem of suppressed Mexican wages during at least five of the six negotiating rounds held in 2017 and early 2018.[131] Labor unions pressed to include wage issues in a NAFTA 2.0 labor chapter as a way of inducing Mexico to raise minimum wages and reduce wage disparities with its NAFTA partners.[132] Leading Democratic congressional allies of the U.S. labor movement argued that Mexican wages were "the central issue" in the talks.[133] Similarly, on June 25, 2019, the twenty-seven new Democratic members of the U.S. House of Representatives elected in November 2018 wrote to USTR Lighthizer to argue that:

> Unless the current [USMCA] text's labor and environmental standards are strengthened, and swift and certain enforcement mechanisms are added, [U.S.] corporations will continue to outsource jobs and pollution to Mexico where they can violate international labor rights and pay workers unconscionably low wages. Disincentivizing that practice is good for North American workers.[134]

In this same letter, the Democratic lawmakers openly called for "linkage between market access and wage levels." Representatives Blumenauer and Neal raised the wage issue with senior Mexican government officials during their trips to Mexico City in, respectively, July and October.[135] And during his trip to Mexico City to meet with President López Obrador in September 2019, AFL-CIO president Trumka declared, "No [trade] treaty will be successful if Mexican wages don't rise. . . . There should be equal wages for equal work [between Mexico and the United States]."[136]

Of course, Mexican government officials and business leaders strongly resisted pressures to align salaries with U.S. and Canadian wage levels. Mexico's trade negotiators actually dismissed as a "purple cow" (an issue placed on the negotiating table with little real expectation that it would find traction) a U.S. proposal that the Mexican federal government set salaries by executive decree in order to ensure that they rose quickly.[137] In fact, despite many strong, insistent pressures on the issue, U.S. and Canadian negotiators never proposed a general wage provision in the USMCA, nor did they make an explicit demand on the Mexican government for wage increases of a particular amount. Instead, they focused on the wage-depressing effect of employer protection contracts and the importance of ensuring freedom of association and the right to collective bargaining so that Mexican trade unions could themselves decide how hard to push for wage increases, how long to strike in support of their demands, and so forth.[138] In effect, then, U.S. and Canadian negotiators viewed Mexican wage increases as, in the word employed by a senior U.S. congressional trade advisor closely involved in the talks, "complementary" to the trade agreement text.[139]

One of López Obrador's signature pledges during his 2018 presidential campaign had, in fact, been to significantly increase Mexico's national minimum wage, which preceding governments had systematically repressed since the mid-1980s as a means of enhancing the country's international comparative economic advantage.[140] He promised that he would increase the minimum wage in stages, doubling its value by the end of his six-year presidential term. López Obrador demonstrated his commitment in this regard by quickly introducing a 16.2 percent increase in January 2019.[141] This was the largest nominal increase in the national minimum wage since January 1997, at a time of high inflation in the aftermath of Mexico's 1994–1995 financial crisis, and the highest inflation-adjusted increase (11.8 percent) during the entire 1997–2019 period.[142] Economic analysts had anticipated a January 2020 increase equal to that of the previous year, but the federal government raised the national minimum wage by a full 20 percent.[143] Annual increases of 15 percent and 22 percent followed in, respectively, January 2021 and January 2022.[144]

The Negotiations Endgame and Outcome

Pressures to reach an agreement on labor rights enforcement measures and other controversial USMCA issues mounted on all sides in late Autumn 2019. Congressional Republicans and U.S. business organizations pushed hard for a final resolution, but it was politically difficult for Republicans to oppose Democrats' demands for reliable enforcement mechanisms.[145] For their part, Speaker Pelosi and other House Democrats felt compelled to demonstrate that they could still enact important legislation at a time when congressional attention was increasingly focused on the beginning of the House of Representatives' first impeachment proceedings against President Trump.[146] The U.S. labor movement, however, kept up its public pressure. On November 5, 2019, the twelve-member AFL-CIO Industrial Relations Council released a public letter arguing that no final USMCA implementation legislation should be brought before the House of Representatives until organized labor's concerns (especially guarantees for Mexican workers' rights to organize and bargain collectively and adequate Mexican budgetary resources for effective labor reform implementation) had been fully resolved: "An agreement that does so ["reflects our core recommendations" to the USTR] will be worthy of our support."[147] Bolstered by labor's stance, House Democrats remained intent on using their political leverage (Speaker Pelosi formally had wide discretion in determining when the agreement would go to the full House for a vote) to extract final concessions on labor enforcement.[148]

President López Obrador also pushed for quick action by the U.S. House of Representatives. Following passage of the Mexican federal government's 2020 budget with the allocations for labor justice reform that he had promised Representative Neal, López Obrador again wrote Speaker Pelosi "respectfully lobbying" for passage of the USMCA implementation legislation.[149] Serious concerns that further delay might jeopardize U.S. ratification of the USMCA (and thus prolong economic uncertainty for Mexico) did not, though, translate into greater Mexican flexibility regarding U.S. demands for onsite labor inspections.

At his October meeting with the Neal congressional delegation, López Obrador had pledged to adopt "a joint evaluation mechanism," and in Neal's presence, he had instructed Ambassador Seade "to work with you [Neal] to develop the compliance mechanism."[150] However, Ambassador Seade consistently and strenuously opposed, both publicly and in lengthy private discussions with USTR Lighthizer, the idea of plant-level labor inspections outside regular USMCA dispute-settlement procedures or checks on Mexican products entering the United States.[151] He also firmly rejected a proposal from Representative Andy Levin (Democrat-Michigan, son of retired Representative Sander Levin) calling for the final U.S. congressional vote on USMCA implementation legislation to be postponed until the Mexican government had actually overseen democratic union elections and contract signing procedures in a "representative sample" of five hundred firms in leading export industries (automobile vehicle assembly, automotive parts, aerospace, industrial bakery, electronics, and call centers), thereby demonstrating its commitment to labor rights enforcement.[152] Seade argued that attaching any such condition to U.S. ratification of the USMCA violated the "contract" that Mexico had agreed with the United States when it accepted annex 23-A, which the Mexican government was in practice honoring.[153]

The Mexican private sector, certainly motivated by its own interests, strongly backed the government's position on labor enforcement issues. The influential Private Sector Coordinating Council (Consejo Coordinador, Empresarial, CCE), which claimed to represent 1.3 million Mexican firms, condemned the Brown-Wyden approach. It argued that any such provision in the final agreement would violate national sovereignty and severely undercut private firms' economic competitiveness.[154] The U.S. Chamber of Commerce in Mexico opposed this possibility on the same grounds.[155] Mexican business resistance mainly focused on U.S. proposals for plant-level labor inspections. However, the CCE also opposed earlier changes in the agreement text that eased the conditions under which labor rights investigations could be triggered, amendments that Ambassador Lighthizer had made in response to U.S. labor demands.[156]

The USTR, reflecting the core concerns of U.S. labor organizations and their Democratic congressional allies, pressed hard for direct U.S. inspections of Mexican production sites and expedited procedures for addressing labor rights violations until near the very end of the USMCA negotiations—in essence, framing these as sine qua non, "all or nothing" demands that Mexico would have to accept in order to bring the negotiations to conclusion.[157] There was great pressure on Mexico to reach final agreement on labor enforcement and other questions because, with U.S. House of Representatives impeachment proceedings against President Trump underway and the approaching January 2020 start of the U.S. presidential election process, any further delay placed in doubt the political likelihood of U.S. congressional ratification of the USMCA and required implementation legislation.[158] Nevertheless, there was strong consensus opposition among senior Mexican government officials and even staunch labor rights advocates to direct U.S. onsite labor inspections on the grounds that it would compromise Mexico's national sovereignty.[159] López Obrador administration officials also opposed the outright blocking of Mexican export products as a penalty for documented labor violations.[160]

The most intense negotiations took place in Washington, DC, in late November and early December 2019. Controversial, still-unresolved issues included labor inspections, patent protection for biologic drugs, immigration, and the question of cross-border trucking, which had been a perennial controversy in Mexico-U.S. relations since the original NAFTA.[161] Representative Neal and Ambassador Lighthizer, sometimes with Speaker Pelosi present, continued their discussions during the week of November 25.[162] Final bargaining came down to intense one-on-one exchanges between Ambassadors Lighthizer and Seade, including a seven-hour meeting on December 4 in which the form that onsite labor inspections might take was a key issue.[163] On December 10, 2019, they reached agreement on a protocol of amendment to the USMCA.[164]

One indication of the importance that labor rights enforcement issues had in the phase II negotiations was that seventeen pages of the twenty-seven-page protocol addressed labor matters. On the crucial issue of production site inspections, the USTR succeeded in establishing procedures that permitted such inspections. However, Mexico successfully defended its demands that the new facility-specific rapid response panels constitute a specific instance of regular dispute-settlement procedures and that only these panels could, as part of their regular evidence-gathering procedures, request plant-level inspections. Ambassador Seade's apparent confidence that he had protected national sovereignty concerns in this area was such that he publicly recognized that the Mexican government or a private company could still reject a rapid-response panel's request.[165] He did, however, agree that the new enforcement provisions benefited Mexico by reinforcing the López Obrador administration's own labor reforms.[166]

Reforms to Dispute-Settlement Procedures and Protected Labor Rights

The protocol of amendment made two significant changes in the USMCA in order to strengthen dispute-settlement procedures and protect labor rights in Mexico. First, in essence, it made the installation of a dispute-settlement panel automatic whenever a dispute could not be resolved within a specified time period through consultations between the signatory parties. The protocol precluded a country from blocking panels by preventing the Free Trade Commission from meeting, either by declining to name lists of potential panel members or failing to meet procedural deadlines.[167] In the event that one or more of the parties failed to meet the obligation to name rosters of potential panelists "by the date of entry into force of the Agreement [USMCA]" or attempted to delay or block a panel's operations through other obstructionist actions (or inactions), the protocol laid out alternative procedures to ensure that panel deliberations could nonetheless proceed.[168]

Second, the protocol further strengthened articles 23.3 (Labor Rights) and 23.7 (Violence Against Workers) by inserting a new footnote in each article that reversed the burden of proof between contending parties in instances of alleged violations of covered labor rights:

> For the purposes of dispute settlement, a panel shall presume that a failure is in a manner affecting trade or investment between the Parties, unless the responding Party demonstrates otherwise (item 4[a][ii]).

Finally, in a further significant amendment to article 23.7, the protocol deleted the "through a sustained or recurring course of action or inaction" language (including the qualifying footnote stipulating that "a course of action or inaction does not include an isolated instance or case") that in the 2018 USMCA had conditioned signatory parties' obligation to address the problem of violence against workers.[169] In principle, this change made it easier to enforce the prohibition.

The Facility-Specific Rapid Response Labor Enforcement Mechanism

Certainly, the most original—and hotly debated—part of the protocol negotiated by the U.S. and Mexican governments was the Facility-Specific Rapid Response Labor Mechanism (annex 31-A) added to USMCA chapter 31 on dispute settlement.[170] Under the terms established by the annex, a respondent government had forty-five days in which to seek to remediate a complainant's "good faith" allegation that specified labor rights had been violated at a covered production facility (article 31-A.4.2). If, after further discussions over a mutually agreed period, the parties could not reach a settlement, the complainant could petition the USMCA Free Trade Commission's secretariat (article 30.6) to establish a three-member rapid-response panel, the third member of which (and the deciding vote in formulating the panel's final recommendation) had to be a nonnational of either Mexico or the United States.[171] The panel was then to take steps to verify that the petition fulfilled certain requirements (that it identified a covered facility, specified the respondent government's relevant laws, and indicated the substantive grounds for alleging a violation of rights; article 31-A.6). When it had done so, it was to request verification from the respondent government concerning the alleged violations and any investigation or remediation of them it had taken. However, the panel could only proceed to conduct onsite inspections if the respondent government agreed to them—a crucial constraint based on the exercise of state sovereignty. If the respondent refused the request for verification, the complainant government could still request that the panel issue a decision concerning the alleged rights violations, but it would be forced to do so without direct evidence gathered at the production site in question (article 31-A.7.6-9).

Both the Mexican and U.S. governments also set other significant limitations on the use of the mechanism. By mutual agreement, it could, in the first instance, only be applied in cases involving the alleged denial of freedom of association and the right to collective bargaining (article 31-A.2). Where Mexico was concerned, "a claim can be brought only with respect to an alleged Denial of Rights under legislation that complies with Annex 23-A (Worker Representation in Collective Bargaining in Mexico)." Where the United States was concerned, the restriction was even more limiting: "A claim can be brought only with respect to an alleged Denial of Rights owed to workers at a covered facility under an enforced order of the National Labor Relations Board" (article 31-A.2, footnote 1). In other words, the protocol precluded Mexico from using the mechanism to investigate labor rights violations allegedly occurring in the United States; Mexico could only seek to enforce a binding decision already taken by U.S. national labor authorities.[172] Moreover, the absence of clear U.S. national legislation regulating union elections and contract signings meant that a rapid-response panel requested by Mexico could not easily investigate such matters in the United States.[173]

Limitations concerning the priority economic sectors in which the mechanism could be applied were also skewed in favor of the United States. These sectors included those producing manufactured goods (including, but not limited to, aerospace products and components, automobiles and automobile parts, cosmetic products, industrial baked goods, steel and aluminum, glass, pottery, plastics, forgings, and cement), supplying services, or involving mining (article 31-A.15). Low-wage Mexican production in all these manufacturing activities had posed competitive challenges to U.S. producers.[174] Mexican and U.S. negotiators agreed to review the list annually in order to determine whether any additional sectors should be added to (but not deleted from) the priority list (article 31-A.13). Agriculture was, however, notably absent from the original list. This meant that Mexico could not apply the rapid-response mechanism in defense of Mexican migrant workers employed in U.S. agriculture—a significant limitation given the high proportion of Mexican NAALC public communications focused on this subject (see chapter 4). The Mexican government could, however, presumably still file such a case through the USMCA's regular dispute-settlement procedures.

In establishing the terms under which these special dispute-settlement panels would operate, the protocol responded to long-standing complaints from U.S. labor stakeholders by setting procedural time limits that would, in principle, lead to much more rapid resolution of labor rights complaints than under the NAALC.[175] For example, following receipt of a complainant's request to establish a rapid-response panel, the secretariat had only three business days in which to select the panelists by lot from the list of five Mexican, five U.S., and five international experts established when the USMCA took effect (article 31-A.5.3). There remained, however, some ambiguity regarding just how quickly the new dispute-settlement procedures could be concluded. Much could still depend on whether the respondent government and/or the owner(s) of the production site in question refused to cooperate by declining to authorize, or failing to cooperate with, a panel's onsite inspections and on how quickly those inspections could actually be undertaken. Senator Brown himself estimated that the entire rapid-response process would take approximately 150 days.[176]

Finally, the protocol took significant steps to address the U.S. labor movement's long-standing demand for enforcement procedures with substantial potential penalties. The protocol affirmed the overarching commitment of both Mexico and the United States to trade only in goods produced in compliance with the USMCA's labor chapter (article 31-A.12), and it gave the complainant government discretion to impose "the most appropriate" penalties required to remedy labor rights violations in cases where violations had been proved.[177] These included either the suspension of preferential tariff treatment for goods manufactured at the sanctioned production facility or the imposition of penalties on goods or services produced at the facility, in proportion to the severity of the rights violations that had occurred. The protocol also explicitly authorized the complainant to extend penalties to a sanctioned company's entire national operations in cases in which one of its facilities had previously been found to have violated protected labor rights. If rapid-response panels had documented labor rights violations on two prior occasions, the complainant state could outright bar entry of the company's entire production to its market, thus giving form to a long-standing U.S. labor demand that the potential sanctions for serious labor rights violations include a product importation ban.[178] Moreover, if one of the USMCA's regular labor dispute-settlement panels determined that a signatory country had, in fact, breached any of its overall USMCA labor obligations in a particular instance, the complainant government was authorized to employ the rapid-response mechanism "with regard to the relevant law or laws at issue in that dispute" in an unrestricted manner—that is, not limited to the freedom of association and the right to collective bargaining—for a minimum of two years (article 31-A.12, Expansion of Claims).

In all these ways, the facility-specific rapid response mechanism significantly strengthened U.S. actors' capacity to enforce USMCA labor provisions in Mexico. However, although the Mexican government was obliged to accept the mechanism, the final terms of the protocol of amendment also reflected Mexican negotiators' success in deflecting some of the most intrusive U.S. demands. For instance, whereas a November 2019 version of the Brown-Wyden proposal stated that it would apply to "all labor obligations under USMCA," the final agreement restricted (except under the multiple-violations circumstances detailed above) use of the rapid-response mechanism to alleged denials of freedom of association and the right to collective bargaining. Whereas the U.S. labor movement lobbied hard during the phase II negotiations to include export product-certification requirements (which would have implied prior verification that Mexican exporters of goods and services complied with broad USMCA labor obligations), in the final agreement investigations of alleged labor rights violations remained incident-specific. Most important, whereas the Brown-Wyden proposal gave the complainant government unilateral authority to decide whether to dispatch a "verification team" to one or more production facilities in another party's territory (without any intermediate period in which the respondent government could conduct its own assessment of the alleged labor rights violations or attempt to negotiate a resolution of the problem), the final terms of the protocol firmly embedded both the decision to appoint a rapid-response labor panel and any onsite inspections within regular dispute-settlement procedures. And in notable contrast to the April version of the Brown-Wyden proposal, U.S. officials could only participate in onsite inspections in Mexico as observers—and then only if the Mexican government agreed that they could do so (article 31-A.7.7).[179]

U.S. LEGISLATION IMPLEMENTING THE USMCA: ADMINISTRATIVE ARRANGEMENTS TO SUPPORT LABOR RIGHTS ENFORCEMENT IN MEXICO

The U.S. House of Representatives approved legislation implementing the USMCA on December 19, 2019, by an overwhelming 385–41 majority.[180] In an outcome that reflected Ambassador Lighthizer's commitment to negotiating an agreement capable of winning bipartisan congressional support, 193 House Democrats supported the bill, and only 38 opposed it.[181] In endorsing the agreement, AFL-CIO president Trumka stated, "We have pushed them hard and have done quite well"; "President Trump may have opened this deal, but working people closed it."[182] He called the protocol of amendment "a new standard for future trade negotiations," and Speaker Pelosi hailed it as "a victory for America's workers.[183] After a short, pro forma debate, the U.S. Senate approved the agreement by an eighty-nine to ten vote on January 16,[184] and President Trump signed it into law on January 29, 2020.

Of particular note, the United States-Mexico-Canada Agreement Implementation Act (hereinafter H.R. 5430) created a new U.S. administrative apparatus directly charged with ensuring Mexico's enforcement of both its USMCA labor obligations and its May 2019 Federal Labor Law, which had been directly linked to the trade agreement by annex 23-A. The centerpiece was an Interagency Labor Committee for Monitoring and Enforcement (ILCME) cochaired by the U.S. Trade Representative and the U.S. Secretary of Labor and comprised of "representatives of such other Federal departments or agencies with relevant expertise as the President determines appropriate."[185] Although the committee's written mandate was diplomatically framed in terms of coordinating U.S. efforts to monitor the implementation and maintenance of agreed labor obligations "with respect to each USMCA country" (section 711.a), it focused squarely on Mexico.

As part of its broad responsibility for coordinating U.S. government efforts to ensure that Mexico complied with its agreed labor obligations, the ILCME's duties included: reviewing relevant information and assessments from USMCA countries, public sources, and labor attachés attached to the U.S. embassy in Mexico City; "establishing an ongoing dialogue with appropriate officials of the Government of Mexico regarding the implementation of Mexico's labor reform and compliance with its labor obligations" and "coordinating visits to Mexico as necessary"; monitoring the financial and technical support Mexico received for labor justice reform from the Inter-American Development Bank, the ILO, and the Government of Canada; and identifying priority areas for U.S. government support for capacity-building in Mexico (section 712).

The ILCME was specifically required to make formal assessments (biannually for the first five years of its operation and annually for the next five years) of "the extent to which Mexico is in compliance with its obligations under Annex 23-A of the USMCA" (section 714.a).[186] Here, the authors of H.R. 5430 wrote into

U.S. law in almost verbatim terms the various promises that Mexican officials had made to House Democrats and U.S. labor leaders during the intense phase II USMCA negotiations. The issues that the committee was obliged to address were defined in minute detail:

> (1) Whether Mexico is providing adequate funding to implement and enforce Mexico's labor reform, including specifically whether Mexico has provided funding consistent with commitments made to contribute the following amounts for the labor reform implementation budget: (A) [US] $176,000,000 for 2021. (B) $325,000,000 for 2022. (C) $328,000,000 for 2023. (2) The extent to which any legal challenges to Mexico's labor reform have succeeded in that court system. (3) The extent to which Mexico has implemented the federal and state labor courts, registration entity, and federal and state conciliation centers consistent with the timeline set forth for Mexico's labor reform, in the September 2019 policy statements by the Government of Mexico on a national strategy for implementation of the labor justice system, and in subsequent policy statements in accordance with Mexico's labor reform (section 714.c.1-3).

The ILCME was, moreover, charged with requesting U.S. government enforcement actions regarding labor issues in Mexico (section 711.a.3). One of its responsibilities in this regard was to review both the list of priority economic activities included in annex 31-A (and update it on an annual basis) and "priority facilities within such priority subsectors for monitoring and enforcement" (section 713.3). The committee was then to make, within delimited time periods and based on reports from the Forced Labor Enforcement Task Force and the Independent Mexico Labor Expert Board (section 712.6-9; see below), recommendations to the USTR regarding the initiation of dispute-settlement actions when "a USMCA country" failed to meet its labor obligations (section 715.a).[187] Committee procedures permitted the public both to submit information concerning general failures to implement labor obligations in "a USMCA country" and to file facility-specific petitions alleging a denial of labor rights at a covered facility (section 716.a, b). Furthermore, the committee was responsible for establishing and operating a web-based hotline (monitored by the U.S. Department of Labor) to receive confidential information concerning labor issues from "interested parties, including Mexican workers" (section 717).

To support the work of the Interagency Labor Committee, H.R. 5430 also created a Forced Labor Enforcement Task Force (Sections 741–744) and an Independent Mexico Labor Expert Board (Sections 731–734). The central mandate of the task force, chaired by the secretary of homeland security,[188] was to monitor and strengthen overall U.S. enforcement of the long-standing prohibition against the importation of goods produced by child or forced labor.[189] It was, however, enjoined to develop a specific enforcement plan for goods produced by or with forced labor in Mexico. The Independent Mexico Labor Expert Board, in turn, was responsible for both monitoring and evaluating Mexico's compliance with its labor obligations and advising the ILCME on capacity-building initiatives. The board's twelve members were appointed to six-year terms. Four of its members were appointed by the USTR Labor Advisory Committee for Trade Negotiations and Trade Policy (comprised of leaders of major U.S. unions), and the House of Representatives and the Senate each appointed four more members (divided evenly between the majority and minority parties in each chamber).[190] Of particular note, the board's annual report to the ILCME and relevant congressional committees was to address not just overall Mexican compliance but also "*the efforts of Mexico*" (emphasis added) to implement labor reform and "the manner and extent to which labor laws are generally enforced in Mexico" (section 734.1).

Several provisions of the implementation legislation offered U.S. labor organizations and other domestic stakeholders opportunities to play a direct role in overseeing Mexico's enforcement of its labor obligations. As noted above, the ILCME was specifically authorized to receive relevant information "from the public" (section 712.1.A). The process through which it made recommendations to the USTR regarding dispute-settlement actions incorporated a petition process "for submissions by the public of information with respect to potential failures to implement the labor obligations of a USMCA country," including allegations of a denial of rights at specific production facilities (section 716.a, b). During its first five years of operation, the ILCME was required to meet biannually (and annually for five years thereafter) with the Labor Advisory Committee for Trade Negotiations and Trade Policy to consult and provide opportunities for input with respect to (A) the implementation of Mexico's labor reform; (B) labor capacity-building activities in Mexico funded by the United States; (C) labor monitoring efforts; (D) labor enforcement priorities (section 712.5).

As noted, the Labor Advisory Committee (by statute comprised of up to thirty representatives of major U.S. labor organizations[191]) named one-third of the members of the new Independent Mexico Labor Expert Board. Moreover, the 2019 legislation authorizing financial support for U.S. monitoring of labor enforcement in Mexico required the USTR and the U.S. secretary of labor to report to the Labor Advisory Committee (and simultaneously to the House Committee on Ways and Means and the Senate Committee on Finance) on their handling of any request the committee might make to investigate specific labor rights matters in Mexico.[192] No previous U.S. trade legislation had provided the U.S. labor movement with representation and authority of this kind.

All these provisions were designed to ensure that the U.S. federal government maintained a concentrated focus on labor rights in Mexico. The range of departments and agencies involved (USTR, Labor, State, Homeland Security, Commerce, Treasury, Agriculture, and the U.S. Agency for International Development, USAID) and tight administrative decision-making deadlines underpinned this goal.[193] In effect, H.R. 5430 procedures institutionalized the intense scrutiny that had in the past arisen mainly during U.S. debates about whether to enter into a trade agreement with Mexico or through NAALC public communications. By doing so, these provisions implicitly addressed a long-standing U.S. labor complaint that, in practice, worker organizations bore the principal costs of enforcement efforts by undertaking the necessary background research required to file public complaints protesting labor rights violations in U.S. trade partners.[194]

The substantial differences in congressional reporting requirements between previous U.S. trade agreements and H.R. 5430 further illustrate this point. For instance, the Trade and Tariff Act of 1984, which made observance of core labor rights an eligibility requirement for the U.S. Generalized System of Preferences program, required the president to make an annual report to Congress on labor rights in each beneficiary country.[195] There was, however, no requirement that the executive report to Congress on its handling of individual complaints filed by U.S. unions or labor rights advocates alleging rights violations in the country in question. The NAALC public communications process had included no congressional reporting provisions at all. In marked contrast, H.R. 5430 required both the Interagency Labor Committee and the USTR to submit an explanatory report to "the appropriate congressional committees" whenever either body decided not to act favorably on a report or petition recommending enforcement actions against alleged labor rights violators.[196] Moreover, each report by a rapid response labor panel was to be submitted "immediately" to both the appropriate congressional committees and the USTR Labor Advisory Committee, and the USTR was to make it publicly available (section 751).

These administrative arrangements for enforcing the USMCA's labor provisions were bolstered by significant U.S. financial commitments. On December 9, 2019, Congress initiated legislation that substantially increased funding for the Trade Enforcement Trust Fund in order to support U.S. monitoring activities and capacity-building and technical assistance programs in Mexico.[197] Beginning in 2020, the U.S. Department of Labor was to receive US$180 million over four years for these purposes. Its Office of Trade and Labor Affairs (in the Bureau of International Labor Affairs, ILAB) was to use its special funding to monitor Mexico's implementation of its USMCA labor obligations and domestic labor laws, including "to inspect facilities in Mexico to determine whether those facilities are complying with those labor laws." Some of these funds were to support development of a Mexican government digital platform that would make collective bargaining agreements in both federal- and local (state)-jurisdiction economic activities, union registrations, and worker-employer grievance filings available online, with the goal of eliminating administrative discretion and possible corruption in these areas.[198] Funds allocated to the Office of Child Labor, Forced Labor, and Human Trafficking (ILAB) were to help combat child and forced labor in Mexico. In both instances, some of the allocated funds could be expended through grants to nongovernmental organizations engaged in labor rights advocacy in Mexico. Most remarkably, one purpose of the expanded funding was "to support a long-term commitment by the Bureau of International Labor Affairs to promote sustainable, independent worker organizations in Mexico."[199]

Overall, the U.S. implementation and funding legislation was notable for the ways in which it charged U.S. governmental agencies with exercising close oversight over Mexico's domestic affairs. Indeed, a part of H.R. 5430 (Title VII, subtitle B) became the focus of intense bilateral controversy even before the House of Representatives formally adopted it. The provision in question called on the Department of Labor to recruit up to five additional full-time labor attachés assigned to the U.S. embassy (or consulates) in Mexico "to monitor and enforce the labor obligations of Mexico." They were charged with submitting quarterly reports on Mexico's compliance to the new Interagency Labor Committee.[200]

The first public word of this provision came from a summary overview of the protocol of amendment (titled "Improvements to the USMCA") released by the House of Representatives Committee on Ways and Means on December 10, 2019.[201] Ambassador Seade, who had only days earlier claimed public credit for the omission of overly intrusive labor inspections language in the final USMCA text, immediately denounced the measure as a violation of good-faith diplomacy.[202] He claimed that labor attachés had never been discussed during the lengthy bilateral negotiations concerning labor enforcement and that the U.S. government was, in effect, inserting into an international agreement a "redundant" and "unnecessary" mechanism that was really directed at a domestic political audience. He argued, moreover, that any attempt by U.S. labor attachés to conduct plant-level inspections would constitute a violation of Mexican law and sovereignty.[203] Seade, backed publicly by Secretary of Foreign Relations Marcelo Ebrard,[204] laid out these objections in a public letter to Ambassador Lighthizer and immediately flew to Washington, DC, to discuss the matter with him in person.[205] Lighthizer quickly released his written response, stating that the U.S. government did not envision the attachés as anything more than what was standard diplomatic practice by both the U.S. and Mexican governments.[206] He explained that the labor attachés would primarily be devoted to providing technical assistance and disbursing capacity-building funds, and he confirmed that only special rapid response mechanism investigative panels established under the terms of the protocol of amendment would undertake plant-level inspections.[207]

Seade's public denunciations were apparently based on sincerely held principle. However, by hoisting the banner of Mexican nationalism, he also helped protect the López Obrador administration against the criticisms lodged by some Mexican business organizations that Seade had conceded too much by agreeing to annex 31-A provisions permitting onsite inspections under any conditions. At a minimum, the short-lived but intense controversy surrounding the appointment of U.S. labor attachés ensured that the issue would remain a sensitive political issue during USMCA implementation. In the end, however, Mexico's Senate ratified the protocol of amendment by a vote of 107–1 on December 12, 2019, and President López Obrador issued an official enactment decree on January 21, 2020.[208]

CONCLUSION

The renegotiation of the NAFTA between 2017 and 2019 constituted a critical point of inflection in the North American labor rights experience. Labor issues were at the center of U.S. domestic and international bargaining over a revised continental free-trade agreement, as they had been in the 1991–1993 debates over the NAFTA and the NAALC. The main state and nonstate actors engaged in these interactions also generally remained the same. Nonetheless, the bargaining outcomes differed substantially.

The USMCA's labor chapter responded to the NAALC and the NAALC experience in two different ways. First, its contents quite naturally reflected the principal adaptations made after 1994 in the labor rights provisions the U.S. government embedded in free-trade agreements, with the TPP as the most proximate model. For instance, ILO declaration-centered covered rights were subject to chapter 31 dispute-settlement procedures; signatory countries were committed to nonderogation of labor rights; provisions concerning workplace equality and migrant workers' rights were fully enforceable; and grievance procedures (with tight timelines) were significantly strengthened.[209] Amendments to the language identifying the conditions under which alleged rights violations trigger dispute-settlement proceedings ("in a manner affecting trade or investment between the Parties") specifically responded to the widely shared frustration produced by the 2017 Guatemala international arbitral panel decision against the United States.

Second, the most politically significant parts of the USMCA's labor provisions responded to the broader NAALC experience in the sense that they addressed labor rights problems in Mexico that the NAALC had failed to remedy.[210] This was the U.S. government's explicit goal in demanding the inclusion of annex 23-A, a provision that reflected the more general post-2007 U.S. practice of requiring prospective developing country trade partners to adopt required labor reforms before the FTA took effect and exactly paralleled the TPP labor contingency plans that Mexico had previously avoided. The Brown-Wyden rapid response mechanism, which held private companies responsible for any rights violations occurring at their production facilities and included possible onsite inspections as part of dispute-settlement procedures, was an especially important innovation in labor rights enforcement provisions that in all likelihood, set a new bar for any later U.S. FTAs. Both the inclusion of a sunset clause in the final trade agreement and the creation of new U.S. administrative oversight bodies bolstered U.S. leverage in addressing labor rights issues in Mexico over the long term.[211]

The legacies of the NAALC, then, materialized in USMCA labor rights provisions of historic importance, even though there were a number of U.S. labor demands that found no traction during the negotiations.[212] Two distinct but reinforcing factors explain this outcome.

First, U.S. negotiators were highly effective at deploying sovereignty leverage to positive effect in their interactions with Mexican government officials. At the outset of the NAFTA 2.0 negotiations, USTR Lighthizer openly asserted the U.S. advantage in this regard, telling the U.S. House of Representatives' Committee on Ways and Means Subcommittee on Trade that the U.S. domestic market was large enough to "muscle anyone to our desire."[213] Yet in the cases examined in chapter 5, the United States' sovereignty leverage and its effective capacity to advance worker rights declined following the implementation of a bilateral free-trade agreement, regardless of underlying power disparities between the signatory countries. It was certainly possible that efforts to renegotiate the long-established NAFTA would have conformed to this pattern. What decisively reestablished the U.S. government's leverage in the NAFTA 2.0/USMCA context were Donald Trump's unbalanced but credible, repeated threats simply to cancel "the worst trade deal maybe ever signed anywhere." In bargaining terms, those threats, in effect, returned the NAFTA partners closer to their status quo ante positions. Trump's posturing, in conjunction with the fact that Mexico's overall economic dependence on continental free trade had significantly deepened in the quarter century since the adoption of the NAFTA, determined the dynamics of U.S.-Mexican negotiations over labor questions such as annex 23-A and other controversial issues.[214] As two Mexican presidential administrations with very different political profiles and policy agendas demonstrated over the course of the negotiations, the country's strategic economic dependence on the U.S. market was so great that no Mexican government could refuse to make whatever concessions were required to defend its stake in the trade agreement.

The character of important portions of the NAFTA 2.0 / USMCA negotiations over labor rights also reinforced U.S. sovereignty leverage. In contrast to the 1993 NAALC negotiations, from mid-2018 onward, U.S. officials conducted international bargaining sequentially, first winning concessions from the Mexican government on labor issues and then presenting the resulting bilateral agreements to Canadian negotiators as a fait accompli.[215] Although this bargaining approach was in line with Trump's expressed personal preference for bilateral over multi-lateral negotiations, it mainly reflected the facts that the main labor questions under discussion involved Mexico and that uncertainties concerning ratification of a final trade agreement were centered in Washington, DC. In the end, however, the de facto exclusion of the Canadian government from negotiations over annex 23-A and the facility-specific rapid response mechanism probably made little sub-stantive difference. Canadian negotiators were unlikely to have disagreed with either the content of the annex or the final design of the rapid response labor mechanism.[216] Even had Canadian negotiators formed part of those discussions, they almost certainly would not have seriously contested positions adopted by U.S. officials because, in the last analysis, the Canadian government gave higher priority to other issues in the trade agreement.

Second, an unanticipated alignment of sociopolitical actors in the United States propelled forward the USMCA's historically important labor provisions. In noted contrast to the NAALC negotiations, a politically contingent coalition of trade union leaders, labor-allied Democratic congressional representatives, and Republican trade officials worked together effectively in favor of enhanced labor rights protections. This coalition was sustained by the post-NAALC legit-imacy of the labor rights/trade link, the consensus that (ineffective) NAALC public communications procedures had forged among U.S. unions and their Mexican allies concerning the essential content of meaningful labor reform in Mexico, and Democrats' majority in the U.S. House of Representatives. Since the first adoption of labor rights-conditionality provisions in U.S. trade legislation in the early 1980s, no previous Republican presidential administration had taken such a flexible position on these questions. The terms on which labor rights advocates politically defined the debate over the USMCA's labor enforcement provisions—the importance of requiring the Mexican government to enforce in practice its agreed labor rights obligations and establishing a "level playing field" for U.S. workers—made Republican congressional resistance difficult. For U.S. business associations that might have otherwise opposed the facility-specific rapid response mechanism, acquiescence was the price of securing approval of the trade agreement as a whole.

Although U.S. labor rights advocates and the U.S. government were the principal proponents of the USMCA's labor provisions, Mexican negotiators did influence their final content. The positions that the Mexican government took on key topics during the NAFTA 2.0 / USMCA labor negotiations changed over time. Having failed first to pursue the democratizing labor law reform initiative negotiated with the United States in 2015 and then to secure passage of the more conservative González-Medina alternative legislation in 2018, the Peña Nieto administration was vulnerable to U.S. pressures over annex 23-A. Mexican negotiators, reflecting intense opposition from national business organizations and the interests of their old-guard labor allies based on the workplace control they exercised under the established state-labor relations regime, vigorously opposed the annex because its priority focus on collective-action rights directly challenged Mexico's Weberian sovereignty. In the end, however, the outgoing Peña Nieto administration ceded to U.S. demands in order to secure final agreement on a revised NAFTA before its term in office ended. In doing so, it found political cover in the incoming López Obrador administration's endorsement of annex 23-A, whose content was congruent with its own domestic reform agenda and the long-term goals of labor organizations such as the National Union of Workers (UNT). Even then, however, Mexican officials strongly resisted the link established in the annex between adoption of a progressive labor law reform and implementation of the trade agreement.[217] The compromise reached by U.S. and Mexican negotiators was artfully worded:

> It is the *expectation* of the Parties that Mexico shall adopt legislation described above before January 1, 2019. It is further understood that entry into force of the agreement <u>may be</u> delayed until such legislation becomes effective. (Annex 23-A.8, emphasis added)

In their drive to insert annex 23-A in the NAFTA 2.0 text in 2018, U.S. negotiators and U.S. and Mexican labor rights proponents benefited substantially from López Obrador's presidential election victory and his transition team's support for far-reaching labor reforms. In contrast, initial U.S. proposals in 2019 for a facility-specific rapid response labor enforcement mechanism met unified Mexican resistance because of the challenges the arrangement posed to Mexico's Westphalian sovereignty. Mexican trade negotiators, national business organizations, and even pro-union democracy reformists all opposed direct U.S. intervention in Mexico's domestic affairs in the form of onsite company inspections involving U.S. government officials. Labor-allied Democratic legislators in the United States advocated the rapid response mechanism because, within the institutional and political constraints of an existing free-trade agreement with an important U.S. strategic ally, it established for the first time in a U.S. FTA—at least at the company level—the possibility of a Generalized System of Preferences-style suspension of market access as a sanction for serious violations of collective-action rights. Of course, Mexican government officials and national business associations strenuously opposed the measure for that same reason. In the end, the López Obrador government was compelled to accept the rapid response mechanism because it was the necessary price to bring the USMCA negotiations to conclusion and secure U.S. congressional approval of the continental free-trade agreement on which Mexico depended so heavily. Mexican negotiators' persistent defense of national sovereignty did, however, lead to important restrictions on the terms under which the mechanism could be employed.

CHAPTER 7

Labor Rights, Trade Agreements, State Sovereignty

Past Record and Future Prospects

S ince the founding of the International Labour Organization (ILO) in 1919, both the scope of internationally recognized labor rights and the range of arenas in which they are promoted and defended have expanded substantially. Only with the post–World War II declarations of universal human rights did the conventions adopted by the ILO shift in focus from individual worker rights, employment conditions, and wages to more explicitly political issues, such as the freedom of association and the rights to organize and bargain collectively. The 1998 ILO Declaration on Fundamental Principles and Rights at Work consolidated an international consensus concerning core labor rights. Similarly, although there had long been a prominent tradition of cross-border union solidarity actions, trade agreement–linked labor rights provisions and corporate social responsibility campaigns only emerged in the 1980s and 1990s as important alternative arenas for advancing worker rights.

The debate over linking labor standards to trade agreements has also evolved significantly since the mid-twentieth century. For several decades after the adoption of the General Agreement on Tariffs and Trade (GATT) in 1947, attempts by labor organizations and their political allies to establish a labor rights/trade link focused on attaching a "social clause" to the GATT. Repeated failures to achieve this goal eventually led U.S. labor rights advocates to shift their focus to national legislation, leading to the first labor-conditionality provisions in the 1983 Caribbean Basin Initiative and the 1984 amended Generalized System of Preferences (GSP) program. The growing success during and after the 1990s that U.S. labor organizations had in embedding labor rights provisions in free-trade agreements, often during Republican presidential administrations that resisted or sought to minimize labor rights/trade linkage, was somewhat paradoxical; this was, after all, the same period when the labor movement's aggregate size and overall policymaking influence were generally in decline. In part, it was that very decline and the increasing challenges posed by international economic competition that spurred trade unions and their political allies to greater action in the labor rights/trade field. There was an immense political distance between the U.S. labor movement's somewhat indifferent response to inserting fair labor standards provisions in the Havana Charter (Cuban delegates to the 1947–1948 Havana Conference were more active in this regard than their U.S. counterparts) and what leading U.S. trade unions sought and achieved in the labor chapter of the 2020 United States-Mexico-Canada Agreement (USMCA). Mexico played an important role in inducing this change because it was a very proximate focus of the low-standards, low-wage competitive challenges that U.S. unions faced. However, part of the explanation for the significant evolution that occurred also lies in the broader internationalization of labor rights and policy issue maturation over time, which resulted in a more widely shared perceived legitimacy of labor rights/trade linkage.

The evolution of trade agreement–linked labor rights provisions in the United States has, in this sense, been path-dependent in character. The adoption of the North American Agreement on Labor Cooperation (NAALC) in 1993 was a key contingent event—an occurrence that was not expected to take place but which set in motion "institutional patterns or event chains that have deterministic properties"[1]—because, by explicit mutual agreement, it breached the sovereignty barrier and made labor rights in the three North American Free Trade Agreement (NAFTA) signatory countries subject to institutionalized external scrutiny.[2] As chapter 3 showed, the NAALC provisions were hard-fought political compromises among Canada, Mexico, and the United States. None of the governments that negotiated the NAFTA envisioned such an institutional arrangement. Nor was the administration of President William J. (Bill) Clinton (1993–1997, 1997–2001) compelled to proceed with a Republican-negotiated trade agreement; in fact, some of Clinton's closest advisers argued that he should invest his political capital in his domestic policy agenda. Moreover, U.S. labor organizations, which were nominally the NAALC's principal beneficiaries, did not actively promote it, and U.S. business interests were strongly opposed. Yet once adopted, despite its very limited record of practical achievement and U.S.

(and Canadian) trade unions' continued opposition to free-trade agreements (FTAs), the NAALC became the point of departure and benchmark for the negotiation of labor rights provisions in all subsequent FTAs promoted by the United States. These arrangements (and parallel provisions concerning environmental protection) were, in the first instance, symbolically important ways of addressing the often-negative social consequences of free trade. The ILO's 1998 declaration and the May 10, 2007, U.S. executive-legislative accord over the inclusion of labor rights protections in the main text of U.S. FTAs consolidated their political legitimacy, and subsequent debates focused on the institutional design of these provisions rather than the merits of labor rights/trade linkage per se. In the terms employed by Mahoney (2000), this was, then, an instance of institutional replication through legitimation rather than through utilitarian, cost-benefit assessment by the sociopolitical actors involved.[3]

It is because the NAALC has held a special place in labor rights/trade linkage policy debates that this book focuses principally on the North American labor rights experience. This experience demonstrates that, despite major advances in recognition of workers' rights as human rights and considerable evolution in the strategies employed to advance them, the international defense of labor rights remains fundamentally conditioned (and often constrained) by state sovereignty, particularly where collective-action rights are concerned. How the tensions between state sovereignty and rights promotion shape government-to-government interactions over the adoption and implementation of labor provisions in trade agreements, how rights advocates navigate this arena, and the outcomes of governmental and nongovernmental actions in the context of the NAALC and other U.S. trade agreements have been principal axes of analysis.

This concluding chapter proceeds in two parts. The first section assesses the evidence presented in this book concerning the efficacy of U.S. trade agreement–linked labor provisions as a strategy for defending labor rights internationally, focusing on the interplay between state sovereignty and labor rights promotion in two different political moments: U.S. pretrade agreement bargaining over labor rights and the implementation of labor rights provisions in U.S. trade agreements. With regard to the latter subject, the discussion considers three possible explanations for the limited effectiveness of labor complaints filed under U.S. FTA dispute-settlement procedures: shifts over time in U.S. presidential policy and political commitment to employing these provisions to advance workers' rights; differences in the institutional design of U.S. trade agreements' labor rights provisions; and variations in the strength of the local sociopolitical alliances mobilized by U.S. unions and labor rights advocates in support of their complaints. The second part of this chapter examines possible future directions in the configuration of trade agreement–linked labor rights provisions. In particular, it highlights the USMCA's innovative facility-specific rapid response labor mechanism that makes rights violations by private companies potentially subject to trade sanctions.

SOVEREIGNTY LEVERAGE AND LABOR RIGHTS IN TWO POLITICAL MOMENTS: A COMPARATIVE ASSESSMENT

The central research question addressed in this book is whether sovereignty leverage exercised through U.S. trade agreements is an efficacious strategy for advancing labor rights internationally. In line with the conceptual framework developed in chapter 1, this summary discussion examines the question in two different political moments, distinguishing between pretrade agreement state-to-state bargaining over labor rights (the content of the agreement's labor provisions and/or the legal and policy reforms that prospective trade partners adopt prior to their accession to the agreement) and the subsequent implementation of a U.S. trade agreement's labor provisions.[4] Government-to-government negotiations may, of course, also feature prominently in the postagreement resolution of specific labor complaints.

U.S. Preagreement Bargaining Over Labor Rights

Because this book focuses primarily on the North American labor rights experience, preceding chapters examined state-to-state bargaining over trade agreement–linked labor provisions principally through case studies of U.S.-Mexican interactions over the NAALC and the labor chapter in the United States-Mexico-Canada Agreement (USMCA). There were no international negotiations over the labor-conditionality provisions in either the Caribbean Basin Initiative (Caribbean Basin Economic Recovery Act [CBERA], 1983), a program that offered duty-free entry into the U.S. market for most exports from designated Caribbean and Central American countries, or the 1984 amended Generalized System of Preferences program because these were both preferential trade agreements in which the U.S. government designated beneficiaries based on its own specified eligibility criteria. Bargaining between the United States and one or more prospective trade partners over labor rights provisions was, however, central in the NAALC and in several post-NAFTA U.S. free-trade agreements, including the USMCA. Chapters 3, 5, and 6 examine these negotiations and their outcomes in detail.

Where the United States is concerned, a comparison of bilateral preagreement bargaining with Mexico over labor rights questions across the NAFTA, Trans-Pacific Partnership (TPP) agreement, and NAFTA 2.0/USMCA cases—one mixed and two positive cases, respectively, in terms of U.S. success in achieving its main goals—indicates significant political adaptation and issue evolution. The U.S. organized labor movement's core issue agenda remained relatively constant over time. However, once the NAFTA took effect, labor leaders shifted their focus from outright rejection of a continental free-trade agreement to prolonged political bargaining over bolstering its labor rights provisions and those included in later U.S. FTAs as well. By actively pursuing public communications under the NAALC, U.S. trade unions, albeit less concerned about the policy agenda-setting legacies of their actions than with their inability to achieve meaningful results at the workplace level through NAALC grievance processes, helped shape a wider U.S. understanding regarding how labor dispute-settlement procedures might be strengthened. Among U.S. sociopolitical actors more generally, a broad consensus slowly emerged concerning the essential legitimacy of labor rights/trade linkage, which was manifested both in the May 10, 2007, executive-legislative accord and bipartisan agreement among Democratic and Republican congressional representatives during the NAFTA 2.0/USMCA negotiations about the importance of robust enforcement measures. In marked contrast to the 1993 NAALC negotiations, domestic political concurrence on these questions underpinned the U.S. successes in exercising sovereignty leverage vis-à-vis Mexico in both the TPP and NAFTA 2.0/USMCA negotiations. Moreover, for the U.S. government, the NAALC experience shifted the terms of debate from enforcement of national labor laws to securing constitutional and legislative changes during the TPP and NAFTA 2.0/USMCA negotiations that redefined the institutional bases of Mexico's state-labor relations regime. The constitutional amendments that Mexico adopted in 2017 in response to insistent U.S. demands during the TPP negotiations laid the required foundations for a far-reaching federal labor law reform in 2019, and the USMCA's annex 23-A made Mexico's effective enforcement of collective-action rights a continuing obligation under the terms of the trade agreement.

Mexico's overall political stance in its interactions with the United States over labor questions did not differ much between 1993 and 2019. The Mexican government was finally forced to make major concessions in bilateral bargaining over the country's accession to the TPP, and its initial NAFTA 2.0 negotiating goals indicated a greater willingness among some officials to accept labor rights/trade linkage than had characterized its position during the NAALC negotiations. Nonetheless, presidential administrations with different partisan identities and policy agendas all staunchly defended national sovereignty and resisted intrusive U.S. scrutiny of Mexico's labor rights record. Indeed, Mexican officials publicly denied any connection between U.S. diplomatic pressures over the TPP and the adoption of constitutional labor reforms in 2017. Had U.S.-Mexican negotiations over labor rights in the context of the TPP not been followed quickly thereafter by intense bilateral bargaining over revision of the NAFTA, the Mexican government might have succeeded in backing away from some of the concessions it had previously made.

Mexico did, however, experience important changes in three areas. First, growing consensus among U.S. sociopolitical actors in favor of efforts to promote significant labor reform in Mexico reduced the Mexican government's room for maneuver vis-à-vis the United States. During the 1993 NAALC negotiations, the Mexican government's resistance to more expansive side-agreement provisions found de facto political support among U.S. business interests and congressional Republicans opposed to labor rights/trade linkage. By the time the TPP and NAFTA 2.0/USMCA negotiations took place, there was no major domestic opposition to U.S. government pressures on Mexico.

Second, the principal sources of domestic opposition to altering Mexico's established state-labor relations regime shifted over time. Whereas the old-guard labor movement had posed the most visible resistance to the NAALC, during the TPP and NAFTA 2.0/USMCA negotiations, it was the Mexican private sector that most actively opposed any substantial change in trade agreement provisions that would affect enforcement of collective-action rights. In fact, Mexican trade unions were largely marginalized during the NAFTA 2.0/USMCA labor negotiations.[5] It was not until 2018 and the election of President Andrés Manuel López Obrador (2018–2024), whose domestic policy agenda included a commitment to far-reaching labor reform, that the Mexican government accepted the USMCA's annex 23-A. López Obrador's presidential transition team concurred in doing so both to ensure that the crucial trade negotiations were concluded before López Obrador took office and because it calculated that U.S. support might prove politically advantageous in pushing through labor justice reforms against stiff private-sector opposition. Even then, however, Mexican negotiators worked hard to protect national sovereignty by constraining the terms on which the U.S. government could employ the USMCA's rapid response labor mechanism.

Third, and most important, progressively closer economic integration with the United States compromised Mexico's capacity to resist U.S. pressures for major labor reforms. Even though Mexico's already high export dependence on the United States did not vary greatly between 1993 and 2019, total trade (exports plus imports) as a proportion of gross domestic product did expand substantially. Even more significant, the deepening of Mexico-U.S. economic ties under the NAFTA transformed the Mexican economy. The export manufacturing of automotive vehicles and parts, for example, grew substantially in economic importance, and the industry became tightly integrated into North American production networks, whose disruption would have had serious negative consequences for the entire economy. The overall difference in the economic stakes for Mexico between the NAFTA negotiations (when the Mexican government doggedly and successfully resisted U.S. demands for a NAALC that would have made violations of collective-action rights subject to fines and/or trade-linked sanctions) and the NAFTA 2.0/USMCA negotiations (when the government acceded to annex 23-A and its detailed requirements for extensive legal reforms in how Mexico implemented collective-action rights) can be characterized as a shift from sensitivity to vulnerability interdependence vis-à-vis the United States.[6] Failing to secure final approval of the NAFTA would have been a major political setback with at least a short-term negative impact on the country's currency exchange rate and foreign investment climate,[7] but collapse of the NAFTA 2.0/USMCA negotiations was an outcome that no Mexican government could risk. Mexico's vulnerability was particularly acute in interactions with the United States over the TPP and the NAFTA 2.0/USMCA because these were "up-or-down" negotiations in which the U.S. government held a much stronger hand.

The convention of U.S. bargaining over the domestic labor reforms that prospective trade partners were to effect as a condition for accession to a trade agreement, a strategy that the United States employed very effectively vis-à-vis Mexico in the TPP and NAFTA 2.0/USMCA cases, began with the Caribbean Basin Initiative (CBI) in 1983.[8] There were no such negotiations with Mexico surrounding the NAFTA because Mexico's constitutional and legal protections of workers' rights were, at face value, strong and because the three center-right governments involved were not inclined to include social provisions in a free-trade agreement. However, in significant part because of the lessons that U.S. sociopolitical actors drew from the NAFTA/NAALC experience, the U.S. government regularly engaged in preaccession bargaining over labor rights with prospective partners when negotiating post-NAFTA FTAs. The most high-profile international interactions of this kind involved those with Colombia over the formulation of an "action plan"; with Brunei, Malaysia, Mexico, and Vietnam over so-called labor consistency plans during the TPP negotiations; and with Mexico over the USMCA's annex 23-A.

The principal contribution of case studies of U.S.-Mexican interactions concerning labor issues in preagreement bargaining over the TPP and the NAFTA 2.0/USMCA (chapters 5 and 6, respectively) is that they illuminate the inherent complexity of these negotiations. Without carefully tracing causal processes in selected case studies such as these, it is difficult to characterize preagreement negotiations between two states or to specify the form and strength of U.S. pressures—with U.S. market-access leverage as the fulcrum—and the domestic and international political and economic calculations that lead prospective trade partners to make significant concessions on labor issues. Nonetheless, there are a number of documented cases in which bargaining of this kind did yield commitments to substantial labor reforms in developing countries. Even in 1983, when the Office of the United States Trade Representative (USTR) and the U.S. Department of Labor had no prior experience in this area, U.S. preaccession negotiations with several potential participants in the Caribbean Basin Initiative addressed both general and specific labor reforms that the applicant states agreed to undertake as an accession condition.[9] For instance, the Dominican Republic promised to take a number of steps to end what were, in effect, forced-labor working conditions for Haitian immigrant workers in the sugar industry. El Salvador committed to curtailing violence against, and the illegal detention of, trade unionists. Haiti agreed to modify several legal provisions that had restricted unionization.[10] Similarly, as discussed in chapter 5, a number of the developing countries negotiating free-trade agreements with the United States during the 2000s agreed to undertake substantial labor reforms, some of which focused on collective-action rights. Colombia and several Central American countries were prominent examples.[11] These cases show, then, that despite variations over time in the partisan identity of U.S. presidential administrations, the specific labor issues in contention, differences in political regime type (authoritarian versus democratic), the structure of domestic sociopolitical coalitions, and the economic interests of the countries seeking expanded access to the U.S. marketplace, U.S. sovereignty leverage can be deployed in ways that promote international labor rights.

However, as difficult as even the most successful of these labor rights negotiations might have been, the postagreement implementation of trade partners' expressed commitments to labor reforms—although undoubtedly important politically on their own terms—has consistently constituted an even greater challenge.[12] One measure of the scale of this problem is that all five of the countries that were the focus of concentrated U.S. reform pressures as prospective CBI participants (Dominican Republic, El Salvador, Guatemala, Haiti, Honduras) were subsequently the object of labor rights complaints filed under the U.S. GSP program and (in the cases of the Dominican Republic and Guatemala) the Dominican Republic-Central America-United States Free Trade Agreement (DR-CAFTA). These complaints often focused on the same kinds of labor rights problems that the U.S. government worked to resolve in 1983.[13] The U.S. government often lacks adequate resources to conduct long-term monitoring of trade partners' compliance with agreed labor standards.[14] Yet, despite regular U.S. monitoring and some efforts by the Colombian government to fulfill its reform commitments under the action plan the two countries signed in 2011, major obstacles to freedom of association and the rights to organize and bargain collectively (including persistent judicial impunity in cases involving threats and violence against trade unionists) persisted.[15] Similarly, as noted above, had U.S.-Mexican negotiations over labor rights ended in 2016, the Mexican government would almost certainly have succeeded in implementing labor law reform legislation that would have significantly undercut the democratizing potential of the 2017 constitutional reforms it had adopted under strong U.S. pressures. It was only because labor rights issues returned to the fore in bilateral negotiations over revising the NAFTA that the Mexican government's elusive maneuvering failed.

In all these cases, without an explicit link between actual reform implementation and formal accession to the trade agreement in question, the capacity of the U.S. government to ensure trade partners' compliance with agreed commitments was very limited once preaccession negotiations ended. It is possible that the labor consistency plans the United States signed with Brunei, Malaysia, and Vietnam might have produced more positive results because these accords did directly link reform implementation to accession to the Trans-Pacific Partnership's trade benefits. However, those bilateral agreements lapsed when the United States withdrew from the TPP in January 2017.[16]

THE IMPLEMENTATION OF LABOR RIGHTS PROVISIONS IN U.S. TRADE AGREEMENTS

At a second political moment, the outcomes of the complaints filed under U.S. trade agreements' labor provisions constitute a critical test of the efficacy of these institutional arrangements as a means of protecting worker rights internationally. Chapters 2, 4, and 5 examine this issue in the contexts of, respectively, the U.S. GSP program, the NAALC, and post-NAFTA U.S. free-trade agreements. In each of these instances, the analysis focuses principally on the ability of U.S. labor organizations and labor rights advocates to employ complaint procedures to effect reforms in labor law and government policy in developing countries concerning collective-action rights (freedom of association and the rights to organize and bargain collectively). Among the U.S. GSP cases from the 1985–1995 period, there were positive observed policy impacts in five of the fifteen countries examined; policy changes in three countries were coded 2, and reforms in two countries were scored 3 on a five-point scale (table 2.1). Under the NAALC, complaints involving freedom of association, the rights to organize and bargain collectively, and the right to strike were not subject to full dispute-settlement procedures, but a number of the public communications filed on these grounds became the focus of high-level negotiations among the three NAFTA signatory countries. Nonetheless, only two of the twenty-six (7.7 percent) Canadian and U.S. communications addressing collective-action rights in Mexico led to policy outcomes coded 3 on a five-point scale (table 4.2), and, in practice, the Mexican government's implementation of the agreed policy change was delayed and partial. Similarly, for post-NAFTA FTAs, only two of the eight complaints lodged between 2008 and 2016 ended with any positive observed policy impact, and in both cases, the result was only coded 1 on a five-point scale (table 5.1).

Taken together, these findings raise serious questions about the efficacy of trade agreement-linked labor provisions as a mechanism for protecting worker rights. (Table 7.1 compares U.S. trade agreement-based complaint actions with labor rights complaints undertaken in the three alternative international arenas discussed in chapter 1 in terms of the principal actors generally involved; whether the objects of complaint actions are governments, private firms, or both; the overall frequency of such actions; whether collective-action rights are a priority of focus of these complaints; and their typical impact on law and policy in developing countries.[17]) One might object that the priority focus on

TABLE 7.1 Comparing alternative international arenas for advancing collective-action rights: Actors, processes, and policy impact

	Union-to-union solidarity actions	ILO	CSR campaigns	U.S. trade agreement labor provisions
Principal actors	Unions	Unions, governments	NGOs, sometimes unions	Unions, NGOs, governments
Target of compliant actions	Private firms, governments	Governments	Private firms	Governments
Frequency of actions	High	Moderate	High	Low to moderate
Collective-action rights as priority focus	Frequent	Frequent	Infrequent	Frequent
Impact of complaints on law and government policy	Very limited	Limited	Very limited	Limited (FTAs) to moderate (GSP)

Source: Author's assessment of empirical materials presented in chapters 1, 2, 3, and 5.

Notes: Collective-action rights are freedom of association and the rights to organize and bargain collectively. The U.S. trade agreements referenced in this table include the Generalized System of Preferences (GSP) program since 1984, the North American Free Trade Agreement (NAFTA) and the North American Agreement on Labor Cooperation (NAALC), and all post-NAFTA free-trade agreements (FTAs) except the United States-Mexico-Canada Agreement (2020). ILO = International Labour Organization; CSR = corporate social responsibility; NGOs = nongovernmental organizations.

collective-action rights yields unduly pessimistic conclusions in this regard. As outlined by the double-helix model described in chapter 1, there has historically been strong Westphalian and Weberian sovereign resistance in developing countries both to the formal recognition and actual implementation of these rights because they pose much greater potential challenges than individual worker rights to state officials' exercise of their public authority. Collective-action rights lie at the heart of national political economy because they are invoked in struggles over the organization of economic production in the workplace, linking both the public and the private sectors. Yet, these are precisely the reasons why trade unions and labor rights advocates consider collective-action rights to be fundamentally important. It is no coincidence that ILO conventions nos. 87 (freedom of association) and 98 (the rights to organize and bargain collectively) top the list of core labor rights in both the 1998 ILO declaration and the protected rights in trade agreements' labor provisions. No thorough examination of the efficacy of these provisions could ignore them. Indeed, for the labor organizations and rights-advocacy groups that file complaints under these institutional arrangements, they constitute a litmus test.

One might, moreover, argue that external labor rights promoters should not expect to bring about broad reform of a target country's collective-action rights legislation and policy practices through a single U.S. GSP, NAALC, or U.S. FTA submission. However, these complaints are both framed by rights advocates and perceived in the target country in precisely these terms. The public submissions examined in this book employed documented instances of labor abuses in particular work sites, companies, and/or industries to illustrate broader patterns of rights violations, legislative lacunae, and weaknesses in policy implementation. In fact, the essential requirement for the U.S. government to accept these submissions for formal review was that they addressed a serious, persistent pattern of action or inaction in a trade partner's implementation of its labor rights commitments. Individual complaints were, then, specifically designed as vehicles to address broader rights issues.

How, then, might we explain the different but generally negative policy outcomes summarized above? Three possible explanations, focusing on distinct but interacting intervening variables, merit close examination: shifts over time in U.S. presidential policy and political commitment to employing trade agreement-linked labor provisions to advance workers' rights internationally; differences in the institutional design of U.S. trade agreements' labor rights provisions; and variations in the strength of the local sociopolitical alliances mobilized by U.S. unions and rights advocates in support of their complaints. Although the specific focus here is on the U.S. trade agreements examined in this book, these factors framed more broadly would be relevant to the evaluation of the efficacy of labor rights provisions linked to any country's trade agreements.

U.S. Presidential Policy and Political Commitment

The fact that the U.S. government is responsible for pursuing complaints filed under trade agreement–linked labor provisions makes U.S. officials' commitment to the process a necessary condition for success. There is, however, no linear relationship between the political will they bring to these procedures and the outcomes they achieve. At least in principle, in some circumstances, relatively limited U.S. pressure might have a significant impact on the target government's willingness to effect labor rights reforms, while in other cases, even strong, persistent U.S. diplomatic pressures may fail to achieve the desired results. What is more certain is that, because trade agreements are state-to-state accords, U.S. government officials will necessarily weigh concerns about labor rights against competing foreign policy priorities in managing U.S. relations with the target country.[18] The United States negotiated some free-trade agreements more for strategic than for trade-promotion reasons per se (for instance, the U.S. FTAs with Bahrain, Israel, Jordan, Morocco, Oman, and even Colombia). In such cases, U.S. geopolitical interests may easily override concerns about labor rights violations alone. Even when geopolitical considerations are not predominant, U.S. officials may hesitate to strong-arm a valued commercial partner unless domestic U.S. political considerations or egregious labor rights violations in the partner country make it imperative to do so. Yet on occasion, these different policy interests can also overlap. In October 2021, U.S. government officials announced their intention to toughen enforcement of the DR-CAFTA's labor provisions as a way of reducing pressures for undocumented out-migration from Central American countries to the United States.[19]

Except by undertaking detailed process-tracing analysis of individual cases, it is often difficult in practice to determine how much political will U.S. government officials bring to the resolution of labor rights complaints or to assess the relative importance of this factor versus other possible explanations for the outcome of a particular grievance case. There is, nonetheless, some evidence that

U.S. government policy in this area has varied broadly by presidential administration. The examination of U.S. GSP labor rights petitions in chapter 2 found that under two preceding Republican administrations, the USTR accepted for review—the first test of political commitment—a lower proportion of the petitions filed than under the Clinton administration. In the case of NAALC public communications as well, the proportion of submissions involving Mexico that the U.S. National Administrative Office accepted for formal review declined between the Clinton administration and the administration of President George W. Bush (2001–2005, 2005–2009). The Clinton administration did, of course, have an especially strong interest in demonstrating that NAALC procedures offered an effective means of addressing labor rights problems in Mexico, but the difference in acceptance rates was nevertheless notable. Similarly, during the administration of President Barack Obama (2009–2013, 2013–2017), the Department of Labor's Office of Trade and Labor Affairs accepted for review and actively pursued all of the labor rights submissions filed under U.S. FTAs between 2010 and 2016. One can, then, conclude that Democratic presidential administrations, with the U.S. organized labor movement as a traditional electoral constituency, have generally been more committed to trade agreement-linked labor grievance procedures than their Republican counterparts.

In some instances, strong U.S. government pressure on a developing country over collective-rights issues has produced positive policy change. Among the U.S. GSP cases, the United States won modifications of labor code provisions regarding unionization and collective bargaining rights in El Salvador, Panama, and Paraguay, and in the Dominican Republic and Guatemala, these more favorable provisions were extended to the public sector and any export-processing zones in these countries. Among the NAALC public communications, Clinton administration pressures over the 1997 Han Young and Echlin/Itapsa cases, with parallel lobbying by the Canadian government, led Mexican government officials to agree for the first time to employ secret-ballot procedures to resolve future conflicts over legal title to collective bargaining agreements. However, of the twenty U.S. NAALC public communications concerning Mexico that addressed freedom of association and the rights to organize and bargain collectively (table 4.2), these were the only communications in which there was an observed policy impact scored 3 on a scale of 0–4. And as noted above, in practice, the Mexican government's implementation of the agreed policy change was slow and only partial.

The case record examined in this book includes far more instances in which even substantial pressures from U.S. officials over a sustained period of time failed to secure their objectives. The Obama administration brought very firm commitment to its interactions with Bahrain, Colombia, the Dominican Republic, and Peru over U.S. FTA labor rights submissions, including lobbying by President Obama himself with the president of Peru. Yet, the U.S. government won minor policy concessions only from Honduras and Peru (both rated 1 on a 0–4 scale). The most notorious example was, of course, the U.S. defeat in the prolonged 2008–2017 Guatemala grievance proceedings in which Obama administration officials demonstrated strong political will over the course of several years. On balance, then, although variations in U.S. presidential policy and differences in the degree of political commitment evidenced by U.S. government officials have, at times, influenced the outcome of particular labor rights grievance cases, these considerations do not explain the overall paltry record of success. Constraints based in the institutional design of the labor dispute-settlement procedures included in U.S. FTAs from the NAFTA/NAALC up until the USMCA appear to be more important in this regard.

The Institutional Design of Labor Rights Provisions

Chapter 1 highlighted the importance of the institutional design of trade agreement-linked labor provisions and hypothesized that differences in these arrangements might account for variations in their observed policy impact. The relevant sections of the U.S. trade agreements examined here (the GSP program, NAFTA/NAALC, and post-NAFTA FTAs) all recognized a broadly similar range of core labor rights, and they all featured complaints procedures that were (within some resource constraints) widely accessible to trade unions and other nongovernmental organizations (NGOs). However, one obvious difference between the NAFTA and later U.S. FTAs was that the NAALC was only a supplemental agreement (that is, it did not form part of the trade agreement text) with three tiers of recognized labor rights. Ending disparities between the treatment of labor rights and, for example, intellectual property rights, immediately became a central goal of U.S. trade unions and labor rights advocates. As a result of insistent lobbying by these groups, the U.S. trade agreements (re) negotiated after 2007 included a special labor chapter in the body of each accord. In addition, they made all covered labor rights, including collective-action rights, subject to dispute-settlement procedures.[20] These changes did allow the U.S. government to pursue a labor complaint against Guatemala through the full dispute-settlement process established by the DR-CAFTA, but the result was, if anything, more disappointing than what rights advocates achieved under the NAALC.

The objects of labor rights–violation penalties in the U.S. trade agreements discussed in this section were the same: national governments. However, the nature and severity of the penalties that could be levied against target governments for proven rights violations differed significantly between the U.S. GSP program, on the one hand, and the NAALC and post-NAFTA U.S. FTAs, on the other. Only in the former can a beneficiary country's export access to the U.S. market be suspended or terminated as a sanction for severe, persistent violations of protected labor rights.[21] In the NAALC and in the dispute-settlement provisions of all subsequent FTAs the United States negotiated between 2003 and 2019, penalties for proven labor rights violations in the first instance consisted of fines of different amounts. The U.S. government could suspend an equivalent amount of the sanctioned country's trade benefits only if it failed to pay the assessed fines in a timely manner. Under no circumstances could the U.S. government suspend the country from the agreement itself for labor rights abuses, even had it been prepared to set aside broader foreign policy considerations and take such a momentous step.

One way of assessing the practical importance of these differences in penalty structure is to compare the observed policy impact of labor rights complaints filed under different U.S. trade agreements. Among the country cases examined in this book, six countries were the object of complaints under both the U.S. GSP program and U.S. FTAs: Colombia, Costa Rica, the Dominican Republic, Guatemala, Honduras, and Peru.[22] None of the complaints against Colombia produced any positive results concerning collective-action rights (tables 2.1, 5.1). However, labor rights petitions lodged under U.S. GSP procedures between 1985 and 1995 produced at least some positive policy change in all five of the other countries. In Costa Rica and Honduras, the results were coded only 1 on a 0–4 scale, but policy outcomes were coded 2 or 3 in the Dominican Republic, El Salvador, and Guatemala (table 2.1). In marked contrast, the public submissions filed under U.S. FTAs between 2008 and 2016 produced very modest policy changes (coded 1 on a 0–4 scale) in only two (Honduras and Peru) of the seven countries that were the object of these complaints (table 5.1).

There are several reasons why this can only be an approximate comparison. The GSP and FTA complaints cited above were filed in different time periods and under different presidential administrations in both the United States and the target countries. One might argue that U.S. officials could have been more hesitant to pressure FTA partner countries than countries with "only" GSP beneficiary status. Yet, broad foreign policy considerations were always part of U.S. GSP sanctions deliberations. Moreover, the Obama administration did, in fact, bring strong pressures to bear on FTA partners during labor dispute-settlement procedures,[23] although U.S. officials could not threaten to exclude them from the agreement. Nor were there any substantial changes over time in these countries' overall trade dependence on the U.S. market.[24] There are plausible reasons to conclude, then, that the U.S. GSP program—under which the U.S. government exercises greater sovereignty leverage based on suspension or termination of market access as a maximum possible sanction—was a more effective vehicle for promoting labor rights internationally than U.S. free-trade agreements. One possible explanation for this difference is that the absence of a market-exclusion penalty option in FTAs might lower target governments' perceived cost of sovereign resistance to U.S. pressures for significant labor policy change.[25]

Comparing Guatemala's responses to U.S. pressures over labor rights issues exercised through the GSP program and the DR-CAFTA offers further insight into this issue. In the GSP cases, a combination of external pressures (multiple GSP complaints filed over an extended period of time by U.S. trade unions and labor-rights advocacy groups, followed by strong, persistent lobbying by U.S. government officials) and more favorable domestic political conditions surrounding the 1996 peace settlement that ended a long civil war, initially led to improved implementation of collective-action labor rights. The fact that the national business community took very seriously the threat posed to the country's international reputation by the possible loss of its GSP beneficiary status—a unilateral U.S. action that Guatemala could have contested only ex post facto— was an important factor in producing this outcome. In contrast, multiple rounds of government-to-government consultations and the Guatemalan government's proposals for corrective actions failed to resolve the U.S. concerns articulated in a labor complaint filed under the DR-CAFTA. When the U.S. government persisted in what was widely understood to be a test case of the viability of FTA labor dispute-settlement procedures, Guatemalan officials responded by availing themselves of the institutional options available under the agreement and actively (and successfully) contested U.S. charges—and the explicit threat of trade-linked sanctions—before the independent arbitral panel requested by the U.S. government. The severity of labor rights violations in the country had not substantially changed over time, but the DR-CAFTA's labor provisions offered Guatemalan officials what proved to be powerful means of defending national interests that had not previously been available to them.

The unilateral market-access suspension and termination penalty options available to the U.S. government under the GSP program may have made it more effective than pre-2020 U.S. FTA sanctions provisions as a means of defending worker rights in developing countries.[26] Yet, the available evidence suggests that it has more often been the *threat* of such action, rather than the actual suspension or termination of market access, that counted most in terms of applying U.S. sovereignty leverage.[27] Again, it is only possible to draw tentative conclusions in this regard because the secondary literature that forms the basis of the U.S. GSP labor petitions analysis in chapter 2 did not always examine in depth U.S. bilateral negotiations with target country governments. The potential threat of losing beneficiary status was certainly important in the cases of Guatemala and Honduras. This risk may, in fact, have been more significant in securing policy concessions from other target countries than the available documentary record indicates because it was always an implicit part of bilateral bargaining over changes in labor law and policy. What is also clear, however, is that the actual loss of partial or full GSP trade benefits did not immediately produce significant policy change in the cases of Chile, Nicaragua, Pakistan, and Paraguay. One explanation for the U.S. failures to win meaningful policy concessions from these countries may simply be that a target government that consistently resists strong U.S. diplomatic pressures to adopt and/or implement collective-action rights guarantees may be so committed to preserving a repressive domestic labor regime that it is willing to pay some actual economic cost to avoid significant reforms.

Sociopolitical Alliances in Target Countries

The analysis of U.S. GSP labor rights petitions in chapter 2 found a close association between the strength of domestic political support that U.S. labor organizations and labor-rights NGOs were able to mobilize in target countries and the observed policy outcomes of these petitions. Local allies were important in helping external petitioners formulate well-documented cases that accurately reflected the specificities of national labor legislation and workplace practices. Evidence of support for GSP petitions within the target country may have been especially valuable in persuading U.S. government officials to take the claims of labor rights violations seriously and to invest political capital in pursuing them. More broadly, even in countries where both the organized labor movement and democratic political institutions were comparatively weak, the engagement of local trade unions and/or labor-rights NGOs in U.S. GSP processes sometimes increased pressures on national governments to accept legal and policy reforms.

In contrast, in the NAALC and U.S. FTA public submissions examined in chapters 4 and 5, respectively, there was no correlation between the extent of sociopolitical support in the target country and what these labor rights complaints achieved. In a very high proportion of the U.S. NAALC public communications addressing labor rights problems in Mexico and in all the U.S. FTA submissions filed between 2008 and 2016, the complainants successfully mobilized significant numbers of local trade unions and labor-rights NGOs. These allies frequently played vital roles in helping the U.S.-based petitioners compile an extensive documentary record and thereby demonstrate the severity of alleged rights violations to U.S. Department of Labor and USTR officials. These alliances were, moreover, important instances of social capital formation that held the promise to promote progressive change over the longer term.

Nonetheless, in essence, these were all instances in which sociopolitical actors in target countries had not yet been capable, acting on their own, of effectively ensuring workers' core rights. The NAALC public communications illustrated particularly well the great difficulties that pro-union democracy elements frequently face in their efforts to compel national government officials to alter an established state-labor relations regime in any significant way. In Mexico, the organizational strength and political influence of the old-guard labor organizations that benefited most directly from the legal status quo declined between the early 1990s and the 2010s. The formation of the National Union of Workers (Unión Nacional de Trabajadores, UNT) in 1997 also created a new pole of labor opposition that became the basis for a formal alliance with the American Federation of Labor-Congress of Industrial Organizations (AFL-CIO) and regular collaboration with leading U.S. and Canadian unions in NAALC public communications. Yet, the repeated failure of the UNT's legislative proposals for democratizing labor reforms from the late 1990s through the 2010s, and the fact that the 2012 federal labor law reform did not include changes in its collective-rights and labor justice provisions, showed the limits of UNT influence even after Mexico's successful transition to electoral democracy in 2000.

The notable stability of Mexico's postrevolutionary state-labor relations regime over almost ninety years may have made it a somewhat exceptional case. However, the broader question remains: How does one account for the fact that, in contrast to the U.S. GSP record, there was no close association between the strength of the local sociopolitical alliances that external actors mobilized in target countries and the policy outcomes of the labor rights complaints filed under the NAALC and pre-2020 U.S. FTAs?

The answer may lie in differences between the U.S. GSP program on the one hand, and the NAALC and U.S. free-trade agreements on the other, in the character of complaint procedures and sanctions provisions. Under the former, the U.S. executive retains full discretion in the decision to suspend or terminate a beneficiary country's preferential export access to the U.S. market. A target country government can present its point of view during the USTR's review of its labor rights record, and it retains the right to appeal a negative U.S. decision. However, the center of political gravity is squarely in Washington, DC. Perhaps equally important, the prospect of losing U.S. GSP market access and suffering the associated negative reputational and/or economic consequences may make a target government more sensitive to domestic reform pressures than it would be during the course of U.S. FTA complaints procedures. These pressures may have less impact in U.S. FTA cases because labor dispute-settlement procedures involve more institutionalized state-to-state interactions that give a target government considerable capacity to delay resolution of the matter. In principle, in the worst case, a target country potentially faces comparatively minor financial or trade-linked penalties; in practice, in the period between 1994 and 2022, the U.S. government never levied economic sanctions against an FTA partner country for labor rights violations. Moreover, as illustrated by the 2008–2017 Guatemala case, in the last instance, the final decision concerning the possible application of monetary or trade-linked sanctions in FTA labor rights cases is not in the hands of U.S. government officials. Rather, the decision is within the purview of an independent arbitral panel whose views can be influenced by the relative professional talents of the attorneys representing the contesting parties.

NEW HORIZONS IN THE INTERNATIONAL DEFENSE
OF LABOR RIGHTS

By focusing on the tension between state sovereignty and the international promotion and defense of workers' rights, this book highlights both the contributions of and the limits to efforts by U.S. governmental and nongovernmental actors to employ trade agreement-linked labor provisions to advance collective-action rights in developing countries. The leverage that the U.S. government can bring to bear in state-to-state negotiations with prospective trade partners is greatest when future access to the U.S. market—the fulcrum point of its sovereignty leverage—is at stake. In that political moment, during bargaining over the content of the agreement's labor provisions and/or the legal and policy reforms that the prospective partner might be required to make before acceding to the trade agreement, the United States has sometimes been able to win significant concessions. Yet, securing subsequent implementation of agreed labor reforms has often proved difficult because the U.S. government has markedly less leverage over a free-trade partner government once an agreement is in place.

The labor provisions in U.S. FTAs institutionalize government-to-government interactions over signatory countries' compliance with their labor rights obligations, processes in which U.S. bargaining leverage is also constrained. For instance, even though the U.S. government actively supported a number of NAALC public communications identifying systemic barriers to Mexican workers' rights to associate freely and bargain collectively, it never succeeded in persuading the Mexican government to adopt legislative or policy reforms remotely similar to those it won in bilateral negotiations over Mexico's accession to the TPP and the USMCA. Rather than the sovereign decision-making authority that the U.S. government exercises in investigating and sanctioning rights violations under the GSP program, under FTAs, the United States is ultimately bound by the decision of an international arbitral panel. The reverses that the U.S. government suffered in its attempts to sanction Guatemala for serious, persistent labor rights violations illustrate this point. The arbitral panel convened to review the case declined on procedural grounds to address obstacles to the legal registration of trade unions in Guatemala because the U.S. government had not specifically included that issue in its call for formation of the panel.

Although U.S. trade unions and labor-rights NGOs had very limited success in achieving positive policy outcomes in the grievance cases they filed under the NAALC and pre-2020 U.S. FTAs, their actions did make several important contributions to the overall goal of defending workers' rights in Mexico and other developing countries. First, public submissions filed under these agreements proved to be an important way of focusing international attention on labor rights violations in signatory countries.[28] Second, the process of identifying potential cases for review, formulating petition documents and preparing public testimony, and sometimes coordinating support campaigns stimulated the formation of binational and trinational labor rights coalitions that constructed valuable transnational social capital. Third, the combination of U.S. government pressures in support of worker rights and domestic sociopolitical mobilization in alliance with external rights advocates sometimes provided an important impulse to reform efforts in target countries. For instance, the 1997 NAALC public communication concerning mandatory pregnancy testing of women workers increased public awareness of this issue in Mexico and bolstered growing domestic pressures for policy change. This example is of double significance: external governmental and nongovernmental actors can be invaluable allies, but in the final analysis, securing the recognition and implementation of core labor rights in developing countries fundamentally depends on the balance of domestic sociopolitical forces.[29]

These conclusions speak to the broader debate regarding the presumed merits of "hard law" human rights provisions in international agreements.[30] Chapter 1, in contrasting alternative international arenas for promoting worker rights, argued that trade agreement-linked labor provisions such as those examined in this book theoretically constitute the most efficacious way of defending labor rights because they directly address the issue of collective-action rights, focus government-to-government interactions on these issues, and establish binding penalties for proven rights violations. Yet, in-depth analysis of the actual implementation of the labor provisions in U.S. trade agreements has shown that, contrary to the assumption that is sometimes made in this regard, simply agreeing to legally binding, penalty-backed enforcement mechanisms is often insufficient to alter signatory countries' labor practices. In evaluating international arrangements of this kind, it is, at minimum, necessary to distinguish between the effectiveness of "hard law" provisions in addressing violations of individual worker rights (including child and forced labor, which is widely condemned) and collective-action rights, where enforcement efforts are much more likely to encounter sovereign resistance. Moreover, because so many different factors—contextual political circumstances, the calculations and responses of key socio-political actors, variations in the content of different trade agreements' sanctions provisions—interact in determining the outcome of enforcement efforts, careful process-tracing analysis of selected cases is essential to formulating empirically based conclusions regarding the efficacy of "hard" rights protections embedded in international agreements.[31]

The question then becomes whether the design of free-trade agreements' labor provisions might be altered so as to improve their overall efficacy.[32] The U.S. GSP cases examined in chapter 2 indicate that the prospects of a developing country improving its labor rights practices rise when the retention of its trade benefits is at stake. It is highly unlikely, however, that any developing country government negotiating an FTA with the United States would ever agree to U.S. GSP-style conditions that would allow the U.S. government to suspend or ter-minate unilaterally the country's participation in the agreement because of labor rights violations. A penalty structure of that nature would violate the principle of equality among sovereign states. A "sunset clause" such as that included in the USMCA might periodically bolster U.S. leverage vis-à-vis a signatory country over its labor rights record.[33] Yet even then, it is difficult to envision the circum-stances under which the U.S. government would set aside multiple foreign policy interests and abrogate a major free-trade agreement in response to persistent labor rights violations in a partner country—and, under the terms of existing FTAs, the United States cannot force a partner country to withdraw from the agreement on those grounds.

One innovative way forward would be to modify the focus of labor rights enforcement arrangements to engage both national governments and private companies, thereby expanding the scope of potential U.S. sovereignty lever-age based on control over market access. The USMCA's facility-specific rapid response labor mechanism (RRLM) was ground-breaking in this regard. In parallel to U.S. GSP sanctions provisions, the U.S. government could suspend or exclude imports from individual Mexico-based companies implicated in collective-action labor rights violations.[34] The U.S. congressional authors of this provi-sion explicitly sought to shift the focus of enforcement efforts from exclusive attention to "a pattern of action or inaction" by a national government and cre-ate a means of immediately addressing specific workplace rights violations.[35]

Making private companies directly responsible for rights abuses taking place in their production facilities responded to a long-standing demand by the U.S. labor movement. In fact, U.S. labor organizations had called for company-level sanctions during the NAALC negotiations.[36] The most important precedent was the 1999 U.S.-Cambodia Bilateral Textile Trade Agreement, which offered garment companies operating in Cambodia progressively greater access to the U.S. market if close, regular ILO monitoring of factories confirmed improvements in workplace conditions over time. Only those companies that participated in the monitoring program received government permits that gave them access to Cambodia's enhanced textile export quotas.[37]

Although the USMCA's RRLM set a benchmark against which to assess other U.S. FTAs' enforcement mechanisms, there was no certainty that it would serve as a template for other agreements because the contents of U.S. FTA labor provisions have often varied as a result of the different state-to-state negotiations that produce them. Nonetheless, one advantage of shifting the terms of enforcement away from an exclusive focus on national government conduct and toward the actions of private companies is that arrangements like the RRLM may somewhat dilute the weight of broad foreign policy considerations in U.S. government decisions regarding whether, and how hard, to pressure a trade partner over labor rights issues.[38] Close attention to the labor relations practices of transnational companies might also increase the likelihood of overlap between two distinct rights-promotion arenas, corporate social responsibility campaigns and grievance petitions filed under the USMCA. Of course, the lessons that could be drawn from the RRLM experiment depended on how the mechanism performed in practice over time. It did, however, receive positive reviews in its debut in the General Motors-Silao case.

THE GENERAL MOTORS-SILAO TEST CASE

The first test of the USMCA's facility-specific rapid response labor mechanism (annex 31-B) and a transnational corporation's sensitivity to potential USMCA trade penalties came at General Motors Corporation's vehicle manufacturing plant in Silao, Guanajuato, in 2021. General Motors (GM) opened the plant in 1995 as part of a general shift by transnational automobile companies toward opening new, "greenfield" manufacturing facilities in central and northern

Mexico, away from older, mostly democratically unionized automobile plants in and around Mexico City.[39] Two different unions affiliated with the nationally dominant Confederation of Mexican Workers (Confederación de Trabajadores de México, CTM) legally represented the GM-Silao workforce between 1995 and 2022, the second of which was the "Miguel Trujillo López" National Union of Metalworking, Steel-Metallurgical, Automobile and General Autoparts Suppliers, Energy, and Related Industry Workers (Sindicato Nacional de Trabajadores de la Industria Metal-Mecánica, Sidero-Metalúrgica, Automotriz y Proveedores de Autopartes en General, de la Energía, sus Derivados y Similares de la República Mexicana "Miguel Trujillo López").[40] This union, whose secretary-general Tereso Medina Ramírez had as a federal senator cosponsored the 2017–2018 legislative initiative that threatened to undercut the democratizing effects of Mexico's 2017 constitutional labor reforms,[41] signed a collective contract with General Motors that granted the company unrestricted flexibility to hire temporary workers to meet fluctuations in market demand, allocate workers to different production tasks as needed, and redistribute work shifts in order to meet production requirements.[42] The incumbent union's persistent failure to address rank-and-file workplace concerns, or to ever hold a union general assembly meeting,[43] gave rise to an internal opposition movement, Generating Movement (Generando Movimiento), in April 2019.[44]

On April 20–21, 2021, the "Miguel Trujillo López" union organized a membership vote to legitimate the existing collective contract, as it was required to do under the terms of Mexico's 2019 Federal Labor Law (and USMCA annex 23-A). However, the Ministry of Labor and Social Welfare (Secretaría del Trabajo y Previsión Social, STPS) immediately suspended the process when labor inspectors discovered destroyed ballot papers at the incumbent union's headquarters and observed other serious irregularities, and on May 11, the STPS formally canceled the first legitimation vote and determined that a second vote would be required.[45] The U.S. Interagency Labor Committee for Monitoring and Enforcement, acting on its own initiative, then triggered the USMCA rapid response labor mechanism and, on May 12, 2021, the USTR requested that the Mexican government investigate further to determine whether there had been a "denial of rights" at GM-Silao plant.[46] On June 21, 2021, the STPS ordered the incumbent union to hold a second contract legitimation vote before August 20, 2021, and on July 7, the Mexican and U.S. governments jointly announced a five-page, single-spaced remediation plan that stipulated in detail the terms under which the vote would be held.[47]

There were reports that in April, some local GM managers pressured Silao workers to vote in favor of the existing contract and even barred STPS-accredited observers from entering the facility.[48] From the outset, therefore, General Motors corporate management came under intense pressure to ensure that the company would maintain strict neutrality during the second contract legitimation process. On May 11, 2021, three members of the U.S. House of Representatives Committee on Ways and Means wrote to Mary Barra, GM's chief executive officer, to list their objections to the way in which the April 2011 vote had been conducted. For instance, in violation of Mexican law, plant managers had not made the collective contract widely available to workers for their inspection prior to the vote.[49] The legislators demanded written company responses to detailed questions concerning possible management complicity in the flawed voting process, and they insisted that General Motors remain neutral.

> We understand that the Mexican government has a significant role to play in upholding workers' legal right to unionize, but companies like yours do as well. As one of America's most iconic companies, GM should be an active participant in respecting labor rights.[50]

In response, a General Motors spokesperson declared that "GM condemns violations of labor rights and actions to restrict collective bargaining," and the Mexican manager of the Silao plant pledged that the second vote would be "impeccable."[51]

Underpinning these General Motors responses was a USMCA provision that, in effect, extended U.S. market-access sovereignty leverage to private companies and structured GM management's incentives to resolve the conflict as quickly as possible.[52] Under USMCA article 31-A.4.3, upon delivery of a denial-of-rights enquiry to the respondent government, the complainant government could delay final settlement of customs accounts related to entries of goods from the production facility involved until the parties reached agreement that there was no denial of rights or until an international arbitral panel reached that conclusion.[53] In 2021, the U.S. tariff rate on the full-size, light-duty pickup trucks produced at the GM-Silao manufacturing facility (the Chevrolet Silverado and the GMC Sierra) was 25 percent, and the plant was producing approximately one thousand of these vehicles each day. At the time, the average U.S. retail price of those trucks was approximately US$40,000 each, yielding anticipated daily GM revenues of about US$40 million. Facing a potential tariff of 25 percent, General Motors was therefore required to place in escrow approximately US$10 million per day from the date on which the U.S. government requested that Mexican authorities review whether a denial of rights had occurred (May 12, 2021) until the case was resolved (September 22, 2021). Thus, over a period of 132 days, General Motors placed in escrow approximately US$1.32 billion.

The available evidence indicates that GM management did, in fact, remain impartial in both the second contract legitimation vote and in a later election to determine the trade union recognized as legal bargaining representative of the GM-Silao workforce.[54] With intense international attention focused on the Silao case and with so much potentially at stake financially in terms of the plant's exports to the United States, the company had no real alternative course of action. In addition to posting in the workplace public notices of corporate neutrality and pledging not to retaliate against workers who voted against the existing contract and the incumbent CTM union, the company allowed workers to take time off during their regular work shifts, at full pay, to cast their ballots. Moreover, company managers cooperated fully with intensive onsite monitoring by the STPS, which dispatched a progressively larger number of inspectors to the plant as the dates of the scheduled votes drew closer.[55] In both votes, the five onsite polling places were located in areas distant from GM's administrative offices (and the "Miguel Trujillo López" union's headquarters) in order to underscore the company's neutrality.

In the second legitimation vote held on August 17–18, 2021, GM-Silao workers rejected the existing collective contract by a total of 3,214 to 2,623 votes, with thirty-nine null ballots.[56] Under Mexican law, the contract terms remained in effect while a second vote was scheduled to determine whether the incumbent "Miguel Trujillo López" union or another labor organization would be recognized as the legal bargaining representative of the labor force. That election was finally held on February 1–2, 2022. A politically independent union with roots in Generating Movement, the National Independent Union of Automotive and Related Industry Workers (Sindicato Independiente Nacional de Trabajadores y Trabajadoras de la Industria Automotriz y las Adhesivas, SINTTIA, formed in August 2021), handily won the election with 4,182 (77.6 percent) of the 5,389 valid votes cast. In doing so, it defeated two different CTM affiliates (the incumbent "Miguel Trujillo López" union did not contest the election[57]) and a third rival union linked to the old-guard Revolutionary Confederation of Workers and Peasants (Confederación Revolucionaria de Obreros y Campesinos, CROC).[58]

These outcomes promised to redefine workplace relations at GM-Silao, and they drew applause from pro-union democracy labor organizations and labor rights advocates in all three USMCA countries.[59] The results were also cited by U.S. officials as evidence that USMCA enforcement mechanisms were effective in practice.[60] However, the GM-Silao outcome was not representative of initial contract validation processes nationwide,[61] and there was some reason to doubt whether the closely monitored conditions surrounding the contract legitimation and workplace representation votes at GM-Silao could be reproduced consistently throughout Mexico. On both occasions, the STPS and the National Electoral Institute (Instituto Nacional Electoral, INE) invested considerable human and financial resources in ensuring that GM-Silao employees were fully informed of the voting options available to them and the legal and practical consequences of the choices they made. Approximately sixty domestic and international observers from the INE, the National Commission on Human Rights (Comisión Nacional de Derechos Humanos), the ILO's Mexico and Cuba office, and trade unions and labor-rights advocacy organizations from the United States, Mexico, Canada, Brazil, and Colombia witnessed the February 2022 election.[62]

Yet, even if the GM-Silao circumstances were exceptional, a key legacy of the SNTTIA's resounding electoral victory in February 2022 was the message it sent to transnational corporations with major manufacturing facilities in Mexico: Under the terms of Mexico's 2019 Federal Labor Law and the USMCA, the rules governing employer-worker relations had changed. The overall pattern established by the seven (including GM-Silao) rapid response submissions that Mexican and U.S. trade unions and labor- and human-rights NGOs filed with the U.S. Department of Labor's Office of Trade and Labor Affairs (OTLA) during 2021 and 2022 strongly reinforced this message. (Appendix D summarizes RRLM submission procedures and the facility-specific rapid response labor mechanism petitions filed with the OTLA during this period.) As required by RRLM procedures, all the petitions alleged violations of collective-action rights. All seven of the 2020–2021 submissions involved automobile manufacturing companies or automotive parts producers. Six of the labor conflicts addressed by the petitions (85.7 percent, $N = 7$) ended with democratically organized local unions displacing incumbent, company-aligned labor unions (all but one of which was affiliated with the CTM) winning workforce representation rights at the production facilities in question.[63] Most important, because of the political will demonstrated by both U.S. and Mexican trade and labor officials, during the 2021–2022 period, the RRLM submission process proved capable of promptly resolving individual workplace conflicts over collective-action rights in important Mexican manufacturing facilities, sometimes with direct remedial benefits for employees who had been fired for attempting to organize a democratic union responsive to workers' interests.[64]

In summary, the General Motors-Silao case was selected for detailed examination because it points to an important new area of research: the relative merits of company-focused sanctions mechanisms as a way of protecting workers' rights through trade agreement–linked labor provisions. More broadly, however, this case manifests well one of the main arguments developed in this book: Although the U.S. government can sometimes employ its sovereignty leverage successfully to promote significant labor reforms in a trade-partner country, effective implementation of reform measures over the longer term requires a national government committed to the workplace enforcement of protected labor rights. The USTR, under pressure from U.S. labor organizations to employ the USMCA's labor provisions to combat so-called employer protection contracts and promote union democracy in Mexico, quickly activated the RRLM in the GM-Silao case. However, it was Mexican labor authorities—certainly sensitive to U.S. scrutiny but operating under the requirements established by the May 2019 Federal Labor Law—who identified and condemned faults in the April 2021 contract legitimation vote. Similarly, although international observers had a prominent presence during both the August 2021 recount and the February 2022 workplace representation vote, it was the STPS and a phalanx of Mexican observers that had principal responsibility for ensuring open and free workplace elections. The elections themselves were highly contested because a democratically organized union, the SNTTIA, had demonstrated its credibility and won the support of GM-Silao employees. The most important lesson of the GM-Silao case was, then, that although international actors can undoubtedly make important contributions to advancing labor rights, in the final analysis, the successful defense of workers' rights is a matter of national commitment.

Acknowledgments

Abook of this length and complexity could not have been completed without the extensive cooperation and support of many people. J. Fernando Franco González Salas has, over several decades, warmly welcomed me into his home, shared with me his unrivaled knowledge of Mexican labor law and politics, and, not least, helped arrange interviews with a broad range of senior Mexican government officials and public figures—access to whom was vital to my research. Graciela Bensusán, a valued friend and colleague and frequent collaborator, has for many years shared with me research materials and her in-depth expertise on Mexican labor law. Jonathan Fox, a close friend and engaged colleague whose judgments I trust, helped me clarify my thinking on a number of the issues addressed in this book.

I am particularly grateful to a number of academic and professional colleagues who took the time to read and comment extensively on the full manuscript while it was in preparation: Lance Compa, Ben Davis, Paulo Drinot, Jonathan Fox, Sandra Polaski, and three anonymous reviewers for Columbia University Press. Other colleagues commented perceptively on one or more chapters: Graciela Bensusán, Néstor Castañeda, Par Engström, Fernando Franco, Héctor González Graf, Nadia Hilliard, Bob Jeffcott, Susan L. Kang, Lewis Karesh, Tom Long, Layna Mosley, Jorge Pérez-López, and Carol Pier. It is difficult to express just how important it was to have constructive feedback on a work in progress.

This book would not have been possible without the cooperation and good will of many labor rights advocates, trade unionists, contemporary and former government officials, and other public figures whom I interviewed in Mexico, the United States, and Canada. They were patient and generous with their time in responding to endless questions posed by an insatiably curious university researcher. I will always be especially grateful for the insights offered by trade unionists and knowledgeable practitioners in the Mexican, U.S., and Canadian labor rights communities.

Special thanks go to Sam Kelly for truly outstanding research assistance, particularly with regard to the topics examined in chapters 1, 2, and 5, and to Kazuma Mizukoshi for the expert statistical analysis presented in chapters 2 and 4. I am also grateful for valuable research support at different times from Remy Roberts, Druscilla Scribner, Caterina Perrone, Ary Moshe Boltansky, William Hopcroft, Franco Diaz, Daniel Park, and Janet Stiles, the talented and resourceful senior librarian at the Woodrow Wilson International Center for Scholars. Archivists at the Office of the United States Trade Representative, the U.S. Department of the Treasury, the William J. Clinton Presidential Library all responded efficiently to document requests I filed through the Freedom of Information Act.

The Nuffield Foundation and the Institute of the Americas, University College London, provided financial support for portions of my field research in Canada, Mexico, and the United States. During 2018 and 2019, I greatly benefited from residential fellowships at, respectively, the Woodrow Wilson International Center for Scholars and the Center for U.S.-Mexican Studies, University of California-San Diego.

With all this help, any omissions or errors are certainly my own responsibility.

I acknowledge permission from El Colegio de México to draw on material previously published in Graciela Bensusán and Kevin J. Middlebrook, "Cambio político desde afuera hacia adentro: Influencia comercial estadounidense y reforma de los derechos laborales en México," *Foro Internacional* LX (3), no. 241 (July–September 2020): 985–1039.

Unless otherwise noted, all translations of material originally written in Spanish are by the author. Similarly, unless otherwise noted, all monetary amounts reported in the text are at their contemporaneous (not inflation-adjusted) value.

This book is dedicated to the memory of my parents, Harlan and Wilda Middlebrook, and my paternal grandparents, Roy and Della Middlebrook, whose lifetimes of hard work on the family farm created the space for me to do my schoolwork; to Helga, *compañera* and colleague, and to Mariel, a third-generation teacher, in lasting gratitude for their love and unquestioning support over many years; and to those people everywhere who struggle for union democracy and workplace rights.

APPENDIX A

Statistical Analysis of U.S. Generalized System
of Preferences Cases, 1985–1995

This appendix reports the results of Bayesian logit and ordered-logit regression analyses of the observed outcomes of the U.S. Generalized System of Preferences (GSP) labor rights petitions examined in chapter 2. Bayesian techniques were employed to overcome the problem of separation encountered in attempting estimations with frequentist logit and ordered-logic regressions. The Bayesian approach assumes a weakly informative prior distribution of values even when working with a limited number of observations, which makes it particularly appropriate for this study. The principal difference between the Bayesian theorem and frequentist statistics is its approach to probability; it investigates whether the probability of an event (for instance, the outcome observed in collective-action labor rights) can be accurately predicted by a particular independent variable (for example, the strength of domestic political support in the target country) compared to the probability of an event without the presence of a particular predictor variable. The Bayesian theorem thus relaxes frequentist assumptions about the probabilistic distribution of values in the dataset under examination.

Because the number of cases for examination is small ($N = 14$; Colombia is omitted from this analysis because the Office of the United States Trade Representative did not accept for review any of the GSP petitions alleging labor-rights violations in the country), the observed outcomes reported in the final column of table 2.1 were grouped in three different ways in order to maximize variation on the dependent variable: dataset A (0 = observed outcome 0; 1 = observed outcomes 1, 2, or 3), dataset B (0 = outcome 0; 1 = outcomes 1 or 2; 2 = outcome 3), and dataset C, in which outcomes ranged from 0 to 3. The analysis then tested the impact of a range of independent variables: the aggregate number of petitions filed against a country, the extent of domestic political support in the target country ("political support"), the two measures of the target country's export sensitivity reported in table 2.1, column 6 ("GSP" and "GSP +"), whether the country experienced democratic regime change ("regime change"), the target country's economic size and level of socioeconomic development at the time GSP petitions were filed against it, and dummy variables indicating whether the country is (or is not) located in the Caribbean Basin or in the larger Latin American region.

Preliminary analysis found that there was no statistically significant relationship between many of these variables and observed outcomes. Similarly, the analysis identified no statistically significant impact of interaction effects among different independent variables. Results for three models featuring potential explanatory variables of particular interest, tested in each of the three datasets described above, are reported in table A.1 on the next page. These models are:

Model 1: *Outcome = f(political support, GSP + exports)*
Model 2: *Outcome = f(political support, Regime change)*
Model 3: *Outcome = f(political support, GSP + exports, regime change)*

Variable	Mean	Standard deviation	Minimum value	Maximum value
Political support	0.714	0.914	0	2
GSP + exports	0.122	0.195	0.007	0.756
Regime change	0.286	0.469	0	1

The reported coefficients represent the mean of the distribution of the "observed outcome" variable after adding each explanatory variable. These results indicate that there is consistently a statistically significant relationship between "political support" and "observed outcomes," regardless of how the dependent variable is ordered in the three datasets. The DIC values indicate that the three models employed best fit the distribution of data in dataset A.

Figure A.1 visually depicts the regression estimates reported in table A.1. The dot at the center of each vertical bar represents the estimated mean coefficient of each independent variable, while the thin lines show the posterior

TABLE A.1 Analysis of observed outcomes of U.S. Generalized System of Preferences labor rights petitions, 1985–1995

	Model 1			Model 2			Model 3		
	Dataset A	Dataset B	Dataset C	Dataset A	Dataset B	Dataset C	Dataset A	Dataset B	Dataset C
Intercept	-0.75			-1.00			-0.88		
	(0.76)			(0.82)			(0.84)		
Political support	2.30*	2.39*	2.41**	2.37*	2.36*	2.36**	2.54*	2.37*	2.37**
	(1.13)	(1.04)	(0.88)	(1.18)	(1.05)	(0.89)	(1.25)	(1.05)	(0.89)
GSP + exports	-0.61	-0.29	-0.38				-2.35	-0.40	-0.65
	(1.88)	(1.57)	(1.60)				(3.17)	(1.59)	(1.66)
Regime change				0.70	0.49	1.02	1.20	0.53	1.11
				(1.27)	(1.03)	(1.11)	(1.47)	(1.05)	(1.15)
AIC	15.94	33.12	42.26	15.62	32.93	41.42	16.45	37.16	45.55
BIC	17.86	35.68	45.46	17.54	35.49	44.62	19.01	40.35	49.38
DIC	9.94	25.12	32.26	9.62	24.93	31.42	8.45	24.93	33.55
Chi-square	9.47**	7.68**	9.37**	8.80*	7.23**	8.69**	9.54**	7.25**	8.76**
Number of observations	14	14	14	14	14	14	14	14	14

**p < 0.01; *p < 0.05.

Notes: The table reports estimated coefficients (median point estimates) for each independent variable in models 1, 2, and 3; standard deviations from the means of coefficients appear in parentheses below each estimate. The *p*-value of regression estimates was calculated from Z tests in which an alternative hypothesis is that the mean of the posterior distribution given parameters is different from zero (no effect). The Akaike information criterion (AIC) is an estimator of the relative quality of a statistical model for a given dataset. The Bayesian information criterion (BIC) is a criterion for model selection among a finite set of models; the model with the lowest value is preferred. The deviance information criterion (DIC) is a hierarchical modeling generalization of the AIC and BIC.

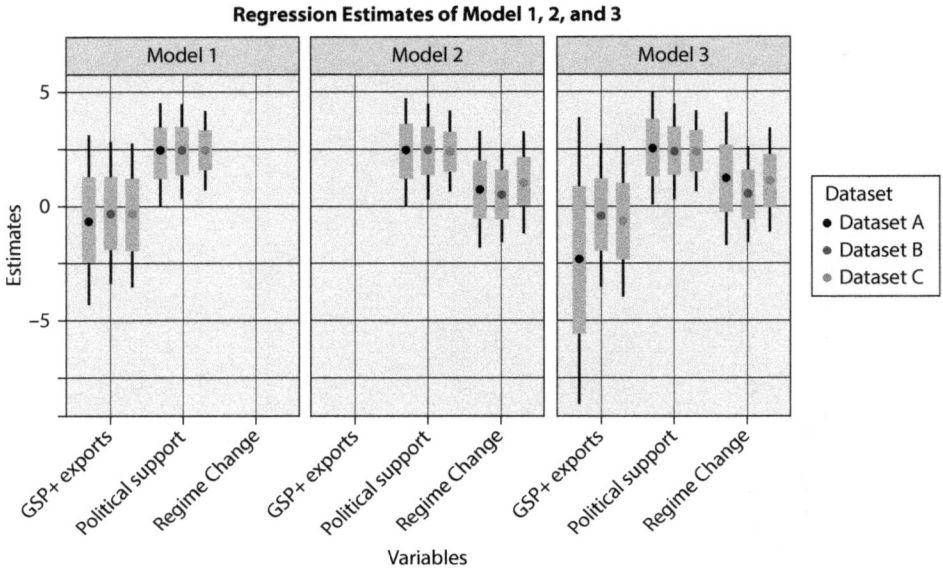

A.1 Visual representation of Bayesian regression estimates of models 1, 2, and 3

densities of each explanatory variable within a 95 percent confidence interval. Only the "political support" variable is statistically significant in all models (that is, both the dots and the vertical space defined by the thin lines are above 0) across all datasets.

Annotated List of NAALC Public Communications Submitted to the Canadian, Mexican, and U.S. National Administrative Offices (NAOs), 1994–2020

T his appendix summarizes the main issues raised in public communications submitted under the North American Agreement on Labor Cooperation (NAALC). It is based on a review of both the communications themselves and any public report(s) issued following NAO review of the submissions. The principal sources were: for Canada, Employment and Social Development Canada (Labour Affairs) and U.S. Department of Labor (Bureau of International Labor Affairs); for Mexico, Ministry of Labor and Social Welfare (STPS, Unidad de Asuntos Internacionales) and U.S. Department of Labor (Bureau of International Labor Affairs); and for the United States, U.S. Department of Labor (Bureau of International Labor Affairs, https://www .dol.gov/agencies/ilab/submissions-under-north-american-agreement-labor-cooperation-naalc). The other sources employed were: Compa and Brooks 2019: 112–17, 120–22, 126–29, 133–36, 138, 140, 142–43; González Graf 2009: 149, 152–53; Brower 2008: 174; Human Rights Watch/Americas 2001: 27–28, 31.

In those cases in which there were discrepancies between a communication and the NAO public report(s) regarding the NAALC articles and principles the submission addressed, the articles and principles listed here were drawn from the NAO public report(s). In MEX 9804, US 9802, and US 2018-01, the author identified the NAALC principles based on information included in the public communication.

The total number of labor unions endorsing a communication does not include individual union locals or sections listed in the submission documents if the corresponding national union endorsed the communication. However, in those cases in which Canadian and U.S. national divisions of the same union endorsed a communication, both divisions were counted as separate submitters.

Principal acronyms: AFL-CIO (American Federation of Labor-Congress of Industrial Organizations), ANAD (National Association of Democratic Lawyers), CAW (Canadian Auto Workers), CJM (Coalition for Justice in the Maquiladoras), CLC (Canadian Labour Congress), CROC (Revolutionary Confederation of Workers and Peasants), CTM (Confederation of Mexican Workers), CWA (Communications Workers of America), FAT (Authentic Labor Front), FESEBS (Federation of Unions of Goods and Services Enterprises), FTQ (Quebéc Workers' Federation), IAMAW (International Association of Machinists and Aerospace Workers), IBT (International Brotherhood of Teamsters), ILRERF/ILRF (International Labor Rights Education and Research Fund / International Labor Rights Forum), JFCA (Federal Conciliation and Arbitration Board), LyFC (Central Light and Power Company), MSN (Maquila Solidarity Network), OCAW (Oil, Chemical, and Atomic Workers), PACE (Paper, Allied-Industrial, Chemical, and Energy Workers), SEIU (Service Employees International Union), SME (Mexican Electricians' Union), SNTMMSRM (Mexican Mining and Metalworkers Union), STIMAHCS (Union of Workers in the Metal, Iron, Steel, and Related and Similar Industries), STRM (Mexican Telephone Workers' Union), UAW (United Automobile, Aerospace, and Agricultural Implement Workers Union of America), UE (United Electrical, Radio, and Machine Workers of America), UFCW (United Food and Commercial Workers), UNITE! (Union of Needletrade, Industrial, and Textile Workers)/UNITE HERE!, UNT (National Union of Workers), UPIU (United Paperworkers International Union), USLEAP (U.S. Labor Education in the Americas Program), USW (United Steelworkers), WOLA (Washington Office on Latin America). For other acronyms and organizations' full names in English and Spanish, see the list of acronyms.

CANADIAN NAO

98-1 (Echlin/Itapsa): In parallel with their submission to the U.S. NAO (US 9703), the CAW, IBT, UNITE!, UE, UPIU, USW (Canadian and U.S. divisions), IAMAW, AFL-CIO, CLC, FAT, UNT, seventeen additional Mexican unions, and fourteen nongovernmental organizations (NGOs) (Canadian, seven; Mexican, two; U.S., five) filed a public communication targeting Echlin, Inc. (a Connecticut-based manufacturer of automobile replacement parts), its Mexican subsidiaries Itapsa and American Brakeblock, Mexico's Federal Conciliation and Arbitration Board (JFLA), and the CTM and its local affiliates representing Itapsa and American Brakeblock employees. They charged that workers at Itapsa, S. A. de C. V., Echlin's brake-system manufacturing plant in Ciudad de los Reyes, state of México, were subject to serious occupational safety and health risks, including exposure to asbestos and other toxic substances without adequate personal protective equipment. Moreover, they alleged that plant managers and the incumbent CTM union had seriously obstructed STIMAHCS in an election contest to determine which of the two unions would hold collective bargaining rights at the facility. Workers involved in the STIMAHCS campaign were fired. NAALC articles 2–5; principles 1, 9.

98-2 (Yale / Immigration and Naturalization Service): In parallel with their submission to the Mexican NAO (MEX 9804), the Yale Law School Workers' Rights Project, ILRF, fifteen additional U.S. human- and immigrant-rights NGOs, SEIU, and UNITE! filed a public communication challenging a U.S. Department of Labor and U.S. Immigration and Naturalization Service joint enforcement memorandum (June 11, 1992) that deterred undocumented migrant workers from filing wage and working hours (overtime) complaints because doing so exposed them to the risk of deportation. NAALC articles 2–4, 7; principles 6, 11.

99-1 (Labor Policy Association / EFCO Corporation): The Labor Policy Association, a U.S. lobbying group representing human resource officers in the private sector, and the EFCO Corporation, an Iowa-based manufacturer of commercial architecture products (doors, windows, and so forth), filed a communication in which they charged that the U.S. National Labor Relations Board's enforcement of a legal prohibition against employer domination of labor organizations unreasonably prevented EFCO, an ununionized company, from adopting effective labor-management cooperation policies, including employee involvement programs addressing safety and health issues. NAALC principle 9.

2003-1 (Puebla garment producers): In parallel with their submission to the U.S. NAO (US 2003-1), United Students Against Sweatshops and the Center for Worker Support (Centro de Apoyo al Trabajador), joined later by MSN, filed a complaint against Matamoros Garment and Tarrant México, two garment producers in the State of Puebla that supplied Puma and other international brand-name clothing companies. They charged that workers at the facilities faced occupational safety and health risks and that plant managers and the state's labor conciliation and arbitration board blocked workers' attempts to form independent unions that would be more responsive to their interests than the incumbent CROC and CTM affiliates. NAALC articles 2–5, 7; principles 1, 6, 9.

2005-1 (Aviacsa pilots): In parallel with its submission to the U.S. NAO (US 2005-02), the Mexican Airline Pilots' Association (ASPAM) filed a public communication stemming from a five-year conflict with Aviacsa Airlines (Consorcio Aviacsa, S.A. de C. V.), a passenger and cargo airline, over the organization of a craft union. NAALC articles 1–5; principles 1, 2.

2008-1 (North Carolina public employees): In parallel with their submission to the Mexican NAO (MEX 2006-1), the FAT, UE, CLC, UNT, fifty-two other unions (Canadian, nine; Mexican, thirty-five; U.S., eight), and two NGOs (one each from Canada and the United States) filed a public communication protesting the absence of U.S. federal legal protection for the collective-action rights of state and municipal workers, focusing on North Carolina's prohibition (Statute 95-98) against public sector workers entering into collective bargaining agreements. NAALC articles 3–7; principles 1, 2, 6–10.

2011-1 (SME): In parallel with their submission to the U.S. NAO (US 2011-01), the Mexican Electricians' Union (SME), joined by fifty-six other North American unions (Canadian, thirteen; Mexican, thirty-two; U.S., eleven), twenty-three NGOs (Canadian, three; Mexican, six; U.S., fourteen), and six international labor organizations, filed a public communication condemning the Mexican government's abrupt decision in October 2009 to close the state-subsidized and heavily indebted Central Light and Power Company (LyFC). The action led to the immediate dismissal of some forty-four thousand unionized workers and the de facto elimination of the SME, one of Mexico's oldest democratic unions. NAALC articles 1–6; principles 1–3, 9.

MEXICAN NAO

9501 (Sprint Corporation): The Mexican Telephone Workers' Union (STRM) filed a complaint against Sprint Corporation for blocking a CWA organizing campaign among Latino workers at La Conexión Familiar, a San Francisco-based telemarketing facility, and closing the facility just before to a scheduled CWA union representation election. NAALC principle 1.

9801 (Solec International): The OCAW International Union, Support Committee for Maquiladora Workers, "6 of October" Union of Industry and Commerce (the Tijuana, Mexico-based union that had organized Han Young workers; see US 9702), and a Tijuana-based labor rights NGO filed a public communication alleging that Solec International, Inc., a Japanese-owned and California-based manufacturer of solar panels, systematically obstructed an OCAW organizing campaign and had committed occupational safety and health and working conditions violations. NAALC articles 1, 3–5; principles 1, 6, 7, 9, 10.

9802 (Washington State apple growers and packers): The UNT, FAT, STIMAHCS, and the Chihuahua, Mexico-based Peasant Democratic Front (Frente Democrático Campesino) filed a communication charging that Washington State apple growers and warehouse operators had engaged in antiunion campaigns, antimigrant worker discrimination, and occupational safety and health violations. They also criticized the U.S. federal government for failing to adequately protect unionization and collective bargaining by migrant agricultural workers. NAALC articles 2–5, 7; principles 1, 2, 6, 7, 9–11.

9803 (DeCoster Egg Farm): The CTM and the Government of Mexico (as cosubmitter) filed a class-action complaint against a large Maine egg producer (at the time, supposedly the largest egg producer in the United States) for violations of migrant workers' labor rights and minimum employment standards, employment discrimination, and occupational safety and health violations. NAALC articles 3–5, 7; principles 6, 7, 9–11.

9804 (Yale / Immigration and Naturalization Service): Yale Law School Workers' Rights Project, ILRF, fifteen other U.S. human- and immigrant-rights NGOs, SEIU, and UNITE! filed a public communication challenging a U.S. Department of Labor and U.S. Immigration and

Naturalization Service joint enforcement memorandum (June 11, 1992) that discouraged undocumented migrant workers from filing wage and working hours (overtime) complaints because doing so exposed them to the risk of deportation. NAALC articles 2–4, 7; principles 6, 11.

2001-1 (New York State workers' compensation): The Chinese Staff and Workers' Association, National Mobilization Against Sweat Shops, Workers' Awaaz, Tepoyac Association (Asociación Tepoyac), and thirteen individual immigrant workers submitted a public communication charging that the U.S. federal government and the State of New York failed to enforce effectively laws governing compensation to workers who suffered occupational injuries. NAALC articles 3–7; principles 9–11.

2003-1 (H-2A visa migrant workers in North Carolina): The Independent Central of Agricultural Workers and Peasants (CIOAC) and the Farmworker Justice Fund (Washington, DC) filed a communication alleging that the U.S. federal and North Carolina state governments failed to enforce labor laws concerning the recruitment, hiring, transportation, and employment of, and housing and working conditions for, H-2A visa migrant agricultural workers recruited by the North Carolina Growers Association. NAALC articles 2–5; principles 1, 2, 4. 6, 7, 9–11.

2005-1 (H-2B visa migrant workers in various states): The Northwest Workers' Justice Project, Brennan Center for Justice (New York University), Andrade Law Office (Boise, Idaho), FAT, Mexican Action Network Against Free Trade (RMALC), UNT, seven other migrant- and human-rights NGOs (Mexican, three; U.S., four), and sixteen individual H-2B visa (temporary nonagricultural work) migrant workers filed a public communication in which they alleged that forestry and food-processing companies in Idaho, Colorado, and six other U.S. states widely violated minimum employment standards, the prohibition against forced labor, and occupational safety and health injury compensation requirements. NAALC articles 4, 5; principles 4, 6, 9–11.

2006-1 (North Carolina public employees): The FAT, UE, CLC, UNT, fifty-two other unions (Canadian, nine; Mexican, thirty-five; U.S., eight), and two NGOs (one each from Canada and the United States) submitted a communication protesting the absence of U.S. federal legal protection for the collective bargaining rights of state and municipal workers, focusing on North Carolina's prohibition (statute 95–98) against public sector workers entering into collective bargaining agreements. NAALC articles 3–7; principles 1, 2, 6–10.

2011-1 (H-2B visa migrant carnival and fair workers): The binational Center for Migrant Rights (Centro de los Derechos del Migrante), twelve other migrant-rights NGOs (Mexican, five; U.S., seven), the AFL-CIO, and three individual Mexican migrant workers filed a public communication arguing that the United States failed to enforce laws ensuring minimum employment standards for H-2B migrant workers or provide them with the same legal protections as its nationals. The submission focused specifically on migrant workers employed in traveling carnivals and fairs. NAALC articles 2–4; principles 6, 11.

2012-1 (Alabama anti-immigrant law): The SEIU and ANAD filed a communication challenging a 2011 Alabama state law (H. B. 56) that barred undocumented immigrant workers from all legal employment, thereby creating a coercive climate in which workers could not organize, bargain collectively, or pursue occupational safety and health claims. NAALC principles 1, 2, 6, 7, 9–11.

2015-1 (U.S. Department of Labor): A former U.S. Department of Labor employee confidentially filed a public communication alleging widespread discrimination against minority employees in hiring and promotion practices. NAALC articles 1–4, 7; principle 7.

2016-1 (gender discrimination in the recruitment of female migrant workers for H-2A and H-2B visa programs): The binational Center for Migrant Rights (Centro de los Derechos del Migrante) and two individual Mexican women petitioners, joined by twenty-four other migrant-rights NGOs (El Salvadoran, one; Mexican, seven; U.S., sixteen) and three labor federations (U.S., two; Mexican, one), submitted a public communication alleging systematic discrimination against women in the recruitment, hiring, and employment of H-2A and H-2B visa migrant workers in the United States. NAALC articles 1, 3, 4; principles 7, 8.

2016-2 (gender discrimination in the recruitment of female migrant workers for the Seasonal Agricultural Workers Program, Canada): The UFCM-Canada, UNT, seven migrant-rights NGOs (El Salvadoran, one; Mexican, five; U.S., one), and six Mexican women petitioners filed a communication charging that the Government of Canada failed to enforce domestic laws, and thus violated NAALC provisions, barring discrimination on the basis of gender in the recruitment of Mexican workers through its Seasonal Agricultural Workers Program. NAALC articles 1–3, 7; principles 7, 8.

U.S. NAO

940001 (Honeywell, Inc.): The IBT filed a public communication targeting Honeywell, Inc., a Minneapolis-based manufacturer of electronic equipment. It charging that managers at Honeywell's Ciudad Chihuahua, Chihuahua, plant had fired workers who had engaged in a STIMAHCS-led unionization campaign and forced them to accept severance payments. NAALC principles 1, 2.

940002 (General Electric Company): Simultaneous with the IBT's 940001 submission, the UE submitted a communication alleging that managers at the General Electric Company's electric motor plant (Compañía Armadora, S.A.) in Ciudad Juárez, Chihuahua, had blocked a STIMAHCS-led unionization campaign, firing the workers involved and compelling them to accept severance payments. NAALC principles 1, 2.

940003 (Sony Corporation): The ILRERF, ANAD, CJM, and the American Friends Service Committee submitted a public communication charging that Sony Corporation's manufacturing plants in Nuevo Laredo, Tamaulipas (Magnéticos de México) violated minimum employment standards with regard to work schedules, and that plant managers blocked employees' attempts to form a new union that better represented their interests. NAALC articles 4, 5; principles 1, 2.

940004 (General Electric Company): The UE filed a second communication focused on the General Electric Company's electric motor plant in Ciudad Juárez, Chihuahua, citing the same issues raised in US 940002. It later withdrew the submission for unspecified reasons. NAALC principles 1, 2.

9601 (General Union of Workers at the Ministry of Fishing, SUTSP): In a public communication addressing the denial of official recognition to a union claiming to represent employees of the newly created Ministry of the Environment, Natural Resources, and Fisheries (Secretaría del Medio Ambiente, Recursos Naturales y Pesca, SEMARNAP), the ILRF, Human Rights Watch/Americas, and ANAD challenged the Mexican federal law prohibiting the recognition of more than one union representing public-sector workers at any particular government agency or department. The submitters also charged the Federal Conciliation and Arbitration Tribunal (Tribunal Federal de Conciliación y Arbitraje) with a conflict of interest in its handling of the case. NAALC articles 2, 3, 5; principle 1.

9602 (Maxi-Switch): The CWA, STRM, and FESEBS filed a complaint against the managers of Maxi-Switch, an electronic equipment manufacturer in Cananea, Sonora, owned by the Taiwan-based Silitek Corporation, for blocking the formation of a FESEBS-affiliated independent union and firing workers involved in the unionization campaign. They also charged the state's labor conciliation and arbitration board with a conflict of interest in its handling of the case. NAALC articles 3, 5; principle 1.

9701 (pregnancy testing): Human Rights Watch (Women's Rights Project and Americas divisions), ILRF, and ANAD filed a public communication in which they alleged widespread discrimination against women job applicants and women workers in Mexico's in-bond manufacturing (*maquiladora*) industry, where employers regularly required women to verify their pregnancy status as a condition of employment and denied employment to (or harassed or discharged) pregnant women. NAALC articles 3, 4, 7; principle 7.

9702 (Han Young de México): The Support Committee for Maquiladora Workers, ILRF, ANAD, and STIMAHCS, later joined by two U.S. NGOs and three industrial unions (Canadian, one; U.S., two) submitted a public communication concerning Han Young de México, S. A. de C. V., a truck welding and assembly facility in Tijuana, Baja California, that assembled truck chassis for a U.S. subsidiary of the Korean-owned Hyundai Corporation. They charged that there were extensive workplace safety and health problems at the plant, and that plant managers conspired with officials of the state's labor conciliation and arbitration board to block STIMAHCS attempts to organize an independent union at the facility. NAALC articles 3, 5; principles 1, 9.

9703 (Echlin/Itapsa): The CAW, IBT, UAW, UNITE!, UE, UPIU, USW
(Canadian and U.S. divisions), FAT, sixteen other unions (Mexican,
fifteen; U.S., one), and fourteen NGOs (Mexican, six; U.S., eight)
submitted a communication focused on Echlin, Inc. (a Connecticut-
based manufacturer of automobile replacement parts), its Mexican
subsidiaries Itapsa and American Brakeblock, and the CTM and
its local affiliate representing Echlin/Itapsa employees. They
charged that workers at Itapsa, S. A. de C. V., Echlin's brake system
manufacturing plant in Ciudad de los Reyes, State of México, were
subject to serious occupational safety and health risks, including
exposure to asbestos and other toxic substances without adequate
personal protective equipment. Moreover, they alleged that plant
managers and the incumbent CTM union had seriously obstructed
STIMAHCS in an election contest to determine which of the two
unions would hold collective bargaining rights at the facility. Workers
involved in the STIMAHCS campaign were fired. NAALC articles 1, 2,
3, 5; principles 1, 9.

9801 (Aeroméxico flight attendants): The AFL-CIO-affiliated Association of
Flight Attendants (AFA) submitted a public communication in which it
charged that the Government of Mexico violated Aeroméxico (Aerovías
de México) workers' right to strike when President Ernesto Zedillo Ponce
de León (1994–2000) issued an executive order barring a scheduled strike
by flight attendants. NAALC article 1; principle 3.

9802 (child labor in tomato production): The U.S. NAO opened this case
based on information the Florida Tomato Exchange (FTE) had provided
to the U.S. Department of Labor concerning the use of child labor in the
production of fruits and vegetables in Mexico. However, the FTE did not
pursue the case, and after a year the U.S. NAO closed the file. NAALC
principle 5.

9803 (St.-Hubert McDonald's): The IBT (Canadian and U.S. divisions),
FTQ, and ILRF filed a public communication protesting against the
antiunion actions taken by the franchisee of a McDonald's restaurant
in St.-Hubert, Québec. The U.S. NAO ended its review when the
complainants reached agreement with the Government of Québec that it
would examine the issue of antiunion-motivated plant closings. NAALC
articles 2, 4, 5; principles 1, 2.

9804 (Canadian rural mail carriers): Two Canadian (Organization of Rural Route Mail Carriers, Canadian Union of Postal Workers) and one U.S. (National Association of Letter Carriers) mail carrier unions, along with fifteen other unions (Canadian, six; Mexican, two; U.S., seven) and five NGOs (Canadian, three; Mexican, one; U.S., one), challenged provisions of the Canada Post Corporation Act that denied rural mail carriers the right to bargain collectively. As a consequence, the carriers did not have adequate protections for occupational illnesses and injuries or against employment discrimination. NAALC articles 1–3; principles 1, 2, 7, 9, 10.

9901 (TAESA flight attendants): The AFA and the Union Association of Mexican Aviation Flight Attendants (ASSAM) submitted a public communication in which they charged that Mexico's privately-owned Executive Air Transport, Inc. (Transportes Aéreos Ejecutivos, S.A., TAESA) systematically violated occupational safety and health and minimum employment standards for flight attendants. Company managers and an incumbent CTM union also repeatedly blocked the UNT-affiliated ASSAM's efforts to hold an election to determine which of the two unions would hold collective bargaining rights at the company. ASSAM supporters were fired. NAALC articles 1–5; principles 1, 2, 6, 9.

2000-01 (Auto Trim / Custom Trim): The CJM, 20 other NGOs (Canadian, one; Mexican, five; U.S., fourteen), three U.S. unions, and contemporary and former workers filed a communication charging that Mexican federal government agencies had repeatedly failed to enforce occupational safety and health laws or provide adequate compensation in cases of occupational injuries and illnesses to workers at Auto Trim de México (Matamoros, Tamaulipas) and Custom Trim / Breed Mexicana (Valle Hermoso, Tamaulipas). The two plants were owned by Florida-based Breed Technologies, Inc., and they produced leather-covered automobile steering wheels and gear shift knobs. Workers suffered repetitive-movement injuries, and they were exposed to toxic chemicals without adequate ventilation or personal protective equipment, leading to miscarriages, birth defects, and other serious health problems. NAALC articles 1, 3–5, 7; principles 9, 10.

2001-01 (Duro Bag Manufacturing Corporation): The AFL–CIO and PACE International Union submitted a public communication testing the Mexican government's May 2000 commitment (based on a Mexico-U.S.

ministerial agreement following U.S. NAO submissions US 9702 and US 9703) to support the use of secret ballots in elections to determine workers' choice of union representation. The petitioners alleged that workers were denied this right in a union representation election at a Río Bravo, Tamaulipas, plant owned by Duro Bag Manufacturing Corporation, a Ludlow, Kentucky-based producer of premium shopping bags for retail sales. NAALC articles 2–5; principles 1, 2.

2003-01 (Puebla garment producers): The United Students Against Sweatshops and the Center for Worker Support (Centro de Apoyo al Trabajador), joined later by MSN, filed a communication focused on Matamoros Garment and Tarrant México, two garment producers in the State of Puebla that supplied Puma and other international clothing companies. They charged that workers at the facilities faced occupational safety and health risks, and that plant managers and the state's labor conciliation and arbitration board blocked workers' attempts to form independent unions that would be more responsive to their interests than the incumbent CROC and CTM affiliates. NAALC articles 4, 5; principles 1, 2, 6, 9.

2004-01 (Yucatán apparel producers): UNITE HERE! and the Support Center for Yucatán Workers (Centro de Apoyo a los Trabajadores de Yucatán) filed a communication alleging violations of minimum employment standards and occupational safety and health standards at two apparel-manufacturing plants in Mérida, Yucatán. The petitioners initially withdrew the communication in order to gather further supporting information, but they never resubmitted it. Instead, they pursued the complaint under the OECD Guidelines for Multinational Enterprises and eventually reached a settlement with the U.S. corporation operating the Mexican plants. NAALC articles 5, 7; principles 6, 9.

2005-01 (Federal Labor Law reform, 2002): WOLA, another U.S. NGO, and twenty unions (Canadian, six; Mexican, three; U.S., eleven) failed a public communication in which they alleged that a December 2002 labor law reform initiative under consideration by the administration of President Vicente Fox Quesada (2000–2006) would in several important ways "violate the letter and spirit" of the NAALC. NAALC articles 1–4, 6; principles 1–3.

2005-02 (Aviacsa pilots): The Mexican Airline Pilots' Association (ASPAM) filed a communication stemming from a five-year conflict with Aviacsa Airlines (Consorcio Aviacsa, S.A. de C. V.), a passenger and cargo airline, over the organization of a craft union. NAALC articles 1–5; principles 1, 2.

2005-03 (Rubie's de México): A CROC-affiliated textile workers' union, USLEAP, and WOLA filed a complaint against Rubie's de México, a subsidiary of New York-based Rubie's Costume Company in Tepeji del Río, Hidalgo, that produced costumes, masks, and pet outfits, often under license to Mattel, Inc. They charged that biased labor conciliation and arbitration board authorities had illegally blocked both the registration of an alternative union at the plant and the union's attempt to strike to compel the company to recognize a collective bargaining agreement that better protected workers' interests. The submitters also alleged that company managers had failed to correct occupational safety and health problems, hired underage workers, and discriminated against women employed at the plant. NAALC articles 3, 5; principles 1–7, 9, 10.

2006-01 (SNTMMSRM and Pasta de Conchos): The USW submitted a public communication contesting the Mexican government's decertification of the elected leadership of the Mexican Mining and Metalworkers Union (SNTMMSRM) and its failure to conduct workplace inspections that might have prevented a methane gas explosion and the partial collapse of the Pasta de Conchos coal mine near Nueva Rosita, Coahuila, a major accident that led to the death of sixty-five miners. NAALC articles 3–5; principles 1, 6, 9.

2011-02 (SME): The Mexican Electricians' Union (SME), joined by sixty-one other North American unions (Canadian, ten; Mexican, thirty-two; U.S., nineteen), twenty-three NGOs (Canadian, three; Mexican, six; U.S., fourteen), and seven international labor organizations, filed a public communication condemning the Mexican government's abrupt decision in October 2009 to close the state-subsidized and heavily indebted Central Light and Power Company (LyFC). The action led to the immediate dismissal of some forty-four thousand unionized workers and immobilized the SME, one of Mexico's oldest democratic unions. NAALC articles 1–6; principles 1–3, 9.

2015-04 (Chedraui retail stores): The UFCW International Union (local 770), FAT, and two U.S. NGOs filed a complaint against Grupo Comercial Chedraui, Mexico's third-largest retail chain, charging that the company violated minimum employment standards by relying on unsalaried workers. It also allegedly utilized so-called employer protection contracts to prevent workers from voting for union leaders and asserting their rights. NAALC articles 2, 3, 5; principles 1, 2, 6, 7, 9, 10.

2018-01 (Federal Labor Law reform, 2018): The AFL-CIO and the UNT submitted a public communication in which they charged that a legislative proposal to amend Mexico's Federal Labor Law and thereby implement a 2017 constitutional reform on labor rights in fact threatened to undercut the constitutional reform's democratizing principles, particularly with regard to freedom of association and the right to collective bargaining. NAALC articles 1-4; principles 1, 2, 9.

APPENDIX C

Annotated List of Public Submissions to the U.S. Office of Trade and Labor Affairs (OTLA), 2008–2016

US 2008-01 (Guatemala): The American Federation of Labor-Congress of Industrial Organizations (AFL-CIO) and six Guatemalan labor organizations submitted a complaint focused principally on obstacles to freedom of association and the right to collective bargaining in Guatemala. The submission centered on violations linked to the sustained violence (assassinations, attempted murders, coercion, and intimidation) suffered by union leaders and trade union activists. Although antiunion violence was a long-standing problem in Guatemala, the complaint highlighted developments since the Dominican Republic-Central America-United States Free Trade Agreement (DR-CAFTA) had taken effect on July 1, 2006, by presenting case studies of alleged rights violations in five different companies. These cases were selected to demonstrate that serious violations of core labor rights were common in sectors and firms (apparel manufacturing, export agriculture, food products) that either exported their production to the United States or were otherwise linked to bilateral trade (including the state-owned company managing Puerto Quetzal, the country's principal port on the Pacific Ocean).

Note: These case summaries are based on the author's review of OTLA submissions and public reports (available at https://www.dol.gov/agencies/ilab/our-work/trade/fta-submissions; accessed on February 15, 2021) and *Inside U.S. Trade*, August 13, 2010; May 6, 2011. No case number is available for the 2010 submission concerning Costa Rica.

US 2010 (Costa Rica): The International Longshore and Warehouse Union and two Costa Rican labor organizations, the Union of Atlantic-side Port Administration Workers (Sindicato de Trabajadores de la Junta Administradora Portuaria de la Vertiente Atlántica, SINTRAJAP) and the National Association of Public and Private Employees (Asociación Nacional de Empleados Públicos y Privados), charged that the Government of Costa Rica had violated the SINTRAJAP's freedom of association and right to collective bargaining by illegally ousting its elected leadership in an attempt to undercut the union's opposition to the privatization of the ports of Limón and Moin.

US 2010-03 (Peru): Peru's National Union of United Customs and Tax Administration Workers (Sindicato Nacional de Unidad de Trabajadores de la Superintendencia Nacional de Aduanas y de Administración Tributaria) appealed to the OTLA to compel the Lima-Callao Regional Bureau of Labor and Employment Promotion to engage in collective bargaining over wage issues and, if negotiations failed, to accept binding arbitration as provided for under Peruvian law.

US 2011-01 (Bahrain): The AFL-CIO, working closely with the General Federation of Bahrain Trade Unions, condemned the arrest of trade union leaders and the large-scale firing of labor activists in both the public and private sectors during the Government of Bahrain's repression of "Arab Spring" political protests (including two general strikes) in February–March 2011. It called upon the U.S. government to withdraw from the U.S.-Bahrain Free Trade Agreement if Bahrain did not cease its campaign against unions and fully restore core labor rights.

US 2011-03 (Dominican Republic): Father Christopher Hartley, a British-Spanish Catholic missionary priest then associated with the Madrid-based Mission of Mercy (Misión de la Misericordia), submitted a complaint concerning the egregious labor rights abuses suffered by immigrant Haitian workers employed in the Dominican Republic's sugar cane industry. He listed forced labor, child labor, hazardous working conditions, and employer retaliation against unionization attempts among the labor rights violations at issue.

US 2012-01 (Honduras): The AFL-CIO, twenty-five Honduran labor organizations (including six national federations and confederations), and one Honduran human-rights nongovernmental organization (NGO) filed a submission charging the Government of Honduras with failing to enforce its labor obligations under the DR-CAFTA. The complaint featured a total of eighteen case studies of a broad range of alleged labor violations (the frequent firing of union leaders, employers' abuse of subcontracting arrangements to block unionization, widespread child labor violations, and serious shortcomings in the government's labor inspection and enforcement regimes) in the apparel and autoparts industries, export agriculture, and Puerto Cortez port facilities.

US 2015-01 (Peru): The U.S.-based International Labor Rights Fund, seven Peruvian labor organizations (four national confederations and three sector-specific federations), and one Peruvian indigenous-rights NGO jointly filed a complaint charging that abuses of special legislation allowing employers in nontraditional export sectors to hire workers on an indefinite series of short-term contracts seriously constrained their freedom of association. Citing workers' experiences at eight individual companies in textile and garment manufacturing and in the export agriculture sector, they demonstrated that employers frequently failed to renew the contracts of union leaders and members, thereby blocking unionization efforts.

US 2016-02 (Colombia): The AFL-CIO, four Colombian labor organizations, and one Colombian labor-rights NGO submitted a complaint documenting widespread employer abuses of short-term or temporary labor contracts as a way of avoiding direct employment relationships and thereby blocking unionization, as well as systematic employer resistance to collective bargaining and inadequate inspections and enforcement by the Ministry of Labor. Because employers were not legally required to give any reason for failing to renew short-term or temporary contracts, employers often manipulated them to fire union leaders and members as a way of obstructing union formation. The submission cited examples from the oil and sugar sectors to illustrate the extent of illegal subcontracting practices.

*Annotated List of Rapid Response Mechanism Petitions
Concerning Mexico Submitted to the U.S. Interagency Labor
Committee for Monitoring and Enforcement, 2021–2022*

REVIEW PROCEDURES

All the rapid response labor mechanism (RRLM) petitions listed below were reviewed by the U.S. Interagency Labor Committee for Monitoring and Enforcement (ILCME, cochaired by the Office of the United States Trade Representative and the U.S. Department of Labor) under the interim procedural guidelines published by the Office of the United States Trade Representative (USTR), "Interagency Labor Committee for Monitoring and Enforcement Procedural Guidelines for Petitions Pursuant to the USMCA," *U.S. Federal Register* 85, no. 126 (June 30, 2020): 39257-60. The U.S. Department of Labor's (U.S. DOL) Office of Trade and Labor Affairs (OTLA) received petitions on behalf of the ILCME.

Acting under these guidelines (annex: USMCA Procedural Guidelines, section D), the ILCME reviewed a petition and any supporting materials within thirty days after the OTLA received them. If the ILCME decided to proceed with the case, the USTR then notified Mexico's Ministry of the Economy (Secretaría de la Economía, SE) that there was a good faith basis on which to believe that a denial of rights involving freedom of association and/or the right to collective bargaining had occurred at the designated production facility. The SE, acting under the United States-Mexico-Canada Agreement's (USMCA) article 31-A.4 (2), then notified the USTR within ten days whether Mexican trade and labor officials intended to conduct a review of the matter. If Mexican authorities agreed to do so, they had forty-five days within which to attempt to remediate the situation. The available evidence indicates that, in the six cases summarized here, both the U.S. and Mexican governments acted within the stipulated time periods.

PETITIONS

Tridonex, S. de R.L. de C.V.: In a RRLM petition filed with the OTLA on
May 10, 2021, the AFL-CIO, Service Employees International Union
(SEIU), Public Citizen (a Washington, DC-based nongovernmental
organization, NGO), and the "Movement 20/32" Independent National
Union of Industrial and Service Workers (Sindicato Nacional
Independiente de Trabajadores de Industrias y Servicios 'Movimiento
20/32'," SNITIS) charged the managers of Tridonex, an aftermarket
automotive parts subsidiary of Pennsylvania-based Cardone Industries,
Inc. employing some 3,800 workers at three manufacturing plants in
Matamoros, Tamaulipas, with violating their employees' freedom of
association and right to collective bargaining. They alleged that the
company, in addition to denying employees access to the existing
collective contract and a secret-ballot contract ratification vote, had
over a sustained period seriously harassed SNITIS leaders and fired
approximately six hundred workers in an effort to block their challenge
to the incumbent, CTM-affiliated Industrial Union of Matamoros
Maquiladora and Assembly Plant Workers (Sindicato Industrial de
Trabajadores en Plantas Maquiladoras y Ensambladoras de Matamoros
y su Municipio, SITPME). The ILCME accepted the case on June 9, and
the USTR then submitted a request to Mexico's Ministry of the Economy
asking that Mexican authorities review the matter. However, Mexican
trade and labor officials announced on August 11, 2021, that they declined
to proceed with the case on the grounds that the events in question had
transpired before the USMCA had taken effect on July 1, 2020. In the
interim, U.S. officials had worked with their Mexican counterparts to
negotiate a private settlement with Tridonex that resolved the conflict.
Under the terms of the five-page, single-spaced agreement, Tridonex
management agreed to make augmented severance payments to 154
dismissed workers; reform the company's personnel practices and not
suspend or fire any workers on the basis of their union affiliation or
preferences; observe strict neutrality in workers' election of their union
representatives; and cooperate fully with Mexican labor authorities
in advance of a special workplace vote to determine which labor
organization would legally represent Tridonex employees and negotiate
a collective bargaining agreement on their behalf. In the recount election

held on February 28, 2022, the SNITIS defeated the SITPME by an overwhelming margin, 1,126 to 176 votes.[1]

General Motors-Silao: In contrast to the five stakeholder-initiated petitions listed in this appendix, the ILCME itself initiated this case. On May 12, 2021, the USTR requested that Mexican authorities investigate a possible denial of rights at General Motors's vehicle manufacturing plant in Silao, Guanajuato (GM-Silao). The case focused on irregularities that had occurred during a legally required contract legitimation vote held at the facility on April 20–21. Mexico's Ministry of Labor and Social Welfare (STPS) had immediately suspended the vote, and on June 21, it ordered the incumbent, CTM-affiliated "Miguel Trujillo López" National Union of Metalworking, Steel-Metallurgical, Automobile and General Autoparts Suppliers, Energy, and Related Industry Workers (Sindicato Nacional de Trabajadores de la Industria Metal-Mecánica, Sidero-Metalúrgica, Automotriz y Proveedores de Autopartes en General, de la Energía, sus Derivados y Similares de la República Mexicana "Miguel Trujillo López") to hold a second contract legitimation vote before August 20. On July 7, Mexican and U.S. officials reached agreement on a five-page, single-spaced remediation plan that stipulated in detail the terms under which the vote would be held. In that vote, GM-Silao workers rejected the existing collective contract by a total of 3,214 to 2,623 votes. In the special union representation election then called for February 1–2, 2022, the politically independent, grassroots-organized National Independent Union of Automotive and Related Industry Workers (Sindicato Independiente Nacional de Trabajadoras y Trabajdores d la Industria Automotriz y las Adhesivas) decisively defeated two different CTM-affiliated unions and a third rival union linked to the old-guard Revolutionary Confederation of Workers and Peasants (CROC), winning 4,182 (77.6 percent) of the 5,389 valid votes cast.[2]

Panasonic Automotive Systems de México, S.A. de C.V.: On April 18, 2022, the SNITIS and Rethink Trade (part of the American Economic Liberties Project, a Washington, DC-based NGO) filed a petition with the OTLA alleging that Panasonic management and a CTM-affiliated union claiming workplace representation rights at two Panasonic automotive parts facilities employing approximately two thousand workers in Reynosa, Tamaulipas, the Autonomous Industrial Union of Mexican Maquiladora Operators in General (Sindicato Industrial

Autónomo de Operarios en General de Maquiladoras de la República Mexicana, SIAOGMRM), had illegally imposed a contract on the workforce. Company managers had also fired more than sixty protesting workers. Shortly thereafter (April 21–22), the SNITIS defeated the SIAOGMRM in a union representation election by a total of 1,200 to 390 votes. On May 18, the USTR requested that Mexico's SE review the SNITIS complaint. On July 14, U.S. authorities announced that, as a result of that review, Panasonic management had agreed to suspend the SIAOGMRM contract and repay workers the union dues that had been deducted from them for the benefit of the SIAOGMRM.[3]

Teksid Hierro de México, S.A. de C.V.: On May 4, 2022, the AFL-CIO, United Automobile Workers (UAW), and the National Union of Mexican Mineworkers, Metalworkers, and Steelworkers (SNTMMSSRM, previously the SNTMMSRM) filed a RRLM petition in support of the SNTMMSSRM's long-running contest with the CTM-affiliated State Union of Metal-Mechanical Industry Workers (Sindicato de Trabajadores de la Industria Metal Mecánica del Estado, STIMME) over employee bargaining representation at a Stellantis (Fiat Chrsyler Automobiles and Groupe PSA)-subsidiary automobile engine manufacturing plant in Frontera, Coahuila. Both Mexican unions claimed bargaining rights for the workforce, and they both had registered collective contracts for the facility. The submitters noted that, although the SITMMSSRM had won a union representation vote held at the facility in June 2018 and the Federal Conciliation and Arbitration Board (JFCA) had confirmed the result, the company continued to negotiate with the STIMME. Acting in response to the request the USTR made on June 6 to investigate the matter, Mexican authorities announced on August 2 that they had reached an agreement with the employer over the terms of a second union representation election. Teksid Hierro agreed to remain neutral in the voting process, offered reinstatement and/or back pay to thirty-seven workers who had been dismissed over the course of the conflict and promised to transfer to the SITMMSSRM the union dues that the company had withheld from workers' paychecks for the benefit of the STIMME. In the second election held on September 19, 2022, and witnessed by National Human Rights Commission (CNDH) observers, the SNTMMSSRM defeated the STIMME by 642 to 172 votes.[4]

Manufacturas VU, S. de R.L. de C.V.: Two Mexican labor organizations, the Mexican Labor Union League (Liga Sindical Obrera Mexicana, LSOM) and the Frontier Workers' Committee (Comité Fronterizo de Obreras y Obreros), filed a petition with the OTLA on June 20, 2022, in which they claimed that workers at an automotive soft-trim supplier in Piedras Negras, Coahuila, owned by Michigan-based VU Manufacturing had been denied freedom of association and the right to collective bargaining. Specifically, the claimants alleged that company managers had colluded with the CTM-affiliated Coahuila State Union of Workers in the Maquiladora, National Accessory, Heavy Machinery, and Metal Workshop Unit Industries (Sindicato de Trabajadores de la Industria Maquiladora y de la Industria Nacional de Accesorios y Maquinaria Pesada y Manufactura de Muebles Metálicos del Estado de Coahuila) to ensure that only it had access to plant facilities for organizing purposes. Managers had, moreover, pressured many employees to affiliate with the CTM union, and they had suspended, disciplined, or fired four workers who supported the LSOM. On July 21, the USTR requested that Mexico's SE initiate a review of the matter. On the basis of the review, the Federal Center for Conciliation and Labor Registration (CFCRL) scheduled and carefully supervised a special recount election on August 31 that was witnessed by observers from the International Labour Organization and the CNDH. The LSOM won the election with a total of 186 votes, against 101 votes for the CTM affiliate.[5]

BBB Industries: On August 2, 2022, the SNITIS and Rethink Trade (part of the American Economic Liberties Project, a Washington, DC-based NGO) filed a petition with the OTLA charging that the SIAOGMRM, the incumbent union at the aftermarket automotive parts facilities owned by Alabama-based BBB Industries and located in Reynosa, Tamaulipas, had committed fraud in a contract legitimation vote held in early July. The claimants alleged that the workers employed at the four plants had not had the advance access to the collective contract required by Mexican federal labor law. Moreover, several irregularities marred the vote (in which 3,158 ballots were reportedly cast, even though the workers eligible to vote numbered only 2,741). However, the ILCME rejected the filing on September 1, on the grounds that the case did not reach a standard of "sufficient, credible evidence of a denial of rights."[6]

Saint-Gobain de México, S.A. de C.V.: The AFL-CIO, United Steelworkers (USW), and the Independent Union of Free and Democratic Workers of Saint-Gobain México (Sindicato Independiente de las y los Trabajadores Libres y Democráticos de Saint-Gobain México, SITLDSGM, legally registered on January 19, 2022) filed an RRLM petition with the OTLA on September 27, 2022, concerning an alleged denial of rights at an automotive glass manufacturing plant in Cuautla, Morelos, owned by Saint-Gobain Corporation, a French manufacturer of building and high-performance construction materials. They charged that the incumbent Union of Glass Industry Workers (Sindicato de Trabajadores de la Industria de Vidrio, STIV), an affiliate of the Confederation of Workers and Peasants (Confederación de Trabajadores y Campesinos, CTC), had violated Mexican labor law by failing to provide the approximately two thousand workers with copies of union statutes, union financial statements, and the collective bargaining agreement it had negotiated without rank-and-file member participation in March 2022. The petitioners also maintained that some company managers had colluded with the incumbent union to obstruct the SITLDSGM's access to plant facilities for organizing purposes prior to a mandated contract validation vote on July 5–6 , 2022. Workers did not receive the legally stipulated advance notice before the vote was held, and STIV leaders and company managers allegedly conspired in multiple ways to intimidate workers into voting for the existing collective contract. The complainants maintained, furthermore, that after the existing contract was rejected by a total of 814 to 700 votes (with twenty-five annulled ballots), the STIV and some company managers repeatedly harassed and intimidated SITLDSGM leaders in the period before a required union representation vote on September 28–29, 2022. Yet despite the many obstacles the SITLDSGM faced, it defeated the STIV in the representation election by a total of 957 to 587 votes. The USTR and the U.S. DOL then announced on October 27, 2022, that, in view of the independent union's victory, any previous denial of rights no longer had effect and that they would not forward the complaint to Mexican authorities for further investigation. They did, however, state that both the Mexican and U.S. governments would continue working together to monitor developments at the plant in order to ensure that company managers bargained in good faith with the SITLDSGM over new contract terms.[7]

Notes

1. THE INTERNATIONAL DEFENSE OF LABOR RIGHTS: CONCEPTS, POLICY ARENAS, AND THE CHALLENGE OF STATE SOVEREIGNTY

1. Clapham (2007: 6–12) overviews the philosophical and political origins of human rights in the writings of seventeenth- and eighteenth-century authors (including John Locke, Jean-Jacques Rousseau, and Thomas Paine) and in such historically influential eighteenth-century documents as the U.S. Declaration of Independence and the French Declaration of the Rights of Man and of the Citizen. Bates (2014) discusses the concept of human rights and its evolving status in international law.

2. On the historical evolution of the ILO, see Helfer 2006; Hughes and Haworth 2011: chap. 1, *passim*; van der Linden 2019.

3. Simmons (2009: 24–36) analyzes the shifting balance between state sovereignty and international support for human rights over the course of the twentieth century. She emphasizes the importance of democratization and the growing density and influence of international civil society in this process. See also Buergenthal 1997: 714.

4. Chapter 2 discusses in depth the GSP programs developed by the United States and the European Union (EU), which, respectively, provide duty-free or reduced-tariff market access for eligible products from designated less-developed countries on a nonreciprocal basis.

5. Goertz and Mahoney 2012: 185.

6. George and Bennett 2005: chap. 3.

7. See, for example, Finnemore and Sikkink 1998: 895–99; Keck and Sikkink 1998: chaps. 1, 6.

8. Martin and Sikkink 1993 is an important exception in this regard.

9. *Bringing the State Back In* was, of course, the title of a seminal book on state-society relations edited by Evans, Rueschemeyer, and Skocpol (1985).

10. Donnelly 1986: 636.

11. Nimtz 2002: 256; see also Braunthal 1966. The IMWA was founded in 1864; the socialist Second International (1889–1914) succeeded it.

12. Cox 1977: 387; Rodgers et al. 2009: 2–3, 5–6, 27; Symons 2011: 2575–76, 2578. The Preamble of the ILO Constitution included the following statement: "Whereas conditions of labour exist involving such injustice, hardship and privation to large numbers of people

as to produce unrest so great that the peace and harmony of the world are imperilled" (Treaty of Versailles, Part XIII ["Labour"], Section 1, available at https://avalon.law.yale .edu/imt/partxiii.asp; accessed on August 8, 2021).

Rodgers et al. (3–4), whose study was commissioned by the ILO, link the body's founding to nineteenth-century social democratic, Christian democratic, and social liberal debates about the "social question" and particularly to the International Association for Labour Legislation (1900), which promulgated international conventions prohibiting night work for women in industry and the use of white phosphorus in the production of matches. See also Alcock 1971; Ruotsila 2002; Tosstorff 2005; and Van Daele 2005.

13. See Rodgers et al. (2009: 12–14) on the origins of tripartism in the ILO. The ILO sometimes refers to the body of its conventions as "the International Labour Code" (Charnovitz 1995: 168).

14. Clapham 2007: 25; see also Simmons 2009: 36, 38; and Tomuschat 2014: 26. Sikkink (1993: 413) maintains that the decisive shift in international attitudes concerning "the supremacy of the state's absolute authority within its borders" did not occur until World War II; Simmons (2009: 39–40) and Tomuschat (2014: 27–28) concur on this point.

15. Rodgers et al. 2009: 12–13. Donnelly (2013: 182) argues that "the first international human rights regime of any sort was the functional regime of the International Labour Organization."

16. Clapham 2007: 26, 28–29.

17. Convention no. 11 (1921) guaranteed to agricultural workers "the same *rights* of associational combination as to industrial workers" (art. 1, emphasis added here and below); no. 19 (1925) ensured that foreign workers employed in another member state and their dependents would receive "*equality* of treatment" in terms of the industrial accident compensation that country offered to its nationals; and no. 29 (1930) condemned *forced* or compulsory labor. In contrast, all seven of the ILO's core conventions adopted after 1947 (nos. 29, 87, 98, 100, 105, 111, 182) employ terminology of this kind: "freedom," "right," "abolition," "equal," "discrimination," "worst forms." The only core convention not to employ such terminology is no. 138 (Minimum Wage Convention, 1973). International Labour Organization, "C138: Minimum Age Convention, 1973 (No. 138," accessed August 9, 2021, https://www.ilo.org/dyn/normlex/en /f?p=NORMLEXPUB:12100:0::NO::P12100_ilo_code:C138.

18. International Labour Organization, "C138: Minimum Age Convention, 1973 (No. 138," accessed August 9, 2021, https://www.ilo.org/dyn/normlex/en/f?p=NORMLEXPUB:121 00:0::NO::P12100_ilo_code:C138. Table 1.1 later in this chapter lists the eight ILO "fundamental conventions" and the dates on which they were adopted. Rodgers et al. (2009: 250–51) reproduce the general principles from the ILO Constitution (adopted as Part XIII of the 1919 Treaty of Versailles).

19. Rodgers et al. 2009: 95.

20. Clapham 2007: 29, 31–32. The goals articulated in the Declaration of Principles Issued by the President of the United States and the Prime Minister of the United Kingdom included "improved labour standards, economic advancement, and social security" (https://www.nato.int/cps/en/natohq/official_texts_16912.htm; accessed August 10, 2021).

Most authors (see, for example, Donnelly 1986: 614–15 and 2013: 25; Buergenthal 1997: 703–704, 706; Perry 1997: 484; Simmons 2009: 23–24, 36; Tomuschat 2014: 27–28) argue that World War II was the key point of inflection in the development of an international human rights regime. Moyne (2010: 3–4, 7), however, maintains that this shift did not occur until the 1970s.

21. In article 55 of its charter, the United Nations pledged to promote "universal respect for, and observance of, human rights and fundamental freedoms for all without distinction as to race, sex, language, or religion" (North Atlantic Treaty Organization, "The Atlantic Charter," July 2, 2018, https://www.nato.int/cps/en/natohq/official_texts_16912.htm).

22. Rodgers et al. 2009: 7. The Declaration Concerning the Aims and Purposes of the International Labour Organization (reproduced in Rodgers et al. 2009: 251–53) was incorporated into the ILO's constitution in 1946. Mazurek and Betts (2012: 292) argue that this declaration represented the first real linkage between human rights and social rights.

23. Rodgers et al. 2009: 44.

24. Buergenthal 1997: 708.

25. United Nations, "Universal Declaration of Human Rights, accessed August 10, 2021, https://www.un.org/en/universal-declaration-human-rights.

26. In 2005, eleven Nobel Peace Prize laureates commemorated International Human Rights Day (December 10) by publishing a statement in which they cited the UDHR and reaffirmed freedom of association as "an inalienable and fundamental human right" ("A Call for Human Rights": 2005).

27. For overviews of the development of the international human rights regime from World War II until the 1980s, see Buergenthal 1997: 705; Donnelly 2013: 75–92; and Simmons 2009: 39–55. Clapham (2007: 73–80) provides an overview of United Nations' actions on human rights; Whelan (2010: 6) and Tomuschat (2014: 35–36) discuss the origins of the ICCPR and ICESCR.

28. Rodgers et al. 2009: 38, 40–41.

29. United Nations, "No. 14668," December 19, 1966, https://treaties.un.org/doc/Publication /UNTS/Volume%20999/volume-999-I-14668-English.pdf.

30. United Nations, "International Covenant on Economic, Social and Cultural Rights," December 16, 1966, http://www.ohchr.org/EN/ProfessionalInterest/Pages/CESCR.aspx. Articles 6–15 address the rights to work, fair wages, equal remuneration for work of equal value, safe and healthy working conditions, freedom from hunger, education, and so forth. These protections were mirrored in subsequent regional human rights accords. For example, the American Convention on Human Rights (adopted on November 22, 1969 and in effect since July 18, 1978) recognizes the right to associate freely for "ideological, religious, political, economic, labor, social, cultural, sports, or other purposes" (art. 16[1]) (Organization of American States, "Multilateral Treaties," accessed August 12, 2021, https://www.oas.org/dil/treaties_b-32_american_convention _on_human_rights.pdf).

31. Risse and Ropp 2013: 9.

32. Donnelly 1986: 608; see also Tomuschat 2014: 165.

33. Boyle and Shah 2014: 218.

34.   Donnelly (1986: 611n23) maintains that this provision effectively precludes strong international monitoring.

35.   Cited in Clapham 2007: 42; see also Buergenthal 1997: 705-706; Tomuschat 2014: 2-3, 22-23, 26-27. Clapham (42) reports that the UDHR has been "translated into over 300 languages."

36.   The most widely ratified agreement was the International Convention on the Rights of the Child (United Nations, "Convention on the Rights of the Child," November 20, 1989, https://www.ohchr.org/en/instruments-mechanisms/instruments/convention-rights -child).

37.   United Nations, "Convention on the Rights of the Child," November 20, 1989, https:// www.ohchr.org/en/instruments-mechanisms/instruments/convention-rights-child.

38.   Bhagwati (1995: 754) offers a dissenting view on this point.

39.   For a more recent analysis of the evolving debate concerning state sovereignty and human rights, see Hopgood, Snyder, and Vinjamuri 2017.

40.   Sikkink 1993: 440-41; Khagram, Riker, and Sikkink 2000; Risse and Ropp 2013; Barkin and Cronin 1994.

41.   Krasner 1999: 3-4; see pp. 20-25, 51 for a discussion of historical and academic approaches to "Westphalian" sovereignty ("the formal or constitutional autonomy of states"). Krasner (51, 68-69) casts doubt on the extent to which full Westphalian sovereignty has ever been exercised in practice. He also notes that "Westphalian sovereignty does not guarantee domestic control" (226).

42.   This discussion follows Krasner 1999: 26, 30-32, 106, 114; see also Donnelly 1986: 602-603, 608, 616, and 2013: 32-33.

43.   Donnelly 1986: 603-605.

44.   Donnelly 1986: 633. See Krasner (1999: 113-18) for an assessment of several different international human rights agreements in these terms.

45.   Krasner 1999: 8, 119. Krasner (113) notes that the European Convention for the Protection of Human Rights and Fundamental Freedoms (1950), under whose terms the European Court of Human Rights can issue decisions that are binding on member states, "provides the most far-reaching example of infringements on the Westphalian model."

46.   Donnelly 2013: 254-56, 262-63.

47.   United Nations General Assembly Resolution 2625 (Declaration on Principles of International Law concerning Friendly Relations and Co-Operation Among States in Accordance with the Charter of the United Nations, adopted on October 24, 1970 and available at https://www.unoosa.org) stipulates that " no State or group of States has the right to intervene, directly or indirectly, for any reason whatsoever, in the internal or external affairs of another State" (art. XXV). See also Clapham 2007: 60-65; Hopgood 2014: 183, 185.

48.   Donnelly 2013: 33; see also Tomuschat 2014: 323, 325. The first international human rights agreement adopted following the promulgation of the UDHR was the 1948 Convention on the Prevention and Punishment of the Crime of Genocide.

49.   The author gratefully acknowledges insightful comments by Dr. Par Engström on this issue.

50.   United Nations Human Rights Office of the High Commissioner, https://www.ohchr .org; Perry 1997: 481. For academic assessments of this position, see Donnelly 1986: 607 n17; Buergenthal 1997: 714; Nickel 2008; Whelan 2010: 1; van Boven 2014: 143. Tomuschat

(2014: 56, 72) notes that, under pressure from Asian states, the Vienna Declaration references the ICESCR in its operative text but mentions the ICCPR only in its preamble, thus undercutting its claim to the universality of human rights. See also Sen 1994: 32.

51. Meron 1986: 1–4, 10–11, 16; see also Donnelly 2013: 10.

52. Tomuschat 2014: 44. See also Mandel 1989: 457–58; Seiderman 2001: 273–75.

53. Krasner 1999: 4.

54. See Max Weber's classic definition of "the state" and his discussion of domestic political sovereignty in Weber 1978: vol. 1, chap. 17 ("Political and Hierocratic Organizations"), esp. p. 54. Sikkink (1993: 413) argues that "neither the practice nor the doctrine of internal sovereignty has ever been absolute."

55. For example, in the negotiations preceding the creation of the ILO, the United States won a concession stipulating that federal states would treat ILO conventions simply as recommendations. Revisions to the ILO Constitution in 1946 permitted federal states to determine whether conventions fall under federal or local jurisdiction. Haas 1964: 247; Alcock 1971: 29–30.

56. Donnelly (1986: 630–31) identifies racial discrimination and torture as other human rights issues around which there is strong international consensus.

57. Krasner 1999: 33, 106. For instance, Pope Leo XIII's *Rerum novarum* encyclical ("On the Condition of the Workers," May 15, 1891) "emphatically affirmed the right of workers to form and join associations for mutual help" (Dunning 1998: 151).

58. Krasner notes (1999: 113) that such accords "can, but do not necessarily, compromise Westphalian sovereignty by providing external legitimation for certain domestic practices involving relations between rulers and ruled." "The extent to which human rights conventions compromise the Westphalian model is critically dependent on the domestic base of support for such values" (120).

59. Some authors refer to these rights simply as "collective" rights. Rodríguez-Garavito (2005: 215) labels them "enabling" rights; Kang (2012: 3) calls them "trade union" rights.

60. In some developing countries, violations of individual labor rights (for example, egregious abuse of child labor in textile and garment export industries) may be so important to national economic performance that government officials are in practice as reluctant to curtail these abuses as they are violations of the rights to organize and bargain collectively.

61. Dunning (1998: 156–57) discusses the sovereignty-based opposition to freedom of association initiatives that arose within the ILO during the 1920s.

62. Bellace 2014: 30, 34, 47–48; Swepston 1998: 187–90; Novitz 2003: 192. Convention no. 87 (art. 8, para. 2) prohibits restrictions on "the freedom of action of trade union organizations in defence of their occupational interests."

63. The ICESCR (art. 8 [1(d)]) protects "the right to strike, provided that it is exercised in conformity with the laws of the particular country." Similarly, the European Social Charter (first adopted in 1961 and revised in 1996) states (art. 6[4]) that "the Parties undertake . . . and recognise . . . the right of workers and employers to collective action in cases of conflicts of interest, including the right to strike, subject to obligations that might arise out of collective agreements previously entered into" (Council of Europe, "Details of No. 163," July 1, 1999, www.coe.int/en/web/conventions/full-list/-/conventions /treaty/163). The Additional Protocol to the American Convention on Human Rights in

the Area of Economic, Social and Cultural Rights (the Protocol of San Salvador), adopted in 1988 and in force since 1999, explicitly includes the right to strike (art. 8 [1(b)]) (https://extranet.who.int/mindbank/item/1255#:~:text=The%20Additional%20Protocol%20to%20the,and%20the%20right%20to%20education).

64.   Swepston 1998: 186–90. The United Nations Human Rights Committee has held that the right of association recognized by the ICCPR does not include the right to strike (Boyle and Shah 2014: 232).

65.   Bellace 2014: 37.

66.   Bellace 2014: 37–38, 41, 43, 49–52, 55 n59. In 1957 and 1970, the ILO adopted nonbinding resolutions that endorsed workers' right to strike, although the CFA has consistently taken the view that national regulation of the right is appropriate. See Gernigon, Odero, and Guido 1998: 441, 443–71.

67.   In a nonreciprocal preferential trade agreement, a member country unilaterally grants trade preferences (such as lower or zero tariffs) to a trade partner. Free-trade agreements remove tariff and nontariff barriers to trade among member states, but each member retains its own tariff schedule with other countries.

68.   In focusing on *international* arenas for the defense of labor rights, this discussion omits important regional associations of states, including the EU and the Common Market of the South (Mercado Común del Sur). Selected aspects of the EU labor rights experiences are discussed in chapter 2.

69.   Compa 1993a: 177. The author's thematic search (conducted on August 24, 2021) of the United Nations' jurisprudence database (http://juris.ohchr.org/) for the 2000–2020 period confirmed this judgment. Cases typically involved issues such as alleged discrimination against women or persons with disabilities. During this period, the Human Rights Committee heard cases alleging violations of freedom of association in Belarus and Kazakhstan, but they concerned the rights of prodemocracy groups, civic organizations, and political protestors rather than labor organizations per se. Case 3076/2017 involved the murder of a Colombian trade unionist in 2015. At least occasionally, UN committees have also examined cases involving other kinds of labor rights. For instance, between 1991 and 1997, the UN Committee on Economic, Social and Cultural Rights (UNCESCR) actively sought to end the abuses (forced labor, child labor) suffered by Haitian sugarcane cutters working in the Dominican Republic (UNCESCR 1991, 1997).

70.   The author's examination of labor-related cases among the 428 judgments issued by the IACtHR through June 2021 (https://www.corteidh.or.cr./casos_sentencias.cfm; accessed August 24–25, 2021) found that they were mainly concerned with individual rather than collective-action labor rights, including child labor violations, serious workplace safety and health issues, and illegal dismissals. Five of the cases (identified by the year in which the violation occurred) centered on alleged violations of the American Convention on Human Rights (ACHR) guarantee of freedom of association (art. 16): Brazil 1993 (no. 318); Guatemala 1984 (no. 258), 1995 (no. 393); Peru 1989 (no. 340), 1992 (no. 121). These cases usually cited other ACHR guarantees as well, including the rights to life (art. 4), humane treatment (art. 5), personal liberty (art. 7), a fair trial (art. 8), freedom of expression (art. 13), freedom of movement and residence (art. 22), judicial protection (art. 25), and the prohibition against slavery (art. 6). In all five cases, the court found in favor of the plaintiff(s), sometimes awarding material damages to the individual(s) involved.

Other IACtHR cases involved wages, pensions, professional illness, and the large-scale dismissal of public sector employees.

Under the terms of the ACHR, only states that are party to the convention and the Inter-American Commission on Human Rights can submit complaints to the court. In a number of cases examined by the author, national labor organizations and national and/or international human rights organizations supported individual petitioners in commission and court proceedings. On compliance with court rulings and its overall impact, see Engström 2017 and Huneeus 2010.

In contrast to the IACtHR, since 1960, the European Court on Human Rights (ECHR, founded in 1959) has heard a large number of cases alleging violations of those provisions of the European Convention for the Protection of Human Rights and Fundamental Freedoms (1950) regarding trade union rights (freedoms of association and assembly); work-related rights (freedoms of association and expression, protection of property, prohibition against discrimination, safety in the employment context); and prohibitions against forced labor, slavery, and inhuman or degrading treatment. See, respectively, ECHR 2016a, 2016b, 2017. The identity of the complainants (they included both trade unions and individuals) and the outcomes of the cases varied greatly.

71. Compa (1993a: 184–86) cites U.S. court cases involving Costa Rican, Guatemalan, and South Korean labor organizations. See also Compa 2002a: 56–58; Favilla-Silano 1996: 330–32.

72. See, for example, Douglas, Ferguson, and Klett 2004: 26. Similarly, Portela and Orbie (2014: 72) review EU GSP suspension cases and show that ILO reports are important to petitioners' filings. Actual EU suspension of GSP market access in the cases of Belarus and Myanmar depended heavily on critical findings by ILO commissions of inquiry.

73. Author's interview [hereinafter "interview"] with U.S. trade union representative A, July 21, 2004, Mexico City. For example, Compa and Vogt (2001: 208) note that a network formed around U.S. GSP petitions alleging labor rights violations suffered by Guatemalan textile workers was the basis for forming the CSR-focused Commission for the Verification of Codes of Conduct.

74. The great bulk of the literature on cross-border labor solidarity focuses on North-North and North-South union cooperation. The Southern Initiative on Globalization and Trade Union Rights (SIGTUR), a network of democratic unions in the Global South formed in May 1991 (with affiliates in Argentina, Brazil, Cambodia, East Timor, India, Indonesia, Malaysia, Myanmar, Philippines, South Africa, Sri Lanka, and Thailand) is a leading example of South-South international labor cooperation (https://www.sigtur .com; Webster, Lambert, and Bezuidenhout 2008: 199–206; Dobrusin 2014. See also Southall and Bezuidenhout 2004: 143–44 for examples of cooperation among unions in southern Africa.) Recorded instances of South-North labor cooperation are uncommon. Carr (1996: 215), for example, notes the case of the Confederation of Mexican Workers (Confederación de Trabajadores de México, CTM) acting in support of California dockworkers on strike in the 1930s. Chapter 4 cites solidarity actions by Mexico's Authentic Labor Front (Frente Auténtico del Trabajo, FAT) in support of the International Brotherhood of Teamsters and Mexican migrant apple workers in the state of Washington and in collaboration with an organizing campaign by the United Electrical, Radio, and Machine Workers of America in Milwaukee, Wisconsin.

75.　The U.S.-based Knights of Labor also developed a significant international presence in the 1880s, particularly in Great Britain, Belgium, and New Zealand (Parfitt 2015: 136–37, 139).

76.　Association Internationale des Travailleurs 1866: 20–21.

77.　Nimtz 2002: 245, 247, 251, 255, 262–63; Braunthal 1966: 85–105, *passim*; Hansson 1983: 14–15. The IWMA was based in London until 1872 and then transferred its office to New York. Its activities effectively ceased shortly thereafter (Dunning 1998: 152).

78.　Windmuller 2000: 102–3, 105–6, 108–12, 117; Rodgers et al., 2009: 4; Parfitt 2015: 146–47. Dunning (1998: 153, 155) gives examples of other late-nineteenth-century labor organizations.

79.　See Rütters n.d.: table 2.

80.　In chronological order by year of formation, these were the: International Transport Workers Federation (created in 1896); Public Services International (1907); International Union of Food, Agricultural, Hotel, Restaurant, Catering, Tobacco, and Allied Workers' Associations (IUF, 1920); International Federation of Journalists (1926); International Federation of Air Line Pilots' Associations (1948); International Federation of Musicians (1948); Federation of International Civil Servants' Associations (1952); International Federation of Actors (1952); Fédération Internationale des Associations de Footballeurs Professionels (1965); International Affiliation of Writers' Guilds (1986); Education International (1992); International Arts and Entertainment Alliance (1997); UNI (Union Network International) Global Union (2000); Building and Wood Workers' International (2005); International Domestic Workers Federation (2009); IndustriALL Global Union (2012). See Wikipedia, s.v. "global union federation," last modified October 20, 2022, https://wikipedia.org/wiki/Global_union_federation; AFLCIO, "Global Labor Unions and Federations," accessed June 9, 2021, www.aflcio.org/about-us/our-unions-and-allies /global-unions.

81.　Tosstorff 2005: 400; Dunning 1998: 153. The IFTU was a leading lobbyist for the subsequent creation of the ILO.

82.　Dunning 1998: 159.

83.　See Gordon 2000b on the ICFTU. The umbrella ICFTU signed the Milan Agreement with ITSs in 1951 (subsequently revised in 1969 and 1991), which recognized the secretariats' autonomy (Rütters n.d.: 14–15).

84.　Frundt (1996: 388–89, 398–407) discusses the cases of the National Labor Committee Education Fund in Support of Worker and Human Rights in El Salvador (formed in 1981) and the U.S. Guatemala Labor Education Project (formed in 1987), both of which received strong support from major U.S. unions. UNITE HERE! helped form the United Students Against Sweatshops (USAS) (interview with a USAS national coordinator, May 27, 2008, Washington, DC). Waterman (2001: 317) characterizes trade unions that regularly ally with civil society organizations as "social movement unions." See also Kidder and McGinn 1995; Frege, Heery, and Turner 2004.

85.　The International Labor Rights Education and Research Fund was established in 1986; it was renamed in 1996.

86.　Other important labor- and human-rights NGOs active in the 1980s and 1990s included (listed by founding date): Solidar (Brussels; formed as International Workers' Aid in 1948 and renamed in 1995), Asia Monitor Resource Centre (Hong Kong, 1976), Human Rights Watch (New York City, 1978), Human Rights First (New York City, 1978), National

Labor Committee (New York City, 1980), and International Centre for Trade Union Rights (London, 1987) (Compa 2003b: 295–300). See Frundt 1996: 396 on U.S. union support for the CJM.

87. Hale 2004: 159–60.

88. Connor 2004.

89. Eade (2004: 74–76, 78–79) discusses Oxfam's financial and advisory support for Honduran unions during the 1980s.

90. Macfarlane 1967: 132.

91. Southall 1994: 168–71, 189–94; Gordon 2000b: 92–93.

92. Feeley 1990; Reuters 1990; La Botz 1992: 150–52; Carr 1996: 217; McGaughey Jr. et al. 1991. In addition, some 1,200 workers at Ford's Chihuahua, Mexico, plant temporarily suspended production.

93. Jessup and Gordon 2000. For a similar campaign against Phillips Van-Heusen in Guatemala, see Traub-Werner and Cravey 2002.

94. Castree 2000: 281–83.

95. Gordon and Turner 2000: 10, 13; Gordon 2000a: 61. See Johns 1998: 256 for a critique of international solidarity actions that prioritize "accommodative space" ("reasserting the dominance of a particular group of workers within capitalism's spatial structures") over transformatory class solidarity.

96. Anner 2003: 621. For a similar example involving Canadian automobile workers' support for a strike at a General Motors plant in Flint, Michigan, see Herod 2000: 537–38.

From the mid-1960s through the mid-1990s, unions representing workers in the metalworking, electronics, chemical, and food processing industries sought to establish "world company councils" within transnational firms in order to share information on wages and working conditions and thereby increase national unions' bargaining leverage vis-à-vis company subsidiaries (Fetzer 2010: 80–81). For instance, the "Ford Exchange" initiated by the Canadian Auto Workers linked Ford workers in Canada, Brazil, and South Africa (Anner 2003: 623). European Union Directive no. 94/95/CE (September 22, 1994) established works councils in the largest European firms in order to ensure trade unionists' rights to information and consultation. For assessments of their consequences for labor cooperation, see Schulten 1996, Hancké 2000, Wills 2001.

97. For examples, see Herod 1995: 350–51; Jessup and Gordon 2000: 189–90; Zinn 2000: 229, 234–35; Anner 2003: 623.

98. Windmuller 2000: 113–15. See, however, Gordon and Turner 2000: 17–18 (in 1969, the ICEM created a worldwide strike fund to support coordinated bargaining with Compagnie de Saint-Gobin, a French transnational construction materials manufacturer) and Frundt 2007: 102, 104 (the IUF signed the 1999 Guatemalan banana workers' contract with Del Monte Foods). The regional affiliates established by ITSs/GUFs since 1950 are often more directly involved in training union organizers, preparing for collective bargaining in a specific company, and identifying legislative priorities for national unions.

99. Gordon 2000b: 87–89, 91, 93–96. For instance, the ITUC publishes an "Annual Survey of Violations of Trade Union Rights" (https://www.ituc-csi.org/annual-survey-of -violations-of,271; accessed June 28, 2021) and a "Global Rights Index." See Bieler 2012: 369–70 on the ITUC-led transnational solidarity campaign for a "fairer globalization" titled "Decent Work, Decent Life."

100. At the request of the United Mine Workers of America and the International Metal-workers' Federation, the ICFTU became actively involved in resolving the 1989 conflict with the Pittston coal company, a dispute with a multisector international company that directly engaged the principles of freedom of association and the right to collective bargaining (Gordon 2000b: 97).

101. Stevis and Boswell 2007, Schömann et al. 2008, Papadakis 2011. Wills (2002: 686) reproduces the framework agreement between the IUF and Accor, a French-owned international hotel group. The framework agreement that the International Transport Workers Federation negotiated for maritime workers was unusual in that it globally set minimum wage rates, overtime rates, and standards for accommodation and safety (Anner et al. 2006: 16). National unions are sometimes cosignatories to these agreements.

102. Helfen and Fichter 2013: 557; Wills 2002: 682, 684, 691–94. Frundt (2007: 104) discusses the advantages that banana workers in Colombia and Costa Rica (but not Guatemala) gained from the framework agreement that the IUF negotiated with Chiquita Brands International. See also Riisgaard 2005: 718–30. Other assessments of the impact of these agreements include Wills 2002, Niforou 2012, McCallum 2013, Fichter and McCallum 2015.

103. Niforou 2012: 363–64, 370.

104. For studies that illustrate obstacles such as those summarized here, see Cox 1971: 558–59, 567; Johns 1998: 262–66; Castree 2000: 278–79, 281; Fetzer 2010: 82, 83, 85–89; Gordon and Turner 2000: 22–23; Servais 2000: 45–53; Anner and Evans 2004: 38–39; Lillie and Martínez Lucio 2004: 160, 162–64, 175–76; Brecher, Costello, and Smith 2006: 11–15; Young and Sierra Becerra 2014: 252–54; interviews with a senior representative of the United Automobile, Aerospace, and Agricultural Implement Workers of America, August 7, 1995, and U.S. trade union representative A, June 25, 2018, both in Washington, DC. Cox (1971: 554–55, 569) notes that during the Cold War, labor internationalism was sometimes linked to, and subsumed by, national governments' foreign policies.

105. Borgers 1999: 109; Dreiling and Robinson 1998: 180; Hyman 2010: 20, 23; Zweig 2014: 276, 278. See also Brookes 2019: 31–34 on intraunion coordination in transnational labor alliances.

106. See chapters 2 and 4. One such case was the Bibong campaign noted above, in which the American Federation of Labor-Congress of Industrial Organizations (AFL-CIO) cited the ongoing Bibong conflict in its July 1993 U.S. GSP filing against the Dominican Republic (Jessup and Gordon 2000: 194). Similarly, the trinational (United States-Canada-Mexico) Echlin Workers' Alliance initiated a NAALC public submission in 1997 to protest violations of freedom of association and workplace safety and health at Echlin, Inc.'s automotive brake system manufacturing plant in Mexico. See also Armbruster-Sandoval 2003: 567–69 on the protracted labor rights campaign against Kimi de Honduras, a South Korean-owned garment producer.

107. The ILO's chief organs are: the annual International Labour Conference (comprised of four delegates from each member state, two representing its government and one representative each from its most prominent labor and employer organizations); the governing body (comprised of twenty-eight government representatives and fourteen labor and fourteen employer representatives; with the exception of ten government representatives from the member states with the largest economies, all governing body

members are elected to three-year terms by the conference); and the International Labour Office (the secretariat managed by the director-general, who is also elected by the conference). In 2020–2021, the office had a total operating budget of US$796.4 million (in constant 2018–2019 US$) and employed 3,381 officials (1,698 of them in technical cooperation programs) in 107 countries, including some forty field offices (International Labour Organization, "How the ILO Works," accessed July 31, 2021, https://www.ilo.org /global/about-the-ilo/how-the-ilo-works/lang--en/index.htm). For overviews of the ILO's organizational evolution, governance structure, and decision-making processes, see De la Cruz, von Potobsky, and Swepston 1996; Helfer 2006: 671–720; Baccaro and Mele 2012: 197–98.

108.   For the full titles of the ILO conventions cited here, see https://www.ilo.org/global /standards/introduction-to-international-labour-standards/conventions-and -recommendations/lang--en/index.htm.

109.   In 2021, the ILO had 187 members, all but seven of the 193 United Nations member states (Andorra, Bhutan, Democratic People's Republic of Korea, Liechtenstein, Micronesia, Monaco, Nauru) plus the Cook Islands; See Baccini and Koenig-Archibugi 2014 on the factors shaping member states' decisions to ratify ILO conventions. More members have ratified convention number 182 ("Worst Forms of Child Labour," 1999) than any other.

110.   The exception in this regard is international marine transport (Edgren 1979: 527).

111.   The ILO has, for instance, periodically adopted public declarations on major issues, including the Declaration Concerning the Policy of "Apartheid" of the Republic of South Africa (1964), the Declaration on Equality of Opportunity and Treatment of Women Workers (1975), the Tripartite Declaration of Principles Concerning Multinational Enterprises and Social Policy (1977, revised in 2017), and the Declaration on Social Justice for a Fair Globalization (2008). In addition, it has proposed nonbinding codes of practice on such issues as occupational safety and health (Rodgers et al. 2009: 22).

112.   Some of these measures were subsequently withdrawn, and the substantive content of others was updated or replaced by later conventions. For example, the Maritime Labour Convention (2006) consolidated thirty-nine preceding conventions that addressed a range of specific issues affecting seafarers. In 2021, the ILO characterized eighty conventions as "up-to-date" instruments. It classified sixty conventions, adopted between 1919 and 1996, as "outdated." Seventeen others had been abrogated or withdrawn. The remaining conventions required revision or further action, or had an interim, pending, or some other status. See International Labour Organization, accessed August 20, 2021, https://www.ilo.org/wcmsp5/groups/public/---ed_norm /---normes/documents/publication/wcms_413175.pdf.

In 2021, the ILO's own thematic categorization of its "up-to-date" conventions (in alphabetical order, with the number of related conventions in parentheses) was: dockworkers (1); elimination of child labor and protection of children and young persons (5); employment policy and promotion (4); equality of opportunity and treatment (3); final articles (concerning the revision of conventions: (2); fishers (1); forced labor (2); freedom of association, collective bargaining, and industrial relations (6); indigenous and tribal peoples (1); labor administration and inspection (5); maternity protection (1); migrant workers (2); occupational safety and health (13); seafarers (11); social policy (1); social security (7); specific categories of workers (including domestic workers, hotel and

restaurant workers, nursing personnel, and plantation workers: (5); tripartite consultation (1); vocational guidance and training (2); wages (3); and working time (4). See International Labour Organization, accessed August 20, 2021, https://www.ilo.org/wcmsp5
/groups/public/---ed_norm/---normes/documents/publication/wcms_413175.pdf.

113.   The ILC adopted the declaration by a vote of 273 delegates in favor, none against, and
forty-three abstentions (Maupin 2000: 387–88). The ILO took this action following the
defeat in 1996 of proposals calling for the World Trade Organization to adopt a "social
clause" and the WTO's reaffirmation that the ILO was the appropriate international body
to address such questions (Baccaro and Mele 2012: 203–4; chapter 2). For a critical debate
concerning the declaration and its implications for the international labor rights regime,
see Alston 2004 and Langille 2005.

114.   The declaration stated, "In freely joining the ILO, all Members endorsed the principles
and rights set out in its Constitution and in the Declaration of Philadelphia" (point 1).
Most notably, these included the freedom of association and the right to collective
bargaining. In response to concerns raised by developing countries such as Egypt,
Mexico, and Pakistan (Rodgers et al. 2009: 221), the declaration further clarified that
"labour standards should not be used for protectionist trade purposes. . . . The comparative advantage of any country should in no way be called into question by this Declaration and its follow-up" (point 5).

115.   In 1969, the ILO received the Nobel Peace Prize "for creating international legislation
insuring certain norms for working conditions in every country." As of 2021, 147 member
states had ratified all eight of the core conventions cited in the 1998 declaration; another
fourteen states had ratified seven of them.

116.   Even the ILO's staunchest defenders recognize that it is difficult to precisely measure
different states' compliance with ILO-defined international labor standards and that
there is rarely full compliance with ILO conventions (Rodgers et al. 2009: 23).

117.   Member states are required to submit reports every two years on their compliance with
all eight of the fundamental conventions listed in the 1998 declaration.

118.   ILO Constitution (1946), arts. 19.5(b, e), 22, 24(1), 26(1) (International Labour Organization,
accessed August 20, 2021, https://www.ilo.org/dyn/normlex/en/f?p=1000:62:0::NO:62:P62
_LIST_ENTRIE_ID:2453907:NO); von Potobsky 1998: 200–201, 206; Lim n.d.: sect. 5.3.1
(box 4). In the second instance, complaints may be examined by an independent commission of inquiry appointed by the governing body. After reviewing the commission's
recommendations, the government that is the object of the complaint informs the ILO
whether it accepts them or proposes to bring the matter to the International Court of
Justice, whose ruling is final (ILO Constitution, arts. 26(3), 27–29, 31).

　　The ILO has also proactively undertaken practical initiatives to advance the implementation of international labor standards by devoting significant efforts to building
government labor enforcement capabilities in developing countries. In addition, it
assists member states in drafting labor legislation that meets international standards.
On the ILO's wide-ranging technical assistance programs, see Hughes and Haworth 2011:
14–15, 29–31.

119.   These complaints may be filed by either a worker or employer organization in the country concerned, international organizations of workers or employers when one of their
members is directly involved, or international worker and employer organizations and

nongovernmental organizations with consultative status at the ILO. Between 1952 and 2018, the CFA reviewed more than 3,300 complaints (ILO 2019: Annex, p. 2). In 2006, the ILO published a chronological listing (by country) of the cases the CFA had reviewed up until then (ILO 2006).

120. von Potobsky 1998: 212–14.

121. As von Potobsky (1998: 221) observes, "International public pressure is the ILO's most powerful weapon, for the ILO does not have the power to sanction and its Constitution does not allow it to exclude a State in punishment for the violation of international labour standards or principles." However, under the ILO Constitution (arts. 29, 31), a member state that rejects the findings of a commission of inquiry and appeals the matter to the International Court of Justice is bound by the court's final decision.

122. Hall 1997: 594.

123. Simmons 2009: 357, 359–65; Evans 2000: 232.

124. von Potabsky 1998: 214–15.

125. von Potobsky 1998: 215, 217. See also Portela and Orbie 2014: 71 on the ILO's role in Belarus.

126. This discussion draws on Maupin 2005: 95–107.

127. ILO 1999: point 3(a). Under the terms of the resolution, the ILO suspended Myanmar from participation in all ILO meetings and access to its technical assistance programs. At the same time, the ILO requested that member states and international governmental organizations review their relations with Myanmar (Maupin 2005: 99).

128. Helfer 2006: 713; Kryvoi 2008: 232; Portela and Orbie 2014: 67. Following the U.S. ban on imports from Myanmar, more than 130 international clothing retailers adopted policies not to source products from the country (Mathiason 2007).

129. These initiatives included the Organization for Economic Co-Operation and Development's Guidelines for Multinational Enterprises (1976, revised in 2011), the ILO's Tripartite Declaration of Principles Concerning Multinational Enterprises and Social Policy, the ICFTU's Basic Code of Conduct Covering Labour Practices (1977), and, in 2000, the United Nations Global Compact.

130. This discussion focuses on CCCs that address labor rights. Similar initiatives have been undertaken on a range of issues, including broad human rights (including human trafficking) and environmental questions, corruption in business transactions, private investment strategy, the production and sale of antipersonnel mines and cluster munitions, and sustainable food production. Industry-specific CCCs have been formulated to govern electronics manufacturing, forestry, gold and diamond mining, and the cotton, cocoa, and palm oil industries.

131. On the FLA, see Anner 2012: 615–17. Elliott and Freeman (2003: 67) also report initial U.S. government financial support for the FLA. On the ETI, see Blowfield 2002 and Knudsen and Moon 2017: 115–16. For overall assessments of CCCs, see Compa and Hinchliffe-Darricarrère 1995; Jenkins 2002; Bartley 2007.

132. Compa 2003b: 301, 311; O'Rourke 2003: 11–20. Lipschutz (2004: table 2) provides a list of those organizations active in regulatory initiatives in the global apparel industry in early 2000s.

133. For example, although the MSN served as secretariat for Canada's Ethical Trading Action Group (1998–2010), its core members included the Canadian Labour Congress, Canadian

Auto Workers, United Steelworkers-Canada, Canadian Union of Public Employees, and UNITE HERE! (Maquila Solidarity Network, "Ethical Trading Action Group," accessed July 17, 2021, https:// https://en.archive.maquilasolidarity.org/about/etag).

134. Trade unions have often expressed concern that voluntary CCCs will be viewed as a substitute for stronger national labor legislation and clearly defined international labor standards (Jenkins 2002: 14; see also Justice 2002; Braun and Gearhart 2004; Compa 2004: 213). Compa (2004: 211) cites examples of successful union–NGO alliances addressing child labor and occupational safety and health issues and violence against trade unionists. See also Anner 2000: 247–48.

135. Zandvliet and van der Heijden (2015: 177–78) examine references to ILO labor standards in CCCs between 1998 and 2006. They find that references to occupational safety and health and workplace discrimination were most common, while references to wages and freedom of association were least common. Firms adopting CCCs were often very selective in how they framed ILO standards. See also Diller 1999: 112–17; Anner 2012: 610–12, 614.

136. Bair and Ramsay 2003: 59.

137. See, for example, Anner 2000: 242, 248; Anner et al. 2006: 21–22; Seidman 2007: 6, 15, 17, 34. Keck and Sikkink (1998: 27) emphasize the importance of how transnational activists frame the "causal story" in organizing effective campaigns. Elliott and Freeman (2003: table 2.1, p. 30) cite a 1999 Marymount University opinion poll showing greater public opposition to U.S. imports of goods made by children (under force or without the chance of attending school) than those made by workers who are not allowed to unionize.

138. These campaigns constitute examples of what Keck and Sikkink (1998: 24) term "accountability politics"; see also Moran 2002: 87–88. One particularly compelling example of NGO strategy in this regard was the People's Tribunal that the Clean Clothes Campaign organized in Brussels in 1998 to hear evidence about labor rights abuses and exploitative working conditions in suppliers to seven brand-name apparel firms (Shaw 2004: 170).

139. The Rana Plaza accord built upon the precedent established in 2012 by an agreement between PVH Corp., a U.S. apparel company (formerly Phillips-Van Heusen Corporation) whose holdings included the Tommy Hilfiger and Calvin Klein brands, and the ITGLWF, CCC, ILRF, MSN, WRC, and seven Bangladeshi trade unions and NGOs. The agreement established independent building inspections, the public disclosure of inspection reports, worker rights training, and a general review of safety standards in garment factories. See Maquila Solidarity Network 2012a.

140. Reinecke and Donaghey 2015: 257, 263–64, 269; Knudsen and Moon 2017: 124. The ILO chaired the accord's tripartite steering committee, which enhanced the credibility of the agreement. A revised agreement was later formally extended through October 2023 (Cochrane 2021); as of January 2022, a total of 160 brand-name companies had acceded to the new accord (MSN electronic communication, January 10, 2022).

141. Miller 2004: 220–22; Barrientos and Smith 2007: 720. For a summary of the principal points of divergence among multistakeholder CCCs in the mid-2000s, see Maquila Solidarity Network 2008b: 9–11. For an overall assessment of the factors shaping the effectiveness of CCCs and other nongovernmental forms of economic regulation, see Mayer and Gereffi 2010.

142. Shaw 2004: 175; Kearney and Gearhart 2004: 218-21; Compa 2004: 212, 215; Anner et al. 2006: 23; Barrientos and Smith 2007: 720-23; Kim 2013: 287, 289-90; Bartley and Egels-Zandén 2016: 241-48. Greenhill, Mosley, and Prakash (2009: 669, 673, 679-81) identify CCCs and global production networks as important mechanisms for the trade-based diffusion of collective labor rights, but their statistical model does not directly test the impact of these elements.

143. For example, Lipschultz (2004: 204-7) reports that the CSR campaign against Nike led to improvements in working conditions in its global network of some six hundred subcontractors. However, he finds little evidence of "spillover" beyond individual factories, at the sectoral level—that is, improvements in host country enforcement of ILO conventions, increased public and private support for unionization, or reduced restrictions on freedom of association and the right to collective bargaining. Similarly, Vogel (2006: 77-82) concludes that the improvements at Nike principally involved enhanced occupational safety and health protections, increased wages, and reduced reliance on child labor.

144. Vogel 2006: 96-97, 99; Anner 2012: 623; Knudsen and Moon 2017: 113.

145. Vogel 2006: 101; Barrientos and Smith 2007: 720-23; Locke 2013: 18, 20-21. Anner (2012: 615-24) carefully assesses factory audits conducted by the Fair Labor Association (the largest CSR program in the global garment industry) and concludes that its monitoring efforts generally fail to identify violations concerning freedom of association, the right to collective bargaining, and the right to strike. The FLA code of conduct does not characterize freedom of association and the right to collective bargaining as "zero-tolerance" issues as it does prohibitions against child and forced labor.

146. Maquila Solidarity Network 2008b: 9; Pekdemir, Glasbergen, and Cörvers 2015: 220-21. For example, Nike's code of conduct states that, "To the extent permitted by the laws of the manufacturing country, the contractor respects the right of its employees to freedom of association and collective bargaining" (reproduced in Locke 2013: 71). The Nike code contains similar provisions concerning compensation and working hours (71-72).

147. In the case of Bangladesh, extensive CSR campaigns concerning working conditions in the garment industry paralleled the U.S. government's decision to suspend the country's GSP benefits in 2013. The decision, in response to a complaint filed by the AFL-CIO in 2007 but taken in the immediate aftermath of the Rana Plaza tragedy, induced the Bangladeshi government to adopt labor law reforms that somewhat eased restrictions on freedom of association (Greenhouse 2013a, 2013b; International Labor Rights Forum 2015: 31; Knudsen and Moon 2017: 126-28).

148. One could argue that the United States, which since the 1950s has been the most vocal national advocate of linking labor standards to trade agreements, has exercised considerable influence over the international trade policy agenda by insisting on this linkage in the preferential trade agreements it negotiated after 1984. On agenda setting as a form of power, see Bachrach and Baratz 1962: 948-49.

149. Goertz and Mahoney 2012: 87-88.

150. Gerring (2004: 341) defines a case study as an "in-depth study of a single unit (a relatively bounded phenomenon)." See also Gerring 2007: 211.

151. See George and Bennett 2005: 122-23 for a discussion of "most likely" and "least likely" cases.

152.   Falleti and Lynch 2009: 1145-51; Pouliot 2015: 253.

153.   In Gerring's words (2007: 72), "One side of the causal equation is open-ended."

154.   See Gerring 2007: 71-72 and Eckstein 1975: 104-108, respectively, for discussions of exploratory and heuristic case studies.

155.   Dunning (2015: 215) defines process-tracing as "a procedure for developing knowledge of context, sequence, or process." On process-tracing as a research methodology, see George and Bennett 2005: 6, 13, 208-15, 231; Gerring 2007: 173, 178, 216; Bennett and Checkel 2015.

156.   On purposive sampling in qualitative research, see Bryman 2012: chap. 18.

157.   For this reason, the interviews were not recorded.

2. PATHWAYS TO THE NORTH AMERICAN AGREEMENT ON LABOR COOPERATION: FROM MULTILATERAL PROPOSALS TO UNILATERAL ACTIONS LINKING LABOR RIGHTS AND TRADE AGREEMENTS

1.   Advocates of this linkage include Collingsworth, Goold, and Harvey 1994; Elliott 1998a; Howse 1999; Wilkensen 1999: 183-86; Elliott and Freeman 2003: 89-92; and Barry and Reddy 2008; opponents include Bhagwati 1995, 2004: 247-52; Golub 1997; and D. Brown 2001: 107, 110. For overviews of the debate, see Tsogas 2001: chap. 1; van Roozendaal 2002: chap. 3; Trebilcock and Howse 2005; Bhatnagar and Mishra 2008-2009: 195-201, *passim*. Alston (1982: 175-79) and Leary (1996a: 188-96) review debates within the International Labour Organization since the early 1970s concerning the linkage.

2.   Examples include Hansson 1983: 168-73, 183; Organization for Economic Co-Operation and Development 1996; Busse 2002; and Carrère, Olarreaga, and Raess 2017.

3.   The United Nations Conference on Trade and Development (UNCTAD) recognized the GSP concept in 1968. In response, the General Agreement on Tariffs and Trade (GATT) subsequently adopted a ten-year waiver to its underpinning "most favored nation" principle (art. 1) in 1971, and in 1979 it approved an "enabling clause" that made the exception permanent ("Decision on Differential and More Favorable Treatment, Reciprocity and Fuller Participation of Developing Countries"). See Pease and Goold 1985: 360; Jones 2015: 3-5.

4.   See, for example, the May 1970 statement by the United Automobile, Aerospace, and Agricultural Implement Workers of America (UAW) in U.S. House of Representatives 1970 (part 6, May 22 and June 1): 1719, 1722. See also the statement by U.S. Senator Thomas R. Harkin (Democrat-Iowa) as cosponsor of a bill preceding the Omnibus Trade and Competitiveness Act of 1988 (quoted in Ballon 1987: 116).

5.   Charnovitz (1987: 568-70) discusses U.S. tariff legislation adopted in the 1920s and the 1930s that linked trade and various labor issues. For instance, the Tariff Act of 1922 (Fordney-McCumber) and Tariff Act of 1930 (Smoot-Hawley) authorized the president to adjust import tariffs "to equalize the differences in the costs of production [including labor costs] between a domestic article and a similar foreign article from the principal competing country" (568). These provisions were employed extensively in the early 1930s.

Similarly, the United Kingdom's Safeguarding of Industries Act (1921) permitted compensatory tariffs against lower-cost imported goods produced under "inferior conditions of employment of labour, whether as respects remuneration or hours of employment, or otherwise" (United Kingdom Board of Trade 1925, section II, point 5[c]).

6. Since at least 1950, some proponents of international labor standards legislation have argued that such measures would actually promote trade by establishing a floor for worker protection that would challenge a common justification for import restrictions in high-standards countries. The World Bank-sponsored Independent Commission on International Development Issues (the Brandt Commission) adopted this same logic in its final recommendations in 1980. See Hansson 1983: 171, 173–75; Charnovitz 1987: 567.

7. In the words of Ron Blackwell, then the director of corporate affairs at the American Federation of Labor-Congress of Industrial Organizations (AFL-CIO), "Protectionism is a core mission of unions and all sorts of social organizations. They must protect themselves and their members from the brutality of the marketplace. . . . We are obliged to respect the demand of workers to protect their jobs and living conditions" (2002: 71).

8. Hansson 1983: 11–14; Follows 1951.

9. Hansson 1983: 15–22; Charnovitz 1994a: 22; Huberman 2012: table 4.1. For instance, the International Labour Office (established in 1901 in Berne, Switzerland) held international conferences in 1905 and 1906 on the use of white phosphorus and night work by women in attempts to "equalise costs of production and standardize [national] legislation" (Hansson 1983: 17).

10. International Labour Office, "Treaty of Versailles, Part XIII ('Labour'), section 1," accessed July 9, 2023, https://www.ilo.org/wcmsp5/groups/public/---dgreports/---jur /documents/genericdocument/wcms_441862.pdf.

11. Hansson 1983: 19–22; Treaty of Versailles, part XIII, art. 419.

12. Even earlier, the World Economic Conference organized by the League of Nations in 1927 had debated the social problems caused by the export of products whose international competitiveness was based on low labor standards (Charnovitz 1987: 566). See Charnovitz 1987: 567 for references to other proposals from the 1930s through the early 1950s to link trade policy and fair labor standards.

13. Charnovitz 1987: 575. Several Latin American governments made similar proposals at this time (567, 576).

   Emil Rieve, general president of the Textile Workers Union of America, prepared a statement titled "International Labor Standards, a Key to World Security" for the San Francisco Conference on the United Nations Charter that called for an expansive, detailed, and mandatory World Labor Charter ("a basic international code of fair labor practices") that "shall become the qualification for participation in world affairs," including world trade. The pamphlet was reprinted in U.S. House of Representatives 1945: 517–23 (see esp. pp. 522–23).

14. U.S. Department of State 1946: 24; United Nations 1946: 3–4.

15. Charnovitz and Wickham 1995: 112–13.

16. Records from the Preparatory Committee of the United Nations Conference on Trade and Employment (hereinafter PCUNCTE) are available at: https://www.wto.org/gatt _docs/1946_50.htm. See documents E/PC/T/C.I/10, pp. 1–2; E/PC/T/C.I/7, p. 1.

17. See PCUNCTE documents E/PC/T/C.II/16, p. 1; E/PC/T/C.II/PV/9, pp. 9, 11–12, 14–20, 24–26; E/PC/T/C.II/PV/4, p. 10; E/PC/T/C.II/27, p. 3.

18. Cited in Charnovitz 1987: 577.

19. United Nations 1948: chapter 2, article 7(1). The Preparatory Committee had adopted very similar language at its meetings in London (United Nations 1946: part II, chapter 1, section D, and p. 27).

20. Charnovitz 1987: 581; see also U.S. Senate 1947: 120. The exception again involved goods produced by convict or prison labor (United Nations 1948: 33-34). The provision regarding goods produced by prison labor had been part of all ITO deliberations, beginning with the first U.S. draft charter in November 1945 (U.S. Department of State 1945b: 18). The importation of such goods was prohibited by domestic legislation adopted in the United States (1890, 1930), Canada (1894), the United Kingdom (1897), Australia (1901), and other countries. The U.S. Trade Act of 1930 (subtitle II, pt. 1, sec. 307) did, however, exempt those goods for which the import demand could not be met by domestic production—an exemption that was finally removed in 2015 (Urbina 2016).

21. Aaronson 1996: 69-71, 75; Diebold 1952: 6; Toye 2012: 97; Gardner 1980: 374-76; Charnovitz 1987: 581. See also United Nations 1946: 5 and U.S. Senate 1947: 962 (exhibit VI-B), 997 (exhibit VI-C).

22. Aaronson 1996: 114-29; Diebold 1952: 6.

23. Aaronson 1996: 130-31.

24. The GATT's article XXIX did enjoin member states to observe "to the fullest extent of their executive authority" principles articulated in the Havana Charter, including Chapter II, article 7. However, no labor rights complaint was ever lodged under this provision (Charnovitz 1986: 73n54).

25. This discussion focuses principally on multilateral and bilateral trade agreements. It is, however, important to note that, beginning with the International Tin Agreement (1954), there were parallel efforts to embed labor standards provisions in several international commodity agreements. Article XV of the 1954 tin agreement stipulated, "In order to avoid the depression of living standards and the introduction of unfair competitive conditions in world trade, [the signatory parties] will seek to ensure fair labour standards in the tin industry" (https://treaties.fcdo.gov.uk/data/Library2/pdf/1956-TS0050 .pdf). Similarly broad provisions, without specific investigative procedures or sanctions, were included in the International Sugar Agreement after 1968, the International Cocoa Agreement after 1975, and the International Rubber Agreement in 1979 (Kullmann 1980: 527, 529-31).

26. Charnovitz 1987: 574-75; Alben 2001: 1432-38. In a parallel action, in 1954, the U.S. Commission on Foreign Economic Policy (the Randall Commission) recommended that the United States grant no tariff concessions on products made by foreign workers who were paid "substandard" wages (that is, wage levels below the accepted standards in the exporting country) (Charnovitz 1986: 64).

27. The IMF resolution is reproduced as Exhibit Three in U.S. House of Representatives 1970 (part 6): 1726-27. The IMF standard for determining unjustifiably low wage levels was "total hourly labor costs in the exporting firm substantially below the average for its industry in the exporting country; or both hourly and unit labor costs in the exporting firm unjustifiably below those of the same industry in the complaining country." The IMF also called on each GATT member state to file an annual report on "their own development of wages and working conditions in those industries in which tariff

concessions have been granted by other countries or in which increased export trade has resulted in market disruption in an importing nation or nations."

28.   Edgren 1979: 532–33; Hansson 1983: 25–26. In June 1988, the IMF attempted to organize an international campaign in favor of adding a labor rights provision to the GATT (Amato 1990: 92n81).

29.   Mintzes (1960: 1025) reports on a meeting of U.S. and West European trade unionists in March 1960 in which the delegation from the AFL-CIO lobbied for labor standards provisions in the GATT, while West Europeans advocated direct assistance to unions in developing countries to improve labor conditions there. The AFL-CIO representatives argued that GATT provisions of this kind would offset protectionist pressures from U.S. unions affected by imports, particularly in the automobile and textile industries. In order to reassure their West European colleagues that such provisions would not be employed to block exports to the United States, the U.S. unionists affirmed that any GATT provisions would employ moral suasion rather than punitive sanctions. See also Hansson 1983: 24–25; Amato 1990: 92.

30.   Charnovitz 1986: 65.

31.   Testimony by Andres Biemiller (director, Department of Legislation, AFL-CIO) and Nathaniel Goldfinger (director, Department of Research, AFL-CIO) in U.S. House of Representatives 1970 (part 4, May 19 and June 11): 1015, 1017.

32.   Total exports and imports (in constant 1972 U.S. dollars) represented 9.4 percent of U.S. gross national product in 1960 and 12.6 percent in 1970 (U.S. Council of Economic Advisers 1982: table B-2). This proportion was substantially lower than in other advanced industrial countries such as Canada, the Federal Republic of Germany, France, Great Britain, and Japan (Odell 1982: 213n45). Of course, the proportional significance of international trade varied across different U.S. economic sectors and industries.

33.   U.S. House of Representatives 1970 (part 4): 1010. 1014, 1022. See part 5 (20–21 May): 1270, 1273, 1312, 1316, and part 6: 1711, 1718–19, for supporting statements by representatives of several U.S. textile, clothing, and automobile workers' unions on the negative impact of imported goods produced under sweatshop conditions. The UAW statement in support of imposing labor-related conditions on imported goods specifically referred to "Mexican border industries" (part 6: 1723). See also the statements by representatives of U.S. textile, clothing, and garment workers' unions in U.S. House of Representatives 1973a (part 12, June 6–7): 3862, 3871, and Mandel 1989: 452.

34.   U.S. House of Representatives 1970 (part 4): 1014, 1023

35.   U.S. Office of the Special Trade Representative for Trade Negotiations 1969: 44.

36.   U.S. House of Representatives 1970 (part 4): 1022. Representative Wilbur Mills (Democrat-Arkansas), chair of the Committee on Ways and Means, asked, "If there was any way that this factor [fair labor standards] could be written into law in some way so as to bring a degree of compulsion on other countries to do something in the area, in return for access to this [U.S.] market" (U.S. House of Representatives 1970: 1023). See also the parallel comments by U.S. labor union leaders in U.S. House of Representatives 1970, part 6: 1786, 1933, and part 10: 2779, 2903–06, and U.S. House of Representatives 1973a (part 14, June 11): 4800, 4847.

37.   U.S. House of Representatives 1970 (part 4): 1017.

38.   The Trade Act of 1974 (Public Law 93-618) was enacted on January 3, 1975 and became operative on January 1, 1976. At that time, GSP provisions were also part of trade law in the European Community (1971), Japan (1971), Norway (1971) New Zealand (1972), Australia (1974), and Canada (1974) (World Trade Organization, "Preferential Trade Arrangements," accessed November 11, 2016, http://ptadb.wto.org/ptaList.aspx).

39.   U.S. House of Representatives 1973a (part 1, May 9): 84, 86–88; U.S. House of Representatives 1973b: 30. For statements on these issues by the AFL-CIO, the UAW (whose president, Leonard Woodcock, stipulated that the union still supported a liberal international trade regime, but that "to convince delegates elected by the rank and file in convention of the wisdom of that course . . . trade liberalization must be accompanied by measures that will protect workers and their families against victimization"; 849), and other U.S. labor organizations, see U.S House of Representatives 1973a (part 3, May 14–15): 849–52, 874; (part 4, May 16–17): 1275, 1285. For earlier UAW support for such action, see Fetzer 2010: 81.

40.   U.S House of Representatives 1973a (part 3): 874.

41.   U.S House of Representatives 1973a: 907; (part 4): 1285.

42.   U.S. House of Representatives 1973c: 14, 27. The House report maintained that GATT principles should address such issues as earnings, hours and conditions of employment, and complaint procedures through which affected parties (acting through their governments) could address problems of unfair labor practices.

      Nonetheless, the AFL-CIO and other U.S. labor organizations opposed (unsuccessfully) the final bill, both because they considered this provision inadequate protection against the threat that lower-cost imports posed to domestic wages, employment, and living standards and because the bill failed to restrict imports or limit overseas foreign investment by U.S. firms (*U.S. Congressional Record* 119 (1973): 36391, 40542–43).

43.   Some U.S. labor leaders recognized that arbitrarily high labor standards would not be appropriate, given the challenges faced by developing countries. See the statement by UAW President Woodcock in U.S House of Representatives 1973a (part Three, May 14–15): 907.

44.   Still, U.S. government efforts to embed labor standards provisions in the GATT did not cease. In June and September 1986, the U.S. delegation to the Preparatory Committee of the GATT, presumably acting in response to pressures from U.S. labor organizations, "requested the other parties to 'consider possible ways of dealing with worker rights issues in the GATT so as to ensure that expanded trade benefits all workers in all countries' " (Charnovitz 1987: 565; see also Pérez-López 1988: 277–81, 1990: 229) Nevertheless, the subject of worker rights was not addressed in the GATT's so-called Uruguay Round of trade negotiations (Charnovitz 1987: 565).

      In parallel initiatives, on October 28, 1983, and again on September 9, 1986, the European Parliament adopted resolutions calling for a "social clause" in the GATT. The 1983 resolution (art. 12) explicitly invoked article 7 of the Havana Charter as a precedent and model, and it highlighted the ILO conventions on freedom of association and the right to collective bargaining, discrimination in employment, and forced labor (European Parliament 1983: 284). The 1986 resolution reiterated this demand and, like contemporaneous U.S. initiatives regarding the GATT, condemned the "frequently degradingly low wages and lack of satisfactory social security systems in many countries" and the "persistent violation of recognized international labour standards in certain GATT contracting parties as a distortion of fair competition" (European Parliament 1986: 71 [sect. 11], 78 [sect. 64]). These resolutions did not, however, signify lasting regional consensus on the labor rights/trade question; in the mid-1990s, European states were sharply divided over the issue (see below).

45. Senate 1718 (August 1, 1983) in *U.S. Congressional Record* 129 (1983): 21875. In testimony before the Senate Subcommittee on International Trade (Committee on Finance) in January 1984, representatives of the AFL-CIO and Bread for the World (a Christian relief organization) advocated including labor rights provisions in the GSP legislation, but the Senate did not do so (U.S. Senate 1983–1984: 90, 291, 296–98).

46. Pease and Goold 1985: 365.

47. Public Law No. 98-67, sect. 212(c)(8), enacted on August 5, 1983 and in effect from January 1, 1984. The text of the original bill S. 2237 appears in *U.S. Congressional Record* 128 (1982): 4746–50. Labor conditions were one of eleven nonbinding conditions the president was to take into account in granting countries access to the U.S. market (Ballon 1987: 76).

48. House Resolution 5136, "GSP Renewal Act of 1984," March 14, 1984, in *U.S. Congressional Record* 130 (1984): 5544. One historical precedent was the 1942 decision by the United States Board of Economic Welfare to condition the awarding of procurement contracts for strategic materials on the foreign seller's compliance with various labor requirements. Similarly, in 1954, the administration of President Dwight D. Eisenhower (1953–1957, 1957–1961) adopted a policy under which it would "withhold reductions in tariffs on products made by workers receiving wages which are substandard in the exporting country" (Charnovitz 1987: 574, 579).

49. *U.S. Congressional Record* 130 (1984): 23069. Pease also argued that "the tremendous disparity in labor rights between many American workers and the absence of those rights for most workers in other countries is a growing factor in the competitive decline of many of our basic industries like steel, shipbuilding, and auto production as well as in less-skilled intensive industries like footwear, rubber goods, textiles, and electronics" (*U.S. Congressional Record* 130 (1984): 23068). For further comments on Pease's motives, see Pease and Goold 1985: 358–59, 365. In 1986, Pease founded the International Labor Rights Education and Research Fund (after 1996, the International Labor Rights Forum, ILRF) as a monitoring body to oversee the enactment of the trade agreement-linked labor rights provisions that he advocated (author's interview [hereinafter "interview"] with a senior ILRF official, July 6, 2005, Washington, DC).

50. The Bipartisan Trade Promotion Authority Act of 2002 expanded the list of protected labor rights to include a prohibition against the worst forms of child labor (ILO 2016: 31).

51. *U.S. Congressional Record* 130 (1984): 5546.

52. Compa and Vogt (2001: 199n1) list those labor organizations and labor rights groups involved in promoting the GSP initiative. They included the AFL-CIO, UAW, International Association of Machinists and Aerospace Workers, United Steelworkers, United Food and Commercial Workers International Union, and American Federation of Government Employees.

53. U.S. House of Representatives 1984a: 67–69. Critics of the GSP program argued that, by providing developing countries with duty-free access to the U.S. market, it encouraged U.S. companies to move labor-intensive production to lower-wage countries (Harvey n.d.: 1–2).

54.   House Resolution 6023 was approved by voice vote. It was later incorporated into
      House Resolution 3398 (approved on October 9, 1984 by a vote of 386–1, with forty-five
      representatives not voting) and became law on October 30, 1984, as Title V of the
      Trade and Tariff Act of 1984 (Public Law No. 98–573). The labor rights provisions are
      in section 503, amending section 502(a) of the Trade Act of 1974. The House-Senate
      Conference Report specifically recognized that labor standards should be "interpreted
      to be commensurate with the development level of the particular country" (Pérez-López
      1988: 270; see also p. 275).
           Alston (1993: 21) notes that the key phrase employed in the bill ("taking steps toward
      ensuring internationally recognized worker rights") closely paralleled the language used
      in article 2(1) of the United Nations Covenant on Economic, Social and Cultural Rights:
      "to take steps . . . with a view to achieving progressively the full realization of the rights
      recognized."

55.   See, for example, Ballon 1987: 75, 123, 125–26; Alston 1993: 28, 33. Mandel (1989: 460–61)
      argues that the measures were not protectionist because they focused on foreign labor
      conditions and did not require evidence of actual injury to U.S. industry. Amato (1990:
      88, 96–97) notes that programs such as the CBI and GSP granted nonreciprocal benefits
      to developing countries and therefore did not violate the "most favored nation" standard
      underpinning the GATT.

56.   Compa 1995a: 340–41n14; Compa and Vogt 2001: 205–6. The OPIC provides political risk
      insurance to U.S. companies investing internationally. Similar labor rights provisions
      were also included in the Multilateral Investment Guarantee Agency (MIGA) Act of
      1987 (Public Law No. 100–202, sect. 101) (Pérez-López 1990: 226–27).

57.   Kantor 1994: 16.

58.   OTCA (Public Law No. 100–418, enacted on August 23, 1988), sect. 1301/sect. 301(d)(3)(B)
      (iii)(I-V).

59.   Alston 1993: 4, 14; Mandel 1989: 466–68. However, unlike the GSP and OPIC legislation,
      the provisions of the OTCA include an injury requirement (evidence that an unrea-
      sonable act or practice constitutes a burden or restriction on U.S. trade). This could
      include the loss of U.S. jobs when manufacturing facilities relocate to countries whose
      production costs are lower because of lower labor standards. For the earlier legislative
      history of the changes made in section 301 in 1988 (in which Representative Pease and
      Senator Donald W. Riegle Jr. [Democrat-Michigan] played leading roles), see Ballon
      1987: 110–20.
           Under the terms of the OTCA, a foreign country's labor rights violations are not
      considered "unreasonable" and therefore subject to the full range of potential sanctions if
      that country "has taken, or is taking, actions that demonstrate a significant and tangible
      overall advancement" of worker rights, or if "such acts, policies, and practices are not
      inconsistent with the level of economic development of the foreign country" (sect. 1301/
      sect. 301(d)(3)(C)(i)(I, II)).
           The Reagan administration opposed the addition of labor rights provisions to sec-
      tion 301 on the grounds that, in the absence of international consensus regarding what
      constituted "unfair" labor practices and a labor rights provision in the GATT, applying
      the measure might provoke trade retaliation by other countries. The administration did,
      however, support those parts of the Pease and Riegle bills making the promotion of

worker rights a "principal negotiating objective" in the GATT. See Ballon 1987: 113–14, 119–20; Pérez-López 1990: 229; Public Law No. 100–418, sect. 1101(b)(14)(A–C).

60. Section 2202(8). See also sections 2207 and 6306(b)(1–2) concerning required reports by the U.S. Department of Labor on countries' recognition and enforcement of internationally recognized worker rights.

61. Indeed, the OTCA included a separate paragraph on worker rights in the section on "principal trade negotiating objectives." It required the U.S. government "(A) to promote respect for worker rights, (B) to secure a review of the relationship of worker rights to GATT articles, objectives, and related instruments with a view to ensuring that the benefits of the trading system are available to all workers, and (C) to adopt, as a principle of the GATT, that the denial of worker rights should not be a means for a country or its industries to gain competitive advantage in international trade" (section 1101[b][14] [A–C]).

     However, the OTCA requirement that petitions filed under section 301 demonstrate that labor rights violations in a U.S. trade partner produced economic injury (a burden or restriction on trade) to the United States, coupled with U.S. trade union calculations that the president would take maximum advantage of broad executive discretion over the imposition of trade sanctions to avoid the major diplomatic controversies that section 301 actions would involve, have significantly restricted the practical value of the measure as an avenue for addressing worker rights violations in other countries (Mandel 1989: 467–68; van Roozendahl 2002: 93).

62. Charnovitz 1987: 565; Pérez-López 1988: 277–81; Amato 1990: 92–95; Compa 1993a: 187n108; Waer 1996: 25, 27. For a brief discussion of U.S. labor standards initiatives before the GATT during the 1970s, see Pérez-López 1988: 258–59 and Charnovitz 1986: 65–66. For a list of the developing countries that opposed the United States' GATT initiative in 1986, see Pérez-López 1988: 280n79.

63. F. Weiss 1998: 95.

64. Section 131 of the Uruguay Round Agreements Act (Public Law 103–465, December 4, 1994), under which the U.S. Congress approved U.S. membership in the WTO, directed the president to seek creation of a WTO working group on labor rights.

65. Langille 1997: 30–31; Waer 1996: 25–26; Leary 1997: 120; ILO 2917: 19. Leading up to the Singapore conference, the ICFTU strongly endorsed adding a "social clause" to the WTO (Graubart 2008: 13). However, labor organizations in India and Singapore opposed the proposal (Wilkinson and Hughes 2000: 261).

66. Langille 1997: 48.

67. At the Singapore meeting, both supporters and opponents of a WTO labor standards clause found support in a study by the Organization for Economic Co-Operation and Development (OECD), which concluded: "The view which argues that low-standard countries will enjoy gains in export market shares to the detriment of high-standard countries appears to lack solid empirical support. . . . These findings also imply that any fear on the part of developing countries that better core standards would negatively affect either their economic performance or their competitive position in world markets has no economic rationale. On the contrary, it is conceivable that the observance of core standards would strengthen the long-term economic performance of all countries" (OECD 1996: 105).

68.   The text of Point 4 ("Core Labour Standards") of the Singapore Ministerial Declaration (December 13, 1996) is available at: World Trade Organization, accessed April 2, 2017, https://www.wto.org/english/thewto_e/minist_e/min96_e/wtodec_e.htm. Developing countries won a further victory in the WTO ministers' statement: "We reject the use of labour standards for protectionist purposes, and agree that the comparative advantage of countries, particularly low-wage developing countries, must in no way be put into question."

   Some observers maintain that the argument in favor of the ILO, rather than the GATT/WTO, as the appropriate forum for labor rights issues is simply a smokescreen for sovereignty concerns and that many countries prefer that these matters be addressed through the ILO precisely because it is a consensual body whose initiatives do not breach national sovereignty.

69.   Greenhouse and Kahn 1999; Anner 2001: 49, 53–57. For representative statements of the stance taken by developing countries, see Cuts International, "Third World Intellectuals and NGOs' Statement Against Linkage," June 1999, https://cuts-international.org/third-world-intellectuals-and-ngos-statement-against-linkage/; and Amorim 2000.

70.   Sanger 1999; Waer 1996: 33–34; Das 2000: 192. The ICFTU endorsed tariffs on imports from offending countries as a penalty for violations of core labor rights.

   The Seattle ministerial meeting was cancelled because of fears that developing countries, which protested industrialized countries' protection of their agricultural sectors and felt excluded from key decision-making processes, would reject any final agreement (Das 2000: 186–92).

   The controversy over a WTO "social clause" overlapped with an ongoing debate about whether existing GATT/WTO provisions could be employed to defend against unfair labor practices. See, for example, Alben 2001: 1416–23; Moorman 2001: 558–60; de Wet 1995: 456–60.

71.   World Trade Organization 2001: item 8. It was significant in this regard that the ILO's World Commission on the Social Dimensions of Globalization issued a communication in 2004 that omitted any reference to a WTO "social clause" or labor rights/trade linkage (Orbie, Vos, and Taverniers 2005: 169). In October 2021, U.S. congressional Democrats renewed calls for the United States to seek creation of a WTO working group "to examine the linkage of trade and internationally recognized worker rights" (*Inside U.S. Trade*, October 15, 2021).

72.   In 2021, the WTO listed thirty-two preferential trade agreements of different kinds; it classified sixteen of these as GSP programs (World Trade Organization, "Preferential Trade Agreements," accessed September 9, 2021, http://ptadb.wto.org/ptaList.aspx).

   In January 2021, the U.S. program included more than five thousand products (including some 1,500 products from forty-four "least-developed beneficiary developing countries") but excluded textiles, apparel, footwear, leather products, watches, ceramics, and import-sensitive electronic, glass and steel products. Beneficiaries included 119 developing countries and territories. In 2019, U.S. imports under the GSP program (US\$21 billion) accounted for 8.9 percent of imports from GSP-eligible countries and 0.94 percent of total imports (author's calculations based on data presented in Jones and Wong 2021: 1).

73. Countries whose GSP programs do not include specific labor-conditionality provisions may suspend or terminate beneficiaries for human rights abuses. For example, Norway excluded Myanmar from its program in 1997 on human rights grounds (Sekkel 2009: 12).

   Although the European Economic Community established a GSP program in July 1971, it was not until December 1994 that the European Council added labor rights provisions to the legislation. Beginning in 1995, the European Commission could withdraw trade preferences from countries found to have exported goods made by prison labor or to have engaged in "serious and systematic violations" of the ILO conventions (nos. 29 and 105) calling for the prohibition of forced or compulsory labor (Peers 1995: 92). The 1994 reform also introduced an incentive system under which the commission could further liberalize trade preferences for beneficiary countries that complied with ILO conventions nos. 87, 98, and 138 (concerning, respectively, the freedom of association, rights to organize and bargain collectively, and prohibition against child labor). However, when this provision finally came into effect in 1998, the associated trade benefits had been reduced (Orbie, Vos, and Taverniers 2005: 163–64, 166; Peers 1995: 93).

   In 2001, the European Council further expanded the labor rights provisions by requiring that beneficiary countries comply with all eight of the "fundamental" rights conventions highlighted by the ILO in 1998. Yet it was not until the 2005 renewal and modification of the scheme—by which time international consensus on labor rights had evolved considerably—that GSP beneficiary countries were actually required to ratify all eight of the ILO's "fundamental" conventions (Portela and Orbie 2014: 65; the human rights and labor conditions are listed in European Union 2012: annex VIII, part A). The practical impact of this more stringent requirement has been limited because many developing countries enjoy export access to the European Union market under more favorable preferential trade agreements such as the Lomé Convention (1976)/Cotonou Agreement (2000) or reciprocal free-trade agreements (Peers 1995: 81). The 2005 EU program also included a GSP Plus scheme that offers complete removal of tariffs to countries that comply with additional conditions of good governance and environmental protection, which are specified in European Union 2012: annex VIII, part B.

   On EU GSP review procedures, see European Union 2012: art. 19; European Union 2013: art. 7(1); Kryvoi 2008: 229; Portela and Orbie 2014: 66. For case studies of the application of these procedures involving Belarus and Myanmar, see Kryvoi 2008: 230–35; Portela and Orbie 2014: 67–68; Postnikov and Bastiaens 2014. Postnikov (2014) compares the design of social-standards provisions in EU and U.S. preferential trade agreements.

74. At the public hearings convened by the USTR in June 1985, U.S. unions and human rights groups had called for the removal of GSP eligibility from Chile, Guatemala, Haiti, the Republic of Korea, Nicaragua, Paraguay, the Philippines, Romania, Suriname, Taiwan, and Zaire (Pérez-López 1988: 272–73).

75. As noted above, the Generalized System of Preferences Renewal Act of 1984 required the USTR to conduct a two-year review of labor practices in all GSP beneficiary countries. The legislation also authorized the USTR to initiate its own reviews, but, with few exceptions (for example, Guatemala in 2000; DiCaprio 2004: 6n26), in subsequent years, it acted in response to petitions. In October 2017, the agency adopted revised ("proactive") procedures under which all GSP beneficiaries' compliance with eligibility

criteria was to be evaluated every three years. In October 2019, it self-initiated labor rights reviews of Eritrea and Zimbabwe (Jones and Wong 2021: 1, 21).

76. U.S. Code of Federal Regulations (hereinafter U.S. CFR), title 15, subtitle C, chap. XX, pt. 2007. Petition requirements are straightforward in formal terms. Petitioners are required to give their name, identify the country that would be subject to review, indicate the specific worker rights criteria that warrant review, state why the beneficiary country's status should be reviewed, and provide supporting information (U.S. CFR, Title 15, subtitle C, chap. XX, pt. 2007.0[b]).

77. The committee's membership includes the departments of Agriculture, Commerce, Defense, Energy, Health and Human Services, Homeland Security, Interior, Justice, Labor, State, Transportation, and Treasury, as well as the Council of Economic Advisors, Council on Environmental Quality, Environmental Protection Agency, Agency for International Development, National Economic Council, National Security Council, Office of Management and Budget, and International Trade Commission.

78. U.S. Code Title 19 (Customs Duties), chap. 12(V), sect. 2462(b)(2)(G, H) and sect. 2467.

79. Although the statute permits "the duty-free treatment accorded to eligible articles under the GSP to be withdrawn, suspended or limited" (U.S. CFR, Title 15, subtitle C, chap. XX, pt. 2007.2(h)(2)), petitioners generally seek the full withdrawal of a country's eligibility without further specifics (author's email communication with Lewis Karesh, assistant U.S. trade representative for labor affairs, November 26, 2018). However, in 1990, the International Labor Rights Education and Research Fund (ILRERF) filed a sector-specific petition targeting Malaysia's electronics industry (Athreya 2011: 18–19), and in 1995, the U.S. government suspended benefits for Pakistan's handknotted carpets, sports equipment, and surgical instruments industries because of child labor abuses (Elliott 1998b).

80. Ballon 1987: 113; Lyle 1991: 9.

81. Some of the labor rights NGOs and trade unions most actively involved in GSP processes strongly contested these elements of executive discretion, but they failed to alter them. In 1990–1992, the ILRERF led a broad coalition of twenty-three unions and NGOs in legal actions charging that the administration of President George H. W. Bush (1989–1993) had failed to administer the GSP program in accordance with the law and congressional intent. In particular, the plaintiffs challenged the USTR's discretion in determining which groups were qualified to file GSP petitions, what constituted "new information" in the evaluation of a petition, and what was required of a beneficiary country in determining that it was "taking steps" to correct alleged worker rights violations (B. Davis 1995: 1175–76; Compa 1995a: 345n31; Athreya 2011: 57–58). The case was dismissed by a U.S. district court and an appeals court (Cleveland 1997–1998: 1554).

82. U.S. Public Law No. 98-573, sect. 505-6.

83. Author's calculation based on the information in USTR 2005 and Mosley 2011b. The author primarily employs this latter source to establish an historical context for the analysis that follows.

  A significant number of the petitions filed over the 1985-2011 period were multiple filings centered on the same country. For example, over this period, the USTR received at least twenty petitions concerning Guatemala and sixteen petitions regarding El Salvador (author's calculation based on the sources listed in table 2.1). In Bangladesh, the AFL-CIO filed repeat petitions to pressure the government to follow through on its commitment to implement labor laws in export-processing zones (Simpson 2015: 77–80).

In contrast, between 1989 and 2022, there were only two labor rights petitions filed under OTCA section 301, both by the AFL-CIO (in 2004 and 2006) and both alleging that the systematic denial of basic worker rights in China constituted an unfair burden on U.S. commerce and exerted downward pressure on U.S. wages (AFL-CIO 2004b, 2006a; Schwarzenberg 2020). The USTR declined to review both petitions (USTR 2006). In the case of the OPIC, because program officials have consistently followed GSP practice regarding countries whose benefits have been suspended or terminated (Pérez-López 1988: 277; Zimmerman 1991: 613), the secondary literature reports only two instances in which the OPIC has conducted its own worker-rights investigation in countries without GSP standing and then suspended participants: Ethiopia in 1987 and China in 1990 (Lyle 1991: 15–16).

Similarly, there were only six labor rights complaints filed under the EU's GSP program between 1995 and 2021 (Bangladesh, 2016; Belarus, 2003; El Salvador, 2007; Myanmar, 1995; Pakistan, 1995, 1998). Two countries were suspended from the program specifically for labor rights violations: Myanmar in 1997 (forced labor) and Belarus in 2007 (freedom of association). Myanmar was reinstated in 2013. See Kryvoi 2008: 230–35; Portela and Orbie 2014: 67–68; Simpson 2015: 92, 95–97, 100; Kelly 2017: 19–22; International Trade Union Confederation 2018: 13. Sri Lanka was suspended from the GSP Plus program between 2010 and 2017 for multiple labor (child labor, freedom of association) and human rights violations, but it retained access to regular EU GSP benefits (European Commission 2017). Cambodia was partially suspended from the same program for human rights (including labor rights) violations in 2020 (Jones and Wong 2021: 6).

84.   The United Electrical, Radio, and Machine Workers of America; the United Food and Commercial Workers International Union; and the International Union of Electronic, Electrical, Salaried, Machine, and Furniture Workers were actively involved in GSP processes. The NGOs included the ILRERF (renamed the International Labor Rights Forum in 1996), Human Rights Watch and its regional affiliates, Lawyer's Committee on Human Rights, and U.S. Labor Education in the Americas Project (USLEAP). For many of these unions and NGOs, the GSP petition process provided an important incentive to cooperate regularly (Athreya 2011: 4–5).

85.   Mosley and Tello (2014) do not include a substantive classification of the issues raised in the petitions they examine. However, Nolan García (2011a: 10) finds that 67.8 percent of the eighty-seven petitions filed against Latin American countries between 1987 and 2005 alleged violations of collective-action rights (either separately or in combination with other issues), 31 percent addressed minimum standards of employment, 19.5 percent referenced child labor, and 16.1 percent alleged forced labor violations.

86.   Athreya 2011: 50–51; Mosley and Tello 2014: 15–16. Jones and Wong (2021: appendix A) provide a detailed chronology of the GSP program's implementation and renewal between 1975 and 2020. The free-trade agreements adopted by the United States generally state that the reciprocal benefits they contain replace participating countries' GSP eligibility. The only exception is Jordan, which retained its GSP eligibility despite having signed a free-trade agreement with the United States in 2001 (Jones 2015: 11–12).

87.   Author's review of the presidential proclamations published in the *U.S. Federal Register*, various years. The effective date of GSP suspension or termination was sixty days following publication of the proclamation.

Some of these countries were later reinstated in the program: Central African Republic (1991), Chile (1991), Liberia (2006), Maldives (2010), Mauritania (1999), Myanmar (2016), Pakistan (2005), Paraguay (1991), Romania (1994). Nicaragua was not reinstated in the GSP program, but in 1990, President George H.W. Bush acted "in the national security interest of the United States" to waive labor-conditionality requirements and admit it to the Caribbean Basin Initiative preferential trade agreement (*U.S. Federal Register* 55 [230]: 49499).

88.   Elliott 1998b; Nolan García 2011a: 13; Mosley and Tello 2014: 32–35; Hafner-Burton, Mosley, and Galantucci 2019: 1255, 1259–60. Based on her quantitative analysis of the eighty-seven petitions filed against Latin American countries between 1987 and 2005, Nolan García (2011a: 13–15) concludes that the USTR was significantly less likely to review countries that were regional allies (those that received greater amounts of U.S. economic and military assistance) and that the level of labor rights violations was not a statistically significant predictor of the USTR's decision to review a particular petition. She finds that the USTR was more likely to review labor practices in countries with a high export dependency on the United States.

89.   Elliott (1998b: table 7) offers only a binary assessment of petition impact (whether GSP petitions did or did not have a positive impact on labor rights in the targeted country). She identifies thirty-two cases in which the threat of losing GSP benefits might have plausibly produced improvements in labor rights and concludes that only fifteen of these could be judged "successes." She does not specify the criteria on which she bases this judgment.

90.   Goertz and Mahoney 2012: 90, 96.

91.   The geographic distribution of all 122 petitions filed between 1985 and 1995 was: Latin America and the Caribbean (33.3 percent), Asia (26.7 percent), Africa (22.2 percent), the Middle East (11.1 percent), and other (Fiji, Romania, Turkey) (6.7 percent). Author's calculation based on the information in USTR 2005.

92.   There is no evidence that petitioners selected target countries principally on the basis of their anticipated success, which would bias conclusions regarding GSP effectiveness.

93.   See table 2.1 for the complete coding scheme. The focus here is on the extension of collective-action rights in law and practice as a consequence of USTR reviews, without regard to baseline conditions in target countries at the outset. Specific attention to collective-action rights in the public sector and in any export-processing zones (EPZs) reflects the practical importance of these issues in the GSP cases examined here. Attention to developments in these areas does not introduce sectoral bias to the coding scheme, nor did variations in the importance of EPZs among different countries affect how observed outcomes were scored. Table 2.1 reports detailed source materials in order to enhance transparency in the author's coding decisions.

94.   Compared to the changes reported by Mosley (2011b), the "observed outcomes" reported in table 2.1 differ in the cases of Chile, Costa Rica, Dominican Republic, El Salvador, Guatemala, Malaysia, Nicaragua, and Peru. Compared to changes reported by Cingranelli, Richards, and Clay (2014), table 2.1 results differ in the cases of Dominican Republic, El Salvador, Honduras, and Paraguay.

95.   The author chose the petition acceptance date in U.S. GSP cases because, unlike the NAALC and post-NAALC labor complaints examined in chapters 4 and 5, respectively, the readily accessible records to not indicate the date on which the USTR issued its final report.

96.   This total includes twelve instances of de facto USTR acceptance—cases in which, with a formal review of the target country already under way, USTR authorities responded to a new petition by "continuing" it. The target countries were Dominican Republic (1990, 1994), El Salvador (1991, 1992, 1993, 1994), Guatemala (1993, 1995), Haiti (1988, 1989), Indonesia (1993), and Panama (1992).

97.   This finding regarding labor organizations' higher petition success rate concords with the conclusions reached by Elliott (1998b: table 4) and Mosley and Tello (2014: 16–17).

98.   USTR acceptance rates varied depending upon the presidential administration under which petitions were filed, ranging from 50 percent under the Reagan and Bush administrations to 81.3 percent under the Democratic administration of President Clinton (author's calculations based on the dataset compiled for this study). One obvious explanation for this difference would be that the Clinton administration was more broadly sympathetic to labor concerns than were its Republican predecessors. (For example, labor organizations' petition success rate ranged from 53.8 percent under Bush, to 64.3 percent under Reagan, to 90 percent under Clinton.) However, part of the difference in presidential acceptance rates might be explained by the end of the Cold War (and, with it, the inclination of some U.S. officials to view labor rights claims in ideologically divided countries such as El Salvador and Guatemala from an anti-Communist perspective) and evolution in decision criteria as U.S. trade officials gained experience implementing GSP procedures.

99.   B. Davis 1995: 1198–99; Compa and Vogt 2001: 215–16. The USTR responded similarly to petitions alleging violence against trade unionists in Colombia (1990, 1993, 1995) and Guatemala (1991) (USTR 2005).

100.   The USTR rejected 42.2 percent of the petitions it received concerning these fifteen countries between 1985 and 1995 (table 2.1). Moreover, there is evidence that the U.S. embassy personnel involved in GSP reviews were, at times, ideologically or politically biased in their assessments of labor rights conditions in particular countries; see Dorman 1989: 11 (El Salvador) and 13n35 (Malaysia); Frundt 1998: 197–98, 205 (Honduras) and 237, 240–43, 246 (Panama); Athreya 2011: 21–22 (Malaysia). On U.S. Department of State inconsistency in its annual labor rights reports, see Compa 2003b: 304–305 and telephone interview with a former senior U.S. Department of State official [Polaski], July 12, 2018.

101.   Table 2.1; Frundt 1998: 146n36, 147n38; Compa and Vogt 2001: 217n85.

102.   Both U.S. labor rights advocates and USTR officials have generally been careful not to press initiatives that would place local unions at greater risk (interview with former senior U.S. government official A [Karesh], June 14, 2018, Washington, DC). This policy presumably reflects the USTR's experience with countries such as Guatemala, where, in 1992, the acceptance of a petition for review led to death threats against local labor activists. Under the circumstances, the petitioners dropped their demand for the suspension of Guatemala's GSP benefits and accepted a March 1993 USTR decision that the Guatemalan government was "taking steps" to improve its labor practices (Compa and Vogt 2001: 218).

103. See, respectively, Frundt 1998: 255, 266; and Athreya 2011: 17, 19.

104. See Frundt 1998: 98, 254 (Colombia); Athreya 2011: 25–26 (Indonesia) and 61 (Guatemala); Frundt 1998: 254; and Cook 2007: 126 (Peru).

105. Because of unevenness in the available information concerning domestic support in these fifteen countries, this three-level categorization is, of course, only an approximate measure.

106. B. Davis 1995: 1187n105.

107. Frundt 1998: 142, 147, 149, 154, 156.

108. Interview with former senior US government official A [Karesh], June 14, 2018.

109. This conclusion concurs with Frundt's (1998: 254) finding that GSP petitioners were most successful when they engaged with workers in target countries; see also Athreya 2011: 60. It also supports Murillo and Schrank (2005: 987) on the importance of transnational alliances in advancing labor rights in Latin America. However, these latter authors do not examine the relative density of these alliances.

110. In the Dominican Republic in the early 1990s and in Panama in the late 1980s, unionized workers represented approximately 12–15 percent and 15 percent, respectively, of the economically active population (Frundt 1998: 207, 222, 237).

111. Telephone interview with a former senior AFL-CIO official [Lee], July 29, 2021.

112. The sources for this discussion of individual countries are listed in table 2.1. Elliott (1998b) concluded that in eight of forty cases selected for USTR review, improvements in labor rights were mainly due to political opening or regime change.

113. Blanchard and Hakobyan (2015: 400) report that developing countries that lose their GSP eligibility experience significant declines in exports.

114. The trade data are for: Chile/1985, Colombia/1990, Costa Rica/1993, Dominican Republic /1989, El Salvador/1990, Guatemala/1986, Haiti/1988, Honduras/1995, Indonesia/1989, Malaysia/1988, Nicaragua/1985, Pakistan/1993, Panama/1991, Paraguay/1985, and Peru/1993.

115. This conclusion differs from that reached by Tsogas (2000: 358–59), who argues that the impact of GSP pressures varies in line with the proportion of a beneficiary country's exports destined for the U.S. market. Tsogas does not systematically evaluate other factors that might determine the efficacy of USTR labor rights reviews.

116. For instance, El Salvador's principal light-manufactured exports to the United States, textile and apparel products (Shadlen 2008: table 3), were excluded from the GSP program's duty-free treatment. However, these goods did benefit from El Salvador's participation in the CBERA. Haiti benefited from enhanced CBERA trade access under item 807 of the Tariff Schedules of the United States, a provision that permits goods sent abroad for processing or assembly to be reimported into the United States subject only to duty on the value added to the goods abroad.

117. This term should not be confused with the EU's GSP Plus Programme, which offers complete removal of tariffs to countries that comply with additional conditions of good governance and environmental protection.

118. Dorman 1989: 12–13.

119. B. Davis 1995: 1184, 1200–1208; Athreya 2011: 36–39. In June 1995, El Salvador also ratified a bloc of fourteen ILO conventions, including those concerning forced labor, discrimination in employment, and a minimum age for employment. However, it did not ratify conventions nos. 87 and 98 until September 2006 (see below).

120. Elliott (1998b) argues that the negative public attention generated by USTR reviews may be more important in inducing policy change in a target country than the loss of GSP eligibility per se. Considerations of this kind would not be affected by any reduction over time in the difference between preferential (duty-free) GSP and general WTO tariff levels.

121. Frundt 1998: 204–205; Athreya 2011: 48–49.

122. Compa and Vogt 2001: 219–20; Hafner-Burton 2013: 142.

123. Dr. Kazuma Mizukoshi ably performed the statistical analysis reported in appendix A, and Dr. Néstor Castañeda (University College London) generously provided advice concerning how best to structure the analysis.

124. The mean Freedom House aggregate score (an average of the scores for political rights and civil liberties) for these six countries was 2.7 (author's calculation based on Freedom House, *Freedom in the World* reports, various years). The Freedom House scores range from 1 (most free) to 7 (least free).

   Elliott (1998b) also concludes that USTR pressures are more likely to be successful "when the target is relatively more politically open."

   The "smaller" economies in this group of fifteen countries were those with a contemporary gross domestic product (GDP) less than US$20 billion (current US dollars); the "larger" economies (Colombia, Indonesia, Malaysia, Pakistan, Peru) had a GDP greater than US$35 billion. See World Bank, "GDP (Current US$)," accessed July 26, 2017, http://data.worldbank.org/indicator/NY.GDP.MKTP.CD.

125. The mean Freedom House aggregate score for these three countries was 5.2 (author's calculation).

126. There was no statistically significant relationship between observed-outcome scores and a country's level of socioeconomic development. The United Nations classified eleven of these fifteen countries as "lower middle income;" Haiti, Honduras, Indonesia, and Pakistan were classified as "low income." See United Nations, "Least Developed Countries," accessed July 26, 2017, https://www.un.org/development/desa/dpad/least-developed-country-category.html.

127. Colombia was omitted from the regression analysis because the USTR did not accept for review any of the GSP petitions alleging labor rights violations.

128. See, respectively, Frundt 1998: 147, 157 and Athreya 2011: 12–13, 29–31.

129. Frundt 1998: 98.

130. Cook 2007: 127.

131. See, respectively, Athreya 2011: 63 and Frundt 1998: 244–45.

132. Frundt 1998: 214–15, 218–20 (Dominican Republic) and 199, 200–1, 203 (Honduras); Jessup and Gordon 2000: 185 (Dominican Republic); Compa and Vogt 2001: 214–16 (Guatemala); Kernaghan 1993 (Haiti).

133. See Gordon 2000a on the labor rights challenges that EPZs frequently pose.

134. Risse and Ropp (2013: 3) note the more general challenge that "weak or limited statehood" poses for human rights implementation and compliance. See also Risse 2017.

135. Frundt 1998: 110–11, 130–32, 149, 155, 164–66.

136. Frundt 1998: 155, 157–58, 161; Douglas, Ferguson, and Klett 2004: 289. In Guatemala, the USTR "benchmarked" the specific labor reforms that the government was required to enact in order to retain its GSP eligibility.

137.   Athreya 2011: 13. Something similar occurred in Peru following the USTR's review of petitions filed by the AFL-CIO in 1992 and 1993 (Athreya 2011: 56–57).

138.   Krasner 1999: 33; see also pp. 25–26, 74–75.

139.   International Labour Organization, "Normlex," accessed December 1, 2018, www.ilo.org/dyn/normlex/en. Indonesia, which had ratified convention no. 98 in 1957, probably anticipated adoption of the ILO's Declaration on Fundamental Principles and Rights at Work (June 18, 1998) when it ratified no. 87 on June 9, 1998. Chile ratified both these conventions in February 1999. In El Salvador, despite important reforms in labor law and policy, there was persistent resistance to ratifying conventions nos. 87 and 98 based on the claim that they invalidated constitutional provisions regulating the rights of public employees (Frundt 1998: 111, 114). As a result, El Salvador did not ratify them until September 2006, when it did so in order to retain its European Union GSP eligibility (ILO 2015: 101). Despite the ILO's post-1998 convention ratification campaign and growing international consensus around its declaration, as of 2022, Malaysia had still not ratified convention nos. 87 and 98.

140.   The removal of GSP benefits from Chile, Nicaragua, and Paraguay was an element in broader U.S. opposition to authoritarian regimes in these countries, and the U.S. government restored eligibility following democratic regime change based more on expectations regarding future labor policy than any specific short-term actions the target states took (Morley and McGillion 2015: 309; Frundt 1998: 251; Aronson 1991: 192, respectively). The partial suspension of Pakistan's GSP benefits focused on industries in which the abuse of child labor was endemic; the action produced no substantial change in Pakistan's respect for freedom of association and the rights to organize and bargain collectively (Compa and Vogt 2001: 230–31).

    The available indices of collective-rights labor practices support somewhat different conclusions regarding the impact of GSP suspension or termination. At the time of GSP reinstatement, Mosley (2011b, column C, "collective rights overall") records substantial, consistent improvements in Chile, Liberia, Nicaragua, Paraguay, Romania, and possibly Pakistan. In contrast, Cingranelli, Richards, and Clay (2014) indicate that only in the Maldives, Nicaragua, and Romania were there minor improvements in labor practices in the period between suspension or termination and the later restoration of GSP eligibility. Hafner-Burton (2013: 143) reports significant change in Mauritania between the suspension of its GSP eligibility in 1993 and its restoration in 1999.

141.   Drezner (2003: 653–54) argues that the threat of U.S. trade sanctions is generally more effective than actual imposition of them.

142.   Frundt 1998: 231–33 (Costa Rica) and 212–14 (Dominican Republic); B. Davis 1995: 1186n105 (El Salvador); ILO 2005: 6, 12 (Pakistan).

143.   See, for example, Compa and Vogt 2001: 202, 208, 215; Athreya 2011: 25–26, 60–61. See also Caraway 2006b: 282, 296. Keck and Sikkink (1998: 206–207) emphasize the importance of local allies in human rights promotion more generally.

144.   Interviews with former senior U.S. government official A [Karesh] (June 14, 2018), U.S. trade union representative A [Davis] (March 20, 2018), and senior U.S. labor representative A [Feingold] (April 23, 2018), all in Washington, DC; telephone interview with a former senior U.S. Department of State official [Polaski] (May 29, 2018).

145.   This conclusion is based in part on interviews with U.S. trade union representative A and former senior U.S. labor representative A, both cited above.

3. CONTEXT AND CONSTRAINTS: THE ORIGIN AND NEGOTIATION OF THE NORTH AMERICAN FREE TRADE AGREEMENT'S LABOR RIGHTS PROVISIONS

1. For overviews of Canada-U.S. relations, see Lipset 1990, Thompson and Randall 1994, and Lennox 2009.
2. Author's email communication with Professor Eric Van Young (University of California-San Diego), January 24, 2013. Published estimates of Mexico's proportional territorial loss to the United States during this period range from "nearly half" (Cline 1963: 11) to as much as 58.8 percent (one million of 1.7 million square miles; Meinig 1993: 128).
3. For assessments of Mexican foreign policy and Mexico-U.S relations, see especially Ojeda 1976, R. Pastor and Castañeda 1988, and Domínguez and Fernández de Castro 2001.
4. Domínguez and Fernández de Castro 2001: 4, 10. See also Ojeda 1976: 100–106. The so-called La Paz agreement on Mexico-U.S. border environment issues (Agreement on Cooperation for the Protection and Improvement of the Environment in the Border Area), signed in 1983, was an important precedent in the shift toward greater institutionalization in bilateral relations.
5. Finbow (2006: 40–41) argues that the Canadian and Mexican governments sought to limit transnational enforcement authority in the NAALC precisely because they were concerned about power asymmetries vis-à-vis the United States.
6. Beaver 2006: 1. The reported length of the Canada-U.S. border does not include Canada's border with Alaska, which is 1,538 miles long.
7. U.S. Central Intelligence Agency, *1991 World Fact Book*, Project Gutenberg, https://www.gutenberg.org/ebooks/25. The choice of the year in which to anchor this comparison is difficult because Mexico's GDP shrank significantly in the wake of the country's 1982 foreign debt crisis. By 1990 (two years after the signing of the Canada-United States Free Trade Agreement but before the NAFTA negotiations began), Mexico had experienced some degree of economic recovery.
8. Author's calculations based on data from the U.S. Department of Commerce (United States Census Bureau, Foreign Trade Division), "Trade in Goods with Canada," accessed January 16, 2013, http://www.census.gov/foreign-trade/balance/c1220.html; and "U.S. Trade in Goods and Services—Balance of Payments (BOP) Basis," accessed January 16, 2013, http://www.census.gov/foreign-trade/statistics/historical/gands.pdf. The preferred years for these comparisons (1985 and 1989) are immediately prior to the start of bilateral trade agreement negotiations between, respectively, Canada and the United States and Mexico and the United States.
9. Statistics Canada, accessed August 26, 2013 and May 30, 2014, http://www.statcom.gc.ca/cimt-cicm/section-section?lang.
10. Author's calculations based on data from the U.S. Department of Commerce (United States Census Bureau, Foreign Trade Division), "Trade in Goods with Mexico, accessed January 16, 2013, http://www.census.gov/foreign-trade/balance/c2010.html; and "U.S. Trade in Goods and Services—Balance of Payments (BOP) Basis," accessed January 16, 2013, http://www.census.gov/foreign-trade/statistics/historical/gands.pdf.
11. Poder Ejecutivo Federal 1992: 308. See Ojeda 1976: table XI for data concerning the U.S. share of combined Mexican exports and imports for the 1941–1974 period (with a period high of 89.2 percent in 1941 and a low of 58.1 percent in 1972).

12.   In 1989, the United States accounted for 65.6 percent of Canada's stock of inward foreign direct investment (Government of Canada 2003) and 63.1 percent of Mexico's total stock of foreign direct investment (Poder Ejecutivo Federal 1992: 314).

13.   For discussions of Canada-U.S. trade relations from the nineteenth century onward, see Doern and Tomlin 1991: 57–64, 67–69; Smith 1996: 40–41; Stairs 1996: 21–24.

14.   See Orme 1996: 35–36; López Portillo 1988: 859–60; Robert 2000: 23.

15.   Salinas de Gortari 2002: 53; Feld and Brylski 1983: 302; Vaky 1980: 628; Robert 2000: 23–24. Following these Canadian and Mexican reactions, President Reagan subsequently denied (April 1982) that he had suggested "a common market or any kind of formal arrangement" (quoted in Feld and Brylski 1983: 290).

16.   The CUSFTA was only the second bilateral free-trade agreement negotiated by the United States, following an agreement with Israel in 1985 (Truell 1990: 22).

17.   Truell 1990: 22.

18.   Robert (2000: 24–25) discusses Canada-U.S. commercial developments in the early 1980s.

19.   Thompson and Randall 1994: 283–84, 286, 288; Mulroney 2007: 395, 575–77; Doern and Tomlin 1991: 152–53, 272–76; "Timeline of the Progress" (2006). For discussions of the process leading to the CUSFTA, see Doern and Tomlin 1991: 16–35, *passim*; Robert 2000: 24–25; Hart 2002: 367–93.

20.   This overview draws on Middlebrook and Zepeda 2003: 7–8. See also M. Pastor and Wise 1994.

21.   Domínguez and Fernández de Castro 2001: 29.

22.   Mexico had initially applied for GATT membership in December 1978, and by October 1979, the government had negotiated a draft protocol. However, the proposal encountered significant domestic opposition from small and midsize industrial firms and from economic nationalists. In the context of country's petroleum-led economic boom, President José López Portillo (1976–1982) finally rejected the idea—making the announcement on March 18, 1980, the anniversary of Mexico's sensational nationalization of the petroleum industry in 1938. In 1983, President De la Madrid reaffirmed that Mexico would not enter the GATT (Story 1986: 134, 136, 138–42, 145; López Portillo 1988: 941). Cameron and Tomlin (2000: 59) maintain that the terms of Mexico's agreement with the GATT in 1986 were less favorable than those offered in 1979.

23.   Villarreal and Cid 2008: 2–3; Spriggs and Stanford 1993: 504. The 1987 agreement established the first legal framework to govern bilateral commercial relations; led to sectoral agreements liberalizing trade in steel, textiles, and alcoholic beverages; and identified additional areas (agriculture, investment technology transfer, intellectual property rights) for future negotiations. The 1989 agreement established a negotiating process for expanding trade and investment between the two countries.

24.   Cameron and Tomlin 2000: 59. Prior to these liberalizing measures, Mexico's extensive licensing system barred many manufactured imports, and dutiable items incurred tariffs ranging from 35 to 100 percent of their value (Feld and Brylski 1983: 293).

25.   Barr, Honeywell, and Stofel 1991: 7.

26.   Cameron and Tomlin 2000: 59–60; Golob 2003: 377; Salinas de Gortari 2002: 48, 53.

27.   Salinas de Gortari 2002: 12 and 2005: 58. Salinas feared that simultaneously undertaking trade-liberalization and debt-reduction negotiations might force Mexico to make unilateral trade concessions in order to secure its debt-reduction goals.

Salinas rejected Bush's informal proposal even though Mexican government representatives had apparently expressed strong interest in an eventual Mexico-U.S. free-trade agreement during successful bilateral talks in October 1989 concerning how to expand the 1987 framework agreement on trade and investment. Following those talks, U.S. secretary of commerce Robert A. Mosbacher publicly stated, "We should not try to push them [the Mexicans] too fast, too hard, but they are interested, extremely interested in moving toward this [a free-trade agreement]—they want to take it a step at a time" (quoted in Farnsworth 1989).

28. R. Pastor and Castañeda 1988: 65, 69, 71–72, 75, 182–83, 186, 189, 334.

29. Salinas de Gortari 2002: 53; R. Pastor 1990: 16; MacArthur 2000: 89–90.

30. S. R. Golob 2003: 376–78.

31. Salinas de Gortari 2002: 50–51 and 2017: 106–10. The most probable date for the Salinas-Serra Puche exchange is February 2, but the available sources do not specify the precise date.

32. Salinas de Gortari 2002: 46–52, 99–100; von Bertrab 1997: 1–2, 24–25; Cameron and Tomlin 2000: 1–2, 62. See also S. R. Golob 2003: 376–78. In his memoirs, Salinas (2002: 41–42, 45) intimates that he and his principal advisers had begun to consider how Mexico could best adapt to changing global circumstances even prior to his trip to Western Europe. Castañeda (1995: 48, 52–54) argues that one strong incentive for the Salinas administration's decision to pursue closer economic ties with the United States was its pressing need to finance Mexico's substantial current-account deficit. Gruber (2000: 128–38) maintains that the NAFTA proposal was Mexican officials' response to potential market-access challenges posed by the CUSFTA.

33. Long 2014: 138–39, 140.

34. Senior Mexican officials also consulted with the Canadian officials who had negotiated the CUSFTA (Robert 2000: 30).

35. Truell 1990: A3; Salinas de Gortari 2002: 50, 57, 59.

36. Truell 1990.

37. Mayer 1998: 43; Garciadiego et al. 1994: 56; Salinas de Gortari 2002: 60, 69. As late as June 1990, Bush favored informal talks with Mexico, which were to be followed by formal negotiations once the multilateral Uruguay Round of GATT negotiations concluded in December 1990. Following his statement in support of a free-trade agreement with Mexico, Bush announced his goal of signing trade agreements with other Latin American countries as well (R. Pastor 1990: 17, 21).

38. von Bertrab 1997: 4; Cameron and Tomlin 2000: 69.

39. Cameron and Tomlin 2000: 71.

40. Thompson and Randall 1994: 284–85, 292–93; Grayson 1995: 57; Hart 2002: 393–94.

41. Cameron and Tomlin 2000: 6, 63–68, 148; Mayer 1998: 43, 48–49; Robert 2000: 30–33; Mulroney 2007: 228–30, 730–31; Thompson and Randall 1994: 292–93; Grayson 1995: 57–59; Hart 2002: 394; Doern and Tomlin 1991: 226–27. Long (2014: 5) reports that Canadian officials, after initially indicating that they did not wish to join Mexico-U.S. discussions, changed their position and notified Secretary Serra Puche on May 30, 1990 that they wished to do so. It is noteworthy that Mulroney's discussion of the NAFTA in his memoirs is limited to stressing his concern that a separate Mexico-U.S. bilateral agreement might undercut important provisions of Canada's existing trade agreement with the United States.

42. T. Long 2014: 5. In these discussions, U.S. officials argued that any potential agreement should be comprehensive and not exclude any major topics (including the politically sensitive question of foreign investment in the Mexican petroleum industry). They also sought assurances that Mexico would not claim special trade concessions on the basis of its status as a developing country (Mazza 2001: 71; see also MacArthur 2000: 119).

43. Cameron and Tomlin 2000: 71; Mulroney 2007: 731; Salinas de Gortari 2002: 89. For further discussion of U.S. and Canadian positions on this issue, see Grayson 1995: 59–60.

44. The three leaders agreed that any country that later withdrew from the negotiations would do so in a way that did not prejudice the prospects for the other two countries (Robert 2000: 33).

45. Cameron and Tomlin 2000: 185, 193; author's email communication with Dr. Hector Mackenzie (Department of Foreign Affairs, Canada), May 13, 2014.

46. Gerstenzang 1993: 1; PBS, accessed January 11, 2014, http://www.pbs.org/wgbh/americanexperience/features/timeline/clinton/. Executive Order no. 12,889 gave the North American Free Trade Agreement Implementation Act (Congress.gov, "Public Law No. 103-182," December 8, 1993, https://www.congress.gov/103/statute/STATUTE-107/STATUTE-107-Pg2057.pdf) legal force on December 27, 1993.

47. Author's email communications with Lic. J. Fernando Franco González Salas (Suprema Corte de Justicia de la Nación, Mexico), April 6–7, 2014.

48. von Bertrab 1997: 37; Thacker 1999: 69; Cameron and Tomlin 2000: 71, 78.

    There is a substantial literature on the negotiations leading up to the NAFTA, including Grayson 1995, von Bertrab 1997, Mayer 1998, and Golob 2003. Cameron and Tomlin 2000 provide an especially detailed analysis, based on extensive interviews with negotiation participants. Salinas de Gortari (2002: 9–12, 39–196) offers by far the most detailed leadership account of the negotiations. As noted above, Mulroney's memoirs barely mention the NAFTA; in a statement preceding his report of final agreement on the text in August 1992, he observed that "life goes on" (2007: 935). Bush did not write a general memoir of his presidency; Bush and Scowcroft 1998 focuses only on the 1989–1991 period and the end of the Cold War, omitting any reference to Mexico.

    Because the NAFTA incorporated many of the CUSFTA's main provisions, or adopted trilateral agreements to replace bilateral ones, Canada and the United States agreed to suspend the CUSFTA for as long as both countries were parties to the NAFTA (Hart 2002: 395).

49. Grayson 1995: 101; author's email communication with Barry Appleton (Appleton & Associates, Toronto), January 11, 2014. For overviews of the NAFTA, see B. Appleton 1994 and von Bertrab 1997: 51–72.

50. Prior to the NAFTA, the average U.S. tariff on dutiable imports from Mexico was only 3.5 percent. However, in approximately 750 product categories, Mexican exports faced high U.S. tariff barriers, ranging up to 800 percent in exceptional cases (Orme 1996: 71–72).

51. In 1991 and 1992, Mexican democratic reformers and human rights activists sought to attach to the accord a "democracy clause" (or provisions promoting human rights) similar to that established by the European community, under which states seeking membership in the group was required to demonstrate their commitment to democratic governance and basic human rights. The proponents of this approach included several individuals—among them, Jorge G. Castañeda (who later served as Mexico's minister of foreign

relations, 2001–2003) and Adolfo Aguilar Zínser (who later became Mexico's representative to the United Nations, 2002–2003)—who were highly visible critics of the free-trade agreement. See Castañeda 1995: 58; Castañeda 2004: 55–57; Mazza 2001: 95–96. These proposals found modest support in the U.S. Congress (Mazza 2001: 76–77, 86, 94–95; *Inside U.S. Trade* [hereinafter *IUST*], September 10, 1993). On the whole, however, U.S. officials remained reluctant to criticize the Mexican government openly over domestic political matters, in part because they feared that they might undercut the Salinas administration and thus endanger the prospects for a free-trade agreement. For a detailed examination of evolving U.S. policy on this issue, see Mazza 2001, esp. pp. 4–5, 7, 71–72, 75, 87–88, 92–93, 97–99, 103–4, 110–13, 121–22.

52. Environmental and labor rights questions were closely linked in debates about the NAFTA between 1990 and 1993 (Kay and Evans 2018: chap. 4); for brevity, this discussion focuses only on labor issues. A third "side-agreement" was also negotiated during this period (the North American Agreement on Import Surges), even though chapter 8 of the main NAFTA text already addressed the topic.

53. See, for instance, Pomeroy 1996: 772; Grimm 1999: 190n64; DiCaprio 2004: 12.

54. Cameron and Tomlin 2000: 69. See also Mayer 1998: 45–46.

55. For an overview of the widely divergent findings of several employment- and wage-impact studies commissioned during the initial stages of the NAFTA debate, see Housman and Orbuch 1993: 726–29; Taylor 1994: 44–45n208, 77, 81–82; Cowie 1997: 10. Through 2013, the U.S. Department of Labor's Trade Adjustment Assistance Program had certified 845,000 workers as having lost their jobs because of NAFTA, either via the off-shoring of production or due to imports from Canada and Mexico (Bonior 2014).

56. See Miller 1996: 156–61, 166 for a discussion of Congress's constitutional authority over trade agreements and the background to fast-track procedures. See also Grayson 1995: 62–63.

57. Cameron and Tomlin 2000: 74; see also Salinas de Gortari 2002: 79, 88, 92, 95, 99. In an effort to raise the political costs of opposing the NAFTA, the Bush administration sought simultaneous extensions of fast-track authority to negotiate the NAFTA and the Uruguay Round of the GATT (initiated in 1986), on the calculus that congressional opponents of the former initiative would not jeopardize completion of the GATT negotiations (Taylor 1994: 37–8; Mayer 1998: 92).

58. Opponents of a Mexico-U.S. trade agreement made this decision because their experience during the CUSFTA debate had taught them that fast-track procedures limited their capacity to influence the content of the final agreement (Mayer 1998: 73–74, 98).

59. von Bertrab 1997: 22; Mayer 1998: 81–82; Cameron and Tomlin 2000: 73.

60. In addition, Gephardt argued for environmental safeguards in Mexico and various provisions to protect U.S. producers against unfair economic competition (MacArthur 2000: 103–104).

61. President Bush's seventy-eight-page "action plan" (White House 1991), prepared by the Office of the United States Trade Representative (USTR), constituted his formal response to the letters of concern he had received from Representatives Rostenkowski and Gephardt and Senator Bentsen (MacArthur 2000: 117). For a summary of the plan's proposed measures to reduce possible adverse affects of a NAFTA on U.S. workers, see White House 1991: tab 2, pp. 5–7; Miller 1996: 163–64n82.

62.   U.S. Department of State, *Dispatch* 2, no.18 (6 May 1991). For an expanded discussion of these points, see White House 1991: tab 3, pp. 1-16.

　　　　Following up on Bush's announced action plan, in summer 1991, Senator Ernest F. Hollings (Democrat-South Carolina and chair of the U.S. Senate Committee on Commerce, Science, and Transportation) requested that the U.S. General Accounting Office (GAO) assess labor law enforcement in Mexico by examining labor practices in the Mexican autoparts industry. The U.S. GAO published its assessment of workplace safety and occupational health in eight U.S.-owned autoparts maquiladoras in November 1993 (U.S. GAO 1993b).

63.   Cameron and Tomlin 2000: 75; von Bertrab 1997: 74; Housman and Orbuch 1993: 775-76, 793; Taylor 1994: 94-99, 121.

64.   "Labor Secretaries of U.S., Mexico Sign Worker Issues Accord," *Wall Street Journal*, May 6, 1991; Housman and Orbuch 1993: 769; McCaffrey 1993: 474-89; author's email communication with a former senior U.S. Department of Labor official [Pérez-López], June 18, 2018. The Memorandum of Understanding Regarding Cooperation Between the Department of Labor of the United States of America and the Secretariat of Labor and Social Welfare of the United Mexican States (White House 1991: tab 3, pp. 20-24; see also pp. 16-19) was one of the items promised by Bush's action plan. The U.S. and Mexican governments also agreed to an Integrated Environmental Plan for the Border to address the concerns expressed by U.S. environmentalist critics of a trade agreement with Mexico (Grayson 1995: 66-67; see also White House 1991: tab 4).

　　　　The Canadian government sought to join the Mexico-U.S. labor accord and make it trilateral in focus. When U.S. officials demurred, Canada proceeded to negotiate a similar three-year Canada-Mexico Memorandum of Understanding on Co-Operative Labor Activities, which was signed on May 4, 1992 (author's interview [hereinafter "interview(s)"] with a senior Canadian NAALC negotiator [McKinnerey], September 12, 2007, Ottawa). See Government of Canada 1993a: 58 for a summary of the agreement's content.

　　　　The administration of President James E. (Jimmy) Carter (1977-1981) had formulated a similar labor cooperation program with Mexico in 1979, but the Reagan administration abolished it in 1981 (Canadian Labour Congress 1996: 61n3; Charnovitz 1994b: 53).

65.   Housman and Orbuch 1993: 769-70, 772. The U.S. Department of Labor's Labor Advisory Committee for Trade Negotiations and Trade Policy dismissed these activities, one of which was the First Annual United States-Mexico International Law Conference (Secretaría del Trabajo y Previsión Social / U.S. Department of Labor 1993), as "political window dressing."

66.   Housman and Orbuch 1993: 772-74. The full title of this accord was "Agreement Between the Government of the United States of America and the Government of Mexico Complementing the 1991 Memorandum of Understanding on Labor Cooperation, and Regarding the Establishing of a Consultative Commission on Labor Matters." The agreement anticipated (art. 4) an exchange of information on labor standards and working conditions (including workplace safety and health), child labor, labor law and worker rights, procedures for resolving labor disputes, retraining programs, and labor standards for migrant workers.

67. Secretaría de Comercio y Fomento Industrial (SECOFI), "Negociación de asuntos paralelos" (March 10, 1993), p. 4 (a copy of this document is in the author's possession). See also Herzstein 1995: 124n18.

68. Taylor 1994: 49n224; Miller 1996: 164–65; MacArthur 2000: 128; Grayson 1995: 68; Cameron and Tomlin 2000: 75–76. The measure's formal title was Expressing the Sense of the House of Representatives with Respect to the United States Objectives that Should Be Achieved in the Negotiation of Future Trade Agreements (102nd Congress, First Session).

    President Bush's request for an extension of fast-track negotiating authority was, in effect, approved when resolutions opposing it were defeated in the House of Representatives (by a 231–192 vote) on May 23, 1991 and in the Senate (by a 59–36 vote) on May 24, 1991 (MacArthur 2000: 125).

69. Mexican government representatives lobbied behind the scenes to soften the terms of the Gephardt-Rostenkowski resolution (von Bertrab 1997: 33). The Mexican government also presumably encouraged senior leaders of the Confederation of Mexican Workers (Confederación de Trabajadores de México, CTM), the country's largest labor organization and the official labor affiliate of the ruling Institutional Revolutionary Party (Partido Revolucionario Institucional), to publish opinion pieces in the *Wall Street Journal* and the *Washington Post* in May 1991. In these articles (Velázquez Sánchez 1991, Romo 1991), CTM leaders defended the Mexican labor movement's record in protecting worker rights, reassured their Canadian and U.S. counterparts that they favored North American labor solidarity, explained their support for the NAFTA in terms of Mexico's need to improve economic productivity and create employment, and—in Salinas-style language—argued that the legitimate defense of labor interests required a creative response to globalization and de facto North American economic integration.

70. Mazza 2001: 71; Mayer 1998: 73, 206.

71. Mayer 1998: 73, 86.

72. Taylor 1994: 46–47n213, 92; Housman and Orbuch 1993: 776; McCaffrey 1993: 463–64.

73. Two-thirds of Democratic members of the House of Representatives voted against the extension of fast-track trade negotiating authority in May 1991 (Cameron and Tomlin 2000: 76). The Democratic National Committee also opposed the measure (Mazza 2001: 79).

74. Interviews with former senior USTR official B [Hills], March 9, 2018, and a former senior U.S. Department of Labor official [Pérez-López], June 7, 2018, both in Washington, DC. See also Mayer 1998: 85, 207; Mazza 2001: 81–82. The Bush administration's low expectations concerning the U.S. labor movement's stance regarding the NAFTA carried over into the negotiations themselves. Labor concerns on such matters as domestic-content rules for the automobile industry found little support (Mayer 1998: 114, 121, 157).

75. Interview with former senior USTR official B [Hills].

76. Salinas de Gortari 2002: 105. See also Thorup 1991: 17–18, 21; Orme 1996: 81; Mayer 1998: 81–82, 206–207. In February 1992, Canadian officials proposed parallel agreements to the NAFTA on labor and environmental issues, but Bush administration officials were unwilling to pursue those discussions. Statement by Michael Wilson, Canada's minister of international trade, at a joint press conference with USTR Michael (Mickey) Kantor in Washington, DC, on April 2, 1993; see Kukucha 2008: 177.

77.   Hufbauer and Schott 2005: 118.

78.   Salinas de Gortari 2002: 70.

79.   The U.S. negotiating team initially sought to slow the negotiations in order to extract concessions from Mexico, whose government had the strongest interest in securing a free-trade agreement. Canadian representatives felt no urgency because the CUSFTA was their fallback position. As the 1992 U.S. presidential election approached and pressures mounted for the Bush administration to conclude an agreement, Mexican negotiators found bargaining advantages in holding out for better terms on issues of vital importance to them (Cameron and Tomlin 2000: 165; Salinas de Gortari 2002: 70).

80.   Perot 1993: 133, 143; MacArthur 2000: 187; Grayson 1995: 113–17; Orme 1996: 92–97. Perot also strongly criticized the Mexican government's labor policies (Mazza 2001: 86).

    Patrick J. Buchanan, a conservative rival to President Bush during the 1992 Republican presidential primaries, also opposed the NAFTA (Orme 1996: 89; Mazza 2001: 86).

81.   "Bush Acts on Trade Pact," *New York Times*, September 18, 1992; Cameron and Tomlin 2000: 179–80.

82.   von Bertrab 1997: 105; Cameron and Tomlin 2000: 179.

83.   von Bertrab 1997: 119–23.

84.   Cameron and Tomlin 2000: 179–80. Republican efforts to split the Democratic Party over trade issues had begun during the 1991 fast-track debate (MacArthur 2000: 114).

85.   Clinton 2004: 122, 319. Working through Representative Bill Richardson (Democrat-New Mexico), the Salinas administration lobbied to moderate anti-NAFTA language in the Democratic Party's official 1992 platform (von Bertrab 1997: 76). For an analysis of Mexico's overall pro-NAFTA lobbying efforts and the financial resources devoted to this campaign, see Grayson 1995: 153–65; von Bertrab 1997.

86.   Clinton 2004: 432. See also Grayson 1995: 110–12, 117–18.

87.   Mayer 1998: 167–68. The Democratic Party's 1992 electoral program sought to achieve a similar balance. It called for "fair" trade, acknowledging that "multilateral trade agreements can advance our economic interests by expanding the global economy." However, it stressed that in the NAFTA (or GATT) negotiations "our government must assure that our legitimate concerns about environmental, health and safety, and labor standards are included. Those American workers whose jobs are affected must have the benefit of effective adjustment assistance" (quoted in Grayson 1995: 117–18).

88.   Clinton 1992: 4–7. See also Ifill 1992; Grayson 1995: 129–31; Cowie 1997: 24n47.

89.   Clinton 1992: 15. Senior Clinton campaign advisers apparently consulted with Mexican officials as Clinton formulated his position on the NAFTA (*IUST*, September 4, 1992), and through a private channel, Clinton simultaneously reassured Salinas that he was committed to the agreement (Grayson 1995: 121; see also MacArthur 2000: 163, 165–66).

90.   Clinton 1992: 13–15.

91.   Quoted in Cameron and Tomlin 2000: 180.

92.   Grayson 1995: 138–39; Woodward 1994: 314; *IUST*, July 30, 1993a. Given the political salience of the issue, it is remarkable that Clinton's memoirs (2004: 432, 464, 557, 893) include only a short paragraph on final approval of the NAFTA text in August 1992 and three passing references to the environmental and labor side-agreements. He devotes more space (756–57) to his 1997 commencement address at his daughter's school.

93.   MacArthur 2000: 162–63; Cameron and Tomlin 2000: 185.

94. As noted in chapter 2, exports and imports of goods and services represented only 12.6 percent of U.S. gross national product in 1970, a substantially lower percentage than in other industrialized countries such as Canada, the Federal Republic of Germany, Great Britain, France, and Japan. By 1980, this share had risen to 25 percent (Oye 1983: 25, citing *Economic Report of the President*, 1982, table B-2). The cross-national comparison draws on data in Odell 1982: 213n45 (based on United Nations and World Bank data).

95. Donohue (1992: 9-13, 21-28, *passim*) traces U.S. organized labor's support for trade liberalization to the 1934 Reciprocal Trade Adjustment Act.

96. Donohue 1992: 52-63. This legislation established adjustment assistance for U.S. workers who lost their jobs because of import competition.

97. Cowie (1997: 5-6) argues that U.S. labor's position on trade policy began to change by the early 1970s as a result of growing commercial competition from Japan and Western Europe. See also Ahlquist, Clayton, and Levi 2014: 48.

98. Hirsch 2008: 156-58; see also Farber 1990. Hirsch (158-62) discusses the reinforcing structural ("shifts in employment away from occupations, industries, and regions where union density has traditionally been high toward sectors with lower density"), competitive (the effect of unions on companies' financial performance in a competitive national and/or international environment), and institutional (factors affecting union organizing, including the legal environment, management opposition, worker attitudes toward unions, government regulation of the labor market, and so forth) causes of this decline.

99. Grayson 1995: 180.

100. In 1983, the Mexican government extended maquiladora regulations to the entire country (R. Pastor and Castañeda 1988: 227).

101. Van Waas 1981: 91-96.

102. Sklair 1993: tables 3.3, 11.1. For analyses of the evolution of the maquiladora industry, see Mendiola 1999 and Middlebrook and Zepeda 2006.

103. Of the 760 maquiladora plants in operation in 1985, 36.1 percent produced electronic components and equipment, 14.2 percent fabricated apparel, and 8.2 percent manufactured transport equipment. "Other manufactured goods" accounted for a further 13.8 percent of all plants (author's calculations based on data presented in Sklair 1993: table 3.4). Three-quarters of the manufacturing jobs that U.S. firms created in Mexico in the late 1980s and early 1990s were in the transportation equipment (including automobile parts) and electronics sectors (Spriggs and Stanford 1993: 510).

104. Spriggs and Stanford 1993: 512-13.

105. Hirsch 2008: 162, 166-67, 169.

106. Spriggs and Stanford (1993: 513) concluded that, because Mexican wages lagged behind productivity gains, "Mexico has acquired an enormous competitive advantage in unit labor costs (wages relative to productivity)." See Hualde 1996: 305n3 on union density in the maquiladora sector circa 1990.

107. See, for example, Mayer 1998: 88-89; Donohue 1991: 93-94; Anderson 1993: 55-57; Mangone 1993; Kay and Evans 2018: 106. At the time, Donahue served as secretary-treasurer of the AFL-CIO and chaired the USTR's Labor Advisory Committee on International Trade. See Bronfenbrenner 1997: 4, 7 on U.S. employers' threats to move production to Mexico as a bargaining strategy vis-à-vis U.S. workers.

During the intense national debate over the NAFTA, opponents of the agreement played upon these fears by taking U.S. union members and sympathetic U.S. legislators on "educational tours" of maquiladora communities in northern Mexico. There they witnessed first-hand the difficult workplace and living conditions endured by Mexican workers employed in the sector. Both the International Brotherhood of Electrical Workers and the Amalgamated Clothing and Textile Workers' Union published lists of companies that had shifted production to Mexico and calculations of the number of jobs that had been lost as a result (Cowie 1997: 12, 14; Mayer 1998: 225–26).

108. Mexican trade negotiators had remarkably little sympathy for their U.S. trade union opponents. See, for example, the views of Hermann von Bertrab (1997: 9–10, 22–23, 29), head of Mexico's Washington, DC–based Office for the Free Trade Agreement. The response of President Salinas de Gortari to U.S. labor's fears about the employment impact of a free-trade agreement was, in a veiled reference to Mexican out-migration, that "U.S. unions will lose more jobs if Mexicans don't find them in Mexico" (quoted in R. Pastor 1990: 21).

109. Sklair 1993: 47–49; Cowie 1997: 6, 1999: 193; Mayer 1998: 71–72. The AFL-CIO also called for the elimination of foreign tax credits and any trade benefits for U.S. companies that transferred production to Mexico (*IUST*, February 19, 1993a).

110. *IUST*, February 19, 1993b; Kilborn 1993; Marcus and Swoboda 1993; Mayer 1998: 179. Union membership as a proportion of total public-sector employment remained largely unchanged during the 1970s and 1980s (Hirsch 2008: 158).

111. *IUST*, September 17, 1993a.

112. Grayson (1995: 219) calculated that "70.9 percent of the 134 representatives who had received more than $40,000 per year from labor PACs [Political Action Committees] between January 1, 1993, and June 30, 1993, opposed the accord." See also Shoch 2000: 125; Steagall and Jennings 1996. Clinton (2004: 769) attributed the defeat of fast-track trade legislation in 1997 to concern by Democratic members of Congress that, if they voted for the measure, they would lose crucial labor support in the 1998 midterm congressional elections.

113. Orme (1996: 103) cites a poll taken by the *Wall Street Journal* in November 1992 showing that only 21 percent of respondents backed the NAFTA. Secretary of the treasury Lloyd Bentsen feared that strong labor opposition might cause Clinton to abandon the NAFTA (Woodward 1994: 317–18), but Clinton publicly condemned labor's "real roughshod, muscle-bound tactics" and "the raw muscle, the sort of naked pressure that the labor forces have put on" (quoted in Grayson 1995: 209).

114. Wikipedia, s.v. "LV Legislatura del Congreso de la Unión de México," last updated March 13, 2023, http://es.wikipedia.org/wiki/LV_Legislatura_del_Congreso_de_la_Uni%C3%B3n_de_M%C3%A9xico.

115. Lawson 2002: 25–26, 28–30.

116. Salinas de Gortari 2002: 61, 64–66.

117. In late October 1991, Herminio Blanco Mendoza, secretary of trade and industry and Mexico's chief NAFTA negotiator, told participants in an Overseas Development Council conference that labor, environmental, and migration issues were not topics for a free-trade agreement (Robert 2000: 36). Mexico had also been among the leaders

of developing-country opposition to Bush administration efforts to establish a GATT working group on labor rights (Robinson 1993: 31).

118. Interview with a former high-level Mexican elected official [Salinas], July 6, 2006, Mexico City. However, Mexican officials apparently thought that any agreements reached after the end of the main NAFTA negotiations would be "cosmetic" (von Bertrab 1997: 21, 77, 81; see also Mayer 1998: 168).

119. In his March 8, 1990 telephone call to President Bush initiating NAFTA negotiations, Salinas stated that he wished to pursue a free-trade agreement with the United States because "in Mexico I want to consolidate the policies for a market-oriented economy" (accessed May 15, 2018, https://bush4/library.tamu.edu/files/memcons-telcons/1990-03 -08--Salinas.pdf).

120. The Salinas administration made extensive economic contingency plans to prepare for possible rejection of the NAFTA by the U.S. Congress (Salinas de Gortari 2017: 293-94, 298-300).

121. Mexican officials and Clinton's senior foreign policy advisers had established a private channel of communications about the NAFTA as early as September 1992 (Salinas de Gortari 2017: 245-46).

122. Salinas de Gortari 2017: 248.

123. Golden 1992. Of the three topics Clinton had raised in his North Carolina State University campaign address, Salinas commented on environmental and worker-adjustment issues but not on labor law enforcement in Mexico.

    Salinas de Gortari reports (2017: 247) that Clinton confirmed to him on October 28 that he did not intend to reopen negotiations over the NAFTA text.

124. Cameron and Tomlin 2000: 181-82; Garciadiego et al. 1994: 822.

125. Garciadiego et al. 1994: 845-46; Clinton 2004: 464; Mayer 1998: 169; Cameron and Tomlin 2000: 183. Clinton had previously assured Salinas of his support for the NAFTA during their telephone conversation on November 4, 1992 (Garciadiego et al. 1994: 811). As noted above, in his October 4 North Carolina State University campaign speech, Clinton had indicated that he believed his concerns regarding labor and environmental issues could be addressed "without renegotiating the basic agreement."

126. von Bertrab 1997: 80, 82.

127. For detailed examinations of state-labor relations in postrevolutionary Mexico, see Middlebrook 1995 and Bensusán 2000. This overview draws on Bensusán and Middlebrook 2012: chap. 2.

128. This discussion draws on Middlebrook 1995: 62-70. See also Bensusán 1992, 2000.

129. Between 1924 and 1928, CROM leader Luis N. Morones served as minister of industry, commerce, and labor—the only nationally prominent labor leader ever to hold cabinet-level office in Mexico.

130. See Bensusán and Middlebrook 2012: chap. 3 for an examination of these developments.

131. For example, Cowie (1999: 116) documents that U.S. investors found labor peace to be one of the most attractive features of Mexico's maquiladora industry.

132. Salinas de Gortari 2017: 122; Moncayo and Trejo Delarbre 1993: 17, 26.

133. Garciadiego et al. 1994: 834, 843; interview with former Mexican secretary of labor and social welfare A [Palacios Alcocer], June 27, 2012, Mexico City.

134. Middlebrook 1995: 293–94.

135. Other examples of CTM bargaining leverage at the time include its success at blocking both the proposal to eliminate the PRI's established sectoral structure (as noted above, the CTM was the party's official labor sector) in 1990 and 1993 and the Salinas administration's efforts to reform the Federal Labor Law in 1992 (Middlebrook 1995: 297–98).

136. Moncayo and Trejo Delarbre (1993: 16–30) overview Mexican labor leaders' views concerning a North American free-trade agreement.

137. Interview with Canadian Labour Congress international affairs officers, September 12, 2007, Ottawa; Ayres 1998: 123–24. Moncayo and Trejo Delarbre (1993: 22n12) list RMALC coalition members.

138. This discussion draws on Massicotte 2009: 132–41.

139. "Los sindicatos . . . FAT" 1997. Stevenson (1994: 21) estimated a FAT membership of 7,000. See also Hathaway 2000: 117, 176.

140. Chapter 4 discusses the FAT and its role in North American labor alliances.

141. Doern and Tomlin 1991: 110, 210, 212, 234; Brunelle and Dugas 2009: 61–63; interview with Canadian Labour Congress (CLC) international affairs officers. The Network (later renamed Action Canada Network, in deference to the sensitivities of Québec nationalists) linked thirty national organizations and ten provincial groups.

142. Spriggs and Stanford (1993: 528–29) conclude that approximately two-thirds of job losses in Canadian manufacturing industries between 1989 and 1991 were due to firms shifting production to the United States in response to wage and tax advantages available under the CUSFTA.

143. Morisette, Schellenberg, and Johnson 2005: 5–6. The greatest decline in the manufacturing industry (10.9 percentage points) occurred between 1989 and 1998 (7). For a comparison of unionization trends in Canada and the United States, see Riddell 1993.

144. Robinson (1995: 516 [table 1]) lists the Canadian unions and NGOs opposing the NAFTA.

145. The Québec Workers Federation (Fédération des Travailleurs et Travailleuses du Québec), the largest labor federation in Québec, generally supported free trade. However, as a disciplined member, it did not dissent from the CLC's public position (interview with a senior member of Canada's NAALC negotiating team [Morpaw], September 11, 2007, Ottawa).

The strength of the Canadian union-civil society alliance against the CUSFTA also inspired the creation of a North American Worker-to-Worker Network to mobilize broad opposition to the NAFTA (Hecker 1993: 359).

146. Brunelle and Dugas 2009: 68; Thompson and Randall 1994: 294; Doern and Tomlin 1991: 262; Campbell 1993. Canadian concerns about the impact of the NAFTA on expansive domestic social programs was rooted in the CUSFTA experience, in which U.S. negotiators had argued that they constituted non-tariff protectionist barriers (Brunelle and Dugas 2009: 61–62). See Brunelle and Dugas 2009: 72 for an overview of post-NAFTA job losses in Canada.

147. Interview with a senior member of Canada's NAALC negotiating team [Morpaw]; North American Commission for Labor Cooperation 1998a: annex 5, pp. 8–9.

148. Kim Campbell succeeded Mulroney as leader of the Progressive Conservative Party and prime minister on June 12, 1993. Liberal Party leader Jean Chrétien decisively defeated

Campbell in the October 25 general elections, before the NAFTA had been proclaimed law. However, Chrétien, who in opposition had opposed free-trade agreements, finally decided to support the NAFTA, and his government proclaimed it law in mid-November 1993 (Cameron and Tomlin 2000: 193, 203; Hart 2002: 396–97).

149. B. Appleton 1994: 9–10. The 1937 ruling of the British Privy Council (the final court of appeal in Canada before 1949) on federal versus provincial authority over the implementation of treaty obligations came in the *Labour Conventions* case, which concerned the implementation of International Labour Organization conventions in Canada.

150. Doern and Tomlin 1991: 51–52, 126–51, 227–28. The provincial governments of Alberta and Quebéc had supported the NAFTA, but they condemned enforceable labor and environmental side-agreements as "an intolerable affront to provincial jurisdiction" (Robinson 1993: 37).

151. For an overview of the concurrent trilateral negotiations on import surges (a subject already addressed in chapter 8 of the NAFTA), see Grayson 1995: 132–33. For an examination of the negotiations leading to the North American Agreement on Environmental Cooperation, see Grayson 1995: 133–44; Cameron and Tomlin 2000: 183–200.

152. Interview with a former senior U.S. Department of Labor official [Pérez-López], May 27, 2008, Washington, DC. The U.S. government agencies represented in the labor side-agreement negotiations included the departments of labor, state, and commerce; the National Labor Relations Board; and the Federal Mediation and Conciliation Service (telephone interview with a former senior U.S. Department of Labor official [Pérez-López], June 17, 2020.

153. Grayson 1995: 134, 138–40; interview with former senior USTR official A [Roh], May 27, 2007, Washington, DC; telephone interview with a former senior U.S. Department of Labor official [Pérez-López], June 17, 2020. See also U.S. Senate 1993: 4, 14–16, 52; *IUST*, May 7(a), May 28, October 22 1993a; Mayer 1998: 169. The Department of State's reservations focused specifically on new North American environmental institutions, but initially the Clinton administration's labor rights and environmental protection proposals closely paralleled each other in such areas as institutional design and trade-based sanctions for rights violations. Some parts of the U.S. labor movement also had reservations about a supranational body with strong enforcement powers (interview with a former senior U.S. Department of Labor official [Pérez-López], May 27, 2008).

154. Grayson 1995: 140; Mayer 1998: 189–90.

155. Bradsher 1993: 1; Woodward 1994: 318; MacArthur 2000: 174–75, 183, 253, 274.

156. Mayer 1998: 168–69, 178, 183.

157. AFL-CIO 1993a: 5. In this document, the AFL-CIO argued (3–5) that "as a framework for negotiations, the parties should utilize conventions and recommendations of the International Labor Organization," referring specifically to conventions concerning freedom of association and the rights to organize and bargain collectively, forced labor, child labor, minimum wages, hours of work, occupational safety and health, and workplace discrimination.

158. Telephone interview with a former senior U.S. Department of Labor official [Pérez-López], June 17, 2020.

159. Mayer 1998: 178; Cameron and Tomlin 2000: 191, 194.

160. Grayson 1995: 147, 181; Cameron and Tomlin 2000: 197, 199; Mayer 1998: 178–79; interview with a former senior U.S. Department of Labor official [Pérez-López], May 27, 2008. The U.S. negotiators also consulted with the United Automobile, Aerospace, and Agricultural Implement Workers of America (UAW), International Brotherhood of Teamsters, United Steelworkers, International Brotherhood of Electrical Workers, and textile and apparel workers' unions (email communication with a former senior U.S. Department of Labor official [Pérez-López], June 18, 2018).

    As part of the AFL-CIO's strategy, in January 1993, its representatives opened discussions with the confederation's nominal Mexican ally, the CTM, about creating a trinational organization to defend workers' interests under a North American free-trade agreement. Fidel Velázquez, the CTM's leader, responded positively (Garciadiego et al. 1994: 848, 850), but nothing concrete resulted from this initiative (interview with a former UAW senior staff member [Beckman], August 7, 1995, Washington, DC).

161. These initial options were posed in a paper prepared by an interagency group chaired by Jorge Pérez-López, director of the Department of Labor's Office of International Economic Affairs (Bureau of International Labor Affairs). During the 1991 fast-track debate, Pérez-López had coordinated the negotiations with Mexican labor officials that led to a bilateral memorandum of understanding on labor standards (Cameron and Tomlin 2000: 184). See also Kay and Evans 2018: 119.

162. The term *border measures* referred to the NAFTA provisions on intellectual property rights (arts. 1714–1717), which included blocking the importation of illegally produced goods (*IUST*, March 8, 1993).

163. *IUST*, March 8, 1993; Cameron and Tomlin 2000: 190; Grayson 1995: 145; Mayer 1998: 165, 171, 183; Kay and Evans 2018: 120; interviews with a former senior U.S. Department of Labor official [Pérez-López], May 27, 2008, June 17, 2020, and former senior USTR official A [Roh].

    Although Clinton administration officials did not table a formal labor rights proposal until May 1993, some of its main elements had, in fact, been considered during the 1992 presidential campaign. For example, a memorandum on the NAFTA prepared by Clinton advisor Barry Carter on September 28, 1992, discussed trade-based sanctions for rights violations and introduced the idea of a "Commission on Worker Standards" that would have "powers to award money damages or possibly issue injunctions" (quoted in MacArthur 2000: 160; see also p. 161). Clinton's speech at North Carolina State University on October 4 quite accurately signaled the eventual parameters of the NAALC (and the environmental side-agreement as well) by focusing on the effective enforcement of national laws and by calling for the creation of trilateral commissions on labor and environmental issues.

164. *IUST*, March 5, 1993a.

165. Secretaría de Comercio y Fomento Industrial (SECOFI), "Negociación de asuntos paralelos," p. 4 (a copy of this document is in the author's possession).

166. USTR Kantor met with Canadian and Mexican trade ministers on, respectively, February 8 and 17, 1993 in Washington, DC to begin discussions of the labor (and environmental) side-agreements (*IUST*, February 12, 1993; Garciadiego et al. 1994: 858).

167. *IUST*, April 2, 1993; Taylor 1994: 65n305; von Bertrab 1997: 84; Grayson 1995: 146. Some broad similarities in the initial Canadian and U.S. written drafts of a labor side-agreement suggest that this exchange did promote partial consensus regarding the overall institutional design of a North American labor commission.

    Grayson (144–45) names the labor negotiators from the three signatory countries. See also Mayer 1998: 171.

168. *IUST*, April 2, May 14, 1993; Grayson 1995: 146–47; Mayer 1998: 183–86; Cameron and Tomlin 2000: 186, 188. Robinson (1993: 38) compares the different positions taken by U.S. and Canadian negotiators at the April meeting on the authority of any trilateral commission.

169. *IUST*, May 21, 1993d. Domestic political pressures from anti-NAFTA forces led the U.S. bargaining team to harden its position between April and May on such matters as trade-linked penalties for labor rights violations (Mayer 1998: 187, 189; Cameron and Tomlin 2000: 191–92; von Bertrab 1997: 87).

    There are minor discrepancies among the principal published sources concerning the precise dates and specific locations of the negotiation sessions, which initially combined discussions of labor and environmental accords. This discussion draws on Cameron and Tomlin 2000: 186, 192, 194–95; Grayson 1995: 140; von Bertrab 1997: 87; Mayer 1998: 197; *IUST*, March 8, May 14, May 26, June 4(a), August 13(b) 1993.

170. *IUST*, May 21, 1993a. Debates continued within the Clinton administration over its side-agreement positions even after U.S. negotiators presented a draft text at the Hull meeting. See USTR, "Suggested Markup of U.S. Draft Legal Text for NAFTA Labor Pact," June 18, 1993. The author accessed this document and others like it cited in this section through a Freedom of Information Act request to the Office of the United States Trade Representative. They bear no identifying marks and are cited hereinafter simply as "USTR archives."

171. These nine principles included (with illustrative discussion of each one) the following: human resource development, employee voice, distributing the benefits of productivity growth, discouraging the lowering of standards to attract investment, labor-business-government consultation, dialogue among employees "across the border," employment security and career opportunity, social programs (basic health care, workers' compensation, social security), and regional development.

172. Articles 6 and 7 of the U.S. proposal laid out detailed due-process criteria to guide the enforcement of national labor laws. For example, article 6(2b) stipulated that all judicial and administrative proceedings "are open to the public except where the administration of justice requires otherwise."

173. The council could by unanimous vote reject the secretariat's proposed examination of such matters (arts. 9[3], 12[8b]).

174. Article 16(4i) stipulated, "In deciding what sanction is appropriate, the Party shall bear in mind that the purpose of any such suspension should be to encourage enforcement action rather than to create trade protection." To reduce the likelihood that parties might initiate grievances for essentially protectionist reasons, U.S. negotiators apparently took the position that sanctions would not necessarily be applied in the economic sector in which alleged labor rights violations occurred (*IUST*, May 24, 1993).

175. *IUST*, May 21, 1993b. At 11 ¼ pages, the Canadian proposal was longer than either the U.S. (10 ½ pages) or Mexican (8 pages) drafts.

176. Like the U.S. document, the Canadian proposal (arts. 4, 5) contained various stipulations to ensure "effective administrative action" and "effective judicial procedures."

177. Mexican officials viewed this proposal, which was initially supported by U.S. side-agreement negotiators, as an affront to national sovereignty (interview with a then-prominent Mexican labor attorney [de Buen], June 30, 2006, Mexico City). The Canadian proposal did, however, remain under discussion until at least August 6, 1993. See USTR, "Summary of NAFTA Labor Agreement" (August 7, 1993), art. 3 (USTR archives).

178. Interview with a senior Canadian NAALC negotiator [McKinnerey].

179. "A Party may bring to the attention of any other Party any substantial information regarding non-enforcement of that Party's labour laws. The Party so advised shall take appropriate steps to investigate the matter in accordance with its domestic law" (art. 12[1]).

180. Established international practice may have influenced these Canadian formulations. The United Nations Commission on Human Rights can only address "situations of gross, systematic violations," not particular human rights violations, and complaints to the Inter-American Commission on Human Rights are called "communications" (Donnelly 1986: 612, 624).

181. The only limitation was that "the situation concerns workplaces, firms or companies that produce goods and services traded between the Parties or that compete with goods produced or services provided by another Party" (art. 14[1b]).

182. "Any such person or group may also submit information concerning such alleged patterns of which they have indirect knowledge, provided that their communications are accompanied by clear evidence" (art. 15[2]).

183. *IUST*, May 21, 1993c.

184. Even the discussion of potential bilateral or trilateral cooperative programs highlighted Mexico's development status: "Cooperative activities under this Agreement will be undertaken with due recognition of the economic, social, cultural and legislative differences that exist among the Parties"; "The extent to which each Party contributes toward the development of these programs shall be commensurate to that Party's availability of resources" (annex 1[9]).

185. Like the U.S. and Canadian proposals, the Mexican document specified (art. 2) various criteria to ensure due process in labor-related administrative and judicial procedures. The Mexican proposal went further than the U.S. and Canadian documents in this regard by stipulating (art. 2[4]) that, in line with established Mexican institutional arrangements, "The Parties shall maintain or establish a judicial system for the enforcement of labor rights distinct from that Party's system for the enforcement of laws in general."

186. The other examples of potential cooperative activities listed in annex 1 included training programs, labor statistics, work benefits, social programs for workers and their families, and productivity improvement.

187. The Mexican proposal's provisions regarding a secretariat were extremely brief. However, elsewhere the document implied (art. 7[3] stated that a government would submit documents concerning allegations of labor rights violations to "its Section of the Secretariat") that, as in the Canadian proposal, the secretariat would be comprised of national sections. See also Cameron and Tomlin 2000: table 9.1.

188. Annex 2 ("Relationship with the International Labor Organization") noted, "The ILO has extensive experience and has provided technical support and expertise on labor regulation and enforcement systems to members engaged in economic integration processes" (point 4).

     This proposal remained under consideration through at least July 23, 1993 (Government of Canada, "Labour Agreement," July 23, 1993, art. 2[2]; USTR archives), even though U.S. ratification of a comparatively small number of ILO conventions rendered it impractical (interview with a senior Mexican NAALC negotiator, June 9, 2008 [Samaniego], Mexico City). However, later drafts of the side-agreement assigned much more limited roles to the ILO. For instance, in the August 9 draft, the ILO was responsible for defining a roster of experts from which the governing ministerial council would choose the chair of an evaluation committee of experts to resolve a controversy over national labor law enforcement (Government of Canada, "North American Agreement on Labour Cooperation," August 9, 1993, art. 18[3]; see also p. 36; USTR archives).

189. In this regard, article 9(2) stipulated, "Nothing in this Agreement shall be construed to prevent a Party from adopting measures for the purposes of responding to national security matters, national emergencies, and threats of macroeconomic destabilization due to inflation and unemployment."

190. "Industry Letter to Kantor on NAFTA Side Accords," *IUST*, June 11, 1993. With the exception of a fourteen-point list of bilateral or trilateral "cooperative activities" that the NAFTA countries might undertake, most substantive sections of the composite draft included bracketed text indicating the distinct positions still held by one or more of the negotiating teams. Of a total of fourteen such items, six involved Canada (one), Mexico (four), or the United States (one) alone; seven involved Canada and the United States together; and one involved Canada and Mexico together.

191. See, for example, *IUST*, July 23 and 30(b) 1993.

192. Interviews with a senior Mexican NAALC negotiator [Samaniego], June 9, 2008, and a former senior U.S. Department of Labor official [Pérez-López], May 27, 2008.

193. Cameron and Tomlin 2000: 184–85, 188, 198; von Bertrab 1997: 93; interviews with a senior Mexican NAALC negotiator [Samaniego] and a former high-level Mexican elected official [Salinas]; *IUST*, 23 Apr. 1993.

194. von Bertrab 1997: 77.

195. For example, in the composite draft prepared after the May negotiating session, Mexico still held out for an institutional framework in which the ILO would monitor each country's labor law enforcement record ("Composite Draft," art. 2[b]).

196. Interviews with a then-senior CTM leader [Calleja], June 8, 2008, Mexico City, and a then-prominent Mexican labor attorney [de Buen], June 30, 2006.

197. Like the private-sector delegation (comprised of four representatives from the National Confederation of Chambers of Industry [Confederación Nacional de Cámaras Industriales] and the Confederation of National Chambers of Commerce [Confederación de Cámaras Nacionales de Comercio]), the four-member labor delegation had a physical presence in the "side room" (*cuarto de junto* or *cuarto al lado*) at NAALC negotiating sessions. It was comprised of three CTM representatives (Calleja García, Alfonso Reyes Medrano, Netzahualcóyotl de la Vega) and one representative of the Revolutionary Confederation of Workers and Peasants (Confederación Revolucionaria de Obreros y

Campesinos), Roberto Castellanos. The Mexican government also retained Mexico City labor attorney Néstor de Buen Lozano as a special advisor and commissioned him to prepare a study of labor law in the NAFTA countries. Both the business and labor delegations attended the NAALC negotiating sessions at government expense. Interviews with a senior Mexican NAALC negotiator [Samaniego], a then-senior CTM leader [Calleja], and a then-prominent Mexican labor attorney [de Buen]; de Buen 1999: 83n3.

In addition to their "side room" presence, Mexican labor and business organizations were represented on a national Advisory Council (Consejo Asesor) established in September 1990 (M. Fairbrother 2007: 280–81). Six labor representatives participated on the Council (Moncayo and Trejo Delarbre 1993: 25).

198.   Interviews with a former high-level Mexican elected official [Salinas]; a then-senior CTM leader [Calleja]; a former senior U.S. Department of Labor official [Pérez-López], May 27, 2008; and a senior Canadian NAALC negotiator [McKinnerey]. See also Garciadiego et al. 1994: 861, 863–66, 868–69, 886, 890; Cowie 1997: 18; Mayer 1998: 198–99; Cameron and Tomlin 2000: 188–89; Grayson 1995: 147.

199.   Cameron and Tomlin 2000: 196. See also Mayer 1998: 183.

200.   USTR Kantor recognized this point in his first congressional testimony on negotiating side-agreements to the NAFTA (U.S. Senate 1993: 18).

201.   von Bertrab 1997: 81. One measure of the effectiveness of the Mexican government's negotiating position on this issue is that, in postagreement documents promoting the NAALC, the U.S. government lauded the content of Mexican labor law: "Mexico has a comprehensive labor law that provides workers with extensive legal rights. The economic benefits of the NAFTA will provide Mexico with resources to move forward with vigorous enforcement initiatives launched by the Salinas Administration" (White House 1993: 6). For a similar statement by the Canadian government, see Government of Canada 1993b: 48.

202.   Author's analysis of ILO data ("Normlex," accessed February 16, 2016, www.ilo.org/dyn/normlex/en). Over time, both Canada (twelve) and Mexico (eight) had withdrawn from some conventions. In effect, the Salinas administration claimed political credit for the significant number (eighteen) of ILO conventions ratified by the prolabor administration of President Lázaro Cárdenas (1934–1940).

203.   Mexico had not yet ratified convention no. 98 on the right to organize and bargain collectively; it ratified no. 138 (on minimum wages) in 2015 and no. 98 in 2019. By the start of the NAALC negotiations, the only fundamental convention ratified by the United States was no. 105 (on the abolition of forced labor). Canada had ratified four of these conventions (nos. 87, 100, 105, and 111), and it ratified no. 29 (on forced labor) in 2011. The ILO's eighth fundamental convention (no. 182, prohibiting the worst forms of child labor), adopted in 1999, was subsequently ratified by all three NAFTA states. See International Labour Organization, "Normlex," accessed February 16, 2016, www.ilo.org/dyn/normlex/en.

204.   Cowie 1997: 24n48.

205.   Interviews with a former senior U.S. Department of Labor official [Pérez-López], May 27, 2008; former senior USTR official A [Roh]; and a senior Mexican NAALC negotiator [Samaniego]. Von Bertrab (1997: 81) notes that Mexican negotiators were prepared to argue this point from the outset.

206. Mayer 1998: 130; Cameron and Tomlin, 2000: 104, 107, 114, 120–21, 124, 148.

207. von Bertrab 1997: 82; Cameron and Tomlin 2000: 197. The Mexican government's position in this regard reflected lessons the Salinas administration had learned during the final NAFTA negotiations in early August 1992. In those discussions, Mexican negotiators toughened their stance as they came to appreciate that President Bush, who wished to announce the deal at the upcoming Republican National Convention, was under increasingly severe time pressures (Cameron and Tomlin 2000: 165, 197).

208. The PRI announced its 1994 presidential candidate, Luis Donaldo Colosio, on November 28, 1993 (Salinas de Gortari 2017: 305), eight days after the U.S. Senate approved the NAFTA.

209. Interview with a senior Canadian NAALC negotiator [McKinnerey].

210. See "U.S. Draft Legal Text," art. 16[4i] and annex, point 8.

211. Farnsworth 1993; Cameron and Tomlin 2000: 188, 192–93, 198; von Bertrab 1997: 87; Mayer 1998: 192.

212. Interviews with a senior Canadian NAALC negotiator [McKinnerey] and a senior member of Canada's NAALC negotiating team [Morpaw]; Cameron and Tomlin 2000: 193, 195; Grayson 1995: 146.

213. *IUST*, February 19(b), June 4(a), August 13(a) 1993; Cameron and Tomlin 2000: 186, 189, 192; von Bertrab 1997: 93.

214. *IUST*, January 29, March 12, May 7(a), May 26, May 28, and June 11, 1993; Mayer 1998: 181–82, 187–88, 190–93; Cameron and Tomlin 2000: 189, 197; von Bertrab 1997: 86, 88. See *IUST*, June 11, 1993 (letter dated June 4, 1993 from the Business Roundtable and seven other U.S. business associations to USTR Kantor) for a detailed business critique of the initial U.S. proposal for a labor side-agreement.

215. By mid-June, U.S. side-agreement negotiators had moved beyond their initial May proposal and were seriously considering monetary fines rather than trade-based sanctions as penalties in response to "a pattern of persistent and unjustified nonenforcement." See USTR, "Suggested Markup of U.S. Draft Legal Text for NAFTA Labor Pact" (June 18, 1993), pp. 25–26 (USTR archives).

216. Cameron and Tomlin 2000: 193–95; von Bertrab 1997: 93; *IUST*, July 9, 1993. Canada accepted the idea of levying fines for persistent labor rights violations, but, like Mexico, it continued to reject trade-linked sanctions.

217. Cameron and Tomlin 2000: 195–96.

218. USTR, "Labor Issues for Consideration by Ministers," July 29, 1993; Government of Canada, "Structure and Function of Secretariat: Summary of July 8 Discussions," July 8, 1993; "Labour Agreement" (July 23), art. 8(2)(d); "Labour Agreement" (August 7, 1993), part IV, item 4(d); "North American Agreement on Labour Cooperation" (August 9, 1993), pp. 34–35. All the cited documents were located in the USTR archives.

219. Government of Canada, "Structure and Function of Secretariat," item 4 ("Concerns, issues, complaints are first brought to the attention of the National Administrative Unit in the country in which the issue is raised"). See also USTR, "Status of NAFTA Labor Supplemental Talks" (July 13, 1993), p. 2 (USTR archives).

  Mayer (1998: 194) indicates that the U.S. Department of Labor and some U.S. labor unions, in contrast to U.S. environmental groups that pushed for an autonomous trilateral environmental commission, favored national administrative offices. See also interviews with a former senior U.S. Department of Labor official [Pérez-López], May 27,

2008, and former senior USTR official A [Roh]. However, some congressional Democrats preferred an independent trilateral labor commission that would be less vulnerable to influence by national governments (*IUST*, June 4, 1993a).

220. Compare Government of Canada, "Labour Agreement" (July 23, 1993), p. 2; and "Labour Agreement" (August 3, 1993), p. 3 (USTR archives).

221. See, for example, SECOFI, "Proposed Agenda for Labor" (June 7, 1993), point IV (USTR archives); and USTR, "Labor Issues for Consideration by Ministers," July 29, 1993 (USTR archives).

222. The August 9 draft text (Government of Canada, "North American Agreement on Labour Cooperation," USTR archives) specifically defined (p. 39) "technical labor standards" to include eight of the agreed labor principles—all those except freedom of association and protection of the right to organize, the right to bargain collectively, and the right to strike. Mexican negotiators were the probable authors of this provision.

223. See articles 21-24 of the August 9 draft text.

224. This summary draws on Bradsher 1993: 1, 45; von Bertrab 1997: 94; Mayer 1998: 203; Salinas de Gortari 2017: 279; Cameron and Tomlin 2000: 197-98, 202; *IUST*, August 13, 1993b, c.

225. Mayer 1998: 198; Cameron and Tomlin 2000: 197. Final details of the agreement's dispute-settlement provisions were not agreed until after the formal conclusion of the side-agreement negotiations (interview with a former senior U.S. Department of Labor official [Pérez-López], May 27, 2008; "North American Agreement on Labor Cooperation," September 4, 1993, USTR archives).

226. *IUST*, August 13, 1993c; Cameron and Tomlin 2000: 197-98.

227. Grayson 1995: 141; von Bertrab 1997: 94; Mayer 1998: 197-200; Cameron and Tomlin 2000: 198; *IUST*, August 13, 1993c.

228. Mayer 1998: 203; Cameron and Tomlin 2000: 198. Mexican negotiators rejected using the judicial system to enforce penalties on the grounds that such an arrangement would violate national sovereignty (*IUST*, August 13, 1993c).

229. Mayer 1998: 199, 201-202; Cameron and Tomlin 2000: 197.

230. González Graf 2009: 128. A full summary of NAALC provisions appears in chapter 4.

231. Mayer 1998: 201-202; interview with a former senior U.S. Department of Labor official [Pérez-López], May 27, 2008.

232. A "Memorandum from Michael Kantor to Mack McLarty, Chief of Staff" (USTR archives) dated August 9, 1993, indicates that occupational safety and health and child labor were then under discussion as dispute-settlement issues, but it does not mention minimum wage standards. See also Herzenberg 1996a: 25.

233. DePalma 1993; Bradsher 1993: 45; Orme 1996: xvi; von Bertrab 1997: 94; Mayer 1998: 201-2.

234. "Memorandum from Michael Kantor"; *IUST*, March 8, May 7(b) 1993; Herzenberg 1996a: 10-11.

235. The U.S. proposal ("Statement of Labor Principles") was most explicit in this regard: "Equitable distribution of rising productivity in the form of higher compensation for workers at all levels helps maintain the labor-management cooperation necessary to achieve further improvements in productivity and quality. This principle should be reflected, in particular, in the growth of the minimum wage over time." However,

side-agreement negotiators did not consider this proposal after June 18; see USTR, "Suggested Markup of U.S. Draft Legal Text for NAFTA Labor Pact" (June 18, 1993), p. 3 (USTR archives).

236. Interview with senior CTM staff member [Martínez], June 19, 1992, Mexico City; Middlebrook 1995: 298. Instead, Salinas agreed that the government would recognize agreements negotiated company-by-company that linked wage increases to productivity gains (STPS 1992).

237. Salinas de Gortari 2017: 280–81, 283; von Bertrab 1997: 94; Mayer 1998: 201–2; MacArthur 2000: 180.

238. *IUST*, September 17, 1993b. Clinton did not submit the NAFTA implementing legislation to Congress until November 14.

239. The government of Canada apparently joined in this effort. There is documentary evidence that the physical location of the Commission on Labor Cooperation's Secretariat was initially planned for a Canadian city (Government of Canada 1993b: 41). The location was switched to Dallas, Texas, in order to support Clinton's efforts to mobilize final legislative support for the NAFTA (interview with a senior member of Canada's NAALC negotiating team [Morpaw]).

240. Bradsher 1993: 45.

241. *IUST*, July 30, 1993a; MacArthur 2000: 184.

242. Quoted in Bradsher 1993: 1; see also p. 45. See also *IUST*, August 16, September 24, 1993. Taylor (1994: 69n322) gives September 21, 1993 as the date of Gephardt's statement. Gephardt specifically criticized the NAALC for not including "industrial relations" issues in dispute-settlement procedures and for eliminating U.S. Generalized System of Preferences–style penalties for failing to comply with international labor rights (see below). In an interview with MacArthur (2000: 183), USTR Kantor claimed that he had at the time thought that the side accords he had negotiated with Canada and Mexico would be sufficient to satisfy Gephardt's concerns. See also Mayer 1998: 173, 180.

243. *Washington Post*, September 1, 1995 (quoted in Grayson 1995: 177); Kay and Evans 2018: 129. Robert (Bob) White, president of the Canadian Labour Congress, also dismissed the accord as a "toothless tiger" (White 1993).

244. Bradsher 1993: 45; Mayer 1998: 250–51.

245. Clinton, "Remarks on Naming William M. Daley as NAFTA Task Force Chairman and an Exchange with Reporters," August 19, 1983, *Public Papers of the Presidents of the United States: William J. Clinton* (1993), vol. 2, p. 1389. For similar claims by Clinton that the NAALC and Salinas's minimum wage-productivity commitment would over time reduce the wage gap between Mexico and the United States, see vol. 2, pp. 1381–82, 1406, 1497, 1935, 1967.

246. For other examples of such side-deals, see Grayson 1995: 214–18; von Bertrab 1997: 133–38; Mayer 1998: 316–18; MacArthur 2000: 264–66; Salinas de Gortari 2002: 67. Proposals to implement a comprehensive worker assistance and retraining program (the Workforce Security Act) in conjunction with the NAFTA came to naught. However, the Clinton administration did fund a very modest NAFTA-specific expansion of the existing Trade Adjustment Assistance Program (Mayer 1998: 303–5; *IUST*, October 22, 1993b).

247. *IUST*, November 12, 1993.

248. MacArthur 2000: 274. All members of the House of Representatives cast a vote on the NAFTA; one deceased member of the House had not been replaced at the time of the vote. In the Senate, the pro-NAFTA vote included thirty-four Republicans and twenty-seven Democrats (Grayson 1995: 219). For further details concerning NAFTA supporters and opponents in the House and Senate, see Grayson 1995: 219-20.

249. Mazza 2001: 127-28, 132-33, 138.

250. *IUST*, September 3, 1993. Mexico acceded to the U.S. GSP program when it was inaugurated in 1976 (Peñaloza 1978). In 1992, the country accounted for 29 percent of GSP duty-free imports into the United States (U.S. General Accounting Office 1993a: 5). Over the 1991-1993 period, Mexico's GSP-eligible exports as a proportion of its total exports averaged 11.9 percent (Shadlen 2017: table 2.4; author's email communication with Professor Kenneth C. Shadlen, March 27, 2017).

251. Mayer 1998: 171-72, 182-83, 190; interview with former senior USTR official A [Roh]; *IUST*, August 13, 1993b.

252. Cameron and Tomlin 2000: table 9.1; Grayson 1995: 142-43. The conventional explanation for why the final content of the NAALC and the NAAEC differed in significant ways is that, unlike several major U.S. environmental groups, U.S. labor organizations were unwilling to engage fully in the negotiating process and condition their final support for the NAFTA on a stronger labor accord (Mayer 1998: 84, 209; Cameron and Tomlin 2000: 206-207). However, not all U.S. officials involved in the NAALC negotiations were convinced that more active labor involvement would have significantly altered the outcome (interview with a former senior U.S. Department of Labor official [Pérez-López], May 27, 2008).

253. Domínguez and Fernández de Castro 2001: 32, 141-42; Garciadiego et al. 1994: 845 (see also p. 844 for a statement by a senior Mexican official concerning the country's existing environmental commitments).

254. See, in this regard, von Bertrab 1997: 96; Mayer 1998: 191-92. Grayson (1995: 141) reports that Mexico accepted a strong environmental side-agreement in exchange for a weaker labor accord, but the available evidence (the author's review of NAALC negotiating documents and a telephone interview with a former senior U.S. Department of Labor official [Pérez-López], June 17, 2020, who participated in the negotiations) does not support this interpretation.

255. Salinas de Gortari 2002: 170.

256. Interviews with a senior Canadian NAALC negotiator [McKinnerey]; a senior Mexican NAALC negotiator [Samaniego]; and a former high-level Mexican elected official [Salinas]. See also Cameron and Tomlin 2000: 198.

257. In June 1993, Prime Minister Mulroney framed his opposition to trade sanctions in sovereignty terms (*IUST*, June 4, 1993b).

258. Interview with a senior Mexican NAALC negotiator [Samaniego]. See also Herzenberg 1996a: 25.

259. Herzenberg 1996b: 5; see also Kay and Evans 2018: 130, 133. One U.S. participant in the NAALC negotiations discounts this interpretation (interview with a former senior U.S. Department of State official [Pérez-López], May 27, 2008).

260. *IUST*, August 13, 1993b.

261. Interview with a senior Canadian NAALC negotiator [McKinnerey].

4. THE NORTH AMERICAN AGREEMENT ON LABOR COOPERATION IN PRINCIPLE AND IN PRACTICE, 1994–2020

1. Over the years, there have been many (often only partial) assessments of NAALC processes. The most comprehensive are Human Rights Watch/Americas 2001 and especially Compa and Brooks 2019: chap. 4, whose focus is principally on the legal and institutional dimensions of the NAALC experience. Selected examples of other assessments include, in chronological order: Office of the United States Trade Representative (USTR) 1997: 105-7; Damgaard 1999: 99–106; Graubart 2002, 2008: chap. 3; M. Weiss 2003: 730–51; G. Brown 2004a; Delp et. al 2004; Finbow 2006: chaps. 4–8; González Graf 2009: 147–63; Kay 2011a: 111–69; Nolan García 2011b, 2011c, 2012; Aspinwall 2013: 93-135.

   For analyses of the parallel North American Agreement on Environmental Cooperation, see Taylor 1994: 109–14; R. Sánchez 2002; Knox 2004; Graubart 2008: chap. 4; Aspinwall 2013: chap. 2.

2. Compa and Brooks (2019: 44) argue that the NAALC signatory countries, by implicitly stating that they complied with the agreement's eleven principles, " thereby established de facto a supranational normative framework for North American workers' rights, even if they stopped short of creating new enforceable standards." Of the three NAALC signatory states, Canada came closest to embracing this position. In its public report on public communication, CAN 98-1 (Echlin/Itapsa), the Canadian national administrative office observed (part I: 14), "The NAALC is not designed to determine whether or not employers and unions abide by labour legislation. Rather, it creates a framework of values and principles which the signatory countries must respect, notably in adopting and enforcing labour legislation." It took an even stronger position in its final report on CAN 2003-1 (Puebla garment producers, p. 1–1): "It [the NAALC] creates a framework of values, principles, and obligations that the signatory countries must respect."

3. For the NAALC text and annexes, see *International Legal Materials* 32, no. 6 (1993): 1499–1518.

4. See chapter 3 for background discussion of this issue.

5. Annex 46, point 4(b); Compa and Brooks 2019: 63. In the 1990s, workers under federal jurisdiction constituted less than 10 percent of the Canadian labor force (Robinson 1999: 132).

6. Prince Edward Island and Nova Scotia ratified the NAALC in 1998 and 2008, respectively. In matters involving specific industries or sectors, annex 46, point 4(c) required that the labor force in the ratifying provinces comprise at least 55 percent of the total industry or sector workforce.

7. Article 3 listed the government enforcement actions that would realize this goal, including appointing and training labor inspectors, onsite inspections to monitor compliance and investigate possible violations of labor law, encouraging worker-management committees to address labor issues in the workplace, and encouraging mediation, conciliation, and arbitration services.

8. See also article 43 ("Private Rights"): "No Party may provide for a right of action under its domestic law against any other Party on the ground that another Party has acted in a manner inconsistent with this agreement." Diamond (1996: 217-18) notes that this provision sharply contrasted with the legal options available to parties defending intellectual property rights under the NAFTA (arts. 1714, 1715).

9.   In addition to creating the North American Commission for Labor Cooperation and national administrative offices, the NAALC recognized that each member state might convene a national advisory committee with labor, business, and public representation (art. 17) and a governmental committee (art. 18) comprised of representatives of federal, state, and/or provincial governments to advise it on implementation of the agreement. See Pérez-López 1995c: 9–11 concerning the implementation of these provisions.

10.   Pérez-López 1995b. The council of ministers met on six occasions between March 1994 and 1999 (twice in each of the three member countries) and again in 2003 (Secretaría del Trabajo y Previsión Social 2003). However, there were no council meetings after August 2010, even though North American labor ministers continued to meet regularly in other fora (Compa and Brooks 2019: 38, 48).

11.   Author's interviews (hereinafter "interview[s]") with senior U.S. NAO officials [Garza and Shea], August 7, 1995, Washington, DC, and senior Ministry of Labor and Social Welfare (Secretaría del Trabajo y Previsión Social, STPS) official A [C. Franco], July 7, 2004, Mexico City.

12.   Art. 11. In carrying out these cooperative activities, the parties agreed to show "due regard for the economic, social, cultural, and legislative differences between them" (art. 11[3]).

13.   The NACLC was initially based in Dallas, Texas. The secretariat officially began operations on September 27, 1995, with John S. McKinnerey, a senior Canadian diplomat who had played a leading role in the negotiations leading to the NAALC, serving as its first executive director. (Compa and Brooks [2019: 49] provide the names and nationalities of senior NACLC staff members between 1995 and 2009.) During its first three years of operation, the NACLC sponsored cooperative and training activities concerning occupational safety and health, employment, women in the workplace, nonstandard work (part-time employment, independent contracting, home work), freedom of association and the right to organize, child labor, and income security (unemployment insurance, pensions, workers' compensation) (Compa 1997b: 12–13). Over the course of its operation, the secretariat published at least twelve studies on a range of North American labor law, labor market, and worker rights issues. See the bibliographic entries under North American Commission on Labor Cooperation 1996–2005; Samet 2011: table III.1. Compa and Brooks (2019: 64–66) overview their content.

The NACLC relocated to Washington, DC, in June 2000. The secretariat's activities slowed greatly over time both because of staff vacancies produced by the relocation and because of reduced U.S. government support for its mission (interview with senior NACLC official A [Caulfield], July 7, 2005, Washington, DC). In October 2006, the NACLC Council of Ministers forced Executive Director Mark S. Knouse, a U.S. political appointee, to resign after he was accused of misappropriating funds for personal use (Singer 2006; U.S. House of Representatives 2008). The secretariat closed on August 20, 2010, and never reopened; its website ceased to operate in 2016 (Compa and Brooks 2019: 38, 48). See Samet 2011: 20 for the council's statement on the closing.

14.   Canada's NAO (renamed the Office for Inter-American Labour Cooperation following the signing of a free-trade agreement with Chile in 1997) was established effective January 1, 1994. It formed part of Human Resources Development Canada (Labour Branch) and

later Employment and Social Development Canada's Labour Programme (Bilateral and Regional Affairs). Mexico's NAO was established on July 5, 1994; it was renamed the General Coordination of International Affairs (Coordinación General de Asuntos Internacionales) on April 14, 1997, and the International Affairs Unit (Unidad de Asuntos Internacionales) on August 18, 2003 (Secretaría del Trabajo y Previsión Social 2005). The U.S. NAO was established on December 30, 1993, and began operations in January 1994 as part of the Department of Labor's Bureau of International Labor Affairs. On December 17, 2004, it was renamed the Office of Trade Agreement Implementation, reflecting its responsibility for administering labor provisions in U.S. free-trade agreements other than the NAFTA. On December 14, 2006, it became the Office of Trade and Labor Affairs (Compa and Brooks 2019: 53). For simplicity, this chapter employs the original names of all these offices.

15. Interview with Canadian NAO staff members, September 11, 2007, Ottawa. Finbow (2006: table 9.1) lists the seventy conferences, seminars, and technical training sessions the NAOs coordinated over the 1994–2005 period. The largest number of activities (thirty; 42.9 percent) addressed occupational safety and health issues. The other activities focused on industrial relations and worker rights (twelve; 17.1 percent), labor market development (twelve; 17.1 percent), gender discrimination (seven; 10.0 percent), migrant workers (five; 7.1 percent), and children, violence, and labor trafficking issues (four; 5.7 percent) (author's calculations based on information presented in Finbow 2006: table 9.1; see also USTR 1997: 100–104 and Samet 2011: table III.2).

16. Telephone interview with a former senior U.S. Department of Labor official [Pérez-López], June 17, 2020.

17. As noted in chapter 2, the 1984 U.S. Generalized System of Preferences legislation and subsequent U.S. trade law defined "internationally recognized worker rights" as "the freedom of association, the right to organize and bargain collectively, a prohibition on the use of any form of forced or compulsory labor, the prohibition and elimination of discrimination in respect of employment and occupation, the establishment of a minimum age for the employment of children, and the delineation of acceptable conditions of work with respect to minimum wages, hours of work, and occupational safety and health."

18. Compa (1999d: 17n2) notes that the European Union also divides the elements of its social charter into three tiers of treatment. Directives concerning occupational safety and health and equal treatment for men and women can be adopted by a qualified majority vote of the council of ministers, which binds all member states. Middle-tier issues such as dismissal rules and migrant worker rights require a unanimous council vote, giving each member state a veto. However, pay issues and the rights to association and collective bargaining and to strike are excluded from Europe-wide legislation and left exclusively to national law. See also Compa 1997a.

19. This government-to-government grievance mechanism drew strong criticism from trade unions and labor- and human-rights groups because it sharply contrasted with the rights of private investors under the investor-state dispute settlement procedures in NAFTA's chapter 11. Those procedures allowed a foreign investor to act directly in submitting a claim against a host government to binding arbitration (art. 1115).

20.   Art. 21. Any other NAO was entitled to participate in these consultations (art. 21[3]).

Beginning on January 1, 1994, Canada could participate fully in NAALC cooperative activities, and the Canadian NAO could receive public communications, conduct reviews, and issue reports concerning alleged labor rights violations in federal-jurisdiction economic activities in Mexico and/or the United States. However, Canada could not initiate ministerial consultations or dispute-settlement procedures until 1997. NAALC annex 46, point 4; Compa and Brooks 2019: 62–63; Pérez-López 1995c: 15. See also Robinson 1999: 131–42, fig. 1.

21.   Art. 22. The NAALC placed no limit on the time taken to schedule and conduct ministerial consultations.

22.   Art. 23(2, 3). See articles 24–26 and annex 23 for ECE rules of procedure and article 49 for definitions of "technical labor standards," "trade related," and "mutually recognized labor laws."

23.   See articles 30–40 on the selection of panel members, rules of procedure, criteria for assessing the case and making final panel recommendations, and related matters.

24.   Art. 39(5.b), annex 39, point 1. Note that it was the defendant government and not the private employer(s) responsible for labor rights violations that was liable for monetary penalties.

During the first year after the NAALC entered into force, any fine was limited to US$20 million or its currency equivalent (0.007 percent of the estimated US$285 billion in trade among the NAFTA countries in 1992; Robinson 1993: 42). See annex 39, point 2, for the specific criteria to be employed in determining the amount of the fine. Any fines collected were to be placed in an NACLC fund and employed by the council to "improve or enhance the labor law enforcement in the Party complained against, consistent with its law" (annex 39, point 3).

For illustrative purposes, in 1995, the maximum financial penalty for either Mexico or the United States would have been US$8.412 million; in 2015, it would have been US$34.697 million. Author's calculations based on data in Presidencia de la República, *Quinto informe de gobierno, 2016–2017: Anexo estadístico*, accessed August 12, 2020, http://framework-gb.cdn.gob.mx/quintoinforme/5IG_ANEXO_FINAL_TGM_250818.pdf, 467, 471.

25.   Annex 41B specified that the increased tariffs "were not to exceed the lesser of: (a) the rate that was applicable to those goods immediately prior to the date of entry into force of the NAFTA, and (b) the Most Favored Nation rate applicable to those goods on the date the Party suspends such benefits." Wherever practicable, the suspension of NAFTA tariff benefits was to be in the sector(s) in which nonenforcement had occurred.

The NAALC contained language that, in practice, limited the possibility that monetary penalties or trade sanctions would be levied against a defendant government. Article 49(1) stipulated: "For the purposes of this Agreement: A Party has not failed to 'effectively enforce its occupational safety and health, child labor, or minimum wage technical labor standards' or comply with Article 3(1) in a particular case where the action or inaction by agencies or officials of that Party: (a) reflects a reasonable exercise of the agency's or the official's discretion with respect to investigatory, prosecutorial, or compliance matters; or (b) results from *bona fide* decisions to allocate resources to enforcement in respect of other labor matters determined to have higher priorities." This wording closely followed that proposed by Mexican officials during the NAALC negotiations (chapter 3).

At the Canadian government's insistence, the NAALC exempted Canada from any trade-linked penalties for possible labor rights violations (chapter 3). Instead, Canada agreed to make payment of any fines levied against it mandatory by adopting procedures that made a NAALC arbitral panel's final determination a judicial order under Canadian law (and thus enforceable by summary judicial proceedings without further review or appeal) (annex 41a, point 2).

26. Arts. 40, 41. If two complaining parties suspended trade benefits, the combined suspension could not exceed the amount of the monetary enforcement assessment (art. 41[3]). The defendant country could appeal to the arbitral panel to determine whether the suspension of trade benefits was "manifestly excessive" (art. 41[5]).

27. Among many examples, see Compa 2003a: 41; AFL-CIO 2004a: 2–3; Canadian Association of Labour Lawyers 2006: 12.

28. For Canada, "Guidelines for Public Communications Under Articles 16(3) and 21 of the North American Agreement on Labour Cooperation" (published on April 25, 1997, and in effect through 2013 [author's email communication with the Canadian NAO, September 8, 2020]; reproduced in CAN NAO, "Review of Public Communication CAN 98-1 Part I," annex 1, December 11, 1998). For Mexico, Secretaría del Trabajo y Previsión Social, "Reglamento de la Oficina Administrativa Nacional (OAN) de México sobre las Comunicaciones Públicas a que se refiere el artículo 16(3) del Acuerdo de Cooperación Laboral de América del Norte (ACLAN)," *Diario Oficial de la Federación*, primera sección, April 28, 1995. For the United States, Department of Labor, "Bureau of International Labor Affairs; North American Agreement on Labor Cooperation; Establishment of National Administrative Office," *U.S. Federal Register* 58, no. 249 (December 30, 1993): 69410-11; "Revised Notice of U.S. National Administrative Office and Procedural Guidelines," *U.S. Federal Register* 59, no. 67 (April 7, 1994): 16660-62; and "Notice of Reassignment of Functions of Office of Trade Agreement Implementation to Office of Trade and Labor Affairs; Notice of Procedural Guidelines," *U.S. Federal Register* 71, no. 245 (December 21, 2006): 76691-96.

29. For instance, whereas the U.S. NAO's guidelines (1994: sect. C[4]; 2006: sect. C[6]) authorized it to initiate a review of any matter arising under the NAALC (that is, without having received a public communication regarding the issue), the Canadian and Mexican NAO guidelines were silent on this point. In practice, the U.S. NAO never acted under this authority.

The three NAOs also differed in the budgetary and administrative resources available to them. In 1995, the U.S. NAO had an annual budget of US$2 million (from which was drawn the U.S. one-third share of the NACLC secretariat's budget) and nine staff members (with authorization for a total of thirteen staff members), including labor lawyers, labor economists, and public policy analysts. The Canadian and Mexican NAOs had, respectively, five and four staff members. Interviews with senior U.S. NAO officials [Garza and Shea], August 7, 1995, and former senior Canadian NAO official A [Morpaw], September 11, 2007, Ottawa; DePalma 1994; Damgaard 1998: 16.

30. U.S. guidelines 1994: section H (3, 5); Canadian guidelines 1997: point 4(a); Mexican guidelines 1995: point 7. In the revised US NAO guidelines (2006: section H[3]), public hearings became optional. In practice, the Canadian NAO did hold either public hearings (public communication CAN 98-1, Echlin/Itapsa) or public meetings (public communication CAN 2003-1, Puebla garment producers) as part of its review processes.

31. For further discussion of this issue, see Compa and Brooks 2019: 52. Both U.S. NAO (1994: section F[2.d, e]) and Canadian NAO (1997: point 2.a[iii]) guidelines requested information from submitters concerning their efforts to secure domestic relief and the status of such legal actions or any proceedings before international tribunals. The CAN NAO did not formally exclude submissions from consideration on these grounds, but this criterion did constitute a potential basis for rejection by the US NAO (1994: section G[3.c]). (MEX NAO guidelines did not address the issue.) The only known occasion on which the U.S. NAO invoked this provision involved its decision not to consider minimum labor standards issues (NAALC principle no. 6) in its review of public communication US 940003 (Sony Corporation); see US NAO public report 940003: 3n3, and *BorderLines* 2 (4) (December 1994): 7.

32. At least since the suspension of the NACLC internet site in 2016, there is no single repository for NAALC public communications. The author compiled a complete set of NAALC submissions from several sources: for Canada, Employment and Social Development Canada (Labour Affairs) and U.S. Department of Labor (Bureau of International Labor Affairs); for Mexico, Ministry of Labor and Social Welfare (Secretaría del Trabajo y Previsión Social, Unidad de Asuntos Internacionales) and U.S. Department of Labor (Bureau of International Labor Affairs); and for the United States, U.S. Department of Labor (Bureau of International Labor Affairs), "Submissions Under the North American Agreement on Labor Cooperation (NAALC)," accessed July 18, 2023, https://www.dol.gov/agencies/ilab/submissions-under-north-american-agreement-labor -cooperation-naalc; hereinafter http://www.dol.gov).

33. All results reported in the text are the author's calculations based on data presented in table 4.2 and the NAALC case files. The total number of submitters listed in table 4.2 exceeds the number of sociopolitical actors reported here because a significant proportion of them participated in more than one NAO public communication.

    In the CAN 2011-1 / US 2011-02 parallel submissions focused on the Mexican Electricians Union (SME), several international and regional labor organizations appeared as cosubmitters: International Trade Union Confederation (ITUC); Trade Union Confederation of the Americas (the regional affiliate of the ITUC); International Federation of Chemical, Energy, Mine and General Workers' Unions; International Metalworkers' Federation; International Transport Workers' Federation; UNI Global Union (formerly Union Network International, a global union federation representing skilled workers and service employees); and UNI Americas (US 2011-02 only). Similarly, the Independent Monitoring Group of El Salvador (Grupo Monitoreo Independiente de El Salvador) was a cosubmitter in MEX 2016-1 and MEX 2016-2 concerning gender discrimination against migrant workers in, respectively, the United States and Canada.

34. MEX 2015-1 (U.S. Department of Labor) is excluded from this summary because it was filed by a single individual, not by a labor union or NGO.

35. In parallel submissions to two NAOs, the NAOs are listed in the order in which the public communications were received.

36. The proportion of unions among all participating groups ranged from 28.5 percent in the United States to 63 percent in Canada and 76.1 percent in Mexico.

37. Child labor issues featured in only two NAALC submissions (tables 4.2, 4.3), both with the US NAO (US 9802 and US 2005-3) concerning alleged violations in Mexico.

38. In CAN 99-1, this was a tactical decision taken by the submitter (the U.S.-based Labor Policy Association) in order to make possible the formation of an ECE and an arbitral panel (Compa and Brooks 2019: 118).

39. The exception with regard to filing sequence was CAN 2011-1, which was filed shortly before US 2011-02. Of the seven public communications filed with the Canadian NAO, four alleged labor rights violations in Mexico and three concerned the United States (table 4.2, appendix B).

40. The fact that only a limited number of Canadian provinces ratified the NAALC would not have affected the number or focus of CAN NAO submissions because the Canadian NAO was, from the outset, authorized to receive public communications regarding alleged labor rights violations occurring in Mexico or the United States. The restricted jurisdictional scope of the NAALC in Canada might, however, account in part for the fact that there were only two NAO submissions involving alleged rights violations in Canada, both filed with the U.S. NAO (US 9803, US 9804).

41. See appendix 3 for summaries of the individual US NAO and CAN NAO public communications discussed in this section.

42. The U.S. NAO initially accepted US 9803 (St.-Hubert McDonald's) for review in order to demonstrate to Mexican NAO officials that it was evenhanded in its approach to the public communications it received. However, the complainants withdrew their submission before the review began (interview with a former senior US NAO official [Garza], May 28, 2008, Washington, DC).

43. Six ministerial agreements with Mexico addressed: US 940003 (June 26, 1995); US 9601 (September 6, 1997); US 9701 (October 21, 1998); US 9702 and US 9703 (May 18, 2000); US 9901, US 2000-01, and MEX 9804 (June 11, 2002); and US 2003-01 / CAN 2003-1 (April 24, 2008). Canada was a formal signatory to, or endorsed, all these agreements except the one addressing US 9901, US 2000-01, and MEX 9804.

44. The Canadian NAO accepted for review four of the seven public communications it received (57.1 percent), but it issued final reports in only two of these submissions (table 4.2). Although it accepted for review both CAN 2008-1 (submitted in parallel to MEX 2006-1, concerning the labor rights of North Carolina public employees) and CAN 2011-1 (submitted in parallel to US 2011-02, regarding the SME), the office never concluded its reviews of these two politically charged cases. In CAN 2008-1, Canadian NAO officials saw little prospect that bilateral ministerial consultations (the furthest they could take a case involving NAALC principles nos. 1 and 2) would yield any tangible results because the state of North Carolina had long resisted modifying statute 95-98 (appendix B). In CAN 2011-1, SME leaders requested that the Canadian NAO keep the case open in the hope that continuing international attention might strengthen their bargaining position in ongoing negotiations with the Mexican government over the employment rights of SME members. Telephone interview with a confidential Canadian source [Bouchard], September 3, 2020.

The Canadian NAO reportedly declined the parallel submission it received from Mexican Airline Pilots' Association (Asociación Sindical de Pilotos Aviadores de México, ASPAM), CAN 2005-1, because the submitter failed to provide adequate documentation and did not respond to requests for further information (interview with Canadian NAO staff members, September 11, 2007, Ottawa).

45.   Interview with former senior U.S. government official A [Karesh], June 14, 2018, Washington, DC. For example, U.S. NAO officials evidently acted politically in their handling of two complaints concerning controversial proposals to amend Mexico's Federal Labor Law. In US 2005-01, the U.S. NAO declined to review the submission on the grounds that doing so "would not further the objectives of the NAALC" (US NAO summary statement, https://www.dol.gov). By the time the U.S. NAO reached its decision, the Mexican Congress had ended debate on the proposed legislation (Buchanan and Chaparro 2008: 151). In US 2018-01, the U.S. NAO gave public notice that it required additional time to consider the submission (concerning a hotly debated legislative proposal to amend Mexico's Federal Labor Law and thereby implement a 2017 constitutional reform on labor rights in ways that, in fact, threatened to undercut the reform's democratizing principles, particularly with regard to freedom of association and the right to collective bargaining) at a time when the Office of the United States Trade Representative was in dialogue with the Mexican government concerning the significant international opposition the measure had provoked and the risks it posed to the renegotiation of the NAFTA (chapter 5). The U.S. NAO formally declined to review the submission once the legislation had been withdrawn from consideration by the Mexican Senate (Compa and Brooks 2019: 112).

The U.S. NAO also declined to review US 2005-02, a case in which the ASPAM contested the federal government's refusal to recognize a pilots-only craft union. It received the submission on May 27, 2005, but it did not produce a decision until July 7, 2006. In the interim, the Mexican Supreme Court (Suprema Corte de Justicia de la Nación) had sustained (November 25, 2005) a lower court's decision that ASPAM was not entitled to form a craft union.

The U.S. NAO's cautious approach to politically controversial submissions was not restricted to Mexico. In public communication US 9804, a trinational coalition of eighteen major unions (Canadian, eight; U.S., eight; Mexican, two) and five influential NGOs (Canadian, three; U.S., one; Mexican, one) challenged provisions of the Canada Post Corporation Act that denied rural mail carriers the right to bargain collectively. The Canadian law was in prima facie violation of NAALC principle no. 2, but the Supreme Court of Canada had ruled in 1990 that freedom of association guarantees in the Canadian Charter of Rights and Freedoms did not extend to collective bargaining. Here, too, the U.S. NAO declined to review the submission "in accordance with procedural guidelines" (US NAO summary statement, http://www.dol.gov). In a letter to the president of the Organization of Rural Route Mail Carriers, U.S. NAO Secretary Irasema T. Garza further justified the action on the grounds that the case did not "raise questions regarding the application or enforcement of the law" (quoted in Human Rights Watch/Americas 2001: 36n97).

Compa (2019: 282) reports that in 2003, Canadian rural mail carriers finally won the right to bargain collectively, and in 2007, the Supreme Court of Canada reversed its earlier position and ruled that the Charter of Rights and Freedoms did support collective bargaining rights (Kang 2012: 177–80).

46. Bensusán and Middlebrook (2013: 101–8) examine the SME conflict in detail.

47. Author's email communication with former senior U.S. government official B [Pier], February 1, 2021.

48. Interview with former senior U.S. government official A [Karesh], June 14, 2018. In March 2012, U.S. NAO officials did conduct a site visit to Mexico City, where they met with some of the submitters, labor law experts, and Mexican government officials (US NAO public report 2011-02: 5).

49. US NAO public report 2011-02: 10, *passim.*

50. Article 1(b) called upon the signatories to "promote, to the maximum extent possible, the labor principles set out in Annex 1," and article 3(1) affirmed, "Each Party shall promote compliance with and effectively enforce its labor law through appropriate government action." Article 49(1) defined "labor law" to include all eleven NAALC principles.

51. For U.S. private sector opposition, see US NAO public reports 940001 / 940002: 11, 14–15; 940003: 8n8; 9601: 11. In this last submission, the U.S. Council on International Business opposed any change in Mexican labor law concerning exclusive bargaining representation of workers. For the Mexican NAO's opposition, see US NAO public reports 9601: 13–14 and 9701: 10, as well as Finbow 2006: 106 on US 9801.

   In her response to the NACLC's request for comments during its required four-year review of the NAALC, Norma Samaniego de Villarreal, Mexico's lead NAALC negotiator, strongly condemned the U.S. NAO for "detracting from its character" and conducting public hearings that were more appropriate for a court than an administrative unit (NACLC 1998a: annex 5 [Public Comments: Mexico]: 11–13). For the Mexican NAO's own position on these issues, see the Mexican NAO four-year-review comments reproduced in Aspinwall 2013: 148.

52. In its responses to these queries, the Mexican NAO provided clarification and additional information on Mexican labor law and enforcement, but it never addressed the specifics of individual public communications.

53. For example, in US 940003 (Sony Corporation) and US 940004 (General Electric Co.), the U.S. NAO commissioned a detailed, eighty-nine-page analysis (Cuevas 1995) of relevant Mexican labor law provisions and related jurisprudence. Other commissioned studies include Curtis and Gutierrez Kirchner 1994; National Law Center for Inter-American Free Trade 1994, 2000; Torriente 1996; and Middlebrook and Quintero Ramírez 1998.

54. For an example of the U.S. NAO's detailed citation of scholarship on Mexican labor law and dispute settlement, see US NAO public report 940001 / 940002: 22n9.

55. US NAO public report 9901: 5, 12, 33–35, 41–42.

56. US NAO public report 2000-01: 16, 43–44/81.

57. CAN NAO public report 98-1: 4.

58. Over the entire 1994–2020 period, the U.S. NAO held a public hearing and/or conducted a site visit in Mexico in the course of its review of all submissions except 2015-04 (Chedraui). The public hearing held in Washington, DC, on September 12, 1994, examined both US 940001 and US 940002, which had been filed simultaneously.

As previously noted, the Canadian NAO's procedural guidelines did not require it to hold a public hearing as part of its review, but it did so in CAN 2003-1 (in Toronto in May 2004; CAN NAO public report 2003-1: ii). In CAN 98-1, Canadian NAO officials conducted two public meetings in Ottawa on September 14 and November 5, 1998 (CAN NAO public report 98-1: part I, p. 5). They also made two trips to Mexico: in September 1998 to meet with government labor authorities, and in January 1999 to examine more closely the occupational safety and health issues raised in the submission (CAN NAO public report 98-1: part II, p. 4).

59.   US NAO public reports 940001 / 940002: 15–20; 9701: 12; 9702: 14; 9901: 12; 2000-01: 15; 2003-01: 13–14; Alexander 1999: 146, 149, 152–53. At least in some instances, the U.S. NAO paid the travel expenses of witnesses participating in the public hearings (interview with a former senior U.S. NAO official [Garza]).

60.   See, for example, US NAO public reports 940001 / 940002: 10–11, 14; 940003: 11–12; 9703: 10; 2005-03: 8. See also CAN NAO public report 2003-1: 2.1.

61.   The U.S. Council on International Business, the Business Roundtable, and the U.S. National Association of Manufacturers opposed the provision for public hearings in U.S. NAO procedural guidelines (*Inside U.S. Trade* [hereinafter *IUST*], March 4, 1994). The general manager of Han Young de México appeared as a witness at the public hearing held in San Diego, California, as part of the U.S. NAO's investigation of US 9702 (Han Young) (author's contemporary notes on U.S. NAO hearing proceedings, February 18, 1998).
      Both company representatives and attorneys and a Mexican worker participated in the Canadian NAO's public meeting in September 1998 on CAN 98-1 (Alexander 1999: 158–59). The Canadian NAO did not reimburse public hearing participants' travel expenses (interview with former senior Canadian NAO official B [Banks], September 10, 2007, Ottawa).

62.   US NAO public report 2005-03: i, 7. In two cases (US 2000-01, US 2003-01), the U.S. NAO both held public hearings (in, respectively, San Antonio, Texas, and Washington, DC) and conducted site visits in Mexico. In US 2003-01, nine witnesses testified at the public hearing, and during the site visit to the state of Puebla and Mexico City (on April 21–29, 2004), U.S. NAO staff met with Mexican NAO and local conciliation and arbitration board officials, labor lawyers, representatives of both the incumbent and challenger unions, plant managers, the state representative of a national business association, and former workers from Matamoros Garment, Tarrant México, and other garment plants in the area. See US NAO public report 2003-01: 10–14.

63.   The duration of the five submissions the Canadian NAO brought to conclusion ranged from 62 to 586 days (1.6 years) and averaged 278 days (9.3 months) (table 4.2). In three cases, the Canadian NAO met, or came close to meeting, its stipulated deadlines for either reaching a decision about whether to review the submission (sixty days) or publishing its final report (a maximum of 240 days, including the initial review period). See "Guidelines for Public Communications" (1998), points 3(b), 4(a).
      Even though many U.S. and Canadian labor organizations and labor- and human-rights NGOs have complained about the length of NAALC proceedings, no previous analyst has calculated actual NAO case duration times. The AFL–CIO estimated that the time required to move from case submission to the imposition of any monetary or

trade-related sanctions would be 1,225 days; the Canadian Labour Congress estimated that this time span would be 1,320 days. See, respectively, NACLC 1998a: annex 5 (public comments: United States), p. 2, and (public comments: Canada), p. 7.

64.   A number of the US NAO and CAN NAO public reports addressed Mexico's obligations under ILO conventions (especially no. 87) and international human rights treaties. (Mexico did not ratify ILO convention no. 98 until September 2018). See, for example, the reports on US 9601 and US 9703 / CAN 98-1. Only in June 2011 did the Mexican Congress amend article 1 of the constitution to grant binding status to international human rights conventions.

65.   See US NAO public reports 940001 / 940002: 30, 32 and 2015-04: ii–iii.

66.   In addition to the cases summarized in this paragraph, see US NAO public report 2003-01: 85. In CAN NAO public report 2003-1:3.23, Canadian officials recognized it was possible that protesting workers did not always pursue the legal remedies nominally at their disposal because they lacked faith in the impartiality of the Mexican labor justice system. The Puebla garment workers who were the subject of this submission had voiced their grievances informally to Federal Conciliation and Arbitration Board (Junta Federal de Conciliación y Arbitraje, JFCA) and STPS officials, and they had contacted a wide range of other parties, including the state governor and the U.S. embassy labor attaché in Mexico City.

67.   US NAO public report 940003: 23.

68.   CAN NAO public report 98-1: part I, p. 13. See also the Canadian NAO's public report on CAN 2003-1 (v–vi), a submission in which Canadian officials concluded that employees had not requested workplace inspections for alleged occupational safety and health problems or excessive overtime work.

69.   US NAO public report 2005-03: 21.

70.   US NAO public report 2005-03: 29–30. The U.S. NAO's report (2005-03: 54–57) also concluded that the submitters had failed to substantiate their allegations regarding a shortage of appropriate safety and health equipment, working conditions, and work-related injuries.

71.   CAN NAO public report 98-1: part II, p. 34. See also US NAO public report 9901: 44.

72.   US NAO public report 2005-03: 41.

73.   CAN NAO public report 98-1: part II, pp. iii, 36; US NAO public report 2005-03: 20, 29–31. For the U.S. NAO's similar handling of US 2001-1, see US NAO public report 2001-1: 63–67/81.

74.   See also NAALC article 5(1), which stipulated, "Each Party shall ensure that its administrative, quasijudicial, judicial and labor tribunal proceedings for the enforcement of its labor law are fair, equitable and transparent."

Before a major reform of Mexico's federal labor law enacted on May 1, 2019, the STPS's Associational Registry (Registro de Asociaciones) and local (state-level) conciliation and arbitration boards were responsible for legally registering unions in, respectively, federal- and local-jurisdiction economic activities. Federal-jurisdiction activities are generally of strategic economic importance or those that employ particularly large numbers of workers. See Middlebrook 1995: table 2.1 for the progressively longer list of industries that came under federal jurisdiction between 1929 and 1990.

75.   Bouzas Ortiz and Gaitá Riveros 2001: 52–55; Bouzas Ortiz 2010: 113–16, 121–24.

76. A 1980 revision of the Federal Labor Law (art. 923) that permitted conciliation and arbitration boards to reject strike notices demanding the negotiation of a new collective contract in workplaces where an agreement was already registered had the effect of increasing employers' incentives to secure protection contracts (Bensusán 2007: 8 and *passim*). Some analysts estimated that as many as 90 percent of the collecting bargaining agreements registered by state-level conciliation and arbitration boards were, in fact, protection contracts (Bensusán and Middlebrook 2012: 24n16; see also Bensusán 2007).

77. See Middlebrook 1995: 56–62 and Bensusán 2000: 138–41 on the origins and evolution of Mexico's conciliation and arbitration board system.

78. For illustrative examples from NAALC public communications, see US submissions 940003: 11–12; 2003-01: ii, 5, 10; US NAO public report 2005-03: ii, 31; CAN submission 98-1: 37; CAN NAO public report 2003-1: iii, 3.12–13. For instance, in US 2003-01, the reasons the state-level board gave for denying legal recognition to a challenger union included lack of clarity regarding the union's name, a one-name inconsistency in two different union assembly attendance lists, failure to specify on the attendance lists the reasons for creating the union, and lack of proof that all affiliated workers were over the minimum working age of fourteen years (US submission 2003-01: 10).

     In its February 3, 2004, response to the ILO Committee on Freedom of Association's report on the Matamoros Garment case, the government of Mexico acknowledged that the Federal Labor Law required (arts. 685, 686) juntas to correct errors in filings involving worker-employer conflicts and in administrative matters involving individual workers. However, it argued that the requirement did not extend to such collective administrative matters as union registration petitions (cited in US NAO public report 2005-03: 17). See also Cuevas 1995: 6.

79. Before May 2019, union statutes requiring that elections be held in an open general assembly meeting or those that erected other obstacles to rank-and-file challenges had the force of law once they were approved by STPS authorities or state-level conciliation and arbitration boards.

80. On the historical background of what were originally known as "union consolidation clauses," see Middlebrook 1995: 96–98.

81. For an example from the NAALC public communications, see US NAO public report 9703: 10.

82. See US NAO public reports 9702: 5n4; 2003-01: 6; 2005-03: 4; 2015-04: 2–3; US submissions 9602: 4–5; 2001-01: 3; 2005-01: 11; 2005-02: 2. Some public communications did not explicitly raise protection contracts as an issue, even though contract arrangements of that kind were very probably in effect in the Mexican companies and production facilities in question (for example, US 940001, US 940002, US 9703 / CAN 98-1). On the protection contract at Aviacsa Airlines (US 2005-02), see F. Martínez 2001b.

83. See, for example, US NAO public reports 9703: 46 and 2005-03: 6, 11. The Canadian NAO's public report (2003-1) addressed these issues at length: "5.1.4 Information Available to Workers Represented by a Union: As noted above, in accordance with the principle of non-interference by the state in internal union affairs, Mexican labour law allows unions to be formed, registered and to negotiate collective contracts without an election or presenting other evidence to a public authority that they have the support

of a majority of the workers they seek to represent. This absence of regulation creates a risk that those who are represented by a union or covered by a collective contract may have little information about either. This in turn creates a risk that lack of information may impair the ability of workers to ensure that their union is acting on their behalf, to participate in its activities, and to exercise their right under Mexican law to personally enforce their rights under a collective contract. It may also impact on the freedom of workers not to associate with a union, which is protected by Article 538 of the LFT [Ley Federal del Trabajo]. . . .

"There appears to be no legal obligation on unions to provide workers with a copy of a collective contract that covers them. . . . This raises concerns about whether Mexico is meeting its obligations to maintain high labour standards under NAALC Article 2, and its obligations under NAALC Article 4.2 to ensure that persons with a legally recognized interest have recourse to procedures by which they can enforce their rights under a collective contract. Similar concerns were raised in the reports on Public Communications US 94-03 and US 99-01."

The Mexican NAO's defense of the status quo in this regard (quoted in CAN NAO public report 2003-1: 3.30) was: "The Government of Mexico is respectful of such union's internal affairs and therefore does not know whether elections for union representation were held within unions at the said plants."

84. The federal-jurisdiction cases at issue here were US 9703 / CAN 98-1 (Echlin/Itapsa), US 2001-01 (Duro Bag Manufacturing Co.), and US 2005-02 (Aviacsa pilots).

85. US NAO public reports 9702: 44; 9703: 46; 2005-03: 33; CAN NAO public reports 98-1: 38; 2003-1: vii, 6.1. See also US submission 2005-01: 83.

86. U.S. Department of Labor, "Notice of Procedural Guidelines" (2006), section G, 2(f).

87. Interview with former senior U.S. government official B [Pier], April 26, 2018, Washington, DC. See chapter 5 for a detailed analysis of the TPP negotiations.

Because protection contracts were not then illegal under Mexican labor law, and because the U.S. NAO found no evidence that Chedraui workers had mounted legal challenges to protection contracts, it could not determine whether the government of Mexico had failed to enforce its laws in this case. Nor did it, in light of pending 2016 Mexican constitutional and labor law reform proposals, recommend ministerial consultations on the matter (US NAO public report 2015-04: ii–iii, 15–16).

88. US submission 9703:12–27 offered detailed evidence concerning the multiple measures that the employer and the incumbent CTM union (which, at times, employed thugs to harass and attack protesting workers) were prepared to take to block an independent unionization campaign. The US NAO public report on the case cited (p. 32n50) US 940001, US 940002, US 940003, US 940004, US 9501, US 9602, and US 9702 as similar examples. See also US submissions 9901: 8, 10; 2003-01: 4, 8–9; 2005-03: 6 and US NAO public report 9901: 24–26.

89. For discussions of conciliation and arbitration boards' general record addressing both collective and individual labor grievances, see Middlebrook 1995: 185–205 and Middlebrook and Quintero Ramírez 1998.

90. US NAO public report 9901: 17. In US 9901, for unknown reasons, the CTM representative on the JFCA special board voted in favor of the challenger union (US NAO public report 9901: 28).

91.   See US submissions 9601: 1; 9602: 1-2, 5, 10, 14; 2001-01: 1-2; 2003-01: 4, appendix I (p. 44); 2005-01: 11-12; 2005-03: 11-12; and US NAO public reports 940003: 28, 31-32; 9702: 35-36, 41; 9703: 5, 48-49; 9901: 17, 27, 44-45; 2003-1: iii, 31, 34, 36, 83; 2015-04: ii, 8-9; CAN submission 2005-1 (n.p.); CAN NAO public reports 98-1: part I, p. 38; 2003-01: iii, iv, vii, 5.2-4, 6.1. In addition, US submissions 2006-01 (p. 26) and 2011-02 (pp. 28-30) critiqued the role of the STPS Associational Registry in federal-jurisdiction cases.

92.   US NAO public reports 9703: 40n62; 9901: 27. The submitters in US 9703 argued (pp. 36-37) that Mexico's failure to ensure secret-ballot elections violated the right of worker organizations under ILO convention no. 87 (art. 3) "to elect their representatives in full freedom."

93.   The STIMAHCS, an affiliate of the social-Christian Authentic Labor Front (Frente Auténtico del Trabajo, FAT), represented 3,000-3,500 metalworkers in Mexico (Rosenblum 1994: 18; F. Martínez 1998b). Hathaway (2000: 54, 59-89) discusses the origins and development of the FAT, whose slogan was, "For Proletarian Self-Management" ("Por la autogestion proletaria").

94.   US submission 9703: 16-18, 24-25, 28. The independent organizing campaign at Echlin/Itapsa ultimately collapsed (Graubart 2008: 84).

      For other submissions and public reports addressing the question of fairness in union representation elections, see US submission 2005-02: 2; US NAO public reports 9702: 23-25, 29-30, 46; 9901: 5, 24-27; 2015-04: ii; CAN NAO public report 98-1: part I, p. 38.

95.   CAN NAO public report 98-1: part 1, pp. 30-31.

96.   See Middlebrook 1995: 172-85. For personal testimony concerning the obstacles that labor activists faced in their efforts to form an independent union, see U.S. NAO, "U.S. NAO Submission #940003 Follow-Up Report," 1996 (a copy of this document is in the author's possession).

97.   U.S. NAO, "U.S. NAO Submission #940003 Follow-Up Report," 1996: 96 (a copy of this document is in the author's possession). See Englehart 1997: 369-70 for a brief summary of the Mexican legal and political rationale behind this policy. On related Mexican jurisprudence, see Cuevas 1995: 7-9.

98.   Arts. 68, 71-73, 78. Public-sector employees had been subject to a separate legal regime since 1938. This legislation became the basis for article 123's "Section B" in 1960 and the LFTSE in 1963. The Federal Conciliation and Arbitration Tribunal (Tribunal Federal de Conciliación y Arbitraje) was responsible for the registration of unions representing public-sector workers.

99.   The US 940003 submitters argued (p. 3) that, as a member of the ILO, Mexico was bound by convention no. 98's broad guarantee of the right to organize and bargain collectively (art. 2[1]) even though it had not yet ratified it. The US NAO "Follow-Up Report / NAO Submission #940003" also commented on Mexican government policy in this area (pp. 6-7).

100. However, in its public report (9601: 32), the U.S. NAO did not object to the tripartite composition of the TFCA.

101. In December 1997, the US 9601 submitters requested that the U.S. NAO reopen its review, but it declined to do so.

102. Aranda 1999; International Labour Office 2016: 94.

103. US submission 9601: 19. As the U.S. NAO noted in its public report on the case (pp. 29-30), the unanimous SCJN ruling in May 1996 also found unconstitutional a similar law in the state of Oaxaca. As part of its review of the submission, the U.S. NAO commissioned an independent assessment of the SCJN's decisions in these two cases, Amparo Decisions 337/94 (Jalisco) and 338/95 (Oaxaca). See Torriente 1996.

104. Middlebrook 1995: 305. Several independent, pro-union democracy labor leaders criticized the Supreme Court's 1996 and 1999 rulings on the grounds that decisions taken in the name of freedom of association could lead to the fragmentation of workplace representation and the overall weakening of labor organizations (Calderón et al. 1996; Velasco and Martínez 1999).

105. The author published an initial assessment of these two cases as part of his contributions to Bensusán and Middlebrook 2012: chap. 5.

106. As noted above, in 1996, the ILRERF, Human RightsWatch/Americas, and ANAD had collaborated in submitting a complaint to the U.S. NAO (US 9601) concerning freedom of association for Mexican federal government employees. Although it was not a formal signatory in US 9701, the Border Committee of Women Workers (Comité Fronterizo de Obreras) played an important part in building the case (Hertel 2006: 60-61).

107. In 1997, Mexico's National Institute of Statistics, Geography, and Informatics (Instituto Nacional de Estadística, Geografía e Informática, INEGI) reported that 57.7 percent of production workers in the maquiladora industry were women (US NAO public report 9701: 13). For overviews of the maquiladora industry, see Sklair 1993 and Middlebrook and Zepeda 2006.

108. Human Rights Watch/Americas 1996b. Hertel (2006: 59-61, 63) details the contributions that local human- and labor-rights NGOs made to Human Rights Watch's investigation.

109. In cities with high concentrations of maquiladora plants, companies often maintained blacklists of union organizers and other individuals whom they wished to bar from employment.

110. This discussion draws on materials included in US NAO public report 9701.

111. US NAO public report 9701: 10.

112. US NAO public report 9701: 36, 45-46.

113. Secretaría de Gobernación, *Alianza para la Igualdad: Programa Nacional de la Mujer, 1995–2000* (March 1996), pp. 88-90, quoted in US NAO public report 9701: 22-23 (translation by US NAO staff). A 1995 report by the Human Rights Commission of the Federal District similarly found evidence of pre-employment pregnancy testing in several federal agencies located in the Federal District, practices which it judged unconstitutional (US NAO public report 9701: 24-25).

114. Dillon 1998a.

115. Finbow 2006: 95; Hertel 2006: 68. As part of the implementation agreement, the NACLC secretariat produced a report on the employment of women in North America (NACLC 1998b).

116. Interview with senior NACLC official A [Caulfield].

117. Interview with former STPS secretary B [Bonilla], June 28, 2012, Mexico City. See Hertel 2006: 82 for examples of the national and international attention the pregnancy-testing case generated.

118.   F. Martínez 1998a; Velasco 1998a, 1998b; Hertel 2006: 64-68.

119.   U.S. National Administrative Office 1999: 4. Following the trinational conference, in August 1999, the U.S. government organized public information and outreach sessions in McAllen, Texas (August 1999), and Yakima, Washington (July 2000). The Mexican government organized similar events in Reynosa, Tamaulipas (August 1999), and Puebla, Puebla (May 2000), to educate women about their rights in the workplace (NACLC 2005b: 4).

120.   The Robles administration also created an Office for the Defense of Women's Rights (Hertel 2006: 75).

121.   N. Williams 2005: 145.

122.   Hertel 2006: 100, 132n52; "Decreto por el que se expide la Ley Federal para Prevenir y Eliminar la Discriminación." *Diario Oficial de la Federación*, June 11, 2003, www.dof.gob .mx.

123.   Art. 133(XIV). Hertel (2006: 74) reports that some activists also called on the Mexican government to ratify ILO convention no. 158 (Termination of Employment), article 5(d) of which prohibits employment termination on grounds of pregnancy. However, as of 2022, Mexico had not done so.

124.   Human Rights Watch/Americas 1998: summary and appendices B, C, G; Compa 2003a: 22-23; Hertel 2006: 99-100; Graubart 2008: 93; interview with a former senior US NAO official [Garza]. The U.S. NAO found that in 2005, women workers were still required to take pregnancy tests at Rubie's de México (US NAO public report 2005-03: 51), and there was some evidence that the practice persisted in Chedraui retail stores in 2015 (US NAO public report 2015-04: 11, 15). However, by 2011, one knowledgeable observer reported sharply reduced pregnancy testing in the maquiladora industry in general (interview with a senior representative of the Maquila Solidarity Network [Yanz], October 18, 2011, London).

125.   US submission 2005-01: 16-17; US NAO public report 2005-03: 50; Hertel 2006: 100; Aspinwall 2013: 133; González Torres 2018: 32-33, 43-44.

126.   US NAO public report 2015-04: iii.

127.   US NAO public report 9702a (freedom of association): 5n4, 45-46. The available sources (US NAO public report 9702a: 44-45; Bandy 2004a: 315-16, 323) identify only four independent unions in the entire maquiladora sector between the early 1980s and the late 1990s (Solidev, Han Young, Maxi-Switch, Kukdong / Mexmode), even though in December 1997, the sector's 2,867 firms employed 938,438 workers.

    In September 1995, the AFL-CIO published a detailed study (based on data from the U.S. Department of Labor's Trade Adjustment Assistance Office) of Mexican manufacturing facilities linked to U.S. companies shifting production to Mexico and the industries, communities, and number of workers affected, as well as the location of the plants in Mexico. The electronics, garment, and auto parts industries, and the states of Texas, New York, Florida, Pennsylvania, California, and Georgia, were the most affected. The "sister factories" were principally located in Mexico-U.S. border states (Chihuahua, Coahuila, Sonora, Baja California, Tamaulipas, Nuevo León), Durango, and the states surrounding Mexico City. See AFL-CIO 1995; see also Van Waas 1981.

128.   This discussion draws on US NAO public reports 1997a: 4-11, 21-29 and 1997b (occupational safety and health): 2-4, 40-43.

129. In a follow-up visit to the plant on September 5, labor inspectors found that Han Young had corrected seventeen of the twenty-three safety and health deficiencies they had identified in June. They decided against levying fines or other sanctions at that time, although later (shortly after the U.S. NAO accepted a supplemental filing in US 9702 alleging workplace safety and health violations at the plant), they levied fines totalling the equivalent of US$9,400 when they determined that some deficiencies continued to exist. Baja California officials conducted three further inspections of the plant in January and March 1998, finding that some serious workplace hazards had still not been corrected (US NAO public report 1997b: 32–41; Calbreath 1998).

130. The CTM withdrew from the contest on the day of the representation election.

131. *IUST*, November 28, 1997.

132. H. Williams (2003) discusses the SCMW's involvement at Han Young.

133. Kay (2011a: 140) reports that the AFL-CIO also offered behind-the-scenes support for the protesting Han Young workers. The ILRERF was renamed the International Labor Rights Forum in 1996.

134. In the second representation election, a total of thirty Han Young workers voted for the STIMAHCS, twenty-six for a CTM affiliate, and two for the CROC (US NAO public report 1997a: 9; see also Hernández Felix 1999: 11). The Tijuana press reported that the CROC's national secretary-general accepted a substantial payoff in exchange for deferring to the CTM in the case (H. Williams 2003: 536).

135. Dibble and Calbreath 1997. The US NAO public report (9702a: 46n78) cited Mexican government data indicating a larger number (954) of maquiladora plants in the state in 1997.

136. US NAO public report 1997a: 10, 22.

137. US NAO public reports 1997a: 13, 22–23 and 1997b: 7–8.

138. Hyundai Precision America executives also pressured Han Young managers to reinstate fired workers (with full back pay) to facilitate resolution of the conflict. See San Diego Dialogue (Extended Studies and Public Programs, University of California-San Diego) interview with SCMW founder Mary Tong (December 1997), pp. 24, 34 (unedited transcript).

139. US NAO public reports 1997a: 13, 21–33, 45–47 and 1997b: 7–8, 42.

140. US NAO public reports 1997a: 30–33, 41–47 and 1997b: 40–43.

141. US NAO public reports 1997a: 46–48 and 1997b: 43.

142. Dibble 1997: C-3.

143. Kay 2011a: 136.

144. Dillon 1997a; H. Williams 2003: 542–43; Kay 2011a: 136–37. H. Williams (2003: 548n9) provides an extensive list of the solidarity events organized in support of Han Young workers.

145. See chapter 3. Graubart (2008: 80) cites a U.S. union representative who stated that major U.S. trade unions decided to support both the Han Young and the Echlin/Itapsa (US 9703) public communications to highlight, in the context of the fast-track debate, the labor rights violations committed in Mexico by companies producing for the U.S. market.

    One indication of the political sensitivity of the Han Young case is that U.S. NAO officials were in touch with their Mexican counterparts even prior to the formal submission of US 9702 (US NAO public report 9702a: 12).

146. O'Connor 1997; Kay 2011a: 138.

147. Dillon 1997b; *New York Times* 1997; *IUST*, November 28, 1997; H. Williams 2003: 534; Kay 2011a: 137. President Clinton withdrew his fast-track reauthorization bill on November 10, 1997, because it lacked sufficient support in Congress (MacArthur 2000: 299).

148. Calbreath 1997a, 1997b.

149. H. Williams 2003: 535–36, 538; see also Bacon 2004: 85, 113. Baja California state security officers also attempted to disrupt cross-border support for Han Young workers by "shadowing" and intimidating Mary Tong, founder and director of the SCMW, during her visits to Tijuana (statement by Tong at the conference on "NAFTA's Environmental and Labor Institutions: The Road Ahead," Center for U.S.-Mexican Studies, University of California-San Diego, March 20, 1998).

150. Hernández Felix 1999: 11; Calbreath 2000; H. Williams 2003: 538–39.

151. Cornejo 1998a, b; H. Williams 2003: 540.

152. Bandy 2004a: 316.

153. Cornejo 1998b; Bacon 2000a.

154. Hernández Felix 1999: 11; H. Williams 2003: 527, 543; Kay 2011a: 138. Bandy (2004a: 317) reports that the Han Young plant closed in summer 1999.

155. Dillon 1998b.

156. Finbow 2006: 100.

157. The quotations in this paragraph are from the "Agreement on Ministerial Consultations: U.S. NAO Submissions 9702 and 9703," May 28, 2000 (a copy of this document is in the author's possession).

158. The practical steps taken under the action plan included a public seminar conducted by federal and state-level labor authorities in Tijuana, Baja California, on "freedom of association, the registration of trade unions, mechanisms for gaining and challenging title to the collective bargaining contract, and related procedures," and a trilateral NAALC seminar in the state of México on rules and procedures to ensure the impartiality of labor conciliation and arbitration boards and "their role in the processes for gaining the right to a collective bargaining agreement." The Tijuana seminar was convened in June 2000, but it quickly ended in violence. The meeting was disrupted by two dozen protesting Han Young workers carrying banners demanding workplace justice who were physically attacked by CROC affiliates in the audience. These events unfolded in front of STPS Undersecretary Javier Moctezuma Barragán and US NAO Secretary Lewis Karesh (Bacon 2000a; Graubart 2008: 95).

    The May 2000 agreement diplomatically included a reference to the STPS's own "Program for Employment, Training, and Defense of Labor Rights, 1995–2000" and its efforts to improve the professional level of Federal Conciliation and Arbitration Board (JFCA) staff; set "uniform criteria in the interpretation and application of labor law for labor tribunals"; "increase the dissemination of the registry of labor unions in an open manner, including via the Internet"; and promote occupational safety and health compliance, particularly with regard to minors and women in the maquiladora industry.

159. As noted above, the Mexican government's commitment to disseminate union registration information via the internet dated from the STPS's "Program for Employment, Training, and Defense of Labor Rights, 1995–2000."

160. The SEIU took this action following a ruling by the U.S. Supreme Court and a settlement agreement between the U.S. Department of Justice and the state of Alabama that largely resolved the matter in dispute on favorable terms.

161. The Mexican NAO did not issue a public report on MEX 2016-2 (concerning gender discrimination against female Mexican migrant workers in Canada) before July 1, 2020, the date on which the United States-Mexico-Canada Agreement took effect and suspended the NAFTA.

162. The exception was MEX 2001-1 (New York State workers' compensation). Three ministerial agreements with the United States addressed: MEX 9501 (February 13, 1996); MEX 9801, MEX 9802, and MEX 9803 (May 18, 2000); and MEX 2003-1, MEX 2005-1, and MEX 2011-1 (April 3, 2014). Canada subscribed to but was not a formal signatory of the first two of these agreements. As previously noted, MEX 9804 was included in the U.S.-Mexican agreement on US 9901 and US 2000-01.

163. This summary excludes MEX 2015-1 because it was filed by a single individual, not by a labor union or NGO.

164. The UNT was created in November 1997 when twenty-three dissident labor organizations seceded from Mexico's government-allied Labor Congress (Congreso del Trabajo). Its largest founding members were the unions representing telephone, university, and Mexican Social Security Institute workers (Bensusán and Middlebrook 2013: 63).

165. Of these three national labor confederations, the CLC adopted the most distanced position regarding participation in NAALC processes. In May 1995, the CLC Executive Council adopted a statement in which it indicated, "There are no benefits for workers in NAFTA and very few in the side-deals. We will participate in the institutions of NAFTA only to the extent that participation is likely to benefit workers (damage control) or to the extent that we can expose the dangers of NAFTA and the major flaws in the side-deals. . . . Our first aim must be to change NAFTA, principally by having binding social clauses inserted into the text of the Agreement itself, including fundamental labour rights and core labour and environmental standards." (CLC 1996: 67).

166. In MEX 9802 (Washington State apple growers and packers), the International Brotherhood of Teamsters and United Farmworkers of America played key roles in forming the submitter coalition (Compa 2001: 462–63).

167. See appendix B for more detailed summary descriptions of the public communications discussed here.

168. For example, although MEX 2012-1 focused specifically on an Alabama anti-immigrant law, the submitters noted that similar laws were then in effect in Arizona, Georgia, South Carolina, Utah, and other U.S. states.

169. In MEX 2006-1 / CAN 2008-1, the cosubmitter UE simultaneously filed a complaint with the ILO, which condemned the North Carolina law restricting the collective bargaining rights of public employees (author's email communication from Robin Alexander, then the UE Director of International Labor Affairs, April 4, 2007).

170. In total, six of the fourteen (42.9 percent) public communications to the Mexican NAO cited principle no. 1 (table 4.2).

171. The Mexican NAO often engaged in due-diligence consultations with the U.S. NAO as it sought basic information concerning applicable U.S. labor law and policy. See, for example, the final reports on MEX 9501 and MEX 2011-1.

172.   In a number of instances, the submitters requested that the Mexican NAO hold public hearings or public information sessions: MEX 9501 (in San Francisco), MEX 9801 (in Tijuana), MEX 9804 (in New York City and Los Angeles), MEX 2001-1 (presumably in the state of New York), MEX 2005-1 (in New York City; Boise, Idaho; Nashville, Tennessee; Fresno, California; Washington, DC; and Mexico City), MEX 2006-1 / CAN 2008-1 (in North Carolina); MEX 2011-1 (in Mexico City, the states of Zacatecas and Veracruz, and Washington, DC); and MEX 2012-1 (in Alabama). However, because Mexican officials regularly criticized the U.S. NAO for exceeding its authority under the NAALC by holding public hearings or conducting site visits to Mexico, it would have been politically contradictory for the Mexican NAO to have held informative sessions in the United States.

173.   See MEX NAO public reports 9804: 9–10, 12; 2001–1 (November 8, 2002): 9; 2001–1 (November 19, 2004): 5.

174.   Moore 1998; Compa 2001: 463–64; Graubart 2008: 90, 94; Compa and Brooks 2019: 115.

175.   MEX NAO public report 9501: 10.

176.   Indeed, some senior Mexican labor leaders argued that the Mexican NAO should not accept MEX 9501 (Sprint Corporation) for review because doing so would legitimate one NAFTA party's intervention in another's internal affairs and thus undercut the position that the Mexican government and labor movement had taken during the NAALC negotiations (interview with a then-senior CTM leader [Calleja], June 8, 2008, Mexico City).

177.   In two cases, the organizations submitting a complaint to the Mexican NAO filed a parallel submission with the Canadian NAO: MEX 9804 / CAN 98-2, MEX 2006-1 / CAN 2008-1

         The partisan identity of Mexico's federal government apparently did not influence the incidence of public communications submitted to the Mexican NAO. Eight submissions were filed under presidential administrations controlled by the Institutional Revolutionary Party (PRI, 1994–2000, 2012–2018), and six were filed under administrations led by the National Action Party (Partido Acción Nacional, 2000–2006, 2006–2012).

178.   Interviews with former STPS secretaries A [Palacios Alcocer] (June 27, 2012, Mexico City) and B [Bonilla]; interview with a former senior US NAO official [Garza].

179.   The government of Mexico also filed a class-action lawsuit in U.S. federal court on behalf of some 1,500 contemporary and former DeCoster workers, but a U.S. federal appeals court dismissed the action in October 2000 on the grounds that Mexico did not have legal standing in the matter (Compa and Brooks 2019: 115). For details on the settlement of the DeCoster lawsuit, see Finbow 2006: 153.

180.   It is also unlikely that the succeeding administration of President Vicente Fox took any similar initiative. Both Fox and his first minister of labor and social welfare, Carlos Abascal Carranza, were former businessmen who were unlikely to promote NAALC grievance procedures. During Abascal's tenure (2000–2005), neither MEX NAO public communications nor US NAO submissions concerning alleged labor rights violations in Mexico were discussed at regular senior staff meetings (telephone interview with former senior Mexican government official A [F. Franco], October 3, 2019). Indeed, only one of the four submissions filed with the Mexican NAO during Fox's administration (MEX 2001-1) was concluded during his term in office.

181.   For further evidence regarding submitters' autonomy vis-à-vis the Mexican government, see the interviews with a cosubmitter of MEX 2003-1 [Rodríguez] (July 23, 2004, Mexico City) and a then-senior CTM leader [Calleja]. Nevertheless, the government of Mexico was clearly supportive of many of these public communications. For instance, it filed an *amicus curiae* brief with the U.S. district court hearing a legal challenge to the Alabama anti-immigrant law (H. B. 56) that was the focus of MEX 2012-1 (MEX 2012-1 submission: 4).

182.   The three cases with the longest duration times (MEX 2003-1, MEX 2005-1, MEX 2006-1) were all filed during the administration of President Vicente Fox (2000–2006) and not resolved until near the end (November 2012) of the succeeding administration of President Felipe Calderón Hinojosa (2006–2012). If these cases are excluded from the calculation, the mean case duration time falls to 678 days (1.9 years, $N = 9$).

183.   In MEX 2001-1, the Mexican NAO's public report cautiously observed, "The Mexican NAO judges that it is necessary to make more broadly known the labor rights of migrant workers in the United States, as well as the resources available to them" (MEX NAO public report 2001-1 [November 8, 2004]: 27).

        As previously noted, as of July 1, 2020 (the date on which the United States-Mexico-Canada Agreement took effect and suspended the NAFTA), the Mexican NAO had not issued a final report on the sole submission (MEX 2016-2) involving the rights of migrant workers in Canada.

184.   See, for example, MEX NAO public report 2001-1 (November 19, 2004): 2, 10–13; MEX NAO joint public report 2003-1, MEX 2005-1, MEX 2011-1 (November 2012): 30.

185.   MEX NAO joint public report 2003-1, MEX 2005-1, MEX 2011-1 (November 2012): 7–8, 10.

186.   MEX NAO public report 2015-1: 3, 6. The U.S. Department of State, Office of Language Services (Translating Division), prepared the English-language translation of this and several other MEX NAO public reports.

187.   For testimony on this point from those submitting the MEX NAO communications, see Delp et al. 2004: 21.

        Similarly, the Mexico-U.S. ministerial agreement reached in February 1996 in response to MEX 9501 (Sprint Corporation) led to a public forum in San Francisco and the NACLC secretariat's detailed examination of the effect of plant closures or threats of closure on the exercise of freedom of association and the right to organize in the three NAALC signatory states (NACLC 1997c).

188.   See also Compa and Brooks 2019: 121 on this point.

189.   In a similar case (MEX 2005-1), the submitters argued that the United States was also in violation of a 2003 advisory opinion by the Inter-American Court of Human Rights ("Legal Condition and Rights of Migrant Workers") in this regard (MEX 2005-1 submission: 3).

190.   In response to the public attention generated by the MEX 9802 submission, Stemilt Growers accepted union certification procedures that facilitated the International Brotherhood of Teamsters' (IBT) unionization of the workforce. The state of Washington improved enforcement of safety and health regulations for migrant workers, including the distribution of Spanish-language materials outlining migrant workers' rights (Graubart 2008: 77; Nolan García 2011b: 100–101). For its part, the U.S. Department of Labor hosted a trilateral conference on agricultural migrant labor in North America

(February 7–9, 2000, Los Angeles), and during 2000, it organized five outreach sessions and public forums on migrant agricultural workers in the states of California, Florida, New York, Ohio, and Washington (NACLC 2005b: summary; M. Weiss 2003: 746–47).

In contrast to MEX 9802, in MEX 2016-1 the submitters listed in detail the reforms they sought in U.S. law and anti-discrimination enforcement practices affecting migrant workers.

191.   Compa and Brooks 2019: 114, 122. In response to MEX 9801, the U.S. Department of Labor hosted a government-to-government meeting with Mexican officials to discuss union organizing and bargaining rights, the elimination of employment discrimination, minimum wage issues, and occupational safety and health matters (https://www.dol .gov).

192.   Little attention has been devoted to the impact of Mexican NAO submissions on U.S. immigration law and law enforcement.

193.   In MEX 2001-1 (involving the state of New York's often excessive delays in providing compensation to workers who suffered occupational injuries), the U.S. Department of Labor tabled the request for ministerial consultations. In MEX 2006-1 (legal restrictions on the collective bargaining rights of North Carolina public employees), Compa and Brooks (2019: 130) report that the U.S. NAO ignored the Mexican NAO's initial request for ministerial consultations and the UE's subsequent complaint about its inaction.

194.   González Graf 2009: 152; MEX NAO joint public report 2003-1, MEX 2005-1, MEX 2011-1: 8n1; "Work Plan for Activities under the April 2014 Joint Declaration Concerning Public Communications MEX 2003-1, MEX 2005-1, and MEX 2011-1," June 16, 2014 (a copy of this document is in the author's possession).

195.   Between 2004 and 2012, the Mexican and U.S. governments also signed forty-nine agreements (convenios) concerning wages, working hours, and occupational safety and health standards (STPS, "Informe de revisión" [2012], p. 8n1).

196.   Summaries of MEX 9801 and MEX 9802, http://www.dol.gov; Compa and Brooks 2019: 116.

197.   "Work Plan"; "Public Report on Outreach Events Pursuant to U.S.-Mexico Ministerial Consultations on Public Communications MEX 2003-1, 2005-1, and 2011-1 under the North Agreement on Labor Cooperation" (n.d.; a copy of this document is in the author's possession); Compa and Brooks 2019: 122, 133–34. The seventeen-page "Public Report" extensively details activities undertaken under the 2014 joint declaration and the constituencies (workers and employers) they reached. See also Bada and Gleeson 2015b.

Between 2014 and 2019 the U.S. Equal Employment Opportunity Commission signed various binational collaboration agreements with Mexico's Ministry of Foreign Relations and Mexican consulates in the United States to improve migrants' awareness of their labor rights and how they could exercise them. From October 2015 through September 2019, there were more than nine hundred informational activities conducted under the terms of these agreements, reaching a population of more than seventy-five thousand migrant workers (MEX NAO public report 2016-1 [30 June 2020]: 16).

198.   In MEX 9803, Delp et al. (2004: 20) report that DeCoster management subsequently undercut U.S. government enforcement efforts regarding migrant worker housing.

199.   This discussion is based on the author's review of MEX 9804 submission documents and the Mexican NAO's public review of the case.

200. These NGOs were the American Civil Liberties Union Foundation Immigrants' Rights Project; Asian American Legal Defense and Education Fund; Asian Law Caucus (San Francisco); Asian Pacific American Legal Center of Southern California (Los Angeles); Center for Immigrants' Rights; Florida Immigrant Advocacy Center; Korean Immigrant Workers Advocates (Los Angeles); Latino Workers Center (New York City); Legal Aid Society of San Francisco (Employment Law Center); Mexican American Legal Defense and Education Fund; National Employment Law Project; National Immigration Law Center; National Immigration Project of the National Lawyers Guild; National Korean American Service and Education Consortium, Inc.; and National Network for Immigrant and Refugee Rights.

201. "Memorandum of Understanding Between INS and Labor Department on Shared Enforcement Responsibilities, *Daily Labor Report*, 113 DLR C-1, June 11, 1992," attached as exhibit 1 to the MEX 9804 public communication.

202. The submitting organizations noted that several attempts to persuade the U.S. DOL and the INS to rescind the 1992 memorandum and alter their immigration law enforcement policy had been unsuccessful (MEX 9804 submission: 14). See also Singh and Adams 2001: 10; Wishnie 2002: 550–51.

203. Even so, in response to a Mexican NAO enquiry, the submitters called upon the office to complete its review of the case on the grounds that there remained uncertainty regarding implementation of the new policy and considerable ambiguity regarding the difference between complaint-based and noncomplaint-based U.S. DOL inspections. For instance, the Department of Labor reserved the right to report immigration law violations to the INS when they were discovered during a regular (that is, not a complaint-based) workplace inspection (Compa and Brooks 2019: 116). The Mexican NAO issued its final report on November 9, 2000 (citing only NAALC principle no. 11) and called for Mexico-U.S. ministerial consultations on U.S. policies concerning the issues raised by the communication.

　　The Canadian NAO declined to review the parallel submission (CAN 98-2) in April 1999 on the grounds that the November 23, 1998, U.S. DOL-Department of Justice memorandum had resolved the matter (Compa and Brooks 2019: 116–17). Finbow (2006: 178) reports that one factor behind the Canadian NAO's decision was that the submitters did not include any Canadian unions or labor rights organizations.

204. MEX 9801 submission: 4, 20–21.

205. Gutiérrez 2007. For example, STPS Secretary Abascal successfully lobbied U.S. Secretary of Labor Elaine L. Chao to reaffirm the rights of Mexican migrant workers following the U.S. Supreme Court's March 2002 ruling in *Hoffman Plastic Compounds v. NLRB* that undocumented migrant workers who were illegally fired for union organizing activities were ineligible for back pay (interview with senior STPS official A [C. Franco], July 7, 2004). The two labor ministers issued a joint statement on April 15, 2002, in which Chao confirmed that the ruling "will neither deter nor diminish the Department's continued enforcement of applicable labor standards, particularly in guaranteeing a minimum wage and safe and healthy workplaces for all workers in this country, regardless of their immigrant status" (a copy of this statement is in the author's possession).

　　However, the MEX 2006-1 / CAN 2008-1 submissions challenging North Carolina General Statute 95-98, which severely restricted the collective bargaining rights of state and municipal employees, was unsuccessful even though under the NAALC the U.S. federal government was required to enforce agreed labor rights principles throughout U.S. territory.

206. Participating in NAALC procedures also deepened the understanding that U.S. and Canadian trade unions and labor- and human-rights activists had of the legal and political barriers to democratic unionism, collective bargaining, and impartial labor justice in Mexico (telephone interview with a Mexican labor attorney [Alcalde], May 11, 2020). For examples of U.S. unions learning over time how to strengthen their framing of NAALC public communications, see Graubart 2008: 67–68, 71, 75. 79.

207. US NAO public report 940001 / 940002: 31.

208. US NAO public report 940001 / 940002: 31. The seminar was held in Washington, DC, in March 1995 (MEX NAO public report 9501: 10). See footnote 247 for a list of the NAO-sponsored seminars organized on freedom of association and the right to collective bargaining.

209. MEX NAO public report 9501: 2–9.

210. See the bibliographic entries for the North American Commission for Labor Cooperation (NACLC), 1996–2005, esp. NACLC 1996 and 2000b.

211. As noted previously, in US 940003 (Sony Corporation) and US 940004 (General Electric Co.), the U.S. NAO itself commissioned a detailed study of relevant aspects of Mexican labor law and jurisprudence (see Cuevas 1995). For an insightful example of the understanding that U.S. officials gained of Mexican labor law and practice through these activities, see U.S. NAO, "Report on Ministerial Consultations on Submission #940003 under the North American Agreement on Labor Cooperation," June 7, 1996, pp. 7–14 (a copy of this document is in the author's possession).

212. Interview with former senior U.S. government official A [Karesh], June 14, 2018, Washington, DC.

213. US NAO public report 9703: 32n50. See also CAN submission 98–1: 47, 54 and CAN NAO public report 2003-1: ii.

214. Compa 2001: 457, 459–60, 462, 465; Torres 2005: 126; Kay 2011a: 12, 17, 19, 25, 59, *passim*; Aspinwall 2013: 124–27. On the concept of "social capital," see Putnam 1993.

215. In the seven public communications that the U.S. NAO declined for review, there was no correlation between the presence (three cases) or absence (four cases) of binational or trinational submitter coalitions. There was, however, a perfect correlation between the Canadian NAO's decision to accept (four cases) or reject (three cases) public communications for review and the presence or absence of such coalitions. As previously noted, the Mexican NAO accepted for review all the communications it received (table 4.2). This summary excludes from consideration the six communications to the three NAOs that were either withdrawn or not pursued by the submitters.

216. Additional substantial proportions of the sociopolitical actors involved participated in only one parallel communication to two NAOs: Canada, five (18.5 percent); Mexico, sixty-one (56.0 percent); United States, thirty-one (25.2 percent). Author's calculations based on information in the NAALC case files.

217. There was a significant difference between the organizations listed here and other sociopolitical actors in terms of the number of (co)submissions in which they were engaged.

218. See US submissions 940001: 2 (where the IBT states that the Honeywell Corporation had steadily shifted work from Minnesota and other U.S. states to Mexico) and 940002: 4–5 (where the UE reports that the General Electric Co. had shifted production to some fifteen maquiladora plants in or near Ciudad Juárez, Chihuahua). On the especially compelling UE experience, see Cowie 1999.

219. The STIMAHCS was also the local union involved in US 9702 (Han Young) and US 9703 / CAN 98-1 (Echlin/Itapsa) submissions, where it was part of much larger trinational coalitions. On the binational organizing campaigns led by the IBT and UE, see Myerson 1994a; Hathaway 2000: 177–82; Kay 2011a: 124, 127–28. For a detailed presentation of the Honeywell (US 940001) and General Electric (US 940002) cases, see Bazar 1995: 433–52.

220. MEX submission 9501: 2; Shorrock 1995. The US 9804 submission (Canadian rural mail carriers) was another example of occupation-focused cross-border labor solidarity among Canadian and U.S. postal workers' unions.

221. This was, for example, one factor motivating the UE in its initial U.S. NAO communications (interview with a senior UE official, August 8, 1995, Alexandria, Virginia) [Townsend]; Kay 2011a: 127.

222. See appendix 3 for summaries of these submissions.

223. Author's calculations based on information in text box.

224. Alexander 1999: 140; García Urrutia 2002: 79–80; Luján U. 2002: 213; Kay 2011a: 61–62, 88

225. Compa 1995b: 165n49; García Urrutia 2002: 80–85; Alexander 2022: 11. Under the terms of its agreement with the FAT, the UE covered direct expenses incurred in maquiladora organizing efforts, but it purposefully did not provide general financial support to the FAT. The amounts involved (a total of approximately US$20,000 as of August 1995) were modest (interview with a senior UE official; see also Smith and Pearson 1994). For its part, the FAT assisted the UE in its successful efforts to organize workers (a large number of whom were Mexican migrants) at two aluminum manufacturing facilities in Milwaukee, Wisconsin (comments by Lance A. Compa at the "Mexican Labor in Transition" conference organized by the David Rockefeller Center for Latin American Studies, Harvard University, April 19, 1996; T. Davis 1995: 28–29; Kay 2011a: 177).

 In the aftermath of the Han Young and Echlin/Itapsa conflicts, the United Steelworkers (U.S. and Canadian divisions) donated US$70,000 to a "Foundation for FAT / Steelworkers Solidarity and Mutual Support" (Damgaard 1998: 21n35). Canadian Labour Congress sources estimate that Canadian unions together provided approximately C$200,000 to the FAT (interview with Canadian Labour Congress international affairs officers, September 12, 2007, Ottawa). The United Steelworkers-Canada's ties to the FAT also predated the NAALC (interview with a United Steelworkers-Canada representative [Rowlinson], September 14, 2007, Toronto).

226. Xelhuantzi López (2002: 250–51) reproduces (in Spanish) the CWA-STRM-CEWC collaboration agreement. The CEWC's initial contact with the STRM had also been through the Mexico-U.S. Diálogos project (interview with a senior STRM adviser [Sandoval], June 26, 1992, Mexico City). Finbow (2006: 85) reports that the Communication, Energy, and Paperworkers Union's informal support for the Maxi-Switch submission was a Canadian union's first engagement with NAALC processes. On the development of ties among North American telecommunications unions, see Xelhuantzi López 2002: 245–52;

Kay 2011a: 94–97; Cohen and Early 2000: 202–18; interview with a senior STRM adviser [Sandoval].

Similarly, the USW's submission of US 2006-01 (SNTMMSRM and Pasta de Conchos) followed the strategic alliance the union had formed with the National Union of Mexican Mineworkers and Metalworkers (SNTMMSRM) in April 2005 (Kay 2011a: 161).

227. On this general point, see Alexander and Gilmore 1994; Tong 1999: 74; H. Williams 1999: 145, 147–48; Bandy 2004b: 414–16; Delp et al. 2004: 22–23.

228. For twenty-three (65.7 percent) of the thirty-five Mexican unions involved, MEX 2006-1 / CAN 2008-1 were the only NAALC communications they joined. Benedicto Martínez, secretary-general of the STIMAHCS, took the lead in assembling the coalition of Mexican labor organizations joining in the submissions (email communication from Alexander).

229. Some authors have claimed (or strongly implied) that cross-border collaboration was the product of institutional incentives. See, for example: Compa 1997c: 50 ("Trade unionists and their allies are compelled to collaborate across North American borders to use NAALC mechanisms."); Harvey, Collingsworth, and Athreya 2000: 31 ("Trade unionists and their allies are compelled to collaborate across North American borders to use the NAALC."); Finbow 2006: 221 ("The submissions process, which requires bilateral cooperation to bring complaints about a country's practices to the NAO of another NAFTA state . . ."); Graubart 2008: 63 ("the mechanism's encouragement of cross-border collaboration"); Kay 2011a: 10 ("By requiring submitters to file complaints outside their home countries, the NAALC forced labor activists to seek assistance from counterparts in another NAFTA country and thereby catalyzed transnational relationships that had not previously existed"; however, see also p. 118 for a contrasting position); and Aspinwall 2013: 124 ("The principal cause of strengthened cross-border cooperation was the requirement that a complaint be filed with the NAO of a country *different* from the one in which the alleged infraction occurred.").

230. This outcome was, however, anticipated by some of the U.S. and Canadian negotiators involved in drafting the NAALC (Kay 2011a: 120–21).

The revised procedural guidelines that the Canadian NAO adopted in 2014 stipulated (point 3) that, "Public communications may be submitted by any person of Canada," which would have created an incentive for Mexican and U.S. sociopolitical actors to collaborate with Canadian counterparts on submissions to the Canadian NAO. (The 1997 procedural guidelines had stated [point 1(a)] that "Any person or organization may submit a public communication to the Canadian NAO regarding labour law matters arising in the territory of another Party to the Agreement.") However, the Canadian NAO did not receive any NAALC public communications after 2011. See Government of Canada, "Guidelines for Public Communications submitted to the Canadian National Administrative Office under Labour Cooperation Agreements or Chapters," 2014, https://www .canada.ca/en/employment-social-development/services/labour-relations/international /agreements/guidelines.html.

231. These ties were based in part on both confederations' membership in the International Confederation of Free Trade Unions and its regional organization, the Inter-American Regional Workers' Organization. During this period, it was the AFL-CIO's policy to interact only with the CTM in Mexico (Kay 2011: 41, 43).

232. Hufbauer and Schott (2005: 91) found that 1,351 U.S. businesses relocated to Mexico between 1994 and 2002. However, they also concluded (89–90) that expanded employment in the maquiladora sector did not affect inflation-adjusted worker compensation in U.S. industries.

233. Kay 2011a: 71–73, 107, 204–5.

234. One early AFL-CIO response to changing economic conditions was its support for the Coalition for Justice in the Maquiladoras, which was founded in San Antonio, Texas, in 1989 (Graubart 2008: 71; Bandy 2009: 75–87).

 Even though the AFL-CIO generally distanced itself from the CTM after the mid-1990s, in 1998, the two confederations signed an agreement to oppose negative aspects of the NAFTA and to root out employer protection contracts in Mexico (Compa and Brooks 2019: 170). In 2003, the two organizations also collaborated in a joint petition to the ILO's Committee on Freedom of Association that protested the U.S. Supreme Court's 2002 ruling in the Hoffman Plastic Compounds, Inc., case, which barred undocumented workers in the United States from effective remedy if they were unlawfully dismissed for union activity (MEX 2012-1 submission: 6n5).

235. Longtime CTM leader Fidel Velázquez Sánchez initially opposed the AFL-CIO's request in August 1994 to establish an office in Mexico City to investigate alleged labor rights violations by U.S. companies operating in Mexico (SourceMex 1994; interview with senior officials [Donnelly and Jessup] of the American Institute for Free Labor Development, August 8, 1995, Washington, DC).

236. *IUST*, January 22 and February 6, 1998; Damgaard 1998: 21; F. Martínez 2001a; Bensusán 2004b: 258. STPS Secretary Bonilla criticized Sweeney's visit, warning independent labor organizations not to make any agreements with the AFL-CIO that would violate Mexican sovereignty (Dillon 1998a).

237. The AFL-CIO had previously offered informal support to other labor organizations filing US NAO public communications, including US 9602 (Maxi-Switch) and US 9702 (Han Young) (Calbreath 1997c: A-27; Finbow 2006: 85; Kay 2011a: 133, 140–41).

238. The regression coefficient of the "final case outcome" variable was 2.57, with a standard deviation of 1.05 (statistically significant at the $p < 0.05$ confidence interval, $N = 38$). For every one-unit increase in "final case outcome" (that is, moving from "declined" to "reviewed" to "ministerial consultations recommended"), the odds of seeing a one-unit increase in "observed policy impact" increased by 13.08 times. Dr. Kazuma Mizukoshi expertly conducted the statistical analysis, and Dr. Néstor Castañeda (University College London) provided generous advice concerning how best to structure the analysis.

239. The regression coefficient was 1, with a standard deviation of 0.55, $N = 20$.

240. The regression coefficient of the "strategic action" dummy variable was 2.07, with a standard deviation 1.19, $N = 14$.

241. For comments on this issue by major U.S. and Canadian unions, see, respectively, NACLC 1998a: annex 5 (Public Comments: United States), pp. 4, 6, 8, 12, and NACLC 1998a: annex 5 (Public Comments: Canada), p. 7. See also United Steelworkers-Canada 2004: 15, 19–20 and AFL-CIO 2014: 11, 13. Kay (2011a: 20–21) concludes that "unions' inability to get meaningful redress" undermined their commitment to NAALC processes. For critical assessments of the NAALC that took a similar position, see, for example, Economic Policy Institute et al. 1997 (Executive Summary) and Compa 2003a: 45, 48.

It certainly would have been impolitic to voice such criticisms when filing a NAO public communication, but in US submission 2006-01 (SNTMMSRM and Pasta de Conchos), the United Steelworkers applauded the U.S. NAO's efforts to protect the rights of independent unions and enforce occupational safety and health standards in Mexico. The union commented that the "action plans" the U.S. Department of Labor had negotiated with Mexico's STPS "have improved conditions in individual plants" (p. 27). In contrast, the US 2011-02 (Mexican Electricians' Union) submitters concluded their filing by stating, "If these facts do not give rise to the conclusion that Mexico is in violation of the NAALC, then the NAALC is truly of no value whatsoever to the workers of North America" (p. 65). As noted above, the U.S. NAO never took a public position on this communication.

242.   See, for example, the statement by AFL-CIO representative Greg Woodland in "Linking Labor Standards and Rights in Trade Agreements" (1997: 824).

243.   Again, article 42 clearly stipulated that, "Nothing in this Agreement shall be construed to empower a Party's authorities to undertake labor law enforcement activities in the territory of another Party."

244.   See the statements by Irasema T. Garza, the first U.S. NAO secretary ("The institutions of the NAALC are not a substitute for domestic courts, so that we can't enforce individual rights"), and John S. McKinnerey, the first NACLC executive director ("[The NAALC] is not a sort of appeals system . . . it cannot handle specific cases") in "Linking Labor Standards and Rights in Trade Agreements" (1997: 825). See also the interview with former senior U.S. government official A [Karesh], June 14, 2018.

245.   Several of the US NAO communications noted that, because Mexican workers did not have access to unemployment benefits, workers who lost their jobs were almost always compelled by economic necessity to accept termination payments from employers, even if that meant foregoing the right to appeal their dismissal. See, for instance, US NAO public reports 940001 / 940002: 30 and 940003: 27.

246.   Human Rights Watch/Americas 2001: 19; Delp et al. 2004: 36. Complete information concerning the length of time required to conclude NAALC ministerial consultations is not available. However, in CAN 98-1, the public communication was filed on April 6, 1998, and the results of Canadian and Mexican ministerial consultations were not announced publicly until January 29, 2003 (United Steelworkers-Canada 2004: 10).

247.   Following the US 940001 (Honeywell Corporation) and US 940002 (General Electric Co.) submissions, the U.S. NAO organized trinational government-to-government workshops on these issues in Washington, DC, in March and September 1995 and a trinational conference in Montreal in March 1996. Following the US 940003 (Sony Corporation) submission, the U.S. NAO joined with Mexican authorities in convening public seminars on union registration and certification procedures in Mexico City (September 1995), San Antonio, Texas (November 1995), and Monterrey, Nuevo León (February-March 1996) (Compa 1997b: 14–15; for a transcript of the November 1995 seminar, see US NAO 1995b).

248.   US submission 940004: 1; Compa 1997b: 19–20; telephone interview with a Canadian labor attorney [Melançon], April 1, 2022. The Québec government did later revise the provincial labor code to ease delays in union certification.

On the impact of US 940002, see also Kay 2011a: 130. Although the independent organizing campaign at the Sony plant in Nuevo Laredo, Tamaulipas (the focus of US 940003) failed, local organizers credited the U.S. NAO submission with generating favorable international publicity that benefited their movement (Compa 1999a: 193). Similarly, the UNT-affiliated Association of Mexican Flight Attendants (ASSAM) later reported that the ministerial consultations following US 9901 increased its bargaining leverage in a subsequent conflict at Aerocaribe (Compa 2001: 456; Hermanson 2001: 122).

249.   On the Maxi-Switch case, see Finbow 2006: 86; Graubart 2008: 94.

250.   Author's calculation based on data presented in table 4.2 and information in the U.S. and Canadian NAALC public communications.

251.   CAN NAO public report 2003-1: 3.11; US NAO public reports 2003-01: 57, 59–62 and 2005-03: 55; B. Davis 2008: 3–4; Maquila Solidarity Network 2008a. The Kukdong / Mexmode garment manufacturing plant in Puebla was a major exception in this regard. Because of pressure from Nike, Inc., and a large number of international labor rights NGOs, an independent union won legal recognition and successfully negotiated a contract with the employer (Juárez Núñez 2002; Carty 2004: 299–301; Finbow 2006: 133; Nolan García 2013: 113–17).

252.   On the last two cases, see US NAO public reports 2003-01: 57, 60–62 and 2005-03: 55.

253.   In US 940003 (Sony Corporation), the April 21, 1994, report filed by the state of Tamaulipas government representative who was dispatched to end rank-and-file work stoppages at Magnéticos de México referred expressly to "changes taking place in general which characterize the new Tamaulipas, which guarantee labor peace to support more investment and productivity" (a copy of this document is in the author's possession). See also Aspinwall 2013: 103 on the Honeywell case (US 940001).

254.   The June 11, 2002, U.S.-Mexican ministerial agreement resolving public communications US 9901 (TAESA) and US 2000-01 (Auto Trim / Custom Trim), which Canada endorsed in September 2002, led to the creation of the Tri-National Working Group of Government Experts on Workplace Safety and Health. During the period in which it was active (2002–2007), the working group examined diverse occupational safety and health issues, voluntary protection programs, best workplace practices in various industries, and the handling of hazardous substances (G. Brown 2004a: 7, 9–10; interview with Canadian NAO staff members; Compa and Brooks 2019: 89). However, because there is no available information confirming that Mexican government policies changed as a result of the working group's activities, table 4.2 lists the observed policy outcome for both US 9901 and US 2000-01 as "0."

In at least one case, a NAALC communication may have had an indirect positive effect on workplace conditions in Mexico by generating substantially greater public attention to workers' grievances and prompting international brand-name companies to strengthen compliance by local suppliers with their company codes of conduct. See CAN NAO public report 2003-1 (Puebla garment producers): 3.13

255.   US NAO public report 9702a (freedom of association): 44; interview with former STPS secretary B [Bonilla].

256.   Secretaría del Trabajo y Previsión Social 1996: 4.6.3(E).

257.   F. Martínez 1997b.

258. Partido de la Revolución Democrática 1998, art. 516.

259. Nolan García 2010a: 13; telephone interview with former senior Mexican government official A [F. Franco], January 17, 2021.

260. US NAO public report 2003-1: 83–84.

261. US NAO public report 2005-03: 33–34, 58; "Ministerial Consultations Joint Declaration" (US 2003-01 / CAN 2003-1, April 24, 2008; a copy of this document is in the author's possession). See also US NAO public report 2015-04: 6.

262. Ley Federal del Trabajo (2012), art. 365bis. In principle, this information was to be updated every three months. See Bensusán and Middlebrook 2013: 118–30 for a discussion of the 2012 labor law reform process and debates over other proposals to democratize union governance, including a requirement that union leaders regularly provide members with information concerning their management of union dues and assets (art. 373).

263. "Ley Federal de Transparencia y Acceso a la Información Pública Gubernamental," *Diario Oficial de la Federación*, June 11, 2002, arts. 7, 9.

264. International Labour Office 2016: 93; telephone interview with U.S. trade union representative A [Davis], April 21, 2020. In February 2005, the Federal Institute for Access to Public Information (Instituto Federal de Acceso a la Información Pública) ruled that labor conciliation and arbitration boards were required to provide a copy of a registered collective contract to anyone requesting it (Alcalde Justiniani 2010: 167).

265. Becerril 1995. In 1998, the PRD-led Federal District government reformed article 18(XII, XIII, XIV) of the Internal Regulations of Federal District Public Administration (Reglamento interior de la administración pública del Distrito Federal) to require the use of secret ballots in recount elections (Alcalde Justiniani 1998).

266. See, for example, Ley Federal del Trabajo (1978), arts. 389, 462, 604, 621.

267. Partido Acción Nacional 1995, arts. 299, 307.

268. Partido de la Revolución Democrática 1998, arts. 512, 514(IV). The PRD, at times in alliance with the UNT and the Labor Party (Partido del Trabajo), reiterated these proposals in subsequent labor law reform initiatives in 2002, 2010, and 2012 (Bensusán and Middlebrook 2013: 119).

269. Author's email communication with Dr. Graciela Bensusán (Universidad Autónoma Metropolitana-Xochimilco and Facultad Latinoamerica de las Ciencias Sociales-Sede México), November 7, 2020. Bensusán participated in the deliberations that produced the PRD's 1998 reform proposal. See also Graubart 2008: 83, Kay 2011a: 167, and, for supporting evidence on this point, the telephone interview with former senior Mexican government official A [F. Franco], January 17, 2021.

270. Interview with a Mexican labor attorney [Alcalde], July 16, 2004, Mexico City. Although the Mexican government was slow to implement the May 2000 agreement regarding the use of secret ballots in recount elections, high-level attention to the issue had an immediate effect on the conduct of U.S. government agencies engaged with Mexico. On September 11, 2000, the Overseas Private Investment Corporation (OPIC), which under the Trade and Tariff Act of 1984 was prohibited from supporting any project that would contribute to the violation of "internationally recognized worker rights" in the host country, issued a call for consultative research on "certain inadequacies under Mexican labor law with respect to the exercise of the rights of freedom of association, organization and collective bargaining." "A primary concern is the lack of an open,

transparent, and democratic process for union selection . . . [and] a lack of secret ballots and neutral voting places." OPIC solicited the report as part of its review of "applications for finance support for a large retail establishment in Mexico." A copy of the request for proposals (September 11, 2000) is in the author's possession.

271. On the Duro Bag case, see F. Martínez 2000; Bacon 2000b; Campaign for Worker Rights email communication, August 15, 2000 (a copy of this document is in the author's possession).

272. Interviews with former senior U.S. government official A [Karesh], July 7, 2005 (Washington, DC), and (by telephone) June 25, 2021. A U.S. NAO statement justified the decision in these terms: "We remain committed to addressing worker rights in North America. . . . We have forged a strong and deep relationship with the Government of Mexico on labor issues that will lead to a more meaningful collaboration. As we deepen the relationship and build greater trust, we will be even better able to address worker rights issues and find cooperative ways to move them forward" (quoted in Compa 2003a: 50).

273. "Iniciativa de reforma" (2003), art. 931(VII). See also the interviews with senior STPS officials A [C. Franco], August 16, 2002, and B [Valencia], July 27, 2004, Mexico City; Díaz 2004: 428. While labor law reform negotiations were under way, Canadian minister of labor Charlotte Bradshaw continued the ministerial consultations that Canada had initiated around CAN 98-1 (Echlin / Itapsa) by meeting personally with Secretary Abascal on four occasions in 2001–2002 to discuss freedom of association, the right to organize, and occupational safety and health matters (Díaz 2004: 422n4).

274. "Iniciativa de reforma" (2003), art. 893-A(III). The same legislative initiative stipulated (art. 371[IX]) that union statutes indicate how union officers would be elected, authorizing either secret or direct (public) votes. In the course of early Fox administration debates over labor law reform, state governors reportedly expressed strong opposition to secret balloting in union elections (Aspinwall 2013: 181n27).

275. See, for example, US submission 2005-01: 8.

276. Bensusán and Middlebrook 2013: 111–12.

277. Suprema Corte de Justicia de la Nación (hereinafter SCJN) 2008b; SCJN (Segunda Sala) 2008a: 138, 141. Despite the Mexican government's public commitment in the May 2000 bilateral agreement, the Office of the Federal Prosecutor (Procuraduría General de la República) filed a brief in this case arguing that recount votes should not be secret because no part of existing federal labor law required secret ballot procedures (SCJN [Segunda Sala] 2008a: 8).

   In May 2001, the Federal District's labor conciliation and arbitration board publicly agreed to employ secret ballots in recount elections, but in practice it failed to do so (Alcalde Justiniani 2010: 169).

278. SCJN 2008a: 120–21, 124, 131, 136, 138, 141–43, 145, 149–52. Of the international treaties cited by the court, only the Universal Declaration of Human Rights referred specifically to secret balloting (art. 20[3]).

279. In Mexican jurisprudence, *amparo* cases involve constitutional challenges to the enforcement of laws.

280. Nor did the 2012 reform legislation require the use of secret balloting in internal union elections. In nominal deference to union autonomy, the law (art. 371[IX]) permitted each labor organization's general assembly to decide how union officers would be selected.

281. Junta Federal de Conciliación y Arbitraje (JFCA) 2015. The JFCA directive permitted designated employer representatives to be present at the recount election (point 3), and it allowed the election to be held in the workplace if neither/none of the rival unions objected (point 2).

282. Interview with former senior U.S. government official A [Karesh], March 28, 2018, Washington, DC.

283. Interview with former senior U.S. government official A [Karesh], June 14, 2018.

284. Interview with senior U.S. NAO officials [Garza and Shea]; International Labor Rights Education and Research Fund, *Worker Rights News* 10 (summer 1994): 8. Similarly, Deputy Secretary James Shea had previously worked with the AFL-CIO's international division for some twenty years.

      When the U.S. NAO began operations in January 1994, Jorge Pérez-López (then director of the U.S. Department of Labor's Office of International Economic Affairs) served as acting secretary.

285. Levinson 1996: 19. Levinson was the submitters' legal counsel in US 940003.

286. Compa 2019: 273; Myerson 1994b; Nomani 1994.

287. It is an open question whether Clinton administration labor officials would have been prepared to request an Evaluation Committee of Experts (ECE) or call for the creation of an arbitral panel in public communications involving Mexico. At the time, Garza maintained ("Linking Labor Standards" 1997: 828) that the U.S. NAO could not really test ECE procedures because the early U.S. submissions focused mainly on freedom of association issues rather than on NAALC principles nos. 5, 6, or 9. (See also the interview with former senior U.S. government official A [Karesh], June 14, 2018.) When pressed regarding why the U.S. NAO did not self-initiate cases on these actionable principles, Garza pleaded limited staff and budgetary resources. It was, in fact, the case, however, that only one of the public communications submitted during the Clinton administration (US 9901 / TAESA) focused centrally on those NAALC principles (table 4.2).

288. One revealing incident in this regard involved the independent study that the U.S. NAO invited the author (in collaboration with Dr. Cirila Quintero Ramírez, El Colegio de la Frontera Norte-Matamoros) to conduct following the initial public communications it received concerning violations of freedom of association in Mexico. In 1995, the office commissioned a study of state-level conciliation and arbitration boards in the Mexican states of Chihuahua and Tamaulipas, the two states whose labor policies were the focus of US 940001 (Honeywell Corporation), US 940002 (General Electric Co.), US 940003 (Sony Corporation), and US 940004 (General Electric Co.). The final report (based on a random sample of the grievance cases considered by the boards between 1990 and 1994 and subsequently published as Middlebrook and Quintero 1998) found that, despite problems such as administrative delays, the states' labor conciliation and arbitration boards offered individual grievants an effective means of addressing their claims outside the workplace. None of the case files in the random sample concerned the boards' handling of union registration petitions. In a telephone conference call with Middlebrook in December 1995 to discuss the report findings, a frustrated U.S. NAO official called attention to this "absence" by interjecting, "But we didn't get any 'hits'!" (author's contemporary notes of a telephone conversation with U.S. NAO officials, December 15, 1995).

289. Lustig 1995: 20.

290.   The U.S. NAO was, at the time, under pressure from U.S. Department of State (DOS), the Office of the United States Trade Representative (USTR), and even White House officials not to place too much pressure on Mexico. Indeed, the DOS and the USTR lobbied to participate in decisions whether to accept for review public communications regarding Mexico. Nonetheless, the U.S. NAO proceeded to request ministerial consultations with Mexico over US 940003 (Sony Corporation). Interview with a former senior U.S. NAO official [Garza].

291.   Interviews with former STPS secretaries A [Palacios Alcocer] and B [Bonilla].

292.   At the same time, as noted in the preceding discussion of MEX NAO public communications, the same Clinton administration commitment to the success of the NAALC may have made the U.S. government especially responsive to Mexico's use of NAALC procedures to protect the rights of Mexican migrant workers in the United States.

293.   Post, Raile, and Raile (2010: 659) define "political will" as "the extent of committed support among key decision makers for a particular policy solution to a particular problem."

294.   Interviews with former STPS secretaries A [Palacios Alcocer] and B [Bonilla].

295.   Bensusán and Middlebrook 2013: 108–17.

296.   Middlebrook 2004: 21n52; Olvera 2004: 420.

297.   Interview with former STPS secretary B [Bonilla]. President Vicente Fox later took a strategic decision to prioritize political and economic stability by maintaining a de facto alliance with the CTM, CROC, and other government-aligned affiliates of the Labor Congress (Bensusán and Middlebrook 2013: 111).

298.   Indeed, in 1997, the PRI lost its majority in the federal Chamber of Deputies for the first time since its predecessor, the Revolutionary National Party (Partido Nacional Revolucionario) was formed in 1929.

299.   Kay (2011a: table 7.1) notes that the absence of progressive Mexican union allies was an obstacle to the formation of transnational coalitions in some industries.

300.   Given the Clinton administration's strong commitment to the NAALC, the number and identity of the sociopolitical actors engaged in particular US NAO communications may have been relatively less influential in practice than one would otherwise assume.

301.   The communications were: US 940001 (Honeywell Corporation), US 940002 (General Electric Co.), US 940004 (General Electric Co.), US 9702 (Han Young), and US 9703 / CAN 98-1 (Echlin / Itapsa).

302.   The trinational Echlin Workers' Alliance that mobilized around US 9703 / CAN 98-1 was an especially prominent example.

303.   Interviews with former STPS secretaries A [Palacios Alcocer] and B [Bonilla].

304.   Interview with former STPS secretary B [Bonilla].

305.   Interview with former STPS secretary B [Bonilla].

306.   Submissions US 940004 and US 2004-01 are omitted from this calculation because they were withdrawn.

307.   Interviews with senior NACLC official A [Caulfield] and former senior Canadian NAO official B [Banks]; Finbow 2006: 111, 232; Graubart 2008: 57, 96; Aspinwall 2013: 101.

308.   Interviews with senior NACLC officials A [Caulfield] and B [Studer] (July 7, 2005, Washington, DC) and a former senior US NAO official [Garza]; Graubart 2008: 97; Nolan García 2011b: 103–104, 107. The Bush administration also significantly cut the budget of the Bureau of International Labor Affairs (AFL-CIO 2005: 2).

309. Author's calculations based on the data presented in table 4.2 (excluding public communications involving Mexico that were subsequently withdrawn by the submitters or which the submitter failed to pursue). Overall, a Bayesian regression analysis of US NAO submissions found no statistically significant difference in case outcomes between the Clinton and Bush administrations.

   The Clinton and Bush administrations' records with regard to politically high-profile communications were mixed. The U.S. NAO under Clinton declined to review US 9801 (a complaint challenging President Zedillo's executive order barring a scheduled strike by Aeroméxico flight attendants), although it did later publish a commissioned report on how the three NAALC countries reconciled the right to strike with national security and safety concerns (Compa and Brooks 2019: 85; National Law Center for Inter-American Free Trade 2000). However, it reviewed US 9601 (SUTSP), a case with significant national political implications. Under the Bush administration, the U.S. NAO shied away from both US 2005-01 (Federal Labor Law reform, 2002) and US 2006-01 (SNTMMSRM and Pasta de Conchos).

310. US NAO public report 2005-03: 37; Diamond 1996: 217; U.S. Council for International Business 2003: 2; U.S. Chamber of Commerce 2004: 5, 7. This was the rationale cited by the U.S. NAO in declining to review communication US 2006-01 (SNTMMSRM and Pasta de Conchos); see Compa and Brooks 2019: 104.

311. Interviews with a Mexican labor attorney [Alcalde] and U.S. trade union representative A [Davis], July 21, 2004, both in Mexico City; interview with a senior AFL-CIO representative [Lee], May 29, 2008, Washington, DC; Dombois and Winter 2003: 7; Kay 2011a: 21, 154.

   Several of the U.S. and Canadian trade union and U.S., Canadian, and Mexican labor rights NGO representatives the author interviewed expressed concerns regarding the costs they incurred in filing NAALC public communications. For example, the UE and IBT together invested approximately US$50,000 in the US 940001 (Honeywell) and US 940002 (General Electric Co.) submissions. Similarly, the United Steelworkers-Canada spent over C$200,000 on the CAN 98-1 (Echlin/Itapsa) case. The disappointing outcomes in these cases proved to be a turning point in some U.S. and Canadian unions' willingness to engage in NAALC public communications (interviews with a senior UE official [Townsend] and a United Steelworkers-Canada representative [Rowlinson]; author's contemporary notes on a meeting with Canadian union and labor rights NGO representatives, September 10, 2007, Ottawa. For similar views, see the interviews with a Maquila Solidarity Network senior staff member [Jeffcott], September 13, 2007, Toronto, and a U.S. labor rights NGO staff member [Pier], May 27, 2008, Washington, DC. See also the comment by the AFL-CIO in NACLC 1998a: annex 5 (Public Comments: United States), p. 6, and Delp et al. 2004: 25, 30.

312. Brower 2008: 174.

313. Author's email communication with the STPS, January 27, 2021.

314. Compa and Brooks 2019: 129.

315. Interviews with a Mexican labor attorney [Alcalde] and former senior Canadian NAO official B [Banks], September 10, 2007; telephone interview with former senior U.S. government official A [Karesh], June 25, 2021.

316. STPS, "Consulta ministerial-Caso 940003: resoluciones adoptadas" (May 30, 1995) and U.S. NAO, "Ministerial Consultations—Submission 940003 Agreement on Implementation: Statement on Public Release of Documents" (May 10, 1996). All three NAFTA labor ministers signed the agreement on June 26, 1995 (U.S. NAO, "Report on Ministerial Consultations on Submission #940003," p. 3). Copies of these documents are in the author's possession.

317. Maquila Solidarity Network 2008c. The Mexican NAO had strongly protested U.S. NAO officials' onsite visit to Puebla as part of their investigation of the US 2003-01 submission (Nolan García 2011b: 105).

318. US NAO public report 2005-03: 7.

319. Weiss (2003: 724) terms this "effective enforcement of domestic labor law as a supranational obligation."

320. See, for instance, Gacek 1999: 217.

321. In testimony before the Mexican Congress on August 17, 1993, Mexico's secretary of commerce and industrial development and lead NAFTA negotiator Jaime Serra Puche reassured critics of the NAALC's penalty regime that, "The time frame of the process makes it very improbable that the stage of sanctions could be reached" (Negrete 1993).

322. Rapid settlement of the Aeroméxico strike allowed the U.S. NAO to decline the submission and avoid diplomatic conflict with the Mexican government (Compa and Brooks 2019: 84–85).

323. For instance, even though public communication US 940003 (Sony Corporation) focused on freedom of association and the right to collective bargaining in Mexico, the U.S. Department of Labor accepted a bilateral ministerial agreement calling for a public seminar on union registration and certification in the United States as well. (When Canada acceded to the agreement, the parties expanded the program to examine these issues in all three countries.) And as previously noted, the Clinton administration diplomatically agreed to link the public announcement of a ministerial agreement important to the United States (on US 9702 [Han Young] and US 9703 [Echlin/Itapsa]—with one important to Mexico (on MEX 9802, MEX 9803, and MEX 9804, all involving the rights of Mexican migrant workers in the United States).

324. M. Weiss (2003: 750, 752) and Dombois (2006: 752-53, 755) offer similar assessments.

325. Sociopolitical actors' growing disillusionment with the NAALC public communications process, and many rights advocates' commitment to corporate social responsibility campaigns as a principal focus of activity, are the most likely explanations for why there was no renewed interest in NAALC submissions during the Obama administration (telephone interview with a former senior U.S. Department of State official [Polaski], July 12, 2018). From the outset of the Obama administration, however, North American trade unions did pressure for reforms of the NAALC. See, for example, the "Joint AFL-CIO / Canadian Labour Congress Letter on NAFTA" (February 17, 2009) addressed to Obama and Canadian Prime Minister Stephen Harper, and the UNT / AFL-CIO / CLC "Tri-National Labor Declaration on Social and Economic Prosperity for North America" (August 7, 2009) (copies of these documents are in the author's possession).

**5. LEGACIES OF THE NORTH AMERICAN AGREEMENT ON LABOR
COOPERATION: LABOR RIGHTS, U.S. FREE-TRADE AGREEMENTS,
AND U.S.-MEXICAN NEGOTIATIONS OVER THE TRANS-PACIFIC
PARTNERSHIP, 2001–2017**

1. Dewan and Roncini (2018: 40–42) trace the evolution of labor dispute-settlement provisions in U.S. FTAs.

2. As of 2022, the United States formed part of free-trade agreements with six additional countries (in chronological order by the year in which the agreement took effect): Israel (1985), Singapore (2004), Australia (2005), and the Republic of Korea (2012). Canada, Mexico, and the United States completed renegotiation of the NAFTA in 2019 (see chapter 6). The U.S.-Israeli agreement did not include labor provisions.

3. The consensus among U.S. stakeholders on this matter did not immediately extend to Canada. The 1997 Canada-Chile Free Trade Agreement addressed labor issues in a side-agreement, the Canada-Chile Agreement on Labor Cooperation, that replicated the NAALC. See Polaski, Nolan García, and Rioux 2021: 143–44 on Canada's later (post-2008) approach to the issue.

4. U.S. Congress 1992: 78–80; Barr, Honeywell, and Stofel 1991: 11–12; Favilla-Solano 1996: 308–309. See also Bartow 1990.

5. Doumbia-Henry and Gravel 2006: 188.

6. Including labor rights provisions in the U.S.-Jordan agreement provoked considerable political controversy (Kahn 2000). The agreement had been signed on October 24, 2000, near the end of President William J. (Bill) Clinton's administration (1993–1997, 1997–2001), and it was ratified by the U.S. Congress during the first year of George W. Bush's administration (2001–2005, 2005–2009). Because opposition from the U.S. labor movement had contributed to a significant political defeat in 1997 over reauthorization of presidential "fast-track" trade negotiating authority, the Clinton administration included comparatively strong labor provisions in the U.S.-Jordan agreement in a bid for labor's support and to demonstrate its commitment to moving beyond the NAALC (author's interview [hereinafter "interview(s)"] with a senior AFL-CIO representative [Lee], May 29, 2008, Washington, DC; telephone interview with a former senior U.S. Department of State official [Polaski], May 7, 2021). For Republican opposition to the inclusion of labor provisions in the agreement (and in trade agreements in general), see the comments by, respectively, Representatives William Thomas (California) and David Dreier (California) in *U.S. Congressional Record* 147, no. 109 (2001) (107th Congress, first session): H4874, H4875, and by, respectively, Senators Phil Graham (Texas) and Charles E. Grassley (Iowa) in *U.S. Congressional Record* 147, no. 109 (2001): S9685-86, S9688. See also Shoch 2000: 126.

7. All U.S. free-trade agreements finalized following adoption of the 2007 Bipartisan Agreement on Trade Policy (see below) included among the agreed labor provisions the obligation to eliminate discrimination in respect of employment and occupation.

8. Telephone interview with a former senior U.S. Department of State official [Polaski], May 7, 2021.

9. The U.S.-Jordan agreement did not establish a particular penalty or sanctions regime. Its dispute-settlement procedures specified that if, after receiving a settlement panel

report, the joint committee of trade ministers was unable to resolve the controversy within thirty days, then the parties could take "any appropriate and commensurate measure" (art. 17.2[b]). However, in response to Republican congressional pressure, the Bush administration and the Jordanian government exchanged letters prior to ratification of the agreement in which they agreed to resolve potential disputes without resorting to trade sanctions (Bolle 2014: 3). The letters are reproduced in *U.S. Congressional Record* 147, no. 109 (2001): H4874–75.

10.   Shoch 2000: 126–27.

11.   The Bipartisan Trade Promotion Authority Act of 2002 (BTPAA, Public Law 107–210), in designating U.S. trade negotiating objectives, introduced into U.S. law the U.S.-Jordan FTA language regarding "through a sustained or recurring course of action or inaction, in a manner affecting trade." It also called for the future negotiation of agreements in which parties agreed to strive to ensure not to weaken domestic labor laws in order to promote trade and in which labor obligations were given equal treatment in dispute-settlement procedures. See, respectively, 19 U.S. Code 24, sect. 3802, (b) (11) (A) and (a) (7); (b) (12) (G); see also sect. 2102 (a, b, c). See Bolle 2007: 3–5 on the political background to the BTPAA.

The United States negotiated FTAs with Chile and Singapore (2003), Australia and Morocco (2004), and Bahrain, Costa Rica, the Dominican Republic, El Salvador, Guatemala, Honduras, Nicaragua, and Oman (2006) under the terms of this legislation (Bolle 2007: fig. 1). There is an extensive literature on the labor provisions in these agreements; for more general assessments, see Samet 2011 and Bolle 2014.

12.   Office of the United States Trade Representative (USTR) 2007.

13.   On El Salvador, for example, see Greenhouse 2001.

14.   Bolle 2005; American Federation of Labor-Congress of Industrial Organizations (AFL-CIO) 2005: 1; O'Donovan 2005: 6.

15.   The U.S. Congress had previously delayed action on a trade agreement with Bahrain until it reformed its labor laws (Destler 2007: 7).

16.   Hafner-Burton 2009: 60 n28.

17.   Weisman 2007. The quotation is from a letter that recently elected House Speaker Nancy Pelosi (Democrat-California) and twelve other House Democrats sent to President Bush on February 13, 2007 (a copy of which is in the author's possession). The letter focused principally on the large U.S. trade deficit and its impact on employment and wages in the United States.

18.   USTR 2007: 1.

19.   *Inside U.S. Trade* (hereinafter *IUST*), May 10, 2007.

20.   The agreement (p. 2) went on to clarify how the United States was in compliance with the ILO declaration.

21.   This was an important departure from the (post-Jordan) trade agreements that the Bush administration had previously negotiated, all of which limited sanctions arising from proven labor rights violations to a maximum monetary penalty of US$15 million per year (adjusted by the U.S. rate of inflation and paid into a fund dedicated to enhancing labor law enforcement in the territory of the party complained against) or the equivalent amount in reduced trade benefits if the fine was not paid. See, for example, United States-Chile Free Trade Agreement, art. 22.16.2, 4. There were no such limits to sanctions arising from demonstrated violations of commercial or intellectual property rights.

Chilean negotiators had strongly opposed making labor issues subject to trade sanctions (Hornbeck 2003: 15).

22. The Bipartisan Congressional Trade and Accountability Act of 2015 (Public Law 114-26) codified the terms of the 2007 bipartisan agreement in U.S. law.

23. At the time the May 10 agreement was concluded, the United States had already completed free-trade negotiations with Peru (April 2006), Colombia (November 2006), Panama (November 2006), and the Republic of Korea (April 2007). Those agreements were later renegotiated to reflect the terms of the May 10 accord. As an example, see the significant revisions made in the U.S.-Peru Trade Promotion Agreement (Samet 2011: 76–77).

24. In a report published in 2014, the U.S. Government Accountability Office (US GAO) concluded that these bodies were largely inactive in practice (2014: 36–37). None of the post-NAFTA FTAs created an institutional equivalent to the North American Commission on Labor Cooperation.

25. "Notice of Reassignment of Functions of Office of Trade Agreement Implementation to Office of Trade and Labor Affairs; Notice of Procedural Guidelines," *U.S. Federal Register* 71, no. 245 (December 21, 2006): 76691–96.

    None of the post-NAFTA agreements contained a provision equivalent to NAALC article 16(3), which limited the jurisdiction of each party's national administrative office to "labor law matters arising in the territory of another Party." In the United States, this condition was part of the OTLA's 2006 operational regulations cited above (sect. C[5]).

26. Kelly 2016 provides a detailed comparison of the labor rights provisions in U.S. FTAs between 2001 (Jordan) and 2012 (Panama).

27. Chapter 3.

28. US GAO 2009: 52; Hornbeck 2009: 8–9; Samet 2011: 52. Although Heintz and Luce recognize the limitations of the data sources on which they base their analysis, they conclude (2010: 24) that most U.S. FTA partner countries improved their records concerning freedom of association and the right to collective bargaining over an eleven-year period that began before and ended after negotiations over these agreements.

29. El Salvador ratified ILO conventions nos. 87 and 98 in September 2006 in order to retain access to the European Union's Generalized System of Preferences Plus program (Heintz and Luce 2010: 51).

30. DR-CAFTA Ministers of Trade and Economy, "The Labor Dimension in Central America and the Dominican Republic—Building on Progress: Strengthening Compliance and Enhancing Capacity," April 2005.

31. Albertson 2010: 506n43; Bolle 2005: 3–4; Samet 2011: 51. For further details on the DR-CAFTA cases, see Rogowsky and Chyn 2008: 130–33; Heintz and Luce 2010: 53–55; Samet 2011: 52, 55 65–66, 71–72.

    To help win U.S. congressional approval of the agreement, Bush administration officials attached an annex (annex 16.5) that created a "Labor Cooperation and Capacity Building Mechanism." All post-NAFTA U.S. FTAs, including the prior U.S. agreements with Singapore and Chile, also included formal labor cooperation programs. The Washington Office on Latin America (2009) undertook a detailed assessment of U.S.-funded labor reform projects in the DR-CAFTA countries.

32. Samet 2011: 78. On other labor reforms adopted by Peru, including those concerning child labor and the right to strike, see Samet 2011: 79–81 and ILO 2016: 149.

33. ILO 2015: 39; "Public Submission to the Office of Trade and Labor Affairs (OTLA) Under Chapters 17 (Labor) and 21 (Dispute Settlement) of the Trade Promotion Agreement Between the United States and Peru" (July 23, 2015, hereinafter US 2015-01 submission): 19. The U.S. government reports cited in this section are all available at: U.S. Department of Labor, "Submissions Under the Labor Provisions of Free Trade Agreements," accessed February 15–March 24, 2021, www.dol.gov/agencies/ilab/our-work/trade/fta-submissions. See also US GAO 2014: 37.

34. These cases included Bahrain, Chile, Jordan, Morocco, Oman, Panama, and Singapore. See Rogowsky and Chyn 2008: 120, 127, 128, 133; US GAO 2009: 35–38; Hafner-Burton 2009: 148–49; Heintz and Luce 2010: 35–37, 39, 41–44, 47; US GAO 2014: 13, 37–38; ILO 2015: 36–41.

35. See Borkan 2010 on AFL-CIO opposition to the measure.

36. *IUST*, May 10, 2007; Destler 2007: 11.

37. Interview with U.S. trade union representative B [Drake], June 20, 2018, Washington, DC.

38. Villarreal 2014: 25.

39. U.S. DOL, "The Colombian Labor Action Plan: A Five Year Update," April 11, 2016, pp. 6–7. The largest grants were US$9.8 million (2012–2016) for an ILO-coordinated project to strengthen the overall capacity of the Ministry of Labor; US$1.5 million (2012–2017) to the National Union School (Escuela Nacional Sindical) to establish workers' rights centers in four Colombian cities to raise workers' awareness of their rights and enhance their capacity to file complaints with the Ministry of Labor; and US$9.0 million (2013–2017) to combat child labor in the informal mining industry. These grants supplemented extensive earlier U.S. financial assistance to Colombia (White House 2011b: 4, 5).

40. White House 2011a. Even after the action plan was announced, the AFL-CIO continued to oppose the U.S.-Colombian FTA (Villarreal 2014: 28).

41. *U.S. Congressional Record* 157, no 152 (2011) 112th Congress, first session): H6745, H6797, H6799 (comments by, respectively, Representatives Andy Levin [Democrat-Michigan], James McDermott [Democrat-Washington], and Nancy Pelosi).

42. H.R. 3078 became Public Law 112-42 on October 21, 2011. The United States-Colombia Trade Promotion Agreement went into effect on May 15, 2012.

43. *U.S. Congressional Record* 2011: S6413, S6446, H6799 (comments by, respectively, Senator Carl Levin, [Democrat-Michigan], Senator Richard Durbin [Democrat-Illinois], and Representative Pelosi).

44. *U.S. Congressional Record* 2011: H6797.

45. The five Colombian labor and nongovernmental organizations that filed US 2016-02 also submitted, in collaboration with the Canadian Labour Congress, a simultaneous complaint to Canada's Office for Inter-American Labour Cooperation under the Canada-Colombia Labor Cooperation Agreement. For details, see Compa and Brooks 2019: 225–27.

46. The U.S.-Jordan FTA did not fall under OTLA jurisdiction (*U.S. Federal Register* 71, no. 245 (December 21, 2006): 76694 [section A: Designation of Contact Point]).

In September 2006, the AFL-CIO followed up on a May 2006 report by the New York–based National Labor Committee on working conditions in Jordan's export apparel sector by filing a formal complaint with the USTR (AFL-CIO 2006b). The complaint, which focused particularly on abuses suffered by noncitizen workers in garment manufacturing facilities located in so-called qualified industrial zones, alleged widespread violations of national laws and international standards concerning the freedom of association, the right to collective bargaining, the right to strike, and wages, hours, and working conditions. The case was unique in that the U.S. National Textile Association cosubmitted the complaint, the only labor complaint filed under post-NAFTA U.S. FTA procedures by a private-sector organization.

The USTR did not formally consider the complaint for investigation (US GAO 2009: 47). However, between September and December 2006, the U.S. Agency for International Development and the government of Jordan together assessed working conditions in some seventy apparel manufacturing facilities, concluding: "Working conditions in Jordan's garment factories generally fall below the requirements of Jordanian law and international labor standards" (Joint Labor Assessment and Training Project, "Working Conditions in Jordan's Garment Sector," p. 5). In March 2007, Jordan's Ministry of Labor published its own action plan ("Labor Compliance in Jordan's Apparel Sector: Actions to Date and Next Steps") summarizing the steps it had taken to expand workplace inspections, prosecute employers for labor violations and close some factories, raise the minimum wage, increase funding for the Ministry of Labor, and adopt a code of conduct for employers in the export apparel sector. (Copies of these documents are in the author's possession.) In January 2013, the U.S. and Jordanian governments agreed to a subsequent "Implementation Plan Related to Working and Living Conditions of Workers" that outlined further steps to combat employers' anti-union actions and discrimination against foreign workers in garment factories (USTR 2015a: 27). Nevertheless, the U.S. Department of State's 2019 human rights report on Jordan reported continued significant restrictions on freedom of association, collective bargaining, and the right to strike. Foreign workers could legally join trade unions (almost all of which were affiliated with the government-linked General Federation of Jordanian Trade Unions), but they could not form unions or hold union office. U.S. Department of State, "2019 Country Reports on Human Rights Practices: Jordan," accessed March 22, 2021, https://www.state.gov/wp -content/uploads/2020/02/JORDAN-2019-HUMAN-RIGHTS-REPORT.pdf/; section 7: Worker Rights.

47.   The AFL-CIO was the sole submitter in the April 2011 filing against Bahrain, but it acted in close cooperation with the principal Bahraini labor confederation, the General Federation of Bahraini Trade Unions.

48.   US 2016-02 submission: 8–19, 28–38.

49.   For example, managers of Kyungshin-Lear Honduras Electrical Distribution Systems, a South Korean-U.S. joint venture between Kyunghshin Corporation and Lear Corporation producing automotive electrical harnesses for export to the United States, illegally dismissed every union leader ever elected and repeatedly refused to bargain with the union claiming legal representation of its workforce. The company continued its anti-union actions even after the OTLA began its review of the case. Similarly, the union representing workers at Petralax, an apparel producer, was compelled to elect leaders

on five separate occasions because company managers always fired them (OTLA public report 2012-01: 10, 25; for other such cases, see US 2012-01 submission: 6, 8, 9, 11, 13, 15, 22, 28-29, 34, 51).

50. Compa and Brooks (2019: 213) argue that the OTLA set an important precedent by accepting for review a case involving a public employer with a tenuous connection to international trade.

51. No case number is available for the 2010 submission concerning Costa Rica.

52. The legislation in question was the 1978 Non-Traditional Exports Promotion Act and the 2000 Agriculture Sector Promotion Act (US 2015-01 submission: 4, 15-17, 22, 25). At the time of the submission, Peru maintained twelve different labor regimes in the private sector and fifteen different regimes in the public sector (US 2015-01 submission: 24).

53. US 2015-01 submission: 5, 8, 11, 13, 26-27, 31, 35-37,

54. US 2016-01 submission: 8-18; for similar examples from the sugar sector, see pp. 28-38. See also OTLA public report 2016-01: 18-22.

55. OTLA public report 2011-03: iii, 4-5, 8-23. The OTLA reported that two of the Haitian sugarcane workers who spoke to its visiting delegation to the Dominican Republic in April 2012 were subsequently fired. Pressures exerted by U.S. officials later led to their reinstatement (OTLA public report 2011-03: 19, 23-26).

56. The submission against Honduras also cited violence against trade unionists, particularly the repression of union protests against the 2009 military overthrow of President Manuel Zelaya (US 2012-01 submission: 60-63). The OTLA's review of the case did not, however, address this issue (OTLA public report 2012-01: 1).

57. US 2016-02 submission: table 1. In commenting on the trade effects of egregious labor rights violations, the cosubmitters argued (p. 25): "Human rights violations are not a 'natural endowment' nor are they a legitimate basis for trade and investment competition. The GOC's [government of Colombia] failure to ensure workers can freely organize and join trade unions, bargain for better wages and working conditions, and exercise their rights without fear of retaliation or physical violence has distorted the cost of labor in the oil sector, which affects trade and investment between Colombia and the United States."

58. In December 2014, there were 710 union leaders under the protection of the National Protection Unit (US 2016-02 submission: 9).

59. OTLA public report 2016-02: 28-31. Compa and Brooks (2019: 223) report that a total of some three thousand Colombian trade unionists were killed between 1986 and 2014.

60. US 2015-01 submission: 19.

61. US 2016-02 submission: 20-21. Nor had the Colombian government conducted investigations of death threats against trade unionists (US 2016-02 submission: 22); see also OTLA public report 2016-02: 33.

62. See, for example, US 2012-01 submission (Honduras): 4, 24, 46, and US 2015-01 submission (Peru): 9, 13.

63. In August 2010, Costa Rica's Constitutional Court ruled in favor of the SINTRAJAP and ordered the reinstatement of fired union leaders. The ILWU then petitioned the OTLA to postpone its review decision until there was clear evidence that the Costa Rican government would accede to the court's decision. Following reelection of the SINTRAJAP leaders in January 2011, the ILWU withdrew its submission (*IUST*, September 20 and 21, 2010; May 6, 2011).

64. For instance, in its review of US 2011-03 (Dominican Republic), the OTLA's assessment was based on more than four hundred documents, emails, videos, and photographs, including materials it received from the government of the Dominican Republic and other relevant parties (OTLA public report US 2011-03: 2). See also OTLA public report 2012-01 (Honduras): 3, 86. For an example of the use of ILO assessments in OTLA reviews, see OTLA public report 2010-03 (Peru): 2–3.

65. OTLA public reports 2011-03 (Dominican Republic): ii and 2012-01 (Honduras): 3.

66. US 2010 (Costa Rica) is excluded from these calculations.

67. The format of OTLA final public reports on the U.S. FTA cases was the same as that adopted in the NAALC public communications (chapter 4).

68. See, for example, OTLA public report 2012-01 (Honduras).

69. In contrast to the NAALC public communications examined in chapter 4, in which the three NAFTA signatory countries often agreed to address labor problems through such means as trinational seminars, the OTLA reports all focused on legal and policy changes to be undertaken unilaterally by the target country.

70. OTLA public report 2011-01: 40–41.

71. OTLA public report 2011-03: 32–34.

72. OTLA public report 2012-01: 88–91.

73. OTLA public report 2015-01: iii. The 2015-01 submission had called (pp. 37–38) for the outright repeal of specific articles in the laws governing textile and garment production and export agriculture.

74. "Labor Rights Monitoring and Action Plan as Mutually Determined by the Government of the United States and the Government of Honduras," December 9, 2015. (A copy of this document is in the author's possession.) The two governments later agreed to extend the action plan through December 2019.

75. One particularly innovative step was the requirement that the secretariat of labor and social security publish online detailed results of all workplace inspections ("Labor Rights Monitoring and Action Plan," p. 7).

76. OTLA public report 2012-01: 87.

77. In the case of Honduras, these regular exchanges began when the labor complaint was filed (OTLA public report 2012-01: 92–94).

78. "U.S. Department of Labor Statement on the Status of the Implementation of the U.S.-Honduras Labor Rights Monitoring and Action Plan," December 12, 2018, pp. 1–2. Copies of all the documents cited in this discussion are in the author's possession.

79. For example, the U.S. Federal Mediation and Conciliation Service and the U.S. DOL's Wage and Hours Division provided technical advice and training to the Honduran secretariat of labor and social security ("Labor Rights Monitoring and Action Plan," pp. 4, 5). See also "U.S. Department of Labor Statement on the Status of the Implementation of the U.S.-Honduras Labor Rights Monitoring and Action Plan," October 12, 2018, pp. 2–3; Piore and Shrank 2008; USTR 2011. Between fiscal years 2001 and 2013, the United States provided a total of US$275 million in labor-related assistance to DR-CAFTA countries, Colombia, and Peru (US GAO 2014: 15–17).

80. "Second Periodic Review of Progress to Address Issues Identified in the U.S. Department of Labor's Public Report of Review of Submission 2015-01 (Peru)," April 20, 2018, p. 2.

81. "Twelve-Month Review of Implementation of Recommendations in the U.S. Department of Labor's Public Report of Review of Submission 2011-03 (Dominican Republic)," October 16, 2014.

82. "Sixth Periodic Review of Implementation of Recommendations in the U.S. Department of Labor's Public Report of Review of Submission 2011-03 (Dominican Republic)," May 16, 2018, pp. 2–3.

83. OTLA public report 2012-01 (Honduras): 94.

84. "Fifth Periodic Review of Implementation of Recommendations in the U.S. Department of Labor's Public Report of Review of Submission 2011-03 (Dominican Republic)," October 5, 2016, p. 1.

85. "First Periodic Review of Progress to Address Issues Identified in the U.S. Department of Labor's Public Report of Review of Submission 2015-01 (Peru)," December 16, 2016, p. 1.

86. *IUST*, October 29, 2021.

87. OTLA public report 2012-01: 86–87; "Progress Under the U.S.-Honduras Labor Rights Monitoring and Action Plan," March 14, 2016, p. 4. See "U.S. Department of Labor Statement on . . . U.S.-Honduras . . . ," p. 2n2, for the commission's membership.

88. M. Kim's (2012: 710–12, 714) statistical analysis of domestic labor protection in U.S. FTA partner countries found no significant improvement following trade agreement ratification. Dewan and Roncini (2018: 45–48, 50) report that the number of labor inspectors and workplace inspections rose in the Latin American and Caribbean countries that signed free-trade agreements with the United States between 2003 and 2007.

89. OTLA public report 2010-03: iii, 19; Compa and Brooks 2019: 212.

90. "U.S. Department of Labor Statement on . . . U.S.-Honduras . . . ," pp. 3–4. The October 2018 U.S. progress review also noted (p. 4) "significant advancement" by the Honduran government in eliminating child labor, including by reconstituting the National Commission for the Gradual and Progressive Eradication of Child Labor. However, it also restated (p. 5) U.S. concerns about continued threats and violence against trade unionists.

    In February 2015, the US DOL applauded Honduran President Juan Orlando Hernández's (2014–2018, 2018–2022) openness to dialogue and his government's commitment to improved enforcement of labor laws ("Joint Statement of the United States Department of Labor and Honduran Secretariat of Labor and Social Security regarding the Public Report of Review on U.S. Submission 2012-01 (Honduras)," February 27, 2015). However, several years later, the U.S. government accused Hernández of extensive involvement in illegal cocaine smuggling (Parker and Semple 2021).

91. The coding scheme for observed policy outcomes in table 5.1 parallels that employed in table 2.1.

92. U.S. Department of State, "2019 Country Reports on Human Rights Practices: Bahrain," Section 7: Worker Rights; Compa and Brooks 2019: 214.

93. "Second Periodic Review . . . (Peru);" *IUST*, September 28, 2017; April 28, 2018.

94. For the Obama administration's overview of reform measures adopted by the Colombian government in these and related areas, see White House 2011a; 2011b: 3, 4. See also US GAO 2014: 12.

95.   U.S. DOL, "The Colombian Labor Action Plan," p. 2.

96.   OTLA public report 2016-02: 5, 7–8, 10–11, 15–17, 18, 22–26, 34–35.

97.   OTLA public report 2016-02: 31.

98.   OTLA, "First Periodic Review of Progress to Address Issues in the U.S. Department of Labor's Public Report of Review of Submission 2016-02 (Colombia)," January 8, 2018, pp. 1–2.

99.   Compa and Brooks 2019: 227.

100. The six Guatemalan labor organizations were: the Union of Port Quetzal Company Workers (Sindicato de Trabajadores Empresa Portuaria Quetzal), Union of Izabal Banana Workers (Sindicato de Trabajadores del Banano de Izabal), Union of International Frozen Products, Inc. Workers (Sindicato de Trabajadores de la Empresa Internacional Productos Congelados, S.A.), Coalition of Avandia Workers (Coalición de Trabajadores de Avandia), Union of Fribo Company Workers (Sindicato de Trabajadores de la Empresa Fribo), and the Guatemalan Union Federation of Food, Agroindustry, and Similar Activities Workers (Federación Sindical de Trabajadores de la Alimentación, Agro Industria y Similares de Guatemala).

101. US 2008-01 submission: 11, 12, 16, 19, 24.

102. US 2008-01 submission: 2–3.

103. US 2008-01 submission: 8, quoting from ILO CFA report no. 348, case no. 2540, item 813.

104. US 2008-01 submission: 3.

105. US 2008-01 submission: 1.

106. As required by its operating guidelines, OTLA officials also consulted with the U.S. DOL and the USTR concerning the submission.

107. OTLA public report 2008-01: iii.

108. OTLA public report 2008-01: ii, iii, 30–31, *passim*.

109. In their letter (a copy of which is in the author's possession), Secretaries Kirk and Solis closed by stating, "The United States also has grave concerns about the problem of labor-related violence in Guatemala, which is serious and apparently deteriorating." In a separate statement, USTR Kirk argued that the failure of the Guatemalan government to enforce its labor laws "harms U.S. workers by forcing them to compete against substandard labor practices and tilts the playing field away from American workers and businesses" (USTR 2010).

110. The government of Guatemala initially delayed creation of the arbitral panel by claiming that there had been no agreement between the parties regarding the meaning of the provision stipulating they would choose the final panelist "by lot" (*Economist* 2018e).

111. "Mutually Agreed Enforcement Action Plan Between the Government of the United States and the Government of Guatemala" (hereinafter "Enforcement Plan"), April 25, 2013 (a copy of this document is in the author's possession). Even before the action plan was negotiated, the Guatemalan government had taken some steps to improve labor law enforcement. During 2012, the Ministry of Labor hired one hundred additional permanent labor inspectors and another five labor attorneys, as well as purchasing twenty vehicles to enhance the ministry's inspection capacity. The government also created a judicial Unit for Execution and Verification of Reinstatements and Special Procedures related to Labor Matters. See "Enforcement Plan," pp. 2, 3–4.

During the course of U.S.-Guatemalan discussions over the terms of the action plan, a number of international brand-name companies with affiliated production facilities in Guatemala (including Adidas Group, American Eagle Outfitters, Gap, Liz Claiborne, Nike, PVH Group, VF Corporation, and Under Armour) called upon the government to resolve the grievance case quickly (Maquila Solidarity Network 2012b; ILO 2015: 53n76).

In parallel with its negotiations with the United States, in 2013, the government of Guatemala and the ILO reached agreement on a "road map" to address violations of freedom of association, and the government established a National Tripartite Commission on Labor Relations and Freedom of Association to monitor its implementation. However, the ILO later concluded that little was achieved under the plan. U.S. Department of State, "2019 Country Reports on Human Rights Practices," March 11, 2020, www .state.gov/reports/2019-country-reports-on-human-rights-practices/.

112.   USTR 2014; USTR 2015a: 9.

113.   The Guatemalan member resigned in November 2015 and was replaced by a Mexican national.

114.   Copies of these letters ("Submissions of Nongovernmental Entities") are available at: Office of the United States Trade Representative, "In the Matter of Guatemala—Issues Relating to the Obligations Under Article 16.2.1(a) of the CAFTA-DR," April 27, 2015, https://ustr.gov/sites/default/files/enforcement/DS/Submissions%20of%20Non Governmental%20Entities.pdf.

115.   Office of the United States Trade Representative, "U.S. Initial Written Submission, in the matter of, *Guatemala—Issues Relating to the Obligations Under Article 16.2.1(a) of the CAFTA-DR*," November 3, 2014, https://ustr.gov/sites/default/files/US%20Initial%20Written %20Submission.pdf, paras. 17–20, 53–84, 111–13, 132–77, 192, 201–15, 224–40.

116.   Office of the United States Trade Representative, "U.S. Initial Written Submission," para. 96.

117.   Telephone interview with a former senior U.S. Department of State official [Polaski], May 7, 2021; Compa, Vogt, and Gottwald 2018: 5, 30.

118.   Office of the United States Trade Representative, "Initial Written Submission of Guatemala, in the matter of, *Guatemala—Issues Relating to the Obligations under Article 16.2.1(a) of CAFTA-DR*," February 2, 2015, https://ustr.gov/sites/default/files/enforcement/labor /NON-CONFIDENTIAL%20-%20Guatemala%20-%20Initial%20written%20communication %20%202-02-2015.pdf, paras. 3–9, 165–79, 200–69, 273–78, 289–398, 409–50.

119.   Office of the United States Trade Representative, "Initial Written Submission of Guatemala," paras. 10, 451–72.

120.   On September 27, 2016, the panel delivered an initial report to the parties for comment.

121.   International Trade Administration, "Final Report of the Panel, in the Matter of Guatemala—Issues Relating to the Obligations Under Article 16.2.1(a) of CAFTA-DR," June 14, 2017. The considerable length of panel proceedings resulted in part from the parties' requests for postponements as they sought unsuccessfully to resolve the dispute through negotiations (Compa, Vogt, and Gottwald 2018: 7).

122.   International Trade Administration, "Final Report of the Panel," para. 285–432, esp. 426, 428, 430.

123.   International Trade Administration, "Final Report of the Panel," para. 401–5, 491, 497.

124.   International Trade Administration, "Final Report of the Panel," para. 565–86, 588, 591.

125.   International Trade Administration, "Final Report of the Panel," para. 99, 102, 106. Moreover, only one of the union registration cases cited by the U.S. government had arisen before its request to establish the panel (para. 104).

126.   International Trade Administration, "Final Report of the Panel," para. 594.

127.   Compa, Vogt, and Gottwald 2018: 9, 15. See also Polaski 2017.

128.   International Trade Administration, "Final Report of the Panel," para. 168. The panel-lists specifically contrasted the DR–CAFTA language to the phrasing employed ("in a matter that is trade-related") in NAALC articles 29 and 36 (Final Report: 55n126).

129.   International Trade Administration, "Final Report of the Panel," para. 479.

130.   Telephone interview with a former senior U.S. Department of State official [Polaski], May 7, 2021.

131.   "Written Views of the International Trade Union Confederation," April 27, 2015, pp. 2–3 (included in "Submissions of Nongovernmental Entities").

132.   This section draws on some materials, often in revised form, published in Bensusán and Middlebrook 2020.

133.   The United States withdrew from the agreement on January 23, 2017. The remaining countries (Australia, Brunei, Canada, Chile, Japan, Malaysia, Mexico, New Zealand, Peru, Singapore, Vietnam) signed a Comprehensive and Progressive Agreement for Trans-Pacific Partnership on March 8, 2018, in Santiago, Chile.

134.   White House 2016b.

135.   The TPP originated in the Trans-Pacific Strategic Economic Partnership Agreement conceived of by Chile, New Zealand, and Singapore in 2003 and signed (with Brunei) in 2006 (Fergusson, McMinimy, and Williams 2015: 1).

136.   Office of the United States Trade Representative,"Trans-Pacific Partnership," November 5, 2015, https://ustr.gov/trade-agreements/free-trade-agreements/trans-pacific-partnership/tpp-full-text. Cimino-Isaacs 2016 and Charnovitz 2021: 1–5 assess the TPP's labor provisions.

137.   The TPP was the first U.S. trade agreement to call upon signatory states to "encourage enterprises to voluntarily adopt corporate social responsibility initiatives on labour issues that have been endorsed or are supported by that Party" (art. 19.7). It also required signatories to create a national labor consultative or advisory body that included members of the public, including representatives of labor and business organizations (art. 19.14.2). Moreover, the TPP expressly allowed worker and employer stakeholders to participate in identifying cooperative activities that the signatory parties might undertake, including the sharing of information concerning employment conditions in multinational companies operating in two or more member countries (art. 19.10.3, 6[s]). During cooperative consultations to resolve a labor dispute, the complainant could request that the respondent party make available for consultation any of its government officials with relevant expertise (art. 19.15.9).

138.   Available at Office of the United States Trade Representative,"Trans-Pacific Partnership," November 5, 2015, https://ustr.gov/trade-agreements/free-trade-agreements/trans-pacific-partnership/tpp-full-text. For a critical assessment of these agreements, see U.S. House of Representatives 2016: 3–10. All three of these action plans were dropped from the TPP

agreement after the United States withdrew from it. In the case of Malaysia, the concessions that U.S. negotiators won in the labor consistency plan addressed many of the same issues that had featured in U.S. GSP labor complaints (chapter 2).

139. De la Mora 2013: 801–802.

140. *IUST*, December 16, 2011; Barnes 2014: 4.

141. Interview with former senior USTR official A [Cutler], April 30, 2018, Washington, DC.

142. See Silva 2007 on the Colombian case.

143. U.S. House of Representatives 2019b: 5 (statement by Elizabeth Baltzan).

144. USTR 2015c; *IUST*, January 13; February 3 and 19, 2016; Santos 2019: 148n26.

145. Telephone interview with former senior U.S. government official A [Karesh], October 29, 2018.

146. On Obama's and Biden's personal convictions on this matter, see the telephone interview with former senior USTR official C [Holleyman], June 3, 2020.

147. Interviews with former senior U.S. government officials A [Karesh] (March 28) and B [Pier] (April 26, 2018), Washington, DC; Lane 2008; *IUST*, January 11and February 27, 2008. The 2008 Democratic electoral platform committed the party's presidential candidate to incorporating the NAFTA's labor and environmental "side-agreements" into the body of the accord and making their provisions fully enforceable (*IUST*, August 15, 2008). When Obama announced the final TPP text, he did indeed claim that he had fulfilled his campaign pledge because its labor provisions formed part of the main agreement and recognized the core rights articulated in the 1998 ILO Declaration (*IUST*, October 9, 2015b).

148. Telephone interviews with former senior Mexican diplomat A [Sarukhan], October 17, 2018, and former senior Mexican government official C [Videgaray], March 19, 2019; *IUST*, December 16, 2011 and December 14, 2012.

149. Chapter 3.

150. Internal Labour Organization, "Normlex," accessed February 16, 2016, www.ilo.org/dyn /normlex/en.

151. On the issue-specific nature of bargaining power, see Jönsson 1981: 249–50 and Peterson 1986: 188, 198, 201.

152. Bensusán and Middlebrook 2013: 108–36.

153. For examples of successful CTM opposition from the mid-1940s through the early 1990s to proposed electoral and PRI membership reforms that threatened its interests, see Loaeza 2010: 644–46 and Middlebrook 1995: 297–98, 305.

154. Bensusán and Middlebrook 2013: 162–66.

155. IndustriALL 2018; STPS 2015; U.S. House of Representatives 2016: 13.

156. Muñoz Rios 2015.

157. In addition to interviews cited below, this discussion draws on interviews with former senior U.S. government official A [Karesh] (June 14, 2018); former U.S. Department of Labor [Quintana] (May 15, 2018) and Department of State [Polaski] (May 29, 2018) officials; U.S. trade union representative A [Davis] (March 20, 2018); and officials in the Mexican Embassy in the United States [Tamayo] (April 18 [Zabalgoitia] and June 14, 2018) and the U.S. Embassy in Mexico [Wayne] (June 18, 2018), all in Washington, DC, or by telephone.

158. Probably in response to White House guidance, USTR Froman (a former Department of the Treasury official and Citigroup executive) and Secretary of Labor Perez (a former Department of Justice official who had also served as the state of Maryland's secretary of labor) worked closely together in negotiations with Mexico over labor rights.

159. Interviews with senior U.S. trade union representatives A [Feingold], April 23, 2018, and B [Drake]; interview with former senior U.S. government official B [Pier], April 26, 2018, all in Washington, DC. The AFL-CIO had, for example, issued public statements condemning persistent labor rights violations in Mexico to coincide with President-elect Peña Nieto's Oval Office meeting with President Obama on November 27, 2012 (a copy of this statement is in the author's possession) and Peña Nieto's state visit to Washington, DC, on January 6, 2015 (*IUST*, January 6, 2015). See also the joint statement by the AFL-CIO and the National Union of Workers (Unión Nacional de Trabajadores, UNT) concerning the labor reforms Mexico should adopt before it acceded to the TPP ("Declaración sociolaboral de UNT-AFL-CIO," *La Jornada en línea*, August 12, 2015).

160. Mexican labor organizations were not included in "side room" (*cuarto de junto*) consultations, even though the private sector was (De Rosenzweig 2012: 94).

161. Interviews with a former senior Mexican trade negotiator [Guajardo], February 25, 2019, and former senior Mexican diplomat C [Medina-Mora], February 27, 2019, Mexico City. Delay is a well-established Mexican negotiating technique (Torres 2010: 665).

162. "Decreto por el que se reforma la fracción III del Apartado A del artículo 123 de la Constitución Política de los Estados Unidos Mexicanos," *Diario Oficial de la Federación*, June 17, 2014.

163. Interviews with former senior U.S. official B [Pier], April 26, 2018, and with former senior STPS official B [Avante], February 27, 2019, Mexico City.

164. Interviews with former senior U.S. government officials A [Karesh] (March 28) and B [Pier] (April 26, 2018); interviews with a former senior Mexican trade negotiator [Guajardo], a former senior adviser to President Peña Nieto [Nuño], February 25, 2019, and former senior STPS official C [Stein], March 1, 2019, all in Mexico City.

165. *IUST*, May 29, 2014.

166. In Krasner's (1999) terms, Mexican officials rejected this U.S. demand because it threatened both domestic ("the organization of authority within a state," p.10) and Westphalian ("when external actors influence or determine domestic authority structures," p. 20) sovereignty.

167. Interviews with a former senior advisor to President Peña Nieto [Nuño] and former senior STPS official B [Avante].

168. Telephone interviews with former senior Mexican diplomats B [Estivill], January 17, and D [Basañez], March 26, 2019. Although the evidence on this point is not conclusive, Mexican negotiators may have given ground on automotive industry domestic-content rules of origin in exchange for U.S. negotiators' concession on the question of a labor consistency plan (telephone interviews with former senior Mexican diplomat B [Estivill] and former senior USTR official D [Kibria], June 11, 2020; interview with former senior Mexican diplomat C [Medina-Mora]; see also *IUST*, September 25, 2015).

169. The Obama administration drew criticism from U.S. labor unions and congressional Democrats for not negotiating a labor consistency plan with Mexico. Republican legislators opposed such arrangements (*IUST*, October 3 and 7, 2015; January 13 and February 18, 2016).

170. Putnam 1988: 445, 456. Putnam argues (449) that a negotiating party can often gain leverage vis-à-vis its counterpart by asserting that a proposed outcome would face strong domestic opposition. By insisting that bilateral discussions proceed in secret and thereby avoiding public expressions of nationalist opposition, Mexican officials forfeited this theoretical possibility—even though they still argued that constitutional labor reform would be difficult politically. Even though U.S. negotiators largely accepted that claim, it did not deter them (interview with a former senior adviser to President Peña Nieto [Nuño]).

171. Interviews with a former senior Mexican trade negotiator [Guajardo] and former senior STPS official C [Stein].

172. Interview with former senior STPS official B [Avante]. Godoy (2015) details the similar way in which U.S. officials closely monitored domestic legislative change in signatories to the DR-CAFTA.

173. Interview with former senior U.S. government official B [Pier], April 26, 2018.

174. Interview with former senior USTR official A [Cutler].

175. Bipartisan Congressional Priorities and Accountability Act of 2015 (Public Law 114-26), sect. 105(b)(d)(3)(A), June 29, 2015, www.congress.gov/114/plaws/publ26/PLAW-114publ26.pdf.

176. As noted in chapter 3, during the NAALC negotiations, the Clinton administration was significantly constrained by opposition to stronger labor rights provisions from congressional Republicans, whose support was crucial to passage of the NAFTA.

177. Interviews with a former senior advisor to President Peña Nieto [Nuño], former senior STPS official C [Stein], and a former senior Mexican trade negotiator [Guajardo]. Presidents Obama and Peña Nieto spoke personally on several occasions over the course of TPP negotiations.

178. *IUST*, January 14, 2016; interview with former senior Office of the Presidency (Oficina de la Presidencia) official A [Castillejos], February 27, 2019, Mexico City.

179. Because of pressures from Mexican business groups (they argued that the measure would threaten "social peace" by multiplying the number of legally recognized unions in a workplace), the Senate took no action (M. Martínez 2015; Alcalde Justiniani 2018c). After the National Regeneration Movement (Movimiento Regeneración Nacional, MORENA) gained a majority of seats in 2018, the Senate finally ratified the convention on September 20, 2018 (Guzmán 2018).

180. E. Sánchez 2015; Vergara 2016a. The reform would presumably have addressed the issues raised in the Centro de Investigación y Docencia Económicas report (CIDE 2015) concerning tripartite conciliation and arbitration boards (see below).

181. The TPP was formally signed on February 3, 2016 (White House 2016b).

182. In discussions with their Mexican counterparts, U.S. negotiators referred to "labor dumping" (*dumping laboral*) (interview with former senior STPS official B [Avante]).

183. Interview with former senior STPS official B [Avante]. Ambassador Froman never voiced this specific demand during the course of TPP negotiations with Mexico (interview with a former senior Mexican trade negotiator [Guajardo]).

184. Interviews with former senior USTR official A [Cutler] and former Obama administration senior White House official A [González], June 22, 2018, Washington, DC; telephone interview with former senior USTR official C [Holleyman], June 3, 2020; author's email communication with former senior U.S. government official B [Pier], October 27, 2019; White House 2016c.

185. Videgaray served as secretary of finance and public credit between 2012 and 2016 and as secretary of foreign relations between 2017 and 2018.

186. Telephone interview with former senior U.S. government official C [Lew], March 29, 2022.

187. International Monetary Fund (IMF) press release no. 09/130, April 17, 2009.

188. Middlebrook 2010.

189. IMF press release no. 14/543, November 26, 2014.

190. Telephone interviews with former senior Mexican government official C [Videgaray] and former senior U.S. government official C [Lew]; interviews with a former senior Mexican trade negotiator [Guajardo], former senior STPS official B [Avante], former senior Office of the Presidency official A [Castillejos], and former senior Mexican diplomat C [Medina-Mora].

    At about this same time, a campaign spokesperson for Democratic presidential candidate Hillary Clinton contacted Secretary of Foreign Relations Claudia Ruiz-Massieu to urge action on constitutional labor reform (interview with former senior Office of the Presidency official A [Castillejos]).

191. Interview with former senior Office of the Presidency official A [Castillejos]; telephone interview with senior Mexican government official C [Videgaray].

192. Secretary of the Economy Ildefonso Guajardo and Secretary Videgaray also communicated Peña Nieto's decision to their U.S. counterparts, USTR Froman and Secretary Lew, respectively (telephone interview with former senior U.S. government official B [Pier], October 24, 2019).

193. Interviews with former senior STPS officials B [Avante] and C [Stein] and former senior Office of the Presidency official A [Castillejos]; telephone interview with former senior U.S. government official B [Pier], October 24, 2019. See also the interviews with former senior U.S. government officials A [Karesh] (March 28) and B [Pier] (April 26, 2018).

    The probable sequence of these events was: (1) Vice President Biden's private meeting with President Peña Nieto on February 25, 2016, at which Peña Nieto apparently again demurred on the question of constitutional reforms; (2) Lew's telephone call to Videgaray, which coincided closely with word from IMF sources about the Obama administration reservations over Mexico's requested increase in its line of credit; (3) Peña Nieto's decision to reverse his earlier position and undertake reform of article 123; and (4) Obama's confirmatory call to Peña Nieto. The earliest constitutional reform draft among the Office of Legal Counsel to the Presidency (Consejería Jurídica de la Presidencia) documents examined by the author (see below) was dated March 11, 2016.

    Obama (2020) makes no reference to these negotiations in his presidential memoirs. The author reconstructed this series of events on the basis of interviews with former Mexican and U.S. government officials. It is subject to revision if additional information becomes available.

194. Interviews with former senior Office of the Presidency official B [Espeleta], March 1, 2019 (Mexico City), and former senior STPS official B [Avante].
195. Interview with former senior Office of the Presidency official B [Espeleta].
196. Interview with former senior STPS official C [Stein].
197. CJP internal document "XXII," March 16, 2016 (original translation of Spanish text). Of the various internal CJP documents from this period examined by the author, this is the first proposed amendment to article 123 presented in both Spanish and English.
198. The reforms under discussion focused on article 123's section A (Apartado A), which governs labor issues in the private sector and in state-owned enterprises (CJP internal document "Decreto reformas y adiciones Constitucionales," Artículo 99 (B), April 13, 2016). Section B on public-sector workers was not affected.
199. CJP internal document "Opciones con traducción," March 17, 2016 (original translation).
200. CJP internal document "Opciones con traducción: Opción D," March 21, 2016.
201. See, for example, CJP internal document "Reforma Art. 123 (2)" (March 11, 2016), clause XX, and "Iniciativa 10 marzo 16 reforma laboral" (March 11, 2016), pp. 4–6.
202. Examples included the Mexican Social Security Institute (Instituto Mexicano del Seguro Social), National Worker Housing Institute (Instituto de Fondo Nacional de la Vivienda de los Trabajadores), and National Worker Consumption Institute (Instituto del Fondo Nacional para el Consumo de los Trabajadores).
203. Obama administration negotiators were unsuccessful in their push to eliminate any role for state governments and to "federalize" the labor justice system (interview with former senior Office of the Presidency official A [Castillejos].
204. CJP internal documents "Reforma justicial laboral," March 21, and "Reforma justicial laboral," April 13, 2016. Another CJP document dated April 13, "Decreto reformas y adiciones Constitucionales," created a new national labor tribunal as part of the Mexican judiciary. Key aspects of its structure and operation remained undefined.
205. Interview with former senior Office of the Presidency official A [Castillejos]; author's email communication with former senior Mexican government official A [F. Franco], September 30, 2018; CJP internal document "Reforma justicial laboral," clause XXXI (c) (1), April 13, 2016. The April 20, 2016, draft ("Reforma justicial laboral") of this clause specified that it referred to contracts and unions in both state- and federal-jurisdiction economic activities. This draft was also the first to refer to the new specialized agency as "institute."

    The idea of creating a national agency to register all unions and collective contracts had not been part of either the recommendations arising from the "Dialogues for Everyday Justice" ("Diálogos por la Justicia Cotidiana") public consultation coordinated by the CIDE or Peña Nieto's December 2015 announcement regarding reform of the labor justice system, although it had been proposed by the center-left Party of the Democratic Revolution (Partido de la Revolución Democrática, PRD) during earlier debates over labor law reform (CIDE 2015: 44; Bensusán and Middlebrook 2013: 110, 114).
206. Interviews with former senior STPS official B [Avante] and former senior Office of the Presidency official B [Espeleta].
207. "Ley Federal de las Entidades Paraestatales," *Diario Oficial de la Federación* (May 14, 1986), arts. 15(V), 17, 18.

208.   Interview with former senior Office of the Presidency official B [Espeleta].

209.   Interview with former senior Mexican government official A [Franco], March 2, 2019, Mexico City.

210.   Interview with former senior Office of the Presidency official B [Espeleta]; telephone interview with former senior U.S. government official B [Pier], October 24, 2019.

211.   To ensure eventual approval of the constitutional reforms by the required two-thirds majorities in both chambers of the federal Congress, Peña Nieto administration officials also communicated selectively with representatives of the National Action Party (Partido Acción Nacional, PAN) and the PRD. Interviews with a former senior advisor to President Peña Nieto [Nuño] and former senior STPS official C [Stein].

212.   This discussion draws on interviews with former senior STPS official B [Avante] and former senior Office of the Presidency official A [Castillejos].

213.   CIDE 2015: 44; Vergara 2016a.

214.   Interview with former senior Office of the Presidency official A [Castilljeos], February 27, 2019; author's email communication with former senior Mexican government official A [F. Franco], June 16, 2016.

215.   The leaders of these organizations were Isaías González Cuevas (CROC), Rodolfo González Guzmán (CROM), and Francisco Hernández Juárez (UNT). The UNT had long favored the transformation of the labor justice system; see Bensusán and Middlebrook 2013: 114.

216.   Interview with former senior STPS official B [Avante].

217.   Interviews with a former senior adviser to President Peña Nieto [Nuño], former senior STPS official B [Avante] and former senior Mexican government official A [Franco] (March 2, 2019).

218.   Bensusán and Middlebrook 2020: 1016 (Bensusán interview with a Mexican labor attorney, October 1, 2018, Mexico City).

219.   Poder Ejecutivo Federal 2016a. In his opening statement explaining the rationale for these proposed amendments ("Exposición de motivos"), Peña Nieto referred explicitly (p. 5) to the CIDE-coordinated "Dialogues for Everyday Justice" and the recommendations made by the panel on labor justice.

220.   The position that Peña Nieto adopted on questions of union democracy in 2016 contrasted sharply with the stance he took in the 2012 debates about federal labor law reform (Bensusán and Middlebrook 2013: 128).

221.   Poder Ejecutivo Federal 2016b.

222.   Articles 390 bis, 390 ter., 895, 931, 931 bis. For example, if representatives of the new agency responsible for contract registration had any doubts about the validity of workers' signatures on cards ratifying that their procedural rights were fully observed, they could call upon government labor inspectors to conduct confidential interviews (employers or their representatives could not be present) with a representative sample of the workforce. "Fraud, interference, coercion, or any other irregularity" in the contract review process was subject to penal sanction, and public officials who delayed, impeded, or in any way sought to influence the process were also subject to penalties (article 390 ter.).

223.   The submissions may have been timed to coincide with Peña Nieto's meeting with Representative Nancy Pelosi (Democrat-California and minority leader of the U.S. House of Representatives), whose delegation met with him four days later (May 2).

Pelosi reaffirmed to Peña Nieto the importance of the reforms where U.S. congressional approval of the TPP was concerned (interview with former senior USTR official A [Cutler]; Gómez Quintero 2016).

224. USTR 2015c: 83. Peña Nieto's proposed reforms also addressed the principal demands listed in the August 2015 joint UNT/AFL-CIO declaration as well as past ILO concerns (*IUST*, May 12, 2016).

225. IMF press release no. 16/250, May 27, 2016.

226. Parametría 2018. Failing to bring the TPP negotiations to a successful conclusion would presumably have eroded Peña Nieto's support among Mexican elites, who strongly favored participation in the multilateral agreement (Barnes 2014: 2n5).

Mexico did not win TPP concessions from the United States in other areas in exchange for the labor reforms it adopted (interview with a former senior Mexican trade negotiator [Guajardo].

227. To the surprise of some Mexican officials, U.S. officials had raised questions about child labor abuses and union democracy in Mexico even in negotiations over the 2005 Security and Prosperity Partnership Agreement of North America (telephone interview with former senior Mexican diplomat B [Estivill].

228. In this sense, some Mexican decisionmakers may have been sensitive to "wider environmental principles" in modern world society (Meyer 2010: 14). See also Meyer et al. 1997: 145.

229. Interviews with former senior Office of the Presidency official B [Espeleta], former senior STPS officials B [Avante] and C [Stein], and former senior Mexican diplomat C [Medina-Mora]; telephone interviews with former senior Mexican government officials B [Meade] (March 4, 2019) and C [Videgaray] and former senior Mexican diplomat D [Basañez].

230. Telephone interviews with former senior Mexican government officials B [Meade] and C [Videgaray].

231. *IUST*, August 21 and 25, 2015.

232. Telephone interview with former senior Mexican diplomat D [Basañez].

233. Vergara 2016b.

234. Senado de la República 2016a, b; Méndez and Garduño 2016. In the course of their prevote lobbying of PRI-affiliated senators representing labor organizations, STPS officials again denied that the Peña Nieto administration had agreed to the constitutional amendments in response to U.S. pressures (interview with former senior STPS official B [Avante]. Even though Deputy Araceli Damián recognized the reforms' democratizing goals, she opposed the measures because they had been imposed on the federal executive during the TPP negotiations (*Boletín de la Cámara de Diputados* 2477, November 4, 2016).

235. Interviews with a former senior adviser to President Peña Nieto [Nuño] and former senior STPS official B [Avante].

236. Bensusán and Middlebrook 2020: 1017–18 (Bensusán interview with a Mexican labor attorney, October 1, 2018); interviews with former senior STPS official B [Avante] and former senior Mexican government official A [Franco], March 2, 2019. In his negotiations with President Peña Nieto, CTM secretary-general Aceves del Olmo also sought to expand the number of CTM leaders the PRI would nominate for seats in the federal Chamber of Deputies (*diputados obreros*); interview with former senior STPS official B [Avante].

237. Interviews with former senior Office of the Presidency officials A [Castillejos] and B [Espeleta].

238. In applauding the reforms, the UNT claimed credit for the precedents set by its proposals (with the PRD) for labor law reform in 2002, 2010, and 2012 (UNT 2016: 12).

239. Alcalde Justiniani 2020: 12–14; telephone interview with a Mexican labor attorney [Alcalde], May 11, 2020.

240. Interviews with a former senior adviser to President Peña Nieto [Nuño], former senior Office of the Presidency official A [Castillejos], and former senior STPS official A [Quiroga-Quiroga], February 26, 2019, Mexico City.

241. Telephone interview with former Obama administration senior White House official B [Feierstein], June 2, 2020.

242. "Decreto por el que se declaran reformadas y adicionadas diversas disposiciones de los artículos 107 y 123 de la Constitución Política de los Estados Unidos Mexicanos, en materia de Justicia Laboral," *Diario Oficial de la Federación*, February 24, 2017 (primera sección).

243. Ballinas and Becerril 2016.

244. This discussion is based on the interview with former senior STPS official A [Quiroga-Quiroga].

245. STPS officials did not include the center-left UNT in these consultations on the grounds that it did not have a representative in the federal Congress, where the legislation would be debated. They did, however, share the draft legislation's major provisions with Arturo Alcalde Justiniani, a prominent independent labor lawyer. The officials did not follow his recommendation to hold a broadly inclusive national consultation on the proposed legislation, but they did organize more limited consultative fora with a range of legal and labor experts.

246. As the price for his assent, CTM secretary-general Aceves del Olmo demanded (in a private conversation with President Peña Nieto) and received a PRI nomination to a federal Senate seat. Interviews with former senior STPS official A [Quiroga-Quiroga], former senior Office of the Presidency official C [Granados] (February 27), and former senior Mexican government official A [Franco] (March 2, 2019).

247. Interviews with former senior STPS official A [Quiroga-Quiroga] and former senior Mexican government official A [Franco] (March 2, 2019). González was secretary general of the CROC; Medina was secretary general of the CTM federation in the state of Coahuila.

248. "Iniciativa con proyecto de decreto por el que se expide la ley del Instituto Federal de Conciliación y Registro Laborales; y se reforman, adicionan y derogan diversas disposiciones de la Ley Federal del Trabajo, de la Ley Federal de Entidades Paraestatales, de la Ley Orgánica de la Administración Pública Federal, de la Ley del Seguro Social y de la Ley del Instituto del Fondo Nacional de la Vivienda para los Trabajadores, en materia de justicia laboral."

249. See, for example, Alcalde Justiniani 2017b, c.

250. Interview with former senior STPS official A [Quiroga-Quiroga].

251. The number of sectoral council seats was set at four in order to accommodate all the national business organizations involved in consultations concerning the legislation:

CCE, CONCAMIN, CONCANACO, and COPARMEX. The understanding at the time was that the four labor seats would be distributed among the CROC, CROM, CTM, and UNT. Interview with former senior STPS official A [Quiroga-Quiroga].

252. Alcalde Justiniana 2018a.

253. Interview with a former senior Mexican trade negotiator [Guajardo]. Santos (2019: 159) suggests that U.S. withdrawal from the TPP in January 2017 may have encouraged the Mexican government to pursue the González-Medina initiative.

254. "Iniciativa con proyecto de decreto." The center-right PAN introduced its own bill on February 22, 2018 ("Iniciativa con proyecto de decreto."). Like the González-Medina initiative, its governing institutions were tripartite in structure.

255. Chapter 4. See also Kay 2011a and Aspinwall 2013: 123–27.

256. "Public Communication to the U.S. National Administrative Office Under the North American Agreement on Labor Cooperation (NAALC) Concerning the Introduction of Reforms to the Federal Labor Law of Mexico that Would Weaken Fundamental Labor Rights, Including the Right to Freely Associate, to Organize and to Bargain Collectively" (AFL-CIO, "Public Communication to the U.S. NAO," January 25, 2018, https://aflcio.org/sites/default/files/2018-01/NAALC%20submission%20JAN%2025%202018%20with%20UNT.pdf.)

257. A copy of the letter is in the author's possession.

258. Interview with U.S. trade union representative A [Davis], June 25, 2018, Washington, DC.

259. Leo Gerard, president of the United Steelworkers (USW) and chair of the USTR Labor Advisory Committee for Trade Negotiations and Trade Policy, wrote Lighthizer separately on this question (interviews with senior U.S. trade union representatives A [Feingold] and B [Drake]; *IUST*, April 6, 2018b).

260. A copy of the letter is in the author's possession. At least two U.S. industrial unions, the United Electrical, Radio, and Machine Workers of America and the International Brotherhood of Teamsters, wrote similarly worded letters to Cordero at the same time. Copies of these letters are in the author's possession.

261. Fox (2004: 475–77) distinguishes among transnational civil-society networks, coalitions, and movements.

262. *IUST*, March 30, 2018b.

263. A copy of the letter (dated April 18, 2018) is in the author's possession.

264. The individual unions involved in this effort were: USW; United Automobile, Aerospace, and Agricultural Implement Workers of America; International Association of Machinists and Aerospace Workers; Communications Workers of America; American Federation of Teachers; and Service Employees International Union. They were convinced they could have secured even more congressional signatories, but they acted quickly because their Mexican allies persuaded them that approval of the González-Medina bill was imminent. Interview with U.S. trade union representative A [Davis], June 25, 2018.

265. Foro Jurídico 2018. Campa informed Mexican labor leaders of the decision to withdraw the bill from consideration on April 20, the same day that Democratic congressional representatives and senators published their letter to USTR Lighthizer (Muñoz Ríos 2018).

266. Telephone interview with former senior Mexican government official C [Videgaray].
267. Schlesinger 2018.
268. Interview with a senior Mexican trade negotiator [Guajardo]; telephone interview with senior U.S. trade union representative B [Drake], June 20, 2020. Ambassador Lighthizer did not, however, explicitly ask the Peña Nieto administration to withdraw the controversial legislation from Senate consideration.
269. M. Martínez 2018; Hernández 2018.
270. Telephone interview with former senior Mexican official B [Meade].
271. Interview with former Office of the Presidency official C [Granados]; telephone interview with former senior Mexican government official C [Videgaray].
272. Foro Jurídico 2018.
273. "Decreto por el que se reforman, adicionan y derogan diversas disposiciones de la Ley Federal del Trabajo, de la Ley Orgánica del Poder Judicial de la Federación, de la Ley Federal de la Defensoría Pública, de la Ley del Instituto del Fondo Nacional de la Vivienda para los Trabajadores, de la Ley del Seguro Social, en materia de Justicia Laboral, Libertad Sindical y Negociación Colectiva," *Diario Oficial de la Federación*, May 1, 2019. The law took effect on May 2, 2019. See Centro de Investigación Laboral y Asesoría Sindical 2022 for an initial assessment of the new law in operation.
274. In the DR-CAFTA negotiations, Central American countries initially resisted this demand (they sought NAALC-style side-agreements on labor issues), but in the end, they all acceded to the U.S. position (M. Weiss 2003: 723). In the TPP negotiations, Australia and New Zealand initially opposed fully enforceable labor provisions because they were concerned that this requirement would dissuade Brunei, Malaysia, and Vietnam from acceding to the agreement. Canada argued against trade-linked penalties in the TPP for violations of signatory parties' labor obligations (*IUST*, December 14, 2012, May 23, 2013).

    In parallel hemispheric negotiations over a proposed (but never completed) Free Trade Agreement of the Americas, Mexico and the Rio Group of South American states also opposed U.S. proposals to add labor, environmental, and "good governance" provisions to the agreement (Burges 2006: 31; *NAFTA and Inter-American Trade Monitor*, August 22, 1997 and April 3, 1998).
275. Pressures from the United States during FTA negotiations sometimes interacted with domestic calls for labor reform in the prospective partner country. On the Chilean and Moroccan cases, see Rogowsky and Chyn 2008: 128–29; Heintz and Luce 2010: 42–43, 47.
276. The "United States-Viet Nam Plan for the Enhancement of Trade and Labour Relations" (February 4, 2016) required the Communist government of Vietnam to ensure that its laws and regulations provided for broad freedom of association and the rights to collective bargaining and to strike. Had the plan gone into effect, workers would have had, "without distinction," the right to form grassroots unions with full autonomy to elect their own leaders and manage their financial affairs. Grassroots unions were not required to adhere to the official Viet Nam General Confederation of Labor.
277. The U.S. Government Accountability Office (2009: 52) contrasted the U.S. government's capacity to win labor rights improvements in partner countries during FTA negotiations with its ineffectiveness in subsequent efforts to secure these countries' compliance with their labor obligations. See ILO 2015: 30 for a similar assessment.

278. USTR 2015a: 8.

279. U.S. DOL 2012: 19, 21.

280. The OTLA's decision to accept US 2010-03 (Peru) for review was influenced by the timing of the submission. This was the first submission filed during the Obama administration, and some officials believed it was important to signal the administration's commitment to FTA labor rights provisions despite the focus of this particular case (telephone interview with former senior U.S. government official A, June 25, 2021).

   With the exception of the complaint against Guatemala (which was filed near the end of the George W. Bush administration and concluded at the beginning of the Trump administration), all the OTLA review processes began and ended during the Obama administration.

281. Government of Costa Rica 2010; *IUST*, September 21 and 24, 2010. Similarly, during the OTLA review of submission US 2012-01, a senior Honduran government minister appealed to OTLA officials to conclude that Honduras had fulfilled its labor obligations under the DR-CAFTA and to exclude from their final report any recommendation for cooperative consultations (OTLA public report 2012-01: 93).

282. A U.S. Department of Labor review (2012: 4) of the DR-CAFTA experience found that, despite significant U.S. capacity-building efforts, the areas in which it was most difficult to achieve progress were freedom of association, the right to collective bargaining, and the right to strike.

283. As noted previously, table 5.1 employs the same "observed policy impact" coding scheme as table 2.1 in order to enhance comparability in assessments of the U.S. GSP and U.S. FTA labor complaint processes. However, because the principal issue in many FTA cases was the effectiveness of labor law enforcement rather than the formal content of laws regarding freedom of association and the rights to organize and bargain collectively, the coding scheme may, in effect, make it more difficult for U.S. FTA cases to score higher on the 0–4 scale. Nonetheless, a close analysis of policy outcomes based on publicly available sources indicates that, with exceptions such as Honduras, the policy impact of FTA complaints was very limited.

284. Heintz and Luce (2010: 33) also note that resistance to the implementation of labor reforms may increase over time.

   Comparatively few of the OTLA public reports on U.S. FTA submissions called for legislative changes to address the issues in contention. In US 2011-01 (Bahrain), U.S. labor officials sought repeal of the ban on multisector labor federations and the amendment of several emergency laws adopted in response to the country's 2011 political crisis. In US 2008-01 (Guatemala), USTR Kirk included possible legislative reforms among U.S. goals in his request for cooperative consultations in 2010 (USTR 2010), and some portions of the 2013 action plan (for instance, the way in which the Ministry of Labor transmitted its recommendations for fines to the labor courts responsible for sanctioning labor violations) did require legislative approval. However, the action plan did not include any proposals for major legal reforms concerning freedom of association or the rights to organize and bargain collectively; instead, it simply called (item 13.1) on the government of Guatemala to clarify some articles in the existing labor code. Honduras (US 2012-01) was an exception in this regard; the government adopted a new labor inspection law in response to U.S. pressures for policy change.

6. RENEGOTIATING THE NORTH AMERICAN FREE TRADE AGREEMENT: LABOR RIGHTS AND THE UNITED STATES-MEXICO-CANADA AGREEMENT, 2017–2019

1. Labor rights issues were on the agenda for the first day of trilateral discussions over revising the NAFTA (*Economist* 2017: 62).

2. Until Trump's campaign, the other presidential candidates who pledged to renegotiate the NAFTA (particularly its labor and environmental enforcement provisions) had been John Kerry (2004), Hillary Clinton (2008, 2016), and Barack Obama (2008) (Hayden and Wallach 2004, Lane 2008, Carlsen 2009, Kessler 2016).

3. U.S. Senate 2020: 224;Severns 2016.

4. Trump's margins of victory in Michigan, Pennsylvania, and Wisconsin were all less than one percentage point (*New York Times* 2017). Morgan and Lee (2018: 240) conclude that "the white working class was crucial" for his victory.

5. Mauldin and Schlesinger 2017, Schlesinger 2018, Swanson 2019. Trump sought (November 2012) and received (July 2015) trademark protection of the slogan for "political action committee services" (H. Long 2015).

6. See, for example, Wilson 2011.

7. See, for example, *Inside U.S. Trade* (hereinafter *IUST*), October 27, 2017a, b; Decemer 8, 2017a; January 19, 2018c; February 9, 2018; March 30, 2018a; June 22, 2018.

8. Morrow, McKenna, and Nolen 2018; Woodward 2018: 155, 157-58; Swanson 2017.

9. The Canadian and Mexican governments consulted with each other before issuing parallel statements indicating their willingness to renegotiate the agreement (Panetta 2016).

10. In 2017, the United Nations Economic Commission for Latin America and the Caribbean estimated that ending the NAFTA would reduce Mexico's gross national product by 1.9 percent (*IUST*, November 3, 2017b). See also *Economist* 2018d: 42.

11. Mauldin 2018.

12. Swanson 2018a, b; *Economist* 2018d: 41; *IUST*, June 22, 2018; August 31, 2018a. On August 31, 2018, President Trump notified Congress that he was prepared to enter into a trade agreement with Mexico—and with Canada if a deal were concluded by September 29 (*Economist* 2018d: 41). The Canadian and Mexican governments reportedly agreed privately in August 2017 that neither of them would sign a bilateral deal with the United States (Morrow and Nolen 2018), and during most of the NAFTA 2.0 negotiations, they held out for a trilateral agreement (Swanson, Rogers, and Rappeport 2018: 5; Zavala 2018). At times, however, significant tensions surfaced among them over issues such as domestic-content rules of origin in the automobile industry (*Economist* 2018d: 42; Morrow and Nolen 2018).

13. Among the Trump administration labor policies that U.S. unions opposed were those raising the income minimum required to qualify for overtime pay, cutting the number of workplace safety inspections, reducing job protection and cancelling a scheduled salary increase for federal government employees, and reneging on Trump's campaign promise to raise the federal minimum wage (Prescod 2019),

14. Morath 2017

15. Author's telephone interview (hereinafter "interview[s]") with senior U.S. trade union representative B [Drake], June 20, 2020.

16. AFL-CIO 2017: 3. The AFL-CIO consulted with both the Canadian Labour Congress and Mexico's National Union of Workers (Unión Nacional de Trabajadores, UNT) in the preparation of this document (telephone interview with senior U.S. trade union representative B [Drake], June 20, 2020).

    The AFL-CIO (2017: 1) put on record that its opposition to many preceding U.S. free-trade agreements "is not now, and never was, about withdrawal from international commerce or opposition to 'trade' per se." See also USTR (Labor Advisory Committee on Trade Negotiations and Trade Policy) 2018b: 3 ("We view this report as a continuation of the conversation about how to reform the NAFTA and other trade agreements").

17. Hakobyan and McLaren (2016) conclude that Mexican imports substantially lowered wage growth for U.S. blue-collar workers in the most affected industries and localities. Scott (2014: abstract) calculates that rising U.S. trade deficits with Mexico and Canada over the 1993-2013 period displaced 851,700 jobs in the United States, and that, "All the net jobs displaced were due to growing trade deficits with Mexico." Scott (2011: 2) also estimates that 60.8 percent of the U.S. jobs displaced by trade with Mexico were in manufacturing, especially in automobiles, automotive parts, computers, and electronic parts. Total employment in U.S. manufacturing industries fell from 17.265 million workers in 2000 to 12.353 million in 2016, a decline of 28.5 percent (author's calculation based on U.S. Bureau of Labor Statistics data, accessed April 30, 2020, https://data.bls.gov).

18. See, for example, the statement by U.S. Representative Sander Levin (Democrat-Michigan) in *IUST*, July 6, 2018.

19. This examination of the NAFTA 2.0 negotiations relies on press reports, interviews with selected participants, and those documents that were publicly available as of 2023. Before formal discussions began, Canadian, Mexican, and U.S. trade officials agreed not to publicly disclose any documents revealing another party's negotiating positions until four years after the revised trade agreement took effect ("Agreement of Confidentiality," July 26–August 1, 2017; a copy of this document is in the author's possession). The Office of the United States Trade Representative (USTR) declined the author's Freedom of Information Act request to release documents concerning the U.S. government's own negotiating positions (author's email communication with the USTR Freedom of Information Act program manager, June 22, 2022).

20. In compliance with the terms of the Bipartisan Congressional Trade Priorities and Accountability Act of 2015, the USTR notified Congress on May 18, 2017, that it intended to open renegotiations of the NAFTA. The United States, Canada, and Mexico all held public consultations on the matter during May–July 2017.

21. The USTR's published NAFTA 2.0 negotiating objectives on labor questions closely followed the TPP formulation. See USTR, "Summary of Objectives for the NAFTA Renegotiation" (July 17, 2017), pp. 12–13; a copy of this document is in the author's possession. See also *IUST*, September 29, 2017a and February 2, 2018; Vieira 2017.

22. *IUST*, September 22, 2017.

23. *IUST*, September 29, 2017b.

24. *IUST*, November 17, 2017; January 19, 2018b, p. 3.

25. *IUST*, August 25, 2017; December 8, 2017b; Vieira 2017; telephone interviews with senior U.S. trade union representative B [Drake], January 14, 2019, and a Mexican labor attorney [Alcalde], May 11, 2020. The model for Canada's gender equality proposal was the 1997 Canada-Chile Free Trade Agreement (Free Trade Agreement Between the Government of Canada and the Government of the Republic of Chile, appendix II, article N *bis*-01).

26. *IUST*, September 22, 2017b; September 29, 2017b; telephone interview with a confidential Canadian source [Bouchard], September 3, 2020. In its detailed NAFTA renegotiation proposals, the AFL-CIO had also called for framing labor rights obligations in terms of specific ILO conventions and for provisions prohibiting violence against workers (AFL-CIO 2017: 17, 35). UNIFOR (2017: 8) argued that that the three NAFTA countries should be required to ratify the ILO's eight "fundamental" conventions.

27. Challenging U.S. right-to-work laws, including provisions that allow workers to opt out of paying union dues in unionized workplaces, was an explicit Canadian goal (Morrow 2017; telephone interview with a confidential Canadian source [Bouchard]).

28. *IUST*, February 2, 2018.

29. Canadian negotiators' impact on the NAFTA 2.0 labor negotiations was limited because their priority attention focused on other trade issues, especially preservation of the NAFTA's chapter 19 dispute-settlement provisions and removal of the tariffs the Trump administration imposed on imports of Canadian steel and aluminum on May 17, 2018. Telephone interviews with U.S. trade union representative A [Davis], December 18, 2018, and April 21, 2020; senior U.S. trade union representative B [Drake], January 14, 2019; and a confidential Canadian source [Bouchard].

30. *IUST*, October 13, 2017; November 3, 2017a.

31. Althaus 2017a, b. Althaus (2017b) includes a graph comparing the evolution of U.S. and Mexican manufacturing wages between 1994 and 2016. Whereas U.S. wages rose from about $12 to just over $20 per hour, Mexican wages increased only from about US$2 to US$2.50 per hour over this period.

32. Ambassador Lighthizer held at least two personal meetings in 2017 with the presidents of the AFL-CIO, USW, International Brotherhood of Teamsters (IBT), and United Automobile, Aerospace, and Agricultural Implement Workers of America (UAW) (Schlesinger 2018).

33. *IUST*, November 24, 2017; January 5, 2018.

34. *IUST*, February 9, 2018. The USTR and the U.S. Department of Labor often negotiated a labor consistency plan with a potential developing country trade partner. This was an agreement specifying the labor reforms the country would undertake in order to bring its law and policy into line with the FTA's labor rights provisions. In responding to Lighthizer's proposal, Mexican officials declared, "We were not amenable to the idea of a labor consistency plan in the TPP, and we are not amenable to any possibility of having a consistency plan in NAFTA" (*IUST*, February 9, 2018).

35. A copy of the letter is in the author's possession. The signatories critiqued the competitive advantages that Mexico derived from suppressed wages and inadequate enforcement of labor rights, factors that accelerated the outsourcing of U.S. manufacturing jobs and contributed to low U.S. wage growth.

36. *IUST*, January 19, 2018b; January 26, 2018; February 2, 2018.

37. *IUST*, February 23, 2018a. The White House meeting included the presidents of the AFL-CIO, IBT, USW, UAW, International Association of Machinists and Aerospace Workers (IAMAW), and Communications Workers of America (CWA). Trump met with U.S. labor leaders on two further occasions between February and August 2018 in a sustained effort to win their support for a revised NAFTA (*Economist* 2018c).

On January 26, 2018, AFL-CIO, IBT, and USW officials also accompanied a bipartisan congressional delegation to Montreal, Canada, to articulate their position to Mexican government officials and U.S. private sector representatives (*IUST*, February 2, 2018).

38. *IUST*, February 23, 2018b; March 2, 2018; March 9, 2018; Schlesinger 2018.

39. Quoted in Redacción 2017. The objectives also included "incorporating gender perspectives into some parts of the treaty."

40. *IUST*, September 22, 2017c.

41. Author's email communication with a senior Mexican trade official [de la Mora], July 23, 2020.

42. García de León 2017; Villamil 2017; Patiño 2017.

43. Interview with a former senior Mexican trade negotiator [Guajardo], February 25, 2019, Mexico City. See also *IUST*, September 22, 2017a.

44. Patiño 2017; Reuters 2017; Flores 2018; *IUST*, February 9, 2018; February 23, 2018b; March 30, 2018a; April 20, 2018.

Although Mexican negotiators regularly consulted with leading national business organizations and experienced former Mexican trade officials throughout the NAFTA 2.0/USMCA negotiations, major Mexican labor organizations were not closely engaged in these consultations (Smith Ramos 2019; Becerril and Ballinas 2019; telephone interview with a former Mexican trade negotiator [Santos]). Tereso Medina Ramírez, a prominent leader in the Confederation of Mexican Workers (Confederación de Trabajadores de México, CTM), was organized labor's formal representative in Mexico's USMCA *cuarto de junto* ("side room") (interview with former senior STPS official A [Quiroga-Quiroga], February 26, 2019).

45. Interview with a former senior Mexican trade negotiator [Guajardo]; telephone interview with former senior Mexican official C [Videgaray], March 14, 2019; Shaefer Munoz, Harrup, and Whelan 2018; *IUST*, April 6, 2018c, April 20, 2018.

46. *IUST*, February 2, 2018; March 9, 2018.

47. Telephone interview with former senior Mexican official C [Videgaray]. Videgaray's negotiating counterpart was often Jared Kushner—formally a senior White House adviser but, more significantly, President Trump's son-in-law and confidant.

48. *IUST*, April 27, 2018. The labor organizations lobbying for a change in U.S. policy on this point included the AFL-CIO, CWA, IBT, IAMAW, UAW, and USW (telephone interview with U.S. trade union representative B [Dolan], June 29, 2020).

49. *IUST*, May 4, 2018; *Economist* 2018b: 66.

50. Interview with a former senior Mexican trade negotiator [Guajardo]; telephone interview with former senior Mexican official C [Videgaray]; Swanson and Malkin 2018; Alcalde Justiniana 2018b.

51. This was the last possible date for an agreement between the United States and Mexico given the U.S. legislative requirement that the executive give the Congress ninety days' notice between the conclusion of trade agreement negotiations and the date when the agreement is actually signed, and President Peña Nieto's desire to sign the deal before leaving office on November 30, 2018 (Swanson 2018a).

52. Chapter 23 eliminated the TPP provision (art. 19.7) committing signatory parties "to encourage enterprises to voluntarily adopt corporate social responsibility initiatives on labour issues that have been endorsed or are supported by that Party."

53. Article 23.3.1 (a), footnote 5, stated: "For greater certainty, the right to strike is linked to the right to freedom of association, which cannot be realized without protecting the right to strike."

54. Whereas the TPP's article 19.6 stipulated that "each Party shall also discourage" the importation of goods produced in whole or in part by forced or compulsory labor, USMCA article 23.6 stated that "each Party shall prohibit" such imports.

55. The USTR added protections for migrant workers only after successful lobbying by a coalition of migrant worker-rights advocates (Gabriel and Macdonald 2021: 80). In the final USMCA text adopted in 2019, "sex-based" was dropped from the title of article 23.9 (Discrimination in the Workplace), and footnote 15 exempted the United States from any obligation to amend its own laws concerning workplace discrimination.

56. In an additional response to problems that arose during the Guatemala arbitration proceedings, the agreement's dispute-settlement provisions required that arbitration panelists "other than the chair have expertise or experience in labor law or practice" (art. 31.8.3[a]).

      The final 2,082-page NAFTA 2.0 text also contained other provisions designed to win U.S. and Canadian labor support. These included domestic-content rules of origin in the automobile manufacturing industry that were likely to increase production costs in Mexico (and thereby bolster the U.S. and Canadian domestic automobile industries), and limitations on controversial investor-state dispute-settlement procedures that allowed foreign companies to initiate legal actions against host country governments and seek compensation for alleging denying them "fair and equitable treatment" (Swanson and Cochrane 2019a; Swanson, Rogers, and Rappeport 2018: 6; *Economist* 2018a; Mauldin 2018; *IUST*, August 31, 2018a).

57. USMCA, chapter 4, annex 4-B, appendix, art. 7.3.a, footnote 77. For U.S. labor organizations' critiques of the automobile industry wage agreement (especially the absence of any adjustment of the average base wage over time to compensate for inflation, and the fact that US$16.00 per hour was an average rather than a minimum wage), see *IUST*, November 2, 2018a; Thrush 2018b: 7. For an overall summary of the automobile industry rules-of-origin agreement, see *IUST*, October 5, 2018a.

      As a point of comparison, production-line automobile industry workers' wages and benefits averaged US$47 per hour in the United States and US$2.99 in Mexico in, respectively, 2017 and 2018 (Covarrubias Valdenebro 2020: 7).

58. USMCA chapter 4, annex 4-B, appendix, art. 7.3.c. See also *IUST*, October 5, 2018a; October 19, 2018.

59. Office of the United States Trade Representative, Chapter 23 of "Agreement Between the United States of America, the United Mexican States, and Canada 7/1/20 Text,"

July 1, 2020, https://ustr.gov/trade-agreements/free-trade-agreements/united-states-mexico
-canada-agreement/agreement-between.

60. Telephone interviews with senior U.S. trade union representative B [Drake], January 14,
2019; former senior U.S. government official A [Karesh], June 12, 2020; and a former
Mexican trade negotiator [Santos], May 15, 2020. In drafting annex 23-A, USTR officials
consulted with leading U.S. labor organizations (the AFL-CIO, USW, and perhaps other
major U.S. trade unions) and relevant U.S. congressional committee members (U.S.
House of Representatives 2019c: 25), concerning such specific provisions as a four-year
period for the mandatory review of all existing collective bargaining agreements in
Mexico (U.S. House of Representatives 2019c: 84).

All available evidence indicates that the negotiations leading to annex 23-A were
conducted directly between the U.S. and Mexican governments. Although informal communications between the U.S. and Canadian negotiating teams continued, Canadian
officials were absent from the intense U.S.-Mexican negotiations (over more than labor
rights issues) underway from late July through late August. Indeed, Chrystia Freeland,
the chief Canadian trade negotiator, did not return to Washington, DC (where these
final negotiations were held) until August 28, 2018, a day after the U.S.-Mexican deal
was announced. Telephone interviews with U.S. trade union representative A [Davis],
December 18, 2018; senior U.S. trade union representative B [Drake], January 14, 2019;
a confidential Canadian source [Bouchard]; a Mexican labor attorney [Alcalde]; and
former senior U.S. government official A [Karesh], June 12, 2020. See also Morrow and
Nolen 2018; *IUST*, July 27, August 17, August 31, 2018a.

61. Telephone interview with U.S trade union representative A [Davis], December 18, 2018;
interview with former senior STPS official A [Quiroga-Quiroga].

62. On July 29, 2019, the Ministry of Labor and Social Welfare (Secretaría del Trabajo y
Previsión Social, STPS) published a Protocol for the Legitimation of Existing Collective
Bargaining Agreements ("Protocolo para la legitimación de contratos colectivos de
trabajo existentes," *Diario Oficial de la Federación*, July 31, 2019) to guide this process.

63. Telephone interview with former senior U.S. government official A [Karesh], June 12, 2020.

64. Interview with a former senior Mexican trade negotiator [Guajardo]; telephone interviews with a Mexican labor attorney [Alcalde] and a former Mexican trade negotiator
[Santos].

65. Ambassador Jesús Seade Kuri, who later served as Mexico's chief negotiator during
the phase II USMCA negotiations, participated in the final phase I negotiations as
the representative of López Obrador's transition team. He consulted extensively with
President-elect López Obrador, the designated future secretaries of foreign relations
(Marcelo Ebrard) and labor and social welfare (Luisa María Alcalde Luján), and chief-
of-staff designate Alfonso Romo Garza regarding the content of annex 23-A (telephone
interviews with former senior Mexican government official C [Videgaray]; a Mexican
labor attorney [Alcalde]; a former Mexican trade negotiator [Santos]). Seade also reportedly consulted with incoming Mexican congressional leaders, presumably regarding the
practical feasibility of the requirement that Mexico enact a new labor reform bill by the
target deadline of January 1, 2019 (*IUST*, October 19, 2018).

66. The content of annex 23-A remained under discussion as late as August 25, 2018
(interview with a Mexican labor attorney [Alcalde]).

67. Telephone interviews with a senior Mexican trade official [de la Mora]; a Mexican labor analyst [Bensusán], April 28, 2020; and former senior Mexican government official A [Franco], April 26, 2020.

68. Castañeda 2019; telephone interviews with a Mexican labor attorney [Alcalde] and a Mexican labor analyst [Bensusán].

69. See the statements made by representatives of the AFL-CIO, CWA, UAW, and USW at a March 2019 congressional hearing on trade and labor issues (U.S. House of Representatives 2019a: 53–54).

70. See, for example, the statements issued by the AFL-CIO, CWA, IAMAW, UAW, and USW on August 27, 2018 (*IUST*, August 31, 2018b) and by UNIFOR (*IUST*, September 7, 2018).

71. In a historical parallel, it was the Democrats' recovery of a majority in the House of Representatives in November 2006 that led to renegotiation of the labor provisions in pending free-trade agreements with Colombia, Panama, Peru, and the Republic of Kora (see chapter 5).

72. Thrush 2018b.

73. See, respectively, USTR 2018a: 4, 9, 11–12 and 2018b. Both reports were issued on September 27, 2018, thirty days after the U.S.-Mexico agreement was signed.

74. *IUST*, October 5, 2018b.

75. *IUST*, November 2, 2018b. The AFL-CIO's Executive Committee issued a statement on March 14, 2019 ("Trade Must Build an Inclusive Economy for All," https://aflcio .org/about/leadership/statements/trade-must-build-inclusive-economy-all) in which it detailed its critique of the USMCA and laid out its key demands for a revised agreement. These included strong labor rights (including explicit reference to fundamental ILO conventions) and strengthened enforcement provisions, enactment and effective enforcement (with "the upfront guarantee of sufficient resources for enforcement," p. 2) of labor law reforms in Mexico, rules of origin for all manufacturing sectors and appropriate floor wage provisions to promote U.S. domestic content and high-wage production, and other provisions to block outsourcing of U.S. jobs. The statement concluded that "it is possible to have trade rules that lift wages and treat all countries fairly," but "the labor movement is united in our judgment that the new NAFTA does not yet meaningfully address what is wrong with the original NAFTA" (p. 5).

76. This discussion focuses on labor rights questions. The other major issues under debate were, again, investor-state dispute-settlement procedures, patent protection for biologic drugs, and enforcement of the USMCA's environmental provisions (*Economist* 2019: 62).

77. Disagreements concerning appropriate labor rights enforcement arrangements among Democratic members of the House Committee on Ways and Means initially slowed negotiations with the USTR on this issue (telephone interview with U.S. trade union representative A [Davis], April 21, 2020).

78. *IUST*, December 7, 2018a; March 29, 2019b; Cochrane, Swanson, and Tankersley 2019. Lighthizer's negotiating credibility with U.S. labor leaders (several of whom judged him much more willing to consider organized labor's TPP and USMCA concerns than Michael B. G. Froman, USTR during the second administration of President Barack Obama, 2013–2017) was based in part on his personal background and professional experience. The son of a former steel mill worker, he had been born in Ashtabula, Ohio,

an area badly affected by the off-shoring of steel production. Moreover, as a corporate attorney for United States Steel Corporation, he had long interacted with the USW in labor-management negotiations (Thrush 2019; Stockman 2022; interviews with U.S. trade union representative A [Davis], March 20, 2018, and senior U.S. trade union representatives A [Feingold] [April 23, 2018] and B [Drake] [June 20, 2018].) In the USMCA negotiations, Lighthizer "was personally sympathetic to the Democratic demands on labor and enforcement, seeing them as aligned with Trump administration goals" (Cochrane, Swanson, and Tankersley 2019; see also Schlesinger 2018). He reportedly had close working relationships with both Lori Wallach, founder of Global Trade Watch and a long-time critic of the NAFTA, and Senator Sherrod Brown (Democrat-Ohio), who played a central role in phase II USMCA negotiations on labor enforcement issues. Lighthizer repeatedly assured President Trump that he would be able to deliver USW, AFL-CIO, and UAW endorsement of the agreement (telephone interview with senior U.S. trade union representative B [Drake], June 20, 2020; Thrush 2018b: 7).

One indication of Lighthizer's commitment to securing Democrats' support is that some Republican legislators later complained that he had made too many concessions to them (Swanson and Cochrane 2019a; *IUST*, December 13, 2019b). At the conclusion of the USMCA negotiations in December 2020, AFL-CIO President Richard Trumka stated, "I also commend Ambassador Robert Lighthizer for being a straight shooter and an honest broker as we worked toward a resolution" (*IUST*, December 13, 2019e).

Mexican President López Obrador also praised Lighthizer's role as chief U.S. negotiator: "He chose the difficult path, never became politically involved in this, and respected us [his Mexican negotiating counterparts]" ("Eligió el camino difícil, nunca se involucró políticamente en esto y nos respetó"), quoted in Corona 2019.

79.   U.S. Senate 2020: 231 (statement by Senator Rob Portman, Republican-Ohio); U.S. House of Representatives 2019b: 3–4 (statement by Representative Vernon Buchanan, Republican-Florida, ranking member of the Committee on Ways and Means Subcommittee on Trade); telephone interview with U.S. trade union representative B [Dolan].

Congressional Democrats and U.S. labor organizations easily shaped a consensus that employer protection contracts in Mexico constituted a serious labor rights enforcement issue. See, for example, the testimony by Ambassador Lighthizer before the House Committee on Ways and Means on June 19, 2019 (U.S. House of Representatives 2019c: 54): "Well, they [protection contracts] are good for some Mexican businesses, right? And some American businesses, to be honest. But very bad for the workers, and bad for our workers by extension."

80.   U.S. Senate 2020 *passim*. Some Republican legislators were simply unwilling to criticize any part of an agreement that was a high political priority for President Trump (telephone interviews with U.S. trade union representative A [Davis], April 21, 2020; senior former U.S. government official A [Karesh], June 12, 2020; and senior U.S. trade union representative B [Drake], June 20, 2020).

Nor was there any significant public opposition to enhanced labor enforcement provisions from major U.S. business organizations during the phase II negotiations. They apparently accepted that this was what was required to secure congressional approval of the USMCA (telephone interview with U.S. trade union representative A [Davis], April 21, 2020).

81. Thrush 2018b: 7. In any event, the required USITC report on the agreement was not due until mid-March 2019 (*IUST*, November 30, 2018a). The report was released on April 18, 2019 (*IUST*, April 26, 2019b and c). On Trump's initial threat to cancel the NAFTA to force the Congress to adopt the USMCA quickly, see *IUST*, December 7, 2018b; December 14, 2018.

82. *IUST*, November 30, 2018b; January 18, 2019.

83. *IUST*, December 5, 2018; *Economist* 2018e.

84. *IUST*, November 30, 2018c.

85. *IUST*, December 7, 2018a. Lighthizer subsequently acknowledged that, even though both Mexican and Canadian officials had been willing to address the issue of dispute-settlement panels during the initial NAFTA 2.0 negotiations, the United States had been opposed to doing so on the grounds that it might open U.S. trade remedy laws (including antidumping measures) to external challenge (*IUST*, June 21, 2019b; June 28, 2019a; September 13, 2019c; see also U.S. House of Representatives 2019b: 65). Both the DR-CAFTA and the TPP agreements had included language that prevented signatory states from blocking dispute-settlement panels, but the original NAFTA language had been included in the USMCA (*IUST*, March 29, 2019a; July 18, 2019).

86. U.S. House of Representatives 2019c: 104; *IUST*, February 1, 2019; July 5, 2019. Senior Democrats and U.S. labor leaders argued for reopening the USMCA negotiations because they insisted that any amendments to labor-rights enforcement procedures be part of the agreement itself rather than anything like the labor side-agreement appended to the original NAFTA (*IUST*, April 12, 2019a). Not unexpectedly, Mexican officials initially argued that the USMCA chapter 23 provisions agreed in August 2018 were adequate to ensure that Mexico met its labor rights obligations (Thrush 2018b: 8). Mexico was the first country to ratify the USMCA (the Senate approved the agreement on June 19, 2019, by a vote of 114-4, with three abstentions; *IUST*, June 21, 2019a). It did so in an effort to maximize leverage against calls from U.S. unions and congressional Democrats to reopen the negotiations and in the hope of concluding matters quickly and thereby reassuring international investors of Mexico's economic stability (telephone interview with a senior Mexican trade official [de la Mora], July 20, 2020; Smith Ramos 2019; *IUST*, June 21, 2019a).

87. U.S. House of Representatives 2019c: 48, 67-68, 103; *IUST*, April 26, 2019a. The U.S. labor movement's skepticism regarding section 301 remedies was based in part on the fact that the USTR had dismissed the AFL-CIO's section 301 complaints regarding labor rights violations in China in 2004 and 2006 (USTR 2006). See the statement by IAWAW representative Owen Herrnstadt at the May 22, 2019 "Hearing on Enforcement in the New NAFTA" (U.S. House of Representatives 2019b: 7).

88. Telephone interview with senior U.S. congressional trade adviser B [Todd], July 9, 2020. The proposal, a copy of which is in the author's possession, was first reported publicly in *Politico* on April 5, 2019 (Behsudi 2019; *IUST*, April 5, 2019 and April 12, 2019c).

89. The AFL-CIO's 2017 proposal for a new NAFTA labor chapter gave an independent labor secretariat broad authority to conduct workplace inspections, and it focused potential penalties for rights violations on the employer or labor recruiter responsible for them (AFL-CIO 2017: annex II. C.2, 4, 7).

90. Section II, 1, 3–8, 10. Goods produced by forced labor were already barred under U.S. law.

    Under the terms of the Brown-Wyden proposal, the United States could deny entry to a shipment from an enterprise that knowingly provided false information to Mexican or U.S. officials. If Mexico failed to provide the United States with a required verification report, then the United States could "take such actions with respect to the producer's or exporter's products as it considers appropriate" (section II. 10, 11, respectively).

    The AFL-CIO took a stronger position than even Senators Brown and Wyden regarding penalties for labor rights violations: "The AFL-CIO strongly believes that any good found in violation of a trade agreement, not just a violation of forced labor, should be denied entry at the border" (written statement, p. 2, submitted by Catherine Feingold, director, AFL-CIO International Department, to the June 25, 2019 "Hearing on Mexico's Labor Reform," U.S. House of Representatives 2019d).

    Senator Tom Harkin (Democrat-Iowa) and other U.S. senators had advocated a ban on the importation of goods produced by child labor during the 1993 NAALC negotiations (*IUST*, June 18, 1993).

91. U.S.-Peru Trade Promotion Act, chapter 18 (Environment), annex 18.3.4, points 6(b), 7, 10, 11, 13(a). In 2017 and 2019, the USTR had sanctioned two Peruvian companies for illegal logging practices, which Senator Wyden held up as a model for labor enforcement under the USMCA (*IUST*, August 2, 2019c).

92. *IUST*, April 5, 2019.

93. *IUST*, April 26, 2019a. The AFL-CIO's president, Richard Trumka, and other U.S. union leaders supported the idea of bilateral inspections that included the United States. Senator Wyden had initially advocated unilateral U.S. inspections of export facilities in Mexico, but he quickly shifted position and endorsed bilateral inspections (telephone interview with U.S. trade union representative B [Dolan]; *IUST*, May 3, 2019a). A more detailed version of the Brown-Wyden proposal (titled "Brown-Wyden Labor Enforcement Proposal," a copy of which is in the author's possession) circulated on November 5, 2019, explicitly stated that its provisions were "fully reciprocal with Mexico" ("Goal, Objectives, and General Provisions").

94. Cochrane, Swanson, and Tankersley 2019.

95. *IUST*, August 2, 2019a, b.

96. For an overview of reform initiatives such as those proposed by the Party of the Democratic Revolution (Partido de la Revolución Democrática) in 1997, see Bensusán and Middlebrook 2013: 109–14.

97. U.S. House of Representatives 2019c: 125; *IUST*, January 18, 2019; March 22, 2019a; May 3, 2019b; telephone interviews with U.S. trade union representative A [Davis], April 21, 2020; a senior Mexican trade official [De la Mora]; senior U.S. labor representative B [Drake], June 20, 2020; a Mexican labor analyst [Bensusán]; and a Mexican labor attorney [Alcalde]. As they had done during the TPP negotiations, U.S. Department of Labor (U.S. DOL) officials also regularly consulted with independent Mexican labor law experts on the content of the proposed reform initiative (author's email communication with a Mexican labor analyst [Bensusán], May 16, 2019.

    These intensive bilateral interactions continued after the new Federal Labor Law took effect on May 2, 2019. For example, five representatives of the USTR, U.S. DOL, and U.S. embassy in Mexico City participated in a October 3, 2019, meeting of the Mexican government interdepartmental group responsible for coordinating implementation of labor justice reform (author's email communication with former senior Mexican government official A [Franco], October 18, 2019).

98.   Telephone interview with U.S. trade union representative A [Davis], April 21, 2020. Both the AFL-CIO and USW employed senior staff who spoke and read Spanish and who had personal experience and contacts in Mexico. For example, Benjamin Davis, USW Director of International Affairs, headed the AFL-CIO Solidarity Center in Mexico City between 2004 and 2010, where he developed extensive contacts with independent unions and labor activists. For a list of the other U.S. industrial unions involved in these discussions, see footnote 112.

99.   Telephone interview with a Mexican labor analyst [Bensusán].

100.   Telephone interview with U.S. trade union representative A [Davis], April 21, 2020; Centro Federal de Conciliación y Registro Laboral 2021: arts. 11, 30(I)(d). If the employer fails to do so and the union acts in its place, the employer is responsible for the costs.

101.   Telephone interview (May 11, 2020) and the author's email communication (May 13, 2020) with a Mexican labor attorney [Alclade]. See footnote 106 for further details on the direct voting issue.

102.   Ballinas and Becerril 2019. The understanding among senators at the time was that debate would be reopened in September 2019 on some parts of the new labor law. However, this never happened because senior Mexican government officials judged that doing so would introduce new uncertainties about Mexico's commitment to reform at a critical stage in the phase II negotiations.

103.   In April 2019, the MORENA coalition held 308 of 500 seats in the federal Chamber of Deputies and 69 of 128 seats in the Senate (accessed April 27, 2020, http://www.ine.mx). The Chamber of Deputies took two votes on the labor reform bill on April 11, 2019. In the first, the measure was approved by 417 votes in favor and one opposed, with 29 abstentions and 51 absences; in the second, it was approved by 258 votes in favor and 67 against, with 18 abstentions and 155 absences (Cámara de Diputados, Secretaría de Servicios Parlamentarios, April 11, 2019).

104.   Poder Ejecutivo Federal 2019a. A second reform, enacted on the same day, guaranteed freedom of association for public sector workers (Poder Ejecutivo Federal 2019b).

Gustavo de Hoyos, president of the Mexican Employers' Confederation (Confederación Patronal de la República Mexicana, COPARMEX), immediately attacked the new labor law as having been "dictated from the United States" (Ballinas and Becerril 2019). As late as mid-April, the Mexican private sector had still sought to amend the legislation so as to include tripartite representation in the new Federal Center for Conciliation and Labor Registration (Salazar and Martínez 2019). Amendments to the bill proposed by the Institutional Revolutionary Party (Partido Revolucionario Institucional, PRI) would have eliminated the requirement that member votes in union elections be "direct" (see footnote 106), removed term limits for union officials, eliminated the requirement that union leaders provide members with information about the administration of union assets, and reduced the percentage of workers necessary to validate union representation in contract negotiations (IUST, April 12, 2019b). In repelling amendments of this kind, proponents of the reform legislation drew political advantage from the support offered by their U.S. allies and the requirements stipulated by USMCA annex 23-A (telephone interview with a Mexican labor analyst [Bensusán]; *IUST*, April 12, 2019b).

105. As the MORENA labor reform bill (submitted on December 24, 2018) was debated in the federal Chamber of Deputies, labor reformers strengthened its union democracy provisions by stipulating that voting by union members must be not only "personal, free, and secret" (as stipulated by the 2017 constitutional reforms) but also "direct" (Ley Federal del Trabajo, article 371.IX). The Supreme Court (Suprema Corte de Justicia de la Nación, SCJN) had previously validated this wording ("personal, free, direct, and secret" votes) in its 2008 ruling on the terms under which elections to determine legal control over a collective contract (*recuentos*) were to be held (SCJN 2008b; see also chapter 4). Nonetheless, a coalition of at least sixty-six old-guard unions seized on the difference in wording between the constitutional reform (article 123 XXII bis[b]) and the new federal labor law and filed some 460 constitutional challenges (*amparos*) against article 371.X (telephone interview with former senior Mexican government official A [Franco], September 29, 2019). They argued (citing ILO conventions nos. 87 and 98) that the provision violated union freedom and the autonomy of a union's general assembly to select its own statutes (M. Martínez 2019; International Lawyers Assisting Workers Network 2020: 11, 15, annex II).

106. Between April 11 and May 3, 2019, Democratic members of the House Committee on Ways and Means sent USTR Lighthizer four letters outlining their concerns regarding USMCA provisions on enforcement, labor issues, environmental protections, and affordable medicines and patent protection for biologic drugs (Committee on Ways and Means, "Trade," accessed June 27, 2020, waysandmeans.house.gov/subcommittee/trade). The Subcommittee on Trade held hearings on enforcement issues on May 22 (U.S. House of Representatives 2019b).

107. Telephone interview with senior U.S. congressional trade adviser A [Tai], June 26, 2020.

108. The group's members included Representatives Earl Blumenauer (Democrat-Oregon and chair of the House Committee on Ways and Means Subcommittee on Trade), Suzanne Bonamici (Democrat-California), Rosa DeLauro (Democrat-Connectict), Jimmy Gomez (Democrat-California), John B. Larson (Democrat-Connecticut), Jan Schakowsky (Democrat-Illinois), Terri A. Sewell (Democrat-Alabama), and Mike Thompson (Democrat-California).

109. Cochrane, Swanson, and Tankersley 2019.

110. These investigative trips were preceded by the visit that twenty congressional staff members made to Mexico City on June 5-8, where they attended briefing sessions on a range of USMCA topics and met with senior Mexican government officials, congressional leaders, and representatives of the Mexican labor movement, private sector, and civil society. The delegation included both Democratic and Republican staff members representing the leadership and the principal trade-related committees in the House of Representatives and the Senate (author's email communication with U.S. trade union representative A [Davis], April 22, 2020).

111. The House Democratic Working Group on NAFTA 2.0 (2019), pp. 1, 3-5; *IUST*, July 18, 2019; July 26, 2019a; July 26, 2019b. The senior Mexican officials with whom the Blumenauer delegation met in Mexico City included the secretaries of the economy, labor and social welfare, the environment, and foreign affairs, as well as Mexico's chief NAFTA 2.0 negotiator.

112. A copy of this report (House Democratic Working Group on NAFTA 2.0 2019) is in the author's possession.

113. *IUST*, August 2, 2019b; August 9, 2019a. The USTR sent formal counterproposals to the House Democrats on September 11 (*IUST*, September 13, 2019a). USTR Lighthizer had a confidentiality agreement with the Trade Working Group (*IUST*, November 29, 2019a), which limited the author's access to internal U.S. negotiating documents.

114. The U.S. industrial unions most active in these negotiations were the CWA, IAWAW, IBT, UAW, USW, United Food and Commercial Workers International Union, and Bakery, Confectionary, Tobacco Workers, and Grain Millers' International Union (telephone interview with U.S. trade union representative A [Davis], April 21, 2020).

115. *IUST*, March 22, 2019c; September 27, 2019a, b; November 1, 2019a; November 22, 2019; Cochrane, Swanson, and Tankersley 2019.

116. Cano 2019; telephone interview with former senior Mexican government official A [Franco], September 29, 2019. Among the topics Trumka raised with López Obrador were low Mexican wage levels (and the need for equivalent Mexican and U.S. wages for similar work), Mexico's need for far more labor inspectors, and the constitutional challenges that old-guard unions had filed against the new legal requirements for democratic union elections. Trumka later credited López Obrador for having demonstrated good faith. While in Mexico City, Trumka met with senior leaders of the center-left UNT but not with representatives of the CTM, Mexico's largest old-guard labor organization and once a formal ally of the AFL-CIO (*IUST*, November 1, 2019b).

117. *IUST*, October 11, 2019a; November 22, 2019. In a March 2019 statement, the AFL-CIO executive council had stipulated that its criteria for an effective enforcement mechanism included "mandatory monitoring and reporting, assurance that action will be taken promptly when violations occur, and, critically, an avenue by which workers can intervene when governments lack the will to act" and "a guaranteed funding stream to ensure that technical assistance, monitoring, and enforcement occur" (AFL-CIO, "Trade Must Build," p. 3).

118. Telephone interview with former senior U.S. government official A [Karesh], July 20, 2020. See also the interviews with Seade in *IUST*, November 29, 2019a and Corona 2020.

119. *IUST*, March 15, 2019a.

120. *IUST*, March 22, 2019a and b; April 26, 2019a.

121. Langner 2019a.

122. *IUST*, June 28, 2019b. Secretary Alcalde's document (titled "National Strategy for the Implementation of the Labor Justice System") was entered into the official record at the June 25, 2019, hearing the House Committee on Ways and Means Subcommittee on Trade held on Mexican labor reform. The document called for technical cooperation from the U.S. Department of Labor, the Inter-American Development Bank, the United Nations Development Program, and the ILO to support Mexico's labor justice reform, a proposal that was endorsed by Republican members of the committee. Members of the bipartisan House of Representatives delegation that travelled to Mexico in July 2019 discussed the "roadmap" with Secretary Alcalde in detail and were favorably impressed (*IUST*, July 18, 2019; August 2, 2019d).

The STPS did, however, acknowledge that reviewing all existing collective bargaining agreements within the four-year period required by annex 23-A would be a challenging task. In June 2019, the STPS estimated there were as many as 550,000 local-jurisdiction contracts in existence (Gascón 2019).

123. The U.S. congressional delegations visited Mexico on April 25–26, June 6–7 (congressional staff members), July 18–21, and October 7–8, 2019 (author's email communication with U.S. trade union representative A [Davis], April 22, 2020).

124. As early as June 4, 2019, Speaker Pelosi and Representatives Neal and Blumenauer voiced these concerns with Secretary of Foreign Relations Marcelo Ebrard and other senior Mexican officials during their trip to Washington, DC, to discuss Mexico-U.S. immigration issues (Ebrard statement reporting on the trip to leaders of the Mexican Senate, June 2019; a copy of this statement is in the author's possession).

125. *IUST*, September 13, 2019b; September 27, 2019a.

126. "Notes on Neal CODEL [Congressional Delegation] Meeting with GOM [Government of Mexico]," October 8, 2019. (These notes were presumably prepared by a U.S. embassy or congressional staff notetaker. A copy of this document is in the author's possession.) In their meeting with López Obrador, Neal and his colleagues (Jimmy Gomez, Ron Kildee [Democrat-Wisconsin], Jimmy Panetta [Democrat-California], and Bill Pascrell [Democrat-New Jersey]) also voiced their concerns regarding wage levels in Mexico and the implementation schedule for labor justice reform.

The senior Mexican officials attending this meeting included the secretaries of foreign relations, finance, and labor and social welfare; Ambassador Seade; and Ambassador Bárcena (author's email communication with U.S. trade union representative A [Davis], April 22, 2020).

127. Hulse and Cochrane 2019.

128. "Notes on Neal CODEL Meeting," p. 2. In response to a question from Representative Gomez during this same meeting, Secretary Alcalde reassured the Neal delegation regarding the 421 injunctions (*amparos*) that had at that time been filed to challenge the May 2019 federal labor law requirement that union officers be elected directly by members (rather than through any indirect electoral arrangements that might leave incumbent leaders less accountable to rank-and-file members). She reported that, of the 421 injunctions, judges had not admitted 117 and had dismissed 99 others. Only four had been granted on a temporary basis, and their effect did not extend beyond the specific plaintiff union involved.

The matter was finally resolved when the Supreme Court dismissed the injunctions and reaffirmed the validity of Federal Labor Law provisions on November 25, 2020 (SCJN 2020).

129. López Obrador letter to Neal, October 14, 2019 (a copy is in the author's possession). The budget that the Mexican Congress passed in late November 2019 included a supplementary annex that documented line by line the commitments López Obrador made to Neal (*IUST*, November 29, 2019c).

130. *IUST*, November 18, 2019.

131. The negotiating rounds were held on August 16–20 (Washington, DC), September 1–5 (Mexico City), September 23–27 (Ottawa), October 11–15 (Arlington, Virginia), November 17–21, 2017 (Mexico City), and on January 21–29, 2018 (Montreal).

132.   Reuters 2017; García de León 2017; Flores 2018.

In its 2017 NAFTA renegotiation proposals, the AFL-CIO called for region-specific floor wages in the three signatory countries that would guarantee "a decent standard of living for the worker and her or his family." A special expert wages panel would determine whether export producers actually paid wages meeting that standard, and when they did not, an independent NAFTA labor secretariat would require the export goods in question to bear a product notification label stating that the goods (or the components they contained) had been produced "in a facility in which workers receive less than a decent wage." If, after two years, the producer had not remedied the problem, the importing country was authorized to levy a duty equal to the wage gap plus a 20 percent penalty, monies that would be collected and then distributed to the affected workers. See AFL-CIO 2017: annex II ("Proposal for NAFTA Labor Chapter"), A.3, C.3 (a, b), D.9.

133.   Schlesinger 2018. It was presumably this concern that led the U.S. International Trade Commission (USITC) to include in its overall economic assessment of the USMCA an analysis of the agreement's likely impact on wages in Mexico. It estimated (USITC 2019: 221) that enforcement of annex 23-A's collective bargaining provisions would lead to a 17.2 percent increase in wages in Mexico over a six-year implementation period.

134.   Letter from Representative Andy Levin (Democrat-Michigan) and twenty-six other Democratic representatives to USTR Lighthizer, June 25, 2019. A copy of this letter is in the author's possession.

135.   Telephone interview with senior U.S. congressional trade adviser A [Tai].

136.   Cano 2019; telephone interview with former senior Mexican government official A [Franco], September 29, 2019. In March 2019, the AFL-CIO Executive Council had reiterated its call for "appropriate floor wage provisions" in a revised USMCA ("Trade Must Build," p. 4).

President López Obrador assured Trumka that inflation-adjusted wages in Mexico would indeed rise ("Notes on Neal CODEL meeting," pp. 2, 3). He had promised Representative Neal to increase minimum wages "at least two percentage points above the inflation rate each year" (López Obrador letter to Neal, October 14, 2019, p. 4).

137.   Interview with a former senior Mexican trade negotiator [Guajardo]; telephone interview with former senior Mexican official C [Videgaray]. Mexican negotiators also characterized as a "purple cow" issue the U.S. (and AFL-CIO) demand that any Mexican export good carry a "certificate of origin" indicating that workers in the production facility where it originated were unionized and that the facility complied with international labor standards and all relevant national labor laws. Interview with a former senior Mexican trade negotiator [Guajardo]; telephone interview with senior U.S. trade union representative B [Drake], January 14, 2019.

138.   Telephone interviews with a senior Mexican trade official [De la Mora]; former senior U.S. government official A [Karesh], June 12, 2020; and a confidential Canadian source [Bouchard].

139.   Telephone interview with senior U.S. congressional trade adviser A [Tai].

140.   Bensusán and Middlebrook 2013: 49–52. Inflation-adjusted hourly compensation for Mexican manufacturing workers was lower in 2016 than in 1994 (Blecker, Moreno-Brid, and Salat 2018: fig. 3).

141. At the same time, the government doubled the minimum wage in the northern zone along the U.S. border, where costs of living have historically been higher than elsewhere in Mexico.

142. Author's calculations based on minimum wage data from the Comisión Nacional de los Salarios Mínimos, accessed on April 24, 2020, http://www.gob.mx/cms, and inflation (consumer prices) data from Nadal 2003: table 2.2 and the Instituto Nacional de Estadística, Geografía e Informática, *Índice nacional de precios al consumidor*, accessed April 24, 2020, http://www.inegi.org.mx.

143. Sheridan and Agren 2020.

144. Jiménez 2020; Redacción 2022.

145. As early as March, Senator Charles Grassley (Republican-Iowa), chair of the Senate Committee on Finance, had recognized that it was important to "accommodate" Democrats' concerns on enforcement issues (*IUST*, March 8, 2019).

146. Hulse and Cochrane 2019.

147. A copy of the letter is in the author's possession.

148. Cochrane, Swanson, and Tankersley 2019.

149. *IUST*, November 29, 2019b. Presidents López Obrador and Trump spoke by telephone on at least three occasions during the final months of USMCA negotiations (on June 8, September 12, and October 19, 2019). However, their discussions focused primarily on U.S.-Mexico border security issues (undocumented migration from and through Mexico to the United States, and the illegal smuggling of firearms from the United States into Mexico). Press reports on these conversations do not mention USMCA-related issues. See *U.S. News & World Report* (online), June 8, 2018; *Mexico News Daily* (online), September 12, 2019; Esposito 2019.

150. "Notes on Neal CODEL Meeting," pp. 2, 4.

151. Seade described the idea of "putting the law in the hands of some inspectors that would have free rein" as a "horror" (*IUST*, September 13, 2019c). See also *IUST*, October 25 2019; November 8, 2019; November 29. 2019a.

152. Representative Levin wrote to Speaker Pelosi and Representatives Neal and Blumenauer on September 26, 2019, to outline these enforcement conditions. Other preratification conditions in his proposal included an adequate Mexican labor enforcement budget, the resolution of constitutional challenges to the new Federal Labor Law, and USMCA provisions for onsite plant inspections in Mexico (*IUST*, October 4, 2019; October 11, 2019b).

153. *IUST*, October 25, 2019; December 6, 2019b.

154. *IUST*, December 6, 2019b.

155. González G. 2019a.

156. *IUST*, December 6, 2019b; telephone interview with a former Mexican trade negotiator [Santos].

157. Telephone interviews with former senior Mexican government official A [Franco], April 26, 2020, and a senior U.S. congressional trade adviser [Tai]; Smith Ramos 2019. In a meeting with senior STPS officials during his September 2019 trip to Mexico City, AFL-CIO president Trumka had made a similarly forceful demand regarding U.S. labor inspections (telephone interview with a Mexican labor attorney [Alcalde]). Regarding the timing of these discussions, an elaborated version of the Brown-Wyden proposal dated November 5, 2019 ("Brown-Wyden Labor Enforcement Proposal"), bears the

heading "Confidential Negotiating Document." See also López Obrador's statement in late November in which he opposed "strange ideas" ("las ideas peregrinas") that had previously been ruled out in the phase II negotiations (Jiménez and Urrutia 2019).

Seade later captured the intensity of these negotiations when he stated, "The biggest horror for all of us in the last eight to 10 months . . . is the famous labor inspectors. I want to say in the most categorical way that without a doubt that was the most intense topic that did not make it [into the final agreement]" (quoted in *IUST*, December 13, 2019a).

158.   Smith Ramos 2019.

159.   Telephone interview with a Mexican labor attorney [Alcalde]. Ambassador Seade later claimed credit for the omission of problematic labor inspections language in the final agreement, calling it "a gigantic threat" (quoted in Becerril and Ballinas 2019a). Mexican Senate Majority Leader Ricardo Monreal publicly stated that direct U.S. inspections were "frankly unacceptable" to the Senate (Becerril and Ballinas 2019a). Secretary of Foreign Relations Ebrard rejected the possibility outright (Cochrane, Swanson, Malkin, and Haberman 2019). President López Obrador was closely consulted on the issue, and he may have done so as well.

The November 2019 version of the Brown-Wyden proposal did stipulate (step 3) that members of verification teams would be selected from a roster of individuals agreed upon by both parties to a labor violations dispute. The proposal did not address the issue of the nationality(ies) of the panelists.

160.   *IUST*, November 29, 2019a; December 5, 2019.

161.   Swanson and Cochrane 2019b; Cochrane, Swanson, and Tankersley 2019; *IUST*, December 5, 2019; December 6, 2019a; December 6, 2019c.

162.   *IUST*, November 29, 2019d; November 29, 2019e.

163.   *IUST*, December 6, 2019a; Corona 2020. Canadian chief negotiator Freeland participated by telephone in a meeting between Lighthizer and Seade on November 27 that focused on plant-level inspections as part of dispute-settlement procedures (*IUST*, December 6, 2019c).

Lighthizer and Seade reportedly had compatible pragmatic, honest-broker negotiating styles. They had interacted with each other in the late 1980s in difficult U.S.-Mexican negotiations over Mexican canned tuna and cement exports to the U.S. market (Corona 2020; telephone interview with a former Mexican trade negotiator [Santos]).

Some Mexican critics of the final agreement reached concerning labor enforcement measures argued that Seade had been "alone" in the final negotiations (that is, without adequate support from technical staff and trade lawyers), and that as a result, he had failed to protect the country's (and perhaps their) interests (C. Martínez 2019; González G. 2019b; Rodríguez 2019; Corona 2019). Seade's defense was that the final negotiations were one-on-one with Lighthizer, who was also without his advisers (Corona 2020). There were, however, some Mexican observers who noted that the López Obrador government's desire to make a clean break from the preceding Peña Nieto administration may have deprived the Mexican negotiating team of considerable accumulated expertise in trade negotiations and in interacting with the U.S. Congress (*IUST*, March 15, 2019b; telephone interview with former senior Mexican government official A [Franco], December 23, 2019).

164. "Protocol of Amendment to the Agreement Between the United States of America, The United Mexican States, and Canada," accessed March 15, 2020, https://ustr.gov/sites /default/files/files/agreements/FTA/USMCA/Protocol-of-Amendments-to-the-United -States-Mexico-Canada-Agreement.pdf.

165. *IUST*, November 29, 2019a.

166. *Economist* 2019: 63.

167. When the consultation period expired, the complainant was to deliver written notice to the respondent, and "on delivery of the request, the panel is established" (Protocol, item 7[B][ii][4], amending USMCA article 31.6 and deleting the commission's role in this process).

168. Protocol, item 7(C, D).

169. Mexico's Private Sector Coordinating Council opposed elimination of this qualifying footnote, ostensibly because of concerns that it might make Mexican companies liable if their employees were caught up in violence occurring outside the workplace. The compromise language in article 23.7 was that it referred to "cases of violence or threats of violence against workers, directly related to exercising or attempting to exercise the rights set out in Article 23.3 (Labor Rights)" (telephone interview with a former Mexican trade negotiator [Santos]).

    The protocol also slightly modified the language in article 23.3, footnote 4, concerning "in a manner affecting trade or investment between the Parties," and it removed qualifying language in article 23.6 (Forced or Compulsory Labor) concerning how signatory parties might go about prohibiting the importation of goods produced in whole or in part by forced or compulsory labor.

170. Because the United States and Mexico reached bilateral agreement on annex 31-A before the United States and Canada concluded their own negotiations, the protocol also included an annex 31-B, Canada-Mexico Facility-Specific Rapid Response Labor Mechanism. There were no substantive differences between the two agreements. However, because the rapid-response mechanism was governed by two bilateral agreements rather than a single trilateral agreement, neither Canada nor the United States could employ it to investigate alleged labor rights violations occurring in the other country.

    The two annexes comprised fully four-fifths of the protocol devoted to labor issues.

171. Article 31-A.3.2. As with dispute-settlement panels in general, the signatory parties were required to appoint qualified rapid-response labor panelists by the time the USMCA entered into force. Failure to do so could not block establishment of the panels (article 31-A.3).

172. In its bilateral agreement with Mexico, Canada similarly restricted use of the mechanism to "an alleged Denial of Rights owed to workers at a covered facility under an enforced order of the Canada Industrial Relations Board" (article 31-B.2, footnote 1).

173. Langner 2020. In its first report on a public communication under the NAALC (MEX NAO public report 9501: 2; see appendix B), Mexico's National Administrative Office noted the absence of specific U.S. legal provisions concerning union organization.

174. The focus on manufacturing industries reflected the Trump administration's political (and electoral) priorities (telephone interview with U.S. trade union representative A [Davis], April 21, 2020).

175. See, for example, U.S. House of Representatives 2019a: 33 (testimony by Celeste Drake, trade and globalization policy specialist, AFL-CIO). Both the United States and Canada stated their intention to establish domestic processes under which their governments would complete initial reviews of complaints within thirty days, before deciding whether to invoke the rapid-response mechanism (see, respectively, article 31-A.4.1, footnote 2, and article 31-B.4.1, footnote 2).

176. See "Labor Monitoring and Enforcement in USMCA Implementing Bill and Brown-Wyden Rapid Response Mechanism" (prepared by the staff of Senator Brown and the Democratic staff of the Senate Finance Committee, no date; a copy of this document is in the author's possession), p. 4.

177. Some trade-related penalties could be applied conditionally in ways designed to accelerate meaningful action. For instance, the complainant party "may delay final settlement of customs accounts related to goods from the Covered Facility" immediately from the date on which it notified the respondent of alleged rights violations at the production site (article 31-A.4.3), thereby facilitating the complainant's capacity to collect tariffs or penalties on imports that had already entered the complainant's market if it was later determined that they were produced at facilities where labor rights violations had occurred. The key restriction was that, when parties agreed to remediation procedures to correct documented labor rights violations at a facility but later disagreed over whether the violations had been corrected by the respondent, the complainant could not impose penalties without a final determination by the dispute-settlement panel (article 31-A.4.8).

178. Article 31-A.10.3, 4; *IUST*, March 12, 1993. See also U.S. Senate 2020: 229 (statement by Senator Brown) and "Labor Monitoring and Enforcement in USMCA Implementing Bill and Brown-Wyden Rapid Response Mechanism," p. 4. This penalty structure closely paralleled what Harvey, Collingsworth, and Athreya (2000: 60) had advocated two decades earlier.

   If the parties disagreed as to whether a documented problem had been remedied, the respondent could ask a rapid-response labor panel to reassess the situation. However, if the panel determined that the situation had not been remediated, the respondent was barred from requesting further action by the panel for 180 days, leaving in place any penalties imposed by the complainant (article 31-A.10.7).

179. "Brown-Wyden Labor Enforcement Proposal," pp. 1 ("Goal, Objectives, and General Provisions"), 2 (steps 2, 3). Similarly, the Brown-Wyden proposal permitted the verification team, in preparing its final report (step 4), to "make negative inferences if the facility or the respondent Party refuses a verification." However, article 31-A.8.3 of the protocol only allowed a panel to take such a refusal "into account." The Brown-Wyden proposal (step 7) also gave the complainant party much more discretion in deciding whether to deny entry to imports produced at a facility or facilities where labor rights violations had been detected. The AFL-CIO Executive Council's September 12, 2019, statement concerning the ongoing phase II negotiations ("Without Fixes, We Must Oppose the New NAFTA," https://aflcio.org/about/leadership/statements/without-fixes-we-must-oppose-new-nafta) argued that the capacity to block goods produced in violation of the agreement's labor standards "would match the relief afforded to businesses that find their intellectual property rights violated" (p. 1).

180. U.S. House of Representatives (116th Congress, 1st Session), "United States-Mexico-Canada Agreement Implementation Act" (H.R. 5430; Public Law 116-113), December 13, 2019.

181. The dissident Democrats were joined by two Republicans and one Independent representative. In explaining her opposition to the measure, Representative Mary Kaptur (Democrat-Ohio) asked rhetorically, "Why should I believe that Mexico is [going] to enforce anything?" (quoted in *IUST*, December 19, 2019).

182. Cochrane, Swanson, Malkin, and Haberman 2019; Lane 2019. House Speaker Pelosi, in a private meeting with the House Democratic caucus when the final agreement was announced on December 10, was more blunt: "We stayed on this and we ate their lunch" (quoted in Cochrane and Swanson 2019).

183. *Economist* 2019: 62; *IUST*, December 13, 2019e. Other prominent U.S. labor unions supporting the final USMCA agreement included the IBT and USW. The IAMAW, however, condemned the final agreement because it did not sufficiently address the outsourcing of U.S. jobs in the aerospace industry (*IUST*, December 13, 2019c). The United Food and Commercial Workers International Union also opposed the final agreement (U.S. Senate 2020: 234).

184. U.S. Senate 2020; *IUST*, January 17, 2020. The senators voting against the measure included eight Democrats, one Republican, and one Independent. Once approved, the measure became Public Law No. 116-113.

185. Title VII.A, section 711.b.2. The ILCME, which was formally established by executive order on April 28, 2020, was required to meet at least once every ninety days for the first five years and at least once every 180 days for the following five years (sect. 711.c). Its membership initially included the Departments of State, Treasury, Agriculture, Commerce, and Homeland Security and the U.S. Agency for International Development (White House 2020a).

    The creation of the ILCME may have responded indirectly to an AFL-CIO demand for an independent labor secretariat with broad enforcement responsibilities (AFL-CIO 2017: annex II. C). On July 2, 2019, Representative Kaptur had submitted a bill to the House of Representatives calling for enactment of an "Independent Labor Secretariat for Fair Trade Deals Act." The measure would have established a supranational labor secretariat with extensive supervisory, investigative, and enforcement authority. A copy of this bill is in the author's possession; see *IUST*, July 19, 2019, for a summary.

186. See also section 718.c. The protocol did not include a provision permitting U.S. citizens to take legal action against the U.S. federal government if it failed to enforce its obligations, as the AFL-CIO had demanded (*IUST*, March 29, 2019a).

187. The specific enforcement actions cited (sect. 715.a.1-3) included those in USMCA articles 23.13 or 23.17 (cooperative labor dialogue and labor consultations), 31.4 and 31.6 (dispute-settlement consultations), and annex 31-A (rapid response labor mechanism).

188. The task force was formally established by executive order on May 15, 2020. Its membership included the Departments of State, Treasury, Justice, Labor, and the USTR (White House 2020b).

189. Tariff Act of 1930 (19 U.S.C. 1307), sect. 307.

190. If, at the end of its first six years, the board concluded that Mexico was not in full compliance with its labor obligations, its term could be extended (with new members) for a further four years (sect. 732.c).

191. Trade Act of 1974, section 135. The United States Technical Assistance for Mexican Labor Capacity Building Act of 2019 (section 8) required the Labor Advisory Committee to meet at least twice each year.

192. The United States Technical Assistance for Mexican Labor Capacity Building Act (S. 3002), sect. 5.

193. The Department of Commerce, for example, established a special office to assist in the administration of facility-specific rapid response labor panels (The United States Technical Assistance for Mexican Labor Capacity Building Act (S. 3002), sect. 105.a.2[B][i]).

194. See, for example, the testimony of USW representative Holly R. Hart (prepared statement, p. 3) before the March 26, 2019, "Hearing on Trade and Labor" (U.S. House of Representatives 2019a); interviews with senior U.S. trade union representative A [Feingold] and senior U.S. congressional trade adviser A [Tai].

195. Public Law No. 98-573, sect. 505(c). Similarly, the Dominican Republic-Central America-United States Free Trade Implementation Agreement (Public Law No. 109-53 [2005]), sect. 403(a)(3), required the president to report to the Congress every two years on implementation of the signatory countries' labor obligations.

196. For the Interagency Labor Committee, see section 716.b.2; for the USTR, see sections 715.b.2, 716.b.4(B), 716.c.3(B). The legislation (sect. 718.a.3, 5) also required the committee to include in its biannual reports to relevant congressional committees an explanation of when its assessments differed from those of the Independent Mexico Labor Expert Board (and to offer an oral briefing to the committees upon request), as well as a summary of the use of the rapid response labor enforcement mechanism.

197. United States Technical Assistance for Mexican Labor Capacity Building Act of 2019. The discussion below draws on section 3.C.2. See also H.R. 5430, Title IX (USMCA Supplemental Appropriation Act, 2019), for department-by-department details.

    The Trade Facilitation and Enforcement Act of 2015 (Public Law 114-125), sect. 611, established the Trade Enforcement Trust Fund to support costs associated with USTR trade agreement implementation and compliance and litigation before the World Trade Organization.

198. Telephone interview with a Mexican labor analyst [Bensusán].

199. Section 3.C.2 (A)(i)(I)(gg). The legislation also allocated funds to the USAID to monitor Mexico's anticorruption and rule-of-law obligations under the USMCA.

    Canada joined these efforts with C$27.5 million in expanded budgetary support over four years for the Office of Bilateral and Regional Labour Affairs and two Canadian labor attachés in Mexico (Morales and Martínez 2022). To oversee these activities, on August 1, 2019, the governments of Canada and Mexico established a Canada-Mexico Bilateral Labour Working Group that brought specialists together quarterly to assess emergency requests from Mexico for technical assistance with its labor justice reforms (*IUST*, August 9, 2019b).

200. Section 722. The United States Technical Assistance for Mexican Labor Capacity Building Act (sect. 3.C.2 (A)(iii) allocated at least US$900,000 per year to fund three permanent labor attachés stationed in Mexico.

201. This document is attached to *IUST*, December 13, 2019d. The Labor Advisory Committee on Trade Negotiations and Trade Policy report on USMCA 2018 had called for

government-funded labor attachés stationed at the U.S. embassy in Mexico (USTR 2018b: 6).

202. The controversy may have been provoked, in part, by Representative Neal's comment on December 10, 2019, that, under the protocol of amendment, the United States would have the right to send labor inspectors to Mexican facilities—without differentiating between the additional U.S. labor attachés called for by H.R. 5430 and the independent labor experts comprising the investigative teams that might be created under the auspices of rapid response mechanism labor panels (*IUST*, December 13, 2019a). The House Committee on Ways and Means "Improvements to the USMCA" document said only that the additional labor attachés would be "based in Mexico and will provide on-the-ground information about Mexican labor practices."

203. Langner 2019a, b; Redacción 2019a.

204. Méndez and Jiménez 2019.

205. Langner 2019a.

206. Albeit under strict limitations, the USMCA (art. 10.7.7) permitted U.S. officials to participate in duty-evasion verifications on Mexican territory to determine whether export products were in violation of U.S. laws regarding antidumping and countervailing and safeguard duties. In the 2012 bilateral controversy over possible salmonella infection in Mexican tomatoes, the Mexican government successfully lobbied for the U.S. Department of Agriculture to send inspectors to Mexico to verify that tomato exports satisfied sanitary standards (telephone interview with U.S. trade union representative A [Davis], December 18, 2018).

207. See the letters from Seade to Lighthizer (December 14, 2019) and Lighthizer to Seade (December 16, 2019), copies of which are in the author's possession. See also Redacción 2019b, Enciso 2019.

208. Becerril and Ballinas 2019b; *IUST*, January 24, 2020. Canada was the last of the signatory countries to adopt the USMCA. The Canadian House of Commons approved implementation legislation, which had been linked to a motion to close the Parliament temporarily because of the COVID-19 (coronavirus) pandemic, unanimously on March 13, 2020. The Senate adopted it by acclamation that same day, and the governor general also gave royal assent on March 13 (Pinkerton 2020; *IUST*, March 20, 2020).

209. USMCA article 23.11 (Public Submissions) stipulated that "Each Party . . . shall provide for the receipt and consideration of written submissions from persons of a Party on matters related to this Chapter in accordance with its domestic procedures," dropping the NAALC Article 16(3) requirement that public communications address "labor law matters arising in the territory of another Party." For comparisons of the two labor agreements, see Compa and Brooks 2019: 228–45 and Maquila Solidarity Network 2020.

210. The letter demanding major changes in the NAALC that thirty-three U.S., Canadian, and Mexican trade unions and labor rights groups—all of which had participated in NAALC public communications—sent USTR Lighthizer on August 17, 2018, framed the debate precisely in these terms: "We have seen firsthand the weaknesses of the NAALC" (a copy of this letter is in the author's possession). There is perhaps no more telling link between the NAALC experience and the USMCA labor chapter than the fact that the term *protection contracts* figured prominently in U.S. congressional debates over its provisions.

211. Under the terms of article 34.7, the agreement was to terminate sixteen years after its entry into force, unless at the end of a joint review conducted every six years the parties agreed to extend the agreement for another sixteen years. Ambassador Lighthizer's assessment of the provision, in the context of a discussion with U.S. congressional representatives about labor rights in Mexico, was that it "ensures that the United States will never again be in a position where it has permanently given away its economic leverage" (U.S. House of Representatives 2019c: 4).

212. These included: recognition of specific ILO conventions (versus the principles underlying the ILO's 1998 declaration) as the basis of agreed labor standards, which U.S. and Canadian trade unions viewed as a basis for challenging Taft-Hartley "right to work" laws in the United States; a fully autonomous trinational secretariat responsible for overseeing labor enforcement; the right of citizens to undertake legal action in national courts to compel governments to enforce their labor obligations; "certificates of origin" for export goods indicating that the production facilities in which they originate comply with international labor standards and all relevant national labor laws; sector-based equivalent wages in the three USMCA countries; and special protections for cross-border negotiation and unionization activities. See *IUST*, March 22, 2019b; March 29, 2019a; telephone interview with U.S. trade union representative A [Davis], April 21, 2020; statements by Celeste Drake (p. 13) and the CWA (p. 15) in U.S. House of Representatives 2019a; AFL-CIO 2017: annex II: E (on supranational collective bargaining).

213. *IUST*, February 9, 2018.

214. As the negotiations intensified, the Trump administration drove this point home in May 2018 by imposing section 232 (Trade Expansion Act of 1962) tariffs of 25 percent and 10 percent, respectively, on the steel and aluminum the United States imported from Mexico and Canada (*IUST*, March 30, 2018a; August 10, 2018). No previous U.S. administration had adopted a similar tactic in FTA negotiations.

215. In two other ways, negotiations over the USMCA protocol of amendment did parallel those over the NAALC. First, both agreements were the product of shifts in the balance of political power in Washington, DC, Clinton's 1994 presidential election and the Democrats' 2018 midterm electoral victories in the House of Representatives. Second, both of these labor agreements were adopted without reopening trilateral negotiations over the trade agreement to which they were attached. The author thanks Professor Jonathan Fox for highlighting these parallels.

216. UNIFOR (2017: 12) advocated NAFTA 2.0 provisions that closely paralleled the content of annex 23-A.

217. Interview with a former senior Mexican trade negotiator [Guajardo].

7. LABOR RIGHTS, TRADE AGREEMENTS, STATE SOVEREIGNTY: PAST RECORD AND FUTURE PROSPECTS

1. Mahoney 2000: 507, 511, 513.

2. Developing country governments that accede to the U.S. GSP program at least implicitly accept external scrutiny of their labor rights records because the program includes beneficiary country-review procedures.

> The NAFTA itself might be viewed as a contingent event. The United States had adopted free-trade agreements with Israel in 1985 and with Canada in 1989, but the NAFTA was the first such U.S. (or Canadian) agreement with a developing country. It also represented a sharp, unanticipated break with Mexico's established foreign policy.

3.   Mahoney 2000: 517; see also pp. 518, 523–24.

4.   The ILO (2015: 36, 43) and Vogt (2015: 828) also draw this distinction.

5.   In an interview with *Inside U.S. Trade* (hereinafter *IUST*) following the conclusion of the USMCA negotiations, Ambassador Jesús Seade Kuri, Mexico's chief negotiator, mentioned his meetings with President-elect Andrés Manuel López Obrador and private sector representatives to formulate Mexico's bargaining positions, but he made no reference to consultations with labor organizations (*IUST*, December 6, 2019c). Carlos Aceves del Olmo, secretary-general of the Confederation of Mexican Workers (Confederación de Trabajadores de México, Mexico's largest labor confederation), complained that "even though his organization was the largest in Latin America, they had not been consulted on changes concerning labor issues" (Becerril and Ballinas 2019a).

6.   Keohane and Nye (1977: 12–13) distinguish between sensitivity and vulnerability interdependence, defined in terms of "the relative availability and costliness of the alternatives" an actor faces.

7.   Salinas de Gortari 2017: 43, 283. Salinas describes (p. 21) the possible defeat of the NAFTA as a "disaster" (*descalabro*).

8.   The U.S. government designated twenty countries (from a list of twenty-seven potential members) as participants in the CBI in November–December 1983; Bahamas (March 1985) and Aruba (January 1986) followed later (Pérez-López 1988: 263). Bargaining between the U.S. government and prospective CBI participants over labor questions focused principally on the Dominican Republic, El Salvador, Guatemala, Haiti, and Honduras (Charnovitz 1984: 55–56; Pérez-López 1988: 264–65; U.S. House of Representatives 1984b: 5–8; U.S. House of Representatives 1984c: 17, 48–49, 59–60, 78–79, annex B: 24). At the time, seven countries (Anguilla, Guyana, Nicaragua, Suriname, Cayman Islands, Turks and Caicos Islands, Bahamas) declined to be designated under the CBI (Charnovitz 1984: 54n2).

As noted in chapter 2, following the addition of labor-conditionality provisions to the U.S. GSP program in 1984, the Office of the United States Trade Representative conducted a mandatory review of labor practices in all GSP beneficiary countries over the 1985–1986 period. Eleven countries were the objects of in-depth review (Pérez-López 1988: 272–73; DiCaprio 2004: 6), but the available secondary literature does not indicate whether the U.S. government conducted extensive country-by-country negotiations over possible labor reforms as part of this process.

9.   Some of the negotiated commitments were very specific in nature. For instance, the Haitian government agreed to write directly to international trade union organizations to inform them that Haitian unions were free to affiliate with them and that they were welcome to visit the country to build ties with domestic trade unions (U.S. House of Representatives 1984c: 60). The Honduran government committed to sending labor inspectors to all free-trade zones in the country (U.S. House of Representatives 1984c: 78–79).

10. U.S. House of Representatives 1984b: 6–8 (Dominican Republic); U.S. House of Representatives 1984c: 48–49 (El Salvador), 59 (Haiti).

11.   For overall assessments of this question and other examples, see Rogowsky and Chyn 2008: 116–17, 127–33; Luce 2010; ILO 2015: 30, 36–40, 100; Vogt 2015: 837–42. DiCaprio (2004: 8–9) briefly comments on U.S. bargaining over labor rights with several countries participating in preferential trade arrangements established by the African Growth and Opportunities Act (2000) and the Andean Trade Preferences and Drug Eradication Act (2002).

The phenomenon was not limited to U.S. FTAs. As noted in chapter 2, El Salvador finally agreed to ratify ILO conventions nos. 87 (freedom of association) and 98 (the rights to organize and bargain collectively) in 2006 to retain its GSP eligibility with the European Union (EU). Similarly, Canada ratified conventions nos. 138 (minimum age of employment) and 98 in, respectively, 2016 and 2017 in order to satisfy EU requirements for the 2017 EU-Canada Comprehensive and Economic Trade Agreement (Compa 2019: 288).

12.   Krasner (1999: 74–75) notes the relative ease with which target states can rescind the promises they make unless external actors can maintain sufficiently strong pressures to ensure their compliance.

13.   Although the U.S. Department of Labor reportedly planned to monitor implementation of CBI participants' preaccession labor reform commitments, in practice, little was done in this regard (Charnovitz 1984: 56; International Labor Rights Education and Research Fund 1988: 48–49; DiCaprio 2004: 3). In contrast to the other U.S. trade agreements discussed here, the 1983 CBERA made no specific allowance for subsequent reexamination of beneficiary countries' labor conditions. Revised CBI legislation (Caribbean Basin Economic Recovery Expansion Act of 1990) adopted the five "internationally recognized workers' rights" specified by the Trade and Tariff Act of 1984, but it did not specifically incorporate the latter's "country practice" petition procedures to examine alleged labor rights violations (Public Law 101–382, sect. 213-14). Nevertheless, following the conclusion of the 1985-1986 mandatory USTR review of labor practices in all GSP beneficiary countries, all CBI participants were open to labor rights petitions filed under the GSP program (U.S. General Accounting Office 1998: 4–5, 9).

14.   Vogt 2015: 843.

15.   In arguing that Mexico should be compelled to adopt major labor reforms as a condition for accession to the USMCA, U.S. Representative Earl Blumenauer (Democrat-Oregon and chair of the House Committee on Ways and Means Subcommittee on Trade) specifically referred to the earlier failure of Colombia, Guatemala, and Honduras to enact promised labor reforms (U.S. House of Representatives 2019d: 2).

16.   Santos 2019: 150.

17.   The U.S. trade agreements referenced in table 7.1 include the U.S. GSP program since 1984, the NAFTA/NAALC, and all post-NAFTA FTAs except the USMCA.

18.   A similar logic may sometimes shape U.S. trade unions' calculations regarding whether to contest labor rights violations in developing countries through U.S. trade agreement complaint procedures. Union leaders regularly confront tensions between pursuing their international goals and the domestic policy priorities of more immediate interest to many rank-and-file members. The amount of pressure that trade unions bring to bear on a particular U.S. presidential administration to sanction labor rights violations in foreign countries may also depend on their overall policy agenda with that administration.

19.   *IUST*, October 29, 2021.

20.   However, despite equally long-term lobbying, U.S. labor organizations failed to secure trade agreement provisions that would have eliminated the disparity between the protection of worker rights and intellectual property rights where the right of private legal action was concerned. During the NAFTA and the NAALC negotiations, unions pressed the U.S. government strongly on this point (author's interview [hereinafter "interview[s]"] with former senior USTR official B [Hills], March 9, 2018, Washington, DC; American Federation of Labor-Congress of Industrial Organizations [AFL-CIO] 1993a: 5-6). Clinton, in the October 1992 North Carolina State University presidential campaign address in which he outlined future NAFTA side-agreements, promised to include the right of private action (Clinton 1992). The issue was, in fact, debated during the NAALC negotiations (Government of Canada, "Administrative and Judicial Procedures" [June 7, 1993], art. 6 [2] [c]). Yet in the end, the NAALC (art. 43) formally precluded this option, as did the provisions of all post-NAFTA U.S. FTAs.

21.   As noted in chapter 2, the loss of GSP beneficiary status can also affect a country's broader access to U.S. investment protection insurance and financial and development assistance.

22.   It is not possible to compare the policy impact of labor complaints filed against Mexico under the U.S. GSP program and the NAALC because the USTR declined to review the only two GSP filings involving Mexico: McGaughey Jr., Laney, and Quintana, 1991 and International Labor Rights Education and Research Fund (ILRERF) 1993. In the former case, in November 1991, the USTR rejected a petition (Case 001-CP-91 Mexico) filed on May 15, 1991, by three Minnesota-based labor activists, with the support of the ILRERF, on the grounds that they had not demonstrated a "systematic, generalized pattern" of rights violations and that "the proposed North American Free Trade Agreement (NAFTA) will bring Mexico's labor standards up" (ILRERF 1993: 3). On June 1, 1993, the ILRERF filed a second request that the USTR review Mexico's GSP beneficiary status with the explicit goals of bolstering the evidence submitted by McGaughey Jr. Laney, and Quintana (1991) and rebutting the reasons offered by the USTR for rejecting their petition. In October 1993, the USTR, although recognizing that there were extant labor rights problems in Mexico, also declined to review the ILRERF petition on the grounds that "the information found in the petition was insufficient to provide a basis for a full review." It stated, furthermore, that "the negotiation of the North American Agreement on Labor Cooperation, as a supplement to the NAFTA, demonstrates Mexico's determination to improve its worker rights and provides the U.S. with a means for ensuring that Mexico continues to improve its labor standards" (USTR 1993: 2).

23.   See chapter 5.

24.   Chapter 2 concluded that a target country's export sensitivity was not itself a significant determinant of labor rights policy outcomes, at least in the fifteen countries examined over the 1985-1995 period.

25.   In the cases examined in this book, target FTA partner governments presumably did not resist U.S. reform pressures on the calculus that they were invulnerable to sanctions unless it could be proved that labor rights violations occurred "in a manner affecting trade or investment between the parties." They could not have been entirely sure of how an international arbitral panel might interpret that standard U.S. FTA requirement until the Guatemala case was resolved in 2017 (chapter 5).

26.   Even in the U.S. GSP cases, however, the U.S. government often struggled to secure implementation of the legal and policy reforms beneficiary countries agreed to make.

27.   Drezner (2003: 644, 653–54) reaches a similar conclusion regarding the impact of U.S. trade sanctions more generally.

28.   Mexico's NAALC public communications regarding the labor rights violations suffered by migrant workers in the United States and Canada had the same effect.

29.   For parallel assessments, see Simmons 2009: 129, 135–39; Hafner-Burton 2013: 5, 15; Toffel, Short, and Ouellet 2015: 206.

30.   Hafner-Burton (2005: 594–95), following the distinction drawn by Abbott and Snidal (2000), contrasts human rights agreements featuring "soft" standards, with no enforcement mechanisms, and "hard" provisions in preferential trade agreements that condition market access on a beneficiary country's observance of civil and political rights. Shaffer and Pollack (2012) overview the "soft law" versus "hard law" debate.

31.   In practice, the U.S. government frequently complements efforts to enforce a trade agreement's "hard" labor rights requirements with technical cooperation programs and funding to support capacity-building for labor law enforcement in the target country. See ILO 2015: 83 and chapter 5 for selected examples.

32.   Several analysts have considered this question; see Polaski 2003b: 20–21; Pier 2008; ILO 2015: chap. 4. Many labor rights advocates espouse framing signatory countries' labor obligations in terms of more precisely formulated ILO conventions rather than in terms of the principles articulated in the 1998 ILO declaration. However, at least in the post-2007 trade agreements examined in this book, the United States rejected that alternative.

33.   Chapter 6. As noted in chapter 6, USTR Robert E. Lighthizer, in the context of a discussion regarding labor rights in Mexico, argued that the USMCA's sunset clause would allow the United States to preserve its longer-term economic leverage (US House of Representatives 2019c: 4).

34.   Unlike the U.S. GSP program, RRLM sanctions were focused on specific companies in priority industries rather than a country or an entire industry.

35.   Telephone interview with former senior U.S. congressional trade adviser B [Todd], July 9, 2020.

36.   AFL-CIO 1993a: 5. See also Delp et al. 2004: vi; Pier 2008: 2, 12, 20.

37.   The agreement was in effect between 1999 and 2004. For assessments of the program, see Kolben 2004; Polaski 2006b; Oka 2010; Banks 2011: 107–12; Rossi and Robertson 2011.

38.   Interview with a U.S. labor rights advocate [Collingsworth], Washington, DC, July 6, 2005. The change in focus toward the actions of private companies parallels the shift from state responsibility to individual criminal accountability for core human rights violations. Seek Sikkink 2009.

39.   Middlebrook 1991: 275–76.

40.   Huxley 2003: 239.

41.   See chapter 5.

42.   General Motors de México, S. de R. L. de C. V. (Complejo Silao), *Contrato Colectivo de Trabajo, 2020–2022*, points 19, 32, 37, 39–40, 50–51 (a copy of this document is in the author's possession).

43.   Redacción 2021b.

44.   Escalante 2021; Juárez 2022.

45.   Instituto Nacional Electoral (INE) 2021: 6; STPS 2021a.

46.   A senior USTR official reported that the complaint was filed in response to a tip received "a number of months before" via a confidential hotline that GM-Silao management was infringing on workers' rights prior to the May contract legitimation vote (*IUST*, May 14, 2021).

47.   "Course of Remediation to Address Denial of Rights in Connection with the Legitimation Process at General Motors in Silao Agreed between the United States and Mexico," July 7, 2021 (a copy of this document is in the author's possession). Under the plan, General Motors was required to permit employees to vote during regular (paid) working hours and to secure STPS validation of a coordinated voting schedule that accommodated multiple work shifts in different areas of the Silao facility. As required by Mexican labor law, the company provided all Silao workers with a printed copy of the existing collective contract ten days before the vote. In addition, GM publicly posted statements ensuring employees of management's neutrality in the process and that there would be no retaliation against workers who voted down the existing contract. No company personnel could be present at the designated polling stations, and the STPS determined how many (and which) union officials could be present. Both STPS staff and ILO observers were proactive in monitoring the plant before and during the voting, and they were authorized to conduct random interviews with workers on the shopfloor to ensure that they were free from coercion and intimidation. The STPS also circulated audiovisual and printed materials to GM employees to inform them how the vote would be conducted and what its legal and practical implications would be. Finally, STPS created a special email address and a telephone hotline to receive any worker complaints. General Motors was also required to "permanently maintain a mechanism that permits workers to make an anonymous report of any act of intimidation, retaliation, or misinformation."

48.   Redacción 2021a; Gómez Zuppa 2022; INE 2021: 6.

49.   The letter to Barra was signed by William J. Pascrell Jr. (Democrat-New Jersey and chair of the Committee on Ways and Means Subcommittee on Oversight), Earl Blumenaur (Democrat-Oregon and chair of the Committee on Ways and Means Subcommittee on Trade), and Daniel T. Kildee (Democrat-Michigan).

50.   Letter from Reps. Kildee, Pascrell Jr., and Blumenauer to Barra, May 11, 2021 (a copy of this letter is in the author's possession). Members of the U.S. House of Representatives also raised the GM-Silao case with Mexico's ambassador to the United States (Shepardson 2021).

51.   Beggin 2021, Gascón 2021, Kaplan 2021.

52.   This discussion draws on the author's email communication with U.S. trade union representative A [Davis], March 12, 2022. See also LaReau and Lawrence 2022.

53.   This USMCA provision gave form to an AFL-CIO proposal made during initial U.S. debates over the NAALC (AFL-CIO 1993a: 6).

54.   INE 2021: 13, 15; author's email communication with U.S. trade union representative A [Davis], February 3, 2022.

55.   For example, approximately eight STPS inspectors were present at the plant throughout the working day beginning the first week after the joint Mexico-U.S. remediation plan

was announced in June 2021. The number rose to some thirty-two inspectors during the last week before the August contract legitimation vote ("Course of Remediation," point 9).

56.   STPS 2021b. According to the final tally sheet ("Acta de resultados," August 19, 2021), a total of 6,494 GM employees had been eligible to vote.

57.   M. Martínez 2021.

58.   See Centro Federal de Conciliación y Registro Laboral (CFCRL) 2022a: 1 for the full names of these three competitors and CFCRL 2022b for the full election results.

59.   See, for example, statements by the AFL-CIO; the United Automobile, Aerospace, and Agricultural Implement Workers of America; and Canada's UNIFOR (*IUST*, February 4, 2022).

60.   *IUST*, May 4, 2022. In reflecting on the GM-Silao case, U.S. Secretary of Labor Marty Walsh observed, "If we are to succeed in protecting workers' rights at home, we must ensure that those rights will not be undermined by exploitative labor practices and violations of collective bargaining rights around the world" (U.S. Department of Labor 2021).

61.   A study by Maquila Solidarity Network (MSN), a Toronto-based worker rights NGO, found that in only four of the 1,300 (0.3 percent) contract legitimation votes held across Mexico between September 2019 and April 2021 did a majority of workers reject the existing collective bargaining agreement (MSN 2021: 16). In March 2022, more than 4,500 workers at the General Motors assembly and engine manufacturing plants in Ramos Arizpe, Coahuila voted nearly unanimously to retain CTM-negotiated collective contracts (Reuters 2022a).

62.   CFCRL 2022a: 1–3; Chávez-Nava 2022; *IUST*, August 27, 2021.

63.   Mexico's Ministry of the Economy (Secretaría de la Economía) declined the USTR's request in 2021 to investigate alleged violations of collective-action rights at Tridonex (an automotive parts plant in Matamoros, Tamaulipas) because the events in question had transpired before the USMCA came into effect. However, U.S. authorities separately negotiated a settlement agreement with the company, and a democratically organized local union subsequently defeated the CTM incumbent in a workplace representation election (appendix D).

64.   The exception was the BBC Industries case in which the U.S. Interagency Labor Committee for Monitoring and Enforcement declined to take action on the grounds that the submitters had not provided sufficiently compelling evidence in support of their claims (appendix D). The settlement agreements with Tridonex and Teksid Hierro de México provided enhanced severance payments and/or reinstatement to workers who had been dismissed for their union organizing activities (appendix D).

APPENDIX D

This appendix summarizes only those labor rights petitions involving Mexico that were examined under the terms of the rapid response labor mechanism established by the United States-Mexico-Canada Agreement (USMCA); it does not include other public submissions filed under USMCA chapter 23. The petitions are listed in the chronological order in which they were filed or initiated. The full names of the labor unions and other organizations identified here by an acronym appear in the list of acronyms.

1. This summary is based on AFL-CIO, SEIU, Public Citizen, and SNITIS, "Rapid Response Petition" and "Brief in Support of Rapid Response Petition," May 10, 2021 (copies of these documents are in the author's possession); *Inside U.S. Trade* (hereinafter *IUST*), May 14, June 11, August 13, 2021; M. Martínez 2022; USTR / U.S. DOL, "Action Plan," August 10, 2021 (a copy of this document is in the author's possession; Solomon 2022. See Juárez 2021 on the origins of the SNITIS.

2. This case is examined in detail in chapter 7.

3. SNITIS and Rethink Trade, "Rapid Response Petition," April 18, 2022 (a copy of this document is in the author's possession); Gascón 2022; *IUST*, May 20, 2022; Alegría 2022.

4. AFL-CIO, UAW, and SNTMMSSRM, "Brief in Support of Rapid Response Petition," May 4, 2022 (a copy of this document is in the author's possession); *IUST*, June 10, 2022; USTR "Course of Remediation," August 2, 2022 (a copy of this document is in the author's possession); USTR 2022b; Laureles 2022; SNTMMSSRM, *Boletín informativo*, September 20, 2022.

5. LSOM and CFO, "Rapid Response Petition," June 20, 2022 (a copy of this document is in the author's possession); USTR 2022a, U.S. DOL 2022, CFCRL 2022c,

6. SNITIS, "Rapid Response Mechanism Petition," August 2, 2022 (a copy of this document is in the author's possession); Reuters 2022b.

7. AFL-CIO, USW, and SITLDSGM, "Rapid Response Mechanism Petition," September 27, 2022 (a copy of this document is in the author's possession); USTR 2022c; IndustriALL 2022a, b.

Bibliography

Aaronson, Susan Ariel. 1996. *Trade and the American Dream: A Social History of Postwar Trade Policy*. Lexington: University of Kentucky Press.

Abbott, K. W., and Duncan Snidal. 2000. "Hard and Soft Law in International Governance." *International Organization* 54 (3): 421–56.

"A Call for Human Rights in the Workplace." 2005. *International Herald Tribune*, December 7.

Adams, Paul H. 1990. "Suspension of Generalized System of Preferences from Chile–The Proper Use of a Trade Provision?" *George Washington Journal of International Law and Economics* 23 (2): 501–30.

Ahlquist, John S., Amanda B. Clayton, and Margaret Levi. 2014. "Provoking Preferences: Unionization, Trade Policy, and the ILWU Puzzle." *International Organization* 68 (1): 33–75.

Alben, Elissa. 2001. "GATT and the Fair Wage: A Historical Perspective on the Labor-Trade Link." *Columbia Law Review* 101 (6): 1410–47.

Albertson, Paula Church. 2010. "The Evolution of Labor Provisions in U.S. Free Trade Agreements: Lessons Learned and Remaining Questions Examining the Dominican Republic-Central America-United States Free Trade Agreement (CAFTA-DR)." *Stanford Law and Policy Review* 21 (3): 493–512.

Alcalde Justiniani, Arturo. 1998. "Acelerar el paso." *La Jornada*, February 13.

——. 2010. "El sindicalismo, la democracia y la libertad sindical." In *El sindicalismo en México: Historia, crisis y perspectivas*, 2nd ed., ed. José Merced González Guerra and Antonio Gutiérrez Castro, 159–74 (Mexico City: Plaza y Valdés Editores).

——. 2017a. "Dilemas de una histórica reforma laboral." *La Jornada*, May 13.

——. 2017b. "Grotesca iniciativa de reforma laboral." *La Jornada en línea*, December 9.

——. 2017c. "Otra reforma laboral secreta." *La Jornada en línea*, December 10.

——. 2018a. "Se acelera la reforma que da muerte al derecho laboral." *La Jornada en línea*, March 31.

——. 2018b. "Los trabajadores tienen la palabra . . . y el voto." *La Jornada en línea*, April 29.

——. 2018c. "Petición al Senado: Ratificar el Convenio 98 OIT." *La Jornada en línea*, September 1.

——. 2020. *La contratación colectiva y su técnica de negociación* (Mexico City: Editorial Porrúa).

Alcock, Antony. 1971. *History of the International Labour Organisation* (London: Macmillan Press).

Alegría, Alejandro. 2022. "EU felicita a México por resolver conflicto laboral en Panasonic." *La Jornada en línea*, July 14.

Alexander, Robin. 1999. "Experience and Reflections on the Use of the NAALC." In *Memorias: encuentro trinacional de laboralistas democráticos*, ed. José Alfonso Bouzas Ortiz, 139–66. Mexico City: Universidad Nacional Autónoma de México.

—. 2022. *International Solidarity in Action: The United Electrical Workers (UE) and Frente Auténtico del Trabajo (FAT)* (N.p.).

Alexander, Robin, and Peter Gilmore. 1994. "The Emergence of Cross-Border Labor Solidarity." *NACLA Report on the Americas* 28 (1): 42–48.

Alston, Philip. 1982. "International Trade as an Instrument of Positive Human Rights Policy." *Human Rights Quarterly* 4 (2): 155–83.

—. 1993. "Labor Rights Provisions in US Trade Law: 'Aggressive Unilateralism'?" *Human Rights Quarterly* 15 (1): 1–35.

—. 2004. "'Core Labour Standards' and the Transformation of the International Labour Rights Regime." *European Journal of International Law* 15 (3): 457–521.

Althaus, Dudley. 2017a. "Nafta Talks Target Stubbornly Low Mexican Wages." *Wall Street Journal* (online edition), August 29.

—. 2017b. "Mexico's Stubbornly Low Pay Emerges as Target in Nafta Talks." *Wall Street Journal* (online edition), August 30.

Amato, Theresa A. 1990. "Labor Rights Conditionality: United States Trade Legislation and the International Trade Order." *New York University Law Review* 65 (1): 79–125.

American Federation of Labor-Congress of Industrial Organizations (AFL-CIO). 1993a. "Labor Rights and Standards and NAFTA." Task Force on Trade discussion paper, February 14.

—. 1993b. "Statement by the AFL-CIO Executive Council on the North American Free Trade Agreement." February 17.

—. 1995. "Mexico-U.S. NAFTA 'Sister Factories' " (Washington, DC: International Affairs Department, AFL-CIO).

—. 2004a. "Response to Request for Comments on NAALC Review 2004." February 3.

—. 2004b. "AFL-CIO Section 301 Petition Against China." *New Labor Forum* 13 (3): 86–89.

—. 2005. "Latest Administration Labor Promises Do Nothing to Fix the Flaws of CAFTA." Press release.

—. 2006a. "Section 301 Petition of American Federation of Labor and Congress of Industrial Organizations Before the Office of The United States Trade Representative, Section 301 Committee." June 8. .

—. 2006b. "Request by the American Federation of Labor-Congress of Industrial Organizations (AFL-CIO) and the National Textile Association (NTA) to the United States to Invoke Consultations Under the United States-Jordan Free Trade Agreement to Address Jordan's Violations of the Agreement's Labor Rights Provisions." September 21.

—. 2017. "Making NAFTA Work for Working People." Submitted on June 12 to Office of the U.S. Trade Representative in advance of scheduled public hearing on "Negotiating Objectives Regarding Modernization of the North American Free Trade Agreement with Canada and Mexico." Docket No. USTR-2017-0006 (Washington, DC: AFL-CIO).

Amorim, Celso L. N. 2000. "The WTO from the Perspective of a Developing Country." *Fordham International Law Journal* 24 (1–2): 95–106.

Anderson, Mark. 1993. "North American Free Trade Agreement's Impact on Labor." In *The North American Free Trade Agreement: Labor, Industry, and Government Perspectives*, ed. Mario F. Bognanno and Kathryn J. Ready, 238–55 (Westport, CT: Quorum Books).

Anner, Mark. 2000. "Local and Transnational Campaigns to End Sweatshop Practices." In *Transnational Cooperation Among Labor Unions*, ed. Michael E. Gordon and Lowell Turner, 238–55 (Ithaca, NY: Cornell University Press / ILR Press).

—. 2001. "The International Campaign for Core Labor Standards in the WTO." *WorkingUSA* 5 (1): 43–63.

—. 2003. "Industrial Structure, the State, and Ideology: Shaping Labor Transnationalism in the Brazilian Auto Industry." *Social Science History* 27 (4): 603–34.

—. 2012. "Corporate Social Responsibility and Freedom of Association Rights: The Precarious Quest for Legitimacy and Control in Global Supply Chains." *Politics and Society* 40 (4): 609–44.

Anner, Mark, and Peter Evans. 2004. "Building Bridges Across a Double Divide: Alliances Between US and Latin American Labour and NGOs." *Development in Practice* 14 (1/2): 34–47.

Anner, Mark, Ian Greer, Marco Hauptmeier, Nathan Lillie, and Nik Winchester. 2006. "The Industrial Determinants of Transnational Solidarity: Global Interunion Politics in Three Sectors." *European Journal of Industrial Relations* 12 (1): 7–21.

Appleton, Barry. 1994. *Navigating NAFTA: A Concise User's Guide to the North American Free Trade Agreement* (Rochester, NY: Lawyers Cooperative Publishing).

Aranda, Jesús. 1999. "Establecerían hoy jurisprudencia que garantice la libertad sindical." *La Jornada*, May 11.

Armbruster-Sandoval, Ralph. 2003. "Globalization and Transnational Labor Organizing: The Honduran Maquiladora Industry and the Kimi Campaign." *Social Science History* 27 (4): 551–76.

Aronson, Bernard W. 1991. "U.S. Policy and Funding Priorities in Latin America and the Caribbean for FY 1992." *U.S. Department of State Dispatch* 2 (11): 187–94.

Arthur, Charles. 2003. "Haiti's Labour Movement in Renaissance." *International Union Rights* 10 (2) (June 30): http://haitisupportgroup.org/haitis-labour-movement-in-renaissance/.

Aspinwall, Mark. 2013. *Side Effects: Mexican Governance Under NAFTA's Labor and Environmental Agreements* (Stanford, CA: Stanford University Press).

Association Internationale des Travailleurs (International Working Men's Association). 1866. *Congrès Ouvrier de la Association Internationale des Travailleurs*, September 3–8 (Geneva: Imprimerie J.-C. Ducommun et G. Oettinger).

Athreya, Bama. 2011. *Comparative Case Analysis of the Impacts of Trade-Related Labor Provisions on Select U.S. Trade Preference Recipient Countries* (Washington, DC: Bureau of International Labor Affairs, U.S. Department of Labor).

Ayres, Jeffrey M. 1998. *Defying Conventional Wisdom: Political Movements and Popular Contention Against North American Free Trade* (Toronto: University of Toronto Press).

Baccaro, Lucio, and Valentina Mele. 2012. "Pathology of Path-Dependency? The ILO and the Challenge of New Governance." *International Labour Review* 65 (2): 195–224.

Baccini, Leonardo, and Mathias Koenig-Archibugi. 2014. "Why Do States Commit to International Labor Standards? Interdependent Ratification of Core ILO Conventions, 1948–2009." *World Politics* 66 (3): 446–90.

Bachrach, Peter, and Morton S. Baratz. 1962. "Two Faces of Power." *American Political Science Review* 56 (4): 947–52.

—. 2000a. "Strikers Beaten at NAFTA-sponsored Hearing." David Bacon (website), June 23, http://dbacon.igc.org/Mexico/17StrikersBeaten.htm.

——. 2000b. "Just South of Texas, Democracy Faces its Hardest Test." United Students Against Sweatshops communication, August 22.

——. 2004. *The Children of NAFTA: Labor Wars on the U.S./Mexico Border* (Berkeley, CA: University of California Press).

——. 2015b. "The North American Agreement on Labor Cooperation and the Challenges to Protecting Low-Wage Migrant Workers." In *Accountability Across Borders: Migrant Rights in North America*, 83–109 (Austin: University of Texas Press).

Ballinas, Víctor, and Andrea Becerril. 2016. "PRI y PAN aprueban reforma que atenta contra el derecho de huelga." *La Jornada en línea*, October 5.

——. 2019. "Senado tomó puerta falsa al aprobar Reforma Laboral: Coparmex." *La Jornada en línea*, April 29.

Ballon, Ian Charles. 1987. "The Implications of Making the Denial of Internationally Recognized Worker Rights Actionable Under Section 301 of the Trade Act of 1974." *Virginia Journal of International Law* 28 (1): 73–128.

Bandy, Joe. 2004a. "So What Is to Be Done? Maquila Justice Movements, Transnational Solidarity, and Dynamics of Resistance." In *The Social Costs of Industrial Growth in Northern Mexico*, ed. Kathryn Kopinak, 309–42 (La Jolla, CA: Center for U.S.-Mexican Studies, University of California-San Diego).

——. 2004b. "Paradoxes of Transnational Civil Societies under Neoliberalism: The Coalition for Justice in the Maquiladoras." *Social Problems* 51 (3): 410–31.

——. 2009. "Paradoxes of a Transnational Civil Society in a Neoliberal World: The Coalition for Justice in the Maquiladoras." In *Contentious Politics in North America: National Protest and Transnational Collaboration under Continental Integration*, ed. Jeffrey Ayres and Laura Macdonald, 74–91 (Basingstoke, England: Palgrave Macmillan).

——. 2011. "Trade, Labor, and International Governance: An Inquiry into the Potential Effectiveness of the New International Labor Law." *Berkeley Journal of Employment and Law* 32 (1): 45–142.

——. 2021. "Fit for Purpose? The Extent and Enforcement of International Trade Agreement Labor Obligations after the *Guatemala-Labor Obligations* Decision." *Georgetown Journal of International Law* 52 (3): 639–77.

Barkin, J. Samuel, and Bruce Cronin. 1994. "The State and the Nation: Changing Norms and the Rules of Sovereignty in International Relations." *International Organization* 48 (1): 107–30.

Barnes, Joe. 2014. "The Trans-Pacific Partnership Agreement: The Stakes for Mexico and the United States." Issue Brief, September 14, Houston, TX: Baker Institute for Public Policy, Rice University.

Barr, Michael S., Robert Honeywell, and Scott A. Stofel. 1991. "Labor and Environmental Rights in the Proposed Mexico-United States Free Trade Agreement." *Houston Journal of International Law* 14 (1): 1–83.

Barrientos, Stephanie, and Sally Smith. 2007. "Do Workers Benefit from Ethical Trade? Assessing Codes of Labour Practice in Global Production Systems." *Third World Quarterly* 28 (4): 713–29.

Barry, Christian, and Sanjay G. Reddy. 2008. *International Trade and Labor Standards: A Proposal for Linkage* (New York: Columbia University Press).

Bartley, Tim. 2007. "Institutional Emergence in an Era of Globalization: The Rise of Transnational Private Regulation of Labor and Environmental Conditions." *American Journal of Sociology* 113 (2): 297–351.

Bartley, Tim, and Niklas Egels-Zandén. 2016. "Beyond Decoupling: Unions and the Leveraging of Corporate Social Responsibility in Indonesia." *Socio-Economic Review* 14 (2): 231–55.

Bartow, Ann M. 1990. "The Rights of Workers in Mexico." *Comparative Labor Law Journal* 11 (2): 182–202.

Bates, Ed. 2014. "History." In *International Human Rights Law*, 2nd ed., ed. Daniel Moeckli, Sangeeta Shah, and Sandesh Sivakumaran, 15–33 (Oxford: Oxford University Press).

Bazar, Jason S. 1995. "Is the North American Agreement on Labor Cooperation Working for Workers' Rights?" *California Western International Law Journal* 25 (2): 425–58.

Beaver, Janice Cheryl. 2006. *U.S. International Borders: Brief Facts*, Congressional Research Service Report for Congress, RS21729, November 9. https://sgp.fas.org/crs/misc/RS21729.pdf.

Becerril, Andrea. 1995. "Habrá recuento en Saro sobre la afiliación sindical de pilotos." *La Jornada*, February 5.

Becerril, Andrea, and Víctor Ballinas. 2019a. "Ningún punto del T-MEC contrapone intereses de México: Seade." *La Jornada en línea*, December 11.

——. 2019b. "Solo con un voto en contra, ratifica Senado el T-MEC." *La Jornada en línea*, December 12.

Beggin, Riley. 2021. "U.S. Asks Mexico to Review Alleged Labor Violations at GM Plant." *Detroit News* (online edition), May 11.

Behsudi, Adam. 2019. "Wyden, Brown Propose USMCA Labor Enforcement Methods." *Politico* (online), April 5.

Bellace, Janice R. 2014. "The ILO and the Right to Strike." *International Labour Review* 153 (1): 29–70.

Bennett, Andrew, and Jeffrey T. Checkel. 2015. "Process Tracing: From Philosophical Roots to Best Practices." In *Process Tracing: From Metaphor to Analytic Tool*, ed. Bennett and Checkel, 3–37 (Cambridge: Cambridge University Press).

Bensusán, Graciela. 1992. "Institucionalización laboral en México: los años de la definición jurídica, 1917–1931." Ph.D. thesis, Facultad de Ciencias Políticas y Sociales, Universidad Nacional Autónoma de México.

——. 2000. *El modelo mexicano de regulación laboral* (MexicoCity: Facultad Latinoamericana de Ciencias Sociales-Sede México / Universidad Autonoma Metropolitana / Fundación Friedrich Ebert Stiftung / Plaza y Valdés).

——. 2004a. "Labor Regulations and Trade Union Convergence in North America." In *NAFTA's Impact on North America: The First Decade*, ed. Sidney Weintraub, 123–55 (Washington, DC: Center for Strategic and International Studies).

——. 2004b. "A New Scenario for Mexican Trade Unions: Changes in the Structure of Political and Economic Opportunities." In *Dilemmas of Political Change in Mexico*, ed. Kevin J. Middlebrook, 237–85 (London: Institute of Latin American Studies / Center for U.S.-Mexican Studies, University of California, San Diego).

——. 2007. "Los determinantes institucionales de los contratos de protección." In *Contratación colectiva de protección en México: Informe a la Organización Regional Interamericana de Trabajadores (ORIT)*, ed. José Alfonso Bouzas Ortiz and Aleida Hernández Cervantes, 11–48 (Mexico City: Instituto de Investigaciones Económicas, Universidad Nacional Autónoma de México).

Bensusán, Graciela, and Kevin J. Middlebrook. 2012. *Organized Labour and Politics in Mexico: Changes, Continuities and Contradictions* (Institute for the Study of the Americas, University of London).

—. 2013. *Sindicatos y política en México: cambios, continuidades y contradicciones* (Mexico City: Facultad Latinoamericana de Ciencias Sociales-Sede México/Universidad Autónoma Metropolitana-Xochimilco/Consejo Latinoamericana de Ciencias Sociales).

—. 2020. "Cambio político desde afuera hacia adentro: influencia comercial estadounidense y reforma de los derechos laborales en México." *Foro Internacional* LX (3): 985-1039.

Bhagwati, Jagdish. 1995. "Trade Liberalisation and 'Fair Trade' Demands: Addressing the Environmental and Labour Standards Issues." *World Economy* 18 (6): 745-59.

—. 2004. *In Defense of Globalization* (Oxford: Oxford University Press).

Bhatnagar, Harshita, and Vinay V. Mishra. 2008-2009. "Workers' Rights *vis-à-vis* the WTO: Do We Need a Paradigm Shift?" *Hibernian Law Journal* 8: 185-215.

Bieler, Andreas. 2012. "Workers of the World, Unite? Globalization and the Quest for Transnational Solidarity." *Globalizations* 9 (3): 365-78.

Blackwell, Ron. 2002. "Labor Perspectives on Economic Integration and Binational Relations." In *Cross-Border Dialogues: U.S.-Mexico Social Movement Networking*, ed. David Brooks and Jonathan Fox, 69-76 (La Jolla, CA: Center for U.S.-Mexican Studies, University of California-San Diego).

Blanchard, Emily, and Shushanik Hakobyan. 2015. "The US Generalised System of Preferences in Principle and Practice." *World Economy* 38 (3): 399-424.

Blecker, Robert A., Juan Carlos Moreno-Brid, and Isabel Salat. 2018. "La renegociación del TLCAN: Un enfoque alternativo para la convergencia y la prosperidad compartida." *Economía Informa*, 408 (Jan.-Feb.): 5-15.

Blowfield, Mick. 2002. "ETI: A Multi-Stakeholder Approach." In *Corporate Responsibility and Labour Rights: Codes of Conduct in the Global Economy*, ed. Rhys Jenkins, Ruth Pearson, and Gill Seyfang, 184-95 (London: Earthscan).

Bolle, Mary Jane. 2005. "DR-CAFTA Labor Rights Issues." Congressional Research Service Report RS22159 (Washington, DC: Congressional Research Service). CRS Report for Congress.

—. 2007. "Trade Promotion Authority (TPA)/Fast-Track Renewal: Labor Issues." Congressional Research Service Report RL33864 (Washington, DC: Congressional Research Service).

—. 2014. "Overview of Labor Enforcement Issues in Free Trade Agreements." Congressional Research Service Report RS22823 (Washington, DC: Congressional Research Service).

Bonior, David E. 2014. "Obama's Trade Conundrum." *International New York Times*, January 31.

Borgers, Frank. 1999. "Global Unionism—Beyond the Rhetoric: The CWA North Atlantic Alliance." *Labor Studies Journal* 24 (1): 107-22.

Borkan, Bett. 2010. "Colombia Too Far Behind on Labor and Human Rights: US Union." *Colombia Reports*, March 21.

Bouzas Ortíz, José Alfonso. 2010. "Los contratos de protección y el sindicalismo mexicano." In *El sindicalismo en México: historia, crisis y perspectivas*, 2nd ed., ed. José Merced González Guerra and Antonio Gutiérrez Castro, 113-27 (Mexico City: Plaza y Valdés Editores).

Bouzas Ortiz, José Antonio, and María Mercedes Gaitá Riveros. 2001. "Contratos colectivos de trabajo de protección." In *Democracia sindical*, ed. J. Alfonso Bouzas, 49-66 (Mexico City: Instituto de Investigaciones Económicas, Universidad Nacional Autónoma de México).

Boyle, Kevin, and Sangeeta Shah. 2014. "Thought, Expression, Association, and Assembly." In *International Human Rights Law*, 2nd ed., ed. Daniel Moeckli, Sangeeta Shah, and Sandesh Sivakumaran, 217-37 (Oxford: Oxford University Press).

Bradsher, Keith. 1993. "3 Nations Resolve Issues Holding Up Trade Pact Vote: Foes Stand Ground." *New York Times*, August 14.

Braun, Rainer, and Judy Gearhart. 2004. "Who Should Code Your Conduct? Trade Union and NGO Differences in the Fight for Workers' Rights." *Development in Practice* 14 (1/2): 183-206.

Braunthal, Julius. 1966. *History of the International, 1864–1914* (London: Thomas Nelson).

Brecher, Jeremy, Tim Costello, and Brendan Smith. 2006. "International Labor Solidarity: The New Frontier." *New Labor Forum* 15 (1): 9-18.

Bronfenbrenner, Kate. 1997. "Organizing in the NAFTA Environment: How Companies Use 'Free Trade' to Stop Unions." *New Labor Forum* 1 (1): 50-60.

Brookes, Marissa. 2018. "Explaining Employer Responses to Transnational Labor Activism: Indonesia and Cambodia Compared." *Comparative Political Studies* 51 (6): 699-729.

Brower, Adam. 2008. "Rethinking NAFTA's NAALC Provision: The Effectiveness of its Dispute Resolution System on the Protection of Mexican Migrant Workers in the United States." *Indiana International and Comparative Law Review* 18 (1): 153-88.

Brown, Drusilla K., 2001. "Labor Standards: Where Do They Belong on the International Trade Agenda?" *Journal of Economic Perspectives* 15 (3): 89-112.

Brown, Garrett D. 2004a. "NAFTA's 10 Year Failure to Protect Mexican Workers' Health and Safety." December (Berkeley, CA: Maquiladora Health and Safety Support Network).

——. 2004b. "Why NAFTA Failed and What's Needed to Protect Workers' Health and Safety in International Trade Treaties." December (Berkeley, CA: Maquiladora Health and Safety Support Network).

Brunelle, Dorval, and Sylvie Dugas. 2009. "Civil Society Organizations Against Free Trade Agreements in North America." In *Contentious Politics in North America: National Protest and Transnational Collaboration under Continental Integration*, ed. Jeffrey Ayres and Laura Macdonald, 57-73 (Basingstoke, England: Palgrave Macmillan).

Bryman, Alan. 2012. *Social Research Methods*, 4th ed. (Oxford: Oxford University Press).

Buchanan, Ruth, and Rusby Chaparro. 2008. "International Institutions and Transnational Advocacy: The Case of the North American Agreement on Labor Cooperation." *UCLA Journal of International Law and Foreign Affairs* 13 (1): 129-59.

Buergenthal, Thomas. 1997. "The Normative and Institutional Evolution of International Human Rights." *Human Rights Quarterly* 19 (4): 703-23.

Burges, Sean W. 2006. "Without Sticks or Carrots: Brazilian Leadership in South America During the Cardoso Era." *Bulletin of Latin American Research* 25 (1): 23-42.

Bush, George, and Brent Scowcroft. 1998. *A World Transformed* (New York: Alfred A. Knopf).

Busse, Matthias. 2002. "Do Labor Standards Affect Comparative Advantage in Developing Countries?" *World Development* 30 (11): 1921-32.

Calbreath, Dean. 1997a. "Lawmakers Condemn Maquiladora Firings." *San Diego Union-Tribune*, October 30.

——. 1997b. "Informal Talks Held at Plant in Mexico." *San Diego Union-Tribune*, December 10.

——. 1997c. "Baja Union Victory is Seen as a Milestone." *San Diego Union-Tribune*, December 18.

——. 1998. "Mexico Fines Han Young as Hyundai is Drawn into Fight." *San Diego Union-Tribune*, February 21.

—. 2000. "Tijuana Seminar Turns Violent as Workers Clash." *San Diego Union-Tribune*, June 24.

Calderón, Judith, Oscar Camacho, Elena Gallegos, and Georgina Saldierna. 1996. "Rechazan líderes obreros la resolución de la Corte; Hernández Juárez: la medida es una ofensiva del gobierno." *La Jornada*, May 23.

Cameron, Maxwell A., and Brian W. Tomlin. 2000. *The Making of NAFTA: How the Deal was Done* (Ithaca, NY: Cornell University Press).

Campbell, Bruce. 1993. "A Canadian Labour Perspective on the North American Free Trade Agreement." In *The North American Free Trade Agreement: Labor, Industry, and Government Perspectives*, ed. Mario F. Bognanno and Kathryn J. Ready, 61-68 (Westport, CT: Quorum Books).

Canadian Association of Labour Lawyers. 2006. "Submissions Concerning the Proposed Free Trade Agreement between Canada, El Salvador, Guatemala, Honduras, and Nicaragua." Submission to the House of Commons International Trade Committee, June 6.

Canadian Labour Congress (CLC). 1996. "Social Dimensions of North American Economic Integration: Impacts on Working People and Emerging Responses."

Candland, Christopher. 2007. "Workers' Organizations in Pakistan: Why No Role in Formal Politics?" *Critical Asian Studies* 39 (1): 35-57.

Cano, Arturo. 2019. "Seguirá rechazo al T-MEC si no mejora el capítulo laboral: Trumka." *La Jornada en línea*, September 14.

—. 2006b. "Political Openness and Transnational Activism: Comparative Insights from Labor Activism." *Politics and Society* 34 (2): 277-304.

Carlsen, Laura. 2009. "Obama Reaffirms Promise to Renegotiate NAFTA." *Huffpost*, February 12.

Carr, Barry. 1996. "Crossing Borders: Labor Internationalism in the Era of NAFTA." In *Neo-liberalism Revisited: Economic Restructuring and Mexico's Political Future*, ed. Gerardo Otero, 209-31 (Boulder, CO.: Westview).

Carrère, Céline, Marcelo Olarreaga, and Damian Raess. 2017. "Labor Clauses in Trade Agreements: Worker Protection or Protectionism?" Centre for Economic Policy Research (University of Geneva) Discussion Paper No. DP12251, August.

Carty, Victoria. 2004. "Transnational Labor Mobilizing in Two Mexican Maquiladoras: The Struggle for Democratic Globalization." *Mobilization* 9(3): 295-310.

Castañeda, Jorge G. 1995. *The Mexican Shock: Its Meaning for the U.S.* (New York: New Press).

—. 2004. *Somos muchos: ideas para el mañana* (Mexico City: Editorial Planeta Mexicana).

Castree, Noel. 2000. "Geographic Scale and Grass-Roots Internationalism: The Liverpool Dock Dispute, 1995-1998." *Economic Geography* 76 (3): 272-92.

Centro de Investigación Laboral y Asesoría Sindical (CILAS). 2022. *3 años de reforma laboral 2019 y del capítulo 23 laboral del T-MEC* (Mexico City: CILAS/Centro de Apoyo a la Libertad Sindical).

Centro de Investigación y Docencia Económicas (CIDE). 2015. *Informe de resultados de los Foros de Justicia Cotidiana* (Mexico City: CIDE), http://imco.org.mx/wp-content/uploads/2015/04/Documento_JusticiaCotidiana_.pdf.

Centro Federal de Conciliación y Registro Laboral (CFCRL). 2021. "Acuerdo por el que se aprueba el Protocolo para el Procedimiento de Legitimación de Contratos Colectivos de Trabajo Existentes (Acuerdo JGCFCRL-50-18/03/2021." *Diario Oficial de la Federación*, April 30.

—. 2022a. Coordinación General de Registro de Contratos Colectivos. "Acuerdo en el que se determina la acreditación para fungir como observador externo en el proceso de consulta en la empresa 'General Motors de México, S. de R. L. de C. V.'" January 28.

——. 2022b. "Centro Federal Laboral informa sobre los resultados de la consulta en la planta de General Motors, Silao." Comunicado 012, February 3.

——. 2022c. "Resultados de la consulta en la empresa VU Manufacturing." Comunicado 45, August 31.

Charnovitz, Steve. 1984. "Caribbean Basin Initiative: Setting Labor Standards." *Monthly Labor Review* 107 (11): 54–56.

——. 1986. "Fair Labor Standards and International Trade." *Journal of World Trade Law* 20 (1): 61–78.

——. 1987. "The Influence of International Labor Standards on the World Trading Regime: A Historical Overview." *International Labour Review*, 126 (5): 565–84.

——. 1994a. "The World Trade Organization and Social Issues." *Journal of World Trade Law* 28 (5): 17–33.

——. 1994b. "NAFTA's Social Dimension: Lessons from the Past and Framework for the Future." *International Trade Journal* 8 (1): 39–72.

——. 1995. "Promoting Higher Labor Standards." *Washington Quarterly* 18 (3): 167–90.

——. 2021. "The Expanding Labor Dimensions of US-Negotiated Regional Trade Agreements: TPP and USMCA." GW Legal Studies Research Paper No. 2021-14 (Washington, DC: Georgetown University Law School).

Chávez-Nava, Citlalli. 2022. "UCLA Labor Center Researcher Participates in Historic GM Union Election in Mexico." UCLA Institute for Research on Labor and Employment, February 3.

Cimino-Isaacs, Cathleen. 2016. "Labor Standards in the TPP." In *Trans-Pacific Partnership: An Assessment*, Cathleen Cimino-Isaacs and Jeffrey J. Schott, 261–97 (Washington, DC: Peterson Institute for International Economics).

Cingranelli, David L., David L. Richards, and K. Chad Clay. 2014. "The CIRI Human Rights Data Set." Accessed July 18, 2017. http://www.humanrightsdata.com/.

Clapham, Andrew. 2007. *Human Rights: A Very Short Introduction* (Oxford: Oxford University Press).

Cleveland, Sarah H. 1997-1998. "Global Labor Rights and the Alien Tort Claims Act." *Texas Law Review* 76 (6): 1533–79.

Cline, Howard F. 1963. *The United States and Mexico*, rev. ed. (Cambridge, MA: Harvard University Press).

Clinton, Bill. 1992. "Expanding Trade and Creating American Jobs: Remarks by Governor Bill Clinton, North Carolina State University, Raleigh, NC." October 4.

——. 2004. *My Life* (New York: Alfred A. Knopf).

Cochrane, Emily, and Ana Swanson. 2019. "Trump Aides and Democrats Strike Deal in North American Trade Pact." *New York Times* (online edition), December 10.

Cochrane, Emily, Ana Swanson, Elisabeth Malkin, and Maggie Haberman. 2019. "Congress Nears Vote on Revised Trade Pact." *New York Times International Edition*, December 11.

Cochrane, Emily, Ana Swanson, and Jim Tankersley. 2019. "How a Trump Trade Pact Won Over Democrats." *New York Times International Edition*, December 24.

Cochrane, Lauren. 2021. "Welcome for Accord to Protect Bangladesh Garment Workers." *The Guardian*, August 27.

Cohen, Larry, and Steve Early. 2000. "Globalization and De-Unionization in Telecommunications: Three Case Studies in Resistance." In *Transnational Cooperation Among Labor Unions*, ed. Michael E. Gordon and Lowell Turner, 202–22 (Ithaca, NY: Cornell University Press/ILR Press).

Collingsworth, Terry, J. William Goold, and Pharis J. Harvey. 1994. "Labor and Free Trade: Time for a Global New Deal." *Foreign Affairs* (Jan.–Feb.): 8–13.

Compa, Lance A. 1993a. "Labor Rights and Labor Standards in International Trade." *Law and Policy in International Business* 25 (1): 165–91.

——. 1993b. "International Labor Rights and the Sovereignty Question: NAFTA and Guatemala, Two Case Studies." *American University International Law Review* 9 (1): 117–50.

——. 1995a. "Going Multilateral: The Evolution of U.S. Hemispheric Labor Rights Policy Under GSP and NAFTA." *Connecticut Journal of International Law* 10 (2): 337–64.

——. 1995b. "The First NAFTA Labor Cases: A New International Labor Rights Regime Takes Shape." *United States-Mexico Law Journal* 3: 159–81.

——. 1995c. "And the Twain Shall Meet? A North-South Controversy over Labor Rights and Trade." *Labor Research Review* 1 (23): 51–65.

——. 1997a. "Comparing the NAALC and the European Union Social Charter." *American University Journal of International Law and Policy* 12 (5): 837–41.

——. 1997b. "NAFTA's Labor Side Accord: A Three-Year Accounting." *NAFTA: Law and Business Review of the Americas* 3 (3): 6–23.

——. 1997c. "Another Look at NAFTA." *Dissent* 44 (1): 45–50.

——. 1999a. "The North American Agreement on Labor Cooperation and International Labor Solidarity." In *Memorias: encuentro trinacional de laboralistas democráticos,* ed. José Alfonso Bouzas Ortiz, 185–211 (Mexico City: Universidad Nacional Autónoma de México).

——. 1999b. "Is There an Emerging Transnational Regime for Labor Standards? Remarks." *Proceedings of the American Society of International Law* 93 (January 1): 381, http://digitalcommons .ilr.cornell.edu/articles/333/.

——. 1999c. "NAFTA's Labor Side Agreement Five Years On: Progress and Prospects for the NAALC." *Canadian Labor and Employment Law Journal* 7: 2–30.

——. 1999d. "International Labor Rights and NAFTA's Labor Side Agreement." *LASA Forum* XXX (2): 14–17.

——. 2001. "NAFTA's Labor Side Agreement and International Labor Solidarity." *Antipode* 33 (3): 451–67.

——. 2003a. *Justice for All: The Struggle for Worker Rights in Mexico* (Washington, DC: American Center for International Labor Solidarity).

——. 2003b. "Assessing Assessments: A Survey of Efforts to Measure Countries' Compliance with Freedom of Association Standards." *Comparative Labor Law and Policy Journal* 24 (2): 283–320.

——. 2004. "Trade Unions, NGOs, and Corporate Codes of Conduct." *Development in Practice* 14 (1/2): 210–15.

——. 2019. "Trump, Trade, and *Trabajo*: Renegotiating NAFTA's Labor Accord in a Fraught Political Climate." *Indiana Journal of Global Legal Studies* 26 (1): 263–304.

Compa, Lance, and Tequila Brooks. 2019. *NAFTA and NAALC: Twenty-Five Years of North American Trade-Labour Linkage,* 2nd ed. (Alphen aan den Rijn, Netherlands: Kluwer Law International).

Compa, Lance, and Tashia Hinchliffe-Darricarrère. 1995. "Enforcing Labor Rights Through Corporate Codes of Conduct." *Columbia Journal of Transnational Law* 33 (3): 663–89.

Compa, Lance, and Jeffrey S. Vogt. 2001. "Labor Rights in the Generalized System of Preferences: A 20-Year Review." *Comparative Labor Law and Policy Journal* 22 (2/3): 199–238.

Compa, Lance, Jeffrey S. Vogt, and Eric Gottwald. 2018. "Wrong Turn for Workers' Rights: The U.S.-Guatemala CAFTA Labor Arbitration Ruling—And What to Do About It" (Washington, DC: International Labor Rights Forum).

Connor, Tim. 2004. "Time to Scale Up Cooperation? Trade Unions, NGOs, and the International Anti-Sweatshop Movement." *Development in Practice* 14 (1/2): 61–70.

Consejo Coordinador Empresarial. 2015. "Cambio climático y convenio 98 de la OIT." *La voz del CCE*, December 7. https://www.cce.org.mx.

Cook, Maria Lorena. 2007. *The Politics of Labor Reform in Latin America: Between Flexibility and Rights* (University Park: Pennsylvania State University Press).

Cook, Maria Lorena, Morley Gunderson, Mark Thompson, and Anil Verma. 1997. "Making Free Trade More Fair: Developments in Protecting Labor Rights." *Labor Law Journal* 48 (8): 519–29.

Cornejo, Jorge Alberto. 1998a. "Conciliación declare ilegal la huelga de Han Young en BC." *La Jornada*, May 29.

——. 1998b. "La huelga en Han Young es legal, dice una juez de Tijuana." *La Jornada*, May 31.

Corona, Sonia. 2019. "El cierre del tratado de libre comercio da un respiro a la economía mexicana." *El País* (online edition), December 11.

——. 2020. "'El TMEC no salió exactamente como le hubiera gustado a Trump.'" *El País* (online edition), January 20.

Covarrubias Valdenebro, Alex. 2020. *El T-MEC: Escenarios probables para el trabajo y la industria automotriz regional* (Mexico City: Friedrich Ebert Stiftung).

Cowie, Jefferson. 1997. "National Struggles in a Transnational Economy: A Critical Analysis of US Labor's Campaign Against NAFTA." *Labor Studies Journal* 21 (4): 3–32.

——. 1999. *Capital Moves: RCA's Seventy-Year Quest for Cheap Labor* (Ithaca, New York: Cornell University Press).

Cox, Robert W. 1971. "Labor and Transnational Relations." *International Organization*, 25 (3): 554–84.

——. 1977. "Labor and Hegemony." *International Organization*, 31 (3): 385–424.

Cuevas, R. Leticia. 1995. "Analysis of Submissions Nos. 940003 and 940004 Brought Before the U.S. National Administrative Office of the United States Department of Labor." January 21. Unpublished.

Curtis, Paul A., and Alfredo Gutierrez Kirchner. 1994. "Questions on Labor Law Enforcement in Mexico and the Role of the Federal and State Conciliation and Arbitration Boards." Prepared for the U.S. Department of Labor, Bureau of International Affairs. Unpublished.

Damgaard, Bodil. 1998. "Cinco años con el Acuerdo Laboral Paralelo." Paper presented at the international congress of the Latin American Studies Association, Chicago, IL, September 24–26 1998.

——. 1999. "ACLAN: experiencias y tendencias después de cinco años." In *Memorias: encuentro trinacional de laboralistas democráticos*, ed. José Antonio Bouzas Ortíz, 95–121 (Mexico City: Universidad Nacional Autónoma de México).

Das, Dilip K. 2000. "Debacle at Seattle: The Way the Cookie Crumbled." *Journal of World Trade* 34 (5): 181–201.

Davis, Benjamin N. 1995. "The Effects of Worker Rights Protections in United States Trade Laws: A Case Study of El Salvador." *American University Journal of International Law and Policy* 10 (3): 1167–1214.

Davis, Terry. 1995. "Cross-Border Organizing Comes Home: UE and FAT in Mexico and Milwaukee." *Labor Research Review* 1 (23): 23–29.

De Buen, Néstor. 1999. "A cinco años del Acuerdo de Cooperación Laboral anexo al Tratado de Libre Comercio." In *Memorias: encuentro trinacional de laboralistas democráticos*, ed. José Alfonso Bouzas Ortíz, 81–93 (Mexico City: Universidad Nacional Autónoma de México).

De la Cruz, Héctor Bartolomei, Geraldo von Potobsky, and Lee Swepston. 1996. *The International Labor Organization: The International Standards System and Basic Human Rights* (Boulder, CO: Westview Press).

De la Mora, Luz María. 2013. "La política comercial de México durante el gobierno del Presidente Felipe Calderón (2006–2012)." *Foro Internacional* 53 (3/4): 794–815.

Delp, Linda, Marisol Arriaga, Guadalupe Palma, Haydee Urita, and Abel Valenzuela. 2004. "NAFTA's Labor Side Agreement: Fading into Oblivion?" Center for Labor Research and Education, Institute of Industrial Relations, University of California-Los Angeles, March.

DePalma, Anthony. 1993. "Vague Mexico Wage Pledge Clouds Free Trade Accord." *New York Times*, September 29.

——. 1994. "Unions Complain of Delays Involving Trade Pact." *New York Times*, March 21.

De Rosenzweig, Francisco. 2012. "México y su ingreso al Acuerdo de Asociación Transpacífico." *Revista de derecho económico internacional* 3 (1): 89–94.

Destler, I. M. 2007. "American Trade Politics 2007: Building Bipartisan Consensus." Policy Brief PB07-5 (Washington, DC: Institute for International Economics).

Dewan, Sabina, and Lucas Roncini. 2018. "U.S. Free Trade Agreements and Enforcement of Labor Law in Latin America." *Industrial Relations* 57 (1): 35–56.

De Wet, Erika. 1995. "Labor Standards in the Globalized Economy: The Inclusion of a Social Clause in the General Agreement on Tariffs and Trade/World Trade Organization." *Human Rights Quarterly* 17 (3): 443–62.

Diamond, Stephen F. 1996. "Labor Rights in the Global Economy: A Case Study of the North American Free Trade Agreement." In *Human Rights, Labor Rights, and International Trade*, ed. Lance A. Compa and Steven F. Diamond, 199–224 (Philadelphia: University of Pennsylvania Press).

Díaz, Luis Miguel. 2004. "Bill to Reform the Mexican Labor Law." *University of Detroit Mercy Law Review* 81 (4): 421–36.

Dibble, Sandra. 1997. "Vote for Union at Maquiladora Draws Accusations." *San Diego Union-Tribune*, October 11.

Dibble, Sandra, and Dean Calbreath. 1997. "Tijuana Workers Win Right to an Independent Union." *San Diego Union-Tribune*, December 17.

DiCaprio, Alisa. 2004. "Are Labor Provisions Protectionist? Evidence from Nine Labor-Augmented U.S. Trade Arrangements." *Comparative Labor Law and Policy Journal* 26 (1): 1–33.

Diebold, William, Jr. 1952. "The End of the ITO." *Essays in International Finance*, no. 16, Department of Economics and Social Institutions, Princeton University.

Dillon, Sam. 1997a. "Accord Would Oust Union Linked to Government at Tijuana Plant." *New York Times*, December 14.

——. 1997b. "After 4 Years of Nafta, Labor is Forging Cross-Border Ties." *New York Times*, December 20.

——. 1998a. "U.S. Labor Leader Seeks Union Support in Mexico." *New York Times*, January 23.

——. 1998b. "Bias Said to Hurt Independent Mexican Unions." *New York Times*, April 30.

——. 1998c. "Abuses Reported in Mexico at American-owned Plant." *New York Times*, August 5.

Dobrusin, Bruno. 2014. "South-South Labor Internationalism: SIGTUR and the Challenges to the Status Quo." *Working USA* 17 (2): 155–67.

Doern, G. Bruce, and Brian W. Tomlin. 1991. *Faith and Fear: The Free Trade Story* (Toronto: Stoddart Publishing).

Dombois, Ranier. 2006. "La regulación laboral internacional en los tratados de libre comercio: El caso del Acuerdo de Cooperación Laboral de América del Norte entre México, Canadá y los Estados Unidos." *Foro Internacional* 46 (4): 741–61.

Dombois, Ranier, and Jens Winter. 2003. *A Matter of Deficient Design? Observations on Interaction and Cooperation Problems in the NAALC* (Bremen: Institut Arbeit und Wirtshaft, University of Bremen).

Domínguez, Jorge I., and Rafael Fernández de Castro. 2001. *The United States and Mexico: Between Partnership and Conflict* (New York: Routledge).

Donahue, Thomas R. 1991. "The Case Against a North American Free Trade Agreement." *Columbia Journal of World Business* 26 (2): 92–96.

Donnelly, Jack. 1986. "International Human Rights: A Regime Analysis." *International Organization* 40 (3): 599–642.

—. 2007. "The Relative Universality of Human Rights." *Human Rights Quarterly* 29 (2): 281–306.

—. 2013. *Universal Human Rights in Theory and Practice*, 3rd ed. (Ithaca, NY: Cornell University Press).

Donohue, Peter. 1992. "'Free Trade' Unions and the State: Trade Liberalization's Endorsement by the AFL-CIO, 1943–1962." In *Research in Political Economy*, ed. Paul Zarembka, vol. 13, 1–73 (Greenwich, CT: JAI Press).

Dorman, Peter. 1989. *Worker Rights and U.S. Trade Policy: An Evaluation of Worker Rights Conditionality under the Generalized System of Preferences* (Washington, DC: U.S. Department of Labor).

—. 1995. *Policies to Promote International Labor Rights: An Analytical Review* (Washington, DC: U.S. Department of Labor).

Douglas, William A., John-Paul Ferguson, and Erin Klett. 2004. "An Effective Confluence of Forces in Support of Workers' Rights: ILO Standards, US Trade Laws, Unions, and NGOs." *Human Rights Quarterly* 26 (2): 273–99.

Doumbia-Henry, Cleopatra, and Eric Gravel. 2006. "Free Trade Agreements and Labour Rights: Recent Developments." *International Labour Review* 145 (3): 185–206.

Dreiling, Michael, and Ian Robinson. 1998. "Union Responses to NAFTA in the US and Canada: Explaining Intra- and International Variation." *Mobilization* 3 (2): 163–84.

Drezner, Daniel W. 2003. "The Hidden Hand of Economic Coercion." *International Organization* 57 (3): 643–59.

Dunning, Harold. 1998. "The Origins of Convention No. 87 on Freedom of Association and the Right to Organize." *International Labour Review* 137 (2): 149–67.

Dunning, Thad. 2015. "Improving Process Tracing: The Case of Multi-method Research." In *Process Tracing: From Metaphor to Analytic Tool*, ed. Andrew Bennett and Jeffrey T. Checkel, 211–36 (Cambridge: Cambridge University Press).

Eade, Deborah. 2004. "International NGOs and Unions in the South: Worlds Apart or Allies in the Struggle?" *Development in Practice* 14 (1/2): 71–84.

Eckstein, Harry. 1975. "Case Study and Theory in Political Science." In *Handbook of Political Science*, vol. 7, *Strategies of Inquiry*, ed. Fred I. Greenstein and Nelson W. Polsby, 79–137 (Reading, MA: Addison-Wesley Publishing Co.).

Economic Policy Institute, Institute for Policy Studies, International Labor Rights Fund, Public Citizen's Global Trade Watch, Sierra Club, and U.S. Business and Industrial Council Education Foundation. 1997. *The Failed Experiment: NAFTA at Three Years* (Washington, DC: Economic Policy Institute, et al.), June 1. http://www.epi.org/content.cfm/studies_failedexp.

Economist. 2017. "Seconds Out." August 19.

——. 2018a. "Renegotiating NAFTA: A Deal Undone." April 28.

——. 2018b. "Trade Negotiations: Puzzle Pieces." June 2.

——. 2018c. "NAFTA: Wheeler Dealer." September 1.

——. 2018d. "Limiting the Damage from The Donald." September 8.

——. 2018e. "North American Trade: Foul Play." December 8.

——. 2019. "The USMCA: Common Ground." December 14.

Edgren, Gus. 1979. "Fair Labour Standards and Trade Liberalisation." *International Labour Review* 118 (5): 523–35.

Elliott, Kimberly Ann. 1998a. "International Labor Standards and Trade: What Should Be Done?" In *Launching New Global Trade Talks*, ed. Jeffrey J. Schott, 165–77 (Washington, DC: Institute for International Economics).

——. 1998b. "Preferences for Workers? Worker Rights and the US Generalized System of Preference." Paper presented at Globalization and Inequality conference, Calvin College, Grand Rapids, MI, May 28, 1998. https://piie.com/commentary/speeches-papers/preferences -workers-worker-rights-and-us-generalized-system-preference.

Elliott, Kimberly A., and Richard B. Freeman. 2003. *Can Labor Standards Improve Under Globalization?* (Washington, DC: Peterson Institute for International Economics).

Enciso L., Angélica. 2019. "México, satisfecho con explicación de EU sobre agregados: Seade." *La Jornada en línea*, December 16.

Englehart, Fredrick. 1997. "Withered Giants: Mexican and U.S. Organized Labor and the North American Agreement on Labor Cooperation." *Case Western Reserve Journal of International Law* 29 (2): 321–88.

Engström, Par. 2017. "Reconceptualising the Impact of the Inter-American Human Rights System." *Revista Direito e Praxis* 8 (2): 1250–85.

Escalante, Jorge. 2021. "Provoca cacique de la CTM protesta de EU ante T-MEC." *Reforma* (online edition), May 13.

Esposito, Anthony. 2019. "Trump, López Obrador Agree to Take Action to Stem Flow of Weapons to Mexico." *U.S. News and World Report* (online edition), October 19.

European Commission. 2017. "Report on Assessment of the Application for GSP+ by Sri Lanka."

European Court on Human Rights (ECHR). 2016a. "Fact-Sheet: Trade Union Rights." Accessed March 27, 2017, http://www.echr.coe.int/Documents/FS_Trade_union_ENG.pdf.

——. 2016b. "Fact-sheet: Slavery, Servitude, and Forced Labour." Accessed March 27, 2017, http://www.echr.coe.int/Documents/FS_Forced_Labour_ENG.pdf.

——. 2017. "Fact-sheet: Work-related Rights." Accessed March 27, 2017, http://www.echr.coe.int /Documents/FS_Work_ENG.pdf.

European Parliament. 1986. "Resolution on the New Round of Multilateral Trade Negotiations Within GATT." *Official Journal of the European Communities* 29 (C255): 69–78.

European Union. 2012. "Regulation (EU) 978/2012 of the European Parliament and of the Council of 25 October 2012, applying a scheme of generalized tariff preferences and repealing Council Regulation (EC) No 732/2008 (2012)." Accessed July 10, 2023. https://eur-lex.europa .eu/legal-content/EN/TXT/?uri=celex%3A32012R0978.

——. 2013. "Commission Delegated Regulation (EU) No 1083/2013 of 28 August 2013 establishing rules related to the procedure for temporary withdrawal of tariff preferences and adoption of general safeguard measures under Regulation (EU) No 978/2012 of the European Parliament and the Council applying a scheme of generalised tariff preferences (2013)." August 28. https://eur-lex.europa.eu/legal-content/EN/TXT/?uri=CELEX%3A32013R1083.

Evans, Peter B. 2000. "Fighting Marginalization with Transnational Networks: Counter-Hegemonic Globalization." *Contemporary Sociology* 29 (1): 230–41.

Evans, Peter B., Dietrich Rueschemeyer, and Theda Skocpol, eds. 1985. *Bringing the State Back In* (Cambridge: Cambridge University Press).

Fairbrother, Malcolm. 2007. "Making Neoliberalism Possible: The State's Organization of Business Support for NAFTA in Mexico." *Politics and Society* 35 (2): 265–300.

Falleti, Tulia G., and Julia F. Lynch. 2009. "Context and Causal Mechanisms in Political Analysis." *Comparative Political Studies* 42 (9): 1143–66.

Farber, Henry S. 1990. "The Decline of Unionization in the United States: What Can Be Learned from Recent Experience?" *Journal of Labor Economics* 8, 1 [pt. 2]: S75–105.

Farnsworth, Clyde H. 1989. "Mosbacher Sees a Free-Trade Pact with Mexico." *New York Times*, October 19.

——. 1993. "3 Nations Disagree on Trade." *New York Times*, May 22.

Favilla-Solano, Teresa R. 1996. "Legal Mechanisms for Enforcing Labor Rights under NAFTA." *University of Hawaii Law Review* 18 (1): 293–338.

Feeley, Dianne. 1990. "Ford Battles Mexican Workers." *Against the Current*, no. 27 (July/Aug.): www.againstthecurrent.org/atc027/mexican-workers/.

Feld, Werner J., and Cheron Brylski. 1983. "A North American Accord: Feasible or Futile." *Political Research Quarterly* 36 (2): 286–311.

Fergusson, Ian F., Mark A. McMinimy, and Brock R. Williams. 2015. *The Trans-Pacific Partnership (TPP): Negotiations and Issues for Congress*. CRS Report R42694, March 20 (Washington, DC: Congressional Research Service).

Fetzer, Thomas. 2010. "The Late Birth of Transnational Labour Cooperation: Cross-Border Trade Union Networks at Ford and General Motors (1953–2001)." *Labour History Review* 75 (1): 76–97.

Fichter, Michael, and Jamie K. McCallum. 2015. "Implementing Global Framework Agreements: The Limits of Social Partnership." *Global Networks* 15 (supplemental issue): S65–S85.

Finbow, Robert G. 2006. *The Limits of Regionalism: NAFTA's Labour Accord* (Aldershot, England: Ashgate Publishing).

Finnemore, Martha, and Kathryn Sikkink. 1998. "International Norm Dynamics and Political Change." *International Organization* 52 (4): 887–917.

Flores, Zenyazen. 2018. "Capítulo laboral de TLCAN deja fuera tema de salarios: Moisés Kalach." *El Financiero* (online edition), February 15.

Follows, John W. 1951. *Antecedents of the International Labour Organization* (Oxford: Clarendon Press).

Foro Jurídico. 2018. "Culminar la reforma laboral reto de la actual administración: Roberto Campa Cifrián." May 23.

Fox, Jonathan. 2004. "Assessing Binational Civil Society Coalitions: Lessons from the Mexico-U.S. Experience." In *Dilemmas of Political Change in Mexico*, ed. Kevin J. Middlebrook, 466–522 (London: Institute of Latin American Studies, University of London / Center for U.S.-Mexican Studies, University of California, San Diego).

Frege, Carola, Edmund Heery, and Lowell Turner. 2004. "The New Solidarity? Trade Union Coalition-Building in Five Countries." In *Varieties of Unionism: Strategies for Union Revitalization in the Global Economy*, ed. Carola Frege and John Kelly, 137–58 (Oxford: Oxford University Press).

Frundt, Henry J. 1996. "Trade and Cross-Border Labor Strategies in the Americas." *Economic and Industrial Democracy* 17 (3): 387–417.

——. 1998. *Trade Conditions and Labor Rights: U.S. Initiatives, Dominican and Central American Responses* (Gainesville: University of Florida Press).

——. 2007. "Organizing in the Banana Sector." In *Global Unions: Challenging Transnational Capital Through Cross-Border Campaigns*, ed. Kate Bronfenbrenner, 99–116 (Ithaca, NY: Cornell University Press).

Gabriel, Christina, and Laura Macdonald. 2021. "New Architectures for Migration Governance: NAFTA and Transnational Activism around Migrants' Rights." *Third World Quarterly* 42 (1): 65–85.

Gacek, Stan. 1999. "The Political Context for the NAALC: The Viewpoint of the AFL-CIO and the U.S. Labor Movement." In *Memorias: encuentro trinacional de laboralistas democráticos*, ed. José Alonso Bouzas Ortiz, 213–19 (Mexico City: Universidad Nacional Autónoma de México).

García de León, Verónica. 2017. "EU y Canadá arremeten contra México en la tercera ronda del TLCAN." *Expansión* (online edition), September 27.

Garciadiego, Javier. 1994. *El TLC día a día: crónica de una negociación* (Mexico City: Miguel Ángel Porrúa).

García Urrutia, Manuel. 2002. "The Authentic Labor Front in the NAFTA-Era Regional Integration Process." In *Cross-Border Dialogues: U.S.-Mexico Social Movement Networking*, ed. David Brooks and Jonathan Fox, 77–86 (La Jolla, CA: Center for U.S.-Mexican Studies, University of California-San Diego).

Gardner, Richard. 1980. *Sterling-Dollar Diplomacy in Current Perspective: The Origins and the Prospects of Our International Economic Order* (New York: Columbia University Press).

Gascón, Verónica. 2019. "Revisarán 550 mil contratos colectivos." *El Norte* (online edition), June 20.

——. 2021. "Consultation in Silao Will Be Free—GM." *El Norte* (online edition), July 20.

——. 2022. "Gana consulta en Panasonic sindicato independiente." *Reforma* (online edition), April 22.

George, Alexander L., and Andrew Bennett. 2005. *Case Studies and Theory Development in the Social Sciences* (Cambridge, MA: MIT Press).

Gernigon, Bernard, Alberto Odero, and Horacio Guido. 1998. "ILO Principles Concerning the Right to Strike." *International Labour Review* 137 (4): 441–81.

Gerring, John. 2004. "What Is a Case Study and What Is It Good For?" *American Political Science Review* 98 (2): 341–54.

——. 2007. *Case Study Research: Principles and Practices* (New York: Cambridge University Press).

Gerstenzang, James. 1993. "Senate Approves NAFTA on 61-38 Vote." *Los Angeles Times*, November 21.

Godoy, Emilio. 2015. "TPP: Leyes nacionales . . . bajo certificación estadounidense." *Proceso* (9 October 9): https://www.proceso.com.mx/417797/tpp-leyes-nacionales-bajo-certificacion-estadunidense.

Goertz, Gary, and James Mahoney. 2012. *A Tale of Two Cultures: Qualitative and Quantitative Research in the Social Sciences* (Princeton, NJ: Princeton University Press).

Golden, Tim. 1992. "Mexico's Leader Seeks to Address Clinton's Concerns on Trade Pact." *New York Times* (electronic edition), November 21.

Golob, Stephanie R. 2003. "Beyond the Policy Frontier: Canada, Mexico, and the Ideological Origins of NAFTA." *World Politics* 55 (3): 361–98.

Golub, Stephen S. 1997. "International Labor Standards and International Trade." IMF Working Paper 97-37 (Washington, DC: International Monetary Fund).

Gómez Quintero, Natalia. 2016. "Congresistas de EU agradecen diálogo con Peña Nieto." *El Universal*, May 3.

Gómez Zuppa, Willebaldo. 2022. "El movimiento de los trabajadores de General Motors-Silao: Una batalla por la libertad sindical, Parte 2." *Revista Común* (online edition), March 14.

González G., Susana. 2019a. "Cámera de Comercio de EU respalda posición de México ante el T-MEC." *La Jornada en línea*, December 5.

——. 2019b. "IP no tuvo acceso a los nuevos textos del T-MEC: Index." *La Jornada en línea*, December 10.

González Graf, Héctor. 2009. *Regional Collective Bargaining in North America: An Alternative for Balancing Trade and Labor Prerogatives* (Saarbrücken, Germany: VDM Verlag Dr. Müller Aktiengesellschaft).

González Torres, Rosana. 2018. *El examen de no embarazo como requisito en la contratación de mujeres en los centros de trabajo* (Tijuana, Mexico: Ediciones ILCSA).

Gordon, Michael E. 2000a. "Export Processing Zones." In *Transnational Cooperation Among Labor Unions*, ed. Michael E. Gordon and Lowell Turner, 60–78 (Ithaca, NY: Cornell University Press/ILR Press).

——. 2000b. "The International Confederation of Free Trade Unions." In *Transnational Cooperation Among Labor Unions*, ed. Michael E. Gordon and Lowell Turner, 81–101 (Ithaca, NY: Cornell University Press / ILR Press).

Gordon, Michael E., and Lowell Turner. 2000. "Going Global." In *Transnational Cooperation Among Labor Unions*, ed. Michael E. Gordon and Lowell Turner, 3–25 (Ithaca, NY: Cornell University Press / ILR Press).

Government of Canada. 1993a. "Canada-Mexico Environment and Labour Agreements." September.

——. 1993b. "North American Agreements on Environmental and Labour Co-Operation: Questions and Answers." September.

——. 1993c. "Highlights of the North American Agreement on Labour Co-operation." Department of External Affairs and International Trade, September.

——. 2003. *NAFTA@10: A Preliminary Report*, Trade and Economic Analysis Division, Department of Foreign Affairs and International Trade, catalogue E2-4871 (Ottawa, Canada).

Government of Costa Rica. 2010. "Statement by the Government of Costa Rica on the Non-Reviewability Under the Provisions of the CAFTA-DR of the Submission Received by the Office of Trade and Labor Affairs, Bureau of International Labor Affairs, U.S. Department of Labor, from the International Longshore and Warehouse Union, Coast Longshore Division, the Sindicato de Trabajadores de la Junta Administradora Portuaria de la Vertiente Atlántica (SINTRAJAP) and the Asociación Nacional de Empleados Públicos y Privados (ANEP)." September 16.

Graubart, Jonathan. 2002. "Giving Teeth to NAFTA's Labor Side Agreement." In *Linking Trade, Environment, and Social Cohesion: NAFTA Experiences, Global Challenges*, ed. John J. Kirkton and Virginia W. Maclaren, 203–22 (Aldershot, England: Ashgate Publishing).

—. 2008. *Legalizing Transnational Activism: The Struggle to Gain Social Change from NAFTA's Citizen Petitions* (University Park: Pennsylvania State University Press).

Grayson, George W. 1995. *The North American Free Trade Agreement: Regional Community and the New World Order* (Lanham, MD: University Press of America).

Greenhill, Brian, Layna Mosley, and Aseem Prakash. 2009. "Trade-Based Diffusion of Labor Rights: A Panel Study, 1986–2002." *American Political Science Review* 103 (4): 669–90.

Greenhouse, Steven. 2001. "Labor Abuses in El Salvador Are Detailed in Document." *New York Times*, May 10.

—. 2013a. "Bangladesh to Lose U.S. Trade Privileges." *International Herald Tribune*, June 28.

—. 2013b. "Bangladesh Amends Labor Law but Critics See Its Constraints." *International Herald Tribune*, July 18.

Greenhouse, Steven, and Joseph Kahn. 1999. "U.S. Effort to Add Labor Standards to Agenda Fails." *New York Times*, December 3.

Grimm, Nicole L. 1999. "The North American Agreement on Labor Cooperation and its Effects on Women Working in Mexican Maquiladoras." *American University Law Review* 48 (1): 179–227.

Gruber, Lloyd. 2000. *Ruling the World: Power Politics and the Rise of Supranational Institutions* (Princeton, NJ: Princeton University Press).

Gutiérrez, Ramón. 2007. "George W. Bush and Mexican Immigration Policy." *Revue française d'études américaines* 113 (3): 70–76.

Guzmán, Susana. 2018. "Aprueba Senado convenio sobre libertad sindical de la OIT." *El Financiero* (online edition), September 20.

Hafner-Burton, Emilie M. 2005. "Trading Human Rights: How Preferential Trade Agreements Influence Government Repression." *International Organization* 59 (3): 593–629.

—. 2009. *Forced to Be Good: Why Trade Agreements Boost Human Rights* (Ithaca, NY: Cornell University Press).

—. 2013. *Making Human Rights a Reality* (Princeton, NJ: Princeton University Press).

Hafner-Burton, Emilie M., Layna Mosley, and Robert Galantucci. 2019. "Protecting Workers Abroad and Industries at Home: Rights-Based Conditionality in Trade Preference Programs." *Journal of Conflict Resolution* 63 (5): 1253–82.

Hakobyan, Shushanik, and John McLaren. 2016. "Looking for Local Labor Market Effects of NAFTA." *Review of Economics and Statistics* 98 (4): 742–55.

Hale, Angela. 2004. "Beyond the Barriers: New Forms of Labour Internationalism." *Development in Practice* 14 (1/2): 158–62.

Hall, Rodney Bruce. 1997. "Moral Authority as a Power Resource." *International Organization* 51: 591–622.

Hancké, Bob. 2000. "European Works Councils and Industrial Restructuring in the European Motor Industry." *European Journal of Industrial Relations* 6 (1): 35–59.

Hansson, Göte. 1983. *Social Clauses and International Trade: An Economic Analysis of Labour Standards in Trade Policy* (London: Croom Helm).

Hart, Michael. 2002. *A Trading Nation: Canadian Trade Policy from Colonialism to Globalization* (Vancouver, British Columbia: UBC Press).

Harvey, Pharis J. n.d. "U.S. GSP Labor Rights Conditionality: 'Aggressive Unilateralism' or a Forerunner to a Multilateral Social Clause?" (Washington, DC: International Labor Rights Fund).

Harvey, Pharis, Terry Collingsworth, and Bama Athrey. 2000. *Developing Effective Mechanisms for Implementing Labor Rights in the Global Economy* (Washington, DC: International Labor Rights Fund).

Hathaway, Dale A. 2000. *Allies Across the Border: Mexico's "Authentic Labor Front" and Global Solidarity* (Cambridge, MA: South End Press).

Hayden, Tom, and Lori Wallach. 2004. "Kerry's Trade Winds." *Nation* (online edition), September 30.

Hecker, Steven. 1993. "US Unions, Trade and International Solidarity: Emerging Issues and Tactics." *Economic and Industrial Democracy* 14 (3): 355-67.

Heintz, James, and Stephanie Luce. 2010. *Trade Agreements and Labor Standards: The Impact of Trade Negotiations on Country Adoption of Freedom of Association and Collective Bargaining* (Washington, DC: Bureau of International Labor Affairs, U.S. Department of Labor).

Helfen, Markus, and Michael Fichter. 2013. "Building Transnational Union Networks Across Global Production Networks: Conceptualizing a New Arena of Labour-Management Relations." *British Journal of Industrial Relations* 51 (3): 553-76.

Helfer, Laurence R. 2006. "Understanding Change in International Organizations: Globalization and Innovation in the ILO." *Vanderbilt Law Review* 59 (3): 649-726.

Hernández, Érika. 2018. "Cree Campa en extra para ley secundaria." *Reforma* (online edition), May 1.

Hernández Felix, Enrique. 1999. "La alianza del PAN con los charros sindicales." *La Jornada* (*Masiosare* supplement), November 21.

Herod, Andrew. 1995. "The Practice of International Labor Solidarity and the Geography of the Global Economy." *Economic Geography* 71 (October): 341-64.

——. 2000. "Implications of Just-in-Time Production for Union Strategy: Lessons from the 1998 General Motors-United Auto Workers Dispute." *Annals of the Association of American Geographers* 90 (3): 521-47.

Hertel, Shareen. 2006. *Unexpected Power: Conflict and Change among Transnational Activists* (Ithaca, NY: Cornell University Press).

Herzenberg, Stephen A., ed. 1996a. *International Labor Rights and Standards after NAFTA: A Symposium* (New Brunswick, NJ: Rutgers Labor Education Center).

——. 1996b. "Calling Maggie's Bluff: The NAFTA Labor Agreement and the Development of an Alternative to Neoliberalism." *Canadian-American Public Policy* 28: 1-35.

Herzstein, Robert E. 1995. "The Labor Cooperation Agreement Among Mexico, Canada and the United States: Its Negotiation and Prospects." *United States-Mexico Law Journal* 3: 121-31.

Hirsch, Barry T. 2008. "Sluggish Institutions in a Dynamic World: Can Unions and Industrial Competition Coexist?" *Journal of Economic Perspectives* 22 (1): 153-76.

Hoffman, Stanley. 1966. "Obstinate or Obsolete? The Fate of the Nation-State and the Case of Western Europe." *Daedalus* 95 (3): 862-915.

Hopgood, Stephen. 2014. "The Last Rights for Humanitarian Intervention: Darfur, Sri Lanka and R2P." *Global Responsibility to Protect* 6 (2): 181-205.

Hopgood, Stephen, Jack Snyder, and Leslie Vinjamuri, eds. 2017. *Human Rights Futures* (Cambridge: Cambridge University Press).

Hornbeck, John F. 2003. "The U.S.-Chile Free Trade Agreement: Economic and Trade Policy Issues." Congressional Research Service Report RL31144 (Washington, DC: Congressional Research Service).

——. 2009. "Free Trade Agreements: U.S. Promotion and Oversight of Latin American Implementation." Policy Brief IDB-PB-102 (Washington, DC: Inter-American Development Bank). [on US pressures to adopt labor reforms prior to FTAs]

House Democratic Working Group on NAFTA 2.0. 2019. "Status and Progress Report to the Speaker." July 26 (Washington, DC).

Housman, Robert F., and Paul M. Orbuch. 1993. "Integrating Labor and Environmental Concerns into the North American Free Trade Agreement: A Look Back and a Look Ahead." *American University Journal of International Law and Policy* 8 (4): 719–816.

Howse, Robert. 1999. "The World Trade Organization and the Protection of Workers' Rights." *Journal of Small and Emerging Business Law* 3 (1): 131–72.

Hualde, Alfredo. 1996. "Las relaciones laborales en la maquiladora y la búsqueda gerencial del compromiso y la calidad." In *Integración regional y relaciones industriales en América del Norte*, ed. Graciela Bensusán and Arnulfo Arteaga, 303–14 (Mexico City: Universidad Autónoma Metropolitana-Iztapalapa and Facultad Latinoamericana de Ciencias Sociales-Sede México).

Huberman, Michael. 2012. *Odd Couple: International Trade and Labor Standards in History* (New Haven, CT: Yale University Press).

Hufbauer, Gary Clyde, and Jeffrey J. Schott. 2005. *NAFTA Revisited: Achievements and Challenges* (Washington, DC: Institute for International Economics).

Hughes, Steve, and Nigel Haworth. 2011. *The International Labour Organisation (ILO): Coming in from the Cold* (Abingdon, England: Routledge).

Hulse, Carl, and Emily Cochrane. 2019. "Progress that Impeachment May Not Impede." *New York Times International Edition*, October 9.

Human Rights Watch/Americas. 1996a. "Mexico, Labor Rights, and NAFTA: A Case Study." *Human Rights Watch/Americas* 8 (8B), September.

——. 1996b. "No Guarantees: Sex Discrimination in Mexico's Maquiladora Sector." *Human Rights Watch/Americas* 8 (6B), October.

——. 1998. "A Job or Your Rights: Continued Sex Discrimination in Mexico's Maquiladora Sector." *Human Rights Watch/Americas* 10 (1B), December.

——. 2001. "Trading Away Rights: The Unfulfilled Promise of NAFTA's Labor Side Agreement." *Human Rights Watch/Americas*, April 13 (2B).

Huneeus, Alexandra. 2010. "Rejecting the Inter-American Court: Judicialization, National Courts, and Regional Human Rights." In *Cultures of Legality: Judicialization and Political Activism in Latin America*, ed. Javier Couso, Alexandra Huneeus, and Rachel Sieder, 112–38 (Cambridge: Cambridge University Press).

Huxley, Christopher. 2003. "Local Union Responses to Continental Standardization of Production and Work in GM's North American Truck Assembly Plants." In *Multinational Companies and Global Human Resource Strategies*, ed. William N. Cook, 223–47 (Westport, CT: Quorum Books).

Hyman, Richard. 2005. "Shifting Dynamics in International Trade Unionism: Agitation, Organization, Bureacracy, Diplomacy." *Labor History* 46 (2): 137–54.

——. 2010. "Trade Unions, Global Competition and Options for Solidarity." In *Global Restructuring, Labour, and the Challenges for Transnational Solidarity*, ed. Andreas Bieler and Ingemar Lindberg, 16–30 (New York: Routledge).

Ifill, Gwen. 1992. "With Reservations, Clinton Endorses Free-Trade Pact." *New York Times*, 5 October 5.

IndustriALL. 2018. "Se hace justicia: México ratifica C98 de la OIT." September 24, 2018. http://www.industriall-union.org/es/senado-de-mexico-ratifica-por-unanimidad-el-convenio-98-de-la-oit.

——. 2022a. "Trabajadores de Saint Gobain rechazan contrato de protección en México." July 8.

——. 2022b. "Sindicato independiente gana la representación sindical en Saint Gobain México." September 30.

Inside U.S. Trade (IUST) (online and print editions):

—September 4, 1992. "Mexicans Hold Consultations with Clinton-Gore Campaign on Status of NAFTA."

—January 29, 1993. "NAM Proposes Narrow Scope for NAFTA Side Deal on Safeguards."

—February 12, 1993. "Kantor and Serra Puche to Discuss NAFTA Timetable in February 17 Meeting."

—February 19, 1993a. "Text: AFL-CIO NAFTA Statement."

— February 19, 1993b. "AFL-CIO Reiterates Opposition to NAFTA, Calls for Far-Reaching Changes in Text."

—March 5, 1993a. "Confidential White House Draft Details Options for NAFTA Labor Side Pact."

—March 8, 1993. "Confidential White House Draft Details Options for NAFTA Labor Side Pact."

—March 12, 1993. "U.S. Nixes Enforcement Role for NAFTA Panels, Wants Mexican Practices Altered."

—April 2, 1993. "Initial U.S. Presentation on NAFTA Labor Accord Is Silent on Trade Sanctions."

—April 23, 1993. "Drafting of Bracketed Text for NAFTA Side Accords to Begin Early Next Month."

—May 7, 1993a. "NAFTA Deputies Meet to Prepare for Exchange of Draft Legal Texts of Side Pacts."

—May 7, 1993b. "U.S. Backs Link Between Wages, Productivity Gains in North America, USTR Says."

—May 14, 1993. "Canadian Approach on NAFTA Labor Pact Would Use Publicity, Cooperation."

—May 21, 1993a. "U.S. Draft Legal Text for NAFTA Labor Accord."

—May 21, 1993b. "Text: Canadian Draft Text for NAFTA Labor Accord."

—May 21, 1993c. "Text: Mexican Draft Legal Text for NAFTA Labor Pact."

—May 21, 1993d. "U.S. Draft Texts for NAFTA Side Pacts Include Difficult-to-Reach Sanctions."

May 24, 1993, U.S.-Backed Sanctions, Strong Commission Absent from Canadian NAFTA Texts.

—May 26, 1993. "Chamber Criticizes NAFTA Side Deals, Alleges Failure to Consult Business."

—May 28, 1993. "Text: Republican Letter to Clinton on NAFTA Side Accords;" "Text: Republican Follow-On Letter to Clinton on NAFTA Side Pacts."

—June 4, 1993a. "House Democrats to Warn Clinton that NAFTA Side Pacts Must Be Credible."

—June 4, 1993b. "Mexico May Offer New Ideas to Move Toward Compromise on NAFTA Side Deals."

—June 11, 1993. "Industry Letter to Kantor on NAFTA Side Accords."

—June 18, 1993. "Senators to Propose Child-Labor Ban for NAFTA Labor Pact."

—July 9, 1993. "NAFTA Negotiators Seek Breakthrough in Environmental, Labor Talks."

—July 23, 1993. "NAFTA Chiefs Craft Single Text, as Ministers Prepare Final Bargains."

—July 30, 1993a. "Administration Faces Struggle over Timing of NAFTA Implementation."

—July 30, 1993b. "USTR Officials Say Ministerial Will Not Wrap Up NAFTA Side Deals."

— August 13, 1993a. "Gephardt and Baucus Letter on NAFTA Side Pacts."

—August 13, 1993b. "NAFTA Labor Side Agreement Likely to Offer Weak Enforcement."

—August 13, 1993c. "U.S., Canada Attempt to Break Impasse Over NAFTA Side Accords."

—August 16, 1993. "Gephardt Criticizes NAFTA Side Accord as 'Not Supportable.'"

—September 3, 1993. "AFL-CIO Says NAFTA Labor Pact Limits U.S. Enforcement Powers Abroad."

—September 17, 1993a. "Bonior Says Republican Opposition to NAFTA in House on the Rise."

—September 17, 1993b. "Clinton, Ex-Presidents Kick Off Bipartisan Pro-NAFTA Campaign."

—September 24, 1993. "Gephardt Announces Opposition to NAFTA, Plans 'Active' Role."

—October 22, 1993a. "Kantor Letter on NAFTA Effect on U.S. Sovereignty."

—October 22, 1993b. "Labor Dept. Vows NAFTA Worker Package Won't Repeat TAA Mistakes."

—November 12, 1993. "Administration Pledges to Exit NAFTA If Side Pacts Are Abandoned."

—March 4, 1994. "U.S., NAFTA Labor Rules Too Focused on Disputes, Trade Group Says."

—November 28, 1997. "Hotly Disputed Mexican Union Case to be Reviewed by U.S. Officials."

—January 22, 1998. "U.S. Labor Leader Speaks in Mexico City."

—February 6, 1998. "AFL-CIO Chief Seeks New Cooperation with Mexican Labor Unions."

—May 10, 2007. "Congressional Democrats, Republicans Move Close to Deal on Labor, FTA Issues."

—January 11, 2008. "Democratic Presidential Candidates Signal Changes in Trade Policy."

—February 27, 2008. "Clinton, Obama Pledge to Withdraw from NAFTA Unless Renegotiated."

—August 15, 2008. "Democrats in Platform Seek to Finish Doha, Amend NAFTA."

—August 13, 2010. "U.S., Costa Rican Unions Seek CAFTA Consultations for Labor Violations."

—September 20 2010. "Labor Department Notifies Union of Plans to Delay Decision on Costa Rica Labor Complaint to April 2011."

—September 21, 2010. "Costa Rican Labor Minister: U.S. Labor Dept. Delaying Decision on CAFTA Complaint."

—September 24, 2010. "Costa Rican Trade Minister says U.S. Will Delay Decision on Labor Complaint."

—May 6, 2011. "DOL Closes Costa Rica Labor Case After Union Withdraws Petition."

—December 16, 2011. "Mexico Expects TPP Countries to Consider New Entrants at March Round."

—December 14, 2012. "Canada Pushes Alternative Enforcement for TPP Labor Rights Obligations."

—May 23, 2013. "Canada Tables Alternative Enforcement Mechanism in TPP Labor Chapter."

—May 29, 2014. "153 House Democrats Sign Final Letter to Froman Asking for Enforceable Labor Plans in Four TPP Countries."

—January 6, 2015. "Trumka Calls on U.S. TPP Negotiators to Demand Mexican Labor Law Changes in Letter to Obama."

—August 21, 2015. "Mexican Official Says Bilateral Discussions with U.S. on Labor Issues Not Linked to TPP Conclusion."

—August 25, 2015. "Mexican Official Says Possible Labor Reforms Not Tied to TPP Conclusion."

—October 3, 2015. "U.S. Seeking Enforceable Labor Consistency Plans with Select TPP Nations."

—October 7, 2015. "Levin Points to Lack of Mexico Labor Deal in TPP as 'Unsatisfactory,' Says Vote Not Expected Before Spring 2016."

—October 9, 2015a. "Two House Dems Blast TPP in Floor Remarks, Call for Immediate Release of Text."

—October 9, 2015b. "State Dept. Spokesman Shrugs Off Questions about Clinton's Stance on TPP, Reiterates Kerry's Support."

—January 13, 2016. "At ITC Hearing, AFL-CIO Blasts CGE Model; Says TPP's Labor Rules Will Not Be Enforced."

—January 14, 2016. "DeLauro Says TPP Details Will Fuel More Successful Fight Than TPA."

—February 3, 2016. "CWA: Reliance on GOP-Friendly Groups for TPP Undermines 'Progressive' Claims."

—February 18, 2016. "Levin Opposes TPP 'As Negotiated,' Citing Four Key Shortcomings."

—February 19, 2016. "Levin Signals Hope that Clinton Could Get Better TPP Deal for Democrats."

—May 12, 2016. "Mexico Unveils Labor Reforms on Conciliation Boards, Employer Contracts."

—August 25, 2017. "Canadian Unions Expect Government to Push for ILO Ratifications in NAFTA."

—September 22, 2017. "NAFTA TPL Talks to Continue in Ottawa; Supporters Present United Front."

—September 22, 2017a. "Guajardo: As Many as 13 NAFTA Chapters Will Be Difficult to Navigate."

—September 22, 2017b. "USW Executive Slams Right-to-Work Laws, Commends Canadian NAFTA Proposal."

—September 22, 2017c. "Videgaray: Addressing Labor in NAFTA is in Mexico's Best Interest."

—September 28, 2017. "Peruvian Unions Ask U.S. to Convene Labor Consultations under Trade Deal."

—September 29, 2017a. "Mexican Official Says 'Substantive Challenges' Ahead in NAFTA Round Four."

—September 29, 2017b. "Levin Says No Democratic Support for NAFTA without Mexican Labor Reform."

—October 13, 2017. "Lighthizer Meets with Democrats on NAFTA Amid GOP, Business Wariness."

—October 27, 2017a. "Senators Say Trump Called NAFTA Withdrawal Threat a 'Negotiating Tactic.'"

—October 27, 2017b. "Trump: U.S. NAFTA Negotiators Must 'Get Tougher' to Win a Better Deal; Chances are 'Good.'"

—November 3, 2017a. "Pascrell: Lighthizer Meeting with Democrats Was 'Honest Talk About Trade,'"

—November 3, 2017b. "Report: Latin American, Caribbean Trade Rebounding in 2017; All Eyes on NAFTA."

—November 17, 2017. "Senate Democrats Call on USTR to Modify NAFTA Labor Chapter Language."

—November 24, 2017. "USTR Updates NAFTA Objectives, Wyden Lifts Hold on Nominees."

—December 8, 2017a. "Trump Talks NAFTA with GOP Senators as Withdrawal-Threat Concerns Grow."

—December 8, 2017b. "Verheul: Canada 'Struggling' to Figure Out What U.S. Needs for NAFTA 'Win.'"

—January 5, 2018. "Lawmakers, Labor Advocates Call on Trump to Prioritize Enforcement in 2018."

—January 19, 2018a. "NAFTA Ministers Shuffle Sixth Round Schedule, Set Ministerial a Day Later."

—January 19, 2018b. "USTR Nominees Face Questions on NAFTA Proposals, China Trade."

—January 19, 2018c. "Trump Tweets: 'NAFTA is a Bad Joke.'"

—January 26, 2018. "Canada, Mexico Hope for U.S. Flexibility as Auto Negotiators Meet."

—February 2, 2018. "No Indication USTR Will Push for NAFTA Labor Standards that Exceed TPP."

—February 9, 2018. "Lighthizer Defends Engagement with Congress in Ways and Means Briefing."

—February 23, 2018a. "Union Leaders Say Meeting with Trump Was 'Productive.'"

—February 23, 2018b. "Minister: Mexican Labor Standards Will Not Stymie NAFTA Progress."

—March 2, 2018. "Sources: U.S. Won't Make a New Labor Offer during Mexico City Round."

—March 9, 2018. "Labor Discussions Fall Short of Democrats' Expectations in Mexico City."

—March 30, 2018a. "Sources: Lighthizer Pushed NAFTA Parties for Agreement by March 31."

—March 30, 2018b. "Labor Sources: Mexican Bill Could Undermine New NAFTA Standards."

—April 6, 2018a. "USTR Scraps Official NAFTA Round Eight This Week, Hosts Ministerial."

— April 6, 2018b. "USW President Calls on USTR to Oppose 'Regressive' Mexican Labor Bill."

— April 6, 2018c. "NAFTA Auto Rules of Origin Talks Center on 'Focused Value' Approach."

—April 20, 2018. "NAFTA Ministers Gather in DC, But No Major Announcement Expected."

—April 23, 2018. "Labor Department Calls on Peru to Fully Comply with Standards in U.S.-Peru Agreement."

—April 27, 2018. "Sources: New U.S. NAFTA Labor Text Clarifies May 10, CAFTA Language."

—May 4, 2018. "Freeland Extended DC Stay for NAFTA; New Dems Cite Tough Road Ahead."

—June 22, 2018. "Perdue: USTR Aiming for NAFTA Deal with Mexico First, Then Canada."

—July 6, 2018. "Ways and Means Dems Remain Wary of Administration's NAFTA Approach."

—July 27, 2018. "In Letter to Trump, Mexico's President-elect Calls for Resumption of Trilateral NAFTA Talks."

—August 10, 2018. "Sources: U.S., Mexico to Discuss Sector-Specific ISDS Option This Week."

—August 17, 2018. "Kudlow: U.S. 'Getting Close' to a Deal with Mexico."

—August 31, 2018a. "USTR Plans to Notify Congress of Mexico Bilateral if Canada Doesn't Join."

—August 31, 2018b. "Levin: Little Chance of Dem Support for Labor Provisions in Mexico Deal."

—September 7, 2018. "Trudeau: Chapter 19, Cultural Exemptions Are NAFTA Red Lines for Canada."

—October 5, 2018a. "USMCA Auto Rules to be Staged in Over Three Years, Extension Possible."

—October 5, 2018b. "Advisory Panels Cite USMCA Labor Upgrades, Need for Mexican Legislation."

—October 19, 2018. "Seade: Mexico Asked for Cultural Exemption after Canada Got One."

—November 2, 2018a. "Stakeholders Ask ITC to Carefully Consider Impacts of USMCA's Auto Rules."

—November 2, 2018b. "AFL-CIO Has 'Serious Doubts' that Labor Rules in USMCA Will Be Effective."

—November 30, 2018a. "GOP Senators Urge Trump to Trigger USMCA Vote During Lame Duck."

—November 30, 2018b. "After 'Excellent' Meeting with USTR, Pascrell Weighs Prospects for USMCA."

—November 30, 2018c. "AFL-CIO Tells ITC that USMCA's Labor Provisions are 'Weaker' than TPP's."

—December 5, 2018. "Outside Voices: How a Split Congress Might 'Fix' USMCA."

—December 7, 2018a. "Lighthizer: 'No Doubt' Democrats Will Support Passage of USMCA."

—December 7, 2018b. "Trump: 'I Will Be Formally Terminating NAFTA.'"

—December 14, 2018. "Sources: Administration Eyeing NAFTA Withdrawal Any Day."

—January 18, 2019. "Mexico's 2019 Budget Proposal Has No Funds for Labor Reform."

—February 1, 2019. "Ways and Means Trade Panel Members Say USMCA Vote Is Far Off, Uncertain."

—March 8, 2019. "Grassley: Resolve 232 Tariffs First, Then Address Democrats' USMCA Concerns."

—March 15, 2019a. "Mexican Economy, Labor Ministers in DC to Discuss USMCA, 232 with USTR."

—March 15, 2019b. "Analysts: Mexico Not Prepared to Engage with U.S. Congress on USMCA."

—March 22, 2019a. "Sources: Trump Still 'Blocking' Section 232 Steel, Aluminum Resolution."

—March 22, 2019b. "AFL-CIO Opposes Current USMCA, Urges Congress Not to Vote 'Prematurely.'"

—March 22, 2019c. "House Ways and Means Trade Panel to Hold Labor Hearing Next Week."

—March 29, 2019a. "Ways and Means Trade Panel Looks for a USMCA Labor Enforcement Solution."

—March 29, 2019b. "After Meeting with Trump, GOP Lawmakers Eye Summer Passage of USMCA."

—April 5, 2019. "Wyden, Brown Pitch USMCA 'Labor Cooperation' Mechanism."

—April 12, 2019a. "Kind: Dems Need Better Explanation Why USMCA Shouldn't Be Re-opened."

—April 12, 2019b. "Mexican Official: Congress to Pass USMCA Labor Bill This Week."

—April 12, 2019c. "Wyden, Brown Pitch USMCA 'Labor Cooperation' Mechanism."

—April 26, 2019a. "Trumka Says Lighthizer Still Pushing Section 301 as USMCA Enforcement Tool."

—April 26, 2019b. "Democrats Unmoved on USMCA after ITC Projects Moderate Economic Gains."

—April 26, 2019c. "ITC Cites Digital, Auto Provisions in Finding USMCA Will Be Lift to U.S. Economy."

—May 3, 2019a. "Cuellar Touts Comparison of Mexican Labor Reforms to USMCA Commitments."

—May 3, 2019b. "Democrats Laud Mexico's Labor Reform Bill, Remain Wary about Enforcement."

—June 21, 2019a. "Mexico Ratifies USMCA."

—June 21, 2019b. "Senators Press Lighthizer on Use of Section 301, Broader USMCA Concerns."

—June 28, 2019a. "Trump Says He Is Ready to Make 'Minor Changes' to USMCA to Mollify Dems."

—June 28, 2019b. "Mexican Government Outlines Labor Reform 'Roadmap.'"

—July 5, 2019. "Grassley: USMCA Changes Needed for House Approval, Deal Can't Be Re-Opened."

—July 18, 2019. "Blumenauer: USMCA Codel Seeking Clarity on Mexican Labor Roadmap."

—July 19, 2019. "Bill to Establish Independent Labor Secretariat to be Introduced This Week."

—July 26, 2019a. "Rep. Murphy: Mexico Visit Was Productive, Included Seasonal Produce Talks."

—July 26, 2019b. "DeLauro Says Trip to Mexico 'Illuminated' USMCA Concerns."

—August 2, 2019a. "USTR 'Rapid-response' USMCA Plan Pulls from Wyden-Brown Draft."

— August 2, 2019b. "USMCA Working Group to Send Detailed Text to USTR Next Week."

—August 2, 2019c. "USTR, Citing Illegal Logging, Bans Timber from Peruvian Mill."

—August 2, 2019d. "USMCA Working Group Members: Panel-blocking Issues Still Not Resolved."

—August 9, 2019a. "USTR Submits Counterproposals to USMCA Working Group Staff."

—August 9, 2019b. "Mexico, Canada Form USMCA Labor Working Group."

—September 13, 2019a. "USTR Submits Formal Counterproposal to House USMCA Working Group."

—September 13, 2019b. "AFL-CIO: Mexico's Labor Budget Proposals 'Alarming,' Unsatisfactory."

—September 13, 2019c. "Official: Mexico 'Totally' Opposed to Facility Inspections as Part of USMCA."

—September 27, 2019a. "Neal: Working Group Shares AFL-CIO Concerns on Labor Reform Funding."

— September 27, 2019b. "Pelosi Urges Democrats to Continue USMCA Work Amid Impeachment Probe."

—October 4, 2019. "Neal: USTR 'Favorably' Received USMCA Working Group's Counterproposal."

—October 11, 2019a. "AFL-CIO's Trumka Warns Against USMCA Vote Before Thanksgiving."

—October 11, 2019b. "New USMCA Labor Proposal Requires Pre-Ratification Actions by Mexico."

—October 25, 2019. "Mexican President Commits to Increased Spending on USMCA Labor Reforms."

—November 1, 2019a. "Pascrell, Citing Lack of Specifics from Mexico, Says He's 'Leaning No' on USMCA."

—November 1, 2019b. "Trumka Likens Mexican Labor Reform Budget Plan to 'Voodoo Economics.'"

—November 8, 2019. "Seade: Mexico, Canada Must Review Deal Between USTR, House Democrats."

—November 18, 2019. "Mexican Budget Watch."

—November 22, 2019. "McConnell: Democrats Leaving USMCA's Fate to 'Special Interest' Labor Groups."

—November 29, 2019a. "Seade: 'Addendum' to USMCA Will Fix Panel-Blocking Loophole."

—November 29, 2019b. "Mexico to Send Communiqué to Congress Urging No Further UAMCA Delays."

—November 29, 2019c. "Mexico Approves Budget with Boost to USMCA-Required Labor Resources."

—November 29, 2019d. "Trump: Pelosi Being Manipulated by AFL-CIO President."

— November 29, 2019e. "Neal to Send USTR Counterproposals to USMCA, Cites Progress in Talks."

—December 5, 2019. "Rep. Cuellar Hints at New Wrench Thrown into U.S.-Mexico USMCA Talks."

—December 6, 2019a. "Seade: Little Progress on USMCA After a Day of Meetings with Lighthizer."

—December 6, 2019b. "Major Mexican Business Group Rejects Some of U.S. USMCA Labor Proposals."

—December 6, 2019c. "Seade: USMCA Talks 'On the Way to Resolution' After New USTR Proposals."

—December 13, 2019a. "At USMCA Signing, Seade Touts Omission of Labor-Inspections Language."

—December 13, 2019b. "McConnell: Senate USMCA Vote Likely after Impeachment Trial Next Year."

—December 13, 2019c. "PhRMA, Machinists Union Headline List of Groups Opposed to USMCA."

—December 13, 2019d. "Eyeing a Vote Next Week, House Democrats Unveil USMCA Changes."

—December 13, 2019e. "AFL-CIO Endorses Modified USMCA."

—December 19, 2019. "House Overwhelmingly Approves USMCA, Sending Bill to Senate."

—January 17, 2020. "Senate Passes USMCA 89-10."

—January 24, 2020. "López Obrador Issues Decree Approving USMCA Addendum."

—March 20, 2020. "Canada Ratifies USMCA."

—May 14, 2021. "Democrats Laud AFL-CIO USMCA Complaint Against Mexican Auto Factory."

—June 11, 2021. "USTR, Labor to Pursue AFL-CIO USMCA Complaint Against Mexican Auto Plant."

—August 13, 2021. "U.S., Tridonex Reach a Deal Under USMCA Rapid Response Mechanism."

—August 27, 2021. "GM Workers in Mexico Reject 'Protection' Union Following USMCA Action."

—October 15, 2021. "Ways and Means Democrats Urge Tai to Prioritize Labor Protection at MC12."

—October 29, 2021. "Democrats Call for Probe into Reports of Forced Labor in Dominican Sugar."

—February 4, 2022. "AFL-CIO Hails Mexican Union Vote 'Made Possible' by USMCA."

—May 4, 2022. "USTR: USMCA Rapid-Response Tool Key to Future Trade Policy."

—May 20, 2022. "USTR Calls for USMCA Labor Review of Panasonic Facility in Mexico."

—June 10, 2022. "U.S. Wants Mexico to Conduct a Labor Review at Another Auto Parts Facility."

Instituto Nacional Electoral (INE). 2021. "Informe que presenta el Secretario Ejecutivo al Consejo General del Instituto Nacional Electoral sobre la misión de observación en la reposición del procedimiento de legitimación del contrato colectivo de trabajo en la planta de General Motors en Silao, Guanajuato, cuya votación se celebró los días 17 y 18 de agosto de 2021." September 1.

International Confederation of Free Trade Unions (ICFTU). 1997. *Internationally-Recognized Core Labour Standards in Paraguay: Report for the WTO General Council Review of the Trade Policies of Paraguay* (Geneva: ICFTU).

International Labor Rights Education and Research Fund (ILRERF). 1988. *Trade's Hidden Costs: Worker Rights in a Changing World Economy* (Washington, DC: ILRERF).

——. 1993. "To the United States Trade Representative: Petition/Request for Review of the GSP Status of Mexico under GSP Worker Rights Provisions." June 1.

International Labor Rights Forum (ILRF). 2015. *Our Voices, Our Safety: Bangladeshi Garment Workers Speak Out*. December (Washington, DC: ILRF).

International Labour Office (ILO). 2016. *Application of International Labour Standards 2016* (I), 105th session of the International Labour Conference (Geneva: ILO).

—. 2005. *ILO-IPEC in Pakistan: Achievements of a Decade [1994–2004]* (Geneva: ILO).

—. 2015. *Social Dimensions of Free Trade Agreements.* Rev. ed. (Geneva: International Institute for Labour Studies, ILO).

—. 2016. *Assessment of Labour Provisions in Trade and Investment Agreements* (Geneva: ILO).

International Lawyers Assisting Workers Network. 2020. "Amicus Brief Concerning the Amparos against Mexican Labor Law Reforms." June 23.

International Trade Union Confederation. 2018. "Bangladesh: Complaint to the European Ombudsman." June 8. https://www.ituc-csi.org/bangladesh-complaint-to-the.

Jenkins, Rhys. 2002. "The Political Economy of Codes of Conduct." In *Corporate Responsibility and Labour Rights: Codes of Conduct in the Global Economy*, ed. Rhys Jenkins, Ruth Pearson, and Gill Seyfang, 13–30 (London: Earthscan).

Jessup, David, and Michael E. Gordon. 2000. "Organizing in Export Processing Zones: The Bibong Experience in the Dominican Republic." In *Transnational Cooperation among Labor Unions*, ed. Michael E. Gordon and Lowell Turner, 179–201 (Ithaca, NY: Cornell University Press/ILR Press).

Jiménez, Néstor. 2020. "Aprueba Conasami incremento de 15 percent al salario mínimo." *La Jornada en línea*, December 17.

Jiménez, Néstor, and Alonso Urrutia. 2019. "AMLO: México ya cumplió con TMEC; toca ratificar a Congreso de EU." *La Jornada en línea*, November 25.

Johns, Rebecca A. 1998. "Bridging the Gap between Class and Space: U.S. Worker Solidarity with Guatemala." *Economic Geography* 74 (3): 252–71.

Jones, Vivian C. 2015. *Generalized System of Preferences: Background and Renewal Debate*, CRS Report RL33663, August 17 (Washington, DC: Congressional Research Service).

Jones, Vivian C., and Liana Wong. 2021. *Generalized System of Preferences (GSP): Overview and Issues for Congress.* CRS Report RL33663, January 7 (Washington, DC: Congressional Research Service).

Jönsson, Christer. 1981. "Bargaining Power: Notes on an Elusive Concept." *Cooperation and Conflict* 16 (4): 249–57.

Juárez, Blanca. 2021. "El movimiento 20/32 toma fuerza laboral y sindical de la mano del T-MEC." *El Economista* (online edition), August 2.

—. 2022. "Caso GM Silao: Historia de la líder y el movimiento laboral que se impuso a la CTM." *El Economista* (online edition), March 15.

Juárez Nuñez, Huberto. 2002. *Rebelión en el greenfield* (Puebla, Mexico: Siena Editores).

Junta Federal de Conciliación y Arbitraje (JFCA). 2015. "Recuento para determinar la titularidad de un contrato colectivo de trabajo. Buenas prácticas dirigidas a garantizar que, en su desahogo, los trabajadores emitan voto personal, libre, directo y secreto." September 29. http://www.stps.gob.mx/bp/secciones/junta_federal/secciones/documentos/CRITERIO%20APROBADO%202015.pdf.

Justice, Dwight W. 2002. "The International Trade Union Movement and the New Codes of Conduct." In *Corporate Responsibility and Labour Rights: Codes of Conduct in the Global Economy*, ed. Rhys Jenkins, Ruth Pearson, and Gill Seyfang, 90–100 (London: Earthscan).

Kahn, Joseph. 2000. "Labor Praises New Trade Pact with Jordan." *New York Times*, October 25.

Kang, Susan L. 2012. *Human Rights and Labor Solidarity: Trade Unions in the Global Economy* (Philadelphia: University of Pennsylvania Press).

Kantor, Mickey. 1994. "International Labor Standards and Economic Integration: The Perspective of the U.S. Trade Representative." In *International Labor Standards and Global Economic Integration*, ed. Gregory K. Schoepfle and Kenneth A. Swinnerton, 15-17 (Washington, DC: U.S. Department of Labor).

Kaplan, Thomas. 2021. "U.S. Asks Mexico to Investigate Labor Issues at G.M. Facility." *New York Times* (online edition), May 12.

Kay, Tamara. 2011a. *NAFTA and the Politics of Labor Transnationalism* (New York: Cambridge University Press).

——. 2011b. "Legal Transnationalism: The Relationship between Transnational Social Movement Building and International Law." *Law and Social Inquiry* 36 (2): 419-54.

Kay, Tamara, and R. L. Evans. 2018. *Trade Battles: Activism and the Politicization of International Trade Policy* (New York: Oxford University Press).

Kearney, Neil, and Judy Gearhart. 2004. "Workplace Codes as Tools for Workers." *Development in Practice* 14 (1/2): 216-23.

Keck, Margaret E., and Kathryn Sikkink. 1998. *Activists Beyond Borders: Advocacy Networks in International Politics* (Ithaca, NY: Cornell University Press).

Kelly, Sam. 2016. "A Comparative Analysis of the Labor Provisions in U.S. Free-Trade Agreements, 2001-2012." Unpublished.

——. 2017. "GSP Schemes Worldwide and Reviews/Sanctions under the US and EU Schemes." Unpublished.

Keohane, Robert O., and Joseph S. Nye. 1977. *Power and Interdependence: World Politics in Transition* (Boston: Little, Brown).

Kernaghan, Charles. 1993. *Haiti After the Coup: Sweatshop or Real Development?: A Special Delegation Report* (New York: National Labor Committee).

Kessler, Glenn. 2016. "Trump's False Claim that Clinton Only Recently Pledged to Renegotiate NAFTA." *Washington Post* (online edition), August 8.

Khagram, Sanjeev, James V. Riker, and Kathryn Sikkink. 2002. "From Santiago to Seattle: Transnational Advocacy Groups Restructuring World Politics." In *Restructuring World Politics: Transnational Social Movements, Networks, and Norms*, 3-23 (Minneapolis: University of Minnesota Press).

Kidder, Thalia G., and Mary McGinn. 1995. "In the Wake of NAFTA: Transnational Workers' Networks." *Social Policy* 25 (4): 14-21.

Kilborn, Peter T. 1993. "Unions Gird for War Over Trade Pact." *New York Times*, October 4.

Kim, Jee Young. 2013. "The Politics of Code Enforcement and Implementation in Vietnam's Apparel and Footwear Factories." *World Development* 45: 286-95.

Kim, Moonhawk. 2012. "*Ex Ante* Diligence: Formation of PTAs and Protection of Labor Rights." *International Studies Quarterly* 56 (4): 704-19.

Knox, John H. 2004. "Separated at Birth: The North American Agreements on Labor and the Environment." *Loyola of Los Angeles International and Comparative Law Review* 26 (3): 359-87.

Knudsen, Jetta Steen, and Jeremy Moon. 2017. *Visible Hands: Government Regulation and International Business Responsibility* (Cambridge: Cambridge University Press).

Kolben, Kevin. 2004. "Trade, Monitoring, and the ILO: Working to Improve Conditions in Cambodia's Garment Factories." *Yale Human Rights and Development Law Journal* 7: 79-107.

Krasner, Stephen. 1999. *Sovereignty: Organized Hypocrisy* (Princeton, NJ: Princeton University Press).

Kryvoi, Yarastau. 2008. "Why European Union Trade Sanctions Do Not Work." *Minnesota Journal of International Law* 17 (2): 209–46.

Kullmann, Ulrich. 1980. " 'Fair Labor Standards' in International Commodity Agreements." *Journal of World Trade* 14 (6): 527–35.

La Botz, Dan. 1992. *Mask of Democracy: Labor Suppression in Mexico Today* (Boston: South End Press).

Lane, Alexander. 2008. "Obama's Been Critical of NAFTA." *Politifact* (The Poynter Institute, www.politifact.com), October 15.

Lane, Sylvan. 2019. "AFL-CIO Backs Trump's North American Trade Pact." *The Hill* (online edition), December 10.

Langille, Brian A. 1997. "Eight Ways to Think about International Labour Standards." *Journal of World Trade* 31 (4): 27–53.

—. 2005. "Core Labour Rights—The True Story (Reply to Alston)." *European Journal of International Law* 16 (3): 409–37.

Langner, Ana. 2019a. "Reforma laboral cubre demandas de EU de varias décadas: Jesús Seade." *La Jornada en línea*, May 5.

—. 2019b. "México se inconforma con EU por figura de agregados laborales." *La Jornada en línea*, December 14.

—. 2020. "Será difícil resolver quejas contra EU por elecciones sindicales: Seade." *La Jornada en línea*, January 10.

LaReau, Jamie L., and Eric D. Lawrence. 2022. "New Union at GM Mexico Plant Could Benefit US Autoworkers." *Detroit Free Press* (online edition), February 4.

Laureles, Jared. 2022. "Reconoce Teksid Hierro a sindicato minero como titular del CCT." *La Jornada en línea*, July 13.

Lawson, Chappell H. 2002. *Building the Fourth Estate: Democratization and the Rise of a Free Press in Mexico* (Berkeley: University of California Press).

Leary, Virginia A. 1996a. "Workers' Rights and International Trade: The Social Clause (GATT, ILO, NAFTA, U.S. Laws)." In *Fair Trade and Harmonization: Prerequisites for Free Trade?* Vol. 2, *Legal Analysis*, ed. Jagdish Bhagwati and Robert E. Hudec, 177–230 (Cambridge: MIT Press).

—. 1996b. "The Paradox of Workers' Rights as Human Rights." In *Human Rights, Labor Rights, and International Trade*, ed. Lance A. Compa and Steven F. Diamond, 22–47 (Philadelphia: University of Pennsylvania Press).

—. 1997. "The WTO and the Social Clause: Post-Singapore." *European Journal of International Law* 8 (1): 118–22.

Levinson, Jerome I. 1996. "NAFTA's Labor Agreement: Lessons from the First Three Years." November (Washington, DC: Institute for Policy Studies / International Labor Rights Forum).

Lillie, Nathan, and Miguel Martínez Lucio. 2004. "International Trade Union Revitalization: The Role of National Union Approaches." In *Varieties of Unionism: Strategies for Union Revitalization in the Global Economy*, ed. Carola Frege and John Kelly, 159–80 (Oxford: Oxford University Press).

Lim, Hoe. N.d. *The Social Clause: Issues and Challenges*. Accessed on February 16, 2016. http://training.itcilo.it/actrav_cdrom1/english/global/guide/hoelim.htm.

"Linking Labor Standards and Rights in Trade Agreements." 1997. Proceedings of the November 12, 1996 conference co-sponsored by the Washington College of Law, American University, and the U.S. National Administrative Office (Bureau of International Labor Affairs,

U.S. Department of Labor), published in *American University International Law Review* 12 (5): 815-74.

Lipschultz, Ronnie D. 2004. "Sweating it Out: NGO Campaigns and Trade Union Empowerment." *Development in Practice* 14 (1/2): 197-209.

Lipset, Seymour Martin. 1990. *Continental Divide: The Values and Institutions of the United States and Canada* (New York: Routledge, Chapman, and Hall).

Loaeza, Soledad. 2010. "La política de acomodo de México a la superpotencia. Dos episodios de cambio de régimen: 1944-1948 y 1989-1994." *Foro Internacional* 50 (3/4): 627-60.

Locke, Richard M. 2013. *The Promise and Limits of Private Power: Promoting Labor Standards in a Global Economy* (New York: Cambridge University Press).

Long, Heather. 2015. "Donald Trump Trademarks 'Make America Great Again.'" *CNN Business*, October 8, https://money.cnn.com/2015/10/08/investing/donald-trump-make-america-great -again-trademark/.

Long, Tom. 2014. *Echoes of 1992: The NAFTA Negotiations and North America Now* (Washington, DC: Mexico Institute, Woodrow Wilson International Center for Scholars).

López Portillo, José. 1988. *Mis tiempos: biografía y testimonio político* (Mexico City: Fernández Editores).

"Los sindicatos, con menos fuerza de negociación: FAT." *La Jornada*, July 28, 1997.

Luce, Stephanie. 2010. "Labor Standards and Trade Agreements: The Impact of Trade Negotiations on Country Adoption of Freedom of Association and Collective Bargaining" (Washington, DC: Bureau of International Labor Affairs, U.S. Department of Labor).

Luján U., Bertha Elena. 2002. "Citizen Advocacy Networks and the NAFTA." In *Cross-Border Dialogues: U.S.-Mexico Social Movement Networking*, ed. David Brooks and Jonathan Fox, 211-26 (La Jolla, CA: Center for U.S.-Mexican Studies, University of California-San Diego).

Lustig, Nora. 1995. "The Mexican Peso Crisis: The Foreseeable and the Surprise." June (Washington, DC: The Brookings Institution).

Lyle, Faye. 1991. *Worker Rights in U.S. Policy* (Washington, DC: Bureau of International Labor Affairs, U.S. Department of Labor).

MacArthur, John R. 2000. *The Selling of "Free Trade": NAFTA, Washington, and the Subversion of American Democracy* (Berkeley: University of California Press).

Macfarlane, L. J. 1967. "Hands off Russia: British Labour and the Russo-Polish War, 1920." *Past and Present*, ,o. 38 (Dec.): 126-52.

Mahoney, James. 2000. "Path Dependence in Historical Sociology." *Theory and Society* 29 (4): 507-48.

Mandel, Harlan. 1989. "In Pursuit of the Missing Link: International Worker Rights and International Trade?" *Columbia Journal of Transnational Law* 27 (2) 443-82.

Mangone, Joseph. 1993. "International Unions and NAFTA." In *The North American Free Trade Agreement: Labor, Industry, and Government Perspectives*, ed. Mario F. Bognanno and Kathryn J. Ready, 175-79 (Westport, CT: Quorum Books).

Maquila Solidarity Network (MSN). 2008a. "Grupo Navarra Closes Factory to Punish Workers for Joining Union." *Maquila Solidarity Update* 13 (1), February.

—. 2008b. "Who's Got the Universal Code?" Codes Memo, April 23.

—. 2008c. *Maquila Solidarity Wire.* December 10.

—. 2012a. "New Agreement Reached on Worker Safety in Bangladesh." March 22, email circular.

—. 2012b. *Maquila Solidarity Wire.* May 4.

—. 2020. "Labour Rights Enforcement in the USMCA." July.

—. 2021. "Legitimating Collective Bargaining Agreements in Mexico: What Have We Learned to Date?" December.

Marcus, Ruth, and Frank Swoboda. 1993. "President Urges Labor to Support Health Care Plan: In Speech to Union Leaders, Clinton Keeps Discussion of Free Trade Agreement Brief." *Washington Post*, October 5.

Martin, Lisa L., and Kathryn Sikkink. 1993. "U.S. Policy and Human Rights in Argentina and Guatemala, 1973-1980." In *Double-Edged Diplomacy: International Bargaining and Domestic Politics*, ed. Peter B. Evans, Harold K. Jacobson, and Robert D. Putnam, 330-62 (Berkeley: University of California Press).

Martínez, César. 2019. "Advierten desconfianza hacia negociador." *Reforma*, December 16.

—. 1997b. "Exige la Fesebes cambios a la Ley Federal del Trabajo." *La Jornada*, August 19.

—. 1998a. "Piden a autoridades de México y EU acatar las leyes laborales." *La Jornada*, January 17.

—. 1998b. "Protesta la AFL-CIO por violaciones a derechos laborales." *La Jornada*, March 30.

—. 2000. "La UNT, con trabajadores de maquiladoras." *La Jornada*, August 15.

—. 2001a. "Exige central obrera de EU a Abascal precise acusaciones de injerencia." *La Jornada*, February 24.

—. 2001b. "Mito, la libertad sindical en México: expertos." *La Jornada*, June 24.

Martínez, María del Pilar. 2015. "Convenio 98 abre la puerta a más sindicatos." *El Economista* (online edition), December 4.

—. 2018. "Senado abrirá etapa de consulta para reforma laboral." *El Economista* (online edition), May 1.

—. 2019. "Tiene listo CTM amparo en contra de reforma laboral." *El Economista* (online edition), June 16.

—. 2021. "Sindicato 'Miguel Trujillo' no irá por contrato de GM Silao." *El Economista* (online edition), December 14.

—. 2022. "Investigación Mexicana no encuentra violaciones a derechos de los trabajadores de Tridonex." *El Economista* (online edition), August 11.

Massicotte, Marie-Josée. 2009. "Coalition Politics: A Political Analysis of the Strategies, Discourses and Impact of the Mexican Action Network on Free Trade (RMALC)." In *Contentious Politics in North America: National Protest and Transnational Collaboration under Continental Integration*, ed. Jeffrey Ayres and Laura Macdonald, 132-52 (Basingstoke, England: Palgrave Macmillan).

Mathiason, Nick. 2007. "Result: MkOne Forced to Drop Burma Clothing." *Observer* (London), March 18.

Mauldin, William. 2018. "Lawmakers Press Trump Administration on Nafta Dispute Resolution." *Wall Street Journal* (online edition), February 7.

Mauldin, William, and Jacob M. Schlesinger. 2017. "Nafta Flashpoints: Issues to Watch as the Talks Unfold." *Wall Street Journal* (online edition), August 13.

Maupin, Francis. 2000. "International Labor Organization: Recommendations and Similar Instruments." In *Commitment and Compliance: The Role of Non-Binding Norms in the International Legal System*, ed. Dinah Shelton, 372-93 (Oxford: Oxford University Press).

—. 2005. "Is the ILO Effective in Upholding Workers' Rights? Reflections on the Myanamar Experience." In *Labour Rights as Human Rights*, Philip Alston, 85-142 (Oxford: Oxford University Press).

Mayer, Frederick W. 1998. *Interpreting NAFTA: The Science and Art of Political Analysis* (New York: Columbia University Press).

Mayer, Frederick W., and Gary Gereffi. 2010. "Regulation and Economic Globalization: Prospects and Limits of Private Governance." *Business and Politics* 12 (3): n.p.

Mazurek, Malgorzata, and Paul Betts. 2012. "Preface: When Rights Were Social." *Humanity* 3 (3): 291–95.

Mazza, Jacqueline. 2001. *Don't Disturb the Neighbors: The United States and Democracy in Mexico, 1980–1995* (New York: Routledge).

McCaffrey, Shellyn G. 1993. "North American Free Trade and Labor Issues." *Hofstra Labor and Employment Law Journal* 10 (2): 449–94.

McCallum, Jamie K. 2013. *Global Unions, Local Power: The New Spirit of Transnational Labor Organizing* (Ithaca, NY: Cornell University Press).

McGaughey, William, Jr., Thomas J. Laney, and Jose L. Quintana. 1991. "Petition to Review the Eligibility of Mexico as a Beneficiary Developing Country under the Generalized System of Preferences." May 15.

Meinig, D. W. 1993. *The Shaping of America: A Geographical Perspective on 500 Years of History* (5 vols.). Vol. 2, *Continental America, 1800–1867* (New Haven, CT: Yale University Press).

Méndez, Enrique, and Roberto Garduño. 2016. "Diputados eliminan juntas de conciliación; empoderan al trabajador." *La Jornada en línea*, November 5.

Mendiola P., Gerardo. 1999. "Las empresas maquiladoras de exportación, 1980–1995." In *Pensar globalmente y actuar regionalmente: hacia un nuevo paradigma industrial para el Siglo Veintiuno*, ed. Enrique Dussel, Michael Piore, and Clemente Ruiz Durán, 185–226 (Mexico City: Universidad Nacional Autónoma de México/Fundación Friedrich Ebert/Editorial Jus).

Meron, Theodor. 1986. "On a Hierarchy of International Human Rights." *American Journal of International Law* 80 (1): 1–23.

Meyer, John F., John Boli, George M. Thomas, and Francisco O. Ramirez. 1997. "World Society and the Nation-State." *American Journal of Sociology* 103 (1): 144–81.

Middlebrook, Kevin J. 1991. "The Politics of Industrial Restructuring: Transnational Firms' Search for Flexible Production in the Mexican Automobile Industry." *Comparative Politics* 23 (3): 275–97.

——. 1995. *The Paradox of Revolution: Labor, the State, and Authoritariansim in Mexico* (Baltimore, MD: Johns Hopkins University Press).

——. 2004. "Mexico's Democratic Transitions: Dynamics and Prospects." In *Dilemmas of Political Change in Mexico*, 1–53 (London: Institute of Latin American Studies, University of London / Center for U.S.-Mexican Studies, University of California-San Diego).

——. 2010. "Le Mexique et la crise internationale." *Amérique latine*, 87–95.

Middlebrook, Kevin J., and Cirila Quintero Ramírez. 1998. "Protecting Workers' Rights in Mexico: Local Conciliation and Arbitration Boards, Union Registration, and Conflict Resolution in the 1990s." *Labor Studies Journal* 23 (1): 21–51.

Middlebrook, Kevin J., and Eduardo Zepeda. 2003. "On the Political Economy of Mexican Development Policy." In *Confronting Development: Assessing Mexico's Economic and Social Policy Challenges*, 3–52 (Stanford, CA: Stanford University Press and Center for U.S.-Mexican Studies, University of California-San Diego).

——, eds. 2006. *La industria maquiladora de exportación: ensamble, manufactura y desarrollo económico* (Mexico City: Universidad Autónoma Metropolitana-Azcapotzalco).

Miller, Doug. 2004. "Preparing for the Long Haul: Negotiating International Framework Agreements in the Global Textile, Garment and Footwear Sector." *Global Social Policy* 4 (2): 215-39.

Miller, Melissa Ann. 1996. "Will the Circle Be Unbroken? Chile's Accession to the NAFTA and the Fast-Track Debate." *Valparaiso University Law Review* 31 (1): 153-90.

Mintzes, Joseph. 1960. "Union Views on Fair Labor Standards in Foreign Trade." *Monthly Labor Review* 83 (10): 1025-30.

Moncayo, Pablo Pascual, and Raúl Trejo Delarbre. 1993. *Los sindicatos mexicanos ante el TLC* (Mexico City: Sindicato Nacional de Trabajadores de la Educación / Instituto para la Transición Democrática).

Moore, Molly. 1998. "Mexican Farmworkers Accuse U.S. Firms." *Washington Post*, December 3.

Moorman, Yasmin. 2001. "Integration of ILO Core Labor Rights Standards into the WTO." *Columbia Journal of Transnational Law* 39 (2): 555-83.

Morales, Roberto, and María del Pilar Martínez. 2022. "EU y Canadá presionan en legitimación de contratos." *El Economista* (online edition), August 29.

Moran, Theodore H. 2002. *Beyond Sweatshops: Foreign Direct Investment and Globalization in Developing Countries* (Washington, DC: Brookings Institution Press).

Morath, Eric. 2017 "Union Leaders Largely Echo Donald Trump on Nafta." *Wall Street Journal* (online edition), October 25.

Morgan, Stephen L., and Jiwon Lee. 2018. "Trump Voters and the White Working Class." *Sociological Science* 5: 234-45

Morisette, René, Grant Schellenberg and Anick Johnson. 2005. "Diverging Trends in Unionization." *Perspectives on Labour and Income* [published by Statistics Canada] 6 (4): 5-12. http://www.statcan.gc.ca/pub/75-001-x/10405/7827-eng.pdf.

Morley, Morris, and Chris McGillion. 2015. *Reagan and Pinochet: The Struggle over US Policy Toward Chile* (Cambridge: Cambridge University Press).

Morrow, Adrian. 2017. "Canada Demands U.S. End 'Right to Work' Laws as Part of NAFTA Talk." *Globe and Mail* (Toronto) (online edition), September 3.

Morrow, Adrian, Barrie McKenna, and Stephanie Nolen. 2018. "From NAFTA to USMCA: Inside the Tense Negotiations that Saved North American Trade." *Globe and Mail* (Toronto) (online edition), October 5.

Mosley, Layna. 2011a. *Labor Rights and Multinational Production* (Cambridge: Cambridge University Press).

——. 2011b. "Replication Data for Collective Labor Rights Dataset." https://doi.org/10.7910/DVN/WVZC90.

Mosley, Layna, and Lindsay Tello. 2014. "The Politics of Petitions: Interest Groups and Labor Rights in the U.S. Generalized System of Preferences?" Unpublished paper.

——. 2015. "Labor Rights, Material Interests, and Moral Entrepreneurship." *Human Rights Quarterly* 37 (1): 53-79.

Moyne, Samuel. 2010. *The Last Utopia: Human Rights in History* (Cambridge, MA: Harvard University Press).

Mulroney, Brian. 2007. *Memoirs* (Toronto: McClelland and Stewart).

Munck, Ronaldo, and Peter Waterman, eds. 1999. *Labour Worldwide in the Era of Globalization* (London: Macmillan).

Muñoz Rios, Patricia. 2015. "Exigen empresarios a la STPS reformar la ley para eliminar los sindicatos de protección." *La Jornada*, November 9.

—. 2018. "La reforma laboral, detenida en el Senado, será presentada en el próximo periodo." *La Jornada en línea*, April 23.

Murillo, M. Victoria, and Andrew Schrank. 2005. "With a Little Help from My Friends: Partisan Politics, Transnational Alliances, and Labor Rights in Latin America." *Comparative Political Studies* 38 (8): 971–99.

Myerson, Allen R. 1994a. "Big Labor's Strategic Raid in Mexico." *New York Times*, September 12.

—. 1994b. "U.S. Backs Mexico Law, Vexing Labor." *New York Times*, October 13.

Nadal, Alejandro. 2003. "Macroeconomic Challenges for Mexico's Development Strategy." In *Confronting Development: Assessing Mexico's Economic and Social Policy Challenges*, ed. Kevin J. Middlebrook and Eduardo Zepeda, 55–88 (Stanford, CA: Stanford University Press/Center for U.S.-Mexican Studies, University of California, San Diego).

National Labor Committee. 1993. *Haiti After the Coup: Sweatshop or Real Development? A Special Delegation Report* (Pittsburgh, PA: National Labor Committee).

National Law Center for Inter-American Free Trade. 1994. "Labor Law Enforcement in Mexico and the Role of the Federal and State Conciliation and Arbitration Boards." Report submitted to the U.S. National Administrative Office (Bureau of International Labor Affairs), U.S. Department of Labor, July 26.

—. 2000. "Emergency Procedures for Resolving Labor-Management Disputes in the United States, Canada, and Mexico." Report submitted to the U.S. National Administrative Office (Bureau of International Labor Affairs), U.S. Department of Labor, September.

Negrete, Ingrid. 1993. "Mexican Official Defends NAFTA Dispute Process." *Journal of Commerce*, August 20.

New York Times. 1997. "Mexico's Vulnerable Workers." December 6.

—. 2017. "Presidential Election Results: Donald J. Trump Wins." November 9. https://nytimes.com/elections/2016/results/president.

Nickel, James W. 2008. "Rethinking Indivisibility: Towards a Theory of Supporting Relations Between Human Rights. *Human Rights Quarterly* 30 (4): 985–1001.

Niforou, Christina. 2012. "International Framework Agreements and Industrial Relations Governance: Global Rhetoric versus Local Realities." *British Journal of Industrial Relations* 50 (2): 352–73.

Nimtz, August. 2002. "Marx and Engels: The Prototypical Transnational Actors." In *Restructuring World Politics: Transnational Social Movements, Networks, and Norms*, ed. Sanjeev Khagram, James V. Riker, and Kathryn Sikkink, 245–68 (Minneapolis: University of Minnesota Press).

Nolan García, Kimberly A. 2010a. "Norms Socialization and NAFTA's Side Accord on Labor." Serie de Documentos de Trabajo de la División de Estudios Internacionales, Centro de Investigación y Docencia y Docencia Económicas (CIDE), DEI-206 (Mexico City: CIDE).

—. 2010b. "Enforcement by Design: The Legalization of Labor Rights Mechanisms in US Trade Policy." Serie de Documentos de Trabajo de la División de Estudios Internacionales, Centro de Investigación y Docencia y Docencia Económicas (CIDE), DEI-207 (Mexico City: CIDE).

—. 2011a. "Whose Preferences? Latin American Trade Promotion Pacts as a Tool of US Foreign Policy." Serie de Documentos de Trabajo de la División de Estudios Internacionales, Centro de Investigación y Docencia y Docencia Económicas (CIDE), DEI-218 (Mexico City: CIDE).

—. 2011b. "The Evolution of United States-Mexico Labor Cooperation (1994-2009): Achievements and Challenges." *Politics and Policy* 39 (1): 91–117.

—. 2011c. "Transnational Advocates and Labor Rights Enforcement in the North American Free Trade Agreement." *Latin American Politics and Society* 53 (2): 29–60.

—. 2012. "Pressure, Coercion and the Domestic Costs of Compliance: Evaluating the NAALC Resolutions Against Mexico." Serie de Documentos de Trabajo de la División de Estudios Internacionales, Centro de Investigación y Docencia y Docencia Económicas (CIDE), DEI-231 (Mexico City: CIDE).

—. 2013. "Network Dynamics and Local Labor Rights Movements in Puebla, Mexico." In *Transnational Activism and National Movements in Latin America: Bridging the Divide*, ed. Eduardo Silva, 106–40 (New York: Routledge).

Nomani, Asra Q. 1994. "Unions Angry After Administration Rejects Complaints About Mexico Plants." *Wall Street Journal*, October 14.

North American Commission for Labor Cooperation (NACLC). 1996. *Preliminary Report to the Ministerial Council on Labor and Industrial Relations Laws in Canada, Mexico, and the United States* (Dallas, TX: Secretariat of the NACLC).

—. 1997a. *Incomes and Productivity in North America* (Dallas, TX: Secretariat of the NACLC).

—. 1997b. *North American Labor Markets: A Comparative Profile* (Dallas, TX: Secretariat of the NACLC).

—. 1997c. *Plant Closings and Labor Rights: The Effects of Sudden Plant Closings on Freedom of Association and the Right to Organize in Canada, Mexico, and the United States* (Dallas, TX: Secretariat of the NACLC).

—. 1998a. "Review of the North American Agreement on Labor Cooperation, 1994–1997" (Dallas, TX: NACLC).

—. 1998b. *The Employment of Women in North America* (Dallas, TX: Secretariat of the NACLC).

—. 2000a. *Income Security Programs for Workers in North America: A Reference Manual for Workers and Employers* (Washington, DC: Secretariat of the NACLC).

—. 2000b. *Labor Relations Law in North America* (Washington, DC: Secretariat of the NACLC).

—. 2000c. *"Standard" and "Advanced" Practices in the North American Garment Industry* (Washington, DC: Secretariat of the NACLC).

—. 2002. *Protection of Migrant Agricultural Workers in Canada, Mexico, and the United States* (Washington, DC: Secretariat of the NACLC).

—. 2003a. *North American Labor Markets: Main Changes Since NAFTA* (Washington, DC: Secretariat of the NACLC).

—. 2003b. *The Rights of Nonstandard Workers: A North American Guide* (Washington, DC: Secretariat of the NACLC).

—. 2004. *North American Labor Markets: A Graphical Portrait* (Washington, DC: Secretariat of the NACLC).

—. 2005a. *Guide to Labor and Employment Laws for Migrant Workers in North America* (Washington, DC: Secretariat of the NACLC).

—. 2005b. "Public Communications." December 12. Unpublished.

Novitz, Tonia. 2003. *International and European Protection of the Right to Strike: A Comparative Study of Standards Set by the International Labour Organization, the Council of Europe and the European Union* (Oxford: Oxford University Press).

O'Brien, Robert. 2000. "Workers and World Order: The Tentative Transformation of the International Union Movement." *Review of International Studies* 26 (4): 533–55.

O'Connor, Anne-Marie. 1997. "Tijuana Union Fight Highlights NAFTA Fears." *Los Angeles Times*, November 7.

Odell, John S. 1982. *U.S. International Economic Policy: Markets, Power, and Ideas as Sources of Change* (Princeton, NJ: Princeton University Press).

O'Donovan, Michael. 2005. "Labor Standards from NAFTA to CAFTA: Standards that Work, or a Work in Progress?" Working Paper LJA 2005-1 (Boston: Boston College Law School).

Office of the United States Trade Representative (USTR). 1993. "1993 GSP Annual Review: Worker Rights Summary, Case 013-CP-93, Mexico." Generalized System of Preferences Subcommittee of the Trade Policy Staff Committee, October.

——. 1997. *Study on the Operation and Effects of the North American Free Trade Agreement* (Washington, DC: USTR).

——. 2005. "U.S. Generalized System of Preferences (GSP) Program: Worker Rights Case History." June 9 (Washington, DC: USTR).

——. 2006. "Statement from USTR Spokesman Regarding China Labor Petition." July 21. https://ustr.gov/archive/Document_Library/Press_Releases/2006/July/Statement_from_USTR_Spokesman_Regarding_China_Labor_Petition.html.

——. 2007. "Bipartisan Trade Deal." May. https://ustr.gov/sites/default/files/uploads/factsheets/2007/asset_upload_file127_11319.pdf.

——. 2010. "United States Trade Representative Kirk Announces Labor Rights Trade Enforcement Case Against Guatemala." *USTR News*, July 30.

——. 2011. *CAFTA-DR Labor Capacity Building* (Washington, DC: USTR). Accessed May 4, 2020. https://ustr.gov/about-us/policy-offices/press-office/fact-sheets/2011/may/cafta-dr-labor-capacity-building.

——. 2014. "United States Proceeds with Labor Enforcement Case Against Guatemala." Press release, September 18.

——. 2015a. *Standing Up for Workers: Promoting Labor Rights through Trade*. February (Washington, DC: USTR).

——. 2015b. *U.S. Generalized System of Preferences Guidebook*, October (Washington, DC: USTR). https://ustr.gov/sites/default/files/GSP%20Guidebook%20October%202015%20Final.pdf.

——. 2015c. *Labor Advisory Committee on Trade Negotiations and Trade Policy (Labor Advisory Committee) Report on the Impacts of the Trans-Pacific Partnership*, December 2 (Washington, DC: USTR).

——. 2018a. *The Advisory Committee for Trade Policy Negotiations (ACTPN) Committee Report to the President, the Congress, and the United States Trade Representative on the Trade Agreement*, September 27 (Washington, DC: USTR).

——. 2018b. *Labor Advisory Committee on Trade Negotiations and Trade Policy (Labor Advisory Committee) Report on the Impacts of the Renegotiated North American Free Trade Agreement*, September 27 (Washington, DC: USTR).

——. 2022a. "United States Seeks Mexico's Review of Alleged Denial of Workers' Rights at Automotive Components Facility." July 21.

——. 2022b. "United States Announces Successful Resolution of Rapid Response Labor Mechanism Matter at Auto Parts Facility in Frontera, Mexico." August 16.

——. 2022c. "United States Announces Successful Resolution of a Rapid Response Mechanism Petition Regarding a Saint Gobain Facility in Mexico." October 27.

Ojeda, Mario. 1976. *Alcances y límites de la política exterior de México* (Mexico City: El Colegio de México).

Oka, Chikako. 2010. "Accounting for the Gaps in Labour Standard Compliance: The Role of Reputation-Conscious Buyers in the Cambodian Garment Industry." *European Journal of Development Research* 22: 59–78.

Olvera, Alberto J. 2004. "Civil Society in Mexico at Century's End." In *Dilemmas of Political Change in Mexico*, ed. Kevin J. Middlebrook, 403–39 (London: Institute of Latin American Studies, University of London / Center for U.S.-Mexican Studies, University of California-San Diego).

Orbie, Jan, Hendrik Vos, and Liesbeth Taverniers. 2005. "EU Trade Policy and a Social Clause: A Question of Competences?" *Politique Européenne* 3 (17): 159–87.

Organization for Economic Co-Operation and Development (OECD). 1996. *Trade, Employment and Labour Standards: A Study of Core Workers' Rights and International Trade* (Paris: OECD).

Orme, William A., Jr. 1996. *Understanding NAFTA: Mexico, Free Trade, and the New North America* (Austin: University of Texas Press).

O'Rourke, Dara. 2003. "Outsourcing Regulation: Analyzing Nongovernmental Systems of Labor Standards and Monitoring." *Policy Studies Journal* 31 (1): 1–29.

Oye, Kenneth A. 1983. "International Systems Structure and American Foreign Policy." In *Eagle Defiant: United States Foreign Policy in the 1980s*, ed. Kenneth A. Oye, Robert J. Lieber, and Donald Rothchild, 3–32 (Boston: Little, Brown).

Panetta, Alexander. 2016. "Canada, Mexico Talked Before Making NAFTA Overture to Trump." CBC News, November 16. https://www.cbc.ca/news/politics/canada-mexico-trade-nafta-tr ump-1.3853406.

Papadakis, Konstantinos, ed. 2011. *Shaping Global Labor Relations: The Impact of International Framework Agreements* (Basingstoke, England: Palgrave Macmillan).

Parametría. 2018. "¿Estaba el Presidente en la boleta el primero de julio?" *Carta Paramétrica* (online edition), July 26.

Parfitt, Steven. 2015. "The First-and-a-Half International: The Knights of Labor and the History of International Labour Organization in the Nineteenth Century." *International Labour Review* 80 (2): 135–67.

Parker, Emily, and Kirk Semple. 2021. "A Damning Portrait of Presidential Corruption, But Hondurans Sound Resigned." *New York Times* (online edition), March 23.

Partido Acción Nacional. 1995. "Iniciativa de decreto que reforma a la Ley Federal del Trabajo." July 12.

Partido de la Revolución Democrática. 1998. "Anteproyecto de reforma a la Constitución Política de los Estados Unidos Mexicanos y la Ley Federal del Trabajo presentado por el Grupo Parlamentario del Partido de la Revolución Democrática de la LVII Legislatura de la Cámara de Diputados del H. Congreso de la Unión." May.

Pastor, Manuel, and Carol Wise. 1994. "The Origins and Sustainability of Mexico's Free Trade Policy." *International Organization* 48 (3): 459–89.

Pastor, Robert A. 1990. "Post-Revolutionary Mexico: The Salinas Opening." *Journal of Interamerican Studies and World Affairs* 32 (3): 1–22.

Pastor, Robert A., and Jorge G. Castañeda. 1988. *Limits to Friendship: The United States and Mexico* (New York: Alfred A. Knopf).

Patiño, Dainzú. 2017. "Los temas laboral y transporte anteceden la ronda 5 del TLCAN." *Expansión* (online edition), November 15.

Pease, Don J., and J. William Goold. 1985. "The New GSP: Fair Trade with the Third World?" *World Policy Journal* 2 (2): 35–66.

Peers, Steve. 1995. "Reform of the European Community's Generalized System of Preferences: A Missed Opportunity." *Journal of World Trade* 29 (6): 79–96.

Pekdemir, Ceren, Pieter Glasbergen, and Ron Cörvers. 2015. "On the Transformative Capacity of Private Fair Labour Arrangements." In *Global Governance of Labour Rights: Assessing the Effectiveness of Transnational Public and Private Policy Initiatives*, ed. Axel Marx, Jan Wouters, Glenn Rayp, and Laura Beke, 209–29 (Cheltenham, Gloucestershire: Edward Elgar).

Peñaloza, Tomás. 1978. "Efectos del Sistema General de Preferencias de Estados Unidos en América Latina y México: Una evaluación preliminar." *Comercio Exterior* 28 (7): 867–76.

Pérez-López, Jorge F. 1988. "Conditioning Trade on Foreign Labor Law: The U.S. Approach." *Comparative Labor Law and Policy Journal* 9 (2): 253–92.

—. 1990. "Worker Rights in the U.S. Omnibus Trade and Competitiveness Act." *Labor Law Journal* 41 (4): 222–34.

—. 1995a. "The Promotion of International Labor Standards and NAFTA: Retrospect and Prospects." *Connecticut Journal of International Law* 10 (2): 427–74.

—. 1995b. "The Institutional Framework of the North American Agreement on Labor Cooperation." *NAFTA: United States-Mexico Law Journal* 3: 133–47.

—. 1995c. "Implementation of the North American Agreement on Labor Cooperation: A Perspective from the Signatory Countries." *Law and Business Review of the Americas* 1 (4): 3–19.

Perot, Ross. 1993. *Not for Sale at Any Price: How We Can Save America for Our Children* (New York: Hyperion).

Perry, Michael. J. 1997. "Are Human Rights Universal? The Relativist Challenge and Related Matters." *Human Rights Quarterly* 19 (3): 461–509.

Peterson, Nikolaj. 1986. "Bargaining Power Among Potential Allies: Negotiating the North Atlantic Treaty, 1948-9." *Review of International Studies* 12 (3): 187–203.

Pier, Carol J. "A Way Forward for Workers' Rights in U.S. Free Trade Agreements" (New York: Human Rights Watch).

Pinkerton, Charlie. 2020. "USMCA Passes House and Senate as Parliament Shuts Down." *iPolitics*, March 13.

Piore, Michael J., and Andrew Shrank. 2008. "Toward Managed Flexibility: The Revival of Labour Inspection in the Latin World." *International Labour Review* 147 (1): 1–23.

Poder Ejecutivo Federal. 1992. *Carlos Salinas de Gortari: cuarto informe de gobierno, 1992 (anexo)*. Mexico City: Presidencia de la República.

—. 2016a. "Iniciativa de Decreto por el que se reforman y adicionan diversas disposiciones de la Constitución Política de los Estados Unidos Mexicanos, en materia de justicia laboral." Mexico City: Presidencia de la República.

—. 2016b. "Iniciativa de Decreto por el que se reforman y adicionan diversas disposiciones de la Ley Federal del Trabajo." Mexico City: Presidencia de la República.

—. 2019a. "Decreto por el que se reforman, adicionan y derogan diversas disposiciones de la Ley Federal del Trabajo, de la Ley Orgánica del Poder Judicial de la Federación, de la

Ley Federal de la Defensoría Pública, de la Ley del Instituto del Fondo Nacional de la Vivienda para los Trabajadores y de la Ley del Seguro Social, en materia de Justicia Laboral, Libertad Sindical y Negociación Colectiva." *Diario Oficial de la Federación* (online edition), May 1.

——. 2019b. "Decreto por el que se reforman, adicionan y derogan diversas disposiciones de la Ley Federal de los Trabajadores al Servicio del Estado, Reglamentaria del apartado B del Artículo 123 Constitucional." *Diario Oficial de la Federación* (online edition), May 1.

Polaski, Sandra. 2003a. *Trade and Labor Standards: A Strategy for Developing Countries* (Washington, DC: Carnegie Endowment for World Peace).

——. 2003b. "Protecting Labor Rights through Trade Agreements: An Analytical Guide." *U.C. Davis Journal of International Law and Policy* 10 (1): 13–25.

——. 2006a. "Perspectivas sobre el Futuro del TLCAN." In *Diez años del TLCAN*, ed. Mónica Gambrill, 35–56 (Mexico City: Centro de Investigación Sobre América del Norte, Universidad Nacional Autónoma de México).

——. 2006b. "Combining Global and Local Forces: The Case of Labor Rights in Cambodia." *World Development* 34 (5): 919–32.

——. 2017. "Twenty of Years of Progress at Risk: Labor and Environmental Protections in Trade Agreements." GEGI Policy Brief 004 (Boston: Global Development Policy Center, Boston University).

Polaski, Sandra, Kimberly A. Nolan García, and Michèle Rioux. 2021. "The USMCA: A 'New Model' for Labor Governance in North America?" In *NAFTA 2.0: From the First NAFTA to the United States-Mexico-Canada Agreement*, ed. Gilbert Gagné and Michèle Rioux, 139–56 (Cham, Switzerland: Springer Nature).

Pomeroy, Laura Okin. 1996. "The Labor Side Agreement under the NAFTA: Analysis of Its Failure to Include Strong Enforcement Provisions and Recommendations for Future Labor Agreements Negotiated with Developing Countries." *George Washington Journal of International Law and Economics* 29 (3): 769–801.

Portela, Clara, and Jan Orbie. 2014. "Sanctions under the EU Generalised System of Preferences and Foreign Policy: Coherence by Accident?" *Contemporary Politics* 20 (1): 63–76.

Post, Lori Ann, Amber N. W. Raile, and Eric D. Raile. 2010. "Defining Political Will." *Politics and Policy* 38 (4): 653–76.

Postnikov, Evgeny. 2014. "The Design of Social Standards in EU and US Preferential Trade Agreements." In *Handbook of the International Political Economy of Trade*, ed. David A. Deese, 531–49 (Cheltenham, England: Edward Elgar).

Postnikov, Evgeny, and Ida Bastiaens. 2014. "Does Dialogue Work? The Effectiveness of Labor Standards in EU Preferential Trade Agreements." *Journal of European Public Policy* 21 (6): 923–40.

Pouliot, Vincent. 2015. "Practice Tracing." In *Process Tracing: From Metaphor to Analytic Tool*, ed. Andrew Bennett and Jeffrey T. Checkel, 237–59 (Cambridge: Cambridge University Press).

Prescod, Paul. 2019. "Trump's Assault on Labor." *Jacobin* (online edition), October 9.

Putnam, Robert D. 1988. "Diplomacy and Domestic Politics: The Logic of Two-Level Games." *International Organization* 42 (3): 427–60.

——. 1993. "The Prosperous Community: Social Capital and Public Life." *American Prospect* 13: 35–42.

Redacción. 2017. "¿Cuáles son las prioridades de México en el TLCAN?" *Milenio* (online edition), August 2.

——. 2019a. "Agregados laborales, discurso para las 'galerías' de EU, dice Seade." *La Jornada en línea*, December 15.

——. 2019b. "Agregados respetarán ley mexicana, dice EU; descata que sean inspectores." *La Jornada en línea*, December 16.

——. 2021a. "STPS denuncia presunto fraude en consulta para legitimar el contrato colectivo en General Motors." *Proceso* (online edition), April 23.

——. 2021b. "GM y sindicato deben reponer consulta de contrato colectivo: STPS." *Proceso* (online edition), June 21.

——. 2022. "Salario mínimo: ¿A cuánto ascenderá?" *El Financiero* (online), January 1.

Reinecke, Juliane, and Jimmy Donaghey. 2015. "The 'Accord for Fire and Building Safety in Bangladesh' in Response to the Rana Plaza Disaster." In *Global Governance of Labour Rights: Assessing the Effectiveness of Transnational Public and Private Policy Initiatives*, Axel Marx, Jan Wouters, Glenn Rayp, and Laura Beke, 257-77 (Cheltenham, Gloucestershire: Edward Elgar).

Reuters. 1990. "Ford Threatens Cuts in Mexico." *New York Times*, February 3, 1990.

——. 2017. "Diferencias en tema laboral afloren en TLCAN." *Excélsior* (online edition), September 4.

——. 2022a. "GM Workers in Northern Mexico Vote to Keep Union Contract." March 27.

——. 2022b. "U.S. Rejects Mexican Union Petition for Labor Probe at BBB Industries." September 22.

Riddell, W. Craig. 1993. "Unionization in Canada and the United States: A Tale of Two Countries." In *Small Differences that Matter: Labor Markets and Income Maintenance in Canada and the United States*, ed. David Card and Richard B. Freeman, 109-48 (Chicago, IL: University of Chicago Press).

Riisgaard, Lone. 2005. "International Framework Agreements: A New Model for Securing Workers' Rights?" *Industrial Relations* 44 (4): 707-37.

Risse, Thomas. 2017. "Human Rights in Areas of Limited Statehood: From the Spiral Model to Localization and Translation." In *Human Rights Futures*, ed. Stephen Hopgood, Jack Snyder, and Leslie Vinjamuri, 135-58 (Cambridge: Cambridge University Press).

Risse, Thomas, and Stephen C. Ropp. 2013. "Introduction and Overview." In *The Persistent Power of Human Rights: From Commitment to Compliance*, ed. Thomas Risse, Stephen C. Ropp, and Kathryn Sikkink, 3-25 (New York: Cambridge University Press).

Robert, Maryse. 2000. *Negotiating NAFTA: Explaining the Outcome in Culture, Textiles, Autos, and Pharmaceuticals* (Toronto: University of Toronto Press).

Robinson, Ian. 1993. *North American Trade As If Democracy Mattered: What's Wrong with NAFTA and What Are the Alternatives?* (Ottawa: Canadian Centre for Policy Alternatives and International Labor Rights Education and Research Fund).

——. 1995. "The NAFTA Labour Accord in Canada: Experience, Prospects, and Alternatives." *Connecticut Journal of International Law* 10 (2): 475-531.

——. 1999. "El ACLAN y el movimiento obrero canadiense." In *Estándares laborales después del TLCAN*, ed. Graciela Bensusán, 127-64 (Mexico City: Plaza y Valdés Editores).

Rodgers, Gerry, Eddy Lee, Lee Swepston, and Jasmine Van Daele. 2009. *The International Labour Organization and the Quest for Social Justice, 1919–2009* (Geneva: International Labour Organization).

Rodríguez, Sabrina. 2019. "Mexico Fumes over Labor Enforcement Details in Trade Bill." *Politico* (online edition), December 15.

Rodríguez-Garavito, César A. 2005. "Global Governance and Labor Rights: Codes of Conduct and Anti-Sweatshop Struggles in Global Apparel Factories in Mexico and Guatemala." *Politics and Society* 33 (2): 203-33.

Rogowsky, Robert A., and Eric Chyn. 2008. "U.S. Trade Law and FTAs: A Survey of Labor Requirements." *Journal of International Commerce and Economics* 1: 113-36.

Romo, Arturo. 1991. "Brothers, Not Enemies of American Workers." *Washington Post*, May 19.

Rosenblum, Jonathan D. 1994. "GE in Juarez: Union Election Tests NAFTA." *Latin American Labor News* (Center for Labor Research and Studies, Florida International University) 10/11: 11, 18.

Rossi, Arianna, and Raymond Robertson. 2011. "Better Factories Cambodia: An Instrument for Improving Industrial Relations in a Transnational Context." In *Shaping Global Industrial Relations: The Impact of International Framework Agreements*, ed. Konstantinos Papadakis, 220-41 (New York: Palgrave Macmillan and International Labour Organization).

Ruotsila, Markku. 2002. "'The Great Charter for the Liberty of the Workingman': Labour, Liberals, and the Creation of the ILO." *Labour History Review* 67 (1): 29-47.

Russo, Robert. 2011. "A Cooperative Conundrum? The NAALC and Mexican Migrant Workers in the United States." *Law and Business Review of the Americas* 17 (1): 27-38.

Rütters, Peter. N.d. "International Trade Secretariats: Origins, Development, Activities." Friedrich Ebert Stiftung.

Salazar, Claudia, and Martha Martínez. 2019. "Avanza nueva ley laboral." *Reforma* (online edition), April 11.

Salinas de Gortari, Carlos. 2002. *México: Un paso difícil a la modernidad*, 4th ed. (Barcelona: Plaza and Janés).

——. 2017. *Aliados y adversarios: TLCAN, 1988–2017* (Mexico City: Debate).

Samet, Andrew. 2011. "Labor Provisions in U.S. Free Trade Agreements: Case Study of Mexico, Chile, Costa Rica, El Salvador and Peru." Policy Brief No. IDB-PB-172 (Washington, DC: Integration and Trade Section, Inter-American Development Bank).

Sánchez, Enrique. 2015. "Peña alista reforma en justicia laboral." *Excélsior* (online edition), December 5.

Sánchez, Roberto A. 2002. "Governance, Trade, and the Environment in the Context of NAFTA." *American Behavioral Scientist* 45 (9): 1369-93.

Sanger, David E. 1999. "After Clinton's Push, Questions About Motive." *New York Times*, December 3.

Santos, Álvaro. 2019. "The Lessons of TPP and the Future of Labor Chapters in Trade Agreements." In *Megaregulation Contested: Global Economic Ordering After TPP*, ed. David M. Malone, Paul Merten Skotter, Richard B. Stewart, Thomas Streinz, and Atsushi Sunami, 141-74 (Oxford: Oxford University Press).

Schlesinger, Jacob M. 2018, "Trump Officials Court Democrats Amid NAFTA Talks." *Wall Street Journal* (online edition), February 28.

Schoepfle, Gregory K., and Kenneth A. Swinnerton, eds. 1994. *International Labor Standards and Global Economic Integration* (Washington, DC: U.S. Department of Labor).

Schömann, Isabelle, André Sobczak, Eckhard Voss, and Peter Wilke. 2008. "International Framework Agreements: New Paths to Workers' Participation in Multinationals' Governance." *Transfer* 14 (1): 111-26.

Schulten, Thorsten. 1996. "European Works Councils: Prospects for a New System of European Industrial Relations." *European Journal of Industrial Relations* 2 (3): 303-24.

Schwarzenberg, Andres B. 2020. "Section 301 of the Trade Act of 1974: Origins, Evolution, and Use." Congressional Research Service Report R46604, December 14 (Washington, DC: Congressional Research Service).

Scott, Robert E. 2011. "Heading South: U.S.-Mexico Trade and Job Displacement after NAFTA." Briefing Paper #308 (Washington, DC: Economic Policy Institute).

—. 2014. "The Effects of NAFTA on U.S. Trade, Jobs, and Investment, 1993-2013." *Review of Keynesian Economics* 2 (4): 429-41.

Secretaría del Trabajo y Previsión Social (STPS). 1992. "Acuerdo Nacional para la Elevación de la Productividad y la Calidad." May.

—. 1996. "Programa de Empleo, Capacitación y Defensa de los Derechos Laborales, 1995-2000."

—. 2003. "Los Ministros del Trabajo de América del Norte se reúnen para discutir los avances de la Comisión para la Cooperación Laboral de América del Norte." Dirección General de Comunicación Social, Boletín 160, November 13.

—. 2015. "Secretarios del trabajo del país rechazan la práctica de los denominados 'contratos de protección." *Boletín* 435, June 22.

—. 2021a. "STPS resuelve reponer el proceso de legitimación del contrato colectivo de la planta de General Motors en Silao, Guanajuato." Comunicado 0007/2021, May 11.

—. 2021b. "Concluye sin incidentes legitimación del Contrato Colectivo en General Motors de Silao." Boletín 081, August 19.

Secretaría del Trabajo y Previsión Social / U.S. Department of Labor. 1993. "First Annual United States-Mexico International Labor Law Conference." October.

Seiderman, Ian D. 2001. *Hierarchy in International Law: The Human Rights Dimension* (Antwerp: INTERSENTIA).

Seidman, Gay W. 2007. *Beyond the Boycott: Labor Rights, Human Rights, and Transnational Activism* (New York: Russell Sage Foundation).

Sekkel, Julia. 2009. "Summary of Major Trade Preference Programs." April. https://www.cgdev.org /doc/Working_Groups/Summary_of_Major_Trade_Preference_Programs_Final.pdf.

Sen, Amartya. 1994. "Freedoms and Needs." *New Republic* 210 (2/3, January 10): 31-39.

Senado de la República. 2016a. "Dictamen de las Comisiones Unidas de Puntos Constituciona- les; de Justicia; de Trabajo y Previsión Social, y de Estudios Legislativos, Segunda, sobre la iniciativa de decreto por el que se reforman y adicionan diversas disposiciones de la Con- stitución Política de los Estados Unidos Mexicanos, en materia de justicia laboral." LXIII Legislatura, October 5, Mexico City: Senado de la República.

—. 2016b. "Acuerdo de las Comisiones Unidas de Puntos Constitucionales; de Justicia; de Trabajo y Previsión Social, y de Estudios Legislativos, Segunda, por el que se modifica el dictamen con proyecto de decreto por el que se reforman y adicionan diversas fracciones de los artículos 107 y 123 de la Constitución Política de los Estados Unidos Mexicanos, en materia de justicia laboral." LXIII Legislatura, October 13, Mexico City: Senado de la República.

Servais, Jean-Michel. 2000. "Labor Law and Cross-Border Cooperation Among Unions." In *Transnational Cooperation Among Labor Unions*, ed. Michael E. Gordon and Lowell Turner, 44-59 (Ithaca, NY: Cornell University Press / ILR Press).

Severns, Maggie. 2016. "Trump Pins NAFTA, 'Worst Trade Deal Ever', on Clinton." *Politico*, September 26.

Shadlen, Kenneth C. 2008. "Globalisation, Power and Integration: The Political Economy of Regional and Bilateral Trade Agreements in the Americas." *Journal of Development Studies* 44 (1): 1–20.

—. 2017. *Coalitions and Compliance: The Political Economy of Pharmaceutical Patents in Latin America* (Oxford: Oxford University Press).

Shaefer Munoz, Sara, Anthony Harrup, and Robbie Whelan. 2018. "In Nafta Shift, U.S. Focuses on Labor Standards." *Wall Street Journal* (online edition), April 3.

Shaffer, Gregory, and Mark A. Pollack. 2012. "Hard and Soft Law." In *Interdisciplinary Perspectives on International Law and International Relations: The State of the Art*, ed. Jeffrey L. Dunoff and Mark A. Pollack, 197–222 (New York: Cambridge University Press).

Shaw, Linda. 2004. "Beyond Unions: Labour and Codes of Conduct." In *Labour and Globalisation: Results and Prospects*, ed. Ronaldo Munck, 169–80 (Liverpool: University of Liverpool Press).

Shepardson, David. 2021. "U.S. Lawmakers Press GM CEO on California Emissions, Mexico Labor." *U.S. News and World Report* (online edition), June 16.

Sheridan, Mary Beth, and David Agren. 2020. "Mexico is Giving Millions of Workers a Historic Pay Increase. But Will It Have Much Effect?" *Washington Post* (online edition), January 2.

Shoch, James. 2000. "Contesting Globalization: Organized Labor, NAFTA, and the 1997 and 1998 Fast-Track Fights." *Politics and Society* 28 (1): 119–50.

Shorrock, Tim. 1995. "Mexican Trade Union Steps in to Defend U.S. Workers' Rights." *Journal of Commerce*, February 13.

Sikkink, Kathryn. 1993. "Human Rights, Principled Issue-Networks, and Sovereignty in Latin America." *International Organization* 47 (3): 411–41.

—. 2009. "From State Responsibility to Individual Criminal Accountability: A New Regulatory Model for Core Human Rights Violations." In *The Politics of Global Regulation*, ed. Walter Mattli and Ngaire Woods, 121–50 (Princeton, NJ: Princeton University Press).

Silva, Laura Cristina. 2007. "El proceso de negociación del TLC entre Colombia y Estados Unidos." *Colombia Internacional* 65 (January–June): 112–33.

Simmons, Beth A. 2009. *Mobilizing for Human Rights: International Law in Domestic Politics* (New York: Cambridge University Press).

Simpson, Fraser. 2015. "Labour Rights Protections within International Trade: A Study of Free Trade Agreements and Generalised Systems of Preferences." Thesis submitted for L.L.M., International Human Rights Law, Lund University, Sweden. https://papers.ssrn.com/sol3 /papers.cfm?abstract_id=2686050.

Singer, Paul W. 2006. "Allegations of Cronyism, Misdeeds Leave Labor Panel Under Cloud." *Government Executive*, October 31.

Singh, Parbudyal, and Roy J. Adams. 2001. "Neither a Gem nor a Scam: The Progress of the North American Agreement on Labor Cooperation." *Labor Studies Journal* 26 (2): 1–16.

Sklair, Leslie. 1993. *Assembling for Development: The Maquila Industry in Mexico and the United States*, rev. ed. (La Jolla, CA: Center for U.S.-Mexican Studies, University of California-San Diego).

Smith, Gerri, and John Pearson. 1994. "Which Side (Of the Border) Are You On? Well, Both." *Business Week*, April 4.

Smith, Murray G. 1996. "Canada and Economic Sovereignty." In *NAFTA and Sovereignty: Trade-offs for Canada, Mexico, and the United States*, ed. Joyce Hoebing, Sidney Weintraub, and M. Delal Baer, 29–68 (Washington, DC: Center for Strategic and International Studies).

Smith Ramos, Kenneth. 2019. "El desenlace del T-MEC en el Congreso estadounidense." *El Financiero* (online edition), November 14.

Solomon, Daina Beth. 2022. "Update 1: Independent Union Wins Workers' Vote at Mexico's Tridonex Plant." *Reuters*, March 1.

SourceMex. 1994. "U.S. Labor Union AFL-CIO Asks Labor Secretariat for Permit to Establish Office in Mexico City." September 12.

Southall, Roger. 1994. "The Development and Delivery of 'Northern' Worker Solidarity to South African Trade Unions in the 1970s and 1980s." *Journal of Commonwealth and Comparative Politics* 32 (2): 166–99.

Southall, Roger, and Andries Bezuidenhout. 2004. "International Solidarity and Labour in South Africa." In *Labour and Globalisation: Results and Prospects*, ed. Ronaldo Munck, 128–48 (Liverpool: Liverpool University Press).

Spriggs, William E., and James Stanford. 1993. "Economists' Assessments of the Likely Employment and Wage Effects of the North American Free Trade Agreement." *Hofstra Labor Law Journal* 10 (2): 495–536.

Stairs, Denis. 1996. "The Canadian Dilemma in North America." In *NAFTA and Sovereignty: Trade-Offs for Canada, Mexico, and the United States*, ed. Joyce Hoebing, Sidney Weintraub, and M. Delal Baer, 1–38 (Washington, DC: Center for Strategic and International Studies).

Stevis, Dimitris, and Terry Boswell. 2007. "International Framework Agreements: Opportunities and Challenges for Global Unionism." In *Global Unions: Challenging Transnational Capital Through Cross-Border Campaigns*, ed. Kate Bronfenbrenner, 174–94 (Ithaca, NY: Cornell University Press).

Stockman, Farah. 2022. "Biden's Pro-Labor Vision Goes Beyond America." *New York Times International Edition*, March 8.

Story, Dale. 1986. *Industry, the State, and Public Policy in Mexico* (Austin: University of Texas Press).

Suprema Corte de Justicia de la Nación (SCJN). 2008a. "Contradicción de tesis 74/2008-SS, suscitada entre los Tribunales Colegiados Tercero, Cuarto, Noveno, Décimo Segundo, Décimo Tercero y Décimo Cuarto, todos en materia del trabajo del Primer Circuito." Segunda Sala, September 10. Mexico City: SCJN.

——. 2008b. "Tesis de jurisprudencia 150/2008" ("Recuento para determinar la titularidad del contrato colectivo de trabajo previsto en el artículo 931 de la Ley Federal del Trabajo. Las Juntas de Conciliación y Arbitraje deben ordenar y garantizar que en su desahogo los trabajadores emitan voto personal, libre, directo y secreto"). *Seminario judicial del la Federación y su gaceta* 28 (October.): 451.

——. 2020. "Amparo en revisión 28/2020 quejoso y recurrente: Sindicato Nacional de Trabajadores y Empleados del Transporte Aéreo de la República Mexicana." Segunda Sala, November 25, Mexico City: SCJN.

Swanson, Ana. 2017. "Trade Plans Disrupted by Discord in Trump Circle." *New York Times International Edition*, October 23.

——. 2018a. "U.S. and Mexico Nearing Deal on Trade." *New York Times International Edition*, August 6.

—. 2018b. "As Nafta Deal Nears, Canada is Sidelined." *New York Times International Edition*, 20 Aug., p. 7.

—. 2019. "Democrats Vow to Alter Trade." *New York Times International Edition*, August 12.

Swanson, Ana, and Emily Cochrane. 2019a. "Trump's Trade Deal Steals a Page from Democrats' Playbook." *New York Times* (online edition), December 1.

—. 2019b. "Democrats in a Bind over Trade Deal." *New York Times International Edition*, December 4.

Swanson, Ana, and Elisabeth Malkin. 2018. "Chances of Revising Nafta in 2018 Shrink as House Deadline Passes." *New York Times*, May 18.

Swanson, Ana, Katie Rogers, and Alan Rappeport. 2018. "Trade Deal with Mexico Puts Canada in Limbo." *New York Times International Edition*, August 29.

Swepston, Lee. 1998. "Human Rights Law and Freedom of Association: Development Through ILO Supervision." *International Labour Review* 137 (2): 169–94.

Symons, Jonathan. 2011. "The Legitimation of International Organisations: Examining the Identity of the Communities that Grant Legitimacy." *Review of International Studies* 37 (5): 2557–83.

Taylor, Chantell O'Neal. 1994. "Fast Track, Trade Policy, and Free Trade Agreements: Why the NAFTA Turned Into a Battle." *George Washington University Journal of International Law and Economics* 28 (1): 1–132.

Thacker, Strom. 1999. "NAFTA Coalitions and the Political Viability of Neoliberalism in Mexico." *Journal of Inter-American Studies and World Affairs* 41 (2): 57–89.

Thompson, John Herd, and Stephen J. Randall. 1994. *Canada and the United States: Ambivalent Allies* (Athens: University of Georgia Press).

Thorup, Cathryn L. 1991. "The Politics of Free Trade and the Dynamics of Cross-Border Coalitions in U.S.-Mexican Relations." *Columbia Journal of World Business* 26 (2): 12–26.

Thrush, Glenn. 2018a. "Trump's Nafta Plan Could be Upended by Democrats' House Takeover." *New York Times* (online edition), November 12.

—. 2018b. "Election Interrupts Trump Treaty Reset." *New York Times International Edition*, November 14.

—. 2018c. "Trump Claims Nafta Victory but Deal Faces Long Odds in U.S." *New York Times* (online edition), November 30.

—. 2019. "China Truce in Hands of President's Trade Warrior." *New York Times International Edition*, January 3.

"Timeline of the Progress Toward a North American Union." Accessed December 7, 2006, https://www.globalresearch.ca/deep-integration-timeline-of-the-progress-toward-a-north -american-union/4216.

Toffel, Michael W., Jodi L. Short, and Melissa Ouellet. 2015. "Codes in Context: How States, Markets, and Civil Society Shape Adherence to Global Labor Standards." *Regulation and Governance* 9: 205–23.

Tomuschat, Christian. 2014. *Human Rights: Between Idealism and Realism*, 3rd ed. (Oxford: Oxford University Press).

Tong, Mary E. 1999. "Reaching Across the Rio." In *The Maquiladora Reader: Cross-Border Organizing Since NAFTA*, ed. Rachel Kamel and Anya Hoffman, 74–78 (Philadelphia, PA: American Friends Service Committee).

Torres, Blanca. "Transnational Actors and NAFTA: The Search for Coalitions on Labor and the Environment." In *Regionalism and Governance in the Americas: Continental Drift*, ed. Louise L. Faucett and Mónica Serrano, 117–34 (Basingstoke, England: Palgrave Macmillan).

—. 2010. "Estrategias y tácticas mexicanas en la conducción de sus relaciones con Estados Unidos (1945–1970)." *Foro Internacional* 50 (3/4): 661–88.

Torriente, Anna. 1996. "Study of Mexican Supreme Court Decisions Concerning the Rights of State Employees to Organize in the States of Jalisco and Oaxaca." Report submitted to the U.S. National Administrative Office (U.S. Department of Labor), November 11.

Tosstorff, Reiner. 2005. "The International Trade-Union Movement and the Founding of the International Labour Organization." *International Review of Social History* 50 (3): 399–433.

Toye, Richard. 2012. "The International Trade Organization." In *The Oxford Handbook on the World Trade Organization*, ed. Amrita Narlikar, Martin Daunton, and Robert M. Stern, 85–101 (Oxford: University of Oxford Press).

Traub-Werner, Marion, and Altha J. Cravey. 2002. "Spatiality, Sweatshops, and Solidarity in Guatemala." *Social and Cultural Geography* 3 (4): 383–401.

Trebilcock, Michael J., and Robert Howse. 2005. "Trade Policy and Labor Standards." *Minnesota Journal of Global Trade* 14 (2): 261–300.

Truell, Peter. 1990. "U.S. and Mexico Agree to Seek Free-Trade Pact." *Wall Street Journal*, March 27.

Tsogas, George. 2000. "Labour Standards in the Generalized Systems of Preferences of the European Union and the United States." *European Journal of Industrial Relations* 6 (3): 349–70.

—. 2001. *Labor Regulation in a Global Economy* (Armonk, NY: M. E. Sharpe).

UNIFOR. 2017. "Unifor Position Statement on the Renegotiated North American Free Trade Agreement." July.

Unión Nacional de Trabajadores (UNT). 2016. "Informe sobre el exitoso inicio del proceso legislativo relativo a la iniciativa de reformar a los artículos 107 y 123 constitucionales promovida por el Ejecutivo Federal." October 17, Mexico City.

United Kingdom Board of Trade. 1925. *Safeguarding of Industries: Procedure and Enquiries*, Cmd. 2327 (London: H.M. Stationery Office).

United Nations. 1946. *Report of the First Session of the London Preparatory Committee of the United Nations Conference on Trade and Employment*. U.N. Document EPCT/33. London: United Nations (https://www.wto.org/gatt_docs/English/SULPDF/92290037.pdf).

—. 1948. *United Nations Conference on Trade and Employment: Final Act and Related Documents* (Lake Success, NY: Interim Commission for the International Trade Organization). https://www.wto.org/english/docs_e/legal_e/havana_e.pdf.

United Nations Committee on Economic, Social, and Cultural Rights (UNCESR). 1991. "Report on the Fifth Session, November 26–December 14, 1990, Supplement No. 3." UN Doc. E/1991/23-E/C.12/1990/8 (New York: United Nations).

—. 1997. "Report on the Technical Assistance Mission to the Dominican Republic of the Committee on Economic, Social, and Cultural Rights, September 19–27, 1997." In "Report on the Sixteenth and Seventeenth Sessions, May 16–April 28, 1997, November 17–December 5, 1997, Supplement No. 2, Annex VI (pp. 123–57)." UN Doc. E/1998/22-E/C.12/1997/10 (New York: United Nations).

United Steelworkers-Canada. 2004. "In the Matter of Public Communication 2003-01 Before the Canadian National Administrative Office, in Pursuit to the North American Agreement on Labour Cooperation: Submission of the United Steelworkers of America." May 28.

Urbina, Ian. 2016. "U.S. Closing a Loophole on Products Tied to Slaves." *International New York Times* (online edition), February 15.

U.S. Chamber of Commerce. 2004. "Comments by the U.S. Chamber of Commerce on the Operation and Effectiveness of the North American Agreement on Labor Cooperation." *Inside U.S. Trade*, February 5.

U.S. Congress (Office of Technology Assessment). 1992. *U.S.-Mexico Trade: Pulling Together or Pulling Apart?* ITE-545, October (Washington, DC: U.S. Government Printing Office).

U.S. Council of Economic Advisers. 1982. *Economic Report of the President* (Washington, DC: U.S. Government Printing Office).

U.S. Council for International Business. 2003. "Comments on Operation and Effectiveness of the NAALC." December 4. Unpublished.

U.S. Department of Labor (U.S. DOL). 2012. *Progress in Implementing Chapter 16 (Labor) and Capacity-Building under the Dominican Republic-Central America-United States Free Trade Agreement* (Washington, DC: Bureau of International Labor Affairs).

——. 2021. "U.S., Mexico Announce Enforcement of Worker Protection Agreement." July 9.

——. 2022. "Secretary of Labor, US Trade Representative Support Protection of Labor Rights at Mexico's Manufacturas VU Auto Parts Factory." September 14.

U.S. Department of State. 1945a. *Charter of the United Nations: Report to the President on the Results of the San Francisco Conference by the Chairman of the United States Delegation, the Secretary of State.* Department of State Publication 2349, Conference Series 71 (Washington, DC: U.S. Department of State).

——. 1945b. *Proposals for Expansion of World Trade and Employment.* Department of State Publication 2411 (Washington, DC: U.S. Department of State).

——. 1946. *Suggested Charter for an International Trade Organization of the United Nations.* Department of State Publication 2598, Commercial Policy Series 93 (Washington, DC: U.S. Department of State).

U.S. General Accounting Office. 1993a. *North American Free Trade Agreement: Assessment of Major Issues*, GAO/GGD-93-137, 2 vols. (Washington, DC: U.S. General Accounting Office).

——. 1993b. *U.S.-Mexico Trade: The Work Environment at Eight U.S.-owned Maquiladora Auto Plants*, B-243936, November (Washington, DC: U.S. General Accounting Office).

——. 1998. *Caribbean Basin: Worker Rights Progress Made, but Enforcement Issues Remain.* July (Washington, DC: U.S. General Accounting Office).

U.S. Government Accountability Office (US GAO). 2009. *International Trade: Four Free Trade Agreements GAO Reviewed Have Resulted in Commercial Benefits, but Challenges in Labor and Environment Remain*, GAO-09-439 (Washington, DC: U.S. Government Accountability Office).

——. 2014. *Free Trade Agreements: U.S. Partners Are Addressing Labor Commitments, but More Monitoring and Enforcement Are Needed*, GAO-15-160 (Washington, DC: U.S. Government Accountability Office).

U.S. House of Representatives. 1945. "Hearings on H.R. 3240: Extension of the Reciprocal Trade Agreements Act." Committee on Ways and Means, 79th Congress, First Session, May 30–June 5 (Washington, DC: U.S. Government Printing Office).

——. 1970. "Tariff and Trade Proposals." Hearings before the Committee on Ways and Means, 91st Congress, Second Session, May 11–14, 18–22 and June 1–5, 8–12, 15–17, 25 (Washington, DC: U.S. Government Printing Office).

——. 1973a. "Hearings on H.R. 6767, Trade Reform Act." Committee on Ways and Means, 93rd Congress, First Session, May 9–11, 14–18, 21–24, 29–31, June 1, 6–8, 11–15 (Washington, DC: U.S. Government Printing Office).

——. 1973b. "Listing of Amendments Proposed to H.R. 6767: The Proposed Trade Reform Act of 1973." Prepared for the Use of the Committee on Ways and Means in Connection with Hearings on the Subject of Foreign Trade and Tariffs, August (Washington, DC: U.S. Government Printing Office).

——. 1973c. "House Report 93-571: Trade Reform Act of 1973." Report of the Committee on Ways and Means, October 10 (Washington, DC: U.S. Government Printing Office).

——. 1984a. "Hearings on the Possible Renewal of the GSP." Committee on Ways and Means (Subcommittee on Trade). 98th Congress, Second Session, House Hearings 98-59, February 8–9 (Washington, DC: U.S. Government Printing Office).

——. 1984b. *Designating Eleven Caribbean Basin Countries as Beneficiaries: Communication from the President Transmitting Notice of His Intention to Designate Eleven Caribbean Basin Countries and Entities as Beneficiaries for the Purpose of Granting Duty-free Treatment, Pursuant to Public Law 98–67, sec. 212(a)(1)(A).* House Document 151, 98th Congress, 2nd Session (Washington, DC: U.S. Government Printing Office).

——. 1984c. *Designation of Nine Caribbean Basin Countries as Beneficiaries of the Caribbean Basin Economic Recovery Act: Communication from the President Transmitting Notice of His Intention to Designate Nine Caribbean Basin Countries and Entities as Beneficiaries for the Purpose of Granting Duty-free Treatment, Pursuant to Public Law 98–67, sec. 212(a)(1)(A).* House Document 159, 98th Congress, 2nd Session (Washington, DC: U.S. Government Printing Office).

——. 2008. "Former President Bush NAFTA Official, Covered by Diplomatic Immunity, Ducks Criminal Prosecution." Press release by Education and Labor Committee, *U.S. Federal News*, April 17.

——. 2016. "TPP Issue Analysis: Worker Rights." Committee on Ways and Means (Minority Staff Report), 114th Congress, Second Session, February 1 (Washington, DC: U.S. Government Printing Office).

——. 2019a. "Hearing on Trade and Labor: Creating and Enforcing Rules to Benefit American Workers." Committee on Ways and Means (Subcommittee on Trade). 116th Congress, First Session, Serial No. 116-16, 26 Mar. (Washington, DC: U.S. Government Printing Office).

——. 2019b. "Hearing on Enforcement in the New NAFTA." Committee on Ways and Means (Subcommittee on Trade)." 116th Congress, First Session, Serial No. 116-23, May 22 (Washington, DC: U.S. Government Printing Office).

——. 2019c. "Hearing on the 2019 Trade Policy Agenda: Negotiations with China, Japan, the EU, and UK; new NAFTA/USMCA; U.S. Participation in the WTO; and Other Matters." Committee on Ways and Means. 116th Congress, First Session, Serial No. 116-27, June 19 (Washington, DC: U.S. Government Printing Office).

——. 2019d. "Hearing on Mexico's Labor Reform: Opportunities and Challenges for an Improved NAFTA." Committee on Ways and Means (Subcommittee on Trade). 116th Congress, First Session, Serial No. 116-29, June 25 (Washington, DC: U.S. Government Printing Office).

U.S. International Trade Commission (USITC). 2019. "U.S.-Mexico-Canada Trade Agreement: Likely Impact on the U.S. Economy and on Specific Industry Sectors." Publication no. 4889, investigation no. TPA-105-003, April (Washington, DC: U.S. International Trade Commission).

U.S. National Administrative Office (US NAO, Bureau of International Labor Affairs, U.S. Department of Labor). 1995a. *1994 Annual Report*, January (Washington, DC: US NAO).

——. 1995b. "Seminar on Union Registration and Certification Procedures." 2 vols. November.

—. 1999. "Status of Submissions Under the North American Agreement on Labor Cooperation (NAALC)." November 16. Unpublished.

U.S. Office of the Special Trade Representative for Trade Negotiations. 1969. *Future United States Foreign Trade Policy: Report to the President* (Washington, DC: U.S. Government Printing Office).

U.S. Senate. 1947. "Hearings on the Trade Agreement System and Proposed International Trade Organization Charter." Committee on Finance. 80th Congress, First Session, March 20– April 3 (Washington, DC U.S. Government Printing Office).

—. 1983-1984. "Proposed Renewal of the Generalized System of Preferences, 1984." Hearings before the Subcommittee on International Trade (Committee on Finance), 98th Congress, Senate Hearings 98-423 (August 4, 1983) and 98-697 (January 27, 1984) (Washington, DC: U.S. Government Printing Office).

—. 1993. "U.S. Trade Policy and NAFTA." Hearing Before the Committee on Finance, 103rd Congress, First Session, Senate Hearing 103-66, March 9 (Washington, DC: U.S. Government Printing Office).

—. 2020. "United States-Mexico-Canada Agreement Implementation Act" (H.R. 5430/S. 3052), *Congressional Record* 166, no. 9-10 (January 15-16), S224-234 (Washington, DC: U.S. Government Printing Office).

Van Boven, Theo. 2014. "Categories of Rights." In *International Human Rights Law*, 2nd ed., ed. Daniel Moeckli, Sangeeta Shah, and Sandesh Sivakumaran, 143-56 (Oxford: Oxford University Press).

Van Daele, Jasmien. 2005. "Engineering Social Peace: Networks, Ideas, and the Founding of the International Labour Organization." *International Review of Social History* 50 (3): 435-66.

Van der Linden, Marcel. 2019. "The International Labour Organization, 1919-2019: An Appraisal." *Labor* 16 (2): 11-41.

Van Roozendaal, Gerda C. 2002. *Trade Unions and Global Governance: The Debate on A Social Clause* (London: Continuum).

Van Waas, Michael. 1981. "The Multinationals' Strategy for Labor: Foreign Assembly Plants in Mexico's Border Industrialization Program." Ph.D. diss., Department of Political Science, Stanford University.

Velasco, Elizabeth. 1998a. "Revisión de la LFT en torno a mujeres, piden al gobierno." *La Jornada*, July 21.

—. 1998b. "Plantean cambios a la LFT que acaben con discriminación." *La Jornada*, May 22.

Velasco, Elizabeth, and Fabiola Martínez. 1999. "Cuestionan centrales obreras el fallo sobre libre sindicalización." *La Jornada*, May 13.

Velázquez Sánchez, Fidel. 1991. "Mexican Labor Leader's Call for Partnership." *Wall Street Journal*, May 3.

Vergara, Rosalía. 2016a. "Justicia laboral 'cosmética' por presiones de EU." *Proceso*, February 14.

—. 2016b. "La reforma laboral, imposición internacional." *Proceso* 2085 (October 16): 32-33.

Vieira, Paul. 2017. "U.S. Proposes to Boost Nafta's Labor Standards, but Union Officials Say the Language in the Proposal Isn't Strong Enough." *Wall Street Journal* (online edition), September 26.

Villamil, Valente. 2017. "Define EU metas para el TLCAN." *El Financiero* (online edition), July 18.

Villarreal, M. Angeles. 2014. "The U.S.-Colombia Free Trade Agreement: Background and Issues." Congressional Research Service Report RL34470 (Washington, DC: Congressional Research Service).

Villarreal, M. Angeles, and Marisabel Cid. 2008. "NAFTA and the Mexican Economy." Congressional Research Service Report RL34733 (Washington, DC: Congressional Research Service).

Vogel, David. 2006. *The Market for Virtue: The Potential and Limits of Corporate Social Responsibility*, 2nd ed. (Washington, DC: Brookings Institution Press).

Vogt, Jeffrey S. 2014. "Trade and Investment Arrangements and Labor Rights." In *Corporate Responsibility for Human Rights: Impacts, New Expectations, and Paradigms*, ed. Lara Blecher, Nancy Kaymar Stafford, and Gretchen Bellamy, 315–431 (Chicago: American Bar Association).

——. 2015. "The Evolution of Labor Rights and Trade—A Transatlantic Comparison and Lessons for the Transatlantic Trade and Investment Partnership." *Journal of International Economic Law* 18 (4): 827–60.

Von Bertrab, Hermann. 1997. *Negotiating NAFTA: A Mexican Envoy's Account.* The Washington Papers 173 (Washington, DC: Center for Strategic and International Studies).

Von Potobsky, Geraldo. 1998. "Freedom of Association: The Impact of Convention No. 87 and ILO Action." *International Labour Review* 137 (2): 195–221.

Waer, Paul. 1996. "Social Clauses in International Trade: The Debate in the European Union." *Journal of World Trade* 30 (4): 25–42.

Weber, Max. 1978. *Economy and Society: An Outline of Interpretative Sociology.* Ed. Guenther Roth and Claus Wittich. 2 vols. (Berkeley: University of California Press).

Webster, Edward, Rob Lambert, and Andries Bezuidenhout. 2008. *Grounding Globalization: Labour in the Age of Insecurity* (Malden, MA: Blackwell).

Weisman, Steven R. 2007. "Democrats Offer Deal on Foreign Trade Pacts." *International Herald Tribune*, March 29.

Weiss, Friedl. 1998. "Internationally Recognized Labor Standards and Trade." In *International Economic Law with a Human Face*, ed. Friedl Weiss, Erick Denters, and Paul de Waart, 79–107 (The Hague: Kluwer Law International).

Weiss, Marley S. 2003. "Two Steps Forward, One Step Back, or Vice Versa: Labor Rights Under Free Trade Agreements from NAFTA, through Jordan, via Chile, to Latin America and Beyond." *University of San Francisco Law Review* 37 (3): 689–755.

Whelan, Daniel J. 2010. *Indivisible Human Rights: A History* (Philadelphia: University of Pennsylvania Press).

White, Robert. 1993. "NAFTA Side-Deal Changes Nothing for Workers." August 25.

White House. 1991, "Response of the Administration to Issues Raised in Connection with the Negotiation of a North American Free Trade Agreement." May 1.

——. 1993. "The North American Free Trade Agreement: Fact Sheet." August 12.

——. 2011a. "Fact Sheets: U.S.-Colombia Trade Agreement and Action Plan (Leveling the Playing Field: Labor Protections and the U.S.-Colombia Trade Promotion Agreement)." April 6.

——. 2011b. "Fact Sheets: U.S.-Colombia Trade Agreement and Action Plan (Trade and the U.S.-Colombia Partnership)." April 6.

——. 2016a. "Readout of the President's Call with President Enrique Peña Nieto of Mexico." January 15.

——. 2016b. "Statement by the President on the Signing of the Trans-Pacific Partnership." February 3. https://obamawhitehouse.archives.gov/the-press-office/2016/02/03/statement-president-signing-trans-pacific-partnership.

——. 2016c. "Readout of Vice President Biden's Meeting with President Enrique Peña Nieto of Mexico." February 25.

—. 2020a. "Executive Order on the Establishment of the Interagency Labor Committee for Monitoring and Enforcement Under Section 711 of the USMCA Implementation Act." April 28.

—. 2020b. "Executive Order on the Establishment of the Forced Labor Task Force Under Section 741 of the United States-Mexico-Canada Implementation Act." May 15.

Wilkensen, Rorden. 1999. "Labour and Trade-Related Regulation: Beyond the Trade-Labour Standards Debate?" *British Journal of Politics and International Relations* 1 (2): 165–91.

Wilkinson, Rorden, and Steve Hughes. 2000. "Labor Standards and Global Governance: Examining the Dimensions of Institutional Engagement." *Global Governance* 6 (2): 259–77.

Williams, Heather L. 1999. "Mobile Capital and Transborder Labor Rights Mobilization." *Politics and Society* 27 (1): 139–66.

—. 2003. "Of Labor Tragedy and Legal Farce: The Han Young Factory Struggle in Tijuana, Mexico." *Social Science History*, 27 (4): 525–50.

Williams, Natara. 2005. "Pre-Hire Pregnancy Screening in Mexico's Maquiladoras: Is It Discrimination?" *Duke Journal of Gender Law and Policy* 12 (Spring): 131–52.

Wills, Jane. 2001. "Uneven Geographies of Capital and Labour: The Lessons of the European Works Councils." In *Place, Space and the New Labour Internationalisms*, ed. Peter Waterman and Jane Wills, 180–205 (Oxford, England: Blackwell).

—. 2002. "Bargaining for the Space to Organize in the Global Economy: A Review of the Accor-IUT Trade Union Rights Agreement." *Review of International Political Economy* 9 (4): 675–700.

Wilson, Christopher E. 2011. *Working Together: Economic Ties Between the United States and Mexico* (Washington, DC: Mexico Institute, Woodrow Wilson International Center for Scholars).

Windmuller, John P. 2000. "The International Trade Secretariats." In *Transnational Cooperation among Labor Unions*, ed. Michael E. Gordon and Lowell Turner, 102–19 (Ithaca, NY: Cornell University Press / ILR Press).

Wishnie, Michael J. 2002. "Immigrant Workers and the Domestic Enforcement of International Labor Rights." *University of Pennsylvania Journal of Labor and Employment Law* 4 (3): 529–57.

Woodward, Bob. 1994. *The Agenda: Inside the Clinton White House* (New York: Simon and Schuster).

—. 2018. *Fear: Trump in the White House* (New York: Simon and Schuster).

World Trade Organization. 2001. "The Doha Round Texts and Related Documents." November 14. https://www.wto.org/english/res_e/publications_e/doha_decl_e.htm.

Xelhuantzi López, María. 2002. *Sindicalismo internacional* (Mexico City: Sindicato de Trabajadores de la Universidad Nacional Autónoma de México).

Young, Kevin, and Diana C. Sierra Becerra. 2014. "How 'Partnership' Weakens Solidarity: Colombian GM Workers and the Limits of UAW Internationalism." *Working USA* 17 (2): 239–60.

Zavala, Misael. 2018. "Trudeau Asks AMLO to Intervene in NAFTA Renegotiations with the U.S." *El Universal* (online English edition), September 28.

Zimmerman, James M. 1991. "The Overseas Private Investment Corporation and Worker Rights: The Loss of Role Models for Employment Standards om the Foreign Workplace." *Hastings International and Comparative Law Review* 14 (3): 603–18.

Zinn, Kenneth S. 2000. "Solidarity Across Borders: The UMWA's Corporate Campaign Against Peabody and Hanson PLC." In *Transnational Cooperation Among Labor Unions*, ed. Michael E. Gordon and Lowell Turner, 223–37 (Ithaca, NY: Cornell University Press / ILR Press).

Zweig, Michael. 2014. "Working for Global Justice in the New Labor Movement." *Working USA* 17 (2): 261–81.

Index

Italicized page numbers refer to figures or tables.

Abascal Carranza, Carlos, 177, 422n180, 425n205
Abbott, K. W., 486n30
Accor, 359n101
Aceves del Olmo, Carlos, 231–32, 456n246, 483n5
ACHR. *See* American Convention on Human Rights
Acuerdo de Cooperación Laboral de América del Norte (ACLAN), 407n28
Aeroméxico, 186, 334, 436n309, 437n322
AFA. *See* Association of Flight Attendants
AFL-CIO. *See* American Federation of Labor-Congress of Industrial Organizations
African Growth and Opportunity Act of 2000, 47, 484n11
Agency for International Development, 47
Agreement Between the Government of the United States of America and the Government of Mexico Complementing the 1991 Memorandum of Understanding on Labor Cooperation, and Regarding the Establishing of a Consultative Commission on Labor Matters, 386n65
Agriculture Sector Promotion Act of 2000, 443n52
Aguilar Zínser, Adolfo, 384n51
Alcalde Justiniani, Arturo, 177, 456n245, 472n122
Alcalde Luján, Luisa María, 267
Alston, Philip, 370n54
Althaus, Dudley, 462n31

Amato, Theresa A., 370n55
American Center for International Labor Solidarity, 171
American Convention on Human Rights (ACHR), 145, 354n70
American Federation of Government Employees, 369n52
American Federation of Labor, 42
American Federation of Labor-Congress of Industrial Organizations (AFL-CIO), 368n39; Bahrain and, 203, 441n47; Bibong campaign of, 358n106; Canadian NAOs and, 326, 412n63; CJM and, 429n234; Colombia and, 201, 203, 441n40; CTM and, 428n231, 429nn234–35; GATT and, 367n29, 368n42; Guatemala and, 201; Han Young and, 419n133; ILCME and, 479n185; Jordan and, 199, 216; *maquiladora* and, 418n127; Mexican NAOs and, 331; Mexico and, 450n159, 469n90; NAALC and, 44–47, 96, 108, 113, 114, 170, 171–72, 177, 247, 307, 437n325, 438n6; NAFTA and, 79, 84, 248, 251, 252, 390n109, 393n157, 462n26, 468n89, 474n132, 478n179; NGOs and, 199; OTCA and, 374n83; OTLA and, 339, 340, 341; Peru and, 201; RRLM and, 344, 348; TPP and, 223, 238, 239; U.S. FTAs and, 461n16; U.S. GSP and, 369n45, 369n52; USMCA and, 260, 264, 266–71, 278, 466n75; U.S. NAOs and, 334, 335, 338; USTR and, 52, 54, 59, 199, 441n46

American Federation of Teachers, 86
American Friends Service Committee, 332
Americas Watch, 54, 61
ANAD. *See* Asociación Nacional de Abogados Democráticos
Andean Trade Preference Act of 1991, 47
Andrade Law Office, 330
AP. *See* arbitral panel
Apparel Industry Partnership, 30
arbitral panel (AP), 124–25
Asociación Nacional de Abogados Democráticos (ANAD, National Association of Democratic Lawyers), 142, 150; freedom of association and, 417n106; gender discrimination and, 144; Mexican NAOs and, 331; NAALC and, 170; U.S. NAOs and, 332, 333
Asociación Nacional de Empleados Públicos y Privados (National Association of Public and Private Employees), 340
Asociación Sindical de Pilotos Aviadores de México (ASPAM, Mexican Airline Pilots Association): Canadian NAOs and, 328, 409n44; U.S. NAOs and, 337, 410n45
Asociación Sindical de Sobrecargos de Aviación de México (ASSAM, Union Association of Mexican Aviation Flight Attendants), 335
Asociación Tepoyac (Tepoyac Association), 330
ASPAM. *See* Asociación Sindical de Pilotos Aviadores de México
ASSAM. *See* Asociación Sindical de Sobrecargos de Aviación de México
Associational Registry (Registro de Asociaciones), 413n74
Association of Flight Attendants (AFA), 334, 335
Atlantic Charter, 8
Australia, 458n274; Comprehensive and Progressive Agreement for Trans-Pacific Partnership and, 448n133; U.S. FTA with, 438n2, 439n11
Authentic Labor Front. *See* Frente Auténtico del Trabajo

Autonomous Industrial Union of Mexican Maquiladora Operators in General (Sindicato Industrial Autónomo de Operarios en General de Maquiladoras de la República Mexicana, SIAOAGMRM), 345–46, 347
Auto Trim de México, 170, 335, 431n254
Aviasca Airlines, 337

Bahrain: AFL-CIO and, 203, 441n47; NAALC and, 191; OTLA and, 202–3, 208, 340; U.S. FTA with, 191, 199, 202–3, 208, 301, 439n11, 441n47
Baker, James, 73
Banco Obrero (Workers' Bank), 90
Bangladesh, 362n139, 363n147
Bárcena, Martha, 263
Barra, Mary, 314
BATP. *See* Bipartisan Agreement on Trade Policy
Bayesian logit, 61, 321, 324; for Mexican NAOs, 173; for U.S. NAOs, 436n309
BBB Industries, 347
Belarus, 52, 354n69, 355n72, 375n83
Bellace, Janice R., 14
Bentsen, Lloyd M., Jr., 74, 77, 79, 385n61, 390n113
Bibong campaign, of AFL-CIO, 358n106
Biden, Joseph R., Jr.: NAALC and, 219, 226; Peña Nieto and, 226, 452n193; TPP and, 219–20
BIP. *See* Border Industrialization Program
Bipartisan Agreement on Trade Policy (BATP), 194–95, 198, 438n7
Bipartisan Congressional Trade and Accountability Act of 2015, 440n22, 461n20
Bipartisan Trade Promotion Authority Act of 2002 (BTPAA), 194, 369n50, 439n11
Blackwell, Ron, 365n7
Blanco Mendoza, Herminio, 97, 390n117
Blumenauer, Earl, 266, 269, 471n108, 473n124, 475n152, 484n15
Bonamici, Suzanne, 471n108
Bonilla García, Javier, 146, 153–54

Bonior, David, 114, 152
Border Industrialization Program (BIP), 85
border measures, for NAFTA, 97, 394n162
Bosnia, 11
Bracero Program, 85
Brandt Commission (Independent
    Commission on International
    Development Issues), 365n6
Bread for the World, 369n45
Breed Technologies, Inc., 134, 335
Brennan Center for Justice, 330
Brooks, Tequila, 403n2, 443n50, 443n59
Brown, Sherrod, 262–63, 469n93
Brown-Wyden proposal, 476n159; NAFTA
    and, 262, 272; TPP and, 284–85; USMCA
    and, 277
Brunei, 218, 448n133, 448n135
BTPAA. *See* Bipartisan Trade Promotion
    Authority Act of 2002
Bush, George H. W., 57, 71–74, 374n81; action
    plan of, 385n61, 386n62, 386n64; NAFTA
    and, 76–80, 82, 84, 382n27, 383n37,
    384n48, 385n57, 385n61, 386n62, 386n64,
    387n68, 387n74, 391n119, 399n207
Bush, George W.: BATP and, 194;
    DR-CAFTA and, 440n29; Guatemala
    and, 459n280; Jordan FTA and, 438n6;
    Labor Cooperation and Capacity
    Building Mechanism of, 440n29; NAALC,
    164, 184, 195; OTLA and, 204; TPP
    and, 219

Calderón Hinojosa, Felipe, 181, 185
Calleja García, Moisés, 106
Campa Cifrián, Roberto, 239–40
Campbell, Kim, 111, 392n148
Canada: Comprehensive and Progressive
    Agreement for Trans-Pacific Partnership
    and, 448n133; COVID-19 pandemic and,
    481n208; NAOs of, 167, 171, 174, 326–28,
    404n14, 406n20, 407n28, 407n29, 408n31,
    409n44, 411n58, 412n63, 413n66, 414n83,
    428n230; right to work in, 462n27; Trump
    and, 460n12; U.S. FTA with, 438n2, 482n2.
    See also specific topics

Canada-Chile Agreement on Labor
    Cooperation, 438n3
Canada-Chile Free Trade Agreement, 438n3
Canada-Mexico Facility-Specific Rapid
    Response Labor Mechanism, 477n170
Canada-Mexico Memorandum of
    Understanding on Co-Operative Labor
    Activities, 386n64
Canada Post Corporation Act, 335
Canada-United States Automobile Products
    Trade Agreement of 1965, 70–71
Canada-United States Free Trade Agreement
    (CUSFTA), 71, 74, 92, 93, 94, 382n16;
    NAFTA and, 384n48, 388n79, 392n142,
    392nn145–46
Canadian Auto Workers (CAW), 93–94, 150,
    326, 334
Canadian Labour Congress (CLC), 93, 94;
    Canadian NAOs and, 326, 328; Colombia
    and, 210, 441n45; FTQ and, 392n145;
    Mexican NAOs and, 330; NAALC and,
    421n165, 437n325
Canadian Union of Postal Workers, 335
Caribbean Basin Economic Recovery Act of
    1983 (CBERA), 46, 60, 292, 378n116
Caribbean Basin Initiative (CBI), 45–46, 48,
    483n6; DOL and, 494n13; sovereignty
    and, 296, 297; U.S. GSP and, 289. *See also
    specific countries*
Caribbean Trade Partnership Act of 2000, 47
Castañeda, Jorge G., 383n32, 384n51
Castañeda, Néstor, 429n238
CAW. *See* Canadian Auto Workers
CBERA. *See* Caribbean Basin Economic
    Recovery Act of 1983
CBI. *See* Caribbean Basin Initiative
CCC. *See* Clean Clothes Campaign
CCCs. *See* corporate codes of conduct
CCE. *See* Consejo Coordinador Empresarial
CEACR. *See* Committee of Experts on
    the Application of Conventions and
    Recommendations
CEDAW. *See* Convention on Elimination
    of All Forms of Discrimination Against
    Women

Center for Economic Research and Teaching (Centro de Investigación y Docencia Económicas, CIDE), 231
Center for Worker Support (Centro de Apoyo al Trabajador), 328
Central Independiente de Obreros Agrícolas y Campesinos (CIOAC, Independent Central of Agricultural Workers and Peasants), 330
Central Light and Power Company. *See* Luz y Fuerza del Centro
Centro de Apoyo a los Trabajadores de Yucatán (Support Center for Yucatán Workers), 336
Centro de Apoyo al Trabajador (Center for Worker Support), 328
Centro de Investigación y Docencia Económicas (CIDE, Center for Economic Research and Teaching), 231
Centro Federal de Conciliación y Registro Laboral (CFCRL, Federal Center for Conciliation and Labor Registration), 347
CFA. *See* Committee on Freedom of Association
CFCRL. *See* Centro Federal de Conciliación y Registro Laboral
CFR. *See* Code of Federal Regulations
Chamber of Deputies, 470n103, 471n105
Chao, Elaine L., 183, 425n205
Charnovitz, Steve, 364n5
child labor: Bipartisan Trade Promotion Authority Act of 2002 on, 369n50; CCCs on, 32; collective bargaining and, 353n60; in Colombia, 198; CSR and, 31; Declaration of Fundamental Principles and Rights at Work on, 25; in Dominican Republic, 202, 206; in Honduras, 445n90; IACtHR and, 354n70; ILO on, 1, 8, 255; IWMA on, 18; in Mexico, 455n227; NAALC on, 41, 48, 108, 112, 123, 137, 194, 195, 409n37; NAFTA and, 78; NGOs and, 362n134; OTLA and, 341; USMCA on, 262, 282; U.S. NAOs and, 334; USTR on, 51
Chile, 380n140; Canada and, 438n3; Comprehensive and Progressive

Agreement for Trans-Pacific Partnership and, 448n133; NAALC and, 191; Trans-Pacific Strategic Economic Partnership Agreement and, 448n135; U.S. FTA with, 191, 439n11, 439n21
Chinese Staff and Workers' Association, 330
Chrétien, Jean, 392n148
Churchill, Winston, 8
CIDE. *See* Centro de Investigación y Docencia Económicas
Cingranelli, David L., 54
CIOAC. *See* Central Independiente de Obreros Agrícolas y Campesinos
Citizen Observatory on Labor Reform (Observatorio Ciudadano sobre la Reforma Laboral), 237-38
CJM. *See* Coalition for Justice in the Maquiladoras
CJP. *See* Consejería Jurídica de la Presidencia
Clapham, Andrew, 349n1
cláusulas de exclusión de separación (separation exclusion clauses), 139
Clay, K. Chad, 54
CLC. *See* Canadian Labour Congress
Clean Clothes Campaign (CCC), 20, 30, 31, 362n138
Clinton, Hillary, 452n190, 460n2
Clinton, William J. (Bill), 49; Jordan FTA and, 438n6; migrants and, 163; NAALC and, 95-96, 106, 109, 111-14, 117, 152, 163, 179, 180, 184, 194, 268, 302, 401n245, 434n287, 435n292, 435n300, 436n309, 451n176; NAFTA and, 76, 80, 81, 82-84, 87, 88, 290, 291n125, 388n89, 388n92, 390n113, 393n153, 394n163; Salinas de Gortari and, 291n125, 391n123; USTR and, 377n98
CNDH. *See* Comisión Nacional de Derechos Humanos
Coalition for Justice in the Maquiladoras (CJM), 20, 332, 335, 429n234
Code of Federal Regulations (CFR), 374n76
collective-action rights, 299, 299-300; in Costa Rica, 202; CSR and, 17, 31; in EPZs, 63; in EU, 50; ILO and, 13, 65, 300; labor

rights and, 37; in NAALC, 36, 114, 173, 183, 191, 219–20; sovereignty and, 18; U.S. GSP and, 50, 53, 62; USTR and, 54, 59, 62; Weberian sovereignty and, 13. *See also* collective bargaining; freedom of association; right to organize/unionize

collective bargaining, 1, 4; child labor and, 353n60; in Colombia, 209; cross-border union solidarity actions and, 20; in Federal Labor Law, 414n76; ILO and, 161; in Mexico, 174, 416n99, 437n323; NAALC on, 98, 108, 112, 122, 138, 195, 302, 410n45; NAFTA and, 78, 257; at Nike, 363n146; OTLA and, 208; RRLM and, 348; STPS and, 472n122; in TPP, 232; in U.S. FTAs, 201–2; in USMCA, 269–70; USTR and, 54

Colombia, 203–4, 379n127; AFL-CIO and, 201, 203, 441n40; CLC and, 210, 441n45; collective bargaining in, 209; freedom of association in, 297; ILO and, 198, 441n39; NAALC and, 191; National Protection Unit of, 209, 443n58; in Organization of Economic Co-Operation and Development, 219; OTLA and, 209–10, 341; trade unions in, 443n59, 443n61; U.S. and, 443n57; U.S. FTA with, 191, 195, 197–99, 201, 209–10, 301, 440n23, 441nn39–40

Colombian Action Plan Related to Labor Rights, 198

Comisión Nacional de Derechos Humanos (CNDH, National Human Rights Commission), 237, 346, 347

Comisión Nacional de los Salarios Mínimos (National Minimum Wage Commission), 90

Comisión Nacional para la Participación de los Trabajadores en las Utilidades (National Commission for Worker Profit-Sharing), 90

Comité Fronterizo de Obreras y Obreros (Frontier Workers' Committee), 347

Commission on Foreign Economic Policy (Randall Commission), 366n26

Commission on Labor Cooperation, 118

Committee of Experts on the Application of Conventions and Recommendations (CEACR), of ILO, 14, 27, 143

Committee on Economic, Social and Cultural Rights, of UN, 15

Committee on Freedom of Association (CFA), of ILO, 14, 22, 27–28, 414n78, 429n234

Committee on the Application of Standards, of ILO, 216

Committee on the Elimination of Discrimination against Women, of UN, 15

Committee on the Rights of the Child, of UN, 15

Communication Workers of America (CWA), 170, 329, 333

Compa, Lance A., 354n69, 355n73, 362n134, 369n52, 403n2, 405n18, 410n45, 443n50, 443n59

Comprehensive and Progressive Agreement for Trans-Pacific Partnership, 448n133

CONCAMIN. *See* Confederación Nacional de Cámaras Industriales

CONCANACO. *See* Confederación de Cámaras Nacionales de Comercio

conciliation and arbitration boards (*juntas de conciliación y arbitraje*), 138–39, 140, 220

conciliation authorities (*instancias de conciliación*), 230

Confederación de Cámaras Nacionales de Comercio (CONCANACO, Confederation of National Chambers of Commerce), 236

Confederación de Trabajadores de México (CTM, Confederation of Mexican Workers), 81, 90, 91–92, 106, 112, 137, 139, 140, 141; AFL-CIO and, 428n231, 429nn234–35; Canadian NAOs and, 327, 328; GM and, 313, 315, 316; Han Young and, 149–50, 153, 419n134; JFCA and, 415n90; Mexican NAOs and, 329; migrant workers and, 158; NAALC and, 171, 181, 182, 223, 397n197; NAFTA and, 387n69, 392n135, 463n44; PRI and, 449n153, 456n246; RRLM and, 344, 345–46; TPP and, 221, 223, 231–32, 234–35, 236; U.S. NAOs and, 335, 336

Confederación Nacional de Cámaras
Industriales (CONCAMIN, National
Confederation of Chambers of
Industry), 236
Confederación Patronal de la República
Mexicana (COPARMEX, Mexican
Employers' Confederation), 231, 236,
470n104
Confederación Regional Obrera Mexicana
(CROM, Mexican Regional Labor
Confederation), 90, 140, 391n391, 454n215;
TPP and, 231, 236
Confederación Revolucionaria de Obreros
y Campesinos (CROC, Revolutionary
Confederation of Workers and Peasants),
139, 140, 454n215; Canadian NAOs and,
328; GM and, 315; Han Young and, 146,
149, 150, 419n134; NAALC and, 177, 181,
182; RRLM and, 345; TPP and, 231, 234–35,
236; U.S. NAOs and, 336, 337
Confédération des Syndicats Nationaux
(Confederation of National Unions),
93–94
Confederation of Mexican Workers. *See*
Confederación de Trabajadores de
México
Confederation of National Chambers
of Commerce (Confederación de
Cámaras Nacionales de Comercio,
CONCANACO), 236
Confederation of National Unions
(Confédération des Syndicats Nationaux),
93–94
Conference Committee on the Application
of Standards, of ILO, 27
Congress of Industrial Organizations, 42.
See also American Federation of Labor-
Congress of Industrial Organizations
Consejería Jurídica de la Presidencia
(CJP, Office of Legal Counsel to the
Presidency), 228–30
Consejo Coordinador Empresarial (CCE,
Private Sector Coordinating Council),
477n169; TPP and, 231, 236; USMCA
and, 272

Consejo Técnico (Technical Council), 236–37
Constitution Act of 1867, 94
Consular Partnership Program, 162
contratos de protección patronal (employer
protection contracts), 138, 221–22,
415n87
Convention on Elimination of All Forms
of Discrimination Against Women
(CEDAW), of UN, 145
COPARMEX. *See* Confederación Patronal de
la República Mexicana
Cordero Arroyo, Ernesto, 238
Córdoba Montoya, José, 73, 88
corporate codes of conduct (CCCs), 29–30,
32, 361n130, 362n134
corporate social responsibility (CSR), 15, 16;
Bangladesh and, 363n147; collective-action
rights and, 17, 31; cross-border union
solidarity actions and, 29–32; ILO and, 17,
30–31; NAALC and, 437n325; Nike and,
363n143; in TPP, 448n137, 464n52
Costa Rica: collective-action rights in, 202;
ILWU and, 199, 202, 443n63; OTLA and,
340; SINTRAJAP and, 443n63; U.S. FTA
with, 199, 202, 439n11
Cotonou Agreement, 373n73
COVID-19 pandemic, Canada and, 481n208
Cowie, Jefferson, 389n97, 391n131
CROC. *See* Confederación Revolucionaria de
Obreros y Campesinos
CROM. *See* Confederación Regional Obrera
Mexicana
cross-border union solidarity actions, 17–32;
boycotts and, 23; collective bargaining
and, 20; CSR and, 29–32; ILO and, 22,
24–29, 26; NAALC and, 20; strikes and, 23;
U.S. GSP and, 20
CSR. *See* corporate social responsibility
CTM. *See* Confederación de Trabajadores de
México
Cubillas, Arsenio Farell, 78
CUSFTA. *See* Canada-United States Free
Trade Agreement
CWA. *See* Communication Workers of
America

Declaration Concerning the Aims and
Purposes of the International Labour
Organization, 351n22
Declaration Concerning the Policy of
"Apartheid" of the Republic of South
Africa, of ILO, 359n111
Declaration of Fundamental Principles and
Rights at Work, of ILO, 14, 25-26, 49, 122,
189-90, 193, 250-51, 289, 380n139
Declaration of Independence, 349n1
Declaration of Philadelphia, of ILO, 8,
360n114
Declaration of Principles Issued by the
President of the United States and the
Prime Minister of the United Kingdom,
350n20
Declaration of the Rights of Man, of France,
349n1
Declaration on Equality of Opportunity and
Treatment of Women Workers, of ILO,
359n111
Declaration on Principles of International
Law concerning Friendly Relations
and Co-Operation Among States in
Accordance with the Charter of the
United Nations, of United Nations
General Assembly, 352n47
Declaration on Social Justice for a Fair
Globalization, of ILO, 359n111
DeCoster Egg Farm, 156, 158, 161, 329,
422n179
DeLauro, Rosa, 471n108
democracy clause, for NAFTA, 384n51
democracy: in union governance, 23-24, 317;
and worker rights, 190
democratic principles, 41
democratic regime change, 61, 62
democratization, 66, 75, 114
Denial of Rights: GM and, 487n47; USMCA
and, 275
Department of Agriculture, 481n206
Department of Commerce, 480n193
Department of Labor (DOL): CBI and,
494n13; Dominican Republic and,
206-7; Honduras and, 445n90; immigrant

workers and, 423n190; Mexican NAOs
and, 329, 331, 425n203; NAALC and, 184;
NAFTA and, 399n219, 462n32; RRLM
and, 343; TPP and, 224; Trade Adjustment
Assistance Program of, 79, 385n55; U.S.
FTAs and, 206; USMCA and, 279, 282;
U.S. NAOs and, 334; Wage and Hours
Division of, 444n79. *See also* Office of
Trade and Labor Affairs
Department of State (DOS), 435n290;
NAALC and, 204, 438n6; TPP and, 222-23
Dewan, Sabina, 438n1, 445n88
"Dialogues for Everyday Justice" ("Diálogos
por la Justicia Cotidiana"), 231
Discrimination in Respect of Employment
and Occupation, of ILO, 145
DOL. *See* Department of Labor
Dole, Elizabeth, 76
Dominican Republic, 378n110; DOL and,
206-7; forced labor in, 202, 296; ILO and,
207; NAALC and, 191; OTLA and, 340,
443n55, 444n64; U.S. FTA with, 191, 199,
202, 206-7, 439n11. *See also* Caribbean
Basin Initiative
Dominican Republic-Central America-
United States Free Trade Agreement
(DR-CAFTA), 195, 197, 339, 458n274;
G. W. Bush and, 440n29; enforcement
of, 301; Guajardo and, 249; OTLA and,
341; reporting requirements of, 480n195;
sovereignty and, 297; U.S. GSP and, 305-6
Donnelly, Jack, 12
Donohue, Thomas R., 389n95
DOS. *See* Department of State
DR-CAFTA. *See* Dominican Republic-
Central America-United States Free
Trade Agreement
Dreier, David, 438n6
Drezner, Daniel W., 486n27
Dunning, Thad, 364n155
Duro Bag Manufacturing Corporation, 335-36

East Timor, 11
Ebrard, Marcelo, 283, 473n124
ECE. *See* evaluation committee of experts

Echlin/Itapsa, 135, 167, 171–72, 176–77, 180, 302, 427n225; Canadian NAOs and, 326–27; U.S. NAOs and, 334

ECHR. *See* European Court on Human Rights

Economic and Social Council, of UN, 19

EFCO Corporation, 132, 327

Eisenhower, Dwight D., 369n48

Elliott, Kimberly Ann, 376n89, 379n120, 379n124

El Salvador, 378n116; ILO and, 197, 378n119, 440n29, 494n11; NAALC and, 191; U.S. FTA with, 191, 197, 439n11. *See also* Caribbean Basin Initiative

employer protection contracts (*contratos de protección patronal*), 138, 221–22, 415n87

employment discrimination: NAALC on, 123, 157, 195. *See also* gender discrimination

enforcement: of DR-CAFTA, 301; in Guatemala, 446n111; ILO on, 8; of NAALC, 124, 136, 247, 381n15, 403n2, 406n25; of NAFTA, 80, 395n172, 396n185; in Peru, 206; of USMCA, 277–83, 479n187. *See also* rapid response labor mechanism

ente público especializado (specialized public entity), 230

EPZs. *See* export-processing zones

Equal Employment Opportunity Commission, 424n197

equal pay for equal work: Declaration of Fundamental Principles and Rights at Work on, 25; NAALC on, 123, 157; in UDHR, 9

Equity and Gender Policy Unit, at STPS, 147

Ethical Trading Initiative (ETI), 30

EU. *See* European Union

European Convention for the Protection of Human Rights and Fundamental Freedoms, 352n45

European Court on Human Rights (ECHR), 354n70

European Economic Community, 373n73

European Union (EU): collective-action rights in, 50; GSP of, 26, 349n4, 373n73, 374n83, 494n11; GSP Plus Programme of, 378n117; social charter of, 405n18; WTO and, 49

evaluation committee of experts (ECE), 124, 125, 409n38, 434n287

Executive Air Transport, Inc. (Transportes Aéreos Ejecutivos, S.A., TAESA), 134, 335

export-processing zones (EPZs), 32; collective-action rights in, 63; U.S. GSP and, 376n93; USTR and, 54, 63

Facility-Specific Rapid Response Labor Mechanism, in USMCA, 274–77

Fair Labor Association (FLA), 30, 363n145

Fair Wear Foundation, 30

fast-track authorization, 180, 194, 195, 438n6; for NAFTA, 385n57, 387n68

FAT. *See* Frente Auténtico del Trabajo

Federación de Sindicatos de Empresas de Bienes y Servicios (FESEBS, Federation of Unions of Goods and Services Enterprises), 170, 176, 333

Federación de Sindicatos de Trabajadores al Servicio del Estado (FSTSE, Federation of Public Service Workers' Unions), 141–42

Federación Sindical de Trabajadores Salvadoreños (FSTS, Union Federation of Salvadoran Workers), 58, 61

Federal Center for Conciliation and Labor Registration (Centro Federal de Conciliación y Registro Laboral, CFCRL), 347

Federal Conciliation and Arbitration Board. *See* Junta Federal de Conciliación y Arbitraje

Federal Conciliation and Arbitration Tribunal (Tribunal Federal de Conciliación y Arbitraje, TFCA), 142, 333, 416n100

Federal Labor Law of 1931. *See* Ley Federal del Trabajo

Federal Law for Public Service Workers. *See* Ley Federal de los Trabajadores al Servicio del Estado

Federal Law on Parastatal Enterprises (Ley Federal de las Entidades Paraestatales), 230

Federal Law on Transparency and Access to Governmental Public Information of 2002, 176

Fédération des travailleurs et travailleuses du Québec (FTQ, Québec Workers Federation): CLC and, 392n145; U.S. NAOs and, 334

Federation of Public Service Workers' Unions (Federación de Sindicatos de Trabajadores al Servicio del Estado, FSTSE), 141–42

Federation of Unions of Goods and Services Enterprises (Federación de Sindicatos de Empresas de Bienes y Servicios, FESEBS), 170, 176, 333

Feingold, Catherine, 469n90

FESEBS. *See* Federación de Sindicatos de Empresas de Bienes y Servicios

Finbow, Robert G., 381n5, 427n226

First International, 6–7

FLA. *See* Fair Labor Association

Florida Tomato Exchange (FTE), 334

forced labor: CCCs on, 32; CSR and, 31; Declaration of Fundamental Principles and Rights at Work on, 25; in Dominican Republic, 202, 296; ILO on, 1, 7–8, 373n73; in Mexico, 469n90; NAALC on, 98, 122–23, 195, 428n229; USMCA on, 282

Forced Labor Enforcement Task Force, 279, 280

Forced Labour Convention, of ILO, 29

Fordney-McCumber Act (Tariff Act of 1922), 364n5

Foro El Sindicalismo ante la Nación ("Union Movement and the Nation" Forum), 176

"Four Freedoms," of Roosevelt, 8

Fox Quesada, Vicente, 147, 178, 185, 336, 422n180

Framework of Principles and Procedures for Consultation Regarding trade and Investment Relations, 72

France, Declaration of the Rights of Man of, 349n1

Freedom House, 379n124

freedom of assembly: ACHR and, 354n70; in UDHR, 8

freedom of association, 4–6; ANAD and, 417n106; in Colombia, 297; Declaration of Fundamental Principles and Rights at Work on, 25; FLA and, 363n145; at Han Young, 147–54; in Honduras, 206; in ICESCR, 14; in ILO, 14; ILRERF and, 417n106; in Mexico, 174, 437n323; NAALC on, 48, 98, 108, 112, 122, 134–35, 147–54, 156–57, 195; at Nike, 363n146; OTLA and, 208; in Pakistan, 380n140; UDHR and, 8, 351n26; in U.S. FTAs, 440n28; in USMCA, 269–70; U.S. NAOs and, 417n106; USTR and, 53

freedom of expression, 354n70

Freedom of Information Act, 395n170

freedom of movement and residence, 354n70

freedom of speech, 8

Freeland, Chrystia, 465n60, 476n163

free-trade agreements (FTAs), 3; CCC and, 32; ILO and, 16; NAALC and, 291; of NAFTA, 36, 37; of U.S., 438n6, 438n7, 438nn1–2, 439n11, 440n28, 441n46, 441n47. *See also specific examples*

Free Trade Commission, of USMCA, 274

Frente Auténtico del Trabajo (FAT, Authentic Labor Front), 92–93; Canadian NAOs and, 328; Han Young and, 149; Mexican NAOs and, 329, 330; NAALC and, 169, 170, 182; STIMAHCS and, 416n93; UE and, 427n225; U.S. NAOs and, 334, 338

Froman, Michael B. G., 466n78

Frontier Workers' Committee (Comité Fronterizo de Obreras y Obreros), 347

Frundt, Henry J., 356n84, 378n109

FSTS. *See* Federación Sindical de Trabajadores Salvadoreños

FSTSE. *See* Federación de Sindicatos de Trabajadores al Servicio del Estado

FTAs. *See* free-trade agreements

FTE. *See* Florida Tomato Exchange

FTQ. *See* Fédération des travailleurs et travailleuses du Québec

GAO. *See* General Accounting Office

García, Nolan, 375n85, 376n88

Garza, Irasema T., 179, 430n244

GATT. *See* General Agreement on Tariffs and Trade

GDP. *See* gross domestic product

gender discrimination: in *maquiladora*, 144–47; Mexican NAOs and, 331–32, 421n161; with NAALC, 143–47

General Accounting Office (GAO), 386n62; NAFTA and, 440n24; U.S. FTAs and, 458n277

General Agreement on Tariffs and Trade (GATT), 2; AFL-CIO and, 367n29, 368n42; Havana Charter and, 366n24, 368n44; International Monetary Fund and, 366n27, 367n28; labor rights in, 289; Mexico and, 382n22; most favored nation for, 364n3, 370n55; NAALC and, 43, 44, 45, 48; NAFTA and, 69, 76; OTCA and, 370n59, 371n61; Preparatory Committee of, 368n44; social clause in, 69; Uruguay Round of, 368n44, 383n37, 385n57; WTO and, 372n70

General Electric Company, 174, 179, 426n211, 427n218, 430n247; U.S. NAOs and, 332

generalized system of preferences (GSP): of EU, 26, 349n4, 374n83, 494n11; of European Economic Community, 373n73. *See also* U.S. Generalized System of Preferences

Generalized System of Preferences Renewal Act of 1984, 47, 369n48, 373n75

General Motors (GM): CROC and, 315; CTM and, 313, 315, 316; Denial of Rights and, 487n47; OTLA and, 316; RRLM and, 316–17, 345; STPS and, 313–17, 487n47; USMCA and, 312–17

General Union of Workers at the Ministry of Fishing (Sindicato Único de Trabajadores de la Secretaría de Pesca, SUTSP), 142, 332–33

genocides, 11

Gephardt, Richard, 77, 78–79, 95, 109, 112, 113, 152, 385n61

Gerard, Leo, 259–60

Gerring, John, 363n150

global union federations (GUFs), 19, 22; CSR and, 29, 31

GM. *See* General Motors

Gomez, Jimmy, 471n108

González Cuevas, Isaías, 236–39, 257, 454n215

González Guzmán, Rodolfo, 454n215

Gore, Albert, 152, 180

Graham, Phil, 438n6

Grassley, Charles E., 438n6

grassroots solidarity, 22

Grayson, George W., 390n112

gross domestic product (GDP), 379n124; of Mexico, 381n5

Gruber, Lloyd, 383n32

Grupo Comercial Chedraui, 139, 338

GSP. *See* generalized system of preferences

GSP Plus Programme, of EU, 378n117

Guajardo, Ildefonso, 240, 249

Guatemala, 377n102, 379n136; AFL-CIO and, 201; G. W. Bush and, 459n280; ILO and, 446n111; NAALC and, 190, 191–92; Obama and, 303; OTLA and, 205–6; trade unions in, 446n100; U.S. FTA with, 190, 191–92, 199, 201, 205–6, 210–16, 309, 439n11, 485n25; U.S. GSP and, 305–6; USTR and, 377n102, 446n109. *See also* Caribbean Basin Initiative

GUFs. *See* global union federations

H-2A visas, 161, 162, 163, 330, 331

H-2B visas, 160, 162, 330, 331

Haiti, 483n9; migrant workers from, 202; OTLA and, 443n55; right to unionize/organize in, 296. *See also* Caribbean Basin Initiative

Hakobyan, Shushanik, 461n17

Han Young of México, 174, 176–77, 180, 183, 302, 412n61, 419n134, 427n225; AFL-CIO and, 419n133; freedom of association at, 147–54; NAALC and, 420n158; pregnancy tests at, 143–47; reinstatement of fired workers at, 419n138; SCMW and, 420n149; STIMAHCS and, 149–50; U.S. NAOs and, 333; workplace safety and health at, 419n129

Harkin, Tom, 469n90

Harper, Stephen, 437n325

Hart, Holly R., 480n194

Hartley, Christopher, 201, 340

Havana Charter, 42–43, 45, 290; GATT and, 366n24, 368n44

Heintz, James, 440n28, 459n284

Herman, Alexis, 154

Hernández Juárez, Francisco, 454n215

Hertel, Shareen, 418n123

Hills, Carla, 74

Hirsch, Barry T., 389n98

Hispanic Chambers of Commerce, 82

Hoffman, Stanley, 34

Hoffman Plastic Compounds v. NLRB, 425n205

Hollings, Ernest F., 386n62

Honduras, 208, 483n9; child labor in, 445n90; DOL and, 445n90; freedom of association in, 206; NAALC and, 191; OTLA and, 205–6, 340–41; trade unions in, 443n56; U.S. and, 444n79; U.S. FTA with, 191, 199, 205–6, 208, 439n11; U.S. GSP and, 306. *See also* Caribbean Basin Initiative

Honeywell, Inc., 179, 332, 427n218, 430n247

House Resolution 146, 78–79

Hoyos, Gustavo de, 470n104

Hufbauer, Gary Clyde, 429n232

Human Resources Development Canada, 135

Human Rights Committee, of UN, 15, 354n69

Human Rights First, 356n86

Human Rights Watch, 142, 144, 146, 147, 356n86; NGOs and, 417n108; U.S. NAOs and, 333

Hyman, Richard, 18

Hyundai Precision America, 146, 151, 152, 419n138

IACtHR. *See* Inter-American Court of Human Rights

IAMAW. *See* International Association of Machinists and Aerospace Workers

IBT. *See* International Brotherhood of Teamsters

ICCPR. *See* International Covenant on Civil and Political Rights

ICEM. *See* International Federation of Chemical, Energy, Mine and General Workers' Unions

ICESCR. *See* International Covenant on Economic, Social and Cultural Rights

ICFTU. *See* International Confederation of Free Trade Unions

ILAB. *See* Office of Child Labor, Forced Labor, and Human Trafficking

ILC. *See* International Labour Conference

ILCME. *See* Interagency Labor Committee for Monitoring and Enforcement

ILO. *See* International Labour Organization

ILRERF. *See* International Labor Rights Education and Research Fund

ILRF. *See* International Labor Rights Forum

ILWU. *See* International Longshore and Warehouse Union

IMF. *See* International Metalworkers' Federation; International Monetary Fund

Immigration and Naturalization Service (INS), 163, 329–30

in-bond manufacturing. *See maquiladora*

Independent Central of Agricultural Workers and Peasants (Central Independiente de Obreros Agrícolas y Campesinos, CIOAC), 330

Independent Commission on International Development Issues (the Brandt Commission), 365n6

Independent Labor Secretariat for Fair Trade Deals Act, 479n185

Independent Mexico Labor Expert Board, 279, 280, 281

Indonesia, 54, 57, 63, 65, 380n139

IndustriALL Global Union, 19, 31

INE. *See* Instituto Nacional Electoral

INEGI. *See* Instituto Nacional de Estadística, Geografía e Informática

INS. *See* Immigration and Naturalization Service

Inside U.S. Trade, 97

instancias de conciliación (conciliation authorities), 230

Institutional Revolutionary Party. *See* Partido Revolucionario Institucional

Instituto del Fondo Nacional de la Vivienda para los Trabajadores (National Worker Housing Institute), 90, 134

Instituto Mexicano del Seguro Social (Social Security Institute), 90, 134

Instituto Nacional de Estadística, Geografía e Informática (INEGI, National Institute of Statistics, Geography, and Informatics), 417n107

Instituto Nacional de Transparencia, Acceso a la Información y Protección de los Datos Personales (National Institute for Transparency, Access to Information, and Protection of Personal Data), 230

Instituto Nacional Electoral (INE, National Electoral Institute), 316

Integrated Environmental Plan for the Border, 386n64

intellectual property: NAFTA on, 72, 75, 96, 192, 254, 303, 394n162; United States-Chile Free Trade Agreement and, 439n21

Interagency Labor Committee for Monitoring and Enforcement (ILCME): AFL-CIO and, 479n185; RRLM and, 343–48; USMCA and, 278–80

Inter-American Court of Human Rights (IACtHR), 16, 354n70

Inter-American Development Bank, 278

Inter-American Regional Workers' Organization, 428n231

International Association for Labour Legislation, 340n12

International Association of Machinists and Aerospace Workers (IAMAW), 369n52; Canadian NAOs and, 326; USMCA and, 259, 479n183

International Brotherhood of Teamsters (IBT): Canadian NAOs and, 326; immigrant workers and, 423n190; NAALC and, 169; NAFTA and, 394n160; STIMAHCS and, 427n218; USMCA and, 479n183; U.S. NAOs and, 332, 334

International Centre for Trade Union Rights, 356n86

International Confederation of Free Trade Unions (ICFTU), 19, 20–21, 22, 428n231; CSR and, 29; ITSs and, 356n83; NAALC and, 43; WTO and, 49

International Convention on the Rights of the Child, 352n36

International Covenant on Civil and Political Rights (ICCPR), of UN, 9–12, 25, 141, 145

International Covenant on Economic, Social and Cultural Rights (ICESCR), of UN, 9–10, 14, 25, 353n63

International Criminal Court, 11

International Federation of Air Line Pilots' Associations, 356n80

International Federation of Chemical, Energy, Mine and General Workers' Unions (ICEM), 19, 357n98

International Federation of Journalists, 356n80

International Finance Corporation, Performance Standards on Environmental and Social, 26

International Labor Rights Education and Research Fund (ILRERF), 142; freedom of association and, 417n106; Han Young and, 150; NAALC and, 167; U.S. NAOs and, 332; USTR and, 54, 57, 485n22; U.S. U.S. GSP and, 485

International Labor Rights Forum (ILRF), 19; Canadian NAOs and, 327; CSR and, 31; gender discrimination and, 144; migrant workers and, 162–63; Peru and, 199; U.S. NAOs and, 333, 334

International Labour Conference (ILC), 25, 358n107

International Labour Office, 358n107

International Labour Organization (ILO):
CEACR of, 14, 27, 143; CFA of, 14, 22,
27–28, 414n78, 429n234; collective-
action rights and, 13, 65, 300; collective
bargaining and, 161; Colombia and, 198,
441n39; Committee on the Application
of Standards of, 216; complaints to,
360nn118–19; Conference Committee
on the Application of Standards of, 27;
constitution of, 8, 41, 340n12, 349n12,
353n55; conventions of, 359n112; creation
of, 1–2, 7; cross-border union solidarity
actions and, 22, 24–29, 26; CSR and, 17,
30–31; Declaration Concerning the Aims
and Purposes of the International Labour
Organization of, 351n22; Declaration
Concerning the Policy of "Apartheid"
of the Republic of South Africa of,
359n111; Declaration of Fundamental
Principles and Rights at Work of, 14,
25–26, 49, 122, 189–90, 193, 250–51, 289,
380n139; Declaration of Philadelphia of,
8, 360n114; Declaration on Equality of
Opportunity and Treatment of Women
Workers of, 359n111; Declaration on
Social Justice for a Fair Globalization
of, 359n111; Discrimination in Respect
of Employment and Occupation of,
145; Dominican Republic and, 207; El
Salvador and, 197, 378n119, 440n29,
494n11; first two decades of, 7–8; on
forced labor, 1, 373n73; Forced Labour
Convention of, 29; freedom of association
in, 14; FTAs and, 16; fundamental
conventions of, 350n18; Guatemala and,
446n111; ICCPR and, 9; ICESR and, 9;
International Association for Labour
Legislation and, 340n12; members of,
359n109; NAALC and, 40–41, 43, 47, 103,
107–8, 118, 122, 142, 145, 178, 189–90, 193,
197, 291, 397n188, 398nn202–3; NAFTA
and, 252, 254, 393n157; organs of, 358n107;
principal policy statements of, 7; right to
organize and, 161; right to strike and, 14,
354n66; right to work and, 482n212; SCJN

and, 471n105; scope of action of, 2; TPP
and, 217, 218, 220–21, 225, 233, 254, 255,
284; Tripartite Declaration of Principles
Concerning Multinational Enterprises
and Social Policy of, 359n111; UN and,
16, 25; U.S. GSP and, 66; USMCA and,
278; USTR and, 61, 64; Westphalian
sovereignty and, 11–12, 115; World
Commission on the Social Dimensions of
Globalization of, 372n71; WTO and, 49,
360n114, 372n71
International Longshore and Warehouse
Union (ILWU): Costa Rica and, 199, 202,
443n63; OTLA and, 340
International Metalworkers' Federation
(IMF), 19, 43, 358n100
International Monetary Fund (IMF): GATT
and, 366n27, 367n28; NAALC and, 47;
TPP and, 226–27, 233, 234
International Textiles, Garment and Leather
Workers' Federation (ITGLWF), 19, 21
International Tin Agreement, 366n25
International Trade Organization (ITO),
41–43; Preparatory Committee of, 42;
prison labor and, 366n20
international trade secretariats (ITSs), 18–19,
20–21; CSR and, 29; ICFTU and, 356n83
International Trade Union Confederation
(ITUC), 19, 22, 408n33
International Trade Union Secretariat, 19
International Transport Workers Federation,
356n80
International Union of Food, Agricultural,
Hotel, Restaurant, Catering, Tobacco,
and Allied Workers' Associations (IUF),
356n80, 359n101
International Workers' Aid, 356n86
International Workers' Association, 19
International Working Men's Association
(IWMA), 6–7, 18
Israel, 301, 438n2, 482n2
ITGLWF. *See* International Textiles,
Garment and Leather Workers'
Federation
ITO. *See* International Trade Organization

ITSs. *See* international trade secretariats

ITUC. *See* International Trade Union Confederation

IUF. *See* International Union of Food, Agricultural, Hotel, Restaurant, Catering, Tobacco, and Allied Workers' Associations

IWMA. *See* International Working Men's Association

Jacobson, Roberta S., 207

Japan, Comprehensive and Progressive Agreement for Trans, 448n133

JFCA. *See* Junta Federal de Conciliación y Arbitraje

JLCA. *See* Junta Local de Conciliación y Arbitraje

Jordan: AFL-CIO and, 199, 216; NAALC and, 191; OTLA and, 441n46; U.S. FTA with, 191, 192–94, 199, 216, 301, 438n6, 438n7, 439n11, 441n46; USTR and, 199

junta de conciliación y arbitraje (conciliation and arbitration board), 138–39, 140

Junta Federal de Conciliación y Arbitraje (JFCA, Federal Conciliation and Arbitration Board), 137, 141, 434n281; Canadian NAOs and, 327; CTM and, 415n90; LFTSE and, 416n98; NAALC and, 176–77, 178; RRLM and, 346

Junta Local de Conciliación y Arbitraje (JLCA, Local Conciliation and Arbitration Board), 149, 150, 151, 153

juntas de conciliación y arbitraje (conciliation and arbitration boards), 220

Kantor, Michael (Mickey), 95, 401n242

Kaptur, Mary, 479n181, 479n185

Karesh, Lewis, 374n79

Kay, Tamara, 419n133, 435n299

Keck, Margaret E., 362nn137–38

Keohane, Robert O., 483n6

Kerry, John, 460n2

Kirk, Ron, 212, 446n109

Kirkland, Lane, 113

Knights of Labor, 356n75

Knouse, Mark S., 404n13

Kohl, Helmut, 73

Korea: OTLA and, 442n49; U.S. FTA with, 195, 438n2, 440n23

Kosovo, 11

Krasner, Stephen, 64–65, 352n41, 352n45, 494n12

Kuczynski, Pedro Pablo, 207

Kyungshin Corporation, 442n49

Labor Advisory Committee for Trade Negotiations and Trade Policy, 96, 223, 259–60, 386n65, 480n201; USMCA and, 280–81, 282

labor consistency plans, 218, 296

Labor Cooperation and Capacity Building Mechanism, 440n29

Labor Management Relations Act of 1947 (Taft-Hartley Act), 195–96, 252, 482n212

Labor Policy Association, 132, 327

labor reform, democratic, 217–36, 308

labor rights, 289–317; alternative international arenas for, 15–38; collective-action rights and, 37; in GATT, 289; institutional design of, 303–7; international defense of, 1–38, 309–12; internationalization of, 6–10; NAALC and, 119, 164–72, 298–301; NAFTA and, 76–94, 249–88; sociopolitical alliances for, 306–8; sovereignty and, 10–15, 33–38, 292–98; in U.S. FTAs, 191–216, 298–301; U.S. GSP for, 50–64, 55–56, 62; in USMCA, 273–74. *See also specific topics*

labor unions. *See* trade unions

Lague of Nations Covenant, 7

La Paz agreement, 381n4

Larroque, José María, 149

Larson, John B., 471n108

League of Nations, 265n12

Lear Corporation, 442n49

Lee, Jiwon, 460n4

Legal Services Corporation, 161

Leo XIII (Pope), 353n57

Levin, Andy, 271

Levin, Sander, 238, 251, 252

Lew, Jacob, 226, 227
Ley Federal de las Entidades Paraestatales
    (Federal Law on Parastatal Enterprises),
    230
Ley Federal de los Trabajadores al Servicio
    del Estado (LFTSE, Federal Law for
    Public Service Workers), 141, 143; JFCA
    and, 416n98; pregnancy testing and, 147
Ley Federal del Trabajo (Federal Labor
    Law of 1931), 89, 107, 138, 139; collective
    bargaining in, 414n76; NAALC and, 176,
    414n83; NAFTA and, 398n201; TPP and,
    221, 224; USMCA and, 265; U.S. NAOs
    and, 338
LFTSE. *See* Ley Federal de los Trabajadores al
    Servicio del Estado
Liga Sindical Obrera Mexicana (LSOM,
    Mexican Labor Union League), 347
Lighthizer, Robert E., 239–40, 261–66, 269,
    272–73, 277–78, 285, 462n32, 466n78,
    468n85, 471n106, 482n211, 486n33
Lipschultz, Ronnie D., 363n143
Local Conciliation and Arbitration Board
    (Junta Local de Conciliación y Arbitraje,
    JLCA), 149, 150, 151, 153
Locke, John, 349n1
Lomé Convention, 373n73
Long, Tom, 383n41
López Obrador, Andrés Manuel, 239, 258–59,
    283, 287–88, 294–95, 465n65, 466n78,
    475n149, 483n5; USMCA and, 263–73
LSOM. *See* Liga Sindical Obrera Mexicana
Luce, Stephanie, 440n28, 459n284
Luz y Fuerza del Centro (LyFC, Central Light
    and Power Company), 133; Canadian
    NAOs and, 328; U.S. NAOs and, 337

Madrid Hurtado, Miguel de la, 72, 81–82,
    382n22
Magnéticos de México, 179, 431n253
Mahoney, James, 291
Malaysia: Comprehensive and Progressive
    Agreement for Trans-Pacific Partnership
    and, 448n133; labor consistency plan
    for, 218

Mandel, Harlan, 370n55
maquiladora (in-bond manufacturing), 19,
    85, 138; gender discrimination in, 144–47;
    goods manufactured by, 389n103; labor
    peace in, 391n131; NAFTA and, 389n107;
    trade unions in, 418n127; women in,
    417n107
Maquiladora Health and Safety Support
    Network, 150
Maquila Solidarity Network (MSN), 19,
    488n61; Canadian NAOs and, 328; CSR
    and, 31; NAALC and, 170; TPP and, 222;
    U.S. NAOs and, 336
Maritime Labour Convention, 359n112
Márquez Colín, Graciela, 267
Martin, Lynn, 78
Martínez, Benedicto, 428n228
Marx, Karl, 18
Matamoros Garment, 175; Canadian NAOs
    and, 328; U.S. NAOs and, 336
matches, white phosphorus on, 349n12,
    365n9
Maxi-Switch, 174, 333, 427n226
May 10 agreement, 195
Mayer, Frederick W., 399n219
McDermott, James, 199
McDonald's, 174, 334
McDonough, Denis, 225
McKinnerey, John S., 404n13, 430n244
McLaren, John, 461n17
Meade Kuribreña, José Antonio, 240
Medina, Danilo, 207
Medina Ramírez, Tereso, 236–39, 257,
    463n44
Memorandum of Understanding Regarding
    Cooperation Between the Department of
    Labor of the United States of America
    and the Secretariat of Labor and Social
    Welfare of the United Mexican States,
    386n64
Mexican Action Network on Free Trade
    (Red Mexicana de Acción Frente al Libre
    Comercio, RMALC), 92–93, 330
Mexican Air. *See* Asociación Sindical de
    Pilotos Aviadores de México

Mexican-American War, 68

Mexican Ecologist Green Party (Partido Verde Ecologista de México), 177

Mexican Electricians Union. *See* Sindicato Mexicano de Electricistas

Mexican Employers' Confederation (Confederación Patronal de la República Mexicana, COPARMEX), 231, 236, 470n104

Mexican Labor Union League (Liga Sindical Obrera Mexicana, LSOM), 347

Mexican NAOs: DOL and, 425n203; due-diligence and, 421n171; gender discrimination and, 331–32, 421n161; Sprint Corporation and, 329, 422n176

Mexican Regional Labor Confederation (Confederación Regional Obrera Mexicana, CROM), 90, 140, 391n391, 454n215

Mexican Social Security Institute (Instituto Mexicano del Seguro Social), 90, 134

Mexican Supreme Court. *See* Suprema Corte de Justicia de la Nación

Mexican Telephone Workers Union. *See* Sindicato de Telefonistas de la República Mexican

Mexico: AFL-CIO and, 450n159, 469n90; child labor in, 455n227; collective bargaining in, 174, 416n99, 437n323; Comprehensive and Progressive Agreement for Trans-Pacific Partnership and, 448n133; forced labor in, 469n90; freedom of association in, 174, 437n323; GATT and, 382n22; GDP of, 381n5; labor costs in, 389n106; NAOs of, 167–68, 171, 173, 329–32, 404n14, 407n29, 408n31, 409n40, 409n42, 411n51, 412n62, 415n4; National Development Plan of, 175; Obama and, 451n169, 452n193; protection contracts in, 415n87; in TPP, 165–66, 189–244; Trump and, 227, 460n12; U.S. FTA with, 438n2; U.S. GSP of, 402n250, 485n22; U.S. tariffs on, 384n50. *See also* specific topics

Migrant and Seasonal Agricultural Worker Protection Act, 161

migrant workers: gender discrimination against, 421n161; from Haiti, 202; Mexican NAOs and, 330; minimum wage for, 425n205; NAALC on, 123, 154–64, 486n28; right to organize by, 425n205; in TPP, 255; workplace safety and health for, 423n190

Miguel Trujillo López" National Union of Metalworking, Steel-Metallurgical, Automobile and General Autoparts Suppliers, Energy, and Related Industry Workers (Sindicato Nacional de Trabajadores de la Industria Metal-Mecánica, Sidero-Metalúrgica, Automotriz y Proveedores de Autopartes en General, de la Energía, sus Derivados y Similares de la República Mexicana "Miguel Trujillo López"), 313, 315, 345

Mills, Wilbur, 367n36

minimum wage: Declaration of Fundamental Principles and Rights at Work on, 25; in Dominican Republic, 202; for migrant workers, 425n205; NAALC on, 48, 98, 108, 112, 113, 123; NAFTA and, 90; Trump and, 460n13; in USMCA, 464n57

Ministerial Conference, of WTO, 49

Ministry of Labor and Social Welfare. *See* Secretaría del Trabajo y Previsión Social

Mintzes, Joseph, 367n29

Misión de la Misericordia (Mission of Mercy), 201, 340

Mizukoshi, Kazuma, 379n123, 429n238

MORENA. *See* Movimiento Regeneración Nacional

Morgan, Stephen L., 460n4

Morocco, 191, 301, 439n11

Morones, Luis N., 391n391

Mosbacher, Robert A., 382n27

Mosley, Layna, 54, 375n85

most favored nation: for GATT, 364n3, 370n55; for NAFTA, 406n25

Mount Olive Pickle Company, 161

"Movement 20/32" Independent National Union of Industrial and Service Workers (Sindicato Nacional Independiente de Trabajadores de Industrias y Servicios 'Movimiento 20/32', SNITIS), 344-46

Movimiento Regeneración Nacional (MORENA, National Regeneration Movement), 264-65, 267, 470n103, 471n105

MSN. *See* Maquila Solidarity Network

Mulroney, Brian, 71, 74-75, 82, 93, 94, 383n41, 384n48

Myanmar, 361nn127-28, 373n73, 375n83

NAAEC. *See* North American Agreement on Environmental Cooperation

NAALC. *See* North American Agreement on Labor Cooperation

NACLC. *See* North American Commission for Labor Cooperation

NAFTA. *See* North American Free Trade Agreement

NAFTA Accountability Act, 114

NAFTA Labor Cooperation and Enforcement Agreement, 262

NAOs. *See* national administrative offices

National Accord for the Elevation of Productivity and Quality, 112

National Action Party (Partido Acción Nacional, PAN), 454n211

national administrative offices (NAOs), 118-19, 121-22, 124-64, 126-29, 131, 325-38; of Canada, 167, 171, 174, 326-28, 404n14, 406n20, 407n28, 407n29, 408n31, 409n44, 411n58, 412n63, 413n66, 414n83, 428n230; of Mexico, 167-68, 171, 173, 329-32, 404n14, 407n29, 408n31, 409n40, 409n42, 411n51, 412n62, 415n4; of U.S., 168, 171, 174, 182-84, 332-38, 404n14, 407n29, 408n31, 409n40, 409n42, 410n45, 411n51, 411n58, 412n62, 413n66, 414nn82-83, 416n100

National Anticorruption System (Sistema Nacional Anticorrupción), 237

National Association of Democratic Lawyers. *See* Asociación Nacional de Abogados Democráticos; Asociación Nacional de Abogados Demócratios

National Association of Letter Carriers, 335

National Association of Public and Private Employees (Asociación Nacional de Empleados Públicos y Privados), 340

National Commission for the Gradual and Progressive Eradication of Child Labor, 445n90

National Commission for Worker Profit-Sharing (Comisión Nacional para la Participación de los Trabajadores en las Utilidades), 90

National Confederation of Chambers of Industry (Confederación Nacional de Cámaras Industriales, CONCAMIN), 236

National Council of La Raza, 82

National Council of the Maquiladora Industry, 147

National Development Plan, of Mexico, 175

National Economic Council (NEC), 96

National Electoral Institute (Instituto Nacional Electoral, INE), 316

National Human Rights Commission (Comisión Nacional de Derechos Humanos, CNDH), 237, 347

National Independent Union of Automotive and Related Industry Workers (Sindicato Independiente Nacional de Trabajadores y Trabajadoras de la Industria Automotriz y las Adhesivas, SINTTIA), 315, 316, 317, 345

National Institute for Occupational Health and Safety, 134

National Institute for Transparency, Access to Information, and Protection of Personal Data (Instituto Nacional de Transparencia, Acceso a la Información y Protección de los Datos Personales), 230

National Institute of Statistics, Geography, and Informatics (Instituto Nacional de Estadística, Geografía e Informática, INEGI), 417n107

National Labor Committee, 356n86

National Labor Relations Act, 161

National Labor Relations Board (NLRB), 156, 163; Canadian NAOs and, 327; USMCA and, 275

National Minimum Wage Commission (Comisión Nacional de los Salarios Mínimos), 90

National Mobilization Against Sweat Shops, 330

National Protection Unit, 209, 443n58

National Regeneration Movement (Movimiento Regeneración Nacional, MORENA), 264-65, 267, 470n103, 471n105

National Registry of Collective Bargaining Arbitrators, 208

National System for Transparency, Access to Public Information, and Protection of Personal Data (Sistema Nacional de Transparencia, Acceso a la Información Pública y Protección de Datos Personales), 237

National Tripartite Commission on Labor Relations and Freedom of Association, 446n111

National Union of Mexican Mineworkers and Metalworkers (Sindicato Nacional de Trabajadores Mineros, Metalúrgicos y Similares de la República Mexicana, SNTMMSRM), 337, 346, 427n226

National Union of United Customs and Tax Administration Workers (Sindicato Nacional de Unidad de Trabajadores de la Superintendencia Nacional de Aduanas y de Administración Tributaria), 201-2, 340

National Union of Workers. *See* Unión Nacional de Trabajadores

National Worker Housing Institute (Instituto del Fondo Nacional de la Vivienda para los Trabajadores), 90, 134

Natural Resources, and Fisheries (Secretaría del Medio Ambiente, Recursos Naturales y Pesca, SEMARNAP), 333

Navarrete Prida, Alfonso, 222, 227-28

Neal, Richard E., 265-66, 268, 269, 272-73, 473n124, 475n152, 481n202

NEC. *See* National Economic Council

New Zealand: Comprehensive and Progressive Agreement for Trans-Pacific Partnership and, 448n133; TPP and, 458n274; Trans-Pacific Strategic Economic Partnership Agreement and, 448n135

NGOs. *See* nongovernmental organizations

Nicaragua, 380n140; NAALC and, 191; U.S. FTA with, 191, 439n11

night work, for women, 349n12, 365n9

Nike, Inc., 431n251; collective bargaining at, 363n146; CSR and, 363n143; freedom of association at, 363n146

NLRB. *See* National Labor Relations Board

nongovernmental organizations (NGOs), 19-20; AFL-CIO and, 199; Canadian NAOs and, 326-27, 328; child labor and, 362n134; CSR and, 29-30; Human Rights Watch and, 417n108; Mexican NAOs and, 329, 330, 331; migrant workers and, 162-63; NAALC and, 119, 130, 132, 133, 141, 142, 143, 166-67, 182, 410n45, 436n311; OTLA and, 340-41; U.S. GSP and, 66, 374n81; U.S. NAOs and, 334, 335, 336, 337, 338, 410n45; USTR and, 50, 52-54, 57-59; workplace safety and health and, 362n134. *See also specific organizations*

Non-Traditional Exports Promotion Act of 1978, 443n52

North American Agreement on Environmental Cooperation (NAAEC), 115

North American Agreement on Import Surges, 385n52

North American Agreement on Labor Cooperation (NAALC), 3-6, 15, 16, 76, 115-17, 290; AFL-CIO and, 96, 108, 113, 114, 170, 171-72, 177, 247, 307, 437n325, 438n6; ANAD and, 170; AP of, 124-25; G. W. Bush and, 164, 184, 195; CCC and, 32; on child labor, 409n37; CLC and, 421n165, 437n325; B. Clinton and, 95-96, 106, 109, 111-14, 117, 152, 163, 179, 180, 184, 194, 268, 302, 401n245, 434n287, 435n292, 435n300,

436n309, 451n176; collective-action rights in, 36, 114, 173, 183, 191, 219–20; collective bargaining in, 302; conciliation and arbitration board of, 138–39, 140; CROC and, 177, 181, 182; cross-border union solidarity actions and, 20; CSR and, 437n325; CTM and, 171, 181, 182, 223, 397n197; CWA and, 170; DOL and, 184; DOS and, 204, 438n6; ECE of, 124, 125, 409n38, 434n287; enforcement of, 124, 136, 247, 381n5, 403n2, 406n25; FAT and, 169, 170, 182; Federal Labor Law and, 414n83; on forced labor, 428n229; on freedom of association, 156–57; FTAs and, 291; gender discrimination and, 143–47; Guatemala and, 190, 191–92; Han Young and, 420n158; IBT and, 169; ILO and, 40–41, 43, 47, 103, 107–8, 118, 122, 142, 145, 178, 189–90, 193, 197, 291, 397n188, 398nn202–3; ILRERF and, 167; institutional architecture of, 120–25; ITUC and, 408n33; JFCA and, 176–77, 178; labor rights and, 119, 164–72, 298–301; legacies of, 189–244; Ley Federal del Trabajo and, 176, 414n83; Mexican policy impact record with, 173–78; Mexican policy outcomes in, 178–85; on migrant workers, 123, 154–64, 486n28; MSN and, 170; NAAEC and, 115; NAFTA and, 69; negotiation of, 95–114, 105; NGOs and, 119, 130, 132, 133, 141, 142, 143, 166–67, 182, 410n45, 436n311; OTLA and, 191, 196–97, 440n25; PACE International Union and, 177; pathways to, 39–67; PRD and, 177; pregnancy testing and, 143–47, 310; PRI and, 181; in principle and practice, 118–88; Private Rights in, 403n8; public communications in, 125–64, *126–29, 131,* 172–85, 408n32; renegotiation of, 245–88; on right to organize, 156–57; SCJN and, 178; SME and, 167, 408n33; social capital and, 166–72, 296; sovereignty and, 119, 120, 292–95; Statement of Labor Principles for, 98, 400n235; STIMAHCS and, 169, 177, 182, 428n228; STPS and, 175, 184; strikes and, 138; STRM and, 169, 170; technical

labor standards in, 400n222, 406n22; TPP and, 220, 221, 225, 238; trade unions and, 119, 426n206; UDHR and, 178; UE and, 167, 170; UNI Global Union and, 408n33; UNT and, 167, 172, 307–8; U.S. FTAs and, 189–216; U.S. GSP and, 35, 36, 37, 38, 40, 45, 46–47, 114, 401n242; USMCA and, 275–76, 281, 284–85, 286, 481nn209–10, 482n215; USTR and, 95; on workplace safety and health, 431n254; WTO and, 48–49. *See also* national administrative offices

North American Commission for Labor Cooperation (NACLC), 121, 404n9; financial penalties of, 406n24; secretariat of, 404n13

North American Free Trade Agreement (NAFTA), 3, 4, 15, 35; AFL-CIO and, 79, 84, 248, 251, 252, 390n109, 393n157, 462n26, 468n89, 478n179; border measures for, 97, 394n162; G. H. W. Bush and, 76–80, 82, 84, 382n27, 383n37, 384n48, 385n57, 385n61, 386n62, 386n64, 387n68, 387n74, 391n119, 399n207; child labor and, 78; B. Clinton and, 76, 80, 81, 82–84, 87, 88, 290, 291n125, 388n89, 388n92, 390n113, 393n153, 394n163; collective bargaining and, 78, 257; CTM and, 392n135, 463n44; CUSFTA and, 384n48, 388n79, 392n142, 392nn145–46; democracy clause for, 384n51; DOL and, 399n219, 462n32; effective date of, 75; enforcement of, 80, 395n172, 396n185; fast-track authorization for, 385n57, 387n68; Freedom of Information Act and, 395n170; FTAs of, 36, 37; GAO and, 440n24; GATT and, 69, 76; on gender discrimination, 421n161; ILO and, 252, 254, 393n157; on intellectual property, 72, 75, 96, 192, 254, 303, 394n162; International Brotherhood of Teamsters and, 394n160; labor rights and, 76–94, 249–88; Ley Federal del Trabajo and, 398n201; *maquiladora* and, 389n107; most favored nation for, 406n25; NAALC and, 69; negotiations for, 384n48; Obama

North American (*Continued*)
    and, 185, 460n2; origin and negotiation
    of, 68–117, *105*; Overseas Development
    Council and, 390n117; PRI and, 392n135;
    renegotiation of, 245–88; sovereignty
    and, 68–69, 293, 294–95, 296; STPS and,
    258; TPP and, 220, 224, 227, 239, 240,
    253, 255, 257; trade unions and, 290n108,
    389n107; Trump and, 235, 237, 245–46, 247,
    248, 253; UAW and, 394n160; UNT and,
    287; U.S. FTAs and, 249; U.S. GSP and,
    69; USMCA and, 468nn85–86; USTR
    and, 252–53, 254, 285, 461n19, 461n21;
    USW and, 251–52, 394n160; workplace
    safety and health and, 78. *See also*
    North American Agreement on Labor
    Cooperation
North American Labour Commission,
    101, 103
North American Worker-to-Worker
    Network, 392n145
North Atlantic Treaty Organization, 42–43
Northwest Workers' Justice Project, 330
Nye, Joseph S., 483n6

OAN. *See* Oficina Administrativa Nacional
Obama, Barack, 437n325; Colombia and,
    198–99; Guatemala and, 303; Mexico
    and, 451n169, 452n193; NAFTA and, 185,
    460n2; OTLA and, 204, 207, 208; TPP
    and, 219–20, 224–25, 228, 230, 232–33, 235;
    U.S. FTAs and, 302; USMCA and, 466n78
Observatorio Ciudadano sobre la Reforma
    Laboral (Citizen Observatory on Labor
    Reform), 237–38
OCAW. *See* Oil, Chemical, and Atomic
    Workers
occupational safety and health. *See* workplace
    safety and health
Occupational Safety and Health
    Administration, 134
"October 6" Union of Industrial and
    Commercial Workers (Sindicato de
    Trabajadores de la Industria y del
    Comercio "6 de octubre"), 150, 152

OECD. *See* Organization for Economic
    Co-Operation and Development
Office for the Defense of Women's Rights,
    418n120
Office of Child Labor, Forced Labor, and
    Human Trafficking (ILAB), 282
Office of Legal Counsel to the Presidency
    (Consejería Jurídica de la Presidencia,
    CJP), 228–30
Office of Trade and Labor Affairs (OTLA):
    Bahrain and, 202–3, 208, 340; collective
    bargaining and, 208; Colombia and,
    209–10; Dominican Republic and, 443n55,
    444n64; freedom of association and, 208;
    GM and, 316; Guatemala and, 205–6;
    Haiti and, 443n55; Honduras and, 205–6;
    Jordan and, 441n46; Korea and, 442n49;
    NAALC and, 191, 196–97, 440n25; Peru
    and, 201–2, 207, 441n33, 459n280; public
    submissions to, 339–41; right to organize
    and, 208; RRLM and, 343, 348; Tripartite
    Follow-up Commission and, 208; U.S.
    FTAs and, 199, 204–6, 459n284
Oficina Administrativa Nacional (OAN),
    407n28
Oil, Chemical, and Atomic Workers
    (OCAW), Mexican NAOs and, 329
Oman, 191, 301, 439n11
Omnibus Trade and Competitiveness Act
    of 1988 (OTCA), 47, 48; AFL-CIO and,
    374n83; GATT and, 370n59, 371n61
Oñate Laborde, Santiago, 184
OPIC. *See* Overseas Private Investment
    Corporation
ordered-logit regressions, 61
Organization for Economic Co-Operation
    and Development (OECD): Colombia in,
    219; WTO and, 371n67
Organization of American States, 64
Organization of Rural Mail Carriers, 335
Orlando Hernández, Juan, 445n90
Orme, William A., Jr., 390n113
OTCA. *See* Omnibus Trade and
    Competitiveness Act of 1988
OTLA. *See* Office of Trade and Labor Affairs

Overseas Development Council, 390n117
Overseas Private Investment Corporation
(OPIC), 47, 48, 60–61, 431n270

PACE International Union. *See* Paper,
Allied-Industrial, Chemical, and Energy
Workers International Union
PACs. *See* Political Action Committees
Paine, Thomas, 349n1
Pakistan, 380n140
PAN. *See* Partido Acción Nacional
Panama, 191, 195, 440n23
Panasonic Automotive Systems de México,
345–46
Paper, Allied-Industrial, Chemical, and
Energy Workers International Union
(PACE International Union), 177, 335
Paraguay, 380n140
Partido Acción Nacional (PAN, National
Action Party), 177, 454n211
Partido de la Revolución Democrática
(PRD), 432n268; NAALC and, 177; TPP
and, 235, 237
Partido Revolucionario Institucional (PRI,
Institutional Revolutionary Party), 82,
87, 90, 92, 108, 143; CTM and, 449n153,
456n246; NAALC and, 181; NAFTA and,
387n69, 392n135; PRD and, 432n268; TPP
and, 221, 222, 234
Partido Verde Ecologista de México (Mexican
Ecologist Green Party), 177
Pascrell, Bill, 238
Pasta de Conchos, U.S. NAOs and, 337
Pease, Donald, 46–47, 369n49
Pelosi, Nancy, 260, 268, 271, 272, 278, 439n17,
473n124, 475n152, 479n182; Peña Nieto
and, 454n223
Peña Nieto, Enrique, 450n159, 451n170;
Biden and, 226, 452n193; NAFTA and,
253–54, 257, 258, 287; PAN and, 454n211;
Pelosi and, 454n223; TPP and, 222, 225,
227–28, 229, 231–34, 235, 236, 240, 455n226;
USMCA and, 263
Perez, Thomas E., 207, 208, 227–28
Pérez-López, Jorge, 394n161

Performance Standards on Environmental
and Social Responsibility, of
International Finance Corporation, 26
Perot, H. Ross, 82, 84, 117
Peru: AFL-CIO and, 201; Comprehensive and
Progressive Agreement for Trans-Pacific
Partnership and, 448n133; enforcement
in, 206; ILRF and, 199; NAALC and, 191;
OTLA and, 201–2, 207, 340, 341, 441n33,
459n280; U.S. FTA with, 191, 195, 197, 199,
201–2, 206, 207, 440n23, 441n33, 459n280
peso crisis, 114
Petralax, 442n49
Petroleum Industry Workers' Union (Unión
Sindical Obrera de la Industria del
Petróleo), 202
Political Action Committees (PACs), 390n112
PRD. *See* Partido de la Revolución
Democrática
pregnancy testing, 63, 143–47, 310, 417n113,
418n124; U.S. NAOs and, 333
Preparatory Committee: of GATT, 368n44;
of ITO, 42
PRI. *See* Partido Revolucionario Institucional
prison/convict labor, 366n20
Private Rights, in NAALC, 403n8
Private Sector Coordinating Council. *See*
Consejo Coordinador Empresarial
Pro-Canada/Action Canada Network, 92, 93
process-tracing, 37–38, 364n155
Proclamation of Tehran, 10
protectionism, 2, 365n7
Public Advisory Committee, 99
public communications: in NAALC,
125–32––64, 126–29, 131, 172–85, 408n32. *See
also* national administrative offices
Public Services International, 356n80
Putnam, Robert D., 34–35, 451n170

Québec Workers Federation. *See* Fédération
des travailleurs et travailleuses du Québec

Rana Plaza accord, 362n139, 363n147
Randall Commission (Commission on
Foreign Economic Policy), 366n26

rapid response labor mechanism (RRLM):
GM and, 316–17; ILCME and, 343–48; in
USMCA, 343, 477n171; USMCA and,
274–77, 311–12
Reagan, Ronald, 47, 57, 71, 370n59, 377n98,
382n15
recount election (*recuento sindical*), 138–39
Red Mexicana de Acción Frente al Libre
Comercio (RMALC, Mexican Action
Network on Free Trade), 92–93, 330
Registro de Asociaciones (Associational
Registry), 413n74
Registro Público Nacional Sindical (national
public union registry), 176
Reich, Robert B., 97, 109, 184
Rethink Trade, 345, 347
Revolutionary Confederation of Workers
and Peasants. *See* Confederación
Revolucionaria de Obreros y Campesinos
Richards, David L., 54
Rieve, Emil, 365n13
right to organize/unionize: in Colombia, 209;
in Haiti, 296; ILO and, 161; in Mexico,
122, 130, 138, 142, 151–57; by migrant
workers, 425n205; NAALC on, 138,
156–57; OTLA and, 208, 341
right to strike: in ICESCR, 14, 353n63; ILO
and, 14, 354n66; in Mexico, 153, 193, 197,
334; NAALC on, 122, 193
right to work: in Canada, 462n27; ILO and,
482n212; in Taft-Hartley Act, 195–96, 252,
482n212; in UDHR, 9
Risse, Thomas, 10
RMALC. *See* Red Mexicana de Acción Frente
al Libre Comercio
Robles, Rosario, 147, 418n120
Rodgers, Gerry, 340nn12–13, 349n12, 350n15
Romo Garza, Alfonso, 465n65
Roncini, Lucas, 438n1, 445n88
Roosevelt, Franklin D., 8
Ropp, Stephen C., 10
Rostenkowski, Dan, 74, 77, 78–79, 385n61
Rousseau, Jean-Jacques, 349n1
RRLM. *See* rapid response labor mechanism
Rubie's de México, 135, 137, 175, 337, 418n124

Ruiz-Massieu, Claudia, 452n190
Rwanda, 11

Safeguarding of Industries Act of 1921,
364n5
Salinas de Gortari, Carlos, 382n27, 383n32,
384n48, 391n120; B. Clinton and, 291n125,
391n123; NAAEC and, 115; NAALC and,
108, 112, 113, 116, 268; NAFTA and, 72–75,
81–82, 87, 88, 91–92, 246; TPP and, 221
Samaniego de Villareal, Norma, 97, 411n51
Schakowsky, Jan, 471n108
Schott, Jeffrey J., 429n232
SCJN. *See* Suprema Corte de Justicia de la
Nación
SCMW. *See* Support Committee for
Maquiladora Workers
Scott, Robert E., 461n17
script of modernity, 12
Seade Kuri, Jesús, 263, 271, 283, 465n65, 483n5
Secretaría del Medio Ambiente, Recursos
Naturales y Pesca (SEMARNAP, Ministry
of the Environment, Natural Resources,
and Fisheries), 333
Secretaría del Trabajo y Previsión Social
(STPS, Ministry of Labor and Social
Welfare), 89, 134, 135; Equity and Gender
Policy Unit at, 147; GM, 487n47; GM and,
313–14, 315–16, 317, 487n47; Han Young
and, 153–54; migrant workers and, 157;
NAALC and, 175, 184; NAFTA and, 258;
Program for Employment, Training, and
Defense of Labor Rights of, 420nn158–59;
Registro de Asociaciones of, 413n74;
RRLM and, 345; state-level conciliation
and arbitration boards of, 414n79; TPP
and, 222, 223, 224, 227–28, 230–34, 236;
UNT and, 456n245; USMCA and, 264,
267, 268
Security and Prosperity Partnership
Agreement of North America, 455n227
SEIU. *See* Service Employees International
Union
SEMARNAP. *See* Secretaría del Medio
Ambiente, Recursos Naturales y Pesca

separation exclusion clauses (*cláusulas de exclusión de separación*), 139

Serrano, Jorge, 61

Serra Puche, Jaime, 73–74, 111, 383n41, 437n321

Service Employees International Union (SEIU), 154–55; Canadian NAOs and, 327; Mexican NAOs and, 329, 331; migrant workers and, 163; RRLM and, 344

Sewell, Terri A., 471n108

SIAOGMRM. *See* Sindicato Industrial Autónomo de Operarios en General de Maquiladoras de la República Mexicana

SIGTUR. *See* Southern Initiative on Globalization and Trade Union Rights

Sikkink, Kathryn, 350n14, 362nn137–38

Simmons, Beth, 349n2, 349n3

Sindicato de Telefonistas de la República Mexicana (STRM, Mexican Telephone Workers Union): Mexican NAOs and, 329; NAALC and, 169, 170; U.S. NAOs and, 333

Sindicato de Trabajadores de la Industria de Vidrio (STIV, Union of Glass Industry Workers), 348

Sindicato de Trabajadores de la Industria Metal Mecánica del Estado (STIMME, State Union of Metal-Mechanical Industry Workers), 346

Sindicato de Trabajadores de la Industria y del Comercio "6 de octubre" ("October 6" Union of Industrial and Commercial Workers), 150, 152

Sindicato de Trabajadores de la Junta Administradora Portuaria de la Vertiente Atlántica (SINTRAJAP, Union of Atlantic-side Port Administration Workers), 202; Costa Rica and, 443n63; OTLA and, 340

Sindicato de Trabajadores en la Industria Metálica, Acero, Hierro, Conexos y Similares (STIMAHCS, Union of Workers in the Metal, Iron, Steel, and Related and Similar Industries), 141, 345; Canadian NAOs and, 327; FAT and, 416n93; Han Young and, 149–50, 419n134; IBT and, 427n218; Mexican NAOs and, 329;

NAALC and, 169, 177, 182, 428n228; UE and, 427n218; U.S. NAOs and, 332, 333

Sindicato Independiente de las y los Trabajadores Libres y Democráticos de Saint-Gobain México (SITLDSGM, Union of Free and Democratic Workers of Saint-Gobain México), 348

Sindicato Independiente Nacional de Trabajadores y Trabajadoras de la Industria Automotriz y las Adhesivas (SINTTIA, National Independent Union of Automotive and Related Industry Workers), 315, 316, 317, 345

Sindicato Industrial Autónomo de Operarios en General de Maquiladoras de la República Mexicana (SIAOAGMRM, Autonomous Industrial Union of Mexican Maquiladora Operators in General), 345–46, 347

Sindicato Industrial de Trabajadores en Plantas Maquiladoras y Ensambladoras de Matamoros y su Municipio (SITPME, Union of Matamoros Maquiladora and Assembly Plant Workers), 344–45

Sindicato Mexicano de Electricistas (SME, Mexican Electricians Union), 130, 132, 133, 136; Canadian NAOs and, 328, 409n44; NAALC and, 167, 408n33; U.S. NAOs and, 337

Sindicato Nacional de Trabajadores de la Industria Metal-Mecánica, Sidero-Metalúrgica, Automotriz y Proveedores de Autopartes en General, de la Energía, sus Derivados y Similares de la República Mexicana "Miguel Trujillo López" (Miguel Trujillo López" National Union of Metalworking, Steel-Metallurgical, Automobile and General Autoparts Suppliers, Energy, and Related Industry Workers), 313, 315, 345

Sindicato Nacional de Trabajadores Mineros, Metalúrgicos y Similares de la República Mexicana (SNTMMSRM, National Union of Mexican Mineworkers and Metalworkers), 337, 346, 427n226

Sindicato Nacional de Unidad de Trabajadores de la Superintendencia Nacional de Aduanas y de Administración Tributaria (National Union of United Customs and Tax Administration Workers), 201-2, 304

Sindicato Nacional Independiente de Trabajadores de Industrias y Servicios 'Movimiento 20/32' (SNITIS, "Movement 20/32" Independent National Union of Industrial and Service Workers), 344-46

Sindicato Único de Trabajadores de la Secretaría de Pesca (SUTSP, General Union of Workers at the Ministry of Fishing), 142, 332-33

Singapore: Comprehensive and Progressive Agreement for Trans-Pacific Partnership and, 448n133; Trans-Pacific Strategic Economic Partnership Agreement and, 448n135; U.S. FTA with, 438n2, 439n11

Singapore Ministerial Declaration, 372n68

SINTRAJAP. See Sindicato de Trabajadores de la Junta Administradora Portuaria de la Vertiente Atlántica

SINTTIA. See Sindicato Independiente Nacional de Trabajadores y Trabajadoras de la Industria Automotriz y las Adhesivas

Sistema Nacional Anticorrupción (National Anticorruption System), 237

Sistema Nacional de Transparencia, Acceso a la Información Pública y Protección de Datos Personales (National System for Transparency, Access to Public Information, and Protection of Personal Data), 237

SITLDSGM. See Sindicato Independiente de las y los Trabajadores Libres y Democráticos de Saint-Gobain México

SITPME. See Sindicato Industrial de Trabajadores en Plantas Maquiladoras y Ensambladoras de Matamoros y su Municipio

SME. See Sindicato Mexicano de Electricistas

Smoot-Hawley Act (Tariff Act of 1830), 364n5

Snidal, Duncan, 486n30

SNITIS. See Sindicato Nacional Independiente de Trabajadores de Industrias y Servicios 'Movimiento 20/32'

SNTMMSRM. See Sindicato Nacional de Trabajadores Mineros, Metalúrgicos y Similares de la República Mexicana

Soares, Mario, 73

social clause: in GATT, 69; of WTO, 49, 372n70

Solec International, 329

solidarity: actions, 4, 15, 169-70, 289, 299; in Canada, 152-54; cross-border, 1, 3-4, 15, 17-24, 355n74, 357n95, 427n220; in Mexico, 153, 170-71, 266, 387n69; in United States, 152-54. See also Maquiladora Solidarity Network; union-to-union solidarity initiatives

Solis, Hilda L., 212, 446n109

Sony Corporation, 136, 179, 332, 426n211, 431n253, 437n323

Southern Initiative on Globalization and Trade Union Rights (SIGTUR), 355n74

sovereignty: Canada, 108-9; collective-action rights and, 18; effect of, 60; invoking to resist reform, 63-65; labor rights and, 10-15, 16, 33-38, 292-98; leverage, 33-37, 40, 50, 66, 69, 117, 119, 285; Mexico, 87-89, 92, 96, 106, 115, 154; NAALC and, 95, 119, 120, 186-87; NAFTA and, 68-69, 283; obstacles to, 16-17, 63; of the state, 1-10, 40; USMCA and, 292-96; Weber on, 353n54. See also Weberian sovereignty; Westphalian sovereignty

specialized public entity (ente público especializado), 230

Spriggs, William E., 389n106, 392n142

Sprint Corporation, 157, 329, 422n176

Stanford, James, 389n106, 392n142

Statement of Labor Principles, for NAALC, 98, 400n235

State Union of Metal-Mechanical Industry
Workers (Sindicato de Trabajadores de
la Industria Metal Mecánica del Estado,
STIMME), 346
STIMAHCS. *See* Sindicato de Trabajadores
en la Industria Metálica, Acero, Hierro,
Conexos y Similares
STIMME. *See* Sindicato de Trabajadores de la
Industria Metal Mecánica del Estado
STIV. *See* Sindicato de Trabajadores de la
Industria de Vidrio
STPS. *See* Secretaría del Trabajo y Previsión
Social
strikes: by Aeroméxico, 437n322; cross-border
union solidarity actions and, 23; IWMA
on, 18; NAALC and, 138; TPP and, 221.
See also right to strike
STRM. *See* Sindicato de Telefonistas de la
República Mexicana
sunset clause, of USMCA, 486n33
Support Center for Yucatán Workers
(Centro de Apoyo a los Trabajadores de
Yucatán), 336
Support Committee for Maquiladora
Workers (SCMW), 149–50, 152; Han
Young and, 420n149; U.S. NAOs and, 333
Suprema Corte de Justicia de la Nación
(SCJN, Mexican Supreme Court), 142,
433n277; ILO and, 471n105; NAALC and,
178; UDHR and, 433n278; U.S. NAOs
and, 417n103
SUTSP. *See* Sindicato Único de Trabajadores
de la Secretaría de Pesca
Sweeney, John, 171

TAESA. *See* Transportes Aéreos Ejecutivos,
S.A.
Taft-Hartley Act (Labor Management
Relations Act of 1947), 195–96, 252,
482n212
Tariff Act of 1830 (Smoot-Hawley Act),
364n5
Tariff Act of 1922 (Fordney-McCumber Act),
364n5

Tarrant México, 175, 328
Technical Council (Consejo Técnico), 236–37
technical labor standards, in NAALC,
400n222, 406n22
Teksid Hierro de México, 346
Tello, Lindsay, 375n85
Tepoyac Association (Associación Tepoyac),
Mexican NAOs and, 330
Textile Workers Union of America, 42
TFCA. *See* Tribunal Federal de Conciliación
y Arbitraje
Thomas, William, 438n6
Thompson, Mike, 471n108
Tong, Mary, 420n149
TPP. *See* Trans-Pacific Partnership
Trade Act of 1974, 45, 76, 370n54; Han Young
and, 152; U.S. GSP and, 368n38
Trade Adjustment Assistance Program, of
DOL, 79, 385n55
Trade and Tariff Act of 1984, 51; OPIC and,
431n270; USMCA and, 281
Trade Enforcement Trust Fund, 282
Trade Expansion Act of 1962, 84, 482n214
Trade Policy Staff Committee, of USTR,
51–52
trade unions (labor unions): in Colombia,
443n59, 443n61; in Guatemala, 446n100;
in Honduras, 443n56; in *maquiladora*,
418n127; NAALC and, 3, 4, 119, 426n206;
NAFTA and, 290n108, 389n107; Trump
and, 460n13; USTR and, 57. *See also*
specific unions and topics
Trade Working Group, 265–66
Traho Services, 153
Trans-Pacific Partnership (TPP), 35, 140,
448n133; AFL-CIO and, 223, 238, 239;
Australia and, 458n274; CCE and,
231, 236; collective bargaining in, 232;
COPARMEX and, 231, 236; CROC and,
231, 234–35, 236; CROM and, 231, 236; CSR
in, 448n137, 464n52; CTM and, 221, 223,
231–32, 234–35, 236; DOL and, 224; DOS
and, 222–23; ILO and, 217, 218, 220–21, 225,
233, 254, 255, 284; International Monetary

Trans-Pacific Partnership (*Continued*)
Fund and, 226–27, 233, 234; Ley Federal del
Trabajo and, 221, 224; Mexico in, 165–66,
189–244; migrant workers in, 255; MSN
and, 222; NAALC and, 220, 221, 225, 238,
250; NAFTA and, 220, 224, 227, 239, 240,
253, 255, 257; New Zealand and, 458n274;
Peña Nieto and, 222, 225, 227–28, 229,
231–34, 235, 236, 240, 455n226; PRD and,
235, 237; PRI and, 221, 222, 234; social
capital and, 296; sovereignty and, 293–95;
STPS and, 222, 223, 224, 227–28, 230–34,
236; Trans-Pacific Strategic Economic
Partnership Agreement and, 448n135;
Trump and, 248; UNT and, 231, 235,
237; U.S. FTAs and, 217, 219; USTR and,
222–23, 224, 250–51
Trans-Pacific Strategic Economic Partnership
Agreement, 448n135
Transportes Aéreos Ejecutivos, S.A. (TAESA,
Executive Air Transport, Inc.), 134, 335
Treaty of Versailles, 1, 7, 41
Tribunal Federal de Conciliación y Arbitraje
(TFCA, Federal Conciliation and
Arbitration Tribunal), 142, 333, 416n100
Tridonex, 344–45, 488n64
Tri-National Working Group of Government
Experts on Workplace Safety and Health,
431n254
Tripartite Commission, 59
Tripartite Declaration of Principles
Concerning Multinational Enterprises
and Social Policy, of ILO, 359n111
Tripartite Follow-up Commission, 208
Trumka, Richard, 238, 247, 266, 269, 278, 469n93
Trump, Donald J., 459n280, 460n2; Canada
and, 460n12; election victory of, 460n4;
Mexico and, 227, 460n12; minimum
wage and, 460n13; NAFTA and, 235, 237,
245–46, 247, 248, 253; TPP and, 248; Trade
Expansion Act of 1962 and, 482n214; trade
unions and, 460n13; USMCA and, 250,
259, 261, 270, 272, 278, 466n78, 475n149
Tsogas, George, 378n115

UAW. *See* United Automobile, Aerospace,
and Agricultural Implement Workers of
America
UDHR. *See* Universal Declaration of Human
Rights
UE. *See* United Electrical, Radio, and
Machine Workers of America
UFCW International Union, 338
UN. *See* United Nations
UNCTAD. *See* United Nations Conference
on Trade and Development
Understanding Regarding Trade and
Investment Facilitation Talks, 72
UNIFOR, 251–52, 268–69
UNI Global Union, 31, 408n33
Union Association of Mexican Aviation
Flight Attendants (Asociación Sindical
de Sobrecargos de Aviación de México,
ASSAM), 335
Unión de Trabajadores de Oficios
Varios (Union of Workers in Various
Occupations), 149
Union Federation of Salvadoran Workers
(Federación Sindical de Trabajadores
Salvadoreños, FSTS), 58, 61
"Union Movement and the Nation" Forum
(Foro El Sindicalismo ante la Nación), 176
Unión Nacional de Trabajadores (UNT,
National Union of Workers), 421n164,
454n215; Canadian NAOs and, 328;
Mexican NAOs and, 329, 330; NAALC
and, 167, 172, 307–8; NAFTA and, 287;
PRD and, 432n268; STPS and, 456n245;
TPP and, 231, 235, 237; USMCA and, 264,
268–69; U.S. NAOs and, 335, 338
Union of Atlantic-side Port Administration
Workers. *See* Sindicato de Trabajadores
de la Junta Administradora Portuaria de
la Vertiente Atlántica
Union of Free and Democratic Workers
of Saint-Gobain México (Sindicato
Independiente de las y los Trabajadores
Libres y Democráticos de Saint-Gobain
México, SITLDSGM), 348

Union of Glass Industry Workers (Sindicato de Trabajadores de la Industria de Vidrio, STIV), 348

Union of Matamoros Maquiladora and Assembly Plant Workers (Sindicato Industrial de Trabajadores en Plantas Maquiladoras y Ensambladoras de Matamoros y su Municipio, SITPME), 344–45

Union of Needletrade, Industrial, and Textile Employees (UNITE!): Canadian NAOs and, 326, 327; Mexican NAOs and, 329; migrant workers and, 163; U.S. NAOs and, 334

Union of Workers in the Metal, Iron, Steel, and Related and Similar Industries. *See* Sindicato de Trabajadores en la Industria Metálica, Acero, Hierro, Conexos y Similares

Union of Workers in Various Occupations (Unión de Trabajadores de Oficios Varios), 149

Unión Sindical Obrera de la Industria del Petróleo (Petroleum Industry Workers' Union), 202

UNITE!. *See* Union of Needletrade, Industrial, and Textile Employees

United Automobile, Aerospace, and Agricultural Implement Workers of America (UAW), 368n39; Han Young and, 150; NAFTA and, 394n160; RRLM and, 346; U.S. GSP and, 369n52; U.S. NAOs and, 334

United Electrical, Radio, and Machine Workers of America (UE): Canadian NAOs and, 326, 328; FAT and, 427n225; Mexican NAOs and, 330; NAALC and, 167, 170; STIMAHCS and, 427n218; U.S. NAOs and, 332, 334

United Food and Commercial Workers International Union, 369n52

United Mine Workers of America, 358n100

United Nations (UN): CEDAW of, 145; Committee on Economic, Social and Cultural Rights of, 15; Committee on the Elimination of Discrimination against Women of, 15; Committee on the Rights of the Child of, 15; Economic and Social Council of, 19; Human Rights Committee of, 15, 354n69; ICCPR of, 9–12, 25, 141, 145; ICESCR of, 9–10, 14, 25, 353n63; ILO and, 16, 25

United Nations Commission on Human Rights, 396n180

United Nations Conference on Trade and Development (UNCTAD), 364n3

United Nations Conference on Trade and Employment, 41

United Nations General Assembly: Declaration on Principles of International Law concerning Friendly Relations and Co-Operation Among States in Accordance with the Charter of the United Nations of, 352n47; UDHR of, 2, 8–9, 13, 178, 433n278

United Nations Global Compact, 26

United Nations Organization, 8

United Paperworkers International Union (UPIU), 326, 334

United States (U.S.): Colombia and, 443n57; Honduras and, 444n79; NAOs of, 168, 171, 174, 182–84, 332–38, 404n14, 407n29, 408n31, 409n40, 409n42, 410n45, 411n51, 411n58, 412n62, 413n66, 414nn82–83, 416n100; U.S. GSP of, 182, 193, 402n250, 405n17, 485n22. *See also specific topics*

United States Board of Economic Welfare, 369n48

United States-Chile Free Trade Agreement, 439n21

United States-Colombia Trade Promotion Agreement, 198

United States-Mexico-Canada Agreement (USMCA), 3, 4, 5, 35, 245–88, 465n65; AFL-CIO and, 260, 264, 266–71, 278, 466n75; on child labor, 262; collective bargaining in, 269–70; Denial of Rights and, 275; Department of Agriculture

United States-Mexico-Canada (*Continued*)
and, 481n206; DOL and, 279, 282;
enforcement of, 277-83, 479n187; freedom
of association in, 269-70; Free Trade
Commission of, 274; GM and, 312-17;
IAMAW and, 259, 479n183; IBT and,
479n183; ILCME and, 278-80; ILO and,
278; Labor Advisory Committee for
Trade Negotiations and Trade Policy
and, 280-81, 282, 480n201; labor rights in,
273-74; Ley Federal del Trabajo and, 265;
minimum wage in, 464n57; NAALC and,
275-76, 281, 284-85, 286, 481nn209-10,
482n215; NAFTA and, 468nn85-86;
NLRB and, 275; RRLM and, 274-77,
311-12, 343, 477n171; sovereignty and,
292-96; STPS and, 264, 267, 268; sunset
clause of, 486n33; Trump and, 250, 259,
261; United States-Peru Trade Promotion
Agreement and, 262-63; UNT and, 264,
268-69; USAID and, 480n199; U.S.
GSP and, 281; USITC and, 260, 474n133;
USTR and, 259-60, 261, 266-67, 271, 272,
280-82, 464n55; USW and, 259, 264,
466n78, 479n183
United States-Peru Trade Promotion
Agreement, 197, 203, 262-63, 440n23
United States Technical Assistance for
Mexican Labor Capacity Building Act of
2019, 480n197, 480n200
United States Trade Representative (USTR),
50-64, 55–56, 66-67, 376n88; acceptance
rates of, 377n98; AFL-CIO and, 199,
441n46; Bipartisan Congressional Trade
and Accountability Act of 2015 and,
461n20; collective-action rights and,
54, 59, 62; Guatemala and, 377n102,
446n109; ILRERF and, 485n22; Jordan
and, 199; NAALC and, 95; NAFTA
and, 74, 252-53, 254, 285, 461n19, 461n21;
rejections by, 377n100; RRLM and, 343;
TPP and, 222-23, 224, 250-51; Trade
Policy Staff Committee of, 51-52; U.S.
GSP and, 379n120; USMCA and, 259-60,

261, 266-67, 271, 272, 280-82, 464n55;
U.S. NAOs and, 435n290. *See also*
Labor Advisory Committee for Trade
Negotiations and Trade Policy
United Steelworkers (USW): Canadian
NAOs and, 326; Han Young and, 150;
NAFTA and, 251-52, 394n160; RRLM
and, 348; SNTMMSRM and, 427n226;
U.S. GSP and, 369n52; USMCA and,
259, 264, 466n78, 479n183; U.S. NAOs
and, 334
United Students Against Sweatshops
(USAS), 20, 30, 327-28, 336, 356n84
UNITE HERE!, 336, 356n84
Universal Declaration of Human Rights
(UDHR), of United Nations General
Assembly, 2, 8-9, 13, 178, 433n278;
freedom of association and, 351n26;
NAALC and, 178; SCJN and, 433n278
UNT. *See* Unión Nacional de Trabajadores
UPIU. *See* United Paperworkers
International Union
Uruguay Round, of GATT, 368n44, 383n37,
385n57
Uruguay Round Agreements Act of 1994,
371n64
U.S. *See* United States
U.S. Agency for International Development
(USAID), 281, 480n199
USAS. *See* United Students Against
Sweatshops
U.S.-Bahrain Free Trade Agreement, 340
U.S. Council on International Business, 133
U.S. Department of Labor. *See* Department
of Labor
U.S. FTAs, 438n6, 438n7, 438nn1-2, 439n11,
440n28, 441n46, 441n47, 445n88; AFL-
CIO and, 461n16; collective bargaining in,
201-2; DOL and, 206; GAO and, 458n277;
with Guatemala, 485n25; labor rights in,
191-216, 298-301; NAALC and, 189-216;
NAFTA and, 249; Obama and, 302;
OTLA and, 199, 204-6; TPP and, 217, 219;
U.S. GSP and, 288, 308

U.S. Generalized System of Preferences (U.S. GSP), 2, 4, 15, 182, 193, 348, 402n250, 405n17, 485n22; AFL-CIO and, 369n45, 369n52; CBI and, 289; CCC and, 32; collective-action rights and, 50, 53, 62; cross-border union solidarity actions and, 20; DR-CAFTA and, 305–6; EPZs and, 376n93; Guatemala and, 305–6; Honduras and, 306; ILO and, 66; for labor rights, 50–64, 55–56, 62; of Mexico, 402n250; NAALC and, 35–38, 40, 45–47, 114, 401n242; NAFTA and, 69; NGOs and, 66, 374n81; sovereignty and, 292–93; statistical analysis of, 321–24, 323, 324; Trade Act of 1974 and, 368n38; UAW and, 369n52; UNCTAD and, 364n3; U.S. FTAs and, 288, 308; USMCA and, 281; USTR and, 50–64, 55–56, 62, 66–67, 379n120; USW and, 369n52; WTO and, 379n120

U.S. Generalized System of Preferences (GSP), ILRERF and, 485

U.S. High Level Economic Dialogue, 226

U.S. International Trade Commission (USITC), 260, 474n133

U.S. Labor Education in the Americas Program (USLEAP), 326, 337

USMCA. *See* United States-Mexico-Canada Agreement

U.S.-Mexico Bilateral Commission, 78

U.S. NAOs, 429n241, 430n247; Bayesian logit for, 436n309; DOS and, 435n290; freedom of association and, 417n106; *maquiladora* and, 418n127; pregnancy testing and, 417n113, 418n124; SCJN and, 417n103; USTR and, 435n290

U.S. National Association of Manufacturers, 133

U.S. National Textile Association, 441n46

USTR. *See* United States Trade Representative

USW. *See* United Steelworkers

Velázquez Sánchez, Fidel, 91, 106, 429n235

Videgaray Caso, Luis, 226–27, 253, 254, 452n193

Vienna Declaration and Programme of Action, 11

Vietnam: Comprehensive and Progressive Agreement for Trans-Pacific Partnership and, 448n133; labor consistency plan for, 218; U.S. FTA with, 394n276

Vogel, David, 363n143

Vogt, Jeffrey S., 355n73, 369n52

VU Manufacturing, 347

Wage and Hours Division, of DOL, 444n79

Washington Office on Latin America (WOLA), 326, 336, 337

Weber, Max, 353n54

Weberian sovereignty, 12, 13, 15, 115

Westphalian sovereignty, 10–12, 14–15, 65, 352n41, 353n58; ILO and, 115

WFTU. *See* World Federation of Trade Unions

white phosphorus, on matches, 349n12, 365n9

WOLA. *See* Washington Office on Latin America

women: IWMA on, 18; in *maquiladora*, 417n107; NAALC on, 123; night work for, 349n12, 365n9. *See also* equal pay for equal work; gender discrimination; pregnancy testing

Women's Rights Project, 144, 333

Women Working Worldwide, 20

Woodcock, Leonard, 368n39

Workers' Awaaz, 330

Workers' Bank (Banco Obrero), 90

worker rights, 3, 6, 12–13, 40, 46, 54, 69, 79, 200, 289–317, 299, 433n272; in China, 375n83; in developing countries, 190; internationally recognized, 46, 51, 122, 193, 405n17, 432n4; in GATT, 268n44; in Mexico, 69, 79, 88, 387n69; migrant workers, 158–59, 405n18. *See also* North American Agreement on Labor Cooperation; North American Free Trade Agreement

Worker Rights Consortium (WRC), 30, 31

working hours: in Dominican Republic, 202; ILO on, 8; IWMA on, 18; NAALC on, 41, 98; in UDHR, 9; USTR and, 63

workplace (occupational) safety and health, 1; CCCs on, 32; in Colombia, 198; in Dominican Republic, 202; at Han Young, 151, 419n129; IACtHR and, 354n70; for migrant workers, 423n190; NAALC on, 108, 123, 194, 431n254; NAFTA and, 78; NGOs and, 362n134; at Nike, 363n143; Tri-National Working Group of Government Experts on Workplace Safety and Health and, 431n254; U.S. NAOs and, 335

Worksafe! Southern California, 150

World Bank: Brandt Commission of, 365n6; NAALC and, 47

World Commission on the Social Dimensions of Globalization, of ILO, 372n71

World Conference on Human Rights, 10

World Economic Conference, 265n12

World Economic Forum, 73

World Federation of Trade Unions (WFTU), 19, 42

World Labor Charter, 365n13

World Organization of Workers, 19

World Trade Organization (WTO), 2; GATT and, 372n70; ILO and, 49, 360n114, 372n71; Ministerial Conference of, 49; NAALC and, 48–49; OECD and, 371n67; preferential trade agreements of, 372n72; Singapore Ministerial Declaration and, 372n68; social clause of, 49, 372n70; Uruguay Round Agreements Act of 1994 and, 371n64; U.S. GSP and, 379n120

WRC. *See* Workers Rights Consortium

WTO. *See* World Trade Organization

Wyden, Ron, 262, 469n90, 469n93. *See also* Brown-Wyden proposal

Xelhuantzi López, María, 427n226

Yale Law School Workers' Rights Project, 162–63; Canadian NAOs and, 327; Mexican NAOs and, 329

Zedillo Ponce de Léon, Ernesto, 152–53, 158–59, 180–83, 436n309; U.S. NAOs and, 334

Zelaya, Manuel, 443n56

GPSR Authorized Representative: Easy Access System Europe, Mustamäe tee
50, 10621 Tallinn, Estonia, gpsr.requests@easproject.com